Lecture Notes of the Institute for Computer Sciences, Social Informatics and Telecommunications Engineering 384

More information about this series at http://www.springer.com/series/8197

Mulugeta Admasu Delele ·
Mekuanint Agegnehu Bitew ·
Abebech Abera Beyene ·
Solomon Workneh Fanta ·
Addisu Negash Ali (Eds.)

Advances of Science and Technology

8th EAI International Conference, ICAST 2020
Bahir Dar, Ethiopia, October 2–4, 2020
Proceedings, Part I

 Springer

Editors
Mulugeta Admasu Delele
Bahir Dar University
Bahir Dar, Ethiopia

Mekuanint Agegnehu Bitew ⓘ
Bahir Dar University
Bahir Dar, Ethiopia

Abebech Abera Beyene ⓘ
Bahir Dar University
Bahir Dar, Ethiopia

Solomon Workneh Fanta ⓘ
Bahir Dar University
Bahir Dar, Ethiopia

Addisu Negash Ali ⓘ
Bahir Dar University
Bahir Dar, Ethiopia

ISSN 1867-8211   ISSN 1867-822X   (electronic)
Lecture Notes of the Institute for Computer Sciences, Social Informatics
and Telecommunications Engineering
ISBN 978-3-030-80620-0   ISBN 978-3-030-80621-7   (eBook)
https://doi.org/10.1007/978-3-030-80621-7

This Springer imprint is published by the registered company Springer Nature Switzerland AG
The registered company address is: Gewerbestrasse 11, 6330 Cham, Switzerland

Preface

On behalf of the organizing team, it is our pleasure to introduce the proceedings of the 8th EAI International Conference on Advancements of Science and Technology (ICAST 2020), which took place at the Bahir Dar Institute of Technology, Bahir Dar University, Ethiopia, during October 2–4, 2020. The ICAST conference is an annual platform for researchers, scholars, scientists in academia, and practitioners in various industries to share know-how, experiences, challenges, and recent advancements in science and technology. In addition, the conference has continued to show promise in the application of research findings and innovations in all areas of science and technology. ICAST 2020 attracted 200 submissions of which 157 were sent out for peer review, where each paper was evaluated by, on average, three experts in the area. The technical program of ICAST 2020 consisted of 74 full papers in the oral presentation sessions during the main conference tracks. The conference was organized into six tracks: Track 1: Chemical, food, and bio-process engineering; Track 2: Electrical and computer engineering; Track 3: IT, computer science, and software engineering; Track 4: Civil, water resources, and environmental engineering; Track 5: Mechanical and industrial engineering; and Track 6: Material science and engineering. The six tracks were conducted as parallel sessions in six halls. In addition to the high-quality technical paper presentations, the technical program also featured three opening keynote speeches and seven session keynote speeches. The three opening keynote speakers were Prof. Desta Mebratu, University of Stellenbosh, South Africa; Dr. Hirpa G.Lemu, University of Stavanger, Norway; and Dr. Lara Allen, Centre for Global Equality, UK.

Coordination with the Steering Committee chair, Prof. Imrich Chlamtac, the Organizing Committee chair, Prof. Kibret Mequanint (The University of Western Ontario, Canada), the co-chairs, Dr. Abebech Abera, Dr. Mekuanint Agegnehu and Dr. Solomon Workneh, the Technical Program Committee chair, Dr. Mulugeta Admasu was essential for the success of the conference. We sincerely appreciate their constant support and guidance. It was also a great pleasure to team up with such an excellent Organizing Committee who worked hard in organizing and supporting the conference. We are grateful to the Technical Program Committee who were instrumental in organizing the peer-review process of the technical papers, which led to a high-quality technical program. In particular, the Technical Program Committee, led by Dr. Mulugeta Admasu, and the co-chairs, Dr. Belachew Bantyrga, Dr. Addisu Negash , Dr. Gebeyehu Belay, Dr. Hanibal Lemma, Dr. Zerihu Getahun, Dr. Elias Wagari and Prof. A. Pushparaghavan, were instrumental in organizing the peer-review process of the technical papers, which led to a high-quality technical program. We are also grateful to the conference manager, Radka Pincakova, for her support, and to all the authors who submitted their papers to the ICAST 2020 conference.

We strongly believe that ICAST 2020 provided a good forum for all researchers, developers, and practitioners to discuss all science and technology aspects that are relevant to advancements in this area. We also expect that future ICAST conferences will be as successful and stimulating as indicated by the contributions presented in this volume.

October 2020   Kibret Mequanint
                                                                                  Mulugeta Admasu Delele

Organization

Steering Committee

Imrich Chlamtac	University of Trento, Italy
Seifu Tilahun	Bahir Dar University, Ethiopia
Kibret Mequanint	University of Western Ontario, Canada

Organizing Committee

General Chair

Kibret Mequanint   University of Western Ontario, Canada

General Co-chairs

Abebech Abera	Bahir Dar University, Ethiopia
Mekuanint Agegnehu	Bahir Dar University, Ethiopia
Solomon Workneh	Bahir Dar University, Ethiopia

Technical Program Committee Chair and Co-chairs

Mulugeta Admasu	Bahir Dar University, Ethiopia
Belachew Bantyrga	Bahir Dar University, Ethiopia
Addisu Negash	Bahir Dar University, Ethiopia
Gebeyehu Belay	Bahir Dar University, Ethiopia
Hanibal Lemma	Bahir Dar University, Ethiopia
Zerihu Getahun	Bahir Dar University, Ethiopia
Elias Wagari	Bahir Dar University, Ethiopia
Pushparaghavan A.	Bahir Dar University, Ethiopia

Sponsorship and Exhibit Chair

Dagnachew Aklog   Bahir Dar University, Ethiopia

Local Chair

Dagnenet Sultan   Bahir Dar University, Ethiopia

Workshops Chair

Fikreselam Gared   Bahir Dar University, Ethiopia

Publicity and Social Media Chair

Hailu Shimelis   Bahir Dar University, Ethiopia

Publications Chair

Mulugeta Admasu   Bahir Dar University, Ethiopia

Web Chair

Ephrem Dagne   Bahir Dar University, Ethiopia

Posters and PhD Track Chair

Nigus Gabbiye   Bahir Dar University, Ethiopia

Panels Chair

Zenamarkos Bantie   Bahir Dar University, Ethiopia

Demos Chair

Bantelay Sintayehu   Bahir Dar University, Ethiopia

Tutorials Chairs

Mulugeta Azeze   Bahir Dar University, Ethiopia

Technical Program Committee

Abdulkadir Aman	Addis Ababa University, Ethiopia
Abebe Dinku	Addis Ababa University, Ethiopia
Abebech Beyene	Bahir Dar University, Ethiopia
Abraham Asmare	Bahir Dar University, Ethiopia
Addisu Negash Ali	Bahir Dar University, Ethiopia
Addiszemen Teklay	Bahir Dar University, Ethiopia
Amando P. Singun Jr.	University of Technology and Applied Sciences - Higher College of Technology, Oman
Aklog Dagnachew	Bahir Dar University, Ethiopia
Assefa Asmare Tsegaw	Bahir Dar University, Ethiopia
Belachew Bantiyrga	Bahir Dar University, Ethiopia
Belete Yigezu	Addis Ababa Science and Technology University, Ethiopia
Bereket Haile	Bahir Dar University, Ethiopia
Berhanu Assefa Demessie	AAiT/AAU
Berihun Bizuneh	National Taiwan University of Science and Technology, Taiwan
Beteley Tekola Meshesha	Addis Ababa University, Ethiopia
Delele Worku	Bahir Dar University, Ethiopia
Hailu Shimles Gebremedhen	Bahir Dar University, Ethiopia
Abreham Debebe	Addis Ababa Science and Technology University, Ethiopia
Anteneh Mohammed Tahir	Wollo University, Ethiopia

Bedilu Habte	Addis Ababa University, Ethiopia
Bikila Teklu	Addis Ababa University, Ethiopia
Bimrew Tamrat	Bahir Dar University, Ethiopia
Dagninet Sultan	Bahir Dar University, Ethiopia
Ermias Gebrekidan Koricho	Georgia Southern University, USA
Fisha Behulu	Addis Ababa University, Ethiopia
Geremew Sahilu	Addis Ababa University, Ethiopia
Getahun Aklilu	Dire Dawa Institute of Technology, Ethiopia
Mitiku Damtie	National Taiwan University of Science and Technology, Taiwan
Misrak Girma	Addis Ababa Science and Technology University, Ethiopia
Negash Alemu	Addis Ababa Science and Technology University, Ethiopia
Pushparaghavan Annamalai	Bahir Dar University, Ethiopia
Samson Mekbib	Addis Ababa Science and Technology University, Ethiopia
Samuel Tesfaye	Addis Ababa University, Ethiopia
Solomon Addisu	Bahir Dar University, Ethiopia
Tena Alamirew	Water and Land Resource Center, Ethiopia
Yitagesu Yilma	Addis Ababa Science and Technology University, Ethiopia
Daniel Tilahun Redda	Addis Ababa University, Ethiopia
Eduardo Ojito	Addis Ababa University, Ethiopia
Elias Gabisa	Bahir Dar University, Ethiopia
Ephrem Gidey	Addis Ababa Science and Technology University, Ethiopia
Fekade Getahun	Addis Ababa University, Ethiopia
Fekadu Lemessa	Addis Ababa Science and Technology University, Ethiopia
Gebeyehu Belay Gebremeskel	Bahir Dar University, Ethiopia
Geta Kidanemariam	Bahir Dar University, Ethiopia
Getachew Shunki	Addis Ababa Science and Technology University, Ethiopia
Haileleoul Sahle Habte	Addis Ababa University, Ethiopia
Hanibal Lemma	Bahir Dar University, Ethiopia
Hilary Inyang	Bahir Dar University, Ethiopia
Hirut Assaye	Bahir Dar University, Ethiopia
James Geodert	Bahir Dar University, Ethiopia
Kibret Mequanint	University of Western Ontario, Canada
Kumsa Delessa	Addis Ababa University, Ethiopia
Mekuanint Agegnehu Bitew	Bahir Dar University, Ethiopia
Mengiste Abate	Bahir Dar University, Ethiopia
Mesfin Wegayehu	Bahir Dar University, Ethiopia
Metadel Kassahun Abera	Bahir Dar University, Ethiopia

Contents – Part I

Electrical and Computer Engineering

IT, Computer Science and Software Engineering

Contents – Part II

Material Science and Engineering

Chemical, Food and Bio-Process Engineering

Production and Characterization of Sawdust Briquettes for Firewood Substitution

Muluken Mengist[1]([✉]), Belay Woldeyes[2], and Nigus Gabbiye[3]

[1] Institute of Technology, University of Gondar, Gondar, Ethiopia
[2] Addis Ababa Institute of Technology, Addis Ababa University, Addis Ababa, Ethiopia
[3] Bahir Dar Institute of Technology, Bahir Dar University, Bahir Dar, Ethiopia

Abstract. The possibility of substitution of firewood by sawdust briquettes was examined. Easy to operate and portable homemade briquetting machine was fabricated. Three internal diameters of molding cylinder/die diameters specifically 6, 8 and, 10 cm were used to examine the effect of pressure on the quality of sawdust briquettes. For all types of sawdust briquettes, the highest and lowest values of density, porosity index, volatile matter, ash content, fixed carbon, and calorific value are 218.2–322.6 kg/m^3, 34–312.4%, 70.2–90.6%, 2.3–7.3%, 6.7–24.3% and 14.5–18.4 MJ/kg respectively. The figured physical and chemical properties of sawdust briquettes were interesting. The density and porosity index of sawdust briquettes were extensively affected by molding cylinder diameter and waste paper percentage. An interesting quality of sawdust briquettes was attained at lower particle dimension, waste paper percentage and higher pressure. The optimum value of density, porosity index, percentage volatile content, percentage ash content and gross calorific value of 306.1 kg/m^3, 35.9%, 83.9%, 3.1% 17.1 MJ/kg respectively were acquired at a combination of die diameter of 6 cm and waste paper percentage of 25%. The capability of production of sawdust briquettes with good quality using only waste paper as a binder is an encouraging fact and the briquettes can be excellent augments to firewood.

Keywords: Sawdust · Briquette · Density · Calorific value

1 Introduction

Natural resources have a great role and impact on the functioning of an economic system of a country. Because of these, energy which, is usually obtained when all these natural resources are harnessed plays a vital role in the overall development planning of any nation. Energy has been the central cross-sectoral issue, which affects all human activities either directly or indirectly. It is a vital input to economic growth and development of any economic sector. Energy has been seen to be a crucial input in the process of economic, social and industrial development. Apart from the other three classical factors i.e. land, capital and labor, the role of energy cannot be underestimated when it comes to development (Kuti 2007).

© ICST Institute for Computer Sciences, Social Informatics and Telecommunications Engineering 2021
Published by Springer Nature Switzerland AG 2021. All Rights Reserved
M. A. Delele et al. (Eds.): ICAST 2020, LNICST 384, pp. 3–26, 2021.
https://doi.org/10.1007/978-3-030-80621-7_1

Energy resources are generally classified into two namely renewable and non-renewable. Renewable is thought to be a better option since the non-renewable has not a capability to be refilled. Renewable energy sources are more environmentally friendly and are thus better candidates for use in achieving some measures of technological development under a sustainable environment both in the developed and developing nations. The high cost of non-renewable energy sources has made people start deviating to the use of renewable energy sources for domestic cooking (Mahadeo and Dubey 2014). The renewable energy sources should be effectively utilized in order to meet the rapidly increasing energy demand. Biomass energy has greater prospective than the other form of energy (Rajaseenivasan and Srinivasan 2016).

The more comfortable human life is paid by excessive energy increase in all its forms. The reserves of not renewable energy sources (coal, crude oil, natural gas) are not limitless, they gradually get exhausted and their price continually increases (Brožek and Nováková 2012).

Materials, which originate through a conversion process like paper, cellulose, organic residues from wood industries and organic waste materials from industries and houses constitute a large part of the biomass. Wood is the largest potential source of biomass when compared to others. Most of this potential lies in wood processing by-products such as sawdust, spent paper pulping liquor, forest management by-products such as thinning and logging residues. Out of all the various kinds of wood wastes, sawdust is of high importance. Sawdust is always obtained from forest wastes or manufacturing wastes. As a result of growing worldwide concern regarding environmental impacts particularly climate change from the use of fossil fuels coupled with the volatile fossil fuel market and, the need for independent energy supply to sustain economic development, there is currently a great deal of interest in renewable energy in general and biomass energy in particular (Kuti 2007).

Apart from the problems of transportation, storage, and handling, the direct burning of loose biomass in conventional grates is associated with very low thermal efficiency and widespread air pollution. The conversion efficiencies are as low as 40% with particulate emissions in the flue gases in excess of 3000 mg/Nm^2. In addition, a large percentage of unburnt carbonaceous ash has to be disposed of (Maninder 2012). The utilization of biomass waste or residue as energy source could help alleviate dependence on imported energy and its use continues to be a topical issue (Carnaje and Talagon 2018). Briquetting involves the collection of combustible materials that are not usable as such because of their low density and compressing them into a solid fuel product of any convenient shape that can be burned like wood or charcoal. Thus, the material is compressed to form a product of higher bulk density, lower moisture content, and uniform size, shape and material properties. Briquettes are easier to package and store, cheaper to transport, more convenient to use, and their burning characteristics are better than those of the original organic waste material. Briquetting is undergoing renewals, principally due to the convergence of three critical factors. First, the recent developments in briquette processing and binding have dramatically changed the economics of using fuel briquettes as an energy resource. Secondly, a shortage of firewood has become increasingly severe in most of the developing countries. Finally, there has been a steady increase in environmental concerns to address the problem of domestic and urban waste disposal (Katimbo and Kiggundu 2014).

Briquettes made from materials that cost little or no money to obtain such as a newspaper or partially decomposed plant waste or sawdust can be an alternate source of domestic and industrial energy to charcoal, firewood, gas, coal, and electricity. Briquettes production thereby turns waste materials into a fuel source. This is therefore attractive because it is a sustainable process (Emerhi 2011). A sawdust briquette is one of the most preferred briquettes. This involving compressing and extruding sawdust to make a reconstituted log that can replace firewood. The production of briquettes from sawdust exemplifies the potential of appropriate technology for wood waste utilization. It save strees that can prevent soil erosion and desertification by providing an alternative to burning wood for domestic and industrial heating and cooking. Also, it substitutes saw milling waste for a valuable resource (Sivakumar 2011).

1.1 Statement of the Problem

The population of Ethiopia depends on biomass almost for all everyday energy needs. Forest resources in Ethiopia have experienced so much pressure due to the increasing need for wood and wood products. Almost all people in Ethiopia use wood for cuisine purposes and as a source of heat in cold seasons. Highly dependence on wood results in deforestation and environmental pollution. Sawdust is a byproduct of all wood processing activities. It is difficult to store and transport sawdust within a small volume because it is bulky. Due to the requirement of excess land to store and low thermal efficiency of direct burning of sawdust, wood processing industries are forced to dispose of sawdust in an open area far from their working areas. This exercise emanates profit reduction and environmental pollution. Starch is one of the staple foods of carbohydrates in human nourishment. In addition to this, starch is an excellent binder type in briquetting technologies. Even if starch is a well-known binder type, it has to be substituted by easily available, low cost, eco-friendly and non-food materials. Therefore, using waste paper as a binder is an interesting material to replace starch in briquette production activities. Sawdust briquettes can be a good substitution of firewood because sawdust is readily accessible in a considerable abundance. The provision of a choice of energy origin is a means to hand over the best living standard of the community in terms of energy cost and environmental security. Therefore, the production of sawdust briquettes is a better means to have an environmentally sound energy source for the substitution of firewood.

2 Materials and Experimental Methods

The experimental process of characterization of the raw sawdust and briquettes, except gross calorific value which was determined in laboratory of Alternative Energy Development and Promotion Directorate laboratory under Ministry of Water Irrigation and Electricity, Addis Ababa, was carried out in Bahir Dar Institute of Technology, Faculty of Chemical and Food Engineering, Chemical Research grade Laboratory, Bahir Dar. Waste paper (any available paper such as old newspaper, used up exercise book, etc.)

and sawdust of Cupressus Lusitanica were collected for the production of briquettes. The sawdust was sun-dried and of which part's of it was screened to the average particle size of 0.5 mm, 1.5 mm, 3 mm, 4.8 mm and 6.8 mm. Both sieved and raw sawdust were sampled, labeled and stored for briquetting purpose. Waste paper was used as a binder during briquetting of sawdust in different proportions (wt/wt), notably 25%, 30%, 35%, 40%, and 45%.as a binder during briquetting of sawdust in different proportions, notably 25%, 30%, 35%, 40%, and 45%.

2.1 Preparation of Materials

2.1.1 Sawdust

The feedstock (sawdust) was collected, sun-dried for two days to reduce the moisture content. The raw sawdust was characterized in terms of moisture content, density, volatile matter, and ash content. The dried sawdust was used to produce sawdust briquettes. A portion of the dried sawdust was screened by standard mesh sizes of 1 mm, 2 mm, 4 mm, 5.6 mm and 8 mm which were arranged vertically starting from the smallest to the widest sieve size and mounted in an electrical sieve shaker. The sieves were shacked for 10 min using the shaker and sorted based on their particle measurement as presented in Fig. 1.

Fig. 1. Sawdust, A; passed through 1 mm, B; retained on 1 mm, C; retained on 2 mm, D; retained on 4 mm, E; retained on 5.6 mm, F; raw sawdust at the source.

2.1.2 Preparation of Binder

Briquetting of sawdust with rurally available cheap binding material will be best for power generation. The problem constituting the waste paper is enormous. How to dispose of this waste is becoming worrisome and it is generated every day. Mixing waste paper with sawdust briquettes could lead to better briquette performance and cost-effectiveness making this fuel more attractive to both producers and consumers (4).

The binder was prepared from waste paper. The waste paper (used up exercise books, newspapers, old books, and old exam papers) was collected, cut into small pieces, sampled and then soaked in water until it seems like porridge. Five levels of weight-weight percentages notably 25%, 30%, 35%, 40% and 45% on a dry basis, of each were considered.

2.2 Construction of Homemade Briquetting Press Machine

A homemade briquetting machine was constructed. It was constructed mainly from wood while some parts of it were made from metal. It was used to produce sawdust briquettes using waste paper as a binder at different proportions. It has five different parts which includes the main body/stand that supports the rest, four cylinders/molds connected each other by nails with supporting base, a plate base which covers the opening of the cylinders while pressing, the presser having four equal legs which are assembled with circular woods at their bottom ends to press down the well-mixed sample during briquette production and press arm, which is assembled on one side of the stand, to push down the presser by applying pressure on it (Fig. 2).

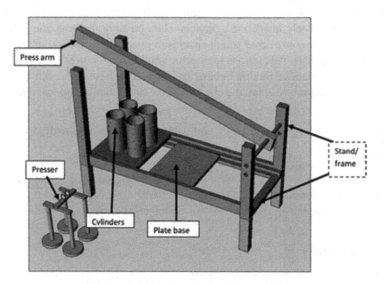

Fig. 2. Cad drawing of briquetting machine

The stand supports the rest parts having a press arm, is made from wood which is milled in size of 4 cm width, 5 cm length, and height of 61 cm on one side and 76 cm on another side. The two sides, 100 cm far from each other, are connected by wood using nails. There are two stages, having 2 cm width and height, on the stand to support and allow the movement of the base and cylinder supporter base to both ends of the briquetting machine. The press arm, which is used to push down the presser and having a dimension of 4 cm * 5 cm * 120 cm, is assembled at a height of 51 cm from the base. The cylinders, 10 cm in internal diameter and 20 cm in height, are made from metal sheets and are connected in a square arrangement. They are 2 cm far from each other and positioned vertically over the supporting base. They are drilled all around so that the water can escape when the feedstock is pressed. A flat wood base/plate which was placed on the first stage of the stand and which was free to move to both ends was used to cover the bottom end of molding- cylinder during compression and moved to one of the ends of the stand during ejection of the briquettes. The base and supporting base with the four cylinders are free to move to both sides of the stand on their own stage provided. The presser, its legs have a square arrangement, is made from pieces of metals. It is constructed in such a way that its legs with assembled circular wood can freely move up and down inside the cylinders during briquette production and ejection. The briquetting press machine is medium in size and all its five parts are not assembled permanently. During briquette production, all the parts are joined together temporarily but during the ejection of briquette, the base will be moved towards either of the two ends and the openings of the cylinders become free. Hence the briquettes will be free to leave out from the cylinders.

The briquetting press machine was constructed in such a way that first the main body/stand is constructed using different wood assembled each other permanently. Secondly, four cylinders were constructed and assembled to a wood base which has four holes to insert and support the cylinders. Thirdly four lids were constructed in such a way that they can move freely inside the cylinders while pushing the briquette downward. Finally, the presser is constructed which enables to press the feedstock inside the four cylinders simultaneously. All motions such as the vertical motion of presser in and out of the cylinders, the horizontal motion of base and supporting base with cylinders: up and down movement of arm press and the ejection of the briquettes are operated manually.

2.3 Determination of Physical and Combustion Properties of Sawdust Briquettes

2.3.1 Density

The mass and volume of briquettes were decided using digital balance and direct measurement of the dimensions of briquettes respectively. The density of briquettes was determined by taking the ratio of the mass of briquettes to their corresponding volume.

2.3.2 Porosity Index

A pre-weighed briquette was immersed in water for 30 s. Then the briquette was taken out of the water and reweighed to obtain the wet weight of briquette. The weight of water absorbed was the difference in the wet weight of the briquette and dry weight of the briquette. The porosity index was computed by dividing the mass of water absorbed into the mass of dry briquette.

2.3.3 Percentage Volatile Matter

A part of a briquette was kept in an oven in order to get the dry weight of the sample. The oven-dried sample was kept in the muffle furnace at a temperature of 550 for 10 min. After which the volatile matter in it has escaped, the crucible and its contents retrieved and cooled in a desiccators and weighed after cooling to obtain the weight of the volatile part of the sample i.e. the change in weight of the sample before and after transfer to the furnace. The analytical balance was used to weigh the weight of the sample. The percentage volatile matter is the ratio of the weight of volatile matter to the weight of the oven-dried sample.

2.3.4 Ash Content

A portion of a briquette was kept in an oven until it is free of moisture content. The oven-dried sample was then placed in a pre-weighed crucible. This was transferred into the furnace set at 900 and left for about 30 min. Then after, the crucible and its contents were transferred to desiccators and cooled. After cooling the crucible and its contents were reweighed to obtain the weight of the ash.

2.3.5 Heating/Calorific Value

The gross heating values of sawdust briquettes were determined using a standard Oxygen Bomb calorimeter (Parr 6200). A predetermined mass of each sample was burnt in the bomb calorimeter until complete combustion was obtained. The 6200 calorimeters will automatically make all of the calculations necessary to produce a gross heat of combustion for the sample.

3 Results and Discussions

Density, porosity index, volatile matter content, ash content and heating/calorific value of sawdust briquettes were examined. Waste paper percentage, molding cylinder/die diameter and particle measurement of raw sawdust were the agents used to estimate the features of sawdust briquettes.

3.1 Density

It is a substantial physical characteristic of briquettes. The maximum density of sawdust briquettes attained in this work was 322.62 kg/m^3. The highest value obtained in this experiment was lower than the lowest value obtained by M. Brožek (Brožek and Nováková 2012). This can be due to the difference in pressure applied resulted from the variation of the molding machine.

3.1.1 Effect of Particle Measurement

The outcome of particle measurement, at constant molding cylinder diameter of 10 cm, on the density of sawdust briquettes, is presented in Fig. 3.

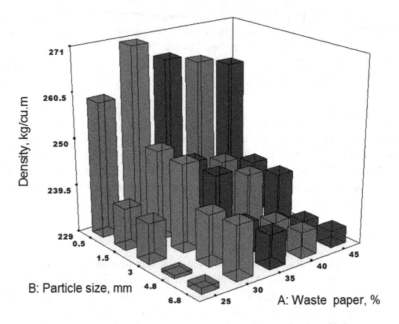

Fig. 3. Outcome of particle measurement of sawdust on density of briquettes.

The highest and lowest density of sawdust briquettes attained in this work was 280.78 kg/m^3 and 218.24 kg/m^3 at particle measurement of 0.5 mm and 4.8 mm respectively. The density of sawdust briquettes was decreased when the average particle size of sawdust increased for each waste paper percentage combinations. The smaller particle size is compact easily leading to a small number of pore spaces while the greater particles have a large number of pore spaces. As the number of pores increased, the void space within the briquette increases, the density will be decreased. That is why the density of briquettes was decreased when the average particle of sawdust was increased.

3.1.2 Effect of Waste Paper Percentage

Different levels of waste paper percentages were combined for each of sawdust of size of 0.5 mm, 1.5 mm, 3 mm, 4.8 mm and 6.8 mm at constant die diameter of 10 cm (Fig. 4).

The density of sawdust briquettes was increased as the percentage by weight of waste paper increased. Nevertheless, density was declined when the waste paper percentage transcended 30%. This implies the effect of waste paper percentage was not a significant factor; however, it has to be at the optimum percentage of 30% on the basis of density of briquettes since it could bring a change in the density of briquettes.

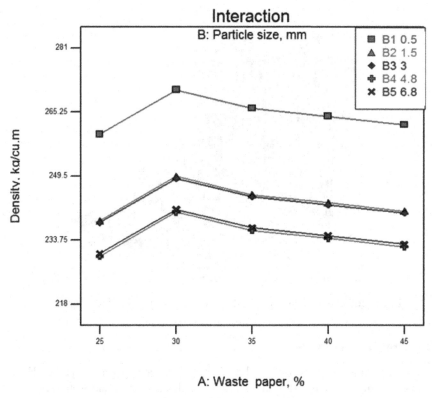

Fig. 4. The consequence of binder percentage on density of sawdust briquettes.

3.1.3 Effect of Molding Cylinder Diameter

The effect of pressure was considered by varying the diameter of the molding cylinders/die. The raw sawdust was sampled and combined with waste paper in different weight percentages. The same combination of sawdust and waste paper was briquettes using the three die-diameters. As can be seen from the Fig. 5, the maximum density (322.62 kg/m^3) was obtained for the die diameter of 6 cm and the least density (246.27 kg/m^3) from dying diameter of 10 cm. The density was decreased when the die diameter was increased. As the die geometry increases the contact area will also increase. Hence the applied pressure will be smaller and smaller because pressure and area have inverse relations.

Lower pressure allows a large number of pores hence the density will be lower. From the result obtained, it can be concluded that the molding cylinder diameter was the basic factor for briquetting and the optimum die diameter on the bases of density was attained at a smaller die diameter of 6 cm.

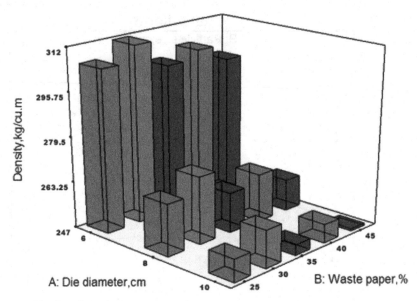

Fig. 5. Effect of molding cylinder diameter on density of sawdust briquettes

3.2 Porosity Index (Weight, %)

A briquette with a higher porosity index has lower water resistance capacity. Hence, briquettes having a low porosity index are desirable to storage and water resistance. The least porosity index (33.97%) was obtained from 0.5 mm particle size of sawdust while the highest (312.24%) was from sawdust of average particle size of 6.8 mm. At constant die diameter and waste paper (binder) percentage, the porosity of sawdust briquettes was raised when particle measurement getting larger and larger. This is due to increasing the average particle size introduces the number of pore space within the briquette by reducing the surface area thereby enhancing the penetration of water into the briquettes. The lower porosity index the higher resistance to water. If briquettes have a higher porosity index, it will absorb more water and will be disintegrated easily and also lowers the calorific value (Fig. 6).

As can be also seen from the figure, sawdust at lower average particle size has a lower porosity index. Hence desirable briquettes can be produced with a relatively smaller particle size of sawdust.

3.2.1 Effect of Waste Paper Percentage

As can be seen from Fig. 7, the porosity index (%) was increased as a waste paper percentage was increased. However, the change was insignificant.

As the percentage of waste paper increased, the amount of water absorbed also increased. This is due to that paper has a higher water holding capacity than sawdust. Therefore, it is better to use lower waste paper percentage and smaller average particle size of sawdust to produce a desirable briquette.

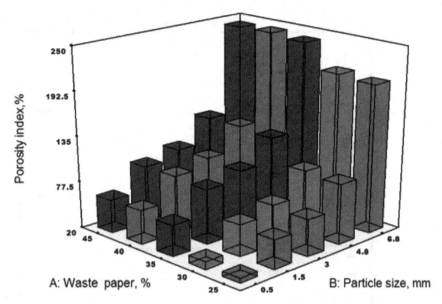

Fig. 6. Effect particle size of sawdust on porosity index of briquettes.

3.2.2 Effect of Die-Diameter

Results from the Fig. 8 shows that for increasing die diameter there was a corresponding increase in porosity index of briquettes.

This resulted from the variation of the pressure because pressure and die diameter have an inverse relationship. When the die diameter gets smaller and smaller, the pressure will become higher leading to fewer pores within the briquettes. Hence, the amount of water absorbed will be lower. This implies die geometry has a marked effect on the porosity index of briquettes. Therefore, briquettes with good quality can be produced at a lower die diameter of cylinders than higher diameters, other things being constant. At constant die diameter and waste paper percentage, the porosity index of briquettes produced from an average particle size of 1.5 mm was higher than that of briquettes produced from unscreened sawdust. This could be the consequence of the interlocking of particles due to the presence of different particle sizes. It can be concluded that it is better to use the raw sawdust instead of using very fine particle size of sawdust because it avoids the task of sieving.

3.3 Percentage Volatile Content

A briquette with a high percentage of volatile content is preferred. Because briquettes with lower percentage volatile content will release a high amount of smoke during burning which leads to environmental pollution.

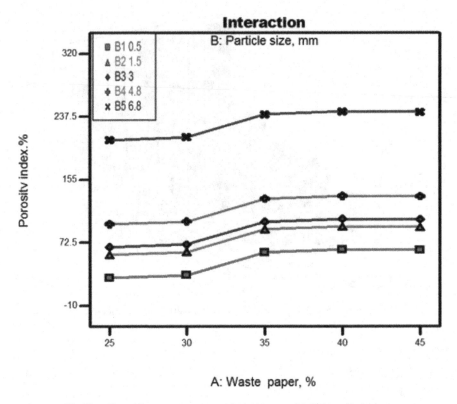

Fig. 7. Effect of waste paper percentage on porosity index of briquettes.

3.3.1 The Outcome of Particle Measurement of Sawdust

As can be seen from the figure, the highest and lowest percentage volatile content obtained was 90.56% and 70.46% respectively. As can be also observed from the figure, the volatile matter was generally increased with the direct proportion of particle size of sawdust. This could be the result of fine particles would be compacted easily compared to larger particles, other things being constant. If particles compacted well, the density will be higher leading to a low rate of mass transfer during the volatilizing phase hence the amount of volatile matter released will be reduced (Fig. 9).

However, it was decreased when the average particle measurement exceeded 3 mm. This can result from the size of individual particles of sawdust. As the average particle size of sawdust increases, the quantity of volatile content within it increases but the mass transfer rate within the particle itself is weak since the contact area is lower. The maximum value of volatile matter (90.56%) was obtained in the average particle size of sawdust of 3 mm. The result shows that briquetting of sawdust can give a better performance based on high volatile matter at 3 mm average particle size of sawdust.

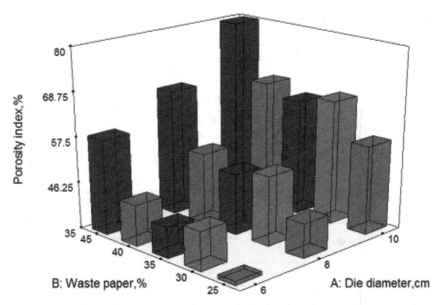

Fig. 8. Effect of die diameter on porosity index of briquettes.

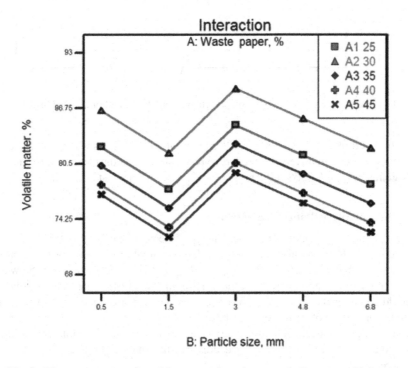

Fig. 9. The consequence of particle extent of sawdust on volatile matter of briquettes.

3.3.2 Effect of Die-Diameter

The raw sawdust was sampled and then bonded with soaked waste paper in five weight percentages notably 25, 30, 35, 40 and 45% at three die diameters.

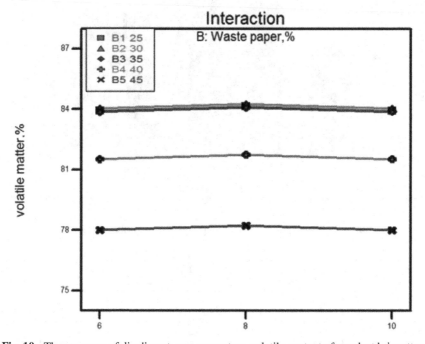

Fig. 10. The sequence of die diameter on percentage volatile content of sawdust briquettes.

As presented from Fig. 10, the volatile content of the briquettes was found to be the same in the three die diameters. The recorded result shows that the effect of die diameter has insignificant (p = 0.3568) effect on volatile matter of sawdust briquettes.

3.3.3 Effect of Waste Paper Percentage

The effect of binder percentage on the percentage of the volatile content of briquettes was displayed in Fig. 11. Generally, percentage volatile content of briquettes was increased when the waste paper percentage was increased from 25% to 30% but when the waste paper percentage was exceeded 30%, the volatile matter of briquettes was decreased. This could be either the waste paper has a lower volatile matter than sawdust or when the weight percentage of waste paper increases, the bond also increases. As a result, the mass transfer rate will be decreased i.e. the rate of volatilization will be hindered. That is why the volatile matter of the briquettes decreases when the weight percentage of waste paper increases.

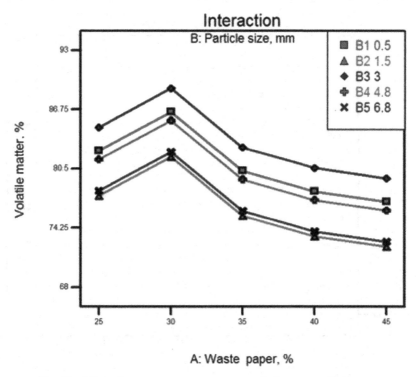

Fig. 11. Effect of waste paper percentage on volatile matter of briquettes.

3.4 Percentage Ash Content

Briquettes with lower ash content are preferred since they have higher calorific value and are suitable for cooking purposes.

3.4.1 Effect of Average Particle Size of Sawdust

The outcome of particle dimension on percentage ash content of briquettes was demonstrated in Fig. 12.

The highest percentage ash content (7.26%) was observed at an average particle size of 6.8 mm while the least (2.33%) was from sawdust of average particle size of 3 mm. Generally, as can be seen from the figure, the percentage ash content of briquettes was decreased when the average particle size of sawdust was increased. This could result from the presence of different pore spaces within the briquette. As the particle size increase, the number of pore space within the briquette will be higher. The smaller particles are less course, compacted easily, a small number of pore spaces leading to incomplete combustion. As the size of particles increases, the number of pore space within the sample will be greater allowing oxygen to flow easily within the sample. Therefore, briquettes with larger particles will be burn completely and the ash content will be smaller.

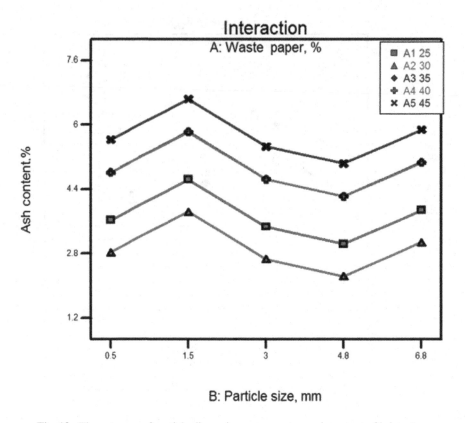

Fig. 12. The outcome of particle dimension on percentage ash content of briquettes.

3.4.2 Effect of Waste Paper Percentage

The highest percentage ash content (7.26%) was observed in 40% of the weight percentage of waste paper while the least value (2.33%) was from 30% waste paper. From Fig. 13, it can be observed that the quality of sawdust briquettes was increased when a percentage of waste paper was increased from 25% to 30%. This is because of the diminishment of the ash content. However, it was increased when the percentage of waste paper was exceeded by 30%. Hence for optimal performance waste paper at 30% could be added to sawdust briquettes.

This could be either waste paper has higher ash content than sawdust or as the percentage waste paper increase, the interparticle bond increases which can reduce the mass transfer rate within the briquette which can hinder the flow of oxygen. Therefore, it is better to use waste paper as a binder at the optimum weight percentage to produce briquettes with low ash content.

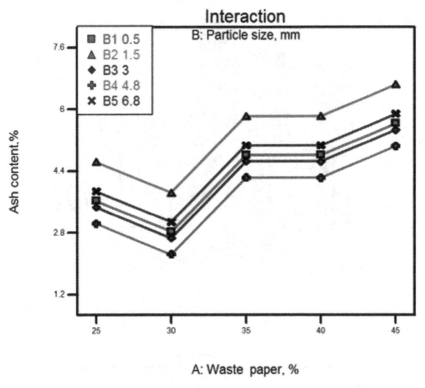

Fig. 13. Effect of percentage of waste paper on the ash content of briquettes.

3.4.3 Effect of Die-Diameter

The briquettes were produced from the raw sawdust using three different die diameters at a constant weight percentage of waste paper. The effect of die diameter on the ash content of briquettes was presented in Fig. 14.

The percentage ash content of briquettes produced at different die diameters shows almost similar values. From this result, it can be concluded that the effect of die diameter on the ash content of sawdust briquettes has an insignificant effect.

3.5 Percentage Fixed Carbon

Fixed carbon percentage is one of the consequential characteristics of briquettes. Briquettes with a smaller quantity of fixed carbon are chosen because they are effortless to burn. The percentage fixed carbon of sawdust briquettes obtained was ranged between 6.63% and 24.26%. The highest fixed carbon was observed in briquettes formed from sawdust of average particle size of 1.5 mm and waste paper percentage of 35%.

3.5.1 Effect of Average Particle Dimensions

The consequence of particle dimension on percentage fixed carbon of sawdust briquettes was presented in Fig. 15.

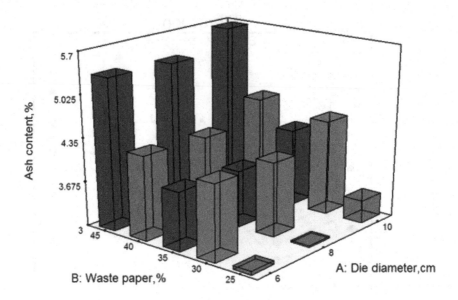

Fig. 14. Effect of die diameter on percentage ash content of briquettes

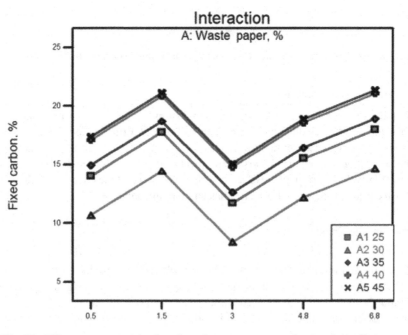

Fig. 15. Effect average particle size of sawdust on percentage fixed carbon of briquettes.

Generally, from the figure, it can be observed that the percentage fixed carbon of sawdust briquettes was increased as the particle dimension was increased. However, the change was not significant. A briquette with a high volatile matter was found to have a lower fixed carbon. Due to this fact the graph of volatile matter and fixed carbon, the effect of average particle size of sawdust, were found to be inverse of each other. The least fixed carbon percentage of briquettes obtained was at 3 mm average particle size of sawdust. Therefore, on the basis of the percentage fixed carbon of briquettes, it is better to use sawdust of average particle size of 3 mm.

3.5.2 Effect of Waste Paper Percentage

Generally, though there was no significant change, the fixed carbon percentage of briquettes was increased when the percentage of waste paper was increased. In the previous section, it was recorded that waste paper percentage and percentage volatile matter show inverse relations. If the volatile matter of the briquette is lower, the fixed carbon will be higher. So as waste paper percentage increases, the fixed carbon percentage also increases (Fig. 16).

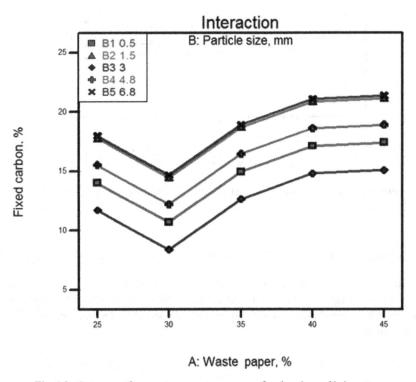

Fig. 16. Outcome of percentage waste paper on fixed carbon of briquettes.

3.5.3   Effect of Die-Diameter

Almost the same values, for each of dying diameters, were recorded for all types of briquettes briquette at different molding cylinder diameters. The effect of molding cylinder/die diameter on fixed carbon of briquettes was insignificant. Therefore, die diameter has not a meaningful effect on the chemical characteristics of briquettes based on the results attained (Fig. 17).

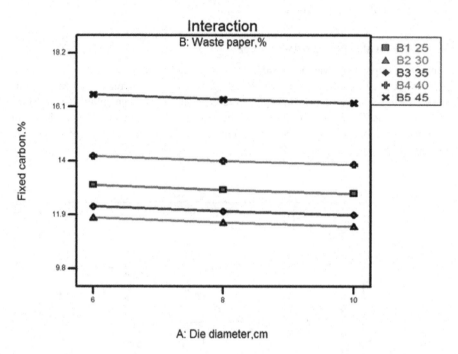

Fig. 17. Consequence of die diameter on percentage fixed carbon of briquettes.

3.6   Calorific Value

Calorific value is the most significant characteristic of briquettes. It is the measure of the amount of energy, in the form of heat, released during the burning of a unit mass of briquettes. Therefore, briquettes with higher calorific value are recommended to use for fuel application.

3.6.1 Effect of Average Particle Dimension of Sawdust

Figure 18 presents the difference in energy content of sawdust briquettes according to the average particle size of sawdust.

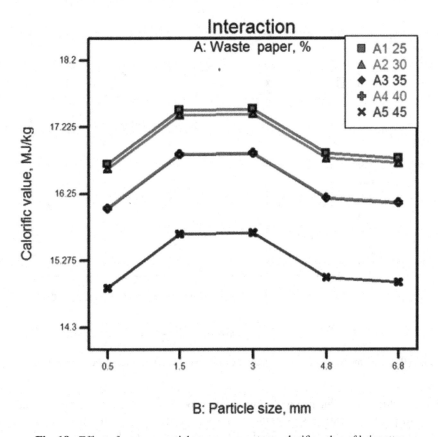

Fig. 18. Effect of average particle measurement on calorific value of briquettes.

The average particle dimension was found to be insignificant on the combustion characteristics of sawdust briquettes. The computed calorific value for all types of sawdust briquettes ranges from 14.5019 to 18.1332 MJ/kg. Therefore, sawdust briquettes are an excellent substituent for firewood for domestic cooking.

3.6.2 Effect of Waste Paper Percentage

As can be observed from the figure, for increasing waste paper percentage, there was a corresponding decrease in the calorific value of briquettes. This shows that the waste paper has to be added as small as possible to get briquettes with high energy content. As presented by Fig. 19, the calorific value of sawdust briquettes was significantly affected by percentage waste paper. Briquettes with low waste paper percentage produce higher

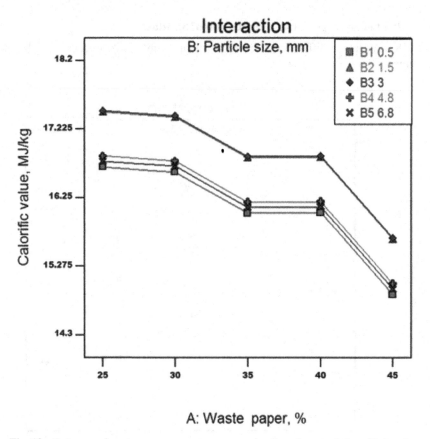

Fig. 19. Outcome of waste paper percentage on combustion characteristics of briquettes.

calorific value than briquettes with high waste paper percentages. It can be concluded that waste paper percentage is a significant factor in briquette production and the increase of waste paper percentage has reduced the calorific value of the briquettes.

3.6.3 Effect of Die-Diameter

The highest and the lowest calorific value of briquettes produced by using the three die diameters was 18.5832 MJ/kg and 15.1165 MJ/kg respectively. The calorific values of briquettes produced in different die diameters were almost constant it was discovered that the diameter of the molding cylinder/die has an insignificant effect (Fig. 20).

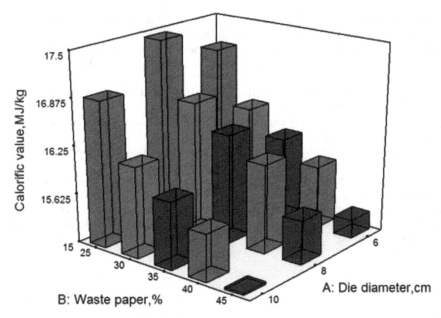

Fig. 20. Effect of die diameter on the calorific value of sawdust briquettes.

4 Conclusion

The paper focused on the very important physical and chemical characteristics of sawdust briquettes. For all types of sawdust briquettes, the highest and lowest values of density, porosity index, volatile matter, ash content, fixed carbon, and calorific value are 218.2–322.6 kg/m^3, 34–312.4%, 70.2–90.6%, 2.3–7.3%, 6.7–24.3% and 14.5–18.4 MJ/kg respectively. The figured physical and chemical properties of sawdust briquettes were interesting. The density and porosity index of sawdust briquettes were extensively affected by molding cylinder diameter and waste paper percentage. A considerable effect of particle size was observed on density, porosity index, and percentage volatile content of sawdust briquettes. The capability of the production of sawdust briquettes with good quality using only waste paper as a binder is an encouraging fact. Sawdust briquettes produced by using waste paper as a binder could be excellent augments to firewood for domestic cooking because it can be easily transported, stored, and used simply. Therefore, the production and utilization of sawdust briquettes using waste paper is sound and enhance environmental security.

References

Katimbo, A., Kiggundu, N.: Potential of densification of mango waste and effect of binders on produced briquettes. J. Agric. Eng. **16**, 146–165 (2014)

Emerhi, E.A.: Physical and combustion properties of briquettes produced from sawdust of three hardwood species and different organic binders. Adv. Appl. Sci. Res. **2**, 236–246 (2011)

Sivakumar, K., Sivaraman, B.: Effectiveness of briquetting bio mass materials with different ratios in 10 kW down draft gasifier. Int. J. Eng. Sci. Technol. 3 (2011)

Mahadeo, K., Dubey, A.K.: Study on physical and chemical properties of crop residues briquettes for gasification. Am. J. Energy Eng. 2(2), 51–58 (2014). https://doi.org/10.11648/j.ajee.201402 02.11

Kuti, O.: Impact of cherred palm kernel shell on the calorific value of composite sawdust briquette. J. Eng. Appl. Sci. 2, 62–65 (2007)

Brožek, M., Nováková, A.: Quality evaluation of briquettes made from wood waste. Res. Agric. Eng. 58(1), 30–35 (2012). https://doi.org/10.17221/33/2011-RAE

Maninder, R.S.: Using agricultural residues as a biomass briquetting: an alternative source of energy. J. Electr. Electron. Eng. 1(1) (2012)

Carnaje, N.P., Talagon, R.B.: Development and characterisation of charcoal briquettes from water hyacinth (Eichhornia crassipes)-molasses blend, 9 November 2018

Rajaseenivasan, T., Srinivasan, V.: An investigation on the performance of sawdust briquette blending with neem powder. Alexandria Eng. J. 55(3), 2833–2838 (2016). https://doi.org/10.1016/j.aej.2016.07.009

Antiviral Activity of *Aloe pirottae* A. Berger Root Extracts Against Influenza A and B Viruses, Picornaviruses and Dengue Virus: An Endemic Plant Species of Ethiopia

Akalu Terfa[1], G. Anuradha[1(✉)], Hailemicahel Tesso[1], Young Sik Jung[2],
Sang Un Choi[3], Sang Ho Lee[3], and J. Sreekantha Kumar[4]

[1] Adama Science and Technology University, Adama, Oromiya, Ethiopia
anuradha.g@astu.edu.et

[2] Cancer and Infectious Diseases Therapeutics Research Group, Korea Research Institute of Chemical Technology, Sinseongno, Yuseong, Daejeon 305-600, South Korea

[3] Bio and Drug Discovery Division, Korea Research Institute of Chemical Technology, Sinseongno, Yuseong, Daejeon 305-600, South Korea

[4] Department of Environmental Sciences, Acharya Nagarjuna University, Guntur, A.P, India

Abstract. This study is aimed to evaluate the antiviral studies of *Aloe pirottae* root extracts in Vitro on Influenza A and B viruses, Picornaviruses, and Dengue virus. During this study, crude methanol extract (MeOH) and its organic solvent fractions including n-hexane (HxF), chloroform (CHF), ethyl acetate (EAF) and n-butanol (BuF) of *Aloe pirottae* root in different concentrations were prepared and evaluated for a cytopathic effect (CPE) inhibitory assay for influenza virus and picornavirus and an immunofluorescence assay (IFA) for dengue virus. In vitro test revealed that *Aloe pirottae* root extracts have shown important effects in reducing both A and B influenza viruses, HRV B14 and EV-71(H) in MDCK cells, and DENV-2 replication in Vero cells. EAF exhibit more potential inhibitory activity with selectivity index >7.2 >17.8 and >8.5 than positive controls AMT with selectivity index not determined (ND), >47.6 and ND and RBV with selectivity index >2.9, >5.3 and >5 against PR8, HK and Lee, respectively. EAF exhibits the strongest anti-HRV B14 and anti-EV-71(H) activity in MDCK cells. Crude MeOH extract, EAF and BuF at both concentrations exhibit strong inhibition of DENV-2 induced CPE where as CHF and HxF at 20 μg/ml exhibit strong inhibition of DENV-2 production. The findings show significant inhibitory effect of *Aloe pirottae* root on influenza A and B viruses, HRV B14 and EV-71(H), and DENV-2 replication.

Keywords: Antiviral · Influenza A and B virus · Picornavirus · Aloe pirottae

1 Introduction

Viruses are generally classified in to DNA viruses and RNA viruses. They are responsible for causing number of diseases in both animals and plants. Influenza virus, Picornavirus

M. A. Delele et al. (Eds.): ICAST 2020, LNICST 384, pp. 27–35, 2021.
https://doi.org/10.1007/978-3-030-80621-7_2

such as rhinovirus and enterovirus-EV68 are examples of the causative agents of respiratory diseases [1, 2] and Dengue virus is one of the causative agents of acute febrile disease [3]. Despite the tremendous progress in human medicine, viral diseases, like SARS, acute febrile disease, acquired immunodeficiency syndrome (AIDS), and hepatitis are still the main cause of mortality in mankind. Emergence of latest drug-resistant viruses like influenza viruses and the lack of promising drugs and vaccines for several viral infections such as dengue viruses, rhinoviruses and enteroviruses have urged a requirement to developing new and effective chemotherapeutic agents to treat viral diseases. Crag and his colleagues have acknowledged that approximately 60% of the anti-tumor and anti-infective agents that are commercially available and utilized in clinical trials today are of natural products in origin [4]. Medicinal plants possess many active compounds, with high chemical diversity and biochemical specificity and offer major opportunities for identifying novel lead structures that are active against a broad range of assay targets. During this study *Aloe pirottae an* endemic medicinal plant of Ethiopia was selected for antiviral studies based on ethno pharmacological knowledge and native healers prescribing folk medicines. This plant features a history of traditional usage and wasn't studied for antiviral activity. *Aloe pirottae* Berger belongs to the family Aloaceae [5] and natively used as a folk medicine for the treatment of inflammation, viral, bacterial and fungal infections, malaria, ulcer, gastro-intestinal parasites, gallstone, eye diseases, constipation, burns, dermatitis, snake bite and as a insectifuge [6]. The target of this work is to assess the anti-viral activity of crude MeOH extract and its four organic solvent fractions of *Aloe pirottea* root against influenza virus strains A/Hong Kong/8/68 (H3N2, HK), A/Puerto Rico/8/34 (H1N1, PR8) and B/Lee/40 (Lee), picornavirus strains: rhino/HRV B14 and HRV A16; entero /EV 68, EV 71(H), CB3, PV3 using Cytopathic effect (CPE) reduction assay and for dengue/DENV-2 strain using an Immunofluorescence assay (IFA) method.

2   Materials and Methods

2.1   Chemicals and Reagents

The commercially available standard antiviral agents used in this study are ribavirin (RBV) and amantadine hydrochloride (AMT) obtained from Sigma (St Louis, MO), arbidol hydrochloride (ARB) from AK Scientific, Inc. (Mountain View, CA) and oseltamivir carboxylate (OSV-C) from US Biological (Swampscott, MA). Rupintrivir was synthesized in-house by I. Y. Lee. All solvents used for preparation of the extracts and purifications are HPLC-grade and obtained from Korea Research Institute of Chemical Technology, South Korea.

2.2   Plant Material

The plant material (root) of *Aloe pirottae* (Voucher No. A004/2017) was collected from Addis Ababa in November 2017 (see Fig. 1). The plant was identified and authenticated by Prof. Teshome Soromesa of the Biology Department, Addis Ababa University. The herbarium sheet of the specimen is preserved in the department of Biology, Addis Ababa University, Ethiopia.

2.3 Preparation of Plant Extract

The roots of *A. pirottae* were cleaned and cut into small pieces and air-dried at room temperature under shade. Then it was grounded to fine powder and was soaked in methanol in 3:1 ratio for 3 days. After 3 days methanol was squeezed out using rotary evaporator under reduced pressure at below 34 °C. This solid or semisolid material is named the crude methanol extract (MeOH). The MeOH is suspended in distilled water in the ratio of 1:10. This water suspension in separating funnel extracted each for 12 h three times with the water immiscible organic solvent in increasing polarity (n-hexane, chloroform, ethyl acetate and n-butanol) and shaken in 30-min interval. Whenever, the quantity of the organic solvent used was an equivalent as that of the water layer. The aqueous layer was extracted with the organic solvent in the order of increasing polarity and the organic layer was dried in the rotary evaporator. Each time, the collected organic solvent layer was combined and evaporated by rotary evaporator to dryness at temperature between 30–33 °C, and the small amounts of wet extracts from each solvent were then lyophilized by using vacuum dryer.

Fig. 1. *Aloe pirottae* Berger

2.4 Cells and Viruses

Influenza virus strains A/Puerto Rico/8/34 (H1N1) (PR8), Lee and A/Hong Kong/8/68 (H3N2) (HK) were obtained from ATCC. Influenza A viral PR8 and HK strains are propagated in 10-day-old chicken embryos at 37 °C for 3 days and influenza B virus (Lee) by infection of MDCK cells under serum-free conditions. Madin-Darby canine kidney (MDCK) cells and C6/36 mosquito cells (ATCC, Manassas, VA) were grown in minimum essential medium (MEM; Gibco/ Invitrogen, Carlsbad, CA) supplemented with 10% fetal bovine serum (FBS; Invitrogen) at 37 °C and 28 °C, respectively [7]. Picorna viruses were grown in RD cells. The cells maintained at 37 °C, 5% CO_2 in Dulbecco's Modified Eagle's Medium (DMEM) with 10% fetal bovine serum (FBS) [8]. The RD-SCARB2 (RDS) cell line stably over expressing hSCARB2 was cultured in 10% FCS-DMEM supplemented with puromycin (0.5 μg/ml; Clontech, Mountain View, CA, USA). Stocks stored at −80 °C until use, as described in the literature. Picornaviruses were provided by the Bio and Drug Discovery Division, Korea Research Institute of Chemical Technology, Korea. DENV-2 (New Guinea C strain) was purchased from the National Collection of Pathogenic Viruses, Culture Collections of Public Health England (Salisbury, Great Britain) and propagated in C6/36 cells. DENV viral titters were quantified by focus-forming assay on Vero76 cells [9].

2.5 Antiviral Assay

Cytopathic Effect (CPE) Reduction Assay: CPE reduction assay was used for influenza and picornavirus antiviral assay. In the CPE reduction assay, MDCK cells are seeded in 96-well plates and either mock-infected or infected with virus at a multiplicity of infection (MOI) of 0.001 50 plaque-forming units (PFU) of given virus per well [7]. After incubation for 1 h at 35 °C, the medium was removed, and test and standard chemicals were added, which were serially diluted in MEM containing 2 µg/ml TPCK-trypsin (Sigma). On day 3 post-infection (p. i.), the cell viability was measured after treatment with fluorescein diacetate (FDA; Sigma), as described by Kim et al. [10] and Schols et al. [11]. The 50% cytotoxic concentration (CC_{50}) and the 50% effective concentration (EC_{50}) values were calculated using Soft Max Pro Software (Molecular Devices, Sunnyvale, CA). The selectivity index (S.I.) is that the ratio of CC_{50} to EC_{50}.

Immunofluorescence Assay (IFA): The assay was used for DENV-2 antiviral assay. Vero cells were seeded on 96-well plates for DENV antiviral assay. After overnight incubation, cells were inoculated with DENV-2 at a multiplicity of infection (MOI) 0.2 for 2 h at 37 °C. Crude extracts were added at two different concentrations (20 µg/ml and 100 µg/ml). An immunofluorescence assay (IFA) used to detect dengue infection is optimized for the dengue high-throughput content imaging assay. Briefly, DENV-infected cells are detected by probing anti-DENV E (4G2) monoclonal antibody and Alexa Fluor 488 (A488)-conjugated goat anti-mouse IgG (H+L) (Invitrogen Molecular Probes, USA) as secondary antibody [7]. Cell nuclei counterstained with 5 µg/ml 4', 5-diamidino-2-phenyl indole (DAPI, Sigma-Aldrich, USA). After washing, digital images are acquired using Operetta® high content imaging system (Perkin Elmer, USA). The digital images were taken from 4 different fields of each well at 20X magnification. The percentage of inhibition was derived by using the formula; [1-(A488-positive cells/total cells)] × 100%.

3 Results and Discussion

There are reports on the antiviral properties of some Aloe species, however there is no reported work and data on antiviral activity of *Aloe pirottae*. Therefore, this is often the primary study of the antiviral activity of *Aloe pirottae* on human influenza A (PR8, BB, and KR; A/H3N2: HK) and B (Lee), viruses, picornaviruses HRV B14, HRV A16, CB3, PV3, EV68, EV 71(H) and DENV-2.In the anti-influenza virus assay, HxF, CHF and EAF exhibited strong antiviral activity against PR8, HK and Lee viral-induced cytopathic effect. Crude MeOH extract showed strong antiviral activity against PR8 and Lee affording 76% and 54% cellular protection, respectively. The most effective antiviral activity was obtained with CHF and EAF, which afforded complete cell protection against influenza A and B viral induced CPE (Table 1).

In cell cytotoxic effect assay, EAF exhibited significantly potent antiviral activity against PR8, HK and Lee with SI values of >7.2, >17.8 and >8.5, respectively, which was nearly 2.5-, 3.5- and 2- fold stronger than the positive control antiviral agent RBV against PR8, HK and Lee, respectively (Table 2). A literature survey indicated some

Table 1. Inhibition by *A. pirottea* root crude Methanol extract and its organic solvent layers of influenza PR8, HK and Lee viral replication. Results are expressed as percent of cell protection relative to control (100%).

S. no	Conc.	20 μg/ml			100 μg/ml		
	Extract/virus	PR8	HK	Lee	PR8	HK	Lee
1	MeOH	41%	44%	21%	76%	25%	54%
2	HxF	67%	73%	76%	−21%	−9%	−7%
3	CHF	117%	60%	97%	17%	24%	33%
4	EAF	69%	33%	65%	117%	100%	126%
5	BuF	10%	18%	12%	22%	6%	28%

extracts of Chinese herbs exhibiting anti-influenza activities in vitro, like Polygonum Chinese methanol extract inhibited PR8, HK and Lee viruses with SI values of 5.5, 7.8 and 5.4; EAF with SI values of 6.4, 13 and 5.9, respectively [12]. Some purified compounds inhibited PR8, HK and Lee viruses such as gallic acid (SI = 5.1, 6.3 and 6.5), ellagic acid (>3.7, >4.8 and >3.8), β-sitosterol (1.1, 1.0 and -), methyl gallate (16.6, 17.5 and 15.5) and caffeic acid (>7.9, >9.4 and >20.4). This study revealed that extracts of *A. pirottae* root showed higher anti-influenza A and B activity than reference antiviral reagent RBV and AMT. Therefore, these plant extracts exhibited significantly potent anti-influenza A and B activities and further study needed to isolate active principles and the exact mechanism underlying behind the activity.

In the anti-picornaviruses assay, EAF exhibit strong antiviral activity with cell viability 50% and 41% against HRV B14 and EV 71 (H) induced CPE. CHF exhibit strong antiviral activity with cell viability 46% against EV 71 (H) induced CPE. HxF exhibit moderate antiviral activity with cell viability 41% against EV68 induced CPE (Table 3). None of the extract/fractions at both concentrations had afforded >10% cellular viability against HRV A16, CB3 and PV3 replication. A literature survey indicated some extracts of Chinese herbs exhibiting anti- EV 71 (H) and coxsackievirus A16 (CVA16) activities in vitro, such as water extract of *H. cordata thumb* inhibited the CPE and plaque formation induced by EV71 and coxsackievirus A16 (CVA16), in Vero cells with an EC_{50} of 125.92 μg/mL. The *H. cordata thunb* extract (125 μg/mL) lowered the 50% viral RNA yield [13]. Geniposide, a primary component of *Fructus gardenia*, protected over 80% of cells against EV71 infection at a concentration of 3 mg/ml [14]. Pure compounds dihydroxy flavone, kaempferol, quercetin, hesperetin, and hesperidin isolated from Chinese herbal medicines *Chrysanthemum morifolium* reduced 80% of EV71-induced CPE at a concentration of 50 μM [15]. This study reveals that extract/fractions of *Aloe pirottae* root exhibited weak antiviral activity compared to some of Chinese herbal medicines against EV68, HRV B14 and EV 71 (H) induced CPE.

In the anti-DENV-2 assay (Table 4), the result demonstrate that when the cell was treated with 20 μg/ml of MeOH, HxF, CHF, EAF and BuF, infectivity by DENV-2 was reduced by 89%, 58%, 69%, 76% and 95% compared with that in untreated cells, respectively. MeOH, EAF and BuF at 20 μg/ml and 100 μg/ml exhibited significant protection

Table 2. Antiviral activity of HxF and EAF of *A. pirottea* root against influenza A and B viruses infecting MDCK cells[a]

	Toxicity $CC^b{}_{50}$ (μg/ml)	Antiviral activity ($EC^c{}_{50}$ μg/ml)			Selectivity index[d]		
		Flu A	Flu A	Flu B	Flu A	Flu A	Flu B
		H1N1	H3N2	-	H3N1	H1N2	H3N2
		PR8	HK	Lee	PR8	HK	Lee
HxF	19.6	7.9	6.5	6.4	2.48	3.01	3.06
EAF	>100.0	13.9	5.7	11.7	>7.2	>17.8	>8.5
AMT	>100.0	>100.0	2.1	>100.0	ND[e]	>47.6	ND
RBV	>100.0	35.0	18.8	20.0	>2.9	>5.3	>5.0
OSV-C	>100.0	0.5	<0.0055	0.6	>204.1	>200.00	>175.4

Solubility: Good, a The data presented are the means ± standard deviations (SD) for three independent experiments. b The CC_{50} is the 50% cytotoxic concentration, which is defined as the compound concentration that produces cellular toxicity of 50%. c The EC_{50} is the 50% effective concentration, which is defined as the compound concentration that reduces the replication of influenza viruses by 50% in the CPE reduction assay. d Selectivity index, CC_{50}/EC_{50}. The 50% cytotoxic (CC_{50}) and 50% effective (EC_{50}) concentrations are calculated from concentration-effect curves after linear regression analysis.

Table 3. Inhibition by *A. pirottea* root crude methanol extracts and organic solvent fractions of picornaviruses replication. Results are expressed as percentages of cellular viability relative to control (100%)[c].

Solvent	HRV B14		HRV A16		CB3		PV3		EV68		EV 71(H)	
	100[a]	20[b]	100	20	100	20	100	20	100	20	100	20
Me	0	0	0	0	0	−1	0	−1	−1	−1	−5	−1
HxF	1	3	−2	0	0	−1	−1	0	41	−6	4	−3
CHF	1	1	−1	0	0	−1	0	−1	−12	−11	46	−5
EAF	50	0	10	1	0	−1	0	−1	−13	4	41	4
BuF	1	0	0	0	0	−1	−1	−1	−1	1	−2	6
Sample conc. in μM	5	1	5	1	5	1	5	1	5	1	5	1
Rupintrivir	104	100	105	102	107	99	103	102	106	99	73	104

a, b concentration in μg/ml, c Results were expressed as the mean value of three independent experiments. The absorbance of the control group was defined as 100%. Sample results are compared with Rupintrivir.

cells against the cytopathic effect of DENV-2 by 82 and 89%, 65 and76%, and 78 and 95%, respectively. HxF and CHF at 100 μg/ml exhibit complete inhibition of DENV-2 replication. In general, the higher concentration was more effective against virus than cells (treatment mode) and the lower concentration was more effective against virus infection (protective mode). A literature survey indicates extracts of plants exhibiting anti- DENV-2 activities. The investigation conducted with *Cladosiphonfucoidan* [16] demonstrated that when the virus was treated with 10μg/ml of fucoidan, infectivity by dengue virus serotype 2 was reduced by 80% compared with that in untreated cells and the determined IC_{50} corresponded to 4.7 μg/ml. Glabranine and 7-O-methylglabranine showed significant inhibitory activity and presented 70% DENV-2 infection inhibition at 25 μmol/l [17]. The cyclohexenylchalcone derivatives pandurantin A and 4-hydroxypanduratin A inhibited DENV-2 by about 27.1 and 52.0% at 40 μg/ml, 66.7 and 78% at 80 μg/ml, 92.2 And 97.3% at 240 μg/ml, and 99.8 and 99.6% at 400 μg/ml, respectively. Pinocembrin was inhibiting by about 60% at μg/ml concentration [18].

Table 4. Inhibition by *A. pirottea* root crude methanol extract and organic solvent fractions of DENV-2 virus. Results are expressed as percentages of cellular viability and viral inhibition relative to control (100%)[a].

S. no	Conc./extracts	100 μg/ml		20 μg/ml	
		% viability	% inhibition	% viability	% inhibition
1	MeOH	82%	−3%	89%	−9%
2	HxF	1%	100%	58%	44%
3	CHF	0%	100%	69%	16%
4	EAF	65%	22%	76%	7%
5	BuF	78%	2%	95%	−16%

[a]Results were expressed as the mean value of three independent experiments

Methyl gallate which was purified from the methanol extract of *Quercus lusitanica* inhibited 98% of DENV-2 NS2B/3 protease at 0.3 mg/ml [19]. Squalamine discovered within the tissues of the dog fish shark (*Squalus acanthias*) was evaluated in vitro on dengue virus infection of human endothelial cells (HMEC-1). At the concentration of 40 μg/mL, dengue infection was inhibited by 60%. The infection was completely suppressed at 100 μg/ml [20]. This study revealed that extracts of *Aloe pirottea* root exhibited stronger anti-DENV-2 activity than extracts of many herbs and the active compounds of natural products in above previous reports. Therefore, these plants extracts exhibited significantly potent anti-dengue virus activities and merit further study to isolate active principles along with testing in vitro and in vivo and the exact mechanism behind their activity.

4   Conclusions

This work shows that MeOH extracts and organic solvent fractions of *A. pirottae* root in vitro exhibit strong anti-influenza A and B, moderate anti-picornavirus and strong anti-dengue-2 activity. The fact that the resulted broad spectrum antiviral activity demonstrates that traditional knowledge of medicinal plant usage and the utility of using ethno botanical leads is an efficient way of identifying biological antiviral activity. Strong anti-influenza A and B virus activity was demonstrated for extracts of *A. pirottae* root, which was stronger than the positive control antiviral agent RBV *A. pirottae* root significantly inhibited DENV-2 production as well as DENV-2 induced CPE and increased the cell viability of Vero cells. This data suggests that the extract and solvent fractions of this plant contains potent components utilized as wide-spectrum antiviral agents and applied to development of a unique herbal medicine. Therefore, further analysis has to be compelled to isolate the bio-active molecules and the exact mechanism underlying behind the activity.

Acknowledgements. The authors are very much grateful to the authority of ASTU for the financial support, Prof. Noah for the arrangement of laboratory works in KRICT, Prof. Jung for supervision and also Dr. Lee for the advice and help throughout the extraction and isolation process.

References

1. Carter, J., Saunders, V.A.: Virology: Principles and Applications, pp. 103–114. Wiley, Hoboken (2007)
2. Melnick, J.L.: Enteroviruses, polioviruses, coxsackieviruses, echoviruses and newer enteroviruses. Fields Virol. **3**, 655–712 (1996)
3. Mukherjee, A.K., Basu, S., Sarkar, N., Ghosh, A.C.: Advances in cancer therapy with plant based natural products. Curr. Med. Chem. **8**, 1467–1486 (2001)
4. Cragg, G.M., Newman, D.J., Snader, K.M.: Natural products in drug discovery and development. J. Nat. Prod. **60**, 623–639 (1997)
5. Demissew, S., Nordal, I.: Aloes and Lilies of Ethiopia and Eritrea, pp. 8–42 (2010)
6. Belayneh, A., Asfaw, Z., Demissew, S., Bussa, N.: Medicinal plants potential and use by pastoral and agro-pastoral communities in Erer Valley of Babile Wereda, Eastern Ethiopia. J. Ethnobiol. Ethnomed. **8**(1), 42 (2012). https://doi.org/10.1186/1746-4269-8-42
7. Kim, M., et al.: Inhibition of influenza virus internalization by (−)-epigallocatechin-3-gallate. Antiviral Res. **100**(2), 460–472 (2013). https://doi.org/10.1016/j.antiviral.2013.08.002
8. Wang, C.Y., et al.: Eupafolin and Ethyl acetate fraction of Kalanchoe gracilis stem extract show potent antiviral activities against Enterovirus 71 and Coxsackievirus A16. Evid. Based Complement. Alternat. Med. (2013)
9. Cos, P., Maes, L., VandenBerghe, D., Hermans, N., Apers, S., Vlietinck, A.J.: Ethnopharmacology – vol. II - Plants and Plant Substances Against AIDS and Others Viral Diseases (2015)
10. Kim, M., et al.: In vitro inhibition of influenza, A virus infection by marine microalga-derived sulfated polysaccharide p-KG03. Antiviral Res. **93**, 253–259 (2012)
11. Schols, D., Pauwels, R., Vanlangendonck, F., Balzarini, J., De Clercq, E.: A highly reliable, sensitive, flow cytometric/fluorometricassay for the evaluation of the anti-HIV activity of antiviral compounds in MT-4 cells. J. Immunol. Methods **114**, 27–32 (1988)
12. Tran, T.T., Kim, M., Jang, Y., et al.: Characterization and mechanisms of anti-influenza virus metabolites isolated from the Vietnamese medicinal plant *Polygonum chinense*. BMC Complement. Altern. Med. **17**, 162 (2017). https://doi.org/10.1186/s12906-017-1675-6

13. Lin, T.Y., et al.: Anti-enterovirus 71 activity screening of chinese herbs with anti-infection and inflammation activities. Am. J. Chin. Med. **37**(1), 143–158 (2009)
14. Lin, Y.J., et al.: Inhibition of enterovirus 71 infections and viral IRES activity by Fruct-us gardeniae and geniposide. Eur. J. Med. Chem. **62**, 206–213 (2013)
15. Tsai, F.J., et al.: Kaempferol inhibits enterovirus 71 replication and internal ribosome entry site (IRES) activity through FUBP and HN RP proteins. Food Chem. **128**(2), 312–322 (2011)
16. Kroeger, A., Nathan, M.B.: Dengue: setting the global research agenda. Lancet **368**, 2193–2195 (2006)
17. Sánchez, I., Garibay, F.G., Taboada, J., Ruiz, B.H.: Antiviral effect of flavonoids on the dengue virus. Phytother. Res. **14**, 89–92 (2000)
18. Kiat, T.S., Pippen, R., Yusof, R., Ibrahim, H., Khalid, N., Rahman, N.A.: Inhibitory activity of cyclohexenylchalcone derivatives and flavonoids of fingerrot, Boesenbergia rotunda (L.), towards dengue-2 virus NS3 protease. Bioorg. Med. Chem. Lett. **16**, 3337–3340 (2006)
19. Rahman, N.A., Hadinur, B., Muliawan, S., Rashid, N.N., Muhamad, M., Yusof, R.: Studies on Quercus. lusitanic extracts on DENV-2 replication. Deng. Bull. **30**, 260–269 (2006)
20. Zasloff, M., et al.: Squalamine as a broad-spectrum systemic antiviral agent with therapeutic potential. Proc. Natl. Acad. Sci. USA **108**, 15978–15983 (2011)

Groundwater Quality Assessment of Chilanchil Abay Watershed: The Case of Bahir-Dar City Waste Disposal Site

Dargie Haile[1](✉) and Nigus Gabbiye[2]

[1] Department of Chemical Engineering, Institute of Technology, Woldia University, P.O. Box 400, Weldiya, Ethiopia
[2] Department of Chemical Engineering, Bahir-Dar Institute of Technology, Bahir-Dar University, Bahir Dar, Ethiopia

Abstract. Groundwater has been under increasing threat of pollution in recent years due to improper management of the vast amount of wastes generated by various human activities. Improper dump sites have served many years as an ultimate disposal site for all types of waste; municipal solid waste, industrial sewage and hazardous waste in developing countries such as Ethiopia. Physical, chemical and biological processes interact simultaneously to bring about the overall decomposition of the wastes. One of the by-products of this mechanism is chemically laden leachate and it is a potentially hazardous waste from waste disposal sites. If not, deal properly, such kind of dumping site can cause pollution to groundwater (because of Leachates) and surface water (through contaminant transportation by flooding and groundwater movements). Therefore, this study investigates the spatial and temporal variation of groundwater quality within the Chilanchil Abay watershed during dry and wet season due to the waste disposal site of the Bahir Dar city. Water samples were collected from 6 sampling points of groundwater from 30th March to 20th August by a monthly period. Over 10 water quality parameters such as pH, TDS, Electrical conductivity, Turbidity, Temperature, DO, BOD, COD, TC, NO3- and PO43-, were analyzed. Moreover, the overall status of the groundwater quality of the study area was evaluated by the Canadian Water Quality Index. Based on the result of this model the status of the groundwater sample points throughout the study area were raged from 42 to 46.2 (marginal status).

Keywords: Bahir-Dar city waste disposal site · CCMEWQI · Chillan Chile Abay watershed · Groundwater · Seasonal variation

1 Introduction

Water is the most bountiful asset on earth, yet just 3% are available for human exercises while the excess is available in the sea as a salt water (Love and Luchsinger 2014). It could be accessible in different structures and amount, yet its utilization for different objects is the subject of value. Of the apparent multitude of ecological worries that non-industrial nations face, the absence of satisfactory and clean water remains the most

M. A. Delele et al. (Eds.): ICAST 2020, LNICST 384, pp. 36–58, 2021.
https://doi.org/10.1007/978-3-030-80621-7_3

difficult issue (Markandya 2006). When tainted, groundwater may everlastingly stay dirtied without cure or treatment. Sicknesses may jump up through water contamination, particularly groundwater pollution, and quickly spread past human desire in view of its stream (Afolayan et al. 2012). Wastesof various sorts, generally strong wastesare the significant contribution of dumpsites/landfills. Concerning the hydrological investigation of groundwater, it streams from regions of higher geology towards zones of lower geography, accordingly achieving the assessment of the degradable material which structures leachate and sully the groundwater of the study area. Sadly, groundwater is very frequently thought to be no longer of any concern except for it requires extraordinary consideration. Groundwater isn't just preoccupied for flexibly or stream-controlled purposes, however it likewise normally takes care of surface - waters through springs and entries into waterways and it is regularly significant in supporting wetlands and their environments. Evacuation or redirection of groundwater can influence all out stream. A decrease in either nature of amount of the releasing groundwater can altogether impact surface water quality and the achievement of water quality norms. Surface water and groundwater are along these lines personally connected in the water cycle, with numerous normal issues. On the off chance that groundwater gets contaminated, it is troublesome, if certainly feasible, to restore. The moderate pace of groundwater stream and low microbiological movement, limit any self-refinement. Open and inappropriate unloading locales have been served numerous years as a definitive removal site for a wide range of waste; metropolitan strong waste, mechanical sewage and dangerous waste in non-industrial nations (Nathanson 2015). Physical, substance and organic cycles connect all the while to achieve the general decay of the squanders. One of the side-effects of this component is artificially loaded leachate and it is a conceivably unsafe waste from garbage removal destinations. If not manage legitimate waste administration, such sort of unloading site can make contamination groundwater (as a result of Leachates) and surface water (through foreign substance transportation by flooding, wind and ground water development from the open dump destinations). The Bahir-Dar city open site is among the inappropriate open dump site and situated in a spot where various individuals are living near. The people group who are living close to the removal site (in a place of downstream and upstream) are utilizing dirtied ground and surface water for their everyday exercises. Because of this it turns into a lot or danger to those networks with respect to the water quality perspective. Subsequently, the focal point of this study was to survey and assess the water quality in that watershed, particularly close to this garbage removal site to inspect its impact on ground and surface water quality.

2 Methodology

2.1 Descriptions of the Study Area

Eriamecharia municipal waste disposal site is 5 km far away from Bahir Dar city, Ethiopia on the highway to Addis Ababa and TIS Abay waterfall. It is part of the territory of the rural community of "sebatamit". As per the Central Statistics Agency of Ethiopia (CSA 2007 G.C), 3,053 females and 3,348 males a total of 6,401 populations are found around the dumpsite. Its geographical coordinates are: latitude 11.54, longitude 37.38 and altitude of 1803 m at 3° and its elevation above sea level is 1801 m. The height and width of this irregular shape disposal site are 384 m (by the side of the agricultural land of Eriamecharia) and 174 m (by the side of the road of sebatamit towards Addis Ababa) respectively. It has neither been equipped with liners nor leachate collection system before ten years up to now. This site has not been designed systematically before being used for disposal/dumping of the waste. Furthermore, no environmental impact assessment has been carried out before the selection of this place to be a waste disposal site. Trucks and separate vehicles from different parts of the city collect and bring the waste to this site and dump in an anarchic way. The waste is dumped as such without segregation. On the other hand, the minimum amount of solid waste which is generated from the city and dumped in the site is, residential waste 12,610 kg/day, commercial 4,202 kg/day, service provider 988 kg/day, municipal waste 1,044 kg/day, total 22,774 kg/day (Source: solid waste characterization and quantification of the Bahir Dar city report, 2007). But currently, the minimum amount of waste dumped to the site is 31,321 kg/day (source: Authors observation).

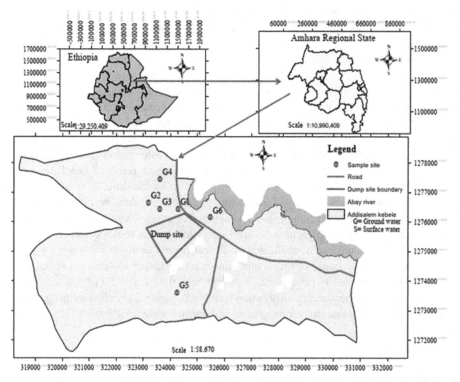

Fig. 1. Topographic map of the study Area.

2.2 Sample Collection, Preservation and Laboratory Analyses

Groundwater samples were collected from the chose test territories close to the dump-site called locally Zebir, to the research facility for the study. Those six inspecting focuses were picked dependent on their availability, closeness to contamination sources, for example, common locales, cabin. Worldwide Positioning System pilot (GPS etrex VISTA HCX) was utilized to decide the genuine places of the inspecting focuses and referred to guarantee consistency in the testing focuses during resulting examining periods. The testing focuses were painstakingly chosen to incorporate the upstream, and the downstream networks. Taking the samples was begun during the dry season from the period of March and proceeded with a wet season up in the long stretch of August from all the six sample points. Groundwater tests were collected from the profundity of 5–12 m drill openings by utilizing an untamed water snatch sampler 3 L limit arranged with a straightforward draw - ring that took into account inspecting at different water profundities of a borehole for groundwater tests [9]. To evaluate the water quality, water samples were kept in 1 L polyethylene plastic bottles cleaned with cleaned with metal-free soap, washed with deionized water lastly drenched by 10% nitric corrosive for 24 h, at long last flushed with super unadulterated water. All water samples were put away in a refrigerator and conveyed around the same time to the research center and kept at a consistent temperature of 4 °C [10]. Water quality boundaries, for example, temperature, pH, electrical conductivity, total dissolved solids, turbidity, salinity were measured with convenient YSI Pro 30 Multiparameter (model HI 98130 HANNA). Other water quality parameters analyzed include, dissolved oxygen (DO) using HI 98193 dissolved oxygen meter BOD5 using BOD5 incubated in the presence of NaOH, COD using COD analysis method within in the presence of standard potassium dichromate, sulfuric acid reagent, ferroin indicator and standard ferrous ammonium sulfate titrant and total coil form was done using a membrane filter method. Phosphates (PO_4^{2-}) and nitrate (NO_3^-) were determined using the method of palintest Spectrophotometer (WAGTECH 8000). All the strategies for lab investigation were directed by the Standard Methods for the Study of Water and Wastewater (Apha Awwa 1998) [11].

2.3 CCME Water Quality Index Procedure

The CCME WQI model comprises of three proportions of fluctuation of chose water quality goals (Scope; Frequency; Amplitude) [12]. The "Scope (F1)" the quantity of factors not meeting water quality objectives. The "Frequency (F2)" the occasions these goals are not met ("bombed tests"). The "Sufficiency (F3)" speaks to the sum by which bombed tests don't meet their destinations. These three elements consolidate to deliver a unitless incentive somewhere in the range of 0 and 100 that speaks to the general water quality. The detailing of the WQI as portrayed in the Canadian Water Quality Index 2001 specialized Report is as per the following. The measure for scope F1 is calculated as follows

$$F1 = \left(\frac{\text{Number of failed variables}}{\text{Total numbers of variables}} \right) * 100 \tag{1}$$

The measure for frequency F2 is calculated as follows:

$$F2 = \left(\frac{\text{Number of failed tests}}{\text{Total numbers of tests}} \right) * 100 \tag{2}$$

The measure for amplitude, F3 is calculated as follows.

The excursion is the number of times by which an individual concentration is greater than (or less than, when the objective is a minimum) the objective. When the test value does not exceed the objective:

$$\text{Excursion} = 100 - \left[\frac{objective}{\text{failed to values}}\right] - 1 \tag{3}$$

For cases in which the test value exceeds the objective.

$$\text{Excursion} = 100 - \left[\frac{\text{failed test value}}{\text{objective}}\right] - 1 \tag{4}$$

The collective amount by which individual tests are out of compliance is calculated by summing the excursions of individual tests from their objectives and dividing by the total number of tests (both those meeting objectives and those not meeting objectives). This variable, referred to as the normalized sum of excursions (nse) is calculated as:

$$nse = \sum_{i=1}^{\infty} \frac{[Excursions]}{number\ of\ tests} \tag{5}$$

F3 is then calculated by an asymptotic function that scales the normalized sum of the excursions from objectives (nse) to yield a range between 0 and 100.

$$F3 = \left(\frac{nse}{0.01_{nse} + 0.01}\right) \tag{6}$$

The water quality index (CCME WQI) is then calculated as:

$$\text{CCMEWQI} = 100 - \left[\frac{\sqrt{F_1^2 + F_1^2 + F_3^2}}{1.732}\right] \tag{7}$$

The divisor 1.732 normalizes the resultant values to a range between 0 and 100, where 0 represents the "worst" water quality and 100 represents the "best" water quality.

3 Results and Discussion

3.1 Spatial and Temporal Variation of Groundwater Quality

3.1.1 Spatial and Temporal Variation in Physical Characteristics of Groundwater

The result of spatial and temporal variation of groundwater physical parameters measured in all six sampling points throughout the study time are presented in below table.

Total dissolved solid (TDS):- The total dissolved solids are a sign of the level of disintegrated substances, for example, metal particles in the water test. In this investigation, the measure of disintegrated strong in the ground water tests were gone from 1294.33 ± 6.35 to 1488 ± 12.12 mg/L With a mean value of 1408.86 ± 25.52 mg/L during the

Table 1. Seasonal and temporal variation in physical parameters of groundwater.

Sampling sites	E.C (µS/m)		TDS (mg/L)		Turbidity (NTU)		Temperature (°C)	
	Dry season	Wet season	Dry season	Wet season	Dry season	Wet season	Dry season	Wet season
SS1	2037 ± 34.1	842.33 ± 32.5	1343.67 ± 32.72	585.83 ± 30.09	6.78 ± 0.705	24.71 ± 4.39	26.4 ± 0.36	21.87 ± 1.76
SS2	2183.33 ± 176.29	804.67 ± 16.80	1294.33 ± 6.35	560.5 ± 44.21	6.98 ± 0.60	27.12 ± 1.40	24.37 ± 3.88	21.63 ± 2.03
SS3	1939.33 ± 36.295	869.667 ± 71.93	1443.33 ± 36.94	717.67 ± 31.501	7.32 ± 0.43	18.94 ± 0.55	26.7 ± 0.56	20.97 ± 2.59
SS4	2211 ± 62.65	805.667 ± 56.37	1427.83 ± 26.71	617.33 ± 69.17	7.83 ± 0.38	22.12 ± 5.63	25.3 ± 2.022	23.23 ± 0.61
SS5	2271 ± 24.02	866.67 ± 37.541	1488 ± 12.12	843.67 ± 89.07	13.85 ± 3.35	32.33 ± 3.512	28.73 ± 1.36	22.3 ± 2.04
SS6	2220 ± 20.66	901.67 ± 114.18	1456 ± 38.31	755.67 ± 110.74	12.4 ± 4.82	31.09 ± 2.87	27.4 ± 1.42	23.503 ± 0.54

dry season while in a wet season from 560.5 ± 44.21 to 843.67 ± 89.07 mg/L with a mean value of 680.11 ± mg/L (Fig. 1). The findings of the investigation showed that the deliberate mean values of total dissolved solid during the dry season (1408.86 ± 25.52 mg/L) and wet season (680.11 ± 62.47 mg/L) were within the WHO's reasonable limit (500–1500 mg/L). Be that as it may, on the base of occasional variety all values of total dissolved solid during the dry season were higher than the values of the wet season (Fig. 1). This might have been because of the higher temperatures saw during the dry season which encouraged disintegration, particle trade limit, desorption and enduring cycles. Additionally, during the dry season borehole water vanished and ionic fixations expanded. The criticalness of this transient variety was upheld by the measurable consequence of single direction ANOVA. On The base of spatial variety in both dry and wet season the most extreme values of all total dissolved solid were seen at SS5 and SS6 though the base an incentive for dry and wet season recorded at SS2 (Fig. 1). This was because of the area of those sample points (SS5 and SS6) were beneath the garbage removal site which is helpless to more farming overflow and released city squander stream openly from the landfill site while for SS2 over the landfill site.

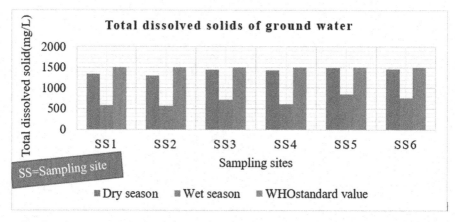

Fig. 2. Seasonal variation in total dissolved solid of ground water quality in the study area

Temperature:- The temperature of ground water samples investigated have a mean temperature values of 26.54 ± 1.58°C during the dry season with the most noteworthy temperature value of 28.73 ± 1.36°C at SS5.The mean temperature during the wet season was 22.25 ± 1.59 °C, with the most elevated value of 23.5033 ± 0.54 °C at SS5 and SS6 (Table 1). From Table 1, one can see that the mean temperature during the dry season was higher than wet season because of the predominant air conditions. A higher number of daylight hours would normally suggest lower relative stickiness, a temperature increments of water bodies because of conduction and convection measures by the earth covering. This shows that the temperature of ground water is lower in the wet season than in the dry season. WHO report (2006), specifies that water for drinking and homegrown purposes ought to have a temperature not surpassing 30–40 °C. Accordingly, temperature esteems recorded for ground water in the study region were inside the WHO passable breaking point. By and large temperature changes influence pH, electrical conductivity, sorption measures, complexation, speciation, precipitation, redox responses, stream rate, particle trade limit, solvency of gases and additionally different accumulates, just to specify however a couple. Additionally, increment in temperature diminishes the measure of disintegrated oxygen, quickens nitrification and oxidation of smelling salts to nitrates and prompting oxygen lacking water climate. This builds harmfulness of pesticides and weighty metals in drinking water. Temperature increment in drinking water prompts a less attractive water taste. By and large, the ANOVA result shows that all the actual properties of ground water quality talked about above were seen to be altogether influenced by the season. This implies the distinction with respect to prepare was genuine however the distinction with respect to the event of test site was because of chance from the part of SPSS.

Electrical conductivity:- Conductivity in groundwater is influenced by the topography of the zone through which the water streams. In this study, the values of electrical conductivity at the six examples of groundwater during dry season went from 1939.33 ± 36.295 to 2271 ± 24.02 µS/cm (Fig. 2) with a mean value of 2143.61 ± 58.999 µS/cm while in a wet season it fluctuates from 804.67 ± 16.80 to 901.667 ± 114.18 µS/cm with a mean value of 848.44 ± 54.88 µS/cm. The outcomes show that the mean values of electrical conductivity for the dry season were higher than the electrical conductivity of the wet season (Fig. 2). Apparently the qualities for the dry season surpasses WHO'S standard constraint of 1000 µS/cm for drinkable water. This could be because of water vanishes during the dry season and grouping of particles increments thus electrical conductivity expands (the expansion in electrical conductivity was because of dissipation of water in under groundwater channels which expanded the centralizations of disintegrated salts or directing substances in the borehole water frameworks) and in the wet season, there is the weakening of the particles because of water expanding under groundwater volumes bringing about an abatement in electrical conductivity [13]. The discoveries of high-esteem E.C in a dry season during the study period was comparative with the investigation of [14] who have done the appraisal of weighty metals in the groundwater wells in the region of Nyanza metropolitan Solid waste in Kigali City-Rwanda and discovered the higher value of E.C during the dry season. From the information of dry season, the greatest qualities were acquired at SS5, SS6 andSS4 separately with a base an incentive at SS3 while in a wet season most extreme qualities were recorded efficient at SS6, SS3 andSS5 with a base an incentive at SS2 (Fig. 2). These distinctions in all values of the dry and wet season were because of the area of the sample points from the garbage removal site and different wellsprings of contamination. By and large, Electrical conductivity esteems give a helpful marker to spatial or potentially worldly changes in deliberation, salt water interruption; energize instrument, and so forth prompting diverse groundwater characteristics in wet and dry seasons.

Turbidity:- The value of turbidity reflects the transparency in water. It is brought about by the substances present in water in suspension. In characteristic waters it is brought about by earth, residue, natural issue, phytoplankton and other tiny life forms. Mean turbidity esteems recorded gave an outline of the varieties in groundwater quality during wet and dry seasons. In the dry season, the value of turbidity at all six samples of groundwater were ranged between 6.78 ± 0.705 to 13.85 ± 3.35NTU with a mean value of 7.25 ± 0.56NTU while in the wet season from 18.94 ± 0.55 to32.33 ± 3.512NTU

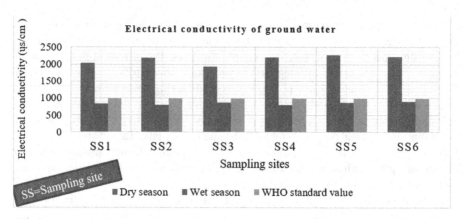

Fig. 3. Seasonal variation in Electrical conductivity of groundwater quality in the study area.

with a mean 26.0517 ± 3.056NTU (Fig. 3). As one can see from Fig. 3 underneath the mean values of turbidity recorded in the wet season(26.0517 ± 3.056NTU) were higher than WHO's (2006) passable constraints of 5-25NTU just as from the mean values of dry season (7.25 ± 0.56NTU). This may have been because of the coagulation of broke down substances in the boreholes, particles from enduring activities in the underground streams and surface overflow from farming fields around the groundwater sources, broken up dirt and mud materials into the groundwater through invasion. This implies during a precipitation, particles from the waste removal site and encompassing area are washed into the water sample points and filtering into groundwater making the water a sloppy earthy colored tone, demonstrating water that has higher turbidity esteems. Additionally, during the wet season, water speeds are quicker and water volumes are higher, which can all the more effectively work up and suspend material from the stream bed, causing higher turbidities. The purpose behind the dry season to be lower was a direct result of the decrease in overflow material, encourages, suspended solids and shaded disintegrated substances which added to the turbidity of the sample points from the waste removal site. This higher value of turbidity in a wet season looks like crafted by [15] who surveys the occasional variety in Physico-substance properties of groundwater around Karu abattoir. Figure 3 shows that, on the base of spatial variety in both dry and wet season the greatest values of turbidity were seen at SS5 and SS6 whereas the base an incentive at SS1 for the dry season and at SS3 for the wet season. This was because of the area of those sample points (SS5 and SS6) were underneath the waste removal site which is helpless for more agrarian spillover and released metropolitan waste stream uninhibitedly and various individuals are utilizing those sample points in like manner for their homegrown reason, accordingly, particles won't get enough habitation time for settling while SS1 and SS3are situated over the landfill site which is normal the impact of waste removal site is non-critical. By and large, the high turbidities establish a wellbeing hazard for the youngsters burning-through this water. High turbidity likewise demonstrates a higher measure of all out suspended solids which may incorporate microorganisms, such as microbes or parasites just as an expansion in the convergence of minerals [16]. Watershed highlights, such as geography, compound manure and pesticide overflow from rural activity metropolitan advancement activity, geology, vegetation and precipitation functions can all significantly impact crude water turbidity in the study area.

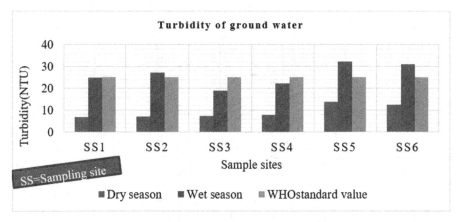

Fig. 4. Seasonal variation in turbidity of groundwater quality in the study area.

3.1.2 Spatial and Temporal Variation in Chemical Characteristics of Groundwater

The result of spatial and temporal variation of groundwater chemical parameters measured in all six sampling points throughout the study time are presented in below table (Table 2).

Groundwater pH:- The value of pH is one of the most habitually utilized tests in water science. The pH results for the groundwater tests from the study area went from 6.67 ± 0.42 to 9.2 ± 0.16 with a mean value of 8.49 ± 0.33 for the dry season and went from 6.48 ± 0.67 to 7.59 ± 0.095 (Fig. 4) with a mean value of 6.88 ± 0.49 for wet seasons. The outcome study of water tests shows the pH of groundwater was over the WHO suitable constraint of 5.5–7.5 for drinking water for both wet and dry season (Fig. 4 below). This could be because of run off from the network (Humans add to raised pH fundamentally as supplement overflow most usually compost). As from the Fig. 4 beneath demonstrated at SS1 and SS5registered the most reduced and the most elevated pH esteems all through the time of study separately. In the base of occasional variety, the mean value of pH in groundwater was lower in the wet season than in the dry season (Fig. 4). This may have been expected to during wet season precipitation consolidates with carbon dioxide can impact the water toward acridity, lower temperature consequently lower TDS esteems, adsorption cycles and lower particle trade limit occurring [17]. The discoveries of lower esteem pH in a wet season during the study period was comparable with crafted by [18] who explores occasional variety in Physico-synthetic attributes of country groundwater of Benue state, Nigeria and discovered lower value of pH during wet season. Hence, carbon dioxide is the most widely recognized reason

Table 2. Seasonal and temporal variation in chemical properties of ground water

Sampling sites	Ph		DO (mg/L)		BOD (mg/L)		COD (mg/L)	
	Dry season	Wet season	Dry season	Wet season	Dry season	Wet season	Dry season	Wet season
SS1	6.67 ± 0.42	6.48 ± 0.67	2.16 ± 0.087	9.18 ± 0.17	2.23 ± 0.10	2.81 ± 0.37	61 ± 2.65	72.33 ± 5.51
SS2	8.67 ± 0.21	6.66 ± 0.61	2.51 ± 0.11	8.97 ± 0.09	2.80 ± 0.04	3.1 ± 0.12	61.67 ± 2.08	77.43 ± 4.18
SS3	8.96 ± 0.03	6.63 ± 0.77	2.34 ± 0.148	7.54 ± 1.14	2.79 ± 0.076	2.98 ± 0.15	60 ± 2	77.3 ± 9.02
SS4	8.65 ± 0.92	6.59 ± 0.61	2.05 ± 0.09	7.83 ± 0.87	2.26 ± 0.06	2.72 ± 0.25	68.13 ± 1.70	73.27 ± 3.26
SS5	9.2 ± 0.16	7.59 ± 0.095	1.58 ± 0.12	2.7 ± 0.58	3.12 ± 0.07	3.91 ± 0.04	71.5 ± 1.10	80.63 ± 6.97
SS6	8.8 ± 0.27	7.32 ± 0.18	2.76 ± 0.08	7.92 ± 0.48	2.85 ± 0.01	3.02 ± 0.23	71.67 ± 1.53	83.1 ± 8.15

for causticity in water. Photosynthesis, breath and disintegration all add to pH changes because of their effects on CO2 levels. The pH esteems inside the scope of 5.5–7.5 were reasonable for the ordinary scope of water system [19]. The pH of the Groundwater falls above FAO and WHO water quality standards for water system and use as crude public water flexibly in dry season (Fig. 4). As per [19] pH surpasses from 7.5 isn't prudent for water system reason. For the most part, the acridity may have been because of high carbon dioxide focuses from eutrophication cycles of natural issue, adsorption of metal anions and presence of some non-metallic mixes, for example, fluorides in the groundwater sources. The low pH esteems which were regular in the wet season are credited to the anaerobic conditions that could prompt the creation of acidic substances, such as natural acids.

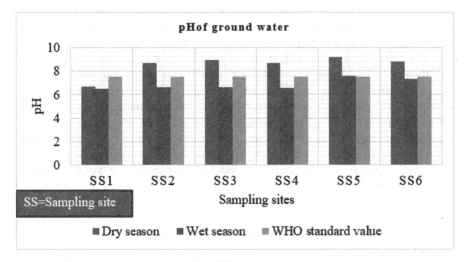

Fig. 5. Seasonal variation in pH of groundwater quality in the study area

Dissolved oxygen:- The findings of the study show that the values of broke down oxygen were ranged between 2.05 ± 0.09 to 2.76 ± 0.08 mg/L during dry season (Fig. 5) with the mean value of 2.24 ± 0.102 mg/L where as in the wet season from 2.7 ± 0.58 to 9.18 ± 0.17 mg/L with the mean value of 7.36 ± 0.56 mg/L (Fig. 5). The recorded outcomes (Fig. 5) show that the measure of disintegrated oxygen during wet season were higher than the value of dry season. This may have been because of temperature and downpour fall. This was in accordance with the investigation of [15] who explores the occasional varieties in physicochemical properties of groundwater around Karuabattoir. As recorded over the measure of temperature estimated in a wet season was lower than dry season and afterward it tends to hold high broke up oxygen which leads disintegrated oxygen to be higher in wet season. Other than to those in wet season oxygen is blended in through downpour, wave and wind subsequently its incentive to be recorded at the example point was increment when contrasted with dry season. Likewise, spatial variety among the six sample points in both dry and wet season was watched. Figure 5 shows that in dry season the base worth was estimated at testing point 5. This was because of testing point 5 was the most noteworthy top to bottom from all. At that point at the most elevated profundity, air was not cooperating all the more moderately and the water that is close to the residue will be drained of oxygen. Then again, the greatest value of broke down oxygen in dry season was estimated at inspecting point 6 (Fig. 5) which is regularly spring water. In spite of the fact that spring waters are considered as ground water, they are basically engrossing oxygen from environmental air therefore testing guide 6 has higher incentive as analyzed toward the other. Where as in the wet season the greatest worth happens at examining point1(Fig. 5) because of this testing point is found far separated from the landfill site the upstream way (over the landfill site) and the base an incentive at inspecting point 5 like dry season. The oxidation of natural substances and diminished inorganic substances prompts lower oxygen content in groundwater. For the most part, a high substance of oxygen penetration water advances the groundwater with oxygen. On account of most groundwater revive happens in the wet season and lower solvency of oxygen in warm water than in chilly water, higher substance of disintegrated oxygen are estimated in the wet season. Notwithstanding, in wet season the deliberate mean value of DO was above WHO water quality reasonable constraint of 5 mg/L. On the record of this the factual investigation of fluctuation (ANOVA) result demonstrates that there was critical contrast in mean DO fixation between and inside seasons during the study period ($p < 0.05$). As broken-down oxygen levels in water dip under 5.0 mg/L, oceanic life is put under pressure. The lower the fixation, the more noteworthy the pressure. Low broke down oxygen (DO) fundamentally results from extreme green growth development brought about by phosphate. As the green growth bite the dust and deteriorate, the cycle devours broke up oxygen. This can bring about lacking measures of broke up oxygen accessible for oceanic life.

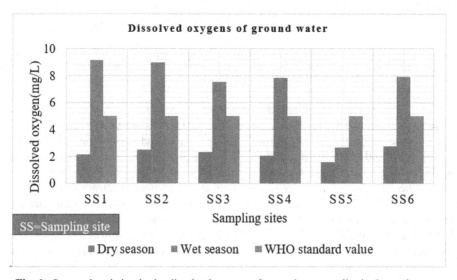

Fig. 6. Seasonal variation in the dissolved oxygen of groundwater quality in the study area.

Biological oxygen demand:- From the stud, the measure of BOD for all samples during the dry season were ranged from 2.23 ± 0.10 to 3.12 ± 0.07 mg/L with a mean value of 2.68 ± 0.07 mg/L while during the wet season the value of BOD fluctuates from 2.72 ± 0.25 to 3.91 ± 0.04 mg/L with a mean value of 3.09 ± 0.202 m/L (Fig. 6). The discoveries of this investigation show that the mean value of the wet season was higher than the mean value of the dry season (Fig. 6). This may have been because of permeation and invasions of biodegradable natural issue and draining of natural iron or potentially manganese into the springs in light of the waste removal site. The higher BOD saw in the wet season inferred that popularity for oxygen was made to help the activity cycle [20] noted comparative circumstances of high BOD and presume that it was because of higher natural waste burden experienced during the blustery season. [21] likewise saw that BOD vacillation between season might be credited to extra natural issue brought into groundwater as the consequence of overflow and soil disintegration brought about by ceaseless precipitation in the downpour season. In the part of spatial variety, the most extreme BOD esteem was recorded at inspecting point 5 and testing point 6 separately for both dry and wet season (Fig. 6). This was because of the profundity of boreholes and the areas of test focuses from the garbage removal site (the toxin source) since in the most elevated top to bottom and downstream from the poison source generally described by an insufficiency of oxygen. Though the base qualities were gotten at testing point 1 and inspecting point 4 (Fig. 6) individually for both dry and wet season because of both are situated over the unloading site which isn't rich with a lot of natural waste that originates from the source (removal site). By and large, the BOD values of groundwater tests all through the study period were beneath the EPA'S/WHO/rule values of 5 mg/l (Fig. 6). This shows that the water was reasonably acceptable between times of BOD for various family exercises, since low BOD is a marker of good quality water, while a high BOD demonstrates dirtied water. From the ANOVA result, there was no conceivable huge variety between the examining focuses just as between the seasons that may lead the BOD past the constraint of WHO. In water with a BOD level of above 5 mg/L, the water is considered fairly contaminated in light of the fact that there is typically natural issue present and microbes are disintegrating this waste. The higher the BOD esteem, the more noteworthy the measure of natural issue or food accessible for oxygen-devouring microbes. Body esteems increment when supplement burdens and amassing of plant rotting matters in examining focuses increment.

Chemical oxygen demand:- COD is a pointer of natural contamination, which is brought about by the inflow of homegrown waste, live stocks and modern waste that contains a raised degree of natural toxins [22]. The study of the investigation show that synthetic oxygen interest in all the six groundwater tests went from 60 ± 2 to 71.67 ± 1.53 mg/L during the dry season with a mean value of 65.67 ± 1.84 while in the wet season it went from 72.233 ± 5.51 to 83.1 ± 8.15 mg/L with a mean value of 77.34 ± 6.18 mg/L (Fig. 7). From this (Fig. 7) one can see that the values of both dry and wet season were beneath the EPA/WHO/rule allowable cutoff. This could presumably be on the grounds that the vast majority of the wastes that are being created from the different networks (accessible at the dumpsite) are biodegradable or the watched contaminations of borehole water tests contemplated may not be because of substance oxidation of toxins present however because of high-impact corruptions of natural issue present by

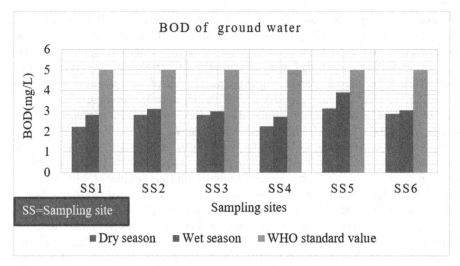

Fig. 7. Seasonal variation in the BOD of groundwater quality in the study area.

microorganism in the water tests. Despite the fact that all values of this study adjust to as far as possible the mean value of COD during the wet season was higher than the value of the dry season (Fig. 10). This may have been because of the impact of family substance items, for example, cleansers, cleansers, shampoos, additives, colors, and cleaners accessible in the dumpsite by the activities of precipitation. Therefore, the delay aggregation of leaked natural leachates in the spring can increment. The disclosures of the high value of COD in a wet season during the assessment time period of this exploration was similar with the study of [23] who have done the assessments of occasional varieties in Physico-compound attributes of Tapi estuary in Hazira modern region and found higher assessment of COD during the wet season than the dry season. In the base of spatial variety most extreme and least qualities were recorded at examining point 6 and inspecting point 1 individually for both dry and wet season (Fig. 7). When contrasted this finding and different studies a higher scope of COD qualities than those in this investigation was acquired in the study that surveyed the nature of boreholes found near the dumpsite in Benin and south-south Nigeria. The COD reach in this study show comparable with COD scope of 55–89 mg/L got in the appraisal of water nature of borehole around chose landfills in Kanometroplis, north Nigeria, just as some chose boreholes in Umiahia in Abia state, southeast Nigeria, in that they are underneath the suggested esteem set by WHO [24].

3.1.3   Spatial and Temporal Variation of Nutrients and Micro Biological Parameters of Groundwater Quality

The result of spatial and temporal variation of groundwater nutrients and microbiological parameters measured in all six sampling points throughout the study time are presented in below table (Table 3).

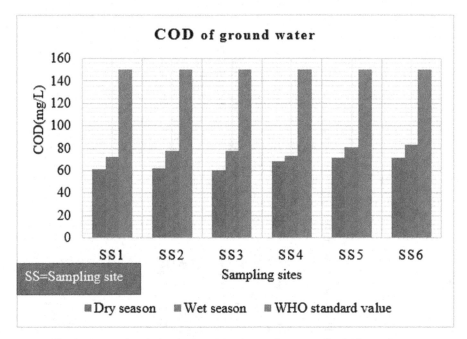

Fig. 8. Seasonal variation in the COD of groundwater quality in the study area.

Dynamics of nitrate in ground water:- From the study, the centralizations of nitrate during dry season changed between 0.071 ± 0.0011 to 0.08 ± 0.0021 mg/L with a mean value of 0.34 ± 0.006 mg/L while in a wet season it went from 0.51 ± 0.02 to 0.94 ± 0.056 mg/L with a mean value of 0.62 ± 0.07 mg/L (Fig. 8). The result of Fig. 8 shows that all values of the dry and wet season were amazingly beneath the WHO standard value of 50 mg/L for groundwater. This could presumably be because of the nonappearance of DO essentially in the wastewater; a more modest measure of nitrate is delivered from alkali just as decay of food wastes and different wellsprings of protein. Generally, factors influencing the event of nitrate in groundwater boreholes are subsurface mud focal points and land use practice. The divulgences/discoveries/of low values of nitrate (beneath WHO standard) during the assessment time span was comparable with crafted by [25] who have evaluated nitrate in wells and springs in the north-focal Ethiopian high terrains and discovered worth which is not as much as WHO standard breaking point all through the investigation period. Despite the fact that all qualities were beneath as far as possible the mean groupings of nitrate acquired during wet season were higher than the value of dry season (Fig. 8). The exposures of the high value of nitrate in a wet season during the study period were like the exploration of [26] who researches groundwater quality in an upland horticultural watershed in the sub-muggy Ethiopian good countries and discovered the higher value of nitrate during the wet season than the dry season. This may have been because of high nitrate fixation in the wet season proposed that expanded flush of nitrate causing segments (blended source, for example, rotting plant or creature material, rural composts, excrement, fertilizer,

Table 3. Spatial and temporal variation in measured values of nutrients and micro biological parameters

Sampling sites	NO_3^- (mg/L)		PO_4^{3-} (mg/L)		TC (CFU/100 ml)	
	Dry season	Wet season	Dry season	Wet season	Dry season	Wet season
SS1	0.071 ± 0.0011	0.53 ± 0.056	0.0058 ± 0.003	0.0018 ± 0.001	8.33 ± 0.1.53	13 ± 3
SS2	0.72 ± 0.023	0.66 ± 0.053	0.0088 ± 0.0029	0.031 ± 0.023	6.33 ± 1.53	13.67 ± 5.132
SS3	0.09 ± 0.003	0.94 ± 0.056	0.048 ± 0.0023	0.0072 ± 0.005	7.33 ± 3.51	18.33 ± 4.51
SS4	0.73 ± 0.01	0.51 ± 0.02	0.039 ± 0.003	0.05 ± 0.0075	5 ± 1	16 ± 1
SS5	0.073 ± 0.0021	0.52 ± 0.16	0.064 ± 0.0042	0.264 ± 0.0.34	11.67 ± 2.52	23 ± 6
SS6	0.08 ± 0.0021	0.55 ± 0.06	0.098 ± 0.001	0.262 ± 0.87	9 ± 2	20 ± 4.583

human or creature waste, and homegrown sewage) got from garbage removal site and the regions around during storm function brought about nitrate focus or the expanded nitrate level was because of freshwater inflow and earthly run-off during the wet season [27]. Another conceivable method of nitrates passage is through oxidation of smelling salts type of nitrogen to nitrite arrangement [28]. For the most part, during the wet season groundwater is revived through precipitation by means of permeation prompting an overall ascent in the degree of the water. This makes them exceptionally powerless to contamination and overflow exercises as components in soils and shakes are effectively delivered into the water. The principle wellspring of nitrate in these groundwater tests could be credited utilization of synthetic composts on ranches, emanating releases and spillover from animal feedlots have been recognized as one of the fundamental drivers of nitrate in groundwater. Also, inappropriate removal of human and creature waste son open land brings about filtering of remaining nitrate subsequently causing high nitrate fixation in groundwater in the wet season. In most case employments of substance manures; ill-advised removal of human and creature wastes and impact of seasons are basic components for wellsprings of nitrogen-containing exacerbates that are changed over to nitrate in the dirt. Then again, the low mean worth was recorded during the dry season because of less freshwater inflow and high saltiness [29] and [30]. In the part of spatial variety, the greatest worth was gotten at inspecting point 4 with a base an incentive at testing point 1 during the dry season while in the wet season the most extreme worth happens at examining point 3 with a base an incentive at testing point1 (Fig. 11). The purpose behind the qualities to be most extreme may have been because of plant rotting, fertilizer, manure, and overflow since testing point 3 and inspecting point 4 borehole tests are found especially at brushing area and nurseries while for the base the converse is valid. From the ANOVA result, there was no conceivable huge variety between the examining focuses just as between the seasons that may lead the centralization of nitrate over the restriction of WHO.

Dynamics of phosphate in ground water:- The grouping of phosphate in the groundwater tests went from 0.0088 ± 0.0029 to 0.098 ± 0.001 mg/L in the dry season and 0.002 ± 0.001 to $0.264 \pm 0.0.34$ mg/L in the wet season (Fig. 9). The discoveries of the investigation show that more significant levels of phosphate focuses were anyway enrolled during the wet seasons contrasted with dry seasons in all the groundwater tests (Fig. 9). This distinction can be clarified as far as expanded dampness in the ground of garbage removal site which contains human squanders, sedated shampoos, food waste and beauty care products that can filter the phosphate into groundwater. By and large, the value of phosphate during the blustery season can increment because of the conceivable contribution of phosphates from the outside climate, inappropriate removal of strong wastes and overflow because of unreasonable utilization of compound composts into the water and normal decay of rocks and minerals that contain phosphates. Phosphates are typically profoundly adsorbed into the dirt and can be shipped into the catchments and the beneficiary water bodies by the activities of downpour and afterward represented the high phosphate focus in nearby water bodies. The base value of phosphate was enlisted during the dry season, this may have been because of the low solvency of local phosphate minerals and the capacity of soils to hold phosphate. This is in accordance with

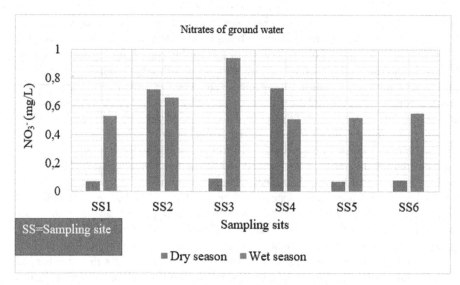

Fig. 9. Seasonal variation in the nitrate of groundwater quality in the study area.

the discoveries of [23] who examines occasional varieties in Physico-substance qualities of Tapi estuary in the Hazira mechanical territory and discovered a higher value of
phosphate during the wet season than dry. From the purpose of spatial variety, the most
elevated centralizations of phosphate were recorded at examining point 5 followed by
inspecting point 6 during the blustery season with a base an incentive at testing point
1 while in the dry season the most elevated level was at testing point 6 with a base an
incentive at inspecting point 2 (Fig. 9). This was because of the areas of boreholes from
the chose garbage removal site. From underneath acquired outcome (Fig. 9) with the
exception of examining point 5 and inspecting point 6 the grouping of PO43-in both dry
and wet seasons were beneath WHO norms limit (PO43- = 0.1 mg/L).On record of this,
the measurable study of change (ANOVA) results demonstrates that there was no huge
contrast in mean phosphate fixation between and inside testing focuses just as seasons
during the investigation period (p < 0.05).

Total coliform:- The results of the bacteriological investigation of borehole water
tests demonstrate that the measure of complete coliform during the dry season was gone
from 5 ± 1 to 11.67 ± 2.52 CFU/100 ml with a mean value of 7.9 ± 2.01 CFU/100 ml
though in a wet season the all-out coliform varied from 13 ± 3 to 23 ± 6 CFU/100 ml
with a mean value of 17.3 ± 4.04 CFU/100 ml (Fig. 10). From the outcome, one can see
that the bacterial settlement checks were all over the WHO rule cutoff of 0 CFU/100 ml
for drinking purposes. Accordingly, groundwater tests were polluted with complete
coliform. This must be because of wastes especially human wastes which are shipped
from Bahir Dar city and released legitimately to the open land (at the open garbage
removal site). It can, thusly, be derived that the boreholes were essentially dirtied by the
channels radiating from the waste site that vacant their substance straightforwardly out
of the dark land. The deliberate mean value of absolute coliform during the wet season
was higher than that of the dry season. This could be because of the released human

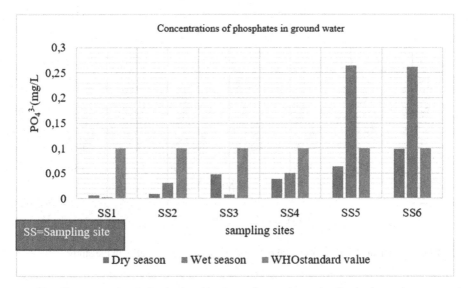

Fig. 10. Seasonal variation in the phosphate of groundwater quality in the study area.

wastes or fecal issues are flushed/washed/away by the activities of precipitation from its source to the diverse water bodies. At that point during its stream, it joins surface waters and open boreholes other than filtering into groundwater through permeation and invasion. The vehicle of exposed soil debased with dung by the breeze/downpour/into open bores just as surface overflow could likewise have represented the high bacterial burden during the wet season when contrasted with the dry season. Test focuses that are closest to the removal site in the downstream like examining point 5 and inspecting point 6 were more influenced by the absolute coliform. Un expectedly test focuses which are situated over the dumpsite were dirtied with absolute coliform. This may have been because of dung and different wastes from anthropogenic sources (open field crap along the boreholes by people and different creatures that eat alongside the groundwater tests) situated in hedges near boreholes. This was inevitably washed by water as spillover towards groundwater tests and afterward spilled into groundwater other than to blend in with the open boreholes and spring water by means of surface stream. The most extreme qualities among the six groundwater tests were found at examining point 5 inspecting point 6, examining point 1 and examining point 3 with a base at inspecting point 4 during the dry season while in a wet season the greatest qualities were gotten at inspecting point 5, testing point 6, testing point 3 and examining point 4 with a base at inspecting point 1. The transient mean value of absolute coliform in the water at the six examining purposes of the investigation zone during the dry and wet season were appeared in Fig. 10.

3.2 Assessing/Evaluating/Changes in Groundwater Quality of Chilanchil Abay Watershed through Water Quality Index (CCMEWQI)

In this investigation, the CCME Water Quality Index was applied and tried for the Chilanchil Abay Watershed quality. The record goes from 0 to 100 and relying upon

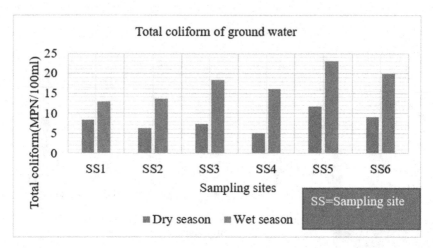

Fig. 11. Seasonal variation in total coliform of groundwater quality in the study area.

the worth; the water quality is portrayed as great, great, reasonable, negligible and poor. The CCME WQI was determined utilizing the technique portrayed by CCME 2001 rules (Eq. 1, 2, 3, 4, 5, 6 and 7). The outcomes got from the utilization of CCME WQI concerning supplements, hefty metals, and physico-synthetic attributes were introduced in Tables and diagrams underneath.

Table 4. Variation of WQI of Chilanchil Abay watershed with different sampling points

Sampling points	Level	Status
SS_1	46.2	Marginal
SS_2	45.53	Marginal
SS_3	45.52	Marginal
SS_4	45.53	Marginal
SS_5	42	Poor
SS_6	42.2	Poor

Study in Chilanchil Abay watershed Table 4 above and Fig. 11 beneath shows the variety of WQI with CCME standard level to assess the status of existing groundwater quality in the investigation territory. The determined outcomes got from all inspecting purposes of groundwater were indicating four sample points as minimal and two sample points as poor for 30th March 2011 to twentieth August 2011. All the negligible status test focuses are found in the upstream of the garbage removal site. This shows that water quality is much of the time jeopardized or disintegrated; conditions regularly stray from normal or attractive levels. This could be come about due to rotting of plants and creatures, farming composts and open abandonment exercises. While the excess two helpless status test focuses were found in the downstream of the garbage removal site.

This demonstrates that the water nature of these testing focuses is constantly imperiled or decayed; conditions normally veer off from regular or attractive levels. Considering all example locales, test site SS5and test site six have demonstrated the most noticeably awful quality with regards to CCMEWQI. The reasons may incorporate the movements of leachate in downstream from the dumpsite towards those two sample points (Fig. 12).

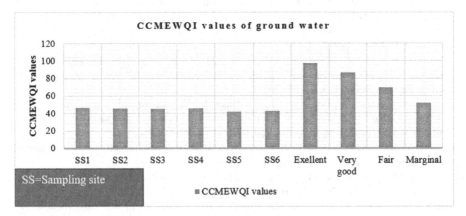

Fig. 12. Figure 11: variations of water quality index in the study area at different groundwater sample sites

4 Conclusion

The temporal and spatial variations of groundwater quality of Chilanchil Abay watershed was assessed following WHO quality parameters and Canadian water quality index. The analysis of physicochemical properties and concentrations of nutrients recorded values, show that BOD, COD, and NO3-were within the acceptable limit for groundwater during the study time while the remains fluctuated with the seasons.

From the findings of the study, it assured that sample points below the dumpsite were more affected than the sample points of upstream.

The total coliform counts detected were above the permissible limits for drinking water in all sample points. Data suggested the importance of greater attention for household contamination, environmental sanitation control and awareness about water contamination since the open waste disposal site and practice of open defecation have actually impacted the watershed of the study area.

According to the Canadian water quality index (CCMEWQI), the water quality of Chilanchil Abay watershed was categorized under poor and marginal status.

Acknowledgments. The authors would like to thank Bahir Dar University, Bahir Dar institute of technology for financial supports of this project.

References

Love, J., Luchsinger, V.: Sustainability and water resources. J. Sustain. Green Bus. **2**, 1–12 (2014)

Markandya, A.: Water quality issues in developing countries. In: López, R., Toman, M.A. (eds.) Economic Development and Environmental Sustainability: New Policy Options, pp. 307–344 (2006)

Afolayan, O., Ogundele, F., Odewumi, S.: Hydrological implication of solid waste disposal on groundwater quality in urbanized area of Lagos state, Nigeria. Int. J. Appl. **2**(5) (2012)

Kola-Olusanya, A.: Impact of municipal solid wastes on underground water sources in Nigeria. Eur. Sci. J. ESJ **8**(11) (2012)

O'riordan, T.: Environmental Science for Environmental Management. Routledge (2014)

Nikbakht, M.: The effect assessment of ahvaz No. 1, 2 water treatment plant on Karoon water quality. Environ. Pollut. B **6**, 51–67 (2004)

Brown, R., McClelland, N., Deininger, R., O'Connor, M.: A water quality index—crashing the psychological barrier. In: Thomas, W.A. (ed.) Indicators of Environmental Quality, pp. 173–182. Springer, Boston (1972). https://doi.org/10.1007/978-1-4684-2856-8_15

Canadian Council of Ministers of the Environment: Canadian environmental quality guidelines: Canadian Council of Ministers of the Environment (2002)

Hamad, O.H.M.: Occupational and Environmental Hazards among Workers in Petroleum Stations, Khartoum State, Sudan (2013–2015), University of Gezira (2018)

Clesceri, L., Greenberg, A., Eaton, A.: Standard Methods for the Study of Water and Wastewater. 20th edition American Public Health Association, Washington, DC (1998)

Apha Awwa, W.: Standard Methods for the Study of Water and Wastewater 20th edition. American Public Health Association, American Water Work Association, Water Environment Federation, Washington, DC (1998)

Khan, A.A., Paterson, R., Khan, H.: Modification and application of the Canadian Council of Ministers of the Environment Water Quality Index (CCME WQI) for the communication of drinking water quality data in Newfoundland and Labrador. Water Qual. Res. J. **39**(3), 285–293 (2004)

Hassan, S.T.: Assessment of groundwater evaporation through groundwater model with spatio-temporally variable fluxes. Thesis. International Institute for Geo-information Science and earth (2008)

Effect of Alkaline Pre-treatment on Fermentable Sugar Yield of Ethiopian Bamboo (Yushania Alpine)

Netsanet Alemayehu[3]($\boxtimes$), Yalew W/Amanuel[2], and Nigus Gabbiye[1]

[1] Faculty of Chemical and Food Engineering, Process-Engineering Stream, Bahir Dar Institute of Technology, Bahir Dar University, Bahir Dar, Ethiopia
[2] College of Biological and Chemical Engineering, Addis Ababa Science and Technology University, Addis Ababa, Ethiopia
[3] Department of Chemical Engineering, Institute of Technology, University of Gondar, Gondar, Ethiopia

Abstract. In the recent years, bioethanol derived from lignocellulosic biomass as an alternative to the conventional fuels is becoming a focus of many researchers. In this study, bamboo is used as a feedstock for the production of bioethanol via alkaline pretreatment followed by, enzymatic and acid hydrolysis process. Specifically, the focus is mainly on the investigation of the effect of alkaline pretreatment on the yield of total fermentable sugar from bamboo (yushania alpine) biomass using sodium hydroxide as a catalyst. Alkali concentration, pretreatment temperature, and reaction time were varied in the alkali pretreatment experiments. Following the pretreatment, enzymatic and dilute sulfuric acid hydrolysis of the pretreated bamboo were carried out separately to measure the success of the alkaline pretreatment in improving the total reducing sugar (fermentable sugar) yields. The composition of raw and pretreated bamboo were characterized using NREL and ASTM protocols. The total reducing sugar concentrations after hydrolysis were determined by DNSA method. It was found that, the raw bamboo has a composition of 42.45% cellulose, 23.6% hemicelluloses, and 32.4% Lignin. The alkali pretreatment resulted in a maximum lignin removal of 35.5% at temperature of 60 °C, contact time of 50 min, and alkali concentration of 4.5% w/v, which leads to an increment of cellulose fraction to 64.93% and reduction of lignin to 20.8%. A maximum total reducing sugar yield of 206.3 mg/g and 351.9 mg/g were obtained for pretreated bamboo by using enzymatic and dilute sulfuric acid hydrolysis, respectively.

Keywords: High land bamboo · Pretreatment process · Delignification · Fermentable sugar

1 Introduction

Lignocelluloses biomass is the primary and most abundant organic material on the earth, which makes it the most promising resource for the alternative energy sources. Among

M. A. Delele et al. (Eds.): ICAST 2020, LNICST 384, pp. 59–67, 2021.
https://doi.org/10.1007/978-3-030-80621-7_4

them, bamboos is receiving a renewed interest due to its high growth rate and better education of carbon footprint compared to an equivalent area of woody plants (Mengistie et al. 2013). Ethiopia shares about 67% of the bamboo resourse in africa (Kindu et al. 2016). Despite its abundance in the country, it has not exploited to use as renewable feedstock for bioethanol production. The most critical step in bioethanol production from lignocellulosic materials is the pretreatment step. Multitudes of pretreatment processes have been developed in the past and each of them has their own advantage and disadvantages. In principle, a pretreatment process has to increase the surface area and pore size, reduce the Crystallinity, remove lignin content, require less chemical dosage and avoid sever process conditions. (Yamashita et al. 2010) have been reported that alkaline pretreatment is generally more effective on agricultural residues and herbaceous crops than on wood materials. However, they cause less cellulose and hemicelluloses hydrolysis and solubilization than acid processes. It has been reported elsewhere (Zhiqiang et al. 2012), (Shangxing et al. 2014), that the dilute alkali treatment was highly effective in delignification of the biomass, at high temperature. There was studied pretreatment of bamboo using at high operating conditions (Megumi et al. 2010). Among the pretreatment processes, alkaline pretreatment can be carried out at mild operating conditions and successful in lignin removal. Thus, the primary aim of the present study is to investigate the effect of mild alkaline pretreatment method on yields of fermentable sugar from bamboo (yushania alpine) biomass.

2 Material and Methods

2.1 Raw Material Preparation

High land bamboo (yushania alpine) sample having an age of 2.5 years was collected from Injibara town, in the district of Awi zone. The raw material was then washed with tap water, dried in sunlight for a week, cut into piece with cutter machines, milled with disc mill, sieved to get a particle size passing through a (0.5–0.71) mm sieve, and stored in a plastic bag at room temperature until used (Fig. 1).

2.2 Method

Alkali Pre-treatment Experiments
Alkaline pretreatment experiments on bamboo (yushania alpine) biomass were performed over a wide range of NaOH solutions (0.5–4.5% (w/v)), reactor temperature (30–80 °C) and contact time of (10–50 min) with SLR a ratio of 1:40 (solid: liquid) respectively (see the experimental design in Table 1).

All experiments were performed in a glass reactor (Atlas syrris reactor) at varying process operating conditions as indicate in Table 1 at constant stirrer speed of 400 rpm and particle sizes of 0.5–0.71 mm. For this 5 g, dried bamboo was immersed in 200 ml distill water with specific amount of NaOH solution. The reaction was allowed to proceed the specified time. The residue was separated from black liquor using vacuum filtration. The solid residue was washed thoroughly until the pH of the washing water becomes neutral.

Fig. 1. Size reduction by manual and Cutter milling setup

Table 1. Experiment design for the

Parameter	Range of values for the parameter		
Temperature (°C)	30	60	80
Alkali Concentration (%w/v)	0.5	2.5	4.5
Time (min)			

The washed residue was dried at 105°C for 12h and milled with ultrafine centrifugal grinder to the required size. NREL and ASTM protocols were used to determine the compositions (Lignin, hemicelluloses, and cellulose) of pretreated and raw bamboo (Sluiter et al. 2012).

Hydrolysis experiments: Pretreated bamboos were hydrolysis by both enzymatic and acid hydrolysis. In enzymatic hydrolysis, the pretreated bamboo was performed using endoglucanase and β-glucosidase enzymes at a pH of 4.9 in a shaking water bath set at 50 °C and 150 rpm for 24 h. Acid hydrolysis was also carried out using 1% sulfuric acid in autoclave reactor set at 121 °C. Then, the lignin removal and the reducing sugar content are determined by using NREL and DNS methods respectively (Sluiter et al. 2012) (Fig. 2).

3 Results and Discussions

The compositional analyses of cellulose, hemicellulose, and lignin were performed for the raw and treated bamboo. The Ethiopian native bamboo (yushania alpine) used in this research was found to be, 42.45% cellulose, 23.6% hemicelluloses, and 32.4% lignin by mass. Moreover, the lignin contents have separated into acid-soluble (3.8% wt/wt of dry biomass) and acid insoluble (28.6% wt/wt of dry biomass) components. However, after pretreatment with 4.5% w/v alkaline solution, at a temperature of 60 °C

Fig. 2. Alkaline pretreatment and hydrolysis equipment setup

for 50 min, the cellulose content of alkaline pretreated bamboo increased particularly (64.93%) but the lignin and hemicelluloses content decreased to 20.8% and 13.56%, respectively. Therefore, in the specified mild alkaline pretreatment, hemicelluloses and lignin contents were partially dissolved and removed which suggest the requirement of further treatment.

3.1 Effect of Alkaline Concentration on Delignification and Total Reducing Sugar

The effect of NaOH concentration on the composition of pretreated bamboo is indicated in Fig. 3. As it can be seen in the figure, delignification rate increases with increasing alkali concentration and less pronounce effect is seen in lower alkali concentration ranges. Such higher rate of delignification with an increase in alkali concentration can be attributed to the fact that hydroxyl ions catalyze the cleavage of ether linkages in the lignin and thus liberate the soluble sodium phenolates in the liquid (Ribeiro et al. 2019). This is because the accessible and soluble lignin type dissolved and removed by alkali pretreatment at 2.5% concentration. But, the highly intact and stable lignin type cannot be dissolved easily, needs high alkalinity of the solution to cause solvation of hydroxyl groups in carbohydrates, and creates the swelling effect in the matrix. Investigation of alkaline pretreatment of lignocellulosic biomass has been found to cause swelling, disruption of the lignin structure and increase in internal surface area by breaking the bond between lignin monomers or between lignin and hemicelluloses components (Cao et al. 2012). This further increases the diffusivity of the NaOH reagent through the capillaries to the biomass structure. In such cases, more hydroxyl ions are in the solution to participate in ether bond breakage and the dissolution of the lignin from the matrix. Furthermore, at higher concentration of alkaline catalyst, there will be more number of hydroxide ions, which can attack the cellulosic bond (glycosidic bond) to release sugar molecules through subsequently protonation of the bond to form carbonium cation (Yan et al. 2014).

The reducing sugar yield of the hydrolysis experiment is also presented in Fig. 4. As the enzymatic hydrolysis yield is also dependent on lignin and hemicelluloses removals,

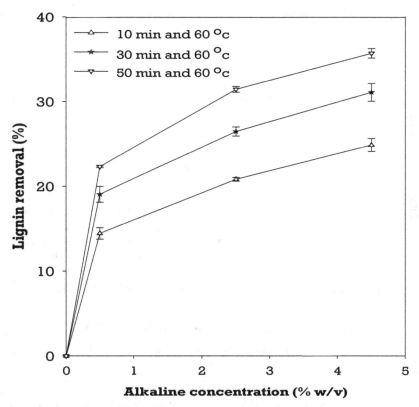

Fig. 3. Effect of alkaline concentration on delignification

higher reducing sugar yield was obtained at high alkali concentration (Fig. 4) for both enzymatic and acid hydrolysis. The presence of less lignin and hemicelluloses components in the biomass facilitated disruption to the biomass matrix, which facilitates enzymatic/acid hydrolysis of the holocellulose (i.e. cellulose and hemicelluloses).

With respect to hydrolysis agents, it appears that dilute sulfuric acid hydrolysis yields higher fermentable sugar than enzymatic hydrolysis with the same bamboo samples pretreated at the same conditions. So, dilute sulfuric acid hydrolysis has highly catalyzed the β - glycosidase bond of the hemicellulose and cellulose to convert them into total reducing sugars. However, the enzymatic (endoglucase and β-glucase) hydrolysis is limited in mass transfer (due to a slow adsorption and desorption processes) as compared to dilute sulfuric acid hydrolysis process. Additional, increase in the NaOH concentration and reaction time in the pre-treatment condition resulted in an increase in reducing sugar due to the removal of lignin.

3.2 Effect of Time on Delignification and Total Reducing Sugar

Previous reports show that delignification occurs in three distinct phases: initial, bulk, and residual lignin reactions (Monica et al. 2009). The bulk phase is normally the reaction

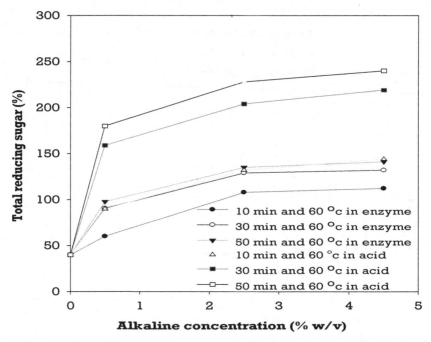

Fig. 4. Effect of alkaline concentration on total reducing sugar

stage in which the largest portion of lignin is removed while the smaller fraction of residual lignin is removed in the residual reaction phase, which is also slower reaction and observable in the later stages of delignification (Macfarlane et al. (2009)).

As shown on Fig. 3, most of the lignin was removed in 10 min and this phase is the bulk delignification phase. Increasing contact time from 10 to 50 min slightly increased the lignin removal, which shows slower reaction phase and can easily be recognized as the residual delignification phase. The residual lignin, which is not accessible by NaOH reagent, was gradually removed over a longer time. However, for higher alkali concentration, solvation of the hydroxyl ions in the biomass swells and opened up the structure, which makes the lignin and hemicelluloses easily dissolved by the reagent. Higher alkali concentration and time increases the internal surface area and porosity by swelling and hemicelluloses degradation. Hence, for longer pretreatment time, the internal surface area, and pores of the biomass increase. These improve the enzyme (endoglucase and β-glucase) and dilute sulfuric acid digestibility of the cellulose.

The effect of reaction time on the total reducing sugar yield is shown in Fig. 4. It shows that, the yield of total reducing sugar increases with an increase in the length of pretreatment time. So, the maximum total reducing sugar yield was obtained by dilute sulfuric acid hydrolysis as compared to enzymatic (endoglucase and β-glucase) hydrolysis.

3.3   Effect of Temperature on Delignification and Total Reducing Sugar

The result presented in Fig. 5 shows that increasing reaction temperature favors lignin and hemicelluloses removals. Sodium hydroxide used in this case as a catalyst is more active at higher temperature and it catalyzes the ether and ester bonds in the lignin matrix and between the hemicelluloses chains, effectively. The more soluble portions of lignin accessible by the alkali can be removed easily by raising the temperature from 30 to 60 °C. Further increment to 80 °C facilitates the removals marginally. On the other hand, hemicelluloses removal continuously increases, as its solubility is more dependent on temperature.

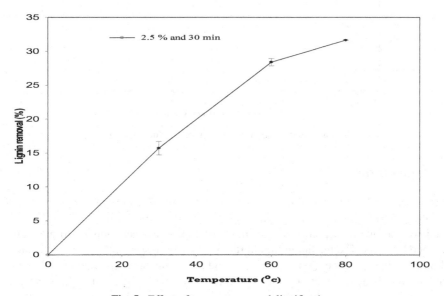

Fig. 5. Effect of temperature on delignification

Eventually, lignin and hemicelluloses removals and creation of more surface areas (porosities) in the biomass are responsible for increasing the acid and enzymatic hydrolysis yield, depicted below in Fig. 6.

As it can be seen in Fig. 6, the total reducing sugar yield of dilute sulfuric acid hydrolysis was higher than in the yield from enzymatic hydrolysis for all range of temperature. Therefore, this indicates that the dilute sulfuric acid hydrolysis has preferable than enzyme (endoglucase and β-glucase) hydrolysis in order to produce high total reducing sugar in alkaline pretreatment at specific condition.

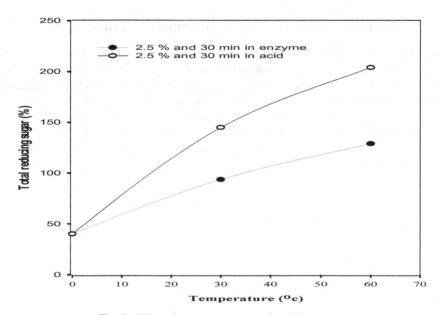

Fig. 6. Effect of temperature on total reducing sugar

4 Conclusions

In this research, the effects of different alkaline pretreatment conditions on lignin removal and their impacts on the subsequent hydrolysis yield have been investigated. Varying alkaline concentration, pretreatment time and temperature were applied to pretreated bamboo biomass. The maximum lignin removal achieved was 35.5% at a temperature of 60 °C, alkali concentration of 4.5% w/v and pretreatment times of 50 min. At these similar pretreatment conditions, the maximum fermentable sugars of 206.3 mg/g raw bamboo from enzymatic hydrolysis and 351.9 mg/g raw bamboo from dilute sulfuric acid hydrolysis were obtained. From the result, acid hydrolysis released higher quantity of reducing sugars than the enzymatic pathways. Therefore, it can be concluded that alkaline pretreatment at such mild operating conditions followed by dilute sulfuric acid hydrolysis is the primary option for production of fermentable sugar from Ethiopian bamboo (yushania alpine). Nevertheless, further experiments is required to improve the fermentable sugar yield to the required level via emerging less energy intensive technologies such ultrasound and micro-wave assisted pretreatments.

Acknowledgment. I would like to thank Bahir Dar University, Bahir Dar Institute of Technology for giving me the scholarship to study my postgraduate study.

References

Cao, L., Bala, G., Caldeira, K.: Climate response to changes in atmospheric carbon dioxide and solar irradiance on the time scale of days to weeks. Environ. Res. Lett. **7**(3), 034015 (2012). https://doi.org/10.1088/1748-9326/7/3/034015

Kindu, et al.: Status of bamboo resource development, utilisation and research in Ethiopia: a review. Ethiopian J. Nat. Resour. 79–98 (2016)

Macfarlane, et al.: Dissolved air flotation: a novel approach to recovery of organosolv lignin. Sciencedirect **5** (2009)

Megumi, et al.: Alkaline Peroxide Pretreatment for Efficient Enzymatic Saccharification of Bamboo. Elsevier.Com/Locate/Carbpol (2010)

Mengistie, et al.: Bioethanol production from bamboo (Dendrocalamus Sp.) process waste. Sciencedirect 142–150 (2013)

Monica, et al.: Pulping chemistry and technology. Sciencedirect (2009)

Ribeiro, et al.: Chemical study of kraft lignin during alkaline delignification of E. Urophylla X E. Grandis hybrid in low and high residual effective alkali. Am. Chem. Soc. Sustain. Chem. Eng. **9** (2019)

Shangxing, et al.: Effects of dilute alkali pretreatment on chemical components and fermentable sugars and structure of bamboo. In: Advanced Materials Research (2014)

Sluiter, et al.: Determination of structural carbohydrates and lignin in biomass. NREL **18** (2012)

Yamashita, et al.: Alkaline peroxide pretreatment for efficient enzymatic saccharification of bamboo. Carbohydrate Polymers 914–920 (2010)

Yan et al.: A comprehensive mechanistic kinetic model for dilute acid hydrolysis of switchgrass cellulose to glucose, 5-HMF and levulinic acid. RSC Adv. **15** (2014)

Zhiqiang et al.: Bioconversion of bamboo to bioethanol using the two-stage organosolv and alkali pretreatment. Bioresources 5691–5699 (2012)

Antimicrobial Activity of Cotton Fabric Treated with Solanum Incanum Fruit and Red Onion Peel Extract

Tesfa Nega Gesese[✉], Solomon Workneh Fanta, and Desalegn Abera Mersha

Faculty of Chemical and Food Engineering, Bahir Dar Institute of Technology, Bahir Dar University, Bahir Dar, Ethiopia

Abstract. The majority of the antimicrobial compounds used for treating textiles are synthetic based and are not considered to be environmentally friendly. Therefore, solanum incanum fruit and onion peel were selected for the current study based on their potent antimicrobial activity. The active substance was extracted from fruit and peel by using the maceration extraction technique for 7 days with mass to solvent ratio of 1:10. The Solanum incanum fruit and red onion peel extracts were applied alone and together, on the cotton fabric samples by the pad-dry-cure method, using citric acid as a cross-linking agent. The antibacterial activity and the wash durability of the treated cotton fabrics were assessed by the American Association of Textile Chemists and Colorists 100-2004 method. Among all treatments, the cotton fabrics treated with 50:50 combinations were found to be more in bacterial reduction. It was 100% and 99.92% bacterial reduction in cotton fabric with 5 g/l concentration for S. aureus and E. coli respectively. The wash durability of fabric treated with 50:50 combinations was 85% for S. aureus and 84.17% was for E. coli bacteria after 15 wash cycle. After treatment, the tensile strength, air permeability, bending length, water absorbency, and soil degradation were tested. Air permeability, water absorbency, and tensile strength were decreased. Soil degradation tests proved the biodegradability of the treated sample. The result recommended that the use of herbal extract could potentially be used as a substituent to a synthetic agent.

Keywords: Antimicrobial · Cotton fabric · Solanum incanum fruit · Red onion peel · Fabric comfort

1 Introduction

The growth of microorganisms on textiles had negative effects not only on the textile itself but also on the wearer. Most of these negative effects are a reduction of mechanical strength in fabrics, discoloration of the fabric, likelihood contamination, generation of bad odor, allergic response, and skin irritation [1–4]. Such a bottleneck problem forced attention towards developing advanced textile-based medical products. The rapid growth in medical and functional textiles provides many opportunities for the application

© ICST Institute for Computer Sciences, Social Informatics and Telecommunications Engineering 2021
Published by Springer Nature Switzerland AG 2021. All Rights Reserved
M. A. Delele et al. (Eds.): ICAST 2020, LNICST 384, pp. 68–82, 2021.
https://doi.org/10.1007/978-3-030-80621-7_5

of innovative functional finishes [5]. Antimicrobial finishes can be applied to textile substrates by the exhaust, pad-dry-cure, coating, spray method, or spinning dope [2, 6]. The growth of microbes on the textile can be controlled by applying antimicrobial agents by various mechanisms like preventing cell production, blocking of enzyme reaction within the cell membrane to the destruction of the cell wall, and poisoning the cell from within [6, 7].

Mostly the textile sector utilized a synthetic antimicrobial agent against bacteria and fungi. But, most of the synthetic antimicrobial agents such as triclosan, formaldehyde have the potential to cause skin irritation, non-biodegradability, and bioaccumulation effect [8]. However, the herbal antimicrobial finishes overcome the disadvantages of the chemical finishes because they are eco-friendly, non-toxic, and non-allergic [9, 10]. The antimicrobial effectiveness of the plant depends on the chemical structure of the active component present in the plant and their concentration [11–13]. Today, numerous herbs and vegetables have been studied to extract the antimicrobial agent. Among the numerous natural herbs and vegetables, Solanum incanum and onion peel are a source of antimicrobial agents.

Solanum incanum L. is one of the most important traditional medicinal plants which belong to the Solanaceae family [12, 14]. Solanum incanum is a plant characterized by thorny leaves, yellow fruits, and blue flowers with yellow pistils which mostly distributed in the Horn of Africa as described by Nalankilli & Tadesse [12].

Onion (Allium cepa L) is a common food plant rich in several phytonutrients associated with the treatment and prevention of several diseases [15]. Allium cepa commonly called onion belongs to the family of Alliaceae and is grown in every part of the world where plants are farmed and exhibit great diversity in a form including color, shape, dry matter content, and pungency [16]. The variety also affects the antimicrobial activity, since the secondary metabolite present in each variety (red variety, green variety, and white variety) are different. The bioactive compound from onion exhibited antibacterial and antifungal activities [15].

The majority of the synthetic antimicrobial agents utilized in the textile industry are leaching type; result in decreasing their concentration and fail to inhibit the growth of harmful microbes and the release of these agents acts as a poison to a wide spectrum of bacteria and fungi [17]. On the contrary, the textile industry looks for non-toxic, non-allergic, and eco-friendly natural antimicrobial agents that do not adversely affect the quality of the textile material and the ecosystem as a substitute for synthetic toxic chemicals [17].

In Ethiopia, cooks will usually use red onion for their kitchen, which results in discarded underutilized parts of the vegetable, and it may cause an environmental problem like a source of unpleasant odor. However, the onion peel has high phenolic and flavonoids content, which act as antimicrobial agents. On the other side, no study has been undertaken to investigate the combined antimicrobial effect of solanum incanum fruit and onion peel extract on cotton fabric. Thus, to overcome these bottles' necked problem applying herb extract on the cotton fabric was taken as an immediate solution. For this study, the two herbs were applied by varying their proportion to examine the combined effects of the antimicrobial agent on the antibacterial activities, wash durability, and physical properties of cotton fabric.

2 Materials and Methods

2.1 Materials and Chemicals

Solanum incanum fruit and red onion peel were used for antimicrobial agent source. The citric acid (99.5%) was used as a cross-linking agent. Chloroform (99.8), hydrochloric acid (37%), ferric chloride (99%), ammonia (35%), aluminum chloride (99%), sulfuric acid (98%), acetic acid glacial (99.5%), potassium iodide (98.5%), phosphoric acid (85%) and sodium hydroxide (98.8) were used for phytochemical analysis. Gallic acid (99%), Folin- Ciocalteau reagent, and sodium carbonate (99.5%) were used for total phenol content determination. Methanol (99.8%) was used for extracting the active component from the peel and fruit of solanum incanum and red onion. Quercetin acid (99.8%), sodium nitrite (99.5%), aluminum chloride, sodium hydroxide was used for total flavonoid content determination. All chemicals used in the current study were analytical grades.

2.2 Equipment Used

Test tubes were used for solution preparation of phenol and flavonoid analysis, padding mangle (Mathis made in Switzerland) for imparting antimicrobial agent onto cotton fabric. Oven dryer was used for removing excess water from the fabric after applying finishing agent, multifunctional grinder (RRH-100g) for reducing the size of the solanum incanum fruit and onion peel into powder form. Universal strength tester (Mesdan, Italy) was used for measuring the tensile strength and elongation of break of the treated fabric, Rotary evaporator (Rota-vapor, RE300, UK) for concentrated the filtrate of the extract, oven (Bernareggio, M40-VF, Italy) for drying of sample, electronics balance for weighing the sample, orbital shaker (Unimax2010, Germany) for extraction.

2.3 Methods

Sample Collection and Pretreatment

The plant material, solanum incanum fruit was collected from Abay Mado, kebele 11, around Gihon secondary and preparatory school, Bahir Dar, Amhara regional state, Ethiopia. The red onion peel was collected from Bahir Dar institute of technology student cafeteria. The collected sample from the available area was washed in tap water and rinsed in distilled water to remove dust and other impurities. Then the rinsed samples were dried in shade; Solanum incanum fruit for five days and onion peel for 14 days by cutting it into the smaller piece-using knife until its moisture content was reduced to 14%.

The dried samples were subjected for size reduction to powder (finely) by high-speed multifunctional grinder (RRH-100g, Hongtaiyang Electrical & Mechanical Service Co. Ltd of the Yongkang City of Zhejiang Province) purchased from the local market, Bahir Dar, Ethiopia. After that, the powder was sieved with a sieve size of 0.5 mm to remove the oversized particles. Finally, the perspective-powdered samples were stored in an airtight glass container at room temperature until used.

Extract Preparation

Extraction was done using a method described by [18]. The dried powder, 50 g of each sample (Solanum incanum fruit and red onion peel) was soaked in 500 ml of absolute methanol with a continuous shaking with an orbital shaker at 172 rpm for one week at room temperature. After a week, the perspective sample was filtered through what man filter paper (125 mm, No.1) using a suction filter apparatus, while the residues were allowed for a second extraction. After filtration, the filtrates were concentrated under reduced pressure using a rotary evaporator at a temperature of 50 °C. The crude extracts were collected and dried in an oven at a temperature of 35 °C for 72 h. The dried concentrate was weighted and scooped into a well-labeled plastic bottle and stored in a refrigerator at 4 °C waiting for bioassay.

Phytochemical Analysis/Screening

Chemical Test: The chemical analysis of both the extracts was performed by following the protocol of [19–22].

Quantification of Total Phenol and Flavonoid Content

Phenol Content Determination: The quantity of total phenolic contents in each extract was determined accordingly to the Folin-Ciocalteau reagent (FCR) method described by [23] using Gallic acid as standard. The absorbance of the reaction mixtures was measured at 765 nm using a UV– Vis spectrophotometer (PerkinElmer UV-Vis spectrometer, Lambda 35) against the blank. The experiments were done in triplicate. The absorbance of the extract was compared with a Gallic acid standard curve using concentrations of 0, 0.050, 0.100, 0.150, 0.200, 0.250, and 0.300 mg/ml for estimating the concentration of phenol content in the sample. The phenolic content was expressed as mg of Gallic acid equivalents (GAE) per ml of sample.

Flavonoid Content Determination: The total flavonoid contents in each extract were determined by the well-known aluminum chloride colorimetric method [24]. The sample absorbance was read at 510 nm using a UV/Vis spectrophotometer. The absorbance of the extract was compared with a quercetin standard curve using concentrations of 0, 0.050, 0.100, 0.150, 0.200, and 0.250 mg/ml for estimating the concentration of flavonoid content in the sample. The flavonoid content was expressed as mg of quercetin equivalents (QE) per ml of sample.

Application of Extract on Fabric Using a Pad-Dry-Cure Method with Standard Combination

Pad-Dry-Cure Method: The cotton fabric was treated with 3 g/l and 5 g/l concentration of Solanum incanum fruit and red onion peel extract and with their standard combination as described in Table 1. The citric acid (6% w/v) was used as cross-linking with a mass liquor ratio of 1:10 (1 g of fabric in 10 ml of active ingredient solution). A two-bowl vertical laboratory padder (pressure 2 bar, speed 1.5 m/s, Mathis made in Switzerland) was used with a two dip and two nip process to get a wet pick up of 95% on the weight of the fabric. After padding, the treated samples were dried at 80 °C for 3 min and cured at 150 °C for 3 min on the lab model-curing chamber. Five solutions were prepared for each concentration and designated sample as shown in Table 1.

Table 1. Fabric treated with different concentrations

Concentration	Type of treatment	Sample code
3 g/l and 5 g/l	25:75 v/v Solanum incanum fruit to red onion peel	S1
	50:50 v/v Solanum incanum fruit to red onion peel	S2
	75:25 v/v Solanum incanum fruit to red onion peel	S3
	100% Solanum incanum fruit	S4
	100% red onion peel	S5
	Unfinished	Untreated

Performance Evaluation of Treated Cotton Fabrics

Tensile Strength Test (ES ISO13934): The tensile strength of fabric was determined on the paramount universal tensile tester (Mesdan, Italy) using the ES ISO 13934 test method. The samples of template size "16 × 5" from the warp and "20 × 5" centimeter from the weft directions of the fabric were cut and mounted between the jaws with approximately 2.54 cm of fabric protruding from each side of the jaws at the distance of 8 cm. The instrument was started; the upper jaw was moved in an upward direction until the sample break. The readings were taken from the digital display at sample break. Two readings of the specimen from both the directions (warp and weft) were taken and the average was calculated.

Bending Length (BS 3356): The fabric stiffness (bending length) was determined according to the method described by BS 3356.

Air Permeability (ES ISO 9237): The air permeability of a fabric is the volume of air, measured in cubic centimeters passed per second through one square centimeter of the fabric at a pressure of 1 cm of water. Air permeability was tested using air permeability tester (FX 3300, Zurich Switzerland) and the result was noted as $cm^3/cm^2 \cdot S$.

Water Absorbency Test (AATCC Test Method 79): The water absorbency of both treated and untreated fabrics was evaluated by the water drop method as per AATCC 79-2000 standard. In brief, a drop of distilled water was dispensed from a dropper onto the fabric surface from a distance of 1 cm. Time was recorded until the water drop absorbs completely. Four readings were taken for each fabric sample and the mean was calculated.

Biodegradability of Finished Fabrics

The soil degradation test was conducted by the burial soil testing method described by [13] with slight modification. Both treated and untreated samples were kept inside the microbial active soil at 10–15 cm depth. The samples were carefully removed from the soil after two weeks and washed with water gently off soil particles, then dried in the sunlight. The degradation (weight loss) of the prescribed samples after two weeks was determined by the following equations.

$$\text{Weight loss} (\%) = \frac{w1 - w2}{w1} * 100 \tag{1}$$

Where w_1 is the initial weight in (gm) and w_2 is the after-burial weight (in gm).

Antibacterial Activity Testing

Antibacterial testing was done by AATCC test method 100:2004 for a quantitative assessment of the antibacterial effectiveness of the antimicrobial agent against Gram-positive bacteria (Staphylococcus aureus) and Gram-negative bacteria (Escherichia coli). Half gram (0.5) of swatches was weighted from the test fabric. The weighted swatches were stacked in 250 ml wide-mouth glass jar with a screw cap followed by sterilization at 121 °C for 15 min. To the sterilized glass jar containing the test fabrics, 1 ml of bacteria culture solution with a cell concentration of 1×10^6 CFU/ml and inoculated individual swatches for 18 h at 37 °C. The inoculated samples were incubated for 24 h at 37 °C. After 24 h incubation, 100 ml of the neutralizing solution prepared by sterilized distilled water was added and shaken vigorously for 1 min. 1 ml of samples were spread on to the agar plate and plates were incubated at 37 °C for 24 h. After incubation, bacterial colonies were counted by a colony counter unit, and the antibacterial activity was determined as follows.

$$\% \text{Reduction} = \frac{A - B}{A} * 100 \tag{2}$$

Where "A" is the number of surviving cells (CFU/ml) for untreated cotton fabric (control), and "B" is the number of surviving bacteria (CFU/ml) for the treated fabrics.

Wash Durability Test

In the present study, the wash durability of the antimicrobial activity of the treated cotton fabric was evaluated at different wash cycles. The treated cotton fabric was washed in a launder –o-meter according to ES ISO 3759 test method with a 5 g/l neutral soap solution at 50 °C for 5 min. The finished fabrics were tested for the retention of antimicrobial activity after 5, 10, 15 launderings by the AATCC-100 test method as described in the above section.

3   Result and Discussion

3.1   Chemical Test Analysis

In the present study, the chemical test analysis was conducted to evaluate the presence of active constituents such as alkaloid, flavonoid, steroid, glycoside, protein, resin, quinone, tannin, anthraquinones and phenols.

The data presented in Table 2, the results of the phytochemical analysis indicate the presence of flavonoids, steroids, glycoside, tannin, protein, quinone, alkaloid, terpenoids, saponins, phenol and the absence of anthraquinone and resin in methanolic fruit extract of Solanum incanum. Whereas the chemical test analysis of a methanolic extract of onion peel indicates the presence of steroids, terpenoids, alkaloids, flavonoids, quinone, anthraquinones, phenols, saponins, tannin, resin but the absence of protein.

Table 2. Chemical test analysis of a phytochemical component of red onion peel and solanum incanum fruit

Phytochemical	Test	Color change observed	Red onion peel	Solanum incanum fruit
Saponins	Frothing test		+	++
Resins	Sulfuric acid test	Violet	+	−
Glycosides	Alkaline reagent test	Yellow	+	+++
Tannins	Ferric chloride test	Blue-black	+++	++
Terpenoids	Salkowski test	Reddish-brown	++	+++
Steroids	Salkowski test	Red	+++	++
Phenol	Ferric chloride test	Blue-black	+++	++
Flavonoids	Alkaline reagent test	Intense yellow	+	++
	Ammonium test	Yellow	+	++
	Aluminum chloride test	Light yellow	−	+
Quinone	Hydrochloric acid test	Yellow	−	+
Anthraquinones	Ammonia test	The red color in the ammonia layer	++	−
Protein	Xanthoproteic	Yellow	−	++
Alkaloid	Wagner's reagent test	Reddish/brown precipitate	++	+++

Key (+++) strongly present, (++) moderately present, (+) weakly present and (−) absent

3.2   Quantification of Total Polyphenol and Total Flavonoid Content

Total Polyphenol Content

The levels of total phenol were quantified from the equation of the regression line: $A = 0.006C + 0.045$ with $R^2 = 0.969$ from calibration curve where A = mean absorbance, C = concentration in mg/L.

The total phenol content can be determined using the formula $TPC = \left(\frac{mgGAE}{ml}\right) = C$ where C = Concentration of Gallic acid in mg/ml and TPC = Total phenol content in mg of Gallic acid equivalents per ml of sample. The level of the total phenol contents of the methanolic extracts of Solanum incanum fruit and red onion peel were presented in the table below (Table 3). It appeared that the methanolic extract of red onion peel had

Table 3. Total phenol content of methanolic extract of red onion peel and solanum incanum fruit

Extracts (mg/ml)	Total phenol content (mg GAE/ml sample)			
	Red onion peel		Solanum incanum fruit	
	Current study	Previous study	Current study	Previous study
1	0.857 ± 0.00078	0.71433 ± 0.06609	0.515 ± 0.00136	No studied

Key, **GAE = Gallic Acid Equivalent (conventional unit for phenolic compound)
All values are mean of triplicate experiments.

the highest phenol content compounds (0.857 ± 0.00078 mg GAE/ml) than that of the same extract of solanum incanum fruit (0.515 ± 0.00136 mg GAE/ml).

Ifesan [25], reported that the total phenol of ethanolic extract of red onion skin was 0.714.33 ± 0.06609 mg GAE/ml from 1 mg/ml concentration. The total phenol content in the present study was 0.857 ± 0.78 mg GAE/ml from 1 mg/ml was higher than that of the total phenol content has been reported by Ifesan [25] which was 0.714.33 ± 0.06609 mg GAE/ml from 1 mg/ml concentration of the sample.

Total Flavonoid Content

The levels of total flavonoid were expressed in terms of quercetin equivalent (QUE), determined by the well-known aluminum chloride colorimetric method described by Viera et al. [24] and quantified from the equation of regression line: $A = 0.0007C + 0.026$ with $R^2 = 0.935$ from calibration curve where A = mean absorbance, C = concentration quercetin in mg/L. The total flavonoid content of the extracts can be determined using the formula $TFC\left(\frac{mgQUE}{ml}\right) = C$ where C = Concentration of quercetin in mg/L of quercetin equivalence and TFC = Total flavonoid content in mg of quercetin equivalence.

Table 4. Total flavonoid contents of methanolic extract of Solanum incanum and red onion peel

Extracts (mg/ml)	Total flavonoid content (mg QUE/ml sample)			
	Red onion peel		Solanum incanum fruit	
	Current study	Previous study	Current study	Previous study
1	0.266 ± 0.0294	0.17733	0.849 ± 0.0067	No studied

Key, **QUE = Quercetin Equivalence (the conventional unit for flavonoid compound)
**All values are mean of triplicate experiments.

The level of the total flavonoid contents of the methanolic extracts of Solanum incanum fruit and red onion peel are presented in the table below (Table 4). It appeared that the methanolic extract of Solanum incanum fruit had the highest flavonoid content compounds (0.849 ± 0.0067 mg QUE/ml sample) than that of the same extract of red onion peel (0.266 ± 0.0294 mg QUE/ml sample).

Ifesan [25], reported that the total flavonoid of ethanolic extract of red onion skin was 0.17733 mg QUE/ml from 1 mg/ml concentration. The total flavonoid content in the present study which was 0.266 ± 0.0294 mg QUE/ml sample from 1 mg/ml was higher than that of the total flavonoid content has been reported by Ifesan [25] which was 0.17733 mg QUE/ml from 1 mg/ml concentration of a sample.

This may due to the type of solvent used, solvent strength, the technique of extraction, and time of extraction. It can be observed that the color change observed for the flavonoid test in solanum incanum fruit extract is confirmed moderately presence of flavonoid compound in solanum incanum fruit extract than the presence of flavonoid compound in red onion peel extract (weakly present). This result reveals that the quantification result from the UV-Vis spectrometer supports the qualitative test.

3.3   Physical Properties and Biodegradability of Treated Cotton Fabric

In the present study, 100% bleached cotton fabric was treated with Solanum incanum fruit and red onion peel extract in the presence of citric acid as a cross-linking agent. The data depicted in Table 5, it was a 4.76% change in the bending length of the treated fabric as compared to the untreated one and the bending length is directly related to the flexural rigidity of the fabric. Thus, the flexibility of the fabric is not changed too much even after the treatment process. [26] Studied the effect crosslinking agent on bending length and observed that the bending length of the treated cotton fabric increased in both warp and weft direction and attributed such an increase in the formation of covalent bonds that held the cellulose molecules together. However, after cross-linking of cellulose, some hydrogen bonds get converted to covalent bonds, therefore, bending length increase. The result published by Mortazavi & Esmailzadeh [27] and Mukthy et al. [26] support the result obtained in the present study.

Air permeability is an indication of the rate of airflow through the fabric. By increasing the concentration of the antimicrobial agent, from 3 to 5 g/l, applied on the cotton fabric, the thickness of the fabric was increased. As a result, the air permeability was slightly decreased.

The test result presented in Table 5 provided that, solanum incanum fruit and red onion peel extract finished fabrics had lower air permeability than that of unfinished fabrics. This is because Solanum incanum fruit and red onion peel extract treatments fill the pore of the fabric. As compared to the air permeability of pure extract finished fabric, fabric treated with pure Solanum incanum fruit extract (S4) had better air permeability than that of pure red onion peel extract finished fabric (S5).

This is due to the better affinity of red onion peel extract towards the fabric than Solanum incanum fruit extract and the coating layer thickness was larger in the case of red onion peel extract-treated fabric compared to Solanum incanum fruit extract treated fabrics.

The result of the present study was similar to the finding of El-Shafei et al. [9] and Mondal et al. [28] who reported that applying herb extract on the fabric surface did not much significantly alert the air permeability of the fabric.

The weight loss of the fabric due to digging soil test after two weeks was calculated by using the Eq. (1). From Table 5, the maximum weight loss because of soil degradation

Table 5. Water absorbency, weight loss (%), stiffness (bending length), and air permeability of Solanum incanum fruit and red onion peel.

Coc. (g/l)	Treatment combination (SIFE: ROPE)	Water absorbency (sec)	Weight loss (%)	Bending length (cm)	Air permeability (cm^3/cm^2/s)
3	S1 (25:75)	8.33 ± 0.57	14.55 ± 0.10	2.05 ± 0.07	38.75 ± 0.30
	S2 (50:50)	7.33 ± 0.57	9.19 ± 0.03	2.02 ± 0.00	40.25 ± 0.69
	S3 (75:25)	5.33 ± 0.57	11.24 ± 0.06	2.01 ± 0.01	40.027 ± 0.870
	S4 (100:0)	4 ± 0.01	15.72 ± 0.27	2.01 ± 0.01	43.42 ± 027
	S5 (0:100)	15.33 ± 0.56	15.98 ± 0.70	2.07 ± 0.02	39.77 ± 0.78
5	S1 (25:75)	12.33 ± 0.57	12.47 ± 0.13	2.09 ± 0.02	38.27 ± 0.01
	S2 (50:50)	10.33 ± 0.54	7.54 ± 0.13	2.04 ± 0.01	37.85 ± 0.09
	S3 (75:25)	10 .1 ± 0.9	10. 12 ± 0.24	2.02 ± 0.02	41.05 ± 0.04
	S4 (100:0)	8 .0 ± 0.01	14.22 ± 0.20	2.02 ± 0.03	41.6 ± 0.97
	S5 (0:100)	18 .0 ± 0.01	15.55 ± 0.24	2.10 ± 0.01	39.32 ± 0.20
	Control	1.33 ± 0.57	30.22 ± 0.04	2 ± 0.00	46.67 ± 0.05

was that of the untreated fabric, this is because microorganisms in the soil attacked the untreated cotton fabric quickly, in the absence of any treatment to inhibit them.

It can be seen from the table (Table 5), the least degradation (7.54%) occurred in the 5 g/l of fifty-fifty combination of Solanum incanum fruit and red onion peel extract-treated fabric, and the second least degradation occurred in the fabric treated with 50% combination with 3 g/l concentration. This proves the strong antibacterial activity of the combinatorial extract of solanum incanum fruit and red onion peel. The present finding was supported by Mondal et al. [28].

As presented in Table 6, the maximum strength loss happened in the fabric treated with pure red onion peel extract in the warp and weft direction of the fabric for both concentrations. The maximum percentage loss of strength was 43.966 ± 2.262% in the warp and 23.576 ± 1.074% in weft direction at 5 g/l concentration and 19.933 ± 0.00% in the warp and 14.6 ± 2.1074% in weft direction at 3 g/l concentration. Whereas the minimum strength loss has happened, the fabric treated with pure Solanum incanum fruit extract in warp and weft direction for both concentrations.

The minimum percentage loss of strength was 10.403 ± 1.074% in the weft and 12.166 ± 0.989% in the warp direction for 3 g/l concentration and 20.033 ± 1.131% and 13.586 ± 1.074% in warp and weft direction for 5 g/l concentration respectively. The loss of strength is mainly due to the stiffening of the molecular backbone after cross-link information Ali et al. [5].

3.4 Antibacterial Activity of Treated Fabric (AATCC Test Method 100-2004)

The bacterial resistance of the fabric finished with pure Solanum incanum fruit and red onion peel extract and their combinations with two different concentrations i.e. 3 g/l

Table 6. Tensile strength of the fabric in warp and weft direction

Concentration in g/l	Treatment combination	Loss of tensile strength (%) (Mean ± SD)	
		Warp direction	Weft direction
3	S1 (25:75)	15.200 ± 1.131	13.620 ± 1.074
	S2 (50:50)	12.700 ± 1.131	12.716 ± 1.074
	S3 (75:25)	15.633 ± 1.131	11.310 ± 1.074
	S4 (100:0)	12.166 ± 0.989	10.403 ± 1.074
	S5 (0:100)	19.933 ± 0.000	14.600 ± 2.142
5	S1 (25:75)	42.333 ± 1.131	23.386 ± 2.138
	S2 (50:50)	36.066 ± 1.131	15.903 ± 1.074
	S3 (75:25)	28.566 ± 2.262	16.610 ± 1.074
	S4 (100:0)	20.033 ± 1.131	13.586 ± 1.074
	S5 (0:100)	43.966 ± 2.262	23.576 ± 1.074
	Control	Nil	Nil

and 5 g/l by pad-dry-cure method, the growth of E. coli (Gram-negative bacteria) and S. aureus (Gram-positive bacteria) was counted quantitatively by the standard test method AATCC 100. As presented in Table 7, after treating the cotton fabric by a pad-dry-cure method with 3 g/l and 5 g/l concentration of red onion peel separately, percentage reduction values were 97.17% and 97.67% for E. coli and 97.50% and 98.00% for S. aureus, respectively.

Table 7. Antibacterial activity of cotton fabric treated by Solanum incanum fruit and red onion peel against S. aureus and E. coli.

Concentration in g/l	Bacteria	Bacterial reduction	Type of treatment				
			Solanum incanum fruit	Red onion peel	Combination of Solanum incanum to onion peel extract		
					50:50	25:75	75:25
3	E.coli	%	97.83	97.17	99.63	98.08	99.00
	S. aureus	%	97.92	97.50	99.83	98.42	99.25
5	E.coli	%	98.00	97.67	99.92	98.92	99.42
	S. aureus	%	98.83	98.00	100	99.08	99.75
Untreated	Confluent growth						

Data (Table 7) also revealed that when Solanum incanum fruit extract was applied by the pad-dry-cure method, percentage reduction values were 97.83% and 98.0% for E. coli and 97.92% and 98.83% for S. aureus. Data (Table 7) also depicted the bacterial reduction against various combinations of Solanum incanum fruit and red onion peel extracts. It was found that 50:50 v/v combinations of Solanum incanum fruit and red onion peel extract had better bacterial reduction i.e. 99.63% for E. coli and 99.83% for S. aureus with 3 g/l.

With 5 g/l concentration of the same extract i.e. combination of Solanum incanum fruit and red onion peel, the bacterial reduction values increased to 99.92%, 99.42%, and 98.92% using 50:50, 75:25 and 25:75 v/v standard combinations on cotton fabric for E. coli bacteria.

The bacterial reduction of the fabric treated with combined extract of solanum incanum fruit and red onion peel was found better than the fabric treated with alone. This is maybe due to the cumulative effect and different chemical composition of Solanum incanum and red onion peel extract in combinatorial treatment. As comparing the bacterial reduction of fabric treated with pure extract, the fabric treated with pure Solanum incanum fruit extract had maximum bacterial reduction than that of red onion peel extract against S. aureus and E. coli test bacteria. This is due to the chemical composition of solanum incanum fruit extract i.e. the presence of a high number of flavonoids, which has known to exhibit a remarkable degree of antibacterial activity.

3.5 Wash Durability Test

As data depicted in Fig. 1, the bacterial reduction of the fabric treated with 50:50 combinations of Solanum incanum fruit and red onion peel extract at 5 g/l concentration shows a slight change after 15 wash cycle for both Gram-positive (S. aureus) and Gram-negative (E. coli) test bacteria. Whereas the bacterial reduction of the fabric treated with pure Solanum incanum fruit and red onion peel had a significant change after a 15-wash cycle at the same concentration.

The decrease in antibacterial activity may be attributed to the slow removal of the extract, due to the breakdown of cross-links between the finishing agent and the cellulose material, which explains the bonding between the finishing agent and the fabric structure. As comparing the wash durability of fabric treated with pure extract, the fabric treated with pure Solanum incanum fruit extract had better efficacy than that of red onion peel extract against S. aureus and E. coli test bacteria. Data also presented in the figure below the wash durability of the synthetic antimicrobial agent (silver nitrate) decrease after 10 wash cycle. Fabric treated with 50:50 combinations of Solanum incanum fruit and onion peel extract had better wash durability than fabric treated with the synthetic antimicrobial agent (silver nitrate). This was due to the leaching property of synthetic agents.

These results are supported by the study conducted by Unango et al. [29] who report on the investigation of biologically active natural compounds on cotton fabrics as an antibacterial textile finishing. Thus, the wash durability test of the present study on antibacterial activity also suggested the study conducted by Singh et al. [30] and Nalankilli & Tadesse [12].

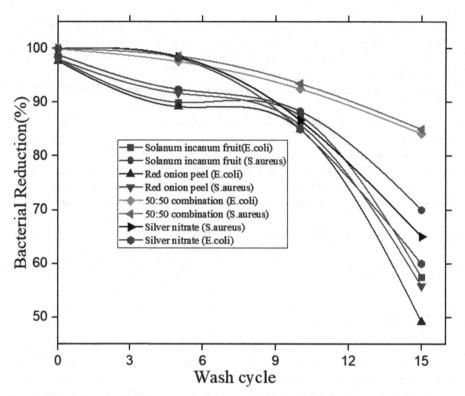

Fig. 1. Effect of wash durability on antibacterial activity of cotton fabric against S. aureus and E. coli

4 Conclusion

Based on the experimental results, it was concluded that the methanolic extract of solanum incanum fruit and red onion peel exhibited a good microbial reduction percentage in both Staphylococcus aureus and Escherichia coli microbes for all treatment. The high antimicrobial effect on cotton fabric was achieved with fifty-fifty combination at 5 g/l concentration for both bacteria. The wash durability of the fabric treated with combined extract exhibit good durability in terms of bacterial reduction percentage even after 15 wash cycles. However, fabric treated with pure extract showed less durability after 15 wash cycles. The physical properties fsuch as weight and bending length increased after the application of extract. Whereas the tensile strength, air permeability, and wetting property of the fabric decreased after the application of extracts.

References

1. Islam, S.U., Mohammad, F.: Natural colorants in the presence of anchors so-called mordants as promising coloring and antimicrobial agents for textile materials. ACS Sustain. Chem. Eng. **3**, 2361–2375 (2015). https://doi.org/10.1021/acssuschemeng.5b00537

2. Purwar, R.: Antimicrobial textiles. In: The Impact and Prospects of Green Chemistry for Textile Technology, pp. 12–30. Elsevier Ltd. (2019)
3. Gao, Y., Cranston, R.: Recent advances in antimicrobial treatments of textiles. Text Res. J. **78**, 60–72 (2008). https://doi.org/10.1177/0040517507082332
4. Kasiri, M.B., Safapour, S.: Natural dyes and antimicrobials for green treatment of textiles. Environ. Chem. Lett. **12**(1), 1–13 (2013). https://doi.org/10.1007/s10311-013-0426-2
5. Ali, S.W., Purwar, R., Joshi, M., Rajendran, S.: Antibacterial properties of Aloe vera gel-finished cotton fabric. Cellulose **21**(3), 2063–2072 (2014). https://doi.org/10.1007/s10570-014-0175-9
6. Dhiman, G., Chakraborty, J.N.: Antimicrobial performance of cotton finished with triclosan, silver and chitosan. Fashion Textiles **2**(1), 1–14 (2015). https://doi.org/10.1186/s40691-015-0040-y
7. Drahansky, M., et al.: Phytochemicals: extraction methods, basic structures, and mode of action as potential chemotherapeutic agents. Intech i:13 (2016). https://doi.org/10.5772/57353
8. Tawiah, B., Badoe, W., Fu, S.: Advances in the development of antimicrobial agents for textiles: the quest for natural products. Rev. Fibres Text East Eur. **24**, 136–149 (2016). https://doi.org/10.5604/12303666.1196624
9. El-Shafei, A., Shaarawy, S., Motawe, F.H., Refaei, R.: Herbal extract as an eco-friendly antimicrobial finishing of cotton fabric. Egypt. J. Chem. **61**, 317–327 (2018). https://doi.org/10.21608/EJCHEM.2018.2621.1209
10. Gopalakrishnan, M., Saravanan, D.: Antimicrobial activity of coleus ambonicus herbal finish on cotton fabric. Fibres Text East Eur. **25**, 106–110 (2017). https://doi.org/10.5604/01.3001.0010.2854
11. Sathianarayanan, M.P., Bhat, N.V., Kokate, S.S., Walunj, V.E.: Antibacterial finish for cotton fabric from herbal products. Indian J. Fibre Text Res. **35**, 50–58 (2010)
12. Nalankilli, G., Tadesse, K.: Antimicrobial cotton textiles by finishing with extracts of an Ethiopian plant (solanum incanum) fruit. Afr. Res. Rev. **12**, 56–65 (2018)
13. Thilagavathi, G., Rajendrakumar, K., Rajendran, R.: Development of eco-friendly antimicrobial textile finishes using herbs. Indian J. Fibre Text Res. **30**, 431–436 (2005)
14. Abebe, H., Gebre, T., Assistant, A.H.: Phytochemical investigation on the roots of solanum incanum, hadiya zone, Ethiopia. J. Med. Plants Stud. **2**, 83–93 (2014)
15. Škerget, M., Majhenič, L., Bezjak, M., Knez, Ž.: Antioxidant, radical scavenging and antimicrobial activities of red onion (Allium cepa L) skin and edible part extracts. Chem. Biochem. Eng. Q. **23**, 435–444 (2009)
16. Griffiths, G., Trueman, L., Crowther, T., Thomas, B., Smith, B.: Onions - a global benefit to health. Phyther Res. **16**, 603–615 (2002). https://doi.org/10.1002/ptr.1222
17. Kumar, M.S.Y., Raghu, T.S., Kumar, P., Varghese, F.V., Kotresh, T.M.: Application of enriched fraction of seabuckthorn leaf extract as antimicrobial finish on technical textile. Def. Life Sci. J. **2**, 428–434 (2017). https://doi.org/10.14429/dlsj.2.12273
18. Harborne, J.B.: Phytochemical Methods a Guide to Modern Techniques of Plant Analysis. Springer, Heidelberg (1998)
19. Pam, C.S., Dahiru, D.: Effect of aqueous extract of Solanum incanum fruit on some serum biochemical parameters. Agric. Bus. Technol. J. **10**, 82–86 (2012)
20. Indhumathi, T., Mohandass, S.: Efficacy of Ethanolic extract of Solanum incanum fruit extract for its antimicrobial activity. Int. J. Curr. Microbiol. Appl. Sci. **3**, 939–949 (2014)
21. Jepkoech, K.E., Gakunga, N.J.: Antimicrobial activity and phytochemical screening of Solanum incanum fruit extract against clinical samples of Staphylococcus aureus collecting from Nakuru Provincial General Hospital Laboratory, Kenya. Int. Res. J. Med. Biomed. Sci. **2**, 1–8 (2017). https://doi.org/10.1111/j.1600-0404.2009.01309.x
22. Kokate, C.K., Purohit, C.K., Gokhale, S.B.: Phytochemical tests. Pharmacognosy **35**, 510–512 (1996)

23. Singleton, V.L., Rossi, J.A.: Colorimetry of total phenolics with phosphomolybdic-phosphotungstic acid reagents. Am. J. Enol. Viticulture **16**(3), 144–158 (1965)
24. Viera, V.B., et al.: Extraction of phenolic compounds and evaluation of the antioxidant and antimicrobial capacity of red onion skin (Allium cepa L.). Int. Food Res. J. **24**, 990–999 (2017)
25. Ifesan, B.O.T.: Chemical composition of onion peel (Allium cepa) and its ability to serve as a preservative in cooked beef. Int. J. Sci. Res. Methodol. **7**(4), 1–10 (2017)
26. Mukthy, A.A., Yousuf, A., Anwarul, M.: Effects of resin finish on cotton blended woven fabrics. Int. J. Sci. Eng. Technol. **990**, 983–990 (2014)
27. Mortazavi, S.M., Boukany, P.E.: Application of mixtures of resin finishing to achieve some physical properties on interlining cotton fabrics: I-effect of stiffening and cross-linking agents. Iran Polym. J. (Engl. Ed.) **13**, 213–218 (2004)
28. Mondal, M.I.H., Saha, J.: Antimicrobial, UV resistant and thermal comfort properties of chitosan- and Aloe vera-modified cotton woven fabric. J. Polym. Environ. **27**(2), 405–420 (2019). https://doi.org/10.1007/s10924-018-1354-9
29. Unango, F.J., Ramasamy, K.M.: A review on the investigation of biologically active natural compounds on cotton fabrics as an antibacterial textile finishing. Int. Res. J. Sci. Technol. **1**, 49–55 (2019)
30. Singh, N., Punia, P., Singh, V.: Bacterial resistance finish on cotton fabric with pomegranate and onion peel extracts. Int. J. Curr. Microbiol. Appl. Sci. **6**, 1075–1079 (2017)

Extraction of Natural Dye from the Root of Rumex Abyssinicus for Textile Dying Application

Melkamu Birlie Genet[✉], Asres Mekonnen Admas, Animaw Gerem Abeje, and Felegush Enyew Melese

Bahir Dar Institute of Technology, Bahir Dar University, Bahir Dar, Ethiopia

Abstract. Dyes extracted from natural sources have emerged as important substitutes to synthetic dyes. In this study, an environmental friendly natural colorant was extracted from the root of Rumex abyssinicus (Mekmeko) by using an aqueous extraction method. The effect of temperature and pH on the extraction of natural dye was studied and the best condition for dye extraction was obtained at pH 10 and temperature of 80 °C. UV-VIS absorption spectrum indicates a λmax peak at 280 nm and this value is associated to anthraquinone dyes. Structural characterization by FT-IR revealed the presence of chromophores compounds like C=O, OH, -C=N- and C=C of aromatic. The coloring potential of the extracted dyes has been studied using selected mordant types, pH, and dyeing techniques. The simultaneous mordanting method at acidic media and iron sulfate mordant type shows very good (4) and very good to excellent (4–5) grade colorfastness characteristics to washing and rubbing.

Keywords: Rumex Abyssinicus · Natural dye · Mordant · Cotton fabric

1 Introduction

Dyeing with natural colorants was one of the oldest techniques practiced since the prehistoric period. Natural dyes extracted from plants, minerals, and insects were used to stain hides, decorate shells, feathers, paint the ancient story on the walls of caves, color food substrate, color natural protein fibers like wool, silk and cotton [1]. Primitive men also used plant dyestuffs to color animal skin and dye their own skin during religious, traditional festivals and wars. Dyes might have found unintentionally, but their advantage has become extremely a part of man's habit that it is hard to think of a civilized world without colorants [2, 3].

Until the end of the 19th century, natural dyes were the major colorants for textile industries. The discovery of first synthetic dye mauveine, a basic dye type, by Sir W. H. Perkin in 1856 led to almost a complete replacement of natural dyes in textile industries [4, 5]. The rapid decline of the use of natural dyes after the introduction of synthetic dyes was due to its drawbacks like the inconsistency of colors, less availability, lack of fastness, etc. [6]. Synthetic dyes are produced from cheap petroleum raw materials

M. A. Delele et al. (Eds.): ICAST 2020, LNICST 384, pp. 83–96, 2021.
https://doi.org/10.1007/978-3-030-80621-7_6

and these dyes are become popular due to its simple production, variety of colors, reproducible application processes, and the consumer's demand for quality products having superior fastness properties at a low price [5, 7]. Currently, there is excessive use of synthetic dyes in numerous industries estimated around 10,000,000 tonnes and approximately 10,000 different types of dyes and pigments are manufactured world-wide annually [8, 9]. The tremendous production rate and use of synthetic dyes in various industries led to the release of a vast amount of colored wastes into the environment. This poses a series health and ecological problem to the world since synthetic dyes are hazardous, toxic and carcinogenic, non-biodegradable, and non-renewable in nature. As a result, its application is slumped tremendously in textile and other dyeing industries in recent times [10]. Textile industries alone uses huge amount of water during the dyeing of fabrics. The effluents released from these factories contain a heavy load of hazardous chemicals including dyes used during textile processing significantly pollutes the natural ecosystem. It is estimated that 10–25% of textile dyes are lost during the dyeing processes [7] and 2–20% of such dyes are directly discharged as aqueous effluents into the environment [11]. It is difficult to remove such effluents that affect aquatic biota [12], rivers, soils, crops, etc. by conventional water treatment methods [6]. Recently, the interest of using natural dyes in textile industries has been growing rapidly due to the stringent environmental standards imposed by many countries in response to toxic and allergic reactions associated with synthetic dyes. Some countries like Germany, USA, India, and Netherland imposed a ban on the use of some synthetic dyes [13–15].

Natural dyes constitute colorants that are obtained from flora, fauna, and minerals without any chemical processing has gained momentum due to increased demand for these dyes by the food, pharmaceutical [16], cosmetic as well as the textile coloration industries [17]. Natural dyes are mostly eco-friendly, biodegradable, less toxic, less allergenic, and renewable [18] dyes. These features and a growing concern for the environment have created a niche market for the industrial-scale use of natural colorants [19, 20]. Nature has gifted us with more than 500 dye-yielding plant species, and all colors of the rainbow are obtained from plants. They can provide not only a rich and varied source of dyestuff, but also the possibility of an income through the sustainable sale of these colorant plants. It has been reported that natural dyes can be successfully extracted from various plant sources like henna leaves, Mahogany, Ketapang, Tamarind, Mangosteen, Mango, Guava, papaya, Banana, and Onion, etc. [21, 22]. Natural colorant from different plant parts such as roots, leaves, barks, twigs, stems, heartwood, bark, wood shavings, flowers, fruits, rinds, hulls, husks, trunks can be extracted through different methods. Natural colorants can be extracted from its source by aqueous extraction, alkali or acid extraction, microwave and ultrasonic-assisted extraction, fermentation, enzymatic extraction, solvent extraction, and supercritical fluid extraction methods [23].

Utilizing natural dyes in textile industries has certain constraints like low dye uptake, low color yield, the complexity of dying process, reproducible results, limited shades and inadequate fastness properties which can be solved using chemicals called mordant [24, 25]. Mordants are metal salts that can escalate the binding efficiency of natural dye on cotton fabrics. Metal ions of mordants act as electron acceptors for electron donors to form coordination bonds with the dye molecule, making them insoluble in water. Copper sulfate, ferrous sulfate, chromium sulfate, stannous chloride, zinc sulfate, alum, etc. are the commonly used mordants that make the fabric to have good colorfastness properties [26, 27]. Colorfastness is the resistance of a material to change any of its color characteristics or extent of transfer of its colorants to adjacent white materials in touch. Generally light fastness, wash fastness and rub fastness are considered for textile fibers.

Natural dyes can be classified based on colors, chemical constitution, application, and origin [28–30]. On the basis of color, natural dye can be classified as red, blue, yellow, green, black, brown, orange, and other derived dye types. Natural dyes have a complex chemical constitution. Unlike synthetic dyes, they are normally not a single entity but a mixture of closely related chemical compounds. On the basis of major chemical constituents present, they are divided into anthraquinone, indigoid, naphthoquinones, carotenoid, flavonoid, and Tannin-based dyes. Natural dyes are also classified based on the method of their application such as mordant dyes, direct dyes, vat dyes, acid dyes, and basic dyes, and disperse dye. There are three major sources from which natural dyes are extracted such as plants, minerals, and animals [31].

Ethiopia is rich in biodiversity and yet it doesn't use its natural resources effectively. Among its natural resources which are not utilized properly is the Rumex Abyssinicus (Mekmeko in local Amharic language) plant. Rumex Abyssinicus is widely spread throughout Ethiopia at altitudes between 1200 and 3300 m and some east African countries. This plant is native to Ethiopia (Abyssinicus means from Abyssinia, Ethiopia) [32]. Rumex abyssinicus is a member of the family of Polygonaceae and most of the species of Polygonaceae genus contain phytoconstituents, namely, flavonoid, anthraquinone, and triterpenoids. Rumex abyssinicus is a perennial herb, which grows up to 3 to 4 m, with the thick and fleshy rhizome. The root of Rumex Abyssinicus mainly consists of anthraquinone and flavonoid based colorant such as red and yellow dyes due to its rhizome [32, 33]. Traditionally Ethiopian Women used this plant root extensively to color their feet and hands during different religious festivals and other events to keep their beauty. This plant has also different antimicrobial activities and used as a cleaning agent to remove wastes. So, it is possible to extract natural dye from this plant for the textile dying application. There are no enough published research works on this indigenous plant for textile dying application and this study tries to fill the gap by providing some information about its dying performance in cotton fabrics.

This study aims to extract eco-friendly natural dye from the root of the Rumex abyssinicus plant for textile dyeing application using aqueous extraction method. The dye was extracted by varying pH and temperature at fixed extraction time (1 h). The coloring performance was studied by applying the extracted dye on the cotton fabrics at different dyeing conditions, pH, and mordants types.

2 Methodology

2.1 Raw Material Collection and Preparation

The roots of Rumex Abyssinicus used in this study were purchased from the market in Bahir Dar city, Amhara national regional state, Ethiopia. Then the root was washed by distilled water to remove mud and impurities. The cover of the cleaned root was peeled and cut into small pieces using a knife manually. The chipped root was dried on open-air by sunlight. Finally, the dried sample was crashed by disc mill and it was sieved to get a uniform particle size passing through 0.5 mm sieve size. Figure 1 shows the root, peeled and powder of the Rumex Abyssinicus plant.

(a)   (b)   (c)

Fig. 1. Rumex Abyssinicus; root (a), chipped root (b) and powder (c)

2.2   Extraction of Dye

The aqueous dye extraction method is used to extract dye from the root of this plant due to its easy and simpler operation. Twenty-five grams of the Rumex abyssinicus root powder was added to the round bottom flasks containing 250 ml of distilled water (1:10 w/v) in acidic (pH-4), neutral (pH-7) and basic media (pH-10) at 40, 60 and 80 °C extraction temperatures at a constant extraction time of one hour. The pH of the acidic and basic medium was regulated by using 0.1M of H_2SO_4 and NaOH. The temperature of each sample was maintained by using a hot water bath. Then, the round bottom flask that contained the extracted dye solution was put on the mechanical shaker for two hours to effectively homogenize it. Finally, the solution was filtered by using a muslin cloth and the filtrate was used for dyeing.

2.3   Characterization of Dye

Identification of the Formation of Anthraquinone Dye: The dye extracted from the root of Rumex abyssinicus mainly contains anthraquinone colorant type [32, 33]. So, the formation of this colorant in the crud extract can be checked using either aqueous ammonia or sodium hydroxide solution. In this study, the presence of the anthraquinone colorant was checked by using sodium hydroxide solution. 3 ml of the crude dye extract from Rumex abyssinicus root powder was added to the test tube containing 1ml of 10% sodium hydroxide solution to confirm the presence of anthraquinone colorant type.

UV - Visible Spectroscopy: The wavelength of the maximum absorbance of an extract was determined by ultraviolet (UV-Vis) spectrophotometer (PerkinElmer, lambda 35). One milliliter of the extracted dye was diluted in 100 ml distilled water for UV analysis. The diluted dye extract was scanned from 200 to 700 nm to generate the characteristic absorption spectra of the sample and the corresponding peaks.

FTIR Spectroscopy: 2 mg of powder extract was mixed thoroughly with 200 mg of potassium bromide (KBr) and homogenized in an agate mortar. The mixture was then placed in the sample compartment of Infrared Fourier Transform Spectroscopy (FT/IR-6600typeA) to determine the main functional groups responsible for light absorption. The measurement was conducted between the ranges from 400 to 4000 cm^{-1} at a resolution of 4 cm^{-1}.

2.4 Dyeing Method

Scouring and Bleaching of Cotton Fabric: The desized cotton fabric samples obtained from Bahir Dar textile share company were washed in a solution containing 3% NaOH, 2.5% soda ash (Na$_2$CO$_3$), and 1% detergent at a temperature of 90 °C for 3 h. before dying of the cotton fabrics by keeping the material to liquor ratio 1:20. The scoured fabric was washed with tap water and it was dried at room temperature. The scoured fabrics were soaked by hydrogen peroxide for 30 min prior to dyeing or mordanting to bleach the fabric effectively [34].

Mordanting and Dying: Chemical mordants have been used to improve the fastness property of the natural dye. In this study, aluminum sulfate, iron sulfate, and copper sulfate mordants were used. Three different mordanting techniques were applied to dye the fabric such as pre mordanting, Simultaneous mordanting, and post mordanting conditions.

Pre-mordanting Method: In this method, the mordants were used to treat the fabrics before dying. Two grams of iron sulfate, aluminum sulfate and copper (II) sulfate mordants were dissolved in 500 ml distilled water separately. The scoured cotton samples were heated at a temperature of 60 °C for 50 min. The pre-mordanted cotton fabrics were allowed to dry without washing. After the mordanted fabrics were dried completely the fabrics were rinsed in the extracted dye to color it.

Simultaneous Mordanting Method: Two grams of iron sulfate, aluminum sulfate, and copper (II) sulfate mordants were added into extracted dye in a separate beaker. Then the scoured cotton fabrics were placed in the mixture and it was allowed to heat at a temperature of 60 °C for 50 min.

Post mordanting method: The dried scoured cotton fabric was immersed in extracted dye. Then, the dried and dyed cotton fabrics were treated with two grams of iron sulfate, aluminum sulfate, and copper (II) sulfate mordants separately in 500 ml distilled water and heated at a temperature of 60 °C for 50 min.

For all the mordanting techniques, the cotton fabrics were dyed directly with the dye extract by keeping the material to liquid ratio of 1:20. All the mordanting methods have done as described [35, 36]. The brine solution was added twice at a time interval of 15 min and finally, sodium carbonate was added for fixing purpose. Figure 2 below shows different dyed cotton fabric samples.

Fig. 2. Dyed cotton fabrics

2.5   Evaluation Method of Color Fastness of the Dyed Fabrics

Fastness to Washing: The washing fastness of the dyed cotton fabrics were conducted out using a Launder-O-meter by following the ISO standard Test No. 3 (ISO 105-C03:1989) procedures [37]. A 4 cm × 10 cm dyed cotton fabric was stitched around the edges of a white cotton sample. The dyed fabric was washed by a mixture of 150 ml water and 75 g of soap with 10 washing balls at a temperature of 60 °C for 35 min. After the treatment, the composite specimen was removed and rinsed in cold water and then dried in an oven. The dried sample was then assessed for change in color of dyed specimen and staining of adjacent fabric with grey scale and grading was given.

Fastness to Rubbing: Colorfastness dyed cotton fabrics to dry rubbing and wet rubbing fastness were tested as per AATCC 8–2007 test method using manually operated Crock meter and grey scale [37]. The specimen to be measured was rubbed against perfectly scoured and bleached fabric of dimension not less than 22 cm × 10 cm. For the determination of dry rub fastness, the sample to be tested was rubbed 10 times in 10 s in a dry condition, whereas for wet rub fastness determination, the same procedure has been adopted by wetting out the rubbing cloth and squeezing it to 100% expression. The staining on the rubbing fabric was assessed with the standard Grey Scale. Figure 3 depicts crock meter, lauder-o-meter, and grey scale.

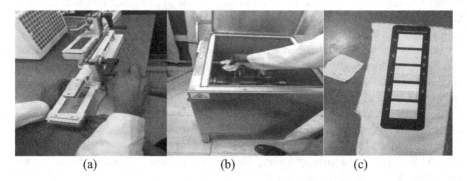

(a)   (b)   (c)

Fig. 3. Crock meter (a), Launder-o-meter (b) and Grey scale (c)

3   Result and Discussion

3.1   The Effect of pH and Temperature on Dye Extraction

Figure 4 shows the effect of extraction pH and temperature on the absorbance of the extracted dye. As the pH changes from acidic to neutral and neutral to basic medium, the absorbance of the extracted dye increased tremendously. The extracted dye at the basic media exhibits a maximum absorbance of 0.783 A. The reason for extracting more coloring components in alkaline solution was due to the presence of acidic phenolic groups in the root of Rumex abyssinicus, which reacted with alkali and form more soluble salts in water. The solubility of the coloring component increased due to an increase in ionization of hydroxyl groups in the alkaline medium. Similarly, the absorbance of the extracted dye increased when the extraction temperature rises from 40 °C to 80 °C. It is obvious that as the temperature increases the ruptures of the root of the Rumex abyssinicus cell wall increase enormously and as a result, more dye components were released into the extract. Higher color absorbance was observed at the extraction temperature of 80 °C. Higher extraction temperature can cause damage to protein-based fiber and so, the extraction temperature of 80 °C can be used as the optimum temperature in order to obtain greater color strength in the root extract.

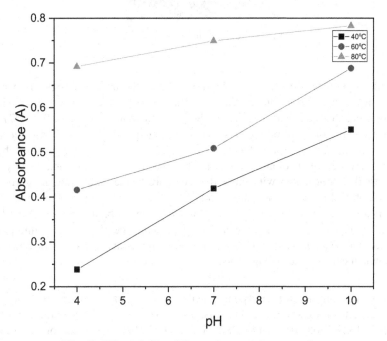

Fig. 4. Effect of pH and Temperature on dye extraction

3.2   Characterization of the Extracted Dye

Identification of Anthraquinone Colorant in Rumex Abyssinicus Root Extract:
Crude extracts of certain plants show color formation when treated with certain chemical compounds. As it is shown in Fig. 5, the formation of red color was observed when the aqueous extract was treated by NaOH. This result confirms the presence of hydroxyl anthraquinones, which is a major color bearing component in Rumex abyssinicus root extract [38]. Anthraquinones are generally yellow, orange, or brown colored pigments. Anthraquinone can be distinguished from benzoquinones and naphthoquinones as they usually give red solutions on a reduction in alkaline solution [39]. This implies that the anthraquinone colorant is the major constituent of the Rumex abyssinicus root extract.

Fig. 5. Anthraquinone colorant test

UV- Visible spectroscopy Analysis: Figure 6 shows the absorption spectrum of the aqueous dye extract from the root of the Rumex abyssinicus plant. A maximum absorbance peak (λmax) was detected at 280 nm with an absorbance of 0.480977 Å in the UV visible region. Anthraquinones shows a strong quinonoid electro transfer at this absorption peak. The absorption band at λmax 280 nm indicate characteristics absorption chromophore center for anthraquinone [33]. But the λmax value obtained by other researchers does not match with those that compare to the anthraquinone derivatives like chrysophanol (λmax = 440 nm), Emodin (λmax = 445 nm) or Physcion (λmax = 433 nm) in the invisible region [32]. This fact shows a bathochromic effect likely caused by co-pigmentation mechanisms. It is a consequence of a typical anthraquinone intermolecular association within flavonoids like tannins and catechins or glucocydic groups, which can act like co-pigments.

FTIR Spectroscopy Result Analysis: The FT-IR spectrum of Rumex abyssinicus root powder extract showed the prominent peaks at 3393.1375, 2918.7346, 2363.3362, 1386.5677, 1324.8568, 1051.0145, 782.9576, and 620.9664 cm^{-1} as shown in Fig. 7. The broad peak appeared at 3393.1375 cm^{-1} assigned to O-H stretching vibrations. This band is caused by the presence of alcoholic and phenolic hydroxyl groups involved in hydrogen bonds [40, 41]. This verifies the presence of poly phenolic groups which are abundantly present in this plant. This polyphenolic compound helps in interlocking majority chromophore to get adhere to fabric and thus increase dye fastness. The

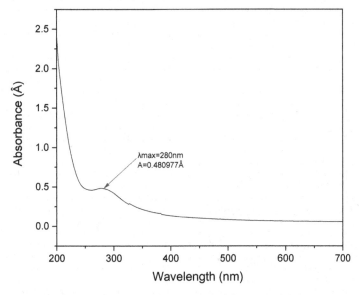

Fig. 6. UV-VIS spectra of Rumex abyssinicus root dye extract

bands at 2918.7346 cm^{-1}assigned to C-H stretching vibrations of the methoxyl group [42]. The peak at 2363 cm^{-1} confirms the presence of Nitriles, Azides, and alkynes. The stretching vibration at 1611 cm^{-1} confirms the presence of -C=O conjugates with the ring double bonds giving a -C=C-, -C=N-, and NH groups [42]. The peak at 1386 and1324 cm^{-1} confirms the presence of nitro-compounds, alkanes and alkenes. The peak at 1051 cm^{-1} emanates from primary and secondary alcoholic groups [42]. The peak at 782 cm^{-1} shows the absorption band caused by deformation vibration of C-H bends on the benzene ring and it indicates the presence of aromatics [42–44]. The peak at 620 cm^{-1} confirms the presence of aromatic compounds. The presence of the main anthraquinone unit is confirmed by the carbonyl and hydroxyl vibrational absorption frequencies.

3.3 Colorfastness Properties of Dyed Cotton Fabrics

The colorfastness grade is equal to the grey-scale step which is judged to have the same color or contrast difference [45]. All the dyed cotton fabric samples recorded acceptable fastness grades except the non-mordanting fabrics. Table 1 shows the colorfastness properties of dyed cotton fabric under different dying conditions, mordant types, and pH. The mordanting methods, the mordant types and pH conditions efficiently improved to washing and rubbing colorfastness on cotton fabrics. The washing fastness (color change and staining) and rubbing fastness (dry and wet) grades of the cotton fabric recorded Good (3), good to very good (3–4), very Good (4) and very good to excellent (4–5) grades in colorfastness were recorded.

The dying of textile fabric at the pre-mordanting condition shows good, good to very good, very good, and very good to excellent grades of washing and rubbing fastness in

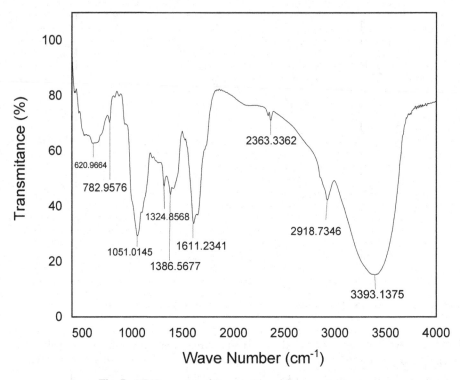

Fig. 7. FT-IR spectra of Rumex Abyssinicus root extract

aluminum sulfate, copper sulfate and iron sulfate with acidic, neutral, and basic media. The washing fastness of cotton fabric was recorded good (3), good to very good (3–4) and very good (4) grades in color changes and staining. Grades of rubbing fastness of the dyed cotton fabric both in wet and dry rubbing exhibit good (3), good to very good (3–4), very good (4) and very good to excellent (4–5) grades. Aluminum sulfate at pH 7 exhibits a very good (4) grade color fastness for both color change and staining washing fastness and very good to excellent (4–5) grade for dry rubbing and good to very good (3–4) for wet rubbing fastness respectively in the pre-mordanting conditions. In simultaneous mordanting condition, all mordant types and dyeing media show a good, good to very good, very good and very good to excellent grade colorfastness to washing and rubbing. Iron sulfate at pH 4 showed a greater colorfastness to washing and rubbing. Both the color change and staining washing fastness recorded a very good to excellent (4–5) colorfastness. Dry and wet rubbing color fastness of the cotton fabric exhibits a very good to excellent (4–5) and very good grade (4) colorfastness respectively. Similar to pre and simultaneous mordanting methods, post mordanting technique yields a good (3) good to very good (3–4), very good (4) and very good to excellent (4–5) grade colorfastness properties. The post-mordanting dyeing condition with iron sulfate at pH 10 shows improved colorfastness to washing and rubbing. Dyeing of cotton fabric by Rumex Abyssinicus extract without the application of mordant shows weak (2), weak to good (2–3) and good grade color fastness properties to washing and rubbing.

Table 1. Dying condition, mordant and pH effect on the performance of dyed cotton fabrics

Dying conditions	Mordant	pH	Fastness			
			Washing		Rubbing	
			Color Change	Staining	Dry	Wet
Pre-mordanting	Aluminum sulfate	4	3–4	4	4–5	3
		7	4	4	4–5	3–4
		10	4	3–4	4	4
	Iron sulfate	4	3	3–4	4	3
		7	3	3	4	3
		10	3–4	4	4	3–4
	Copper Sulfate	4	3	3–4	4	3
		7	3–4	4	4	3
		10	3–4	4	4	3–4
Simultaneous mordanting	Aluminum sulfate	4	4	4	4–5	3–4
		7	4	4	4–5	4
		10	4	3–4	4	3–4
	Iron sulfate	4	4–5	4–5	4–5	4
		7	4–5	4	4–5	4
		10	4	3–4	4	3–4
	Copper Sulfate	4	3–4	3	4	3
		7	4–5	4–5	4	3–4
		10	3–4	3	4	3
Post mordanting	Aluminum sulfate	4	3–4	3	4	3
		7	4	4–5	4–5	3–4
		10	3–4	4	4	4
	Iron sulfate	4	4	3–4	4	3–4
		7	4	3–4	4–5	4
		10	4–5	4	4–5	4
	Copper Sulfate	4	4	3–4	4–5	4
		7	3–4	4	4–5	4
		10	3–4	4	4	3–4
Non mordanting		4	2–3	2	3–4	2
		7	2	2–3	3	2
		10	3	2–3	3	2

Dying of the cotton fabric without mordants at acidic media gives good color fastness behaviors relative to that of the basic and neutral medium. It is difficult to use the Rumex Abyssinicus extract without mordant to dye the cotton fabric. Generally, the simultaneous mordanting method at acidic media and iron sulfate mordant type shows very good and very good to excellent grade colorfastness characteristics to washing and rubbing.

According to the result of this study, the simultaneous mordanting method is excellent dyeing technique, and it is recommended to dye the cotton fabrics in textile industries by the extracts of Rumex abyssinicus root powder. However, there was no significant difference in dry and wet rub fastness for the three mordanting methods. A remarkable improvement in colorfastness was recorded for all mordants and mordanting methods.

4   Conclusion

Natural dye was successfully extracted from the root of Rumex abyssinicus powder by the aqueous method. The best dying extraction condition was found at a basic medium (pH-10) and a temperature of 80 °C with an absorbance value of 0.783. The anthraquinone test of the extracted dye had red rose color and this confirms the presence of hydroxyl anthraquinone group in Rumex Abyssinicus root extract. A maximum absorbance peak (λmax) was detected at 280 nm in the UV region ad it indicates the Rumex abyssinicus plant contains anthraquinone colorant. The FTIR spectrum of the Mekmeko root powder contains O–H, C=O, C=C, C=N, and C-H functional groups, and this carbonyl, hydroxyl, and other aromatic compounds confirms the presence of the anthraquinone dye in the plant. The dye performance of Rumex abyssinicus root extract on cotton fabric tends to perform better with mordants compared to the non-mordanting conditions. Iron sulfate at pH 4 in the simultaneous mordanting technique showed a greater colorfastness to washing and rubbing. Both the color change and staining washing fastness was recorded a very good to excellent (4–5) colorfastness. Dry and wet rubbing color fastness of the cotton fabric exhibits a very good to excellent (4–5) and very good grade (4) colorfastness properties respectively. Generally, the extract of dye from the root of Rumex abyssinicus can be used as a promising source of natural colorant and a potential replacement for synthetic dye applicable for textile industries.

References

1. Janani, L.: Dye for the future: natural dye from Morinda Lucida plant for cotton and silk fabrics. Int. J. Res. Rev. **2**(10), 601–605 (2015)
2. Kafu, E.S., Anzene, S.J.: A review of local dyeing process in Lafia, Nasarawa State, Nigeria. J. Eng. Sci. Technol. **1**(1) (2017)
3. Alemayehu, T., Teklemariam, Z.: Application of natural dyes on textile: a review. Int. J. Res.-Granthaalayah **2**(2), 61–68 (2014)
4. Mussak, R.A., Bechtold, T.: Natural colorants in textile dyeing. In: Handbook of Natural Colorants, pp. 315–335 (2009)
5. Jihad, R.: Dyeing of silk using natural dyes extracted from local plants. Head of the Textile Engineering Department at Kombolcha, Institute of Technology, Wollo University, Ethiopia (2014)

6. Ajmal, M., Khan, A.U.: Effects of a textile factory effluent on soil and crop plants. Environ. Pollut. Ser. A, Ecol. Biol. **37**(2), 131–148 (1985)
7. Kalaiarasi, K., Lavanya, A., Amsamani, S., Bagyalakshmi, G.: Decolourization of textile dye effluent by non-viable biomass of Aspergillus fumigatus. Braz. Arch. Biol. Technol. **55**(3), 471–476 (2012)
8. Ghorpade, B., Darvekar, M., Vankar, P.S.: Ecofriendly cotton dyeing with Sappan wood dye using ultrasound energy. Colourage **47**(1), 27–30 (2000)
9. Iqbal, M.J., Ashiq, M.N.: Adsorption of dyes from aqueous solutions on activated charcoal. J. Hazard. Mater. **139**(1), 57–66 (2007)
10. Jothi, D.: Extraction of natural dyes from African marigold flower (Tagetes erecta L) for textile coloration. AUTEX Res. J. **8**(2), 49–53 (2008)
11. Clark, M.: Handbook of Textile and Industrial Dyeing: Principles, Processes and Types of Dyes. Elsevier, Amsterdam (2011)
12. Walsh, G.E., Bahner, L.H., Horning, W.B.: Toxicity of textile mill effluents to freshwater and estuarine algae, crustaceans and fishes. Environ. Pollut. Ser. A, Ecol. Biol. **21**(3), 169–179 (1980)
13. Kundal, J., Singh, S.V., Purohit, M.C.: Extraction of natural dye from Ficus cunia and dyeing of polyester cotton and wool fabric using different mordants, with evaluation of colour fastness properties. Nat. Prod. Chem. Res. **4**(3), 3–6 (2016)
14. Lee, H.H.W., Chen, G., Yue, P.L.: Integration of chemical and biological treatments for textile industry wastewater: a possible zero-discharge system. Water Sci. Technol. **44**(5), 75–83 (2001)
15. Ranganathan, K., Karunagaran, K., Sharma, D.C.: Recycling of wastewaters of textile dyeing industries using advanced treatment technology and cost analysis—Case studies. Resour. Conserv. Recycl. **50**(3), 306–318 (2007)
16. Gupta, D., Khare, S.K., Laha, A.: Antimicrobial properties of natural dyes against Gram-negative bacteria. Color. Technol. **120**(4), 167–171 (2004)
17. Ali, S.: Evaluation of cotton dyeing with aqueous extracts of natural dyes from indigenous plants (Doctoral dissertation, University Of Agriculture, Faisalabad Pakistan) (2007)
18. Memon, N.: Textile finishing: increased demand for eco-friendly products. Pakistan Text. J. **59**, 46–47 (2010)
19. Ratnapandian, S., Fergusson, S., Wang, L.: Application of acacia natural dyes on cotton by pad dyeing. Fibers Polym. **13**(2), 206–211 (2012). https://doi.org/10.1007/s12221-012-0206-9
20. Ranganathan, K., Lakshmi, G.B.: Processing Growing preference for natural dyes. Text. Mag.-Madras **47**(3), 85 (2006)
21. Fauziyah, N., Hakim, L.: Plants as natural dyes for Jonegoroan Batik processing in Jono cultural tourism village, Bojonegoro, East Java. J. Indonesian Tour. Dev. Stud. **3**(2), 41–44 (2015)
22. Ado, A., Musa, H., Gumel, S.M., Yahaya, H.: Eco-friendly dyeing of cotton and polyester fabrics with natural dyes extracted from different varieties of Kola nuts. Int. J. Chem. Sci. **1**(1), 6–11 (2015)
23. Ghoreishian, S., Maleknia, L., Mirzapour, H., Norouzi, M.: Antibacterial properties and color fastness of silk fabric dyed with turmeric extract. Fibers Polym. **14**(2), 201–207 (2013). https://doi.org/10.1007/s12221-013-0201-9
24. Sachan, K., Kapoor, V.P.: Optimization of extraction and dyeing conditions for traditional turmeric dye. IJTK **6**(2), 270–278 (2007)
25. Siva, R.: Status of natural dyes and dye-yielding plants in India. Curr. Sci. 916–925 (2007)
26. Samanta, A.K., Agarwal, P.: Application of natural dyes on textiles. Indian J. Fibre Text. Res. **34**, 384–399 (2009)
27. Vankar, P.S.: Dyeing cotton, silk and wool yarn with extract of Garcinia mangostana pericarp. J. Text. Apparel Technol. Manag. **6**(1) (2009)

28. Yusuf, M., Shabbir, M., Mohammad, F.: Natural colorants; historical, processing and sustainable prospects. Nat. Prod. Bioprospecting **7**(1), 123–145 (2017)
29. Gulrajani, M.L., Gupta, D.B., Agarwal, V., Jain, M.: Some studies on natural yellow dyes, part 1: CI natural Yellow 3 (turmeric). Indian Text. J. **102**(4), 50–56 (1992)
30. Teli, M.D., Paul, R., Pardeshi, P.D.: Natural dyes. Classification, chemistry and extraction methods Part 1-Chemical classes, extraction methods and future prospects. Colourage **47**(12), 43–48 (2000)
31. Mansour, R.: Natural dyes and pigments. Extraction and applications. In: Handbook of Renewable Materials for Coloration and Finishing, pp. 75–102 (2018)
32. Mohammed, S.A., Panda, R.C., Madhan, B., Demessie, B.A.: Rumex abyssinicus (mekmeko) extract as cleaner approach for dyeing in product manufacture: optimization and modeling studies. Asia-Pac. J. Chem. Eng. **13**(2), 2165 (2018)
33. Zinaye, B., Fiseha, A.: Phytochemical investigation on the root of Rumex abyssinicus (MAKMAKO). AAU Electronic Library (2008)
34. Toussirot, M., et al.: Dyeing properties, coloring compounds and antioxidant activity of Hubera nitidissima (Dunal) Chaowasku (Annonaceae). Dyes Pigm. **102**, 278–284 (2014)
35. American Association of Textile Chemists and Colorists, Technical manual. Research Triangle Park, NC: Author (2001)
36. John, F.M., Cannon, M., Cannon, J., Dalby-Quenet, G.: Dye Plants and Dyeing. Timber Press, Portland (1994)
37. AATCC Technical manual: American Association of Textile Chemists and Colorists, (AATCC), Test methods; 61, 2(A), 8 and 181, vol. 83 (2008)
38. Trease, G.E., Evans, W.C.: Pharmacognosy, 11th edn., pp. 373–377. Bailleric Tindal, London (1978)
39. Shibata, S., Fakido, M., Tanaka, O., Jon: Am. Chem. Soc. **72**(2789) (1950)
40. Sarkaen, K.V.: Lignin. Occurrence, formation, structure and reaction. University of Washington: Seattle, Washington (1987)
41. Grushnikov, O.P., Elkin, V.V.: Lignin chemistry. Progress and problems (1973)
42. Hergert, H.L.: Infrared spectra of lignin and related compounds. II. Conifer lignin and model compounds. J. Organ. Chem. **25**(3), 405–413 (1960)
43. Lindberg, J.J.: Finska Kemists. Medd. **68**, 5 (1961)
44. Kavamura, I., Higoushi, T.: Chemical and Biochemical Properties of Lignin, Cellulose and Hemicellulose, pp.196–201. Forest Industry, Moscow (1969)
45. Vankar, P.S., Shanker, R., Dixit, S., Mahanta, D., Tiwari, S.C.: Sonicator dyeing of cotton with the leaves extract Acer pectinatum Wallich. Pigment Resin Technol. (2008)

The Effect of Drying Method on the Texture, Color, Vitamin C and β-Carotene Content of Dried Mango Slices (*Cv. Apple and Kent*)

Tadlo Yitayew$^{(\boxtimes)}$ and Tadesse Fenta

Faculty of Chemical and Food Engineering, Bahir Dar
University, P. O. Box 26, Bahir Dar, Ethiopia

Abstract. Drying is the oldest method of food preservation. However, the drying method can adversely affect the product quality. This work shows the effect of solar, oven and integrated solar-oven drying methods on the texture, color, vitamin C and β-carotene content of dried mango slices (apple and kent variety). The vitamin C and β-carotene content were measured by UV-Vis spectrophotometer, texture by texture profile analyzer (TPA) and color by spectrophotometer. There is a non-significant effect ($p > 0.05$) on the texture and color apple and kent mango, but significant effect ($p < 0.05$) on the vitamin C and β-carotene content. Apple mango had 72.38 mg/100 g vitamin C and 91.05 μg/100 g β-carotene content and kent mango 66.72 mg/100 g vitamin C and 73.80 μg/100 g β-carotene content. The drying method significantly affect ($p < 0.05$) the texture, color, vitamin C and β-carotene content of dried mango slices. The mango slice structure was become harder in texture and darkens in color. The hardness (5.12 N), color change (48.44), browning index (30.67) and the loss of vitamin C (74.57%) and β-carotene (45.74%) were high in oven dryer as compared to the other drying method. The springiness (1.36) and chewiness (2.13 N) were high in solar dyer. Integrated solar-oven drying method is the best method in terms of keeping the product quality and short processing time.

Keywords: Mango · Drying · Texture · Color · Vitamin C · β-Carotene

1 Introduction

Mango (Mangifera indica L.) is a seasonal flesh stone fruit, widely grown in tropical and subtropical regions. Mango is a healthy and nutritious fruit containing a high amount of nutrients, dietary fiber, bioactive compounds (pro-vitamin A, vitamin C, and phenolic compounds), and minerals (potassium, iron, and calcium) [1–3]. Mango is seasonal and highly perishable fruit due to its high moisture content and respiration rate after harvesting [4, 5] affects its availability in the market and causes wastage of this highly nutritious fruit. Mango can be consumed as a fresh or processed form.

Mango can be preserved by processing it into different forms of products such as concentrate, juice, fruit leather, dried slices, chutney and pure [6]. Drying is the oldest

© ICST Institute for Computer Sciences, Social Informatics and Telecommunications Engineering 2021
Published by Springer Nature Switzerland AG 2021. All Rights Reserved
M. A. Delele et al. (Eds.): ICAST 2020, LNICST 384, pp. 97–109, 2021.
https://doi.org/10.1007/978-3-030-80621-7_7

and commonly used preservation method used to extend the shelf life of fruits and reduce postharvest loss. For mango drying, numerous suitable drying technologies are available with their advantage and disadvantages [7]. The choice of drying method depends on the availability of the technology and the required sanitary condition. It is easy to access sun and solar drying in the tropical and sub-tropical regions, oven drying the most available technology in the developing countries.

However, the drying method and conditions (temperature and drying time) adversely affect the quality of the dried foods [8–10], especially the flavour, colour, texture, and heat-sensitive bioactive compounds. Vitamin C and carotenoids are the most heat-sensitive compounds when exposed to heat during drying. Mango is reported as the main source vitamin C (100% daily recommended intake) and pro-vitamin A (36% daily recommended intake). Colour is the primary perceived feature of foods that plays a significant role in consumer acceptance [11, 12]. The colour change of dried fruits is mainly associated with carotenoid degradation during exposure to heat, oxygen and light. In addition to the color of the product, the texture and flavour also play an important role in the consumer acceptance of products [11]. Texture is one of the sensory attributes of foods, in which represents the deformation, disintegration and flow of foods under the applied force by molar teeth. The texture change of dried agricultural products is due to the enzymatic and non-enzymatic changes on the cell wall components of the material [13]. The color and texture can be measured either objectively (instrumental) or subjectively (sensory) test [8, 14, 15]. Nevertheless, the sensory evaluation is often an ambiguous. Because many of the consumers are unable to accurately determine the properties of the material and different people perceives differently [16, 17]. Most of the previous studies conducted on fruit drying mainly use freeze drying, oven drying, microwave drying, etc. and there is lack of information on solar drying and integrated solar-oven drying method. The aim of this research work was to measure the effect of solar, oven and integrated solar-oven drying method on the texture, color, vitamin C and β-carotene content of dried mango slices (Apple and Kent cultivars).

2   Material and Method

2.1   Raw Material Collection and Experimental Site

Two fully ripe mango varieties (Kent and Apple mango) were collected from *Deq Deset* (Deq Peninsula), *Amhara region*, Ethiopia and further processed at Bahir Dar institute of Technology. All the experiments were carried out in the Food Engineering Department laboratories, at the Faculty of Chemical and Food Engineering, Bahir Dar Institute of Technology, Bahir Dar University.

2.2   Raw Material Preparation

The mango samples were washed with tap water to remove foreign matter such as dirt and other contaminates, followed by blanching at 50 °C for 10 min and further cooling. The washed fruits were peeled and sliced manually using a domestic peeler and a knife.

2.3 Drying of Mango Slices

The drying process of mango slices was performed in three different methods (solar drying, integrated solar-oven drying and oven drying method), until the final moisture content of the dried products reached 10 ± 5%. For the solar-oven integrated drying method, solar drying was performed until the intermediate moisture content reached 35 ± 5%, and then placed in oven dryer at 70 °C. The solar dryer prepared in-house by the faculty of Chemical and Food Engineering, Bahir Dar Institute of Technology was used for this purpose. The temperature and the relative humidity (RH) of the solar dryer during the drying time were recorded using Temperature and RH Data logger. Temperature and RH data logger is a device which can measure both the temperature and RH of the solar dryer.

2.4 Experimental Analysis

2.4.1 Moisture Content

The initial, intermediate and final moisture content of the mango slices was determined by the method used by [18] official method of analysis. The moisture content was expressed on a wet basis using the following equation:

$$MC = \frac{Ww}{Ww + Wd} \tag{1}$$

Where:

MC – moisture content, g of water/g of dry matter, in wet basis.
Ww – weight of water, g
Wd – weight of dry matter, g

2.4.2 Vitamin C Content Determination

The extraction and determination of vitamin C was based on the method used by [19, 20]. Ten gram (10g) mango sample was measured in 100 ml test tube containing 50ml of 5% metaphosphoric acid and 10% glacial acetic acid solution. The sample was homogenized and diluted up to the 100 ml with 5% metaphosphoric acid and 10% glacial acetic acid solution. The obtained solution was centrifuged at 4000 rpm for 15 min and filtered through Whatman filter paper no. 42, to obtain clear solution for UV spectrophotometric determination of vitamin C in the sample. About 30 ml of 3% bromine water was added into the clear sample solution to oxidize the ascorbic acid into dehydroascorbic acid, and a few drops of 10% thiourea solution were added to remove the excess bromine. Standard solutions of ascorbic acid (2, 4, 8, 12, 16 and 20 ppm) were prepared from a stock solution of ascorbic acid by proper dilution. Then 1 ml of 2, 4-DNPH solution was added to form osazone. For the completion of the reaction, all the standards, samples, and blank the solution were kept at 37 °c for 3 h in a thermostatic water bath. After this, all of those were cooled in an ice bath for 30min and treated with 5 ml of 85% H_2SO_4 with constant stirring. The absorbance was taken at 521 nm using UV spectrometer (Cary 60 UV – Vis, Malaysia).

2.4.3 β-carotene Content Determination

The extraction and determination procedure of beta-carotene was based on the method used by [21]. A representative sample of 1g was accurately weighed in a glass test tube containing 5 mL chilled acetone, and held it for 15 min with occasional shaking, and finally centrifuged at 1500 rpm for 10 min. The supernatant was collected into another test tube, and the residue was re-extracted with 5 mL acetone followed by centrifugation once again as above. Both of the supernatants were mixed together and filtered thought Whatman filter paper no. 42. Standard solutions of β-carotene (0.125, 0.25, 0.5, 1, 2 and 4 ppm) were prepared from a stock solution of β-carotene by proper dilution. The absorbance of the extract was determined at 449 nm wavelength in UV-spectrometer (Cary 60 UV – Vis, Malaysia).

2.4.4 Texture Profile Analysis

Stable Micro System Texture Analyser (TA.XT Plus, Surrey, UK) was used to measure the texture profile of fresh and dried mango slices. The texture analyser was calibrated by adding 2kg of calibration weight on the top of the texture analyser. According to the method used by [22], the samples were compressed twice to 5mm depth (60% of the original height) by 2 mm cylindrical probe with a trigger force of 5 g at 3 mm/s pre-test, 2 mm/s test and 10 mm/s post-test speed. During the double compression of the mango slices it draws a force vs time graph. From the force vs time curves the maximum force of first cycle (F1), maximum force of second cycle (F2), area under first curve (A1), area under second curve (A2), time elapsed from area 1 above positive y axis (T1) and time elapsed from area 2 above positive y axis (T2) were used for the expression of the texture profile. The texture attributes of the dried mango slices were calculated by the following equation [13]. The fresh mango reading was used for comparison.

$$Hardness, H = F1 \tag{2}$$

$$Springness, S = \frac{T2}{T1} \tag{3}$$

$$Cohessiveness, C = \frac{A2}{A1} \tag{4}$$

$$Chewiness, CW = H * S * C \tag{5}$$

2.4.5 Colour Evaluation

The method used by [13] was used to determine the color of fresh and dried mango slices based on the color scale of Commission International de l'Ecairage (CIE) using Spectrophotometer (CM-600d Spectrophotometer, Konica Minolta Inc., Japan). CIE used L*, a*, b* to express the color of samples and measured against white standard. L* represents lightness (0 for black and 100 for white), a* expresses red (+) or green (−) and b* expresses yellow (+) or blue (−). The experiment was made in six replication and the average value was used to calculate the color change (ΔE), Chroma (ΔC), hue angle (h) and browning index (BI) by the following equation described by [13, 23]. The fresh mango reading was used as a reference and indicated by the subscript 'o'.

$$\text{Change in color } (\Delta E) = \sqrt{\left(L_0^* - L^*\right)^2 + \left(a_0^* - a^*\right)^2 + \left(b_0^* - b^*\right)^2} \tag{6}$$

$$\text{Change in Chroma } (\Delta C) = \sqrt{a^{*2} + b^{*2}} \tag{7}$$

$$\text{Hue Angle(h)} = \tan^{-1}\left(\frac{b^*}{a^*}\right) \tag{8}$$

$$\text{Browing index (BI)} = \frac{100(x - 0.31)}{0.17} \tag{9}$$

$$x = \frac{a^* + 1.75L^*}{5.64L^* + a^* - 0.01b^*} \tag{10}$$

2.5 Data Analysis

The data were measured in triplicates and SAS software (9.1.3 version) was used to analyze the result. Significance was accepted at 0.05 level of probability ($p < 0.05$). Mean separation was performed by Duncan multiple range test for multiple comparisons of means. Microsoft Excel 2013 was used to plot the graph.

3 Result and Discussion

3.1 Temperature, RH and Moisture Content

The solar drying was performed for three different days from May 27–29/ 2019 and the average value was presented in Fig. 1 below. The average maximum solar dryer temperature was measured as 39.51 °C with 33.64%RH, and the lowest average minimum solar dryer temperature was 30.57 °C with 48.91%RH (Fig. 1). The [24] report shows the average actual temperature during the experiment day was 25.65 °C, respectively at the experiment site in Bahir Dar, Ethiopia. During the day of the experiment, there is a significant difference in the daily temperature and RH value. April, May, and June are the sunniest month in Ethiopia. The sliced mango initial, intermediate and final moisture content was 0.84 g/g water, 0.34 g/g water and 0.13 g/g water for apple mango and 0.83 g/g water, 0.35 g/g water and 0.14 g/g water for kent mango as shown in (Fig. 2) in wet basis.

3.2 Calibration Curve

The absorbance of all standards was used to construct a calibration curve, by plotting the concentration versus the corresponding absorbance as shown in Fig. 3 and 4. The limit of detection (LOD) and the limit of quantification (LOQ) of vitamin C were 2.91 μg/ml and 8.81 μg/ml, respectively. The limit of detection (LOD) and the limit of quantification (LOQ) of β-carotene were 0.72 μg/ml and 2.17 μg/ml, respectively.

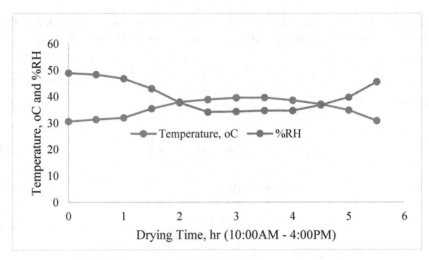

Fig. 1. Temperature and RH of Solar Dryer vs Drying time

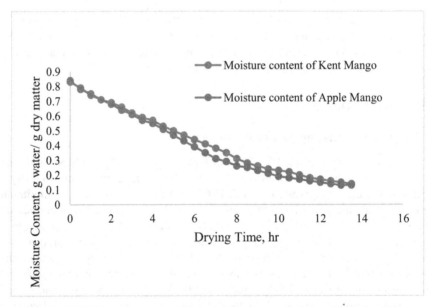

Fig. 2. The Moisture content of Apple and Kent mango variety with Drying Time

3.3 Vitamin C and β-carotene Content

The result in (Table 1) indicates the vitamin C and β-carotene content of fresh apple and kent mango fruit variety, used for comparison of the effect of drying method on the dried sample. Statistically speaking, there is a significant difference ($p < 0.05$) between the fresh apple and kent mango vitamin C and β-carotene content. Apple mango variety has had a high content of vitamin C (72.38 mg/100 g) and β-carotene (91.05 μg/100 g)

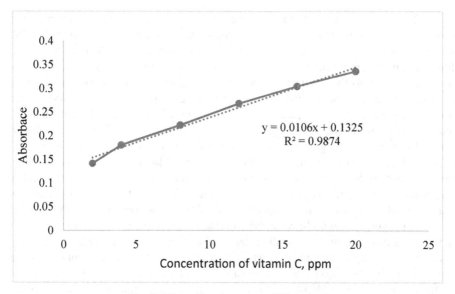

Fig. 3. The calibration curve of Vitamin C

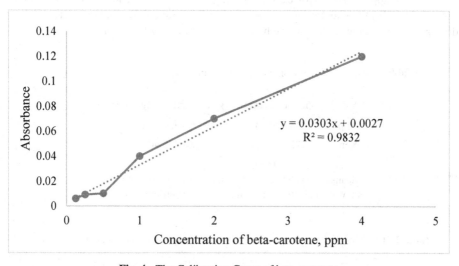

Fig. 4. The Calibration Curve of beta-carotene

content than the kent mango variety (66.72 mg/100 g and 73.80 μg/100 g), respectively. This would be due to that; the nutritional composition would be varied with cultivars [25–28]. The result in (Table 2) indicates the effect of the drying method on vitamin C and β-carotene content of dried mango slices. The vitamin C and β-carotene content of the mango were significantly decreased ($p < 0.05$) with the drying method. The solar dryer was observed higher retention of the vitamin C (83.98%) and β-carotene (71.09%), and lower retention was observed in oven drying method (25.43%) vitamin

C and (28.76%) β-carotene. The retention capacity of the integrated solar-oven drying method was an intermediate value between the solar and oven drying method (60.47% Vitamin C and 54.26% β-carotene). The high drying temperature of the oven dryer also diminishes the vitamin C and β-carotene content of the mango slices greatly. The solar dryer had a minimal effect on the vitamin C and β-carotene content of the mango slices as compared to the oven and integrated solar-oven drying method, but the long drying time (more than 3 days of drying) it takes, contamination with dust and other foreign material, and variability of the solar intensity makes it unsuitable method. The loss of vitamin C and β-carotene of integrated solar-over drying method were 23.51% and 16.83%, respectively, as compared to the solar dryer. This would be due to that; most vitamins are susceptible to heat [29]. The study of [30] indicates the drying of fruit at a higher temperature (100 °C) reduces the vitamin C content significantly. This study indicates that the use of integrated solar-oven drying method can be used as an alternative method to the solar drying method. The result table (Table 3) also indicates the interaction effect of variety and drying method on the vitamin C content and β-carotene content. The result shows drying significantly affects the vitamin C and β-carotene content of the two cultivars dried mango slices as compared to the fresh mango. The average loss of the three drying method (48.68%) was high in kent mango than apple mango variety (38.48%). The highest loss was observed in oven drying method (83.95%) for kent and (65.90%) for apple variety. However, the average loss of β-carotene was higher in apple mango (51.97%) than kent mango variety (44.49%), whereas kent mango variety oven drying method was registered as the highest loss (74.84%) of β-carotene.

Table 1. Effect of variety on the vitamin C and β-carotene content of mango

Variety	Vitamin C, mg/100 g	β-carotene, µg/100 g
Apple	72.38 ± 0.43 a	91.05 ± 0.50 a
Kent	66.72 ± 0.33 b	73.80 ± 0.40 b

Mean ± Standard Deviation
Means followed by different superscripts within column show statistically significant (p < 0.05) differences

Table 2. Effect of drying method on the vitamin C and β-carotene content of mango

Drying method	Vitamin C, mg/100 g	β-carotene, µg/100 g
Solar drying	58.41 ± 4.45 a	58.60 ± 1.11 a
Oven drying	17.69 ± 7.66 c	23.71 ± 5.63 c
Solar-oven integrated	42.06 ± 4.83 b	44.73 ± 2.19 b

Mean ± Standard Deviation
Means followed by different superscripts within column show statistically significant (p < 0.05) differences

Table 3. Interaction effect of variety and drying method on the vitamin C and β-carotene content

Variety	Drying method	Vitamin C, mg/100 g	β-carotene, μg/100 g
Apple	Solar drying	62.46 ± 0.21 a	59.58 ± 0.37 a
	Oven drying	24.68 ± 0.26 e	28.85 ± 0.20 e
	Solar-oven integrated	46.46 ± 0.32 c	42.76 ± 0.53 c
Kent	Solar drying	54.36 ± 0.46 b	57.63 ± 0.33 b
	Oven drying	10.71 ± 0.51 f	18.57 ± 0.14 f
	Solar-oven integrated	37.65 ± 0.28 d	46.70 ± 0.23 d

Mean ± Standard Deviation
Means followed by different superscripts within column show statistically significant ($p < 0.05$) differences

3.3.1 Texture Profile Analysis

The result in (Table 4) indicates variety had no significant effect ($p > 0.05$) on the texture attributes, however, the hardness, cohesiveness, springiness, and chewiness of apple mango had a higher value than the kent mango. The result in (Table 5) indicates that there is a significant effect ($p < 0.05$) of the drying method on the texture attributes of fresh and dried mango slices. The hardness, cohesiveness, springiness, and chewiness were significantly affected by the drying method. The hardness of dried mango slices was significantly increased ($p < 0.05$) with the drying method (1.47 N, 4.93 N and 5.12 N) for solar, integrated solar-oven and oven drying method, respectively as compared to the fresh mango (0.81N). This could be since heating would disrupt the cell wall structure of the mango slices and increases the strength of the mango slices. This was in agreement with the study of [13]. The hardness was higher in oven and integrated solar-oven drying method, due to the higher drying temperature (70 °C). The study of [16] shows that increasing the drying temperature by 10 °C increases the hardness. Similarly, the chewiness also increased with respect to the hardness. The cohesiveness (1.08) and springiness (1.36) of solar-dried increased significantly ($p < 0.05$), as compared to that of the fresh mango slices (0.83 and 1.06), respectively. However, the cohesiveness (0.47) and springiness (0.56) of integrated solar-oven dried and that of oven-dried (0.39 and 0.48), respectively, decreased significantly as compared to that of the fresh mango slices (0.83 and 1.06). This could be due to drying at a lower temperature (solar drier 36.37 °C, average), which is not enough to break the cellular structure of mango slices. This would increase the elasticity and the mastication energy under a given force. In the integrated solar-oven and oven drying methods, the drying process was fast relatively at a higher temperature, which was enough to break the structure of the mango slices. The study of [13] was in agreement with this result but does not show a significant effect ($p > 0.05$) for springiness. The study of [11] indicates the hardness and chewiness were decreased while the cohesiveness and springiness were increased.

Table 4. Effect of Variety on the Texture attributes of two mango varieties

Variety	Hardness, N	Cohesiveness	Springiness	Chewiness, N
Apple	3.09 ± 2.05 a	0.73 ± 0.37 a	0.89 ± 0.39 a	1.38 ± 0.79 a
Kent	3.08 ± 2.00 a	0.65 ± 0.29 a	0.84 ± 0.36 a	1.18 ± 0.57 a

Mean ± Standard Deviation
Means followed by different superscripts within column show statistically significant (p < 0.05) differences

Table 5. Effect of drying method on the texture profile of dried mango slices

Drying method	Hardness, N	Cohesiveness	Springiness	Chewiness, N
Fresh	0.81 ± 0.11 c	0.83 ± 0.22 b	1.06 ± 0.06 b	0.71 ± 0.21 c
Solar drying	1.47 ± 0.29 b	1.08 ± 0.26 a	1.36 ± 0.14 a	2.13 ± 0.65 a
Oven drying	5.12 ± 0.35 a	0.39 ± 0.10 c	0.48 ± 0.08 d	0.94 ± 0.29 c
Solar-oven integrated	4.93 ± 0.42 a	0.47 ± 0.12 c	0.56 ± 0.08 c	1.32 ± 0.45 b

Mean ± standard deviation
Means followed by different superscripts within column show statistically significant (p < 0.05) differences

3.4 Color Analysis

The result in (Table 6) shows the effect of mango variety on the color parameters. It was observed that mango variety has no significant effect (p > 0.05) on the color parameters. However, the result in (Table 7) indicates there is a significant effect (p < 0.05) of the drying method on the color parameter of mango slices. The lightness (L*) of fresh mango (65.28) significantly decreased (p < 0.05) to 57.33 for solar, 47.68 for integrated solar-oven and 36.77 for oven drying. This indicates that the mango slices go through darker as drying proceeds.

Table 6. Effect of variety on the CIE colour scale and colour parameter of dried mango slices

Variety	L*	a*	b*	Colour change	Chroma change	Hue angle	Browning index
Apple	51.01 ± 11.71 a	19.77 ± 4.33 a	40.31 ± 15.93 a	34.58 ± 14.63 a	28.23 ± 11.44 a	89.35 ± 0.15 a	29.66 ± 4.23 a
Kent	52.47 ± 11.85 a	17.55 ± 2.16 a	43.30 ± 16.87 a	31.03 ± 16.43 a	26.11 ± 13.29 a	89.46 ± 0.21 a	25.72 ± 6.83 a

Mean ± standard deviation
Means followed by different superscripts within column show statistically significant (p < 0.05) differences

The oven-dried samples were going through the darkness (L* < 50). Drying of high moisture content foods (~85%) at a higher temperature (70 °C) causes the darkness of the foods due to non-enzymatic reactions [13]. The mango slices were slightly light-colored in integrated solar-oven drying (L* ~ 50) and in the solar drying method (L* >

Table 7. Effect of drying method on the CIE colour scale and colour parameter of dried mango slices

Drying method	L*	a*	b*	Colour change	Chroma change	Hue angle	Browning index
Fresh	65.28 ± 2.39 a	18.36 ± 1.80 a	61.71 ± 3.00 a	–	–	–	–
Solar	57.33 ± 6.79 b	19.44 ± 4.55 a	48.86 ± 10.48 b	16.92 ± 9.10 c	14.31 ± 7.61 c	89.58 ± 0.14 a	23.81 ± 6.71 b
Oven	36.77 ± 3.28 d	16.94 ± 3.28 a	22.73 ± 5.51 d	48.44 ± 6.71 a	39.12 ± 5.42 a	89.24 ± 0.11 c	30.67 ± 4.15 a
Integrated Solar-Oven	47.68 ± 4.86 c	19.89 ± 3.73 a	33.90 ± 5.86 c	33.06 ± 9.41 b	28.11 ± 7.40 b	89.39 ± 0.12 b	28.58 ± 4.81 a

Mean ± standard deviation
Means followed by different superscripts within column show statistically significant ($p < 0.05$) differences

50), as the majority of the moisture was removed at a lower temperature. Similarly, this can affect the redness (a*) and yellowness (b*) value of the dried mango slices. The a* value of fresh mango (18.36) was increased in solar drying (19.44) and integrated solar-oven drying (19.89) and decreasing in the oven drying method (16.94). Similarly, the b* value of fresh mango (61.71) decreased in solar drying (48.86), integrated solar-oven (33.90) and oven drying (22.73). The result in (Table 7), also indicates that the drying method has a significant effect ($p < 0.05$) on the change in color, chroma, hue angle, and browning index. The color, chroma and browning index of dried mango slices were significantly increased ($p < 0.05$) in the solar drying (16.92, 14.31 and 23.51), integrated solar-oven drying (33.06, 28.11 and 28.58) and oven drying (48.44, 39.12 and 30.67) methods, due to none-enzymatic browning reaction. However, the hue angle significantly decreased ($p < 0.05$) from solar drying (89.58) to integrated solar-oven (89.39) and to oven drying (89.24). The study of [11, 13, 31] shows the L* and b* values were decreased significantly, and the value of a* increased significantly with increasing the convective air-drying temperature. The study also shows the color and chroma changes were increased, while the hue angle was decreased which is in agreement with this study. The study of [32] indicates the dried fruit tends darker (redder) as the drying proceeds, due to the increasing of a* values without change of L* values.

4 Conclusion

It was found that mango variety have a significant difference ($p < 0.05$) on the vitamin C and β-carotene content while no significant effect ($p > 0.05$) on the texture attribute and color value. However, the drying method significantly affects ($p < 0.05$) the vitamin C and β-carotene content, texture, and also color. Different drying methods have different retention capacity of vitamin C and β-carotene. The solar dying has a very good retention capacity of vitamin C and β-carotene, while the long drying time makes it unacceptable but oven drying was observed lowest retention capacity. The integrated solar-oven drying method plays a very important role in reducing the long-time taken by the solar dryer and loss of vitamin C and β-carotene in oven drying. The hardness and chewiness were increased significantly ($p < 0.05$) with the drying method (solar, solar-oven integrated and oven) respectively while the cohesiveness and springiness decreased significantly ($p < 0.05$). Similarly, the color scale result shows a significant decrease in the L* and b* value, with an increase in a* value in solar, solar-oven integrated and oven drying method as compared to the fresh mango sample. The change in color and chroma and the browning index was high in the oven drying method and low in the solar drying method, whereas the hue angle was high in solar drying and low in the oven drying method.

Acknowledgment. All experimentations and study were conducted with the help of Bahir Dar Institute of Technology (BiT) for research funding and the authors thankfully acknowledge the mentioned institution for providing all kinds of possible laboratory facilities and funding during the study in Bahir Dar, Ethiopia.

References

1. Singh, N.I., Dhuique-Mayer, C., Lozano, Y.: Physico-chemical changes during enzymatic liquefacttion of mango pulp (cv. Keitt). J. Food Process. Preserv. **24**, 73–85 (2000)
2. Bally, I.S.E.: Mangifera indica (mango) Anacardiaceae (cashew family) kangit, Species Profile Pacific Isl. Agrofor. **25**(5), 938–941 (2006). www.traditionaltree.org
3. Akoy, E.O.M.: Experimental characterization and modeling of thin-layer drying of mango slices. Int. Food Res. J. **21**(5), 1911–1917 (2014)
4. Kabiru, A.A., Joshua, A.A., Raji, A.O.: Effect of slice thickness and temperature on the drying kinetics of mango (Mangifera Indica). IJRRAS **15**(1), 41–50 (2013)
5. Babarinde, G.O., Olatunde, S.J., Adebiyi-Olabode, A.: Quality attributes and phytochemical properties of fresh juice produced from selected mango varieties. Ceylon J. Sci. **48**(1), 31–36 (2019)
6. Azeredo, H.M.C., Brito, E.S., Moreira, G.E.G., Farias, V.L., Bruno, L.M.: Effect of drying and storage time on the physico-chemical properties of mango leathers. Int. J. Food Sci. Technol. **41**, 635–638 (2006)
7. Izli, N., Izli, G., Taskin, O.: Influence of different drying techniques on drying parameters of mango. Food Sci. Technol. **37**(4), 604–612 (2017)
8. Martynenko, A., Janaszek, M.A.: Texture changes during drying of apple slices. Dry. Technol. **32**, 567–577 (2014)
9. Ling, B., Tang, J., Kong, F., Mitcham, E.J., Wang, S.: Kinetics of food quality changes during thermal processing: a review. Food Bioprocess. Technol. **8**(2), 343–358 (2014). https://doi.org/10.1007/s11947-014-1398-3
10. Santos, V.O., Rodrigues, S., Fernandes, F.A.N.: Improvements on the stability and vitamin content of acerola juice obtained by ultrasonic processing. Foods **7**(68), 1–10 (2018)
11. Guine, R.P.F., Barroca, M.J.: Effect of drying treatments on texture and color of vegetables (pumpkin and green pepper). Food Bioprod. Process. **90**, 58–63 (2012)
12. Ismail, O.M., Nagy, K.S.A.: Characteristics of dried mango slices as affected by pre-treatments and drying type. Aust. J. Basic Appl. Sci. **6**(5), 230–235 (2012)
13. Chong, C.H., Law, C.L., Cloke, M., Abdullah, L.C., Daud, W.R.W.: Drying kinetics, texture, color, and determination of effective diffusivities during sun drying of chempedak. Dry. Technol. **26**, 1286–1293 (2008)
14. Nishinari, K., Kohyama, K., Kumagai, H., Funami, T., Bourne, M.C.: Parameters of texture profile analysis. Food Sci. Technol. Res **19**(3), 519–521 (2013)
15. Paula, A., Conti-Silva, A.: Texture profile and correlation between sensory and instrumental analyses on extruded snacks. J. Food Eng. **121**, 9–14 (2014)

16. Marzec, A., Kowalska, H., Zadrozna, M.: Analysis of instrumental and sensory texture attributes of microwave-convective dried apples. J. Texture Stud. **41**, 417–439 (2010)
17. van Dalen, G., Osman, F., Don, A.: Colour and appearance analysis of fruit and vegetable soup using a digital colour imaging system. In: CGIV, Unilever Research & Development, pp. 399–406 (2010)
18. AOAC: Association of Official Analytical Chemist. Official method of analysis. No. 920.149149(c).17th ed.: AOAC International (2000)
19. Kapur, A., et al.: Spectrophotometric analysis of total ascorbic acid contetnt in various fruits and vegetables. Bull. Chem. Technol. Bosnia Herzegovina **38**, 39–42 (2012)
20. Rahman, M.M., Khan, M.M.R., Hosain, M.M.: Analysis of Vitamin C (ascorbic acid) contents in various fruits and vegetables by UV-spectrophotometry. Bangladesh J. Sci. Ind. Res. **42**(4), 417–424 (2007)
21. Biswas, A.K., Sahoo, J., Chatli, M.K.: A simple UV-Vis spectrophotometric method for determination of β-carotene content in raw carrot, sweet potato and supplemented chicken meat nuggets. LWT-Food Sci. Technol. **44**, 1809–1813 (2011)
22. Al-Hinai, K.Z., Guizani, N., Singh, V., Rahman, M.S., Al-Subhi, L.: Instrumental texture profile analysis of date-tamarind fruit leather with different types of hydrocolloids. Food Sci. Technol. Res **19**(4), 531–538 (2013)
23. Kasim, R., Kasim, M.U.: Biochemical changes and color properties of fresh-cut green bean (Phaseolus vulgaris L. cv.gina) treated with calcium chloride during storage. Food Sci. Technol. **35**(2), 266–272 (2015)
24. AccuWeather: Bahir Dar, Amara, Ethiopia Monthly Weather | AccuWeather (2019). https://www.accuweather.com/en/et/bahir-dar/127186/may-weather/127186
25. Ara, R., Motalab, M., Uddin, M.N., Fakhruddin, A.N.M., Saha, B.K.: Nutritional evaluation of different mango varieties available in Bangladesh. Int. Food Res. J. **21**(6), 2169–2174 (2014)
26. Londono, M.B.Z., Chaparro, D., Rojano, B.A., Arbelaez, A.F.A., Betancur, L.F.R., Celis, M.E.M.: Effect of storage time on physicochemical, sensorial, and antioxidant characteristics, and composition of mango (cv. Azukar) juice. Emirates J. Food Agric. **29**(5), 367–377 (2017)
27. Okoth, E.M., Sila, D.N., Onyango, C.A., Owino, W.O., Musyimi, S.M., Mathooko, F.M.: Evaluation of chemical and nutritional quality attributes of selected mango varieties at three stages of ripeness, grown in lower Eastern province of Kenya – part 2. J. Anim. & Plant Sci. **17**(3), 2619–2630 (2013)
28. Nixwell, M.F., Johanna, M.P., Ngezimana, W.: Proximate, chemical compositions and sulphur concentrations on quality of selected dried mango (Mangifera indica L.). African J. Biotechnol. **12**(19), 2678–2684 (2013)
29. Rajwan, I.A., Malik, A.U., Khan, A.S., Saleem, B.A., Ahmed, M.S.: A new mango hybrid shows better shelf life and fruit quality. Pakistan J. Bot. **42**(4), 2503–2512 (2010)
30. Diamante, L., Durand, M., Savage, G., Vanhanen, L.: Effect of temperature on the drying characteristics, colour and ascorbic acid content of green and gold kiwifruits. Int. Food Res. J. **17**, 441–451 (2010)
31. Akoy, E.-A.O.M., Von Horsten, D., Luecke, W.: Drying kinetics and colour change of mango slices as affected by drying temperature and time. In: Tropentag International Conference on "Competition for Resources in a Changing World: New Drive for Rural Development", pp. 1–7 (2008)
32. Ramallo, L.A., Mascheroni, R.H.: Quality evaluation of pineapple fruit during drying process. Food Bioprod. Process. **9**, 275–283 (2012)

Quantitative Postharvest Loss Assessment of Tomato Along the Postharvest Supply Chain in Northwestern Ethiopia

Eskindir E. Tadesse[1]([✉]), Hirut Assaye[1], Mulugeta A. Delele[1], Solomon W. Fanta[1], Dawit F. Huluka[1], Melkamu Alemayehu[3], Getachew Alemayehu[3], Enyew Adgo[3], Jan Nyssen[4], Pieter Verboven[2], and Bart M. Nicolai[2]

[1] Faculty of Chemical and Food Engineering, Bahir Dar Institute of Technology, Bahir Dar University, P.O. Box 26, Bahir Dar, Ethiopia
eskindir.endalew@bdu.edu.et
[2] BIOSYST-MeBioS, KU Leuven, Willem de Croylaan 42, 3001 Leuven, Belgium
[3] College of Agriculture and Environmental Sciences, Bahir Dar University, P.O. Box 5501, Bahir Dar, Ethiopia
[4] Department of Geography, Ghent University, Krijgslaan 281 S8, 9000 Gent, Belgium

Abstract. The aim of this study was to determine postharvest loss of tomatoes along the postharvest supply chain in Northwest Ethiopia. The study was conducted on tomato fruits produced in three productive kebeles (Chimba, Gumara, and Kudmi) of Northwest Ethiopia following the FAO load tracking and sampling assessment method. Postharvest losses of tomatoes ranged from 6.17 to 8.62%, 1.23 to 8.24%, 3.35 to 4.30%, and 9.38 to 12.58% at the farm, transportation, wholesale, and retail levels, respectively. The mean total postharvest loss of tomatoes was $25.91 \pm 1.04\%$ along the supply chain in the study area with in a period of 5 days. Storage and handling of tomatoes at ambient temperature and low relative humidity for a relatively long period of time were the main causes of postharvest losses of tomatoes along the supply chain. Besides, inappropriate postharvest handling practices, lack of storage facilities at wholesale and retail levels, and lack of reliable market system and market information were also identified as contributors for the high postharvest losses of tomatoes observed in our study.

Keywords: Load tracking method · Tomato · Postharvest loss · Supply chain

1 Introduction

Tomato (Lycopersicon esculentum Mill.) is one of major horticultural crops with an estimated total world production of 182.30 million tones [1]. Tomato is also one of the most commonly grown vegetable crops in Ethiopia and has a significant contribution to food and nutrition security [2]. Its production is dominated by small scale farmers with annual production of 23,583.75 tones, which are produced on more than 4000 hectares of land [3]. It is consumed in Ethiopian in various modes [4].

M. A. Delele et al. (Eds.): ICAST 2020, LNICST 384, pp. 110–122, 2021.
https://doi.org/10.1007/978-3-030-80621-7_8

The quality and quantity of harvested fruit and vegetables is reduced rapidly, which is associated with inherent biological nature and very high water loss after harvesting. Since tomato fruit is perishable and poorly managed in developing countries such as Ethiopia, it may suffer significant postharvest losses along the supply chain [5]. Postharvest losses of fruits and vegetables in developing countries can occur at all stages throughout the marketing and distribution chain and it varies between 20 to 50% [6], and even up to 62.5% for tomato [7].

Few reports are available in Ethiopia regarding the cause and extent of postharvest losses of tomato along the supply chain; 45.32% in the Dire Dawa region [8] and losses ranging from 18 to 22% in South Wollo [9]. However, there are no reports regarding the extent as well as cause of tomato quantitative postharvest loss in Northwest Ethiopia specifically along the supply chain. Therefore, the aim of this study was to assess effects of growing location and postharvest supply chain on quantitative postharvest losses of tomato in Northwest Ethiopia.

2 Materials and Methods

2.1 Description of the Study Areas

The study was conducted in three tomato producing kebeles, Chimba, Gumara, and Kudmi which are found in North Achefer, Fogera, and Mecha woredas, respectively as well as Bahir Dar city in Amhara region, Northwest Ethiopia. North Achefer is one of the woredas in the West Gojam zone of the Amhara region, Ethiopia with the capital of Liben, which is found about 100 km away from Bahir Dar. Liben is located at 11°41'53.9"N latitude and 36°56'31.6"E longitude. It has an altitude of 2033 m above sea level. Chimba is one of the kebeles in North Achefer which is found in about 30 km away from Bahir Dar. Fogera is one of the woredas in the South Gondar zone of the Amhara region, Ethiopia with the capital of Wereta, which is found about 61 km away from the regional capital, Bahir Dar. Wereta is located at 11°55'27.2"N latitude and 37°41'46.3"E longitude. It has an altitude of 1819 m above sea level and receives an average annual rainfall of 1321 mm. Gumara is one of the kebeles in Fogera woreda which is found in about 40 km away from Bahir Dar. Mecha is one of the woredas in the West Gojam zone of the Amhara region, Ethiopia with the capital of Merawi, which is found about 35 km away from Bahir Dar. Merawi is located at 11°24'49.4"N latitude and 37°09'10.7"E longitude. It has an average elevation of 2010 m above sea level and receives an average annual rainfall of 1487 mm. Kudmi is one of the kebeles in Merawi which is found in about 42 km away from Bahir Dar. Bahir Dar is the capital of Amhara regional sate, Ethiopia. Bahir Dar is located at 11°35'33.5"N latitude and 37°20'45.9"E longitude. It has an altitude of 1800 m above sea level and receives an average annual rainfall of 1419 mm. The three kebeles used different growing practices of tomato. In Chimba and Kudmi kebeles, tomato plants are supported (staked) (Fig. 1A), whereas in Gumara kebeles they are not supported (Fig. 1B).

2.2 Treatments and Experimental Design

The treatments consisted of three growing locations (Chimba, Gumara, and Kudmi) and four postharvest supply chains (Farm, Transportation, Wholesale, and Retail) which

A   **B**

Fig. 1. Tomato cultivation practice in Chimba and Kudmi (A) and Gumara (B) kebele, Northwest Ethiopia

were arranged in Randomized Complete Block Design (RCBD) with four replications (Table 1). The major tomato postharvest supply chain activities consisted of harvesting, sorting and loading, transportation, storage, wholesale and retail as illustrated in Fig. 2.

Table 1. Treatment combination used to assess quantitative postharvest losses of tomato

Location	Supply chain	Treatment Combination
Chimba (C)	Farm	CF
	Transportation	CT
	Wholesale	CW
	Retail	CR
Gumara (G)	Farm	GF
	Transportation	GT
	Wholesale	GW
	Retail	GR
Kudmi (K)	Farm	KF
	Transportation	KT
	Wholesale	KW
	Retail	KR

Note: C = Chimba, G = Gumara, K = Kudmi, F = Farm,
T = Transportation, W = Wholesale, R = Retail

2.3 Data Collection

Key Informant Interview. Key informant interviews were performed to collect a comprehensive set of information and data related to postharvest management practices and causes of postharvest losses of tomatoes in the study kebeles along the supply chain. Key informants (15 in number) were selected from Woreda Agricultural Offices, Agricultural Extension at Kebele level, producers, wholesalers and retailers.

Observation. An observation of all the activities and processes along the supply chain was also made during data collection.

Load Tracking. Load tracking and sampling method was used to quantify quantitative postharvest losses of tomato along the supply chain as described by FAO [10]. Representative samples of tomato cultivar (Galilea) were collected from farmers in each kebele, which were produced during the dry season of March to May 2019 using irrigation.

Tomato producing kebeles were selected purposively. From each kebele, one potential producer who has a relatively large farm and major supplier to wholesalers in Bahir Dar fruit and vegetable market was selected. From the producer, six wooden boxes that were filled with tomato fruits were collected from Gumara and Kudmi kebeles which were transported with Toyota Minibus Hiace and animal cart (farm to main asphalt road in Kudmi kebele). Moreover, eighty-four wooden boxes that were filled with tomato fruits were collected from Chimba kebele and transported with ISUZU NPR track. From this load at the first sampling stage, five boxes were randomly selected and labeled. Out of the selected five boxes, four boxes (approximately 65 kg each) were randomly selected and their initial quantitative data were collected. While following the samples in the supply chain, the necessary quantitative postharvest losses of tomato were estimated at each point of the supply chain.

2.4 Estimation of Quantitative Postharvest Losses of Tomato

Postharvest losses of tomatoes were estimated by percentage in weight basis at each of the following stages of the different supply chains: farm (harvesting, sorting and field packing), transportation (during transport and arrival at market), wholesale (after two days of handling and storage of tomatoes before selling to retail), and retail (selling and handling of tomatoes to customers with maximum of three days storage). Any tomato fruits that had visible decay or severe injury were regarded as a loss. Quantitative postharvest losses were estimated the equation described below (1):

$$Quantitaive\ Postharvest\ Loss\ (\%) = \frac{Q_{unmarkatable}}{Q_T} \times 100 \tag{1}$$

Where, $Q_{unmarkatable}$ = Quantity of unmarketable tomato due to physical damage, damage by diseases and insect pests, bruising and wilting (kg).
Q_T = Total tomato quantity (net quantity + discarded quantity) (kg).

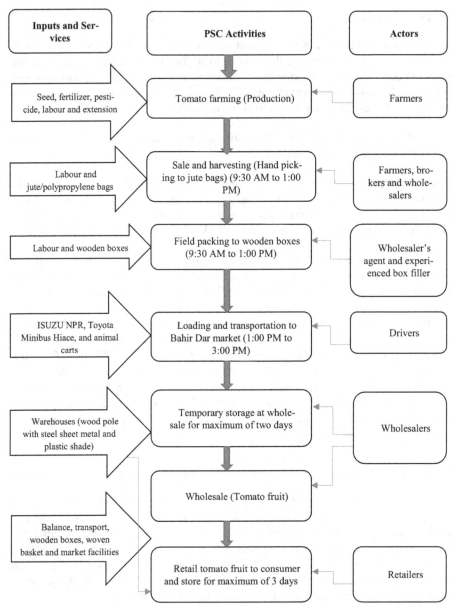

Fig. 2. Tomato postharvest supply chain (PSC) activities and waiting periods in the study kebeles, Northwest Ethiopia

2.5 Weather Conditions (Temperature and Relative Humidity)

Weather conditions such as temperature and relative humidity were measured along the supply chain where temperature were measured using HOBO Temp Data Logger (UX100-001, Range: −20 °C to 70°C, Accuracy: ±0.21 °C from 0° to 50 °C) while relative humidity using HOBO Temp/RH 2.5% Data Logger (UX100-011, Range: 1% to 95%, Accuracy: ±2.5% from 10% to 90%).

2.6 Data Analysis

All data recorded were subjected to statistical analysis. Two way analysis of variance (ANOVA) was carried out using SAS software version 9.2 (Cary, NC, USA) to detect significant effects of growing locations and postharvest supply chain on quantitative postharvest losses of tomato. Treatments were considered as significantly different at p < 0.05. Tukey HSD test was used to compare significance differences between means. Graphs were plotted using SigmaPlot software Version 14.0.

3 Results and Discussion

3.1 Weather Condition

The temperature recorded at the farm, transportation, wholesale, and retail levels ranged from 23.94 to 25.19 °C, 22.94 to 24.39 °C, 22.49 to 24.10 °C, and 22.90 to 25.51 °C, respectively (Fig. 3). The relative humidity recorded at the farm, transportation, wholesale, and retail in our study ranged from 33.40 to 57.24%, 30.46 to 37.82%, 38.45 to 46.54%, and 34.88 to 54.90%, respectively (Fig. 4). The temperature and relative humidity conditions recorded in this study throughout the supply chain were suboptimal as such high handling temperature and low relative humidity accelerates the processes that lead to the quality and quantity deterioration of tomatoes.

3.2 Growing Locations and Harvesting Practices

Quantitative postharvest losses (QPHL) of tomato at different stages of the supply chain and growing location are shown in Fig. 5. The study revealed that the interaction effect among growing locations and supply chain significantly (P < 0.0001) altered the percentage of postharvest losses of tomatoes. Quantitative postharvest loss at the farm level soon after harvesting of tomato was in the range of 6.17 to 8.62% with an average loss of 7.31%. The mean postharvest loss of tomatoes at the farm were 8.62%, 7.15%, and 6.17% in Gumara, Kudmi, and Chimba kebele, respectively (Fig. 5). Lack of harvesting skills and inappropriate packaging like use of wooden crates with hard and sharp surfaces which causes mechanical injuries on harvested fruits, diseases, and insect pests were the prominent factors causing losses at the farm level in the study kebeles.

The highest postharvest loss (8.62%) of tomatoes at the farm level was recorded in Gumara kebele may be associated with the growing practices employed in this kebeles. In this growing location, tomato plants were not staked and thus most of the tomatoes were in direct contact with the soil (Fig. 2B), which predisposes the fruits for disease infection and decay and mechanical damages as indicated in Fig. 6A. Findings of present study are comparable with the findings reported by Genova II, et al. [11] in Vietnam where postharvest losses of tomato at farm level is about 8%. On the other hand, postharvest losses of tomatoes recorded in the present study were relatively lower than those reported by Robert, et al. [12] where it was about 15 to 19%.

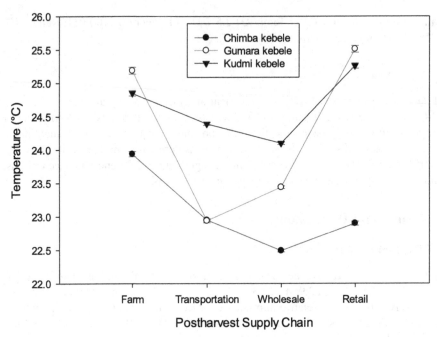

Fig. 3. Temperature in °C (Mean ± standard error) along the postharvest supply chain, Northwest Ethiopia

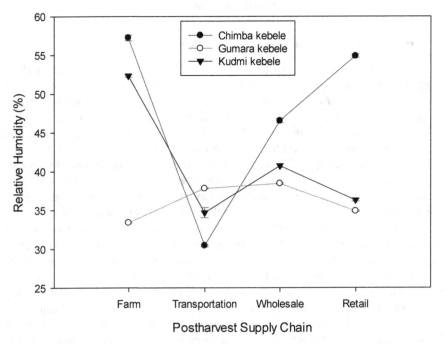

Fig. 4. Relative humidity in % (mean ± standard error) along the postharvest supply chain, Northwest Ethiopia

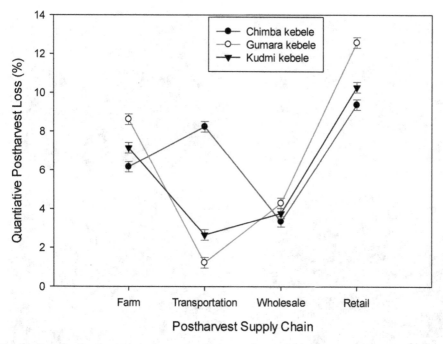

Fig. 5. Quantitative postharvest losses in % (mean ± standard error) of tomatoes along the postharvest supply chain, Northwest Ethiopia

Tomatoes were harvested in the study kebeles at different harvesting stages including turning, pink and light red stages, which was depending on the intended use or mar-ket. Harvesting was almost done by hand without using any special equipment where daily laborers (young male and females) mostly employed. Harvester moved through the planting rows and handpicked the fruits that were ready for harvesting and throw it into the jute/polypropylene bags. Such type of harvesting and handling causes bruising and mechanical damages. Therefore, postharvest losses of tomato fruits begins in the field and continues in the supply chain due to the high possibility of compression stresses during postharvest handling practices such as harvesting, sort-ing, field packing, transportation, and subsequent handling [13, 14]. The harvesting time of tomato was from morning to afternoon (9:30 AM to 1:00 PM) in the study area. Harvesting during the warmer part of the day results in faster senescence, shriv-eling and wilting of fruit through high transpiration rate and losses of water [15, 16].

3.3 Transportation

Quantitative losses of tomatoes during transportation were ranged from 1.23 to 8.24%. The mean losses of tomatoes during transportation were 1.23%, 2.66%, and 8.24% in Gumara, Kudmi, and Chimba kebeles, respectively (Fig. 5). Loading and transportation was done immediately after harvesting and completed from 1:00 PM to 3:00 PM where Bahir Dar city fruit and vegetable market was the destination. Toyota Minibus Hiace

Fig. 6. Damaged tomatoes at the farm (A), during transportation (B), at wholesale (C), and retail (D) level in Northwest Ethiopia

was used to transport tomatoes from Gumara and Kudmi kebeles while ISUZU NPR for tomatoes from Chimba kebele. About 1:35, 1:50, and 2:00 h were required to transport tomatoes from Gumara, Kudmi, and Chimba kebeles, respectively, to Bahir Dar fruit and vegetables market.

The results of the present study showed that postharvest loss during transportation of tomatoes in Chimba kebele (8.24%) was higher than those in Kudmi and Gumara kebeles. This is due to the relatively poor packaging (wooden box), poor road access, and use of poor means of transportation methods like donkeys, public transport and rented trucks which leads to high mechanical damage and high postharvest losses (Fig. 6B). Chimba kebele is 30 km away from the market place (Bahir Dar fruit and vegetable market) and of which about 25 km of the road was bumpy. On the other hand, Kudmi kebele 42 km away from the market place and of which 7 km was bumpy. Gumara kebele was 40 km away from the market place where the road was relatively good. In addition, 84 wooden boxes of tomatoes were loaded in one ISUZU NPR truck in Chimba kebele while in Kudmi and Gumara kebeles only 6 wooden boxes of tomatoes were loaded in one Toyota Minibus Hiace. Similar tomato transportation practices for local market were also reported in Nigeria and Tanzania in line with present study [7, 17]. Vibration during transport because of road bumpiness is one of the major causes of postharvest losses of fruits and vegetables, especially tomatoes [18].

3.4 Wholesaler and Retailer

Immediately after arrival at the market place, tomato fruits in wooden boxes were unloaded by daily laborers (young males) and stored in the warehouses of wholesalers. The warehouses of wholesaler and retailer were constructed from wooden pole covered with stainless steel sheet metal and thick polythene. The warehouses did not have essential storage facilities like cooling. Moreover, the stores are too small and not clean (Fig. 7). Tomatoes in wooden boxes and woven cane baskets were stored for two and three days by wholesaler and retailer, respectively.

Fig. 7. Handling and storage conditions of tomatoes at wholesale (A) and retail (B) levels in Bahir Dar city fruit and vegetable market

Quantitative postharvest losses of tomato at wholesale, and retail levels ranged from 3.35 to 4.30%, and 9.38 to 12.58%, respectively (Fig. 5). The mean postharvest losses of tomatoes at wholesale level sourced from Gumara, Kudmi, and Chimba kebeles were 4.30%, 3.78%, and 3.35% for tomatoes, respectively with an average loss of 3.81%. The mean postharvest losses at retail level were 12.58%, 10.28%, and 9.38% for tomatoes from Gumara, Kudmi, and Chimba kebele, respectively with an average loss of 10.75% (Fig. 5).

The study showed that postharvest losses of tomatoes sourced from Gumara kebele at wholesale and retail levels from were higher compared to those from Kudmi and Chimba kebeles which may be associated with production practices, and suboptimal handling practices (high temperature and low relative humidity storage) which accelerate physiological deterioration of tomatoes than tomatoes from Kudmi and Chimba kebeles. In the present study, tomatoes at the wholesale and retail levels were stored at temperatures ranging from 22.49 to 24.10 °C and 22.90 to 25.51 °C, respectively and with relative humidity ranging from 30.46 to 57.24% (Fig. 3 and 4). However, the recommended transport and storage temperatures for tomatoes are 10 to 18°C depending on the maturity stages of fruits. Temperature below these ranges will cause chilling injuries, while too warm conditions promote transpiration and ripening and thus hastened deterioration and reduces postharvest lives [6, 19, 20].

According to the results of the present study the main causes of postharvest losses of tomatoes at wholesale and retail levels were perhaps associated with inappropriate handling and packaging, inadequate storage facilities, and poor sanitary conditions at local open-air markets (Fig. 6C and D). Such condition lead to the damages of tomatoes by rodents and accelerates physiological and microbial damages, which is in line with the findings of other authors [21–23]. Similar with the present study, postharvest loss of tomato at wholesale level in Vietnam was about 4% as reported by Genova II, et al. [11]. The losses of tomatoes at retail level observed in this study were also comparable with the results reported by Kitinoja and Cantwell [24] in Rwanda which was about 14.7%.

4 Conclusion

The production practices of tomatoes in Northwest Ethiopia varies from location to location, where some farmers used staking (Chimba and Kudmi Kebeles), while others produced tomatoes without staking (Gumara kebele), which increases postharvest losses.

High temperatures and low relative humidity during handling and storage had a significant effect on the quantitative postharvest losses of tomatoes. Tomatoes sourced from Gumara kebele exhibited the highest amount of postharvest losses (12.58%), followed by those from Kudmi (10.28%), and Chimba kebeles (9.38%) at retail level which is associated with high temperatures and suboptimal handling practices. On the other hand, tomatoes sourced from Gumara kebele exhibited the lowest amount of postharvest loss during transportation (1.23%) because of relatively good asphalt-concrete road. The total postharvest losses of tomatoes produced in Chimba, Gumara, and Kudmi kebeles were 27.21%, 26.72%, and 23.88%, respectively, with an average total loss of 25.91% along the postharvest supply chain. These losses were only for the first five days from harvesting up to selling to customers at Bahir Dar fruit and vegetable market. The retail practice was one of the highest and serious postharvest loss points of tomato along the postharvest supply chain next to harvesting, which is associated with the cumulative effects of all pressures exerted on tomatoes from time of harvesting, box filling, loading, transporting, unloading and storage conditions.

Generally, the high postharvest losses of tomatoes in the study were associated with lack of knowledge and skills in postharvest management and handling practices along the supply chain, which includes improper harvesting stage, inappropriate harvesting methods and time, inappropriate harvesting containers and packaging materials, unsuitable transportation system including methods of transport and bumpy roads, inappropriate loading and unloading practices, lack of cold storage facilities at farm, wholesale and retail levels. The information from this study could be used as a basis to minimize the postharvest losses of tomato by policymakers to emplace appropriate policies that minimize postharvest losses of perishable crops along the supply chain. It can be used as base for provision of extension services given by postharvest experts for different actors in the supply chain of tomato.

Acknowledgements. We express our gratitude to Faculty of Chemical and Food Engineering, Bahir Dar Institute of Technology, Bahir Dar University for its support in access all necessary materials for the successful completion of this research work. Authors would like to thank BDU-IUC project (Post-harvest and Food Processing in Northwest Ethiopia) for the financial support and collaboration for accomplishment of the work.

References

1. FAOSTAT: Agricultural data. Provisional Production Indices Data. Crop Primary (2017). http://apps.fao.org/default.jsp. Accessed 20 Sept 2019
2. Emana, B., Afari-Sefa, V., Nenguwo, N., Ayana, A., Kebede, D., Mohammed, H.: Characterization of pre- and postharvest losses of tomato supply chain in Ethiopia. Agric. Food Secur. **6**(1), 1–11 (2017). https://doi.org/10.1186/s40066-016-0085-1
3. CSA: The Federal Democratic Republic of Ethiopia, Agricultural Sample Survey, Volume I, Report on Area and Production of Crops, (Private Peasant Holdings, Meher Season), Addis Ababa, Ethiopia: Central Statistical Agency (CSA) (2019)
4. Gemechis, A., Struik, P.C.O., Emana, B.: Tomato production in Ethiopia: constraints and opportunities. In: International Research on Food Security, Natural Resource Management and Rural Development. Resilience of Agricultural Systems against Crises: Book of Abstracts, p. 373 (2012)
5. Opara, U., Al-Ani, M., Al-Rahbi, N.: Effect of fruit ripening stage on physico-chemical properties, nutritional composition and antioxidant components of tomato (Lycopersicum esculentum) cultivars. Food Bioprocess Technol. **5**(8), 3236–3243 (2012). https://doi.org/10.1007/s11947-011-0693-5
6. Kader, A.A.: Postharvest technology of horticultural crops, vol. 3311. University of California Agriculture and Natural Resources (2002)
7. Olayemi, F., Adegbola, J., Bamishaiye, E., Awagu, E.: Assessment of postharvest losses of some selected crops in eight local government areas of rivers state. Nigeria. Asian J. Rural Dev. **2**(1), 13–23 (2012)
8. Kasso, M., Bekele, A.: Post-harvest loss and quality deterioration of horticultural crops in Dire Dawa Region. Ethiopia. J. Saudi Soc. Agric. Sci. **17**(1), 88–96 (2018)
9. Hussen, S., Beshir, H., Hawariyat, Y.W.: Postharvest Loss assessment of commercial horticultural crops in South Wollo, Ethiopia 'challenges and opportunities.' Food Sci. Qual. Manag. **17**, 34–39 (2013)
10. FAO: Food Loss Analysis: Causes and Solutions. Case studies in the Small-scale Agriculture and Fisheries Subsectors. Methodology (2015)
11. Genova II, C., Weinberger, K., An, H.B, Dam, D.D., Loc, N.T.T., Thuy, N.T.T.: Postharvest loss in the supply chain for vegetables–The case of chili and tomato in Vietnam: AVRDC-World Vegetable Center (2006)
12. Robert, A., Rita, A.D., James, O.M.: Determinants of postharvest losses in tomato production in the Offinso North district of Ghana. J. Dev. Agric. Econ. **6**(8), 338–344 (2014)
13. Ferreira, M.D., Franco, A.T.O., Kasper, R.F., Ferraz, A.C.O., Honório, S.L., Tavares, M.: Post-harvest quality of fresh-marketed tomatoes as a function of harvest periods. Sci. Agric. **62**(5), 446–451 (2005)

14. Mditshwa, A., Magwaza, L.S., Tesfay, S.Z., Opara, U.L.: Postharvest factors affecting vitamin C content of citrus fruits: a review. Sci. Hortic. (Amsterdam) **218**, 95–104 (2017)

15. García, J., Ruiz-Altisent, M., Barreiro, P.: Factors influencing mechanical properties and bruise susceptibility of apples and pears. J. Agric. Eng. Res. **16**(1), 11–17 (1995)

16. Abbott, B., Holford, P., Golding, J.B.: Comparison of 'Cripps Pink' apple bruising. In: ISHS Acta Horticulturae 880: International Symposium Postharvest Pacifica 2009 - Pathways to Quality: V International Symposium on Managing Quality in Chains + Australasian Postharvest Horticultural Conference, pp. 223–229 (2009)

17. Kereth, G., Lyimo, M., Mbwana, H., Mongi, R.J., Ruhembe, C.C.: Assessment of post-harvest handling practices : knowledge and losses of fruits in Bagamoyo District of Tanzania. Food Sci. Qual. Manage. **6088**, 8–16 (2013)

18. Idah, P.A., Ajisegiri, E.S.A., Yisa, M.G.: Fruits and vegetables handling and transportation in Nigeria. Aust. J. Technol. **10**(3), 176–183 (2007)

19. Toor, R.K., Savage, G.P.: Changes in major antioxidant components of tomatoes during postharvest storage. Food Chem. **99**(4), 724–727 (2006)

20. Nunes, M.C.N., Emond, J.P., Rauth, M., Dea, S., Chau, K.V.: Environmental conditions encountered during typical consumer retail display affect fruit and vegetable quality and waste. Postharvest Biol. Technol. **51**(2), 232–241 (2009)

21. Kader, A.A., Rolle, R.S.: The role of post-harvest management in assuring the quality and safety of horticultural produce, vol. 152. Food and Agriculture Organisation (2004)

22. Bollen, A.F.: Major factors causing variation in bruise susceptibility of apples (malus domestica) grown in New Zealand. New Zeal. J. Crop Hortic. Sci. **33**(3), 201–210 (2005)

23. Mbuk, E.M., Bassey, N.E., Udoh, E.S., Udoh, E.J.: Factors influencing postharvest loss of tomato in urban market in Uyo. Nigeria. Niger. J. Agric. Food Environ. **7**(2), 40–46 (2011)

24. Kitinoja, L., Cantwell, M.: Identification of appropriate postharvest technologies for improving market access and incomes for small horticultural farmers in SubSaharan Africa and South Asia. WFLO Grant Final Report to the Bill & Melinda Gates Foundation. Grant number 52198. pp. 234–1848 (2010)

Electrical and Computer Engineering

Reserved Distance and Significant Parameter Determination in Incumbent and TV White Space System Coexistence

Tessema T. Terefe[3]($\boxtimes$), Habib M. Hussien[2], and Sultan F. Meko[1]

[1] College of Electrical and Mechanical Engineering, Department of Electrical and Computer Engineering, AASTU, Addis Ababa, Ethiopia
[2] School of Electrical and Computer Engineering, Addis Ababa Institute of Technology (AAiT), AAU, Addis Ababa, Ethiopia
[3] Addis Ababa Science and Technology University (AASTU), Addis Ababa, Ethiopia
tessema.tariku@aastu.edu.et

Abstract. In the bandwidth demanding world, TV white space is becoming one of the promising options. Its use as a secondary system with incumbent system must be managed in order not affect the primary users. This can be done by determining first the incumbent coverage and then the spatial variation that should be kept in order to maintain unaffecting region. Our primary concern is keeping the incumbent users safe. This is accompanied by different methods to keep the secondary device non interfering. The interference can be avoided by efficient cognitive radio technique or spatial variation between the two systems. The later technique requires efficient signal modeling and planning. The secondary system should be deployed in an area that is out of primary coverage. This is done by first determining the incumbent coverage. To determine this coverage, different factors must be taken in to account. Frequency and antenna height are of the significant factors. After the signal range of primary transmission with receivable quality is determined, we have determined another reserved distance that a secondary device should be kept away in its active status, without affecting the incumbent system. This is what is known to be reserved distance. From the significant factors in determining the spatial variations, we have found transmitter antenna height to be the most significant factor in white space system planning.

Keywords: Antenna height · Contour coverage · Reserved distance · Secondary system

1 Introduction

The TV white space is a vacant space in time or space of the terrestrial TV transmission channels. It is part of the radio communication spectrum, which is vacant at a given time in a given geographical area on noninterfering basis with regard to primary and other services [1]. These vacant portions of spectrum became available as a key research topic

© ICST Institute for Computer Sciences, Social Informatics and Telecommunications Engineering 2021
Published by Springer Nature Switzerland AG 2021. All Rights Reserved
M. A. Delele et al. (Eds.): ICAST 2020, LNICST 384, pp. 125–133, 2021.
https://doi.org/10.1007/978-3-030-80621-7_9

and future technology and business development area. There have been different standards developed to manage this availability of free channels for secondary use [2]. It is a very effective technological option in providing a broadband internet with advantage of good bandwidth quality, large bandwidth, long distance coverage capability and greater signal penetration [3]. To gain these advantages, there must be a good management of the secondary system deployed to exploit the free bands. To have effective management then, efficient cognitive radio technique must be guaranteed which include time or spatial variation of use [4].

The spatial variation uses to keep the secondary device some place out of the signal range of the incumbent system at its minimum receivable signal quality. For this placement determination, signal quality and propagation characteristics are necessary. Using the propagation models, we can calculate the coverage area and hence the range of primary signal [5]. Determining the primary coverage is insufficient in planning the secondary system deployment. The secondary device must be some distance away from the coverage range of the primary system, called reserved distance. This is because the secondary device is transmitting, so that it causes interference [6]. So, the reserved distance must exist between the contour coverage of the primary system and secondary device in order to give sufficient working area in its full transmission power [7]. Different factors determine this distance [6]. Assuming the white space device (WSD) is operating with its maximum power, 36 dBm [8], frequency and transmitter antenna height are the most significant factors. In the deployment of secondary system, the vendor must take care of providing non interfering system to the primary user. Therefore, the most significant factor must be known in determining the coverage and reserved distance. Which one is most significant? Operating frequency or antenna height? We have tried to identify it. Different researchers tried to find different ways to determine the coexistence of the two systems [4, 6–12]. They have shown ways to manage the coexistence. Denkovska et al. [9] used Monte carlo simulation method to calculate the separation distance that should be kept between the LTE mobile technology and Digital Video Broadcasting-Terrestrial (DVB-T) without interference to the television system. Suh et al. [10], studied ways to determine the minimum receivable field strength which in turn is used to determine the protection ratio and reserved distance. K. Kang [11] on the other hand provides a methodology to calculate the reserved distance as well. It implements the geolocational database technique. However, these are not researches made to determine the most significant factor in determining the coverage and reserved distance.

The main purpose of this study resides on determining the reserved distance for the separation of the secondary device (white space device) and the primary or incumbent system (Digital Terrestrial Television). And we studied the most significant factors in determining this reserved distance and separation distance, where this in turn helps during secondary system deployment to protect the primary system from unwanted signal interference. To determine this, we have used geolocational database implementation method, among the three cognitive radio techniques. It works on spatial variation basis. The most significant factor which determines these parameters in secondary system planning and deployment is determined by taking test points. The rest of this paper is arranged in a way like, after the introduction System Model and Problem Formulation follows. Section 3 focuses on Results and Discussion. Finally, a conclusion is given in Sect. 4.

2 System Model and Problem Formulation

The secondary system or TV white space system must be non-interfering to the incumbent system. The licensed user, who pays for the national regulatory body, should not be affected by the secondary system. This is the guiding principle in TV white space system installation. One way to protect the incumbent system is by providing sufficient spatial variation between the primary and the secondary systems. This spatial variation is supported by installing the white space device (WSD) out of the incumbent coverage. In other words, there must be a separation distance from the digital terrestrial TV (DTT) transmitter that the WSD must be kept away. The contour coverage of incumbent system is affected by different factors [1]. These factors include DTT transmitter antenna height, frequency of operation and the minimum allowable field strength value for the DTT receiver below which the receiver can't have acceptable quality of signal. Each of these factors, on the other hand, may be dependent on other factors. In some cases, different selected propagation models may depend on the terrain coverage around the transmitter; this implies the antenna height is better described by Height Above Average Terrain (HAAT). The minimum median field strength is the value which is limited by the national authorized body by considering different factors. These factors contribute in determining the minimum receivable signal quality of the DTT receiver. For one country, the limiting equation is given by [6, 8].

$$E_{min} + F_D + G_D + F_{Da} - L_1 - N_t - N_F = C/N \tag{1}$$

Where E_{min} is the minimum field strength and in this equation, FD is dipole factor with its formula [6]:

$$F_D = -75.05 - 20logf_c \tag{2}$$

Here fc is the channel mid frequency. G_D is dipole antenna gain of the incumbent transmitter. F_{Da} is dipole antenna gain adjustment factor which is given by:

$$F_{Da} = 20log(615/f_c) \tag{3}$$

where in this case f_c is the channel midfrequency. According to Ethiopian Broadcast Authority, the geometric mean frequency is given by 69 MHz for low VHF, 194 MHz for high VHF and 615 MHz for UHF. F_{Da} has the value as defined in the formula for UHF frequencies only; otherwise, it is zero [2]. L_l is the downlead line loss of the transmitter antenna to its receiver antenna. N_t is thermal noise given by:

$$N_t(dBm) = 10log(kTB) \tag{4}$$

where k is Boltzmann constant given by k $= 1.38 \times 10^{-23} J/K$, T is system temperature and B is the bandwidth of the channel. N_F is the noise figure and C/N is carrier to noise ratio. With these values identified, the planning is done to limit the contour coverage of the primary system. The figure below represents the sample system arranged in such a way that a TV white space device is placed not to affect the primary system. The primary system is kept non-interfered by the WSD if it is placed at a certain reserved

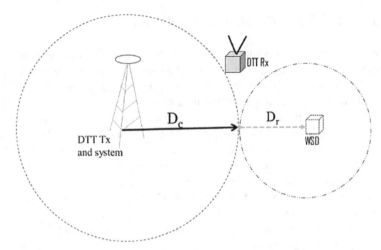

Fig. 1. TV white space device placement and reserved distance

distance, *Dr*. As shown in Fig. 1, the DTT receiver is assumed to be put at the edge of the incumbent contour coverage. It is to receive the minimum receivable signal quality.

Dc is the contour coverage distance when measured from the center of the DTT transmitter, and Dr is reserved distance between the white space device and the DTT coverage contour. Each of these distances must be determined well in order the two systems to coexist. So, the coexistence of the TV white space system with the incumbent system is determined by designing the system which separates the WSD at sufficient distance from the incumbent coverage contour [4, 6]. To determine the contour coverage radius, we have to limit the minimum field strength value, E_{min} from Eq. (1). After the E_{min} value is calculated, appropriate propagation model is used to find at which distance the E_{min} value is met. For this analysis, we have selected Okumura Hata model.

2.1 Okumura Hata Model

It is a propagation model designed to cover a distance up to 100 km. The operating frequency ranges from 150 MHz up to 1.5 GHz [3]. The loss for urban areas is given by:

$$L_{urban} = 69.55 + 26.16log(f) - 13.82log(h_t) - a(h_r) + (44.9 - 6.55log(h_t))log(d) \tag{5}$$

Where L_{urban} is signl loss for urban areas, f is operating frequency, h_t and h_r are transmitter and receiver antenna heights above the ground in m, and correction factor $a(h_r)$ for middle and small cities is given by:

$$a(h_r) = (1.1log(f) - 0.7)h_r - (1.56log(f) - 0.8) \tag{6}$$

For open or rural areas, it become:

$$L_{rural} = L_{urban} - 4.78(log(f))^2 + 18.33log(f) - 40.94 \tag{7}$$

The pathloss for a given minimum field strength is given by a formula:

$$E_{min}\left(dB\mu\frac{v}{m}\right) = P_t(dBm) - P_l(dB) + 20logf(MHz) + 77.2 \tag{8}$$

Where E_{min} is the minimum receivable field strength. This value is what is determined in Eq. (1). F is the working frequency and others are transmitted and loss powers respectively. By equating the loss calculated from the pathloss model and this loss, we will find coverage radius.

Also, for the D_r, we have a field strength value given by:

$$E_r = E_{min} - P_{WSD} - D/U + G_{Dis} + 64.25 \tag{9}$$

Where E_r is the field strength which is at a location where a white space device should be located away from the primary system transmitter. P_{WSD} is the transmitted white space device power, mostly it is given to be 36 dBm. G_{dis} is the offset antenna discrimination factor. D/U is the desired to undesired signal ratio. It has a different value for adjacent and co-channels [4]. Also, for this field strength, we can find the pathloss by using Eq. (8). The parameters set for these calculations are set as in Table 1.

From the factors which affect the coverage and reserved distance, and hence the coexistence, we have selected the two main factors i.e. coverage radius and frequency. In designing a TV white space system, there must be a good management to avoid interference. This management is guided by spatial variation of the secondary and primary system. For this comparison we have selected five different test points with different frequency. These points are from different locations of terrestrial TV transmitters in Ethiopia, with an assumption that they represent the ranges of frequency used for the terrestrial TV transmission.

Table.1. Parameters for reserved distance determination [6]

Parameters	Values
f_c	610 MHz
G_D	10 dB
L_l	4 dB
NF	7 dB
P_{WSD}	36 dBm
C/N	23 dB
$D/U_{co-channel}$	23 dB
$D/U_{Adjacent\ channel}$	−33 dB
G_{Dis}	14 dB
N_t	−104.95 dBm

3   Result and Discussion

The minimum field strength is calculated to be $E_{min} = 49.74$ dB(μV/m). For this field strength value and other given parameters, the coverage contour will be at a radius of 36.28 km. For reserved distance calculation antenna height of 10m is used for the same frequency, 610 MHz. The field strength value is calculated to be 69 dB(μV/m) for co-channel. Then the reserved distance is 5.396 km for co-channel. For adjacent channel, the field strength is 104 dB(μV/m). This value declares that the distance from the contour coverage for adjacent channel is 140 m. It is very near to the coverage contour of the DTT transmitter. The values show that to use a co-channel by the white space device, it must be separated with larger separation distance than adjacent channels. As shown in the coverage map, there is sufficient gap for the WSD and DTT transmitter coverage contour. Thus, their coexistence is determined by the reserved distance which should be calculated as in the formula above. For the primary transmitter site taken as a test point at Bedi, which is operating at frequency of 610 MHz, and located near Addis Ababa, Ethiopia, the WSD should be placed at 5.396 km and 140m away from the contour coverage of 36.28 km, in order to reuse the adjacent channels of channel number 38 and the channel 38 itself respectively. These distance values of keeping the WSD are the least allowed distances, below which the WSD causes interference to the incumbent system, as shown in Fig. 2. The figure shows the SPLAT software analysis result of the signal coverage range and reserved distance.

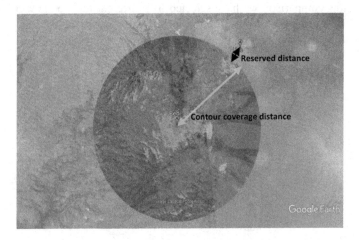

Fig. 2. Contour coverage and reserved distance (adapted from Google Earth)

For different frequency values, the adjacent and co-channel reserved distances from the incumbent system is found as tabulated in Table 2. The site names are incumbent transmitters or the terrestrial TV transmission sites selected based on their different operating frequency.

Table 2. Reserved distances of DTT transmitters for different test points

Site name	Frequency (MHz)	Co-channel D_r(km)	Adjacent channel D_r(km)
Furi	178	7.9684	0.1515
Assosa	220	7.8614	0.1495
Kebridhar	498	7.8096	0.1485
Tendaho	650	7.9155	0.1505
Debark	762	8.0086	0.1523

From Table 2, the variation of reserved distances, with variation of frequency from channel 5 to channel 57 or 178 MHz to 762 MHz, doesn't show a big difference. The difference is in a range of decimal points. For the frequency difference from 178 MHz to 762 MHz, the percentage variation in the reserved distance is only 5%. There is also a non-linear variation, where for co-channel reserved distances it is 7.9684 km for 178 MHz and decreases to 7.8096 km for 498 MHz and this again increases to 8.0086 km for 762 MHz. This characteristic is also noticed in the graph of frequency versus keep out distance for different height values. Keeping the frequency and other parameters constant and varying the antenna height from 1.5 m to 30 m gives a reserved (keep out) distance variation of 5 km or 250%. This analysis indicates that the deployment of TV white space system should be more concerned for antenna heights of the WSD than operating frequency. As it can be seen from Fig. 3, the most significant factor in TVWS system deployment is antenna height. The iterations made for this graphing is in the basis of 0.01.

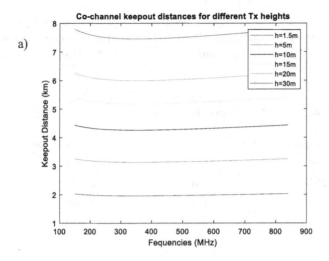

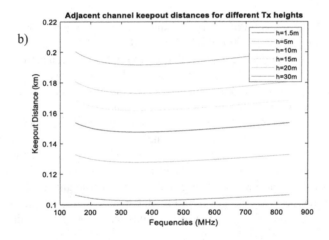

Fig. 3. Reserved (keep out) distance for different antenna heights (a) & (b)

4   Conclusion

In this work, it is tried to analyze the separation distance that a white space device should be kept away from the contour coverage of the primary system. It is the reserved distance to keep the device non interfering to the incumbent system. In the planning of the secondary white space system different factors are taken in to account. Among them, antenna height and operating frequency have been compared in order to identify the most significant factor. Hence, antenna height is found to be the most influencing factor in TV white space system planning and design. So, the planning body must take care of the transmitter antenna heights more than other parameters to have non-interfering and stable system coexistence.

References

1. C. R. 24: Technical considerations regarding harmonisation options for the Digital Dividend. A preliminary assessment of the feasibility of fitting new/future applications/services into nonharmonised spectrum of the digital dividend (namely the so-called "white spaces"between allotments), 27 July 2008
2. Nyasulu, T., Anderson, D., et al.: TV white space for internet access in the developing world. Mawingu Networks, Kenya (2017)
3. Mekonnen, M.: Feasibility study of TV white space for broadband internet services: the case of rural Ethiopia, MSc thesis, AAU (2017)
4. Aji, L.S., Wibisono, G., Gunawan, D.: Analysis of white space coverage area radius to find the equilibrium point between DVB-T2 and IEEE 802.22 WRAN. In: International Conference on Electrical Engineering and Informatics (ICELTICs 2017), Banda Aceh, Indonesia, 18–20 October 2017
5. Stylianos, K.: Modelling and coverage improvement of DVB-T Networks. A thesis submitted for the degree of Doctor of Philosophy, March 2018
6. Mohammed, H., Katzis, K., et al.: Co-existence of TV white space devices and DTV services in Ethiopian Geolocation White Spectrum Database. In: CAMAD IEEE, Liasson, Cyprus, 11–13 September 2019
7. Mfupe, L., Mekuria, F., Mzyece, M.: Geo-location white space spectrum databases: models and design of South Africa's first dynamic spectrum access coexistence manager. KSII Trans. Internet Inf. Syst. **08**(11) (2014)
8. OET BULLETIN No. 69: Longley-Rice Methodology for Evaluating TV Coverage and Interference. FCC, 06 February 2004
9. Dludla, G., Rananga, S., Swart, A.: Co-existence study between analog TV (PAL-I) and LTE in digital dividend band: South African case study. In: 2018 International Conference on Advances in Big Data Computing and Data Communication Systems (icABCD), Durban (2018)
10. Suh, K., Jung, H., Lee, J., Jang, J.-S.: The calculation of field strength for DTV receiver by Rec. ITU-R P.1546. In: 2010 IEEE Asia-Pacific Conference on Applied Electromagnetics (APACE), Port Dickson (2010)
11. Kang, K.: Minimum separation distance of adjacent channel TV band devices from DTV protected contour in TV white space. Electron. Lett. **50**(14), 1024–1025 (2014)
12. Directivity and polarization discrimination of antennas in the reception of television broadcasting, Recommendation BT.419-3 (1999)
13. Song, M., et al.: Dynamic spectrum access: from cognitive radio to network radio. IEEE Wirel. Commun. **19**(1), 23–29 (2012). https://doi.org/10.1109/MWC.2012.6155873
14. Makris, D., Gardikis, G., Kourtis, A.: Quantifying TV white space capacity: quantifying tv white space capacity: IEEE Commun. Mag. **50**(9), 145–152 (2012)
15. Villardi, G.P., de Abreu, G.T.F., Harada, H.: TV white space technology: interference in portable cognitive emergency network. IEEE Veh. Technol. Mag. **7**(02), 47–53 (2012)
16. Denkovska, M., Latkoski, P., Gavrilovska, L.: Optimization of spectrum usage and coexistence analysis of DVB-T and LTE-800 systems. Wirel. Pers. Commun. **87**(3), 713–730 (2015)

Earliest-Arrival Route: A Global Optimized Communication for Networked Control Systems

M. Sundar Rajan[1]($\boxtimes$) (iD), J. R. Arunkumar[2], R. Anusuya[2], and Abraham Mesfin[1]

[1] Faculty of Electrical and Computer Engineering, Arbaminch University, Arba Minch, Ethiopia
sundar.rajan@amu.edu.et

[2] Faculty of Computing and Software Engineering, Arbaminch University, Arba Minch, Ethiopia

Abstract. As per the present switched system theorem, data package-drop ratio decides the strength of NCSs. Through the focal point principle to offer small data package-drop ratio for dispersed NCS under parameter transmission environment, the communication improvement issue is described from universal transmission aspect. Initially, system stimulated break is illustrated function associated with time can be calculated using auto-regressive-moving-average (ARMA) pattern, and the upcoming break is forecasted by the obtained break samples. Subsequently, the widespread referred shortest route of time dependent network(SPTDN) algorithm is described and enhanced by means of introducing waiting-time previous to data packages are dispatched to subsequent unit in a route, in order to get quickly coming time than SPTDN. Subsequently, the concept of earliest-arrival time (EAT) is suggested to calculate the excellence of transmission route, the connected EAT algorithm is intended to look for upcoming EAT and the equivalent route since universal system vigorously. Advantage from the active EAT route, data packages reach at target as early as feasible, it reduces data package-drop ratio. Therefore, EAT route make sure the steadiness of shared NCSs from the opinion of worldwide system. At last, the experiment demonstrates the strength and efficiency of the suggested method.

Keywords: Transmission optimization · Forecasting system-stimulated break pattern · Shortest route system · Networked control system

1 Introduction

Conventional monitor systems are varying from NCS comprises of detecting devices, regulators, and actuators inside a system, consequently, few new procedure constantly happens in the practical system atmosphere. The major issues faced with NCSs are system- stimulated breaks, data package losses and data package disorders. In recent years, many of peoples who is doing research in this field have determined their concentration on removing these breaks, even performing a particular quantity of achievement. Numerous researchers have handled with the agreement issue theoretically by analyzing NCS arrangement [1], The feedback regulators for dynamic system [2], and creating

M. A. Delele et al. (Eds.): ICAST 2020, LNICST 384, pp. 134–142, 2021.
https://doi.org/10.1007/978-3-030-80621-7_10

hypothetical concepts in several agent networks along transmission breaks [3]. Additionally, to these theoretical searching of NCS features, real life analysis were performed in the efficiency of NCS usages in a choice of areas, as like traffic handling [4], mobile detecting device systems [5], unmanned flights and distant manufacturing company monitor [6–8]. Safety issues inbuilt to NCSs have also been analyzed [9]. Modern innovations in NCS study comprises the execution of a direct related-dependent NCS [10] and the expansion of a computerized NCS laboratory, which permits consumers to execute tests distantly, attain pictorial outputs, and scrutinize the testing procedure through the internet [11]. Almost tests are determined on NCSs features, specific disturbs the support capacity of system to NCSs. added by [12], a converted system pattern of NCSs with fixed break was projected. Then both break and confusion issue is transformed into data package-loss issue by placing break edge, and the higher value of data package-drop ratio was specified. Because of the threshold, data packages with more break than threshold will be reduced. It indicates the more greater-break data packages comes into sight in a particular period, the greater the data package-drop ratio turn out to be.

For shared NCSs, numerous routes from regulator to plant may present. Various connects among units present various break feature. With the objective to minimize a dynamic route with reduced data package-drop ratio in time-dependent system, a forecasting system-stimulated break pattern is necessary. In recent times, few comparative researches have been suggested [13] determines pattern through ARMA pattern depends on information concept and except the high computation price creates itself improper to real-time applications. In addition to [14], which suggests a forecasting pattern using different algorithms and the impartiality grey pattern is suggested in [15], but relatively large errors become visible progress to the samples swiftly and extensively. Therefore, ARMA pattern is accepted in this article due to the remaining of handiness and precision.

By ARMA pattern, the present intervals are patterned, then the particular-step ahead breaks are forecasted to compute the improved route. Thus, the key objective of this article is dispatch system components online with the time-varying interval, such that a dynamic low data package-drop ratio route is preserved for signal transmission among regulator and process.

2   System Description

2.1   Forecasting Network Break Pattern

Conversely, theoretical work on NCSs has turn out to be increasingly widespread, there is no satisfying pattern for unfolding system breaks. In engineering, the system stimulated interval among two units at interval k is forever measured the part of the Round-Trip-Time (RTT), where it is indicated by Xk. A nonstop succession of breaks are composed through the sample set {Xk}, for k= 1, 2, 3, by each Xk denotes the time-correlation form of a break. The system break can be explained as time sequence. Thus, to get hold of the break sequence by approving an ARMA pattern.

2.2   Networked Control System Pattern

Assume a widespread constant state-space equation as below,

$$\dot{x}(t) = A_p x(t) + B_p u(t)$$

$x(t) \in \mathbb{R}^{n \times 1}$ and $u(t) \in \mathbb{R}^{m \times 1}$ are state of the system and monitor sign a correspondingly, A_p is state matrix and B_p is monitor matrix of the continuous network (3), $A_p \in \mathbb{R}^{n \times n}$, $B_p \in \mathbb{R}^{n \times m}$, n and m $\in$ N. Subsequently a traditional system below is utilized to portray NCSs [12].

$$S^{(0)} : x(k + 1) = Ax(k) + B_0 u(k) + B_1 u(k - 1)$$
$$S^{(1)} : x(k + 1) = Ax(k) + B_2 u(k - d)$$
$$S^{(2)} : x(k + 1) = Ax(k) + B_0 u(k) + B_1 u(k - d),$$

h- sampling time interval, d - amount of the successive missing data packages at present time, τ is system stimulated break and $A = e^A p^h$,

$$B_0 = \int_0^{h-\tau} .e^A p^s ds B_p$$

$$B1 = \int_{h-\tau}^{h} .e^A p^s ds B_p$$

$$B2 = \int_0^{h} .e^A p^s ds B_p$$

Arrival data packages with break greater than τ will be dropped by system.

3 Earliest Arrival Route of Time Dependent Network

3.1 Shortest Route of TDN

Even if broadly referred SPTDN algorithm [16] already present for resolving the smallest route issue in this network it would not be exact precise whereas the data spreading on a local area network or web.

Figure 1 as per the TDN pattern suggested in [16], once data packages land at a unit vr, they are distributed to next unit vr + 1 instantly, the association is portrayed in (11). It

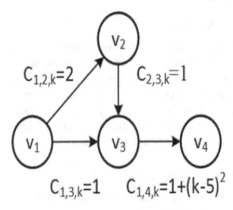

Fig. 1. Counter example of SPTDN

indicates system stimulated break only happens on the data broadcast procedure among units. It is the circumstance creates Theorem 2 correct. But, if vi holds data packages for a particular break ki, it may offer a brief time cost when compare to the smallest specified by 2.

3.2 Algorithm of Look for EAT Route

Stage1: Place the target unit v_n in lineN;

Stage 2: Obtain one component from queue N and remove it from N. Indicate it as v_j.

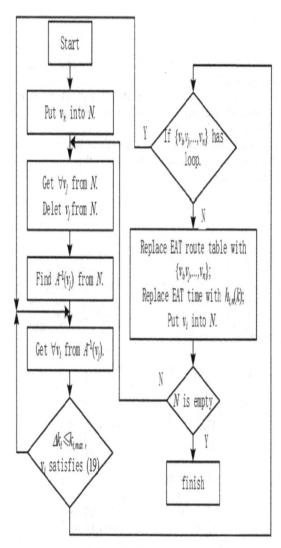

Fig. 2. Flow chart

Stage 3: Obtain $A^{-1}(v_j)$;

Stage 4: Get component from $A^{-1}(v_j)$ by step and label the present value by v_i;

Stage 5: Compute the minimum value from v_j to v_n as per the SPTDN algorithm, and label the output as $\Delta t_{i,max}$. Let $\Delta k_i \le t_{i,max}$, Δk_i is time of delay.

Stage 6: When v_i fulfils the situation, test the path $\{v_i, v_j, ..., v_n\}$ wether has loop route, whose subroute $\{v_j, ..., v_n\}$ has obtained in path. If not, revive path table with path $\{v_i, v_j, ..., v_n\}$ and its coming time $h_{i,n}(k)$, then put v_j in N and move tostage2; if not fall the present component vi and move to stage 4. Until N is vacant, the path performs the output of the suggested algorithm. The flow chart is shown in Fig. 2.

4 Experiments

This part illustrates a test executed out to test the efficiency of the suggested EAT method. The arrangement is shown in Fig. 3. PC-104 regulator serves regulator and the process pattern is compiled to C-language executes in PC-104 Plant. v1 is higher computer of PC-104 regulator, v2 is higher computer of PC-104 plant and v3 is relay computer in the system. Feedback through v3 to v1.

Where the transmission of system depends on UDP. Plant pattern is two-axle grinder, the matching switched method is created in [12], and the information are presented as follows. Matrices of the model (4) are.

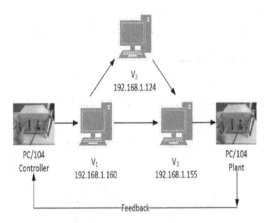

Fig. 3. Experiment topology

$$A = \begin{bmatrix} 10.0461 & 0 & 0 \\ 0 & 0.1624 & 0 & 0 \\ 0 & 0 & 1 & 0.0466 \\ 0 & 0 & 0 & 0.1676 \end{bmatrix}$$

$$B_0 = \begin{bmatrix} 0.7893 & 19.8711 & 0 & 0 \\ 0 & 0 & 0.7965 & 20.1075 \end{bmatrix}$$

$$B_1 = \begin{bmatrix} 0.7394\ 3.8752\ 0 & 0 \\ 0 & 0\ 0.7493\ 3.9907 \end{bmatrix}$$

$$B_2 = \begin{bmatrix} 1.5287\ 23.7463\ 0 & 0 \\ 0 & 0\ 1.5458\ 24.0982 \end{bmatrix}$$

sampling period T = 100 ms, system stimulated break $\tau = 0.3355T$, and the factors are given following:

$$\varepsilon 0 = \varepsilon 3 = \varepsilon 4 = 1.15,$$

$$\varepsilon 1 = \varepsilon 2 = 0.95,$$

$\mu = 1.05$, $\lambda = 1.05$, and the gain matrix of regulator is K, where

$$K = \begin{bmatrix} -0.2038\ -0.011200 \\ 0\ -0.2107\ -0.0118 \end{bmatrix}$$

Their real breaks and forecasted breaks produced by pattern (2). The forecasted breaks in Fig. 4 fundamentally response of the movement. It involves system stimulated break can be patterned and forecasted by ARMA pattern.

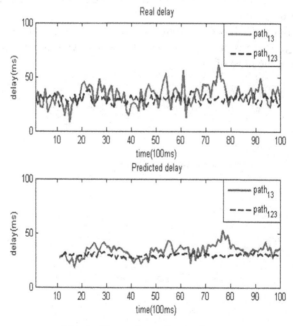

Fig. 4. Comparison of route feature

In Fig. 5, line1 displaying forecasted breaks of earliest route, line2 displaying true breaks.

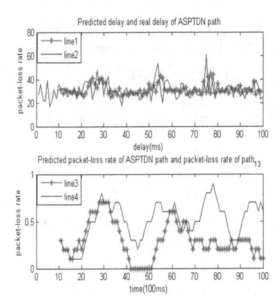

Fig. 5. Break and data package-loss rate

Line3 is the real data package-drop ratio of EAT route and line4 denotes the realdata package-drop ratio of route13.

The Fig. 6 shows the broadcast route of each time, value 1 indicates route$_{13}$, 2 indicates route$_{123}$. This result displays the forecasted EAT route comprises with the actual EAT route at the most of time.

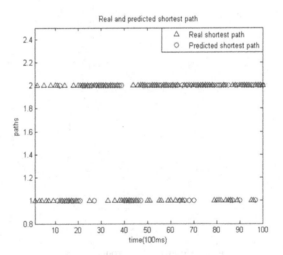

Fig. 6. Real and forecasted EAT route

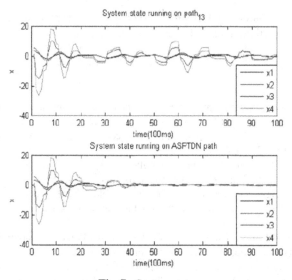

Fig. 7. System state

Figure 7 illustrates state of the system. If the monitor signal is broadcasted via route13, system can't stay stable because data package-drop ratio stimulated by route13transforms to α ∗. When EAT route is adopted, travelling the signal through route13 and route123 alternatively as per the proposed system to the preserve the value of α should be less than α ∗. Figure 7, route123 is to distribute the value predominantly excluding 2 time period from 12th to 21st sampling duration, remaining starts at the 40thand ends at 46thsampling duration complete stable state. Figure 7 reveals that EAT route keeps arrangement basically constant from the 45thsampling duration because of its communication, it offers low data package-drop ratio than α ∗. This shows in the demonstration the strength of EAT route for reducing data package-drop ratio and keep up system steady.

5 Conclusion

This study represents two ground-breaking ideas. At first, from the particularized vision, ARMA pattern is utilized to portray the system-stimulated break. After recognizing the factors, the upcoming breaks are forecasted for specific action. This linear pattern reproduces the tendency of system-stimulated break happens on each link in system, offers forecasted breaks with the given algorithm. Subsequently, proposed system is suggested for the active route from universal system, it makes sure data packages get there as early as possible. Because of the association of data package-drop ratio and steadiness of NCSs, data packages pass through along with EAT route in order to reduce data package-drop ratio, and then assure the steadiness of NCSs. This article is dedicated to suggest an optimized monitor of NCSs. Even though the analysis has specific accomplishment, several issues are faced in the while doing the experiment. Our future work as following parts: 1) to process the pattern of system-stimulated break and enhance its precision; 2) to transferring data streams by means of parallel multiple-routes; 3) to build a NCS with multiple units and on an inter-city scale.

References

1. Wang, Z., Liu, G.-P.: Design and implement of multi-agent transmission platform based on system break forecastion. In: Proceedings of the 33rd Chinese Control Conference (2014)
2. Gao, C., Zhang, X., Yue, Z., Wei, D.: An accelerated physarum solver for network optimization. IEEE Trans. Cybern. (2020)
3. Tang, B., Wang, J., Zhang, Y.: A break-distribution approach to stabilization of networked control systems. IEEE Trans. Control Network Syst. 2(4), (2015)
4. Caruntu, C.F.: A less conservative condition for flexible control lyapunov functions used in networked forecastive control systems. In: 20th International Carrouteian Control Conference (ICCC) (2019)
5. Liu, Z.-Q., Wang, Y.-L., Chen, P., Oi, A.-C., Yang, X.-F.: Forecastive control-based consensus of networked unmanned surface vehicle formation systems. In: IEEE 27th International Symposium on Industrial Electronics (ISIE) (2018)
6. Caruntu, C.F., Lazar, C., Vargas, A.N.: Chance-constrained pattern forecastive monitor for vehicle drive trains in a cyber-physical framework. Int. Conf. Eng. Technol. Innovation (ICE/ITMC) (2017)
7. Ying, L., Chen, Q., Zhu, H.: Robust pattern forecastive monitor for a class of systemed monitor systems with time-varying breaks. IEEE Workshop Electr. Comput. Appl. (2014)
8. Rajan, M.S., Mesfin, A., Sando, S.: An effective and active bandwidth distribution in networked control system. Int. J. Eng. Adv. Technol. (2020)
9. Henrik, S., Saurabh, A., Karl, H.J.: Cyberphysical security in networked control systems. IEEE Control Syst. Magazine 19(1), 20–23 (2015)
10. Lai, C.L., Pau-lo, H.: Design the remote control system with the time-delay estimator and the adaptive smith predictor. IEEE Trans. Control Industr. Inform. 6(1), 73–80 (2010)
11. Hu, W.S., Liu, G.P., David, R., Qiao, Y.L.: Design and implementation of web-based control laboratory for test rigs in geographically diverse locations. IEEE Trans. Control Industr. 55(6), 2343–2354 (2008)
12. Zhang, W.A., Yu, L., Feng, G.: Optimal linear estimation for networked systems with communication constraint. Automatica 47(9), 1992–2000 (2011)
13. Peter, X.L., Meng, Q.H.M., Gu, J.: Internet roundtrip delay prediction using the maximum entropy principle. J. Commun. Netw. 5(1), 65–72 (2003)
14. Sun, C., Young, J.K., Simon, B., Dimitri, M.: Prediction of weather-induced airline delays based on machine learning algorithms. In: Digital Avionics Systems Conference, pp. 1–6, 25–29 September 2016
15. Tu, X., Yang, S., Fei, M.R.: Internet time-delay prediction based on unbiased grey model. In: World Congress on Intelligent Control and Automation, pp. 860–864 (2011)
16. Tan, G.Z., Gao, W.: Shortest path algorithm in timie-dependent networks. Chinese J. comput. 25(2), 165–172 (2002)

Impulsive Noise Mitigation Using Hybrid Nonlinear Preprocessor and Turbo Code in OFDM-PLC System

Fikreselam Gared Mengistu[1(✉)] and Girma Gebeyehu Amlaku[2]

[1] Bahir Dar Institute of Technology, Bahir Dar University, Bahir Dar, Ethiopia
[2] Institute of Technology, University of Gondar, Gondar, Ethiopia

Abstract. Power-line communication (PLC) reuses electric signal carrying power-lines to carry information bearing signals. Since PLC channels are primarily designed to carry low frequency electric signal, they pose harsh conditions for transmission of high frequency communication signals. Impulsive noise (IN) and frequency selective fading, due to multipath characteristic of PLC channels, are the primary challenges in PLC. Orthogonal frequency division multiplexing (OFDM) is successful in reducing the effect of both challenges up to a certain level of noise energy in the system, beyond which it needs to be augmented by other mitigation techniques to reduce error, which is primarily caused by IN. In this paper, Turbo codes and hybrid nonlinear preprocessors are proposed to be applied together to combat IN in OFDM-PLC systems. Error performance of an OFDM-PLC system with the proposed scheme applied is investigated for various levels of PLC channel impulsiveness. It is found that Turbo code plus hybrid preprocessors achieve better error performance than previously applied IN mitigation techniques of Turbo code plus blanking and Turbo code plus clipping nonlinear preprocessors.

Keywords: Blanking · Clipping · Hybrid nonlinear preprocessor · IN · OFDM-PLC · Turbo code

1 Introduction

Power-line communication is a technology which reuses power-lines to carry communication signals. Even though, it enables the reuse of already existing media, power-line channels provide hostile conditions for high frequency communication signals. The primary challenges in PLC are additive noise and multipath induced frequency selective fading [1,2].

Unlike other communication systems, noise in PLC cannot be modeled as additive white Gaussian noise (AWGN), rather it is broadly classified into IN and background noise. Impulsive noise has at least 10–15 dB more power spectral density than the background noise, which can be considered AWGN [3,4].

© ICST Institute for Computer Sciences, Social Informatics and Telecommunications Engineering 2021
Published by Springer Nature Switzerland AG 2021. All Rights Reserved
M. A. Delele et al. (Eds.): ICAST 2020, LNICST 384, pp. 143–156, 2021.
https://doi.org/10.1007/978-3-030-80621-7_11

Middleton class A (MCA) noise model is commonly used to model noise in PLC. MCA noise model gives the probability density function (PDF) of noise in PLC as an infinite series, where each term represents a weighted zero-mean Gaussian distribution [5,6].

IN causes significant error in PLC systems, as a result of which several IN mitigation techniques have been proposed. OFDM, being successful in reducing the effect of multipath induced frequency selective fading and IN, is considered a primary shield against both challenges [2,6,7]. It enables IN mitigation by distributing noise energy among subcarriers, making the noise effect on a single subcarrier minimized. So, it is common practice to use OFDM in PLC, giving rise to OFDM-PLC systems. But, as IN energy in the system exceeds a certain threshold, the noise energy distributing effect of OFDM becomes a disadvantage, as all subcarriers will be affected by significantly high levels of IN energy. In such cases, other IN mitigation techniques are needed alongside OFDM. In General, IN mitigation techniques can be categorized into classes of nonlinear preprocessing, error correcting codes and iterative methods. It is a common practice to combine two or more IN mitigation schemes to achieve a required level of error performance [1].

In [2], blanking/clipping preprocessors, with optimized blanking and clipping thresholds, are proposed to combat IN in OFDM-PLC systems. The proposed nonlinearity, named adaptive hybrid preprocessor (AHP), is shown to perform better than blanking, clipping and conventional blanking/clipping hybrid nonlinear preprocessors. It is found that, with a slight increment in level of complexity, AHP provides the best error performance, considering different levels of channel impulsiveness, compared to the other preprocessors. When it comes to error correcting codes, iteratively decoded codes are of primary choice to combat IN in PLC [1]. In [8], Turbo codes are proposed to combat IN in an impulsive environment. It is found that Turbo codes can achieve a significant improvement in error performance compared to convolutional codes selected for comparison. Low-density parity-check codes are also applied to mitigate IN in OFDM-PLC systems [9,10]. Iterative methods are proposed to reduce the effect of IN in [11,12].

Nonbinary Turbo codes and simple nonlinear preprocessors are applied jointly in [6] to combat IN in OFDM-PLC systems. The nonlinear preprocessors considered are blanking and clipping separately. The performance of the dual IN mitigation schemes is studied for a very impulsive channel condition, and nonbinary Turbo codes are found to perform better than their binary counterparts, both being combined with blanking and clipping. By replacing blanking and clipping by a relatively more complex hybrid blanking/clipping preprocessor, error performance can be improved. In this paper, binary Turbo codes and hybrid nonlinear preprocessors are proposed to be applied together to reduce the effect of IN in OFDM-PLC systems. The relative error performance of the proposed IN mitigation scheme is studied under different levels of channel impulsiveness.

The rest of the paper is organized as follows. In Sect. 2, noise model in PLC is discussed. In Sect. 3, proposed system model is given and components are described. Results and discussions are given in Sect. 4. Finally, in Sect. 5 conclusions are drawn.

2   PLC Noise Model

MCA noise model is commonly used to model noise in PLC systems, and its PDF is defined as [1]

$$p(X) = \sum_{m=0}^{\infty} \frac{e^{-A}A^m}{m!} \cdot \frac{1}{\sqrt{2\pi\sigma_m^2}} exp\left(-\frac{|X|^2}{2\sigma_m^2}\right), \tag{1}$$

Where the variance σ_m^2 is given by

$$\sigma_m^2 = \sigma_u^2 \left(\frac{\frac{m}{A} + \Gamma}{1 + \Gamma}\right), \tag{2}$$

and

$$\sigma_u^2 = \sigma_G^2 + \sigma_I^2, \qquad \Gamma = \frac{\sigma_G^2}{\sigma_I^2}, \tag{3}$$

The parameters σ_G^2 and σ_I^2 are variances of Gaussian noise and IN, respectively. Γ is the background (Gaussian) to IN average power ratio, and A, called impulsive index, represents the density of a certain width pulses in an observation period. It increases the impulsive behavior as it becomes smaller and conversely the noise becomes Gaussian when it is larger [1,6].

The impulsive index A is given as

$$A = \frac{n\tau}{T_0} \tag{4}$$

where n is the number of pulses, τ is the average duration of each pulse and T_0 is the observation period, which is commonly set to unity. A is always less than or equal to one, because it is defined as a fraction of time occupied by pulses in an observation time. Even if $n\tau$ is greater than T_0, the value of A cannot exceed one. Figure 1 [1], shows a simple diagram depicting an impulsive index value which is three times the average duration of impulses.

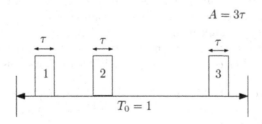

Fig. 1. Impulsive index (A) of three impulses.

3   Noise and System Model

Figure 2 shows the proposed system to mitigate IN. Input bits, arranged in blocks, are Turbo encoded and mapped into baseband symbols S_k using binary phase shift keying (BPSK) modulator. The output symbols of the modulator are then passed to an OFDM modulator, which is commonly executed using Inverse Fast Fourier Transform (IFFT) to result a complex baseband OFDM signal given as [2, 6]

$$s(t) = \frac{1}{\sqrt{N}} \sum_{k=0}^{N-1} S_k e^{\frac{j2\pi kt}{T_s}}, \quad 0 < t < T_s \tag{5}$$

where N is the number of sub-carriers and T_s is the active symbol interval. The resulting complex OFDM signal is then converted into analog form and passed to a PLC channel after proper filtering is performed.

At the receiver side, after filtering and conversion to discrete form by sampling, the received signal is processed by a hybrid nonlinear preprocessor to reduce the effect of IN. Hybrid nonlinear preprocessors combine the effects of blanking and clipping to get enhanced performance in reducing the noise energy, which primarily comes from IN. After preprocessing by hybrid nonlinearities, conversion to digital form is performed followed by OFDM demodulation, which is commonly executed using Fast Fourier Transform (FFT). Next comes BPSK demodulator, which passes soft outputs to the Turbo decoder, which intern detects and corrects as many errors as possible and outputs bits.

The proposed system is basically a PLC system which uses OFDM, to make an OFDM-PLC system, to which hybrid nonlinear preprocessor and Turbo code are applied to reduce the effect of IN.

3.1   Nonlinear Preprocessors

Simple processors which replace received noise affected samples with zero and clip amplitudes of samples when the amplitudes exceed certain thresholds, which are called blanking and clipping respectively, are commonly applied to OFDM-PLC systems to mitigate IN. It is also found that, combined application of the two methods generally results in a better performance. Such combined blanking/clipping nonlinearities are called hybrid nonlinearities, in which two thresholds are used to clip, blank or pass unchanged samples. Two types of hybrid nonlinearities, called conventional and adaptive, can be identified [2]. Below are described nonlinearities commonly used in OFDM-PLC systems.

Blanking: refers to the task of removing or nulling samples whose amplitudes are greater than a certain threshold, while samples with smaller amplitudes are left unchanged. Blanking preprocessors are given as [13]

$$y_k = \begin{cases} r_k, & |r_k| \leq T_b \\ 0, & |r_k| > T_b \end{cases} \tag{6}$$

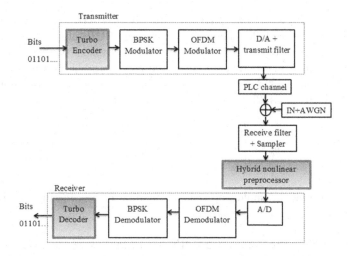

Fig. 2. OFDM-PLC system with the proposed IN mitigation.

Where T_b is blanking threshold, $k = 0, 1, ..., N - 1$, r_k and y_k are input and output of the blanking nonlinear device, respectively.

Clipping: involves replacing samples whose amplitudes are greater than a certain threshold with a sample of fixed amplitude. In other words, samples greater than threshold value are clipped and those with smaller amplitude values are left unchanged. Clipping involves changing amplitudes only with phases of samples unaffected. The operation of clipping preprocessors is given as [13]

$$y_k = \begin{cases} r_k, & |r_k| \leq T_c \\ T_c e^{j\ arg(r_k)}, & |r_k| > T_c \end{cases} \tag{7}$$

where T_c is clipping threshold, and $arg(r_k)$ is angle of the input sample r_k to the clipping preprocessor.

Conventional hybrid preprocessing (CHP): is a hybrid (blanking/clipping) pre-processing scheme in which samples with amplitudes that lie between clipping and blanking thresholds are clipped, and those with sample amplitudes greater than blanking threshold are nulled. Samples with amplitudes less than clipping threshold are passed unchanged. In CHP, blanking threshold value is a constant times clipping threshold, and 1.4 is a commonly used constant. CHP is given as [2]

$$y_k = \begin{cases} r_k, & |r_k| \leq T_c \\ T_c e^{j\ arg(r_k)}, & T_c < |r_k| \leq T_b \\ 0, & |r_k| > T_b \end{cases} \tag{8}$$

Where T_c and T_b are clipping and blanking thresholds, respectively, and usually $T_b = 1.4T_c$.

Adaptive Hybrid Preprocessing (AHP): is similar to CHP in that it employs both clipping and threshold. The difference is, in AHP clipping and blanking thresholds are not related by a fixed value. The constant of proportionality, also called scaling factor, between them is treated as a variable, and it is optimized alongside the clipping threshold to get maximum output signal-to-noise ratio (SRN). AHP is given as [2]

$$
y_k = \begin{cases} r_k, & |r_k| \leq T \\ T e^{j\ arg(r_k)}, & T < |r_k| \leq \alpha T \\ 0, & |r_k| > \alpha T \end{cases} \tag{9}
$$

Where T is clipping threshold and $\alpha > 1$ is scaling factor. In this case blanking threshold is αT.

The output signal to noise ratio (SRN) of a preprocessor is given as [13,14]

$$
SNR_{out} = \frac{E[|K_0 s_k|^2]}{E[|y_k - K_0 s_k|^2]} = \left(\frac{E_{out}}{2K_0^2} - 1\right)^{-1} \tag{10}
$$

where K_0 is an appropriately chosen scaling factor given as $K_0 = E[y_k s_k^*]/E[|s_k|^2]$, $E_{out} = E[|y_k|^2]$ and s_k is the useful OFDM signal.

Since different threshold values of a preprocessor results in different values of SNR_{out}, determining the specific threshold value that maximizes SNR_{out} is a crucial task. In blanking, clipping and CHP, single threshold values are optimized. Whereas, in AHP two optimum threshold values that jointly provide maximum SNR_{out} need to be determined.

In [13], mathematical analysis of different nonlinearities in terms of the maximum SNR_{out} in relation to different threshold values is presented. In the paper, it can be noticed that the mathematical descriptions are well supported by simulation results.

3.2   Turbo Codes

Turbo codes are powerful codes that are known to achieve near Shannon limit performance [15]. They are among the error correcting codes used to mitigate IN in OFDM-PLC systems, due to their enhanced capability to detect and correct errors caused by transmission over the harsh PLC channel.

Turbo encoders are parallel concatenated encoders separated by an interleaver. Recursive systematic convolutional (RSC) encoders are commonly used as component encoders and pseudo-random interleavers are usually chosen over other interleaver types [16]. Figure 3 shows a typical Turbo encoder, which is used in this work.

Just before a block of input bit sequence X_i is encoded, both RSC encoders are brought to the all-zero state by moving the switches downwards, and operating the encoders until the shift registers contain all zeros. Once they are in an initial all-zero state, they are ready to perform Turbo encoding. The upper RSC

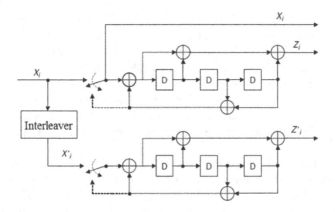

Fig. 3. Turbo encoder

encoder acts on X_i as it is, where as the lower one will encode X_i', which is an interleaved version of input bit sequence X_i. Both encoders act on the same set of bits, but in different order. This difference in sequence reduces the chance of getting low weight encoded outputs from both encoders at the same time. This is one of the key features that make Turbo codes powerful.

The first output of the upper encoder, which is called systematic output, is equivalent to the input sequence X_i. Another output of the same encoder is Z_i, which is a parity sequence. The lower RSC encoder receives X_i', which is X_i interleaved, and outputs parity sequence Z_i'. The systematic output of the lower encoder is suppressed. Thus, the final output of the Turbo encoder is an interleaved version of the three sequences X_i, Z_i and Z_i', giving a coding rate of 1/3.

Turbo decoding is an iterative process to estimate transmitted bits from the received bits that are affected by additive noise in the transmission process. The commonly used decoding algorithm in Turbo codes is called BCJR, which was discovered by Bahl, Cocke, Jelinek and Raviv in 1974. The BCJR algorithm is also called Maximum a Posteriori (MAP) or forward-backward algorithm. Detailed explanation of MAP algorithm can be found in [16] and [17].

4   Results and Discussion

In this section simulation results depicting performance of the proposed dual IN mitigation technique (i.e. Turbo code plus AHP/CHP) are presented, accompanied by respective discussions. To show performance improvement attained by the proposed scheme, error performance of Turbo code paired with blanking and clipping preprocessors separately are also included. Three different channel conditions are considered to show relative performance of the proposed scheme compared to Turbo code combined with blanking and clipping separately under varying channel conditions. As the primary aim of this work is IN mitigation, multipath characteristic of PLC is not considered. Input sequence of bits are divided into Turbo blocks of 1020 bit size, which are encoded by the Turbo encoder shown in Fig. 3. BPSK modulation is used to perform mapping of coded bits into symbols which are then passed to OFDM system with 3072 subcarriers. At the receiver side, after preprocessing, Turbo decoding is performed using MAP algorithm with 5 iterations. Bit error rate (BER) as a function of bit energy per noise power spectral density (Eb/No) are plotted for all Turbo code plus preprocessor combinations for the considered channel conditions, and comparisons are made.

At the receiver side, as processing by a nonlinearity is performed before Turbo decoding, performance of a Turbo code is dependent on performance of a preceding nonlinearity. If a nonlinearity results outputs of higher SNR, a Turbo decoder can detect and correct more errors than when it receives a lower quality signal form the preceding preprocessor unit. Due to this dependence, error performance of preprocessors applied to OFDM-PLC systems is studied first, the results of which are shown in Fig. 4 and Fig. 5, under varying channel conditions. After error performance of nonlinearities is explained, performance analysis of OFDM-PLC systems to which nonlinear preprocessor plus Turbo code IN mitigation techniques are applied is undertaken.

4.1 Error Performance of OFDM-PLC Systems with Preprocessors Applied

Figure 4 shows error performance of blanking, clipping, CHP and AHP applied to an OFDM-PLC system for varying A with fixed values of Γ and SNR. For a fixed value of Γ, channel impulsiveness depends on A, and impulsiveness decreases as A increases. Without any nonlinearity, it is shown that BER remains the same for varying A, because in OFDM error performance depends on the total noise energy in the system, not on how it is distributed [1]. Due to this reason, BER is insensitive to change of A for a fixed Γ and input signal SNR.

Looking at the general trend of error performance of all nonlinearities, it can be noted that all result in lower BER for lower A values which correspond to highly impulsive PLC channels. As channel impulsiveness decreases with increasing A, performance of all preprocessors deteriorates and becomes closer and closer to the case where no nonlinearity is applied to the OFDM-PLC system. The reason can be explained remembering the definition of A. If the observation period is set to one, A is then the product of number of pulses and average duration of pulses. So, A decreasing can result from number of pulses decreasing for a fixed average duration of pulses, pulses becoming narrower with the same number of pulses, or both number and average duration of pulses decreasing. If either or both number and/or average duration of pulses decreases, samples affected by IN become easily identifiable. So for smaller A, nonlinear preprocessors can easily identify and process IN affected samples, resulting in better performance of preprocessors in such channel conditions. On the other hand, as A increases for a fixed Γ, number and/or average duration of pulses increases,

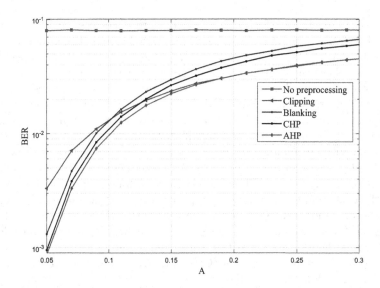

Fig. 4. BER as a function of A of an OFDM-PLC system to which different preprocessors are applied when $\Gamma = 0.1$ and $SNR = 20$ dB.

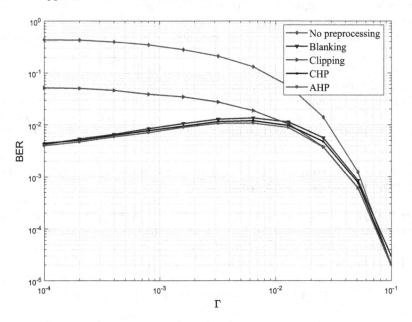

Fig. 5. BER as a function of Γ of an OFDM-PLC system to which different preprocessors are applied when $A = 0.1$ and $SNR = 20$ dB.

making it more difficult for preprocessors to identify samples which are affected
by IN, as a result of which success of all preprocessors declines.

Figure 5 shows error performance of the four preprocessors considered applied to an OFDM-PLC system as a function of Γ for fixed values of A and input signal SNR. Unlike the constant BER curve displayed in Fig.4, there is change in BER for varying Γ, because for a fixed A, change in Γ means change in amplitude of impulses with the distribution of pulses being similar. As Γ increases, IN power in the system decreases assuming a fixed AWGN noise power. This decrement in IN noise energy results in smaller BER, as it is shown in the figure. Considering performance of the nonlinearities, their performance compared to the OFDM-PLC system without nonlinearity decreases as Γ increases, which is shown by a narrowing of the gap between the curves corresponding to nonlinearities and the curve corresponding to the OFDM-PLC system with no preprocessing. The reason for the decline in performance of preprocessors as Γ increases is, IN affected samples become more difficult to distinguish from their IN unaffected neighbors, since higher Γ channels are characterized by pulses with smaller amplitudes.

Comparing the four nonlinearities considered, it can be noted form both Fig. 4 and Fig. 5 that hybrid methods (CHP and AHP) have better performance than blanking and clipping for most channel conditions. In both figures, it can be noted that clipping has the worst performance for highly impulsive channels and it shows improvement as channel impulsiveness decreases. Its performance becomes better than blanking and then CHP for higher values of A and Γ. AHP marks the lowest BER performance for all channel conditions.

Error performance gain by hybrid methods compared to blanking is not significant for very small values of A and Γ. For such highly impulsive channel conditions, samples significantly affected by IN stand out, and get processed by blanking effectively. Adding clipping effect alongside blanking in such cases does not improve performance that much. But, as both A and Γ increase, applying clipping with blanking starts to pay off, as a result of which performance gain by hybrid methods is higher than blanking for higher values of A and Γ.

4.2   Error Performance of OFDM-PLC Systems with Turbo Code Plus Preprocessors Applied

Figure 6 displays error performance of an OFDM-PLC system to which all four preprocessors combined with Turbo code are applied in turn to mitigate IN for three channel conditions, with channel impulsiveness decreasing in order from Fig. 6(a) to Fig. 6(c). Of the three channel conditions considered, $A = \Gamma = 0.05$ is the most impulsive one, and $A = \Gamma = 0.1$ is the least impulsive of all, while $A = 0.1$ and $\Gamma = 0.05$ is used to simulate a channel with impulsiveness that lies between the other two.

From the figure, it can be noted that hybrid preprocessors combined with Turbo code achieve better error performance than previously proposed IN mitigation techniques of Turbo code plus blanking and Turbo code plus clipping for the channel conditions considered. In all three channel conditions considered, AHP plus Turbo code has the least BER followed by CHP plus Turbo code for a given SNR value. Hybrid methods combined with Turbo code are followed by

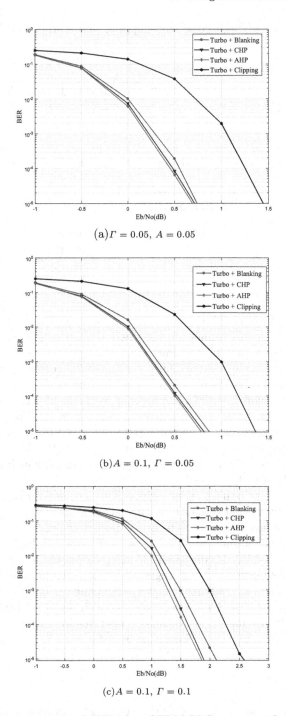

(a)$\Gamma = 0.05$, $A = 0.05$

(b)$A = 0.1$, $\Gamma = 0.05$

(c)$A = 0.1$, $\Gamma = 0.1$

Fig. 6. BER versus input signal SNR of an OFDM-PLC system with different preprocessors plus Turbo code applied for different channel conditions.

blanking paired with Turbo code, and clipping plus Turbo code has the worst performance.

Comparing SNR values required by Turbo code plus preprocessor combinations to achieve a BER value of 10^{-5}, energy saved by the proposed IN mitigation scheme (i.e. Turbo code plus AHP/CHP) compared to Turbo code plus blanking is displayed in Table 1.

Table 1. Energy saved by Turbo code plus hybrid preprocessing compared to Turbo code plus blanking to achieve a BER value of 10^{-5} in an OFDM-PLC system.

PLC channel condition		Energy saved by Turbo code plus AHP	Energy saved by Turbo code plus CHP
A	Γ		
0.05	0.05	0.049	0.027
0.1	0.05	0.086	0.047
0.1	0.1	0.255	0.212

From the table it can be noted that, energy saved by Turbo code plus AHP/CHP increases as channel impulsiveness decreases, and vice versa. As a result, it can be said that performance improvement brought by the proposed scheme over Turbo code plus blanking nonlinearity becomes more significant as channel impulsiveness decreases. This results due to the fact that for very impulsive cases, performance of blanking and hybrid nonlinearities are close to each other, and significant performance difference starts to appear as channel impulsiveness decreases, as can be noted from Fig. 4 and Fig. 5. In those figures, BER curves corresponding to blanking, CHP and AHP start being close to each other for small A and Γ and diverge as A and Γ increase, which correspond to lowering of levels of PLC channel impulsiveness.

Another important point is, clipping plus Turbo code error performance narrows the gap with the performance of Turbo code plus other preprocessors, as channel impulsiveness decreases, which is expected remembering that clipping is suited to channels of lower impulsiveness, as displayed in Fig. 4 and Fig. 5.

The energy saved by the proposed IN mitigation technique will increase as the system employing it operates longer and longer. The reason is, the values presented in a Table 1 are only for relatively small number of bits transmitted, as simulation is run until BER reaches a value of 10^{-5}. As an OFDM-PLC system with the proposed IN mitigation technique operates longer, transmitting more and more bits, the energy saved increases accordingly.

5 Conclusion

In this paper, joint application of Turbo code and a hybrid nonlinear preprocessor (i.e. AHP/CHP) is proposed to combat IN in OFDM-PLC systems. BER performance of the proposed scheme is compared to previously applied Turbo code plus blanking and Turbo code plus clipping IN mitigation techniques for various levels of PLC channel impulsiveness, and it is found that the proposed technique enables performance with reduced BER. It is also found that, comparing the two hybrid preprocessors types, AHP achieves better results than CHP when applied to Turbo-coded OFDM-PLC system, due to its flexibility in combining blanking and clipping to reduce the effect of IN. Obtained simulation results are justified by studying BER performance of different preprocessors applied to OFDM-PLC systems for varying A and Γ values.

References

1. Shongwey, T., Vinck, A.H., Ferreira, H.C.: On impulse noise and its models. In: 18th IEEE International Symposium on Power Line Communications and Its Applications, pp. 12–17. IEEE (2014).https://doi.org/10.1109/ISPLC.2014.6812360
2. Rabie, K.M., Alsusa, E.: Performance analysis of adaptive hybrid nonlinear preprocessors for impulsive noise mitigation over power-line channels. In: 2015 IEEE International Conference on Communications (ICC), pp. 728–733. IEEE (2015). https://doi.org/10.1109/ICC.2015.7248408
3. Anatory, J., Theethayi, N.: Broadband Power-line Communications Systems: Theory & Applications. Wit Press (2010)
4. Zimmermann, M., Dostert, K.: A multipath model for the powerline channel. IEEE Trans. Commun. **50**(4), 553–559 (2002). https://doi.org/10.1109/26.996069
5. Middleton, D.: Statistical-physical models of electromagnetic interference. IEEE Trans. Electromagn. Compat. **3**, 106–127 (1977). https://doi.org/10.1109/TEMC.1977.303527
6. Abd-Alaziz, W., Mei, Z., Johnston, M., Le Goff, S.: Non-binary turbo-coded OFDM-PLC system in the presence of impulsive noise. In: 2017 25th European Signal Processing Conference (EUSIPCO), pp. 2576–2580. IEEE (2017). https://doi.org/10.23919/EUSIPCO.2017.8081676
7. Ghosh, M.: Analysis of the effect of impulse noise on multicarrier and single carrier QAM systems. IEEE Trans. Commun. **44**(2), 145–147 (1996). https://doi.org/10.1109/26.486604
8. Faber, T., Scholand, T., Jung, P.: On turbo codes for environments impaired by impulsive noise. In: 2004 IEEE 60th Vehicular Technology Conference, VTC2004-Fall, vol. 3, pp. 2268–2272. IEEE (2004). https://doi.org/10.1109/VETECF.2004.1400445
9. Nakagawa, H., Umehara, D., Denno, S., Morihiro, Y.: A decoding for low density parity check codes over impulsive noise channels. In: 2005 International Symposium on Power Line Communications and Its Applications, pp. 85–89. IEEE (2005). https://doi.org/10.1109/ISPLC.2005.1430471
10. Hsu, C., Wang, N., Chan, W.-Y., Jain, P.: Improving a power line communications standard with LDPC codes. EURASIP J. Adv. Signal Process. **2007**(1), 1–9 (2007). https://doi.org/10.1155/2007/60839
11. Häring, J., Vinck, A.H.: OFDM transmission corrupted by impulsive noise. In: Proceedings of the 2000 International Symposium on Power-Line Communications and its Applications, Limerick, Ireland, pp. 5–7 (2000)
12. Windyga, P.S.: Fast impulsive noise removal. IEEE Trans. Image Process. **10**(1), 173–179 (2001). https://doi.org/10.1109/83.892455

13. Zhidkov, S.V.: Analysis and comparison of several simple impulsive noise miti-
    gation schemes for OFDM receivers. IEEE Trans. Commun. **56**(1), 5–9 (2008).
    https://doi.org/10.1109/TCOMM.2008.050391
14. Zhidkov, S.V.: Performance analysis and optimization of OFDM receiver with
    blanking nonlinearity in impulsive noise environment. IEEE Trans. Veh. Technol.
    55(1), 234–242 (2006). https://doi.org/10.1109/TVT.2005.858191
15. Vucetic, B., Yuan, J.: Turbo Codes: Principles and Applications, vol. 559. Springer,
    Heidelberg (2012)
16. Andersen, J.D.: A turbo tutorial. TELE (ISSN 1396–1535) (15) (1999)
17. Abrantes, S.A.: From BCJR to turbo decoding: MAP algorithms made easier.
    ResearchGate (2004)

Comparative Analysis of Kalman Filtering and Machine Learning Based Cardiovascular Signal Processing Algorithms

Hiwot Birhanu[(⊠)] and Amare Kassaw

Bahir Dar Institute of Technology, Bahir Dar University, Bahir Dar, Ethiopia
http://www.bdu.edu.et/

Abstract. Cardiovascular (CV) disorder is one of the critical health problem that cause economical and social impacts, even death to lots of peoples globally. Electrocardiogram (ECG) signal is the signal taken from the human body to study the status of CV and heart conditions. Before the introduction of computers, those tasks were done by the experts that cause various mistakes. Currently, the use of advancing signal processing devices manage to reduce these effects. Besides, it allows to develop various signal detection and parameter estimation algorithms. By studying the parameters of ECG signals, it is possible to determine whether the person is in critical condition or not. This helps to take an appropriate action. In the last decades, both classical and machine learning methods have been used to study and characterize the essential properties and parameters of CV signals.

In this work, we study different algorithms that are useful for ECG based CV parameters estimation. We evaluate the performance of both classical (Kalman Filtering) and machine learning algorithms with Butterworth low pass filter, wavelet transform and linear regression for parameter estimation. Besides, we proposed an algorithm that combines adaptive Kalman filter (AKF) and discrete wavelet transform (DWT). In this algorithm, the ECG signal is filtered using AKF. Then segmentation is performed and features are extracted using DWT algorithm. Numerical simulation is done to validate the performances of these algorithms. The results show that the proposed algorithm gives better performance than Kalman filtering and has nearly the same performance with machine learning methods.

Keywords: ECG signal · Cardiovascular parameters · Kalman filter · Machine learning · DWT

M. A. Delele et al. (Eds.): ICAST 2020, LNICST 384, pp. 157–169, 2021.
https://doi.org/10.1007/978-3-030-80621-7_12

1   Introduction

Cardiovascular disease (CVD) is the most widespread chronic disease that cause enormous amount of economic and social problems. It is also one of the main cause for death of lots of people within all age ranges [1]. In order to combat the effect of this disease, a better estimation and prediction of heart state and diagnosis mechanism is required. ECG is one of the devices that capture the electrical activity of the heart, which in turn is used for the diagnosis of cardiac problems [1,2]. The study of cardiovascular parameters from ECG signal is mostly depend on the PQSRT pattern (a cardiac cycle due to the cardiac muscle depolarization and repolarization), which varies from person to person and from time to time. As shown in Fig. 1, one cycle has P-wave (atrial contraction), QRS-complex (contraction of the ventricles) and T-wave (relaxation of the ventricles). The amplitude of these waves and the RR, PR, QT, and QRS complex intervals indicate the condition of the heart. Although the variation of such waves might be visible to the physicians, the time to make the decision may be very long. This endangers the life of the patient at risk since the variation might occur within a fraction of seconds. Hence, due to such variation in addition to the noise and other motion artifacts, having a signal processing system with efficient algorithms is vital to study the condition of the patient, and to make effective and wise decisions [3].

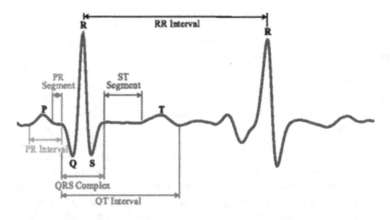

Fig. 1. Heart beat cycle in the ECG waveform [3].

In this work, the performances of Kalman filter and machine learning algorithms based cardiovascular parameter estimation are evaluated and analyzed via simulation. Besides, we propose an algorithm that uses the combination of adaptive Kalman filter and DWT algorithms. Numerical simulation is done to show the performances of the proposed algorithms.

The rest of the paper is organized as follows. In Sect. 2, state of the art and review of related works for cardiovascular signal processing is presented.

The system and signal model is provided in Sect. 3. Performance metrics for cardiovascular parameter estimation is shown in Sect. 4. Simulation results are discussed in Sect. 5 and conclusions are drawn in Sect. 6.

Notations: Vectors and matrices are expressed in lower and upper case boldface letters, respectively. $\mathbf{A}^{\mathrm{T}}$ denotes conjugate transpose of matrix and $\mathbb{E}\{.\}$ is the expectation operator.

2   State of the Art and Review of Related Works

In the past decades, various algorithms with different level of accuracy has been developed and tested for estimating cardiovascular parameters. Stroke volume (SV), cardiac output (CO), and total peripheral resistance (TPR) are some of the parameters that determine the output blood per minute from the heart and give information about the status of patient's heart condition [4].

One of the main problems in ECG signals is the amount of noise which needs noise filtering /denoising to study the characteristics of those parameters. Wavelet is one of the commonly used denoising methods used for ECG signal filtering. In this method, the signal is decomposed in to various bands and each coefficient is processed. Besides, threshold setting and wavelet reconstruction is done to attain the filtered ECG signal [5,6]. This needs an effective thresholding to set the right threshold value that give a better performance. If the ECG signal is too noisy, the wavelet method might not be reliable. Additional signals such as arterial blood pressure (ABP) pulse is used in [7] to study the health condition of the patient in addition to ECG signals. But this adds additional complexity to align the R- peak of ECG signal with ABP pulse, since both are not aligned.

Another recursive denoising method is done by using Kalman filtering. The noise in ECG signals makes it difficult to get a good estimation of time varying cardiovascular state. But, the usage of Kalman denoising, which uses a continual parameter update, enables to attain an estimation of parameters with lower minimum mean square error (MMSE). The extended Kalman filers and adaptive Kalman filters were used for non linear models [8,9]. Empirical mode decomposition (EMD) based adaptive signal processing method has been very essential for non stationary and non linear signal analysis. With the existence of high frequency component in ECG signal, EMD have high probability of filtering the noise but it causes some sort of distortion on the amplitude of the peaks [10,11]. Parameter estimation methods such as Gaussian derivative model [12], autoregressive moving average, Wesseling correlated impedance and other methods were tested [13].

With the classical algorithms, the parameter estimation is mainly based on the shapes of QRS complex, and P and T waves that provide good accuracy for normal ECG signals. However, with the existence of variation in the ECG signal shapes having abnormal rhythms, their performance becomes unreliable. Due to that, data driven approaches including machine-learning models and neural networks have been introduced. Currently, that is more expanded into researches using deep learning algorithms for parameter estimation and classification of

ECG signals. The performance of those algorithms depends on the availability of data besides other factors. That is, with the existence of high amount of training and test data deep learning algorithms are providing good results while other machine learning based algorithms works with better accuracy even with the existence of small amount of data [14, 15].

3   The System and Signal Model

We consider an ECG signal which is contaminated by nose and modeled as [16]

$$\mathbf{y}(n) = \mathbf{x}(n) + \mathbf{v}(n) \tag{1}$$

where the vector $\mathbf{y}(n)$ represents the measured ECG signal, $\mathbf{x}(n)$ is the desired ECG signal, $\mathbf{v}(n)$ is a vector of additive Gaussian noise with $\mathcal{N}(0, \sigma^2)$ due to the sensor and amplifier noise and $n = 0, 1, 2, \cdots, N - 1$ when N is the length of the signal. The sources of noise include movements that affects the skin-electrode interface, muscle contractions or electromyographic spikes, respiration, electromagnetic interference and noise from other electronic devices that couple into the device. With the existence of such noise in the ECG signal, studying and characterizing the health condition of the patient makes it very difficult. Due to that there needs an algorithm that is capable of filtering out the noise while extracting the ECG signal. Having that, the estimation and classification of cardiovascular parameters will be effective. Those algorithms have their different techniques and performances as discussed in the subsequent sections.

3.1   Kalman Filtering Algorithm for Cardiovascular Parameter Estimation

Kalman filter is an estimator of optimal state for systems with random noises. It can be used for filtering, smoothing and state prediction of a linear dynamic system depending on the quantity of information available. For that the Kalman filter has two phases: the prediction and correction of the system which allows to estimate the state of a dynamics system of one information, a priori and the actual measurements using the current state of the system, the estimate of the previous state and current measures. Thus the linear representation of the received ECG signal in Eq. (1) can be reformulated as [17, 18]

$$y_k = \mathbf{H} x_k + v_k \tag{2}$$

where $\mathbf{H}$ is the dynamic constant matrix and v_k is the noise with a covariance matrix Q_k.

Let $\bar{\bar{x}}_k$ be a priori state estimation at step k given the information of the process prior to step k, and $\bar{x}_k$ be a posteriori state estimate at the step k with given measurement y_k. Then, the priori and a posteriori estimation errors can be respectively defined as [17]

$$\bar{\bar{e}}_k \triangleq x_k - \bar{\bar{x}}_k$$
$$\bar{e}_k \triangleq x_k - \bar{x}_k.$$
(3)

And a priori estimate error and posteriori estimate error covariance is given by [17,18]

$$\bar{\bar{P}}_k = \mathbb{E}\{\bar{\bar{e}}_k \bar{\bar{e}}_k^T\}$$
$$\bar{P}_k = \mathbb{E}\{\bar{e}_k \bar{e}_k^T\}.$$
(4)

Then, the posteriori state estimate is given by [17,18]

$$\bar{x}_k = \bar{\bar{x}}_k + K(y_k - \mathbf{H}\bar{\bar{x}}_k).$$
(5)

The difference in the above equation is termed as the measurement residual which shows the discrepancy between actual and predicted state where K is the gain matrix given by

$$K_k = \bar{P}_k \mathbf{H}^T (\mathbf{H}\bar{P}_k \mathbf{H}^T + \mathbf{R})^{-1}.$$
(6)

where $\mathbf{R}$ is the covariance matrix. Hence, with Eq. (5) the filtered ECG signal can be achieved [17,18].

3.2 Machine Learning Algorithm for Cardiovascular Parameter Estimation

Machine learning algorithm is capable to make decisions autonomously without any external support by learning from the data and understanding the patterns that are contained within it. Using that pattern, the machine can perform tasks such as classification and prediction based on the type of algorithm. The three main machine learning algorithms at present includes supervised learning for classification including diagnosis and regression tasks for risk assessment, unsupervised learning for dimensionality reduction and clustering and reinforcement learning for gaming, robot interaction and other applications [19]. The basic building blocks of machine learning algorithms is shown in Fig. 2. The description of each block is outline below.

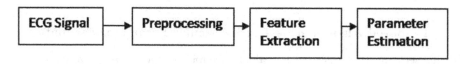

Fig. 2. Basic steps for ECG signal parameter estimation with machine learning algorithm.

- **Preprocessing:** Due to the existence of noise in the ECG signal, first the signal has to be preprocessed in order to extract its features and perform the estimation task. Filtering is one of the techniques used to preprocess the ECG signal. In this work, we use a second order Butter-worth low pass filter to filter the unwanted signal [20].
- **Feature Extraction:** The task of feature extraction for ECG signal starts from feature selection which includes PQRST wave detection using various algorithms. R-peak detection is essential task while other PQST components can be detected by taking the location of R-peak as a reference and tracking to/from R-peak relative position. The features might be time, amplitude, distance, angle and others that can be useful to characterize the ECG signal and estimation. Wavelet transform approach and time domain analysis is used to detect R-peak and others, respectively as in [20].
- **Parameter Estimation:** At this stage the cardiovascular parameters can be estimated based on the extracted features. Linear regression is one of the most known techniques to estimate cardiovascular parameters. The new sequence of the signal to be estimated with linear regression is given by [21]

$$y'(x) = ax + v. \tag{7}$$

The value of the coefficient a and the value of v that describe the best estimated signal, $y'(j)$ from the real $y(j)$ is given by [21]

$$a = \frac{m\sum_{j=l_1}^{l_2} x(j)y(j) - \sum_{j=l_1}^{l_2} x(j)\sum_{j=l_1}^{l_2} y(j)}{m\sum_{j=l_1}^{l_2} x^2(j) - (\sum_{j=l_1}^{l_2} x(j))^2}$$

$$v = \frac{\sum_{j=l_1}^{l_2} x^2(j)\sum_{j=l_1}^{l_2} y(j) - \sum_{j=l_1}^{l_2} x(j)y(j)\sum_{j=l_1}^{l_2} x(j)}{m\sum_{j=l_1}^{l_2} x^2(j) - (\sum_{j=l_1}^{l_2} x(j))^2} \tag{8}$$

with Butterworth filter $H(f) = \frac{b_1(jf)^n + b_2(jf)^{n-1} + b_{n+1}}{a_1(jf)^n + a_2(jf)^{n-1} + a_{n+1}}$ having filter order n (0, 1,..., N−1) and cut-off frequency f = 100 Hz. And $i \in \{w, w+1, ...N - w - 1\}$ where $l_1 = i - \omega$ and $l_2 = i + \omega$, $m = 2\omega + 1$ with window $\omega = 0.03 f_s$ when f_s being the sampling frequency and $j \in \{i - w, i - w + 1, ..., i + w\}$ [21].

3.3   Proposed Algorithm for Cardiovascular Parameter Estimation

In this section, we propose a new algorithm for cardiovascular parameter estimation by combining adaptive Kalman filtering and discreet Wavelet transform as shown in Fig. 3. In this algorithm, first the noise in the ECG signal is filtered using an adaptive Kalman filter (AKF). AKF predicts the state and error covariance ahead, computes the gain, used the estimate with measurement and then update the error until it gets a minimum defined acceptable error that is the difference of desired signal and the filtered noisy signal.

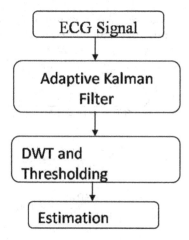

Fig. 3. Block diagram of our algorithm for cardiovascular parameter estimation.

After the noise filtering, the signal is decomposed by Wavelet transform. We use the discrete wavelet transform (DWT) which incorporates low pass filters and high pass filters to reduce the noise that couldn't be filtered with Kalman filter. The DWT signal is given by

$$X[a,b] = \sum_{n=-\alpha}^{\alpha} y(n)\phi_{a,b}(n) \tag{9}$$

where $y(n)$ is the output signal of the Kalman filter to be transformed with n length. And $\phi(n)$ is the window of finite length having a window translation parameter b and dilation/contraction parameter a. The next step is to set the threshold by using hard thresholding approach proposed in [22] to estimate the wavelet coefficients as

$$cD'_j = \begin{cases} cD_j, & |cD_j| \geq t \\ 0, & |cD_j| \leq t \end{cases} \tag{10}$$

where t is obtained by universal threshold selection with a value of $t = \sigma\sqrt{2\log N}$ with the standard deviation of the noise $\sigma = (\text{median}\{|cD_j|/0.6457\})$ where N is the data length, cD_j and cD'_j are wavelet coefficients before and after thresholding [22].

4   Performance Metrics for Cardiovascular Parameter Estimation

To evaluate the performances of cardiovascular parameters estimation algorithms, different parameters are used. Parameters such as True positive Rate (TPR), False Positive Rate (TPR), True positive (TP), False Positive (FP),

False negative (FN), True negative (TN), accuracy, sensitivity and others can be used to check the performance of parameter estimation algorithms. The mathematical expression for accuracy, sensitivity, average FPR and average positive predictive value for N data length is given as follows [7,25]:

$$\text{Accuracy} = \frac{1}{N} \left(\sum_{i=1}^{N} \frac{\text{TP} + \text{TN}}{\text{TP} + \text{FP} + \text{TN} + \text{FN}} \times 100\% \right) \tag{11}$$

$$\text{Sensitvity} = \frac{1}{N} \left(\sum_{i=1}^{N} \frac{\text{TP}}{\text{TP} + \text{FN}} \times 100\% \right) \tag{12}$$

$$\text{FPR} = \frac{1}{N} \left(\sum_{i=1}^{N} \frac{\text{FP}_i}{\text{FP}_i + \text{TN}_i} \times 100\% \right) \tag{13}$$

$$\text{PPV} = \frac{1}{N} \left(\sum_{i=1}^{N} \frac{\text{TP}_i}{\text{TP}_i + \text{FP}_i} \times 100\% \right). \tag{14}$$

Other performance evaluation parameter is mean absolute deviation (MAD) which gives the average absolute deviation of estimated signal, formulated as [26]

$$\text{MAD} = \frac{1}{N} \sum_{i=1}^{N} |e(n)|^2 \tag{15}$$

where the error $e(n)$ is the difference between the estimated signal and the original ECG signal. This error can also be used to determine the signal to noise ratio (SNR).

5   Simulation Results and Discussion

5.1   Simulation Parameters

We use the standard ECG signal dataset from a publicly available dataset, MIT-BIH AR dataset [23,24]. Each ECG signal is sampled at 360 samples per second. The data are used to test the performance of Kalman filter, machine learning and the proposed algorithms for cardiovascular parameter estimation (Table 1).

5.2   Simulation Results

We first show the receiver operating characteristics (ROC) curve of Kalman filter based ECG signal denoising algorithm. As shown in Fig. 4, the estimation of ECG signal parameter estimation is higher at high false positive rate values.

Employing Kalman filter can averaged out the noise from the ECG signal and estimate its necessary parameters. We also show the receiver operating characteristics curve of machine learning based ECG signal parameter estimation algorithm in Fig. 5.

Table 1. Simulation parameters used

Type	Parameter	Methods/Value
Butterworth filter	fs	500 Hz [20]
	Filter length	10 [20]
Machine learning	Preprocessing	Butterworth with length10 [20]
	Feature extraction	Wavelet with hard thresholding [22]
	Parameter estimation	Linear regression [21]
DWT	Window length	0.03 fs [21]

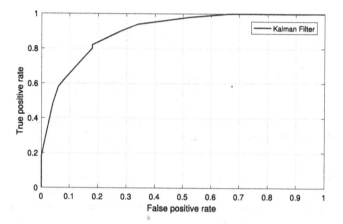

Fig. 4. Receiver operating characteristics (ROC) curve of Kalman filtering based ECG signal denoising.

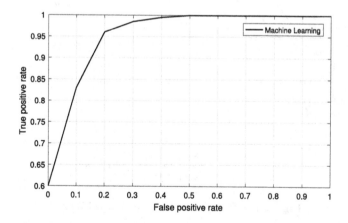

Fig. 5. Receiver operating characteristics (ROC) curve of machine learning based ECG signal parameter estimation method.

The result depicts that by using machine learning algorithm it is possible to achieve an estimation of ECG signal parameter even within a reduced false positive rate. This shows although it has high complexity machine learning algorithms give better performance than classical algorithms.

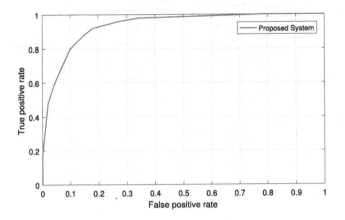

Fig. 6. Receiver operating characteristics (ROC) curve of the proposed algorithm for ECG signal filtering and parameter estimation.

We also plot the receiver operating characteristic curve of our algorithm as shown in Fig. 6. From the ROC curve of the proposed algorithm, it can be seen that a good detection performance can be achieved using classical noise filtering and estimation methods of ECG signal.

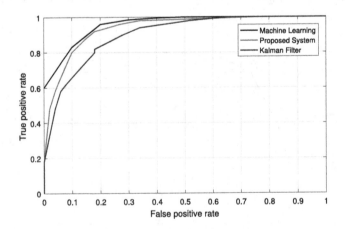

Fig. 7. The ROC for the proposed algorithms.

Finally, we plot the results from the three algorithms together as shown in Fig. 7. The result shows that the proposed classical filtering and prediction algorithm provides better estimation accuracy than Kalman filtering. This is achieved due to additional usage of DWT blocks in the system. Besides, the proposed method gives nearly the same performance as machine learning algorithm with a lower complexity. Note that due to space limitation, we remove results with other performance metrics stated in Sect. 4 (Table 2).

Table 2. Summary of ROC for the three algorithms

FPR	0	0.1	0.2	0.3	0.4	0.5	0.7	0.8	0.9	1
TPR (Kalman Filter)	0.2	0.64	0.82	0.9	0.96	0.97	0.99	1	1	1
TPR (Machine Learning)	0.6	0.81	0.97	0.98	1	1	1	1	1	1
TPR (AKF with DWT)	0.2	0.8	0.95	0.96	0.97	0.97	1	1	1	1

6 Conclusion

In this work, we analyze the comparative performances of classical method (Kalman filtering) and machine learning algorithms for cardiovascular parameter estimation. We also propose an algorithm which uses joint Kalman filtering and DWT and analyze the performance with numerical simulation. The simulation results show that machine learning algorithm outperforms the classical method (Kalman filtering). However, with the proposed method, a better estimation result is attained compared to classical Kalman filtering. Besides, the result from the proposed algorithm shows that we can achieve a better parameter estimation with classical methods. Hence, this algorithm can be used when there is difficult to find enough training data sets. Investigations of other algorithms like deep neural networks will be the future direction of this work.

References

1. Lyon, A., Mincholé, A., Martínez, J.P., Laguna, P., Rodriguez, B.: Computational techniques for ECG analysis and interpretation in light of their contribution to medical advances. J. Roy. Soc. Interface **15**(138), 20170821 (2018)
2. Ghasemi, Z., et al.: Estimation of cardiovascular risk predictors from non-invasively measured diametric pulse volume waveforms via multiple measurement information fusion. Sci. Rep. Nat. Publ. Group **8**(1), 1–11 (2018)
3. Arumugam, M., Sangaiah, A.K.: Arrhythmia identification and classification using wavelet centered methodology in ECG signals. Concurr. Comput.: Pract. Exp. **32**, e5553 (2019)
4. Yao, Y., et al.: Unobtrusive estimation of cardiovascular parameters with limb ballistocardiography. Sensors **19**(13), 2922 (2019)
5. Smital, L., Vítek, M., Kozumplík, J., Provazník, I.: Adaptive wavelet wiener filtering of ECG signals. IEEE Trans. Biomed. Eng. **60**(2), 437–445 (2013)

6. Wang, Z., Zhu, J., Yan, T., Yang, L.: A new modified wavelet-based ECG denoising. Comput. Assist. Surg. **24**, 174–183 (2019)
7. Singh, O., Sunkaria, R.K.: A new approach for identification of heartbeats in multimodal physiological signals. J. Med. Eng. Technol. **42**(3), 182–186 (2018)
8. Vullings, R., Vries, B.D., Bergmans, J.W.M.: An adaptive Kalman filter for ECG signal enhancement. IEEE Trans. Biomed. Eng. **58**(4), 1094–1103 (2011)
9. Kostoglou, K., Robertson, A.D., MacIntosh, B.J., Mitsis, G.D.: A novel framework for estimating time-varying multivariate autoregressive models and application to cardiovascular responses to acute exercise. IEEE Trans. Biomed. Eng. **66**(11), 3257–3266 (2019)
10. Rakshit, M., Das, S.: An efficient ECG denoising methodology using empirical mode decomposition and adaptive switching mean filter. Biomed. Signal Process. Control **40**, 140–148 (2018)
11. Han, G., Lin, B., Xu, Z.: Electrocardiogram signal denoising based on empirical mode decomposition technique: an overview. J. Instr. **12**(3), P03010 (2017)
12. Spicher, N., Kukuk, v: ECG delineation using a piecewise Gaussian derivative model with parameters estimated from scale-dependent algebraic expressions. In: 41st Annual International Conference of the IEEE Engineering in Medicine and Biology Society (EMBC), October 2019
13. Arai, T., Lee, K., Cohen, R.J.: Comparison of cardiovascular parameter estimation methods using swine data. J. Clin. Monit. Comput. **34**, 261–270 (2019)
14. Mykoliuk, I., Jancarczyk, D., Karpinski, M., Kifer, V.: Machine learning methods in Electrocardiography classification. J. Adv. Comput. Inf. Technol. (2018)
15. Al Rahhal, M.M., Bazi, Y., AlHichri, H., Alajlana, N., Melgani, F., Yager, R.R.: Deep learning approach for active classification of electrocardiogram signals. Inf. Sci. **345**, 340–354 (2016)
16. Lastre-Dominguez, C., et al.: ECG Signal denoising and features extraction using Unbiased FIR smoothing. BioMed research international, Hindawi (2019)
17. Reddy, D.V.R., Rahim, B.A., Shaik, F.: Gaussian noise filtering from ECG signal using improved Kalman filter. Int. J. Eng. Res. **3**, 118–126 (2015)
18. Sharma, B., Suji, R.J., Basu, A.: Adaptive Kalman filter approach and Butterworth filter technique for ECG signal enhancement. In: Mishra, D., Nayak, M., Joshi, A. (eds.) Information and Communication Technology for Sustainable Development. Lecture Notes in Networks and Systems, vol. 10, pp. 315–322. Springer, Singapore (2017). https://doi.org/10.1007/978-981-10-3920-1_32
19. Schmidt, J., Marques, M., Botti, S., Marques, M.: Recent advances and applications of machine learning in solid state materials science. Nat. Partner J. **5**, 1–36 (2019)
20. Patro, K.K., Kumar, P.R.: Effective feature extraction of ECG for biometric application. In: 7th International Conference on Advances in Computing and Communications (ICACC), Cochin, India, August 2017
21. Aspuru, J., et al.: Segmentation of the ECG signal by means of a linear regression algorithm. Sensors **19**, 775 (2019)
22. Lina, H.Y., Lianga, S.Y., Hob, Y.L., Linb, Y.H., Maa, H.P.: Discrete-wavelet-transform-based noise removal and feature extraction for ECG signals. Elsevier Masson SAS, November 2014
23. Goldberger, A.L., et al.: PhysioBank, PhysioToolkit and PhysioNet: components of a new research resource for complex physiologic signals. Circulation **101**(23), e215–e220 (2003)
24. Moody, G.B., Muldrow, W.E.: A noise stress test for arrhythmia detectors. Comput. Cardiol. (1984)

25. Plawiak, P.: Novel generic ensembles of classifiers applied to myocardium dysfunction recognition based on ECG signals (2017)
26. Yadav, O.P., Ray, S.: ECG signal characterization using Lagrange-Chebyshev polynomials. Radio Electron. Commun. Syst. Radioelectron. **62**(2), 72–85 (2019)

Modeling and Analysis of Three-Phase Inverter for Induction Motor Drive for Three-Wheel Electric Vehicle Application

Tewodros G. Workineh[1(✉)], Tefera T. Yetayew[2], and Assefa G. Egziabher[2]

[1] Faculty of Electrical and Computer Engineering, Bahir Dar Institute of Technology, Bahir Dar University, Bahir Dar, Ethiopia

[2] School of Electrical Engineering and Computing, Electrical Power and Control Engineering, Adama Science and Technology University, Adama, Ethiopia

Abstract. This paper presents the control scheme Modeling and analysis of three phase voltage switching inverter in using Space vector Pulse Width Modulation (SVPWM) technique for induction motor driven three-wheel electric vehicles. Induction motors are now widely applied in electric vehicle industries as the replacement of internal combustion engine due to the over striking price and environmental concerns. Performance of speed, direction and torque control for three wheel electric drives (Bajaj) has been studied. Better dc utilization for medium performance drive system, more efficient use of DC supply voltage, produce less ripples makes space vector pulse width modulation technique a good choice for this work. By keeping the ratio of stator voltage to frequency constant, this system tipscan adjust the speed of the motor by control the frequency and amplitude of the stator voltage. Transfer model of induction motor, vehicle dynamic model and voltage source inverter type SVPWM model are designed and simulated using matlab Simulink. Control scheme visual realization has been done though Protues and Arduino IDE software. To demonstrate good performance of SVPWM based induction motor for three wheel drive, parameters such has stator current, rotor current, torque and speed as well as switching patter of the inverter waveforms have been displayed and analyzed.

Keywords: SVPWM · Induction motor · Voltage source inverter · Three-wheel electric vehicles · MATLAB/SIMULINK

1 Introduction

Induction Machines is the most widely used motor in industry and also in residential application. Its low cost, high efficiency, wide speed range and robustness makes induction motors to be applied in various applications. Now a day, in the most of the industrial applications, due to their simple and most tough construction without any mechanical commentator, AC motors are more useful than DC machines [1, 2].

In EVs propulsion, three phase AC induction motor drive is fed from three phase inverter with a DC source or battery at approximately constant voltage, through a DC/AC

© ICST Institute for Computer Sciences, Social Informatics and Telecommunications Engineering 2021
Published by Springer Nature Switzerland AG 2021. All Rights Reserved
M. A. Delele et al. (Eds.): ICAST 2020, LNICST 384, pp. 170–183, 2021.
https://doi.org/10.1007/978-3-030-80621-7_13

inverter [3]. The DC/AC inverter is constituted by a fast switching power electronic switches and power diodes. IGBTs and MOSFETs are commonly used in the inverters configurations. A high speed processor in order to produce the proper switching sequence is needed since AC voltage output of the inverter has high frequency square wave forms.

To determine the amplitude and the frequency of the output voltage, various switching schemes are used to generate PWM signal. Space Vector Pulse Width Modulation (SVPWM) one of the various PWM techniques that best suits for electric vehicle application [4].This type of modulation has the following interesting features such as offers better DC-link utilization, more efficient use of DC source voltage, yield less ripples and improved life time of drive [5].

The paper is structured as follows: first system description is discussed, second modeling part is presented, and third power and control issues are demonstrated and finally results obtained are presented along with conclusions.

2   System Descriptions

This paper work consists of the source, the three-phase inverter, the three-phase induction motor, three wheel vehicle (Bajaj) and the Arduino microcontroller. Generally, this proposed system is illustrated in the following Fig. 1. Three phase IGBT based inverter, fed from dc source/battery, converts DC to AC voltage to power three phase induction motor as described in Fig. 1. The controller will generate the pulse width modulation (PWM) to feed the inverter using Arduino and amplified through gate drive circuit.

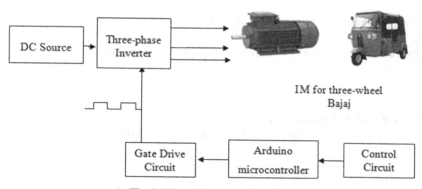

Fig. 1. Block diagram of the paper

The objective of this work is to model and analyze three phase inverter and its controller, Space Vector PWM, using Matlab and Protues with Arduino IDE software.

3   System Modeling and Simulation

3.1   Electric Vehicle Dynamics

Motor rated speed; motor power rating and Maximum speed of the motor are parameters to be considered in designing Electric vehicles [10].

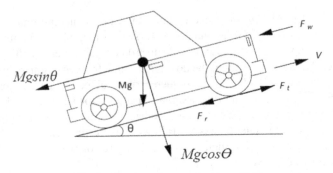

Fig. 2. Forces acting on electric vehicle

Road load is among several forces acting on vehicle while travelling that the vehicle to overcome [6] as shown in Fig. 2. This road load F_l consist of four components drag aerodynamic force F_d, rolling resistance force F_r, gradient or Clamping force F_c and acceleration resistance F_a,

$$F_r + F_d + F_c + F_a \tag{1}$$

Rolling Resistance: Rolling resistance of the tire, the resistive force of vehicle which opposes the rolling of the wheels, is given by:

$$F_r = C_{rr} * M * g * \cos(\theta) \tag{2}$$

where, C_{rr}: rolling resistance Coefficient, $(M * g)$: Vehicle load in N and θ: Inclination angle.

The power (Pr) required to overpowering the rolling resistance is calculated as

$$P_r = F_r * v \left(\frac{m}{sec} \right) \tag{3}$$

Gradient (Climbing) Resistance: The force that tends to pull the vehicle back, gradient resistance, when it is up hilling an inclined surface is given by:

$$F_c = M * g * \sin(\theta) \tag{4}$$

And the climbing power of the Bajaj is given by $P_C = F_C * V_C$. Where $V_c = V_{max}/2$ and v_c is the climbing velocity.

Aerodynamic Drag Force: The force acting on the vehicle body when it is travelling through air, the aerodynamic drag force which consists of the skin friction drags due to air flow in the boundary layer, normal pressure drags depends on the vehicle frontal area and speed and induced drag [5] is expressed by

$$F_d = \frac{1}{2} * V^2 * C_d * A * \rho \tag{5}$$

where,

C_d- the aerodynamic drag coefficient (lies between 0.2 and 1.5),

ρ -the air density in kg/m^3 = 1.23 kg/m,

V -the sum of speed of vehicle and speed of air in m/s.

A is frontal area of the plat form $A = 0.58 * 0.92 = 0.5336$ m^2.

The total power required to drive the Bajaj is given by: $P_t = P_r + P_a + P_c + P_d$

Therefore, the mechanical power output necessary for driving the wheel including transmission losses on the wheel is given by the equation:

$$M_{peak} = \frac{P_{max}}{\text{efficiency of gear}} \qquad (6)$$

To obtain the desired drive characteristics it is important to find the torque on the drive wheel using the following expression:

$$T = F_t \times \frac{r}{G} \qquad (7)$$

Where, T is torque, r is radius of drive wheel and G is gear ratio.

For the calculation of tractive force, total tractive power and total tractive torque needed, at the wheel of the vehicle, the following parameters of the vehicle listed in the Table 1 are considered. To estimate the motor losses and efficiency, the following induction motor parameters shown in the Table 2 are considered.

Table 1. Electric Bajaj specification.

Parameter	Symbol	Value
Maximum power	P	7.52kw
Wheel base	B	1980mm
Total length	L	3030mm
Total width	W	1500mm
Total height	H	1780mm
Coefficient of rolling friction	C_{rr}	0.01
Vehicle mass	m	700 Kg
Air density	ρ	1.23 Kg/m3
Frontal area	A	0.35m2
Aerodynamic drag coefficient	Cd	0.2
Tire radius	R	0.1m
Gravitational acceleration	g	9.81m/s2

3.2 Space Vector Pulse width Modulation

In EVs propulsion, three phase AC induction motor drive is fed from three phase inverter with a DC source or battery at approximately constant voltage through a DC/AC inverter

Table 2. Induction motor specification.

Parameter	Value
Pole	4
Power	8KW
Efficiency	89.5%
Speed	1500-2000RPM
Frequency	50Hz
Slip	2.5%
Voltage	440V
Power factor	0.89
Moment of inertia	0.02
Full load Torque	52.6

with a fast switching power electronic switches and power diodes [3]. Space Vector Pulse Width Modulation (SVPWM), was originally developed as vector approach to Pulse Width Modulation (PWM) scheme for three phase inverters, one of the various PWM techniques that best suits for electric vehicle application [4].It is a more advanced technique with the following merits such as Minimization of harmonics, Minimization switching loss, Maximization of fundamental component, Utilization of DC voltage [3, 4, 7]. The existence of additional zero voltage states such asV0 (000), and V7 (111) is the difference between SVPWM and SPWM in addition to the six possible voltage vectors applied in VSI.

Thus, SVPWM is as an eight state operation with 6 operational vectors as shown in Fig. 3 below [8].

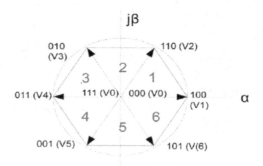

Fig. 3. Space voltage vectors in different sectors

3.3   Three Phases to Two Phase Transformation

The dynamic model of induction motor is studied by driving the equivalency of the transformation from three-phase to two-phase machine. The equivalence is based on the amount of MMF produced in two-phase and three-phase windings as well as equal current amounts. Assuming that each of the three-phase windings have Ns turns per phase and equal currents magnitudes, the two-phase winding will have $3N_s/2$ turns per phase for MMF equality. The direct (d) and Quadrature (q) axes MMF are resolved by using MMF of the three-phase along d and q axes.

The stator voltages of three-phase induction machine under balanced conditions is given by

$$V_a = \sqrt{2}V_{rms}\sin(\omega t) \tag{8}$$

$$V_b = \sqrt{2}V_{rms}\sin(\omega t - 120) \tag{9}$$

$$V_c = \sqrt{2}V_{rms}\sin(\omega t + 120) \tag{10}$$

Where V_a, V_b and V_c are the three line voltages,
The relationship between alpha beta(α_β) and abc is as follows

$$\begin{bmatrix} V_\alpha \\ V_\beta \end{bmatrix} = \frac{2}{3}\begin{bmatrix} 1 & \frac{1}{2} & -\frac{1}{2} \\ 0 & \frac{\sqrt{3}}{2} & -\frac{\sqrt{3}}{2} \end{bmatrix}\begin{bmatrix} V_a \\ V_b \\ V_c \end{bmatrix} \tag{11}$$

Then, the direct and quadrature axes voltages are: -

$$\begin{bmatrix} V_d \\ V_q \end{bmatrix} = \begin{bmatrix} \cos(\theta) & \sin(\theta) \\ -\sin(\theta) & \cos(\theta) \end{bmatrix}\begin{bmatrix} V_\alpha \\ V_\beta \end{bmatrix} \tag{12}$$

The instantaneous values of the stator and rotor currents in three-phase system are ultimately calculated using the following transformation;

$$\begin{bmatrix} i_a \\ i_\beta \end{bmatrix} = \begin{bmatrix} \cos(\theta) & -\sin(\theta) \\ \sin(\theta) & \cos(\theta) \end{bmatrix}\begin{bmatrix} i_d \\ i_q \end{bmatrix} \tag{13}$$

$$\begin{bmatrix} i_a \\ i_b \\ i_c \end{bmatrix} = \frac{2}{3}\begin{bmatrix} -\frac{1}{2} & -\frac{\sqrt{3}}{2} \\ -\frac{1}{2} & -\frac{\sqrt{3}}{2} \end{bmatrix}\begin{bmatrix} i_a \\ i_\beta \end{bmatrix} \tag{14}$$

3.4   MATLAB/SIMULINK Model

The simulation results are given for the induction motor for the following specification [6] (Table 3):

Table 3. Induction motor specifications

No	parameters	values
1	Number of poles [P]	4
2	Frequency [F]	50 Hz
3	Number of phases	3
4	Stator resistance [Rs]	1.115 ohms
5	Rotor resistance [Rr]	1.083 ohms
6	Stator inductance [Ls]	0.00597H
7	Mutual inductance [Lm]	0.2037 H
8	Moment of inertia [J]	0. 02 Kg-m/sec

Figure 4 describes the overall simulation of the system as shown below.

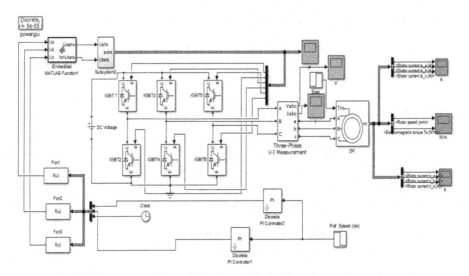

Fig. 4. MATLAB open loop Simulink model of SVPWM based induction motor

3.5 Proteus Simulation

Six IGBT, 4PC40UD, switches is used for the system that are turned on and off by pulse width modulation. The turn on and off of the IGBTs give rise to three phase output from dc source. These are high speed switching devices that turn on and turn off by sequence to produce three phase output. The inverter is simulated and switching of inverter is indicated with LEDs. The switching with LED positions is shown as in Fig. 5 below.

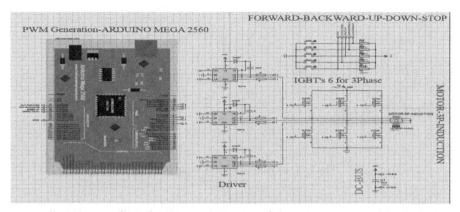

Fig. 5. Inverter with switching sequence

4 Results and Discussions

Switching Pattern of SVPWM Inverter: Figure 6 demonstrated that reduction of the heat of switches by reducing the switching ratio based on carrier. This pattern when compared to high frequency triangular carrier wave produces gating signal to drive the inverter. Because of common mode element in SVPWM compared to SPWM, there is an extra improvement in voltage compared with sinusoidal PWM as clearly indicated.

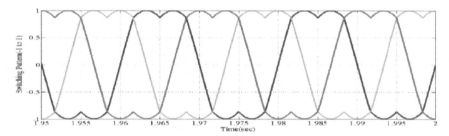

Fig. 6. Switching pattern of SVPWM inverters

Gate Pulse: The output get signal generated based on SVPWM techniques to switching the IGBT sequentially is shown in the Fig. 7, below. The signal that generated from the driver circuit is out phase in one leg. Because in one leg the two switches are on simultaneously a short circuit is happen and cause damage on the inverter. Thus, in order to generate three phase sinusoidal waves the switches are on and off sequentially based on the pattern of sector vectors.

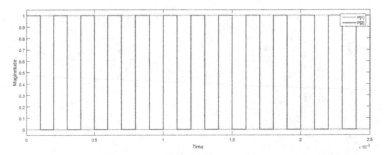

Fig. 7. Gate pulse for IGBT 1 and IGBT 2

Stator Current: The current in that flows through the stator winding of induction motor is shown in Fig. 8. Appropriate control algorithm is applied for motor depending on mechanical load torque so that the stator current should decrease the controller will supply stator with proper voltage and frequency.

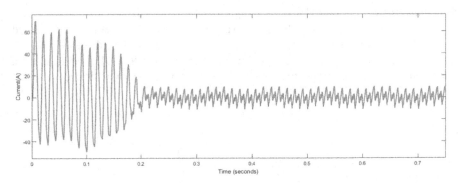

Fig. 8. Stator current

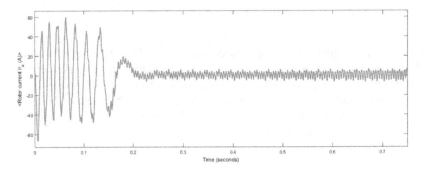

Fig. 9. Rotor current

Rotor Current: The current in the rotor winding of the induction motor is high in the starting. But as the motor accelerates current decreases. The drive automatically decreases the voltage after the motor is smoothly driven (Fig. 9).

Torque: Figure 10 demonstrated that the torque associated with induction motor is high because the starting torque of the induction motor. The torque required by the Bajaj is 52 Nm. After the motor rotate and start drive the vehicle, the torque comes to zero at reduced losses.

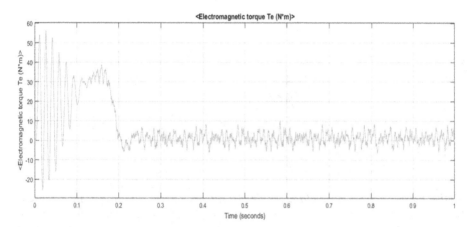

Fig. 10. Electromagnetic torque

The Torque-Speed Curve (At 50 Hz): The combined speed (X-axis) and torque (Y-axis) curve are shown in Fig. 11. The motor is operating at 50 Hz frequency. The speed and torque at 10 Hz are shown below these values are less than initially calculated at 50 Hz.

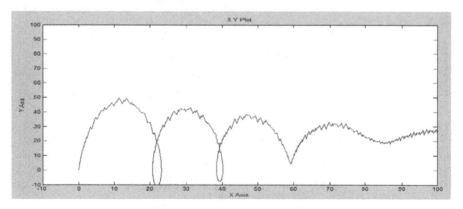

Fig. 11. Torque speed curve at 50 Hz

The Torque-Speed Curve (At 10 Hz): The toque speed curve of induction motor at 10Hz is represented as in shown in Fig. 12. The figure described that the cause reduction magnitude of torque- speed curve is the increase in switching time due to the minimized frequency.

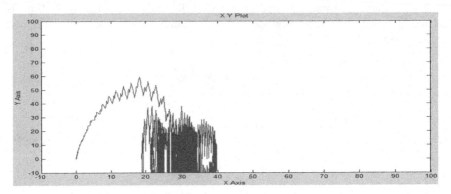

Fig. 12. Torque speed curve at 10 Hz

Motive Force Verses Approaching Angle of Vehicles: There are three main forces which act on the Bajaj when it travels at constant speed. Gradient force increases when the approaching angle is increase. Aerodynamics force is constant at constant speed of the vehicle. The total motive force with each component of the force acting on the vehicle is shown on the Fig. 13. We assumed the vehicle speed when move up is 25 km/h and velocity of the air also assumed equals to zero.

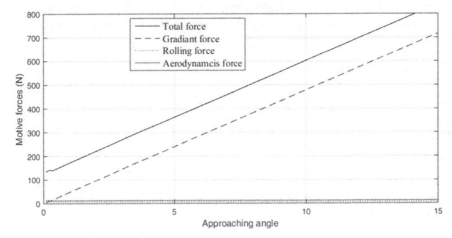

Fig. 13. Motive force verses approaching angle

Motor Power Consumption with Respect to Approaching Angle: The maximum reactive power is supplied when the Bajaj is clamping the hill of maximum approaching angle which is 7.67° at full load with the speed of 25 km/h . The speed of the Bajaj is reduced while clamping the hill is to increase torque with limited power output of the motor. Figure 14 show the power needed to be supplied by the motor to drive the Bajaj at constant speed of 25 km/h with verses approaching angle.

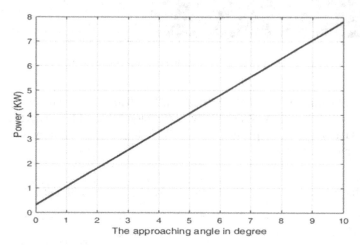

Fig. 14. Motor power consumption with respect to approaching angle

Forward and Reverse Direction Rotate of Motor: The push button in the control circuit is used to run the motor speed up, speed down, forward, reverse direction by due to the changing of switching pulse of IGBT gate signals. The following Fig. 15 and Fig. 16 shows that the output wave result when the motor run forward and reverse direction respectively.

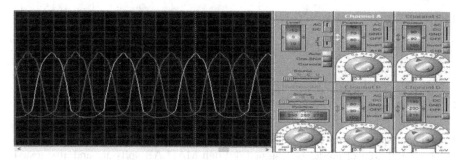

Fig. 15. Wave form when the motor rotate forward direction

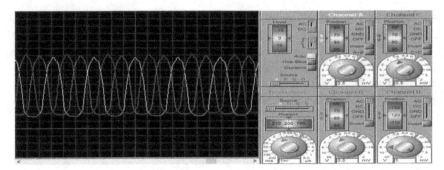

Fig. 16. Wave form when the motor rotate reverse direction

Comparison Simulation Results of SPWM and SVPWM: In the following figures show the wave forms of SPWM and SVPWM techniques using FFT analyzing by varying its modulation index. As per the Table 4, SVPWM gives 15% quality improvement of the fundamental output.

Table 4. Evaluations of SPWM and SVPWM at varying modulation index.

Technique	SPWM		SVPWM	
M. I. (M)	Output line voltage(peak)volt	THD (%)	Output line voltage (peak)volt	THD (%)
0.4	180.80	162.11	192.70	154.07
0.5	266.50	123.35	312.20	108.78
0.6	289.40	117.12	318.10	105.69
0.7	369.20	94.52	436.60	81.19
0.8	396.10	89.73	442.90	78.56
0.9	472.90	70.69	552.30	53.62
1.0	502.40	64.83	567.90	49.15

5   Conclusions

In this paper space vector pulse width modulation-based induction motor with proportional integral control model is designed through MATLAB software and also tested successfully by evaluating the parameters like stator current, rotor current, torque and speed. By keeping the ratio of stator voltage to frequency constant, this system tips can regulate the speed of the motor by controlling the frequency and voltage amplitude of the stator. SVPWM control system design and implementation is simple and trouble free. Besides electric vehicle application, these types of induction motors control system can be used in agricultural and industrial pumps. The modulation technique selected for the paper is space vector pulse width modulation with good exploitation of the DC link voltage and low current ripple. It is also relatively easy to implement in the hardware platform. These features also make it suitable for high-voltage high-power applications.

References

1. Kailaswar, S.V., Keswani, R.A.: Speed control of three induction motor by V/F method for batching motion system. Int. J. Eng. Res. Appl. (IJERA) 3(2), 1732–1736 (2013). ISSN 2248-9622
2. Pawar, H.P., Chavan, N.S., Shinde, A.B., Chavan, Y.S.: Speed control of induction motor using PWM technique. Int. J. Eng. Res. Technol. (IJERT) 4(04), 174–177 (2015). ISSN 2278-0181
3. Soni, S.K., Gupta, A.: Analysis of SVPWM based speed control of induction motor drive with using V/F control based 3 level inverter. IJSET 2(9), 932–938 (2013)
4. Tabbache, B., Kheloui, A., Benbouzid, M.E.H.: Design and control of the induction motor propulsion of an electric vehicle. In: 2010 IEEE Vehicle Power and Propulsion Conference (VPPC), 1–3 September 2010, pp.1–6 (2010)
5. Kumar, K.V., Michael, P.A., John, J.P., Kumar, S.S.: Simulation and comparison of SPWM and SVPWM control for three phase inverter. ARPN J. Eng. Appl. Sci. 5(7), 61–74 (2010)
6. Manivannan, S., Veerakumar, S., Karuppusamy, P., Nandhakumar, A.: Performance analysis of three phase voltage source inverter fed induction motor drive with possible switching sequence execution in SVPWM. Int. J. Adv. Res. Electr. Electron. Instr. Eng. 3(6), 10081–10104 (2014). ISSN (Print): 2320–3765
7. Asma, N.R.L., Suresh, J.: Implementation of space vector pulse width modulation using arduino. Int. J. Sci. Res. (2012). ISSN (online): 2319-7064 Impact factor: 3.358
8. Van Der Broeck, H.W., Skudelny, H.-C., Stanke, G.V.: Analysis and realization of pulse width modulator based on voltage space vectors. IEEE Trans. Ind. Appl. 24(1), 142–150 (1988)
9. Zeraouila, M., Benbouzid, M.E.H., Diallo, D.: Electric motor drive selection issues for HEV propulsion systems: a comparative study. In: 2005 IEEE Conference on Vehicle Power and Propulsion, 7–9 September 2005, pp. 8–15 (2005)
10. Chauhan, S.: Motor torque calculations for electric vehicle. Int. J. Sci. Res. 4(08), 126–127 (2015)
11. Rachid, M.H.: Power Electronics: Circuits, Devices, and Applications. 3rd edn. (2004)
12. El-Saady, G., Ibrahim, E.-N.A., Elbesealy, M.: V/F Control of three phase induction motor drive with different PWM techniques. Innov. Syst. Design Eng. IISTE 4(14), 131–144 (2013)

Performance Analysis of Multicarrier Modulation Techniques for Next Generation Networks

Amare Kassaw[1,2]([✉]), Fikreaddis Tazeb[1], Fikreselam Gared[2], and Dereje Hailemariam[1]

[1] Addis Ababa Institute of Technology, Addis Ababa University, Addis Ababa, Ethiopia
derejeh.hailemariam@aait.edu.et
[2] Bahir Dar Institute of Technology, Bahir Dar University, Bahir Dar, Ethiopia
http://www.aau.edu.et/
http://www.bdu.edu.et

Abstract. Next-generation networks are expected to provide a wide range of services and functionalities. These services impose different requirements on the physical layer. Due to ease of implementation, immunity to interference and high data rate support, orthogonal frequency division multiplexing has been the most promising multicarrier waveform to implement on current wireless networks. Whereas, to provide the expected requirements in next-generation networks, more advanced multicarrier modulation techniques are required. Hence, other alternative multicarrier modulation techniques are proposed to address the challenges of orthogonal frequency division multiplexing.

In this work, we analyze performances of candidate multicarrier modulation techniques for next-generation networks such as filter-bank multicarrier and universal filtered multicarrier. To obtain insightful analysis, we first analyze the basic principles and characteristics of each multicarrier modulation technique. Then, we compare the performances in terms of power spectral density (PSD), bit error rate (BER) and spectral efficiency (SE). Besides, the computational complexity of the proposed multicarrier modulation techniques is evaluated. Finally, numerical simulation is done to validate the theoretical analysis. The results show that FBMC has minimum out-of-band emission and this helps to be almost insensitive to multiuser interference to support different use cases in the same bands. Whereas, UFMC reveals to be the most promising waveform which gives close to OFDM performance with better out-of-band emission.

Keywords: Multicarrier modulation · Next-generation network · Spectral efficiency · Power spectral density · Computational complexity · OFDM · FBMC · UFMC

© ICST Institute for Computer Sciences, Social Informatics and Telecommunications Engineering 2021
Published by Springer Nature Switzerland AG 2021. All Rights Reserved
M. A. Delele et al. (Eds.): ICAST 2020, LNICST 384, pp. 184–199, 2021.
https://doi.org/10.1007/978-3-030-80621-7_14

1   Introduction

Orthogonal frequency division multiplexing (OFDM) is robust against multipath fading, simple to implement due to FFT/IFFT structures, reduce multicarrier interference, easy to integrate with adaptive modulation and multiple antenna systems. Hence, OFDM is widely employed in many wireless systems such as long term evolution (LTE) and IEEE 802.11 families [1,4]. Although OFDM is most employed modulation technique in current wireless networks, it also exhibits intrinsic drawbacks. These include high out-of-band (OOB) interference caused due to rectangular pulse shape, spectral efficiency loss due to cyclic prefix insertion, strict time and frequency synchronization requirement to achieve subcarrier orthogonality and reduce high peak-to-average power ratio (PAPR) which affect the system energy efficiency [1,5]. To mitigate these limitations, several alternative multicarrier modulation techniques have been proposed recently such as filter bank multicarrier modulation (FBMC), universal filter multicarrier modulation (UFMC), filtered OFDM, generalized frequency division multiplexing (GFDM), biorthogonal frequency division multiplexing (BFDM) and time-frequency packing (TFP) [1–3,5,7,10–12,15,22–24].

Many studies are done to evaluate performances of these candidate multicarrier modulation techniques. A comprehensive overview of modulation and multiple access schemes for fifth generation (5G) networks is presented in [8]. The authors provide an overview of orthogonal multiple access (OMA) and non-orthogonal multiple access (NOMA) schemes. Performance comparison is done in terms of OOB leakage and bit error rate. They also propose modulation schemes that are suitable for OMA and NOMA. They show that NOMA provides enhanced throughput and massive connectivity with better spectral efficiency. A comparative study between OFDM and FBMC is provided in [5]. The work analyzes the spectral efficiency and computational complexity of both waveforms. The paper shows drawbacks of OFDM and indicates that FBMC could be an alternative solution. In [7], the authors compare UFMC with OFDM in terms of time-frequency efficiency to transmit small bursts under tight response time requirements. They show that UFMC has better time-frequency efficiency than OFDM.

In [15], performance comparison of UFMC and cyclic prefix based orthogonal frequency division multiplexing (CP-OFDM) is done based on PSD and peak to average power ratio (PAPR). They show that UFMC has better PSD than OFDM and has nearly the same PAPR variation. A performance comparison of FBMC, UFMC and GFDM interms of power spectral density (PSD), spectral efficiency, PAPR and computational complexity is done in [9]. The authors claimed that UFMC gives comparable spectral efficiency to OFDM. They also prove that UFMC preserves backward compatibility with known OFDM algorithms. However, spectral efficiency comparison is done by considering only AWGN channel model. Similar to OFDM, guard interval has to be inserted in UFMC to combat inter symbol interference (ISI) caused by multipath channel. This reduces the spectral efficiency of UFMC compared to the results in [9].

In this work, we analyze the performances of FBMC and UFMC modulation techniques. To obtain insightful analysis, we first analyze the basic principles and characteristics of each waveform. Then, we compare the power spectral density, bit error rate and spectral efficiency of the proposed waveforms. Besides, the computational complexity of the waveforms is analyzed. In line with this, the main contributions of this paper are summarized as follows:

- Review candidate multicarrier waveforms for 5G and beyond networks.
- Formulate mathematical models for the spectral efficiency, BER and computational complexity for OFDM, FBMC and UFMC waveforms.
- Analyze performances of these waveforms theoretically.
- Validate the theoretical analysis via numerical simulation.

The rest of the paper is organized as follows. In Sect. 2, basics of multicarrier modulation techniques for next generation networks are presented. Performance analysis of the proposed multicarrier modulation techniques are provided in Sect. 3. Simulation results are discussed in Sect. 4 and conclusions are drawn in Sect. 5.

2   Multicarrier Modulation Techniques for Next Generation Networks

OFDM, FBMC and UFMC are the most promising multicarrier modulation techniques for next generation networks. The main differences between these modulation techniques are on the multicarrier modulation block, cyclic prefix insertion and filtering operation [1,5,6,18]. In OFDM, implementation of windowing and modulation is achieved by performing N-point FFT operation [5]. Whereas in FBMC the symbols are pulse shaped by a prototype filter that is longer than the number of subcarriers [2,5]. Efficient implementation of this structure is obtained by deploying offset-QAM staggering, FFT operation and polyphase filtering [1,2]. In UFMC, incoming quadrature amplitude modulation (QAM) symbols are grouped into blocks. And each block is modulated and filtered separately and sum up at the end. This is implemented by using N-point IFFT and Dolph-Chebyshev filtering [1,2]. At the receiver side, the inverse operations are executed in reverse order. In all the waveforms, an equalizer has to be deployed to compensate for the channel's frequency selectivity. For OFDM and UFMC, the equalizer is single-tap and for FBMC it is multi-tap [1,5,6]. In subsequent sections, we describe the fundamentals of UFMC and FBMC waveforms.

2.1   FBMC Modulation Techniques

FBMC systems have a group of filters that process common input to give common output. These filters termed as analysis filter banks (AFB) and synthesis filter banks (SFB) [3,5]. The SFB is implemented with IFFT followed by polyphase network structure whereas AFB is implemented with a polyphase network followed by an FFT [3]. The filter bank allows to control the frequency response of the transmitted signal. Due to this, different techniques are proposed to design the filter such as filtered multi-tone (FMT) [13], cosine-modulated multitone (CMT) and staggered multitone (SMT) [3]. In FMT, the subcarriers are separated by guard bands and adjacent subcarriers have not overlapping bands. It is less bandwidth efficient than OFDM, but it does not require the guard interval. Hence, it has better energy efficiency than OFDM [3]. The CMT has high bandwidth efficiency and blind detection capability. However, a 90° phase shift is introduced to adjacent subcarriers [3]. The SMT transmits a set of complex-valued QAM symbols whose real and imaginary parts are separated and time staggered by one half of the symbol duration that results offset QAM (OQAM) symbols. In OQAM-FBMC the data symbols are spaced at $T/2$ in the time domain and the subcarriers are spaced at $1/T$ in frequency domain where T is the symbol time. Therefore, in SMT the symbol rate is doubled and the symbol spacing is halved. Compared to CMT and FMT, OQAM-FBMC has highest stop–band attenuation at fixed filter length and number of subcarriers [3]. Besides, OQAM-FBMC overlaps subcarriers in frequency domain and provides high bandwidth efficiency [3].

FBMC systems can be implemented based on the frequency spreading filter bank multicarrier (FS-FBMC) and the polyphase network filter bank multicarrier (PPN-FBMC) [3]. In FS-FBMC, OQAM symbols are filtered in frequency domain and then feed to the KN-point IFFT where K is the overlapping factor of the prototype filter. At receiver side, a sliding window selects the KN-points at every samples. Then, KN-point FFT is applied and followed by equalization and filtering by prototype filter. Whereas in PPN-FBMC, the OQAM symbols are first fed to N-point IFFT and then pass through the polyphase network for filtering [13].

Thus, the main processing blocks in PPN-FBMC are the OQAM preprocessing, the filter banks and OQAM post-processing. We use the filter proposed by the physical layer for dynamic spectrum access (PHYDYAS) project [2]. Mainly, the N-subchannel filters are designed by complex modulation and the rest subchannel filters are found by frequency shifted versions of the prototype [2]. The transmit filters are modeled based on a specially designed prototype filter and are modulated by the carrier frequency. The OQAM combined with constraints on the prototype filter is used to achieve orthogonality between adjacent symbols and adjacent carriers while giving maximum spectral efficiency [2]. The complex QAM symbol is staggered and changed to real symbols by OQAM preprocessing. The reverse operation is performed at the receiver side. The real to complex conversion decreases the sample rate by a factor of two [13]. Note that the system model and detail mathematical analysis for FBMC transmission are removed due to space limitations.

2.2 UFMC Modulation Techniques

UFMC is a type of subband filtering based waveform where the filtering operation is applied to group of subcarriers [14, 15]. In UFMC transmission, the bit streams are grouped into B-subbands, modulated by QAM modulation and converted to parallel streams. Then, IFFT is performed on each subband and the output is filtered by a filter of length L. Filtering leads to substantial reduction on out-of-band leakage and that helps to minimize harmful interference from adjacent subchannels on neighboring resource blocks [14,15].

UFMC uses Dolph-Chebyshev type filters [16]. The length of the filter depends on the size of subbands. It is characterized by an equi-ripple behavior in which all side lobes have the same height. In some works [7], the guard intervals are discarded. But, this reduces the performance in severe multipath scenarios since the time dispersion of the channel cannot be mitigated [16]. In other works, extra zero padded guard interval blocks of length $L - 1$ are introduced in each UFMC block to mitigate the time dispersion. This adds extra time overhead and results to a UFMC symbol length of $N + L - 1$ samples [1]. But, it helps to mitigate the channel time dispersion using single-tap frequency domain equalizer. The filtered time-domain data is added to form the UFMC waveform. Hence, in contrast to OFDM, separate IFFT operations are done on each frequency block. Besides, windowing is done to suppress the interference. At the receiver side, $2N$-point FFT is taken to demodulate each UFMC symbol. FFT followed by an equalizer and time synchronization is able to estimate the transmitted signal correctly [1].

3   Performance Analysis of Multicarrier Modulation Techniques

Various metrics are used to evaluate the performances of multicarrier modulation techniques. At the transmitter side, power spectral density and spectral efficiency are considered whereas at the receiver side bit error rate (BER) and computational complexity are used to evaluate the performance [1].

3.1   Power Spectral Density (PSD)

The PSD shows the strength of the variations of energy with frequency. It shows at which frequencies the energy variations are strong and at which frequencies the variations are weak. The PSD of multicarrier modulation systems can be calculated by summing the power spectral density of individual subcarriers. Besides, sidelobe radiation can be calculated by the PSD model of the multicarrier signal [1].

3.2   Bit Error Rate (BER)

The main cause of degradation of transmission quality and corresponding BER is the noise and multipath propagation that are random in nature. To analyze the BER characteristics of the proposed multicarrier modulation techniques, we assume the noise follows Gaussian distribution while the propagation model follows Rayleigh distribution [19].

3.3 Spectral Efficiency (SE)

To compare the spectral efficiency of the proposed multicarrier modulation techniques, we use the approach proposed in [14]. It is more applicable for multicarrier modulations and defined the spectral efficiency as the product of time efficiency and modulation efficiency as

$$\text{SE}_{\text{MC}} = \eta_t \eta_m \tag{1}$$

where η_t and η_m are the time and modulation efficiency of multicarrier modulation schemes, respectively. The modulation efficiency depends on the modulation order, the number of active resource blocks and the code rate [9,14]. The time efficiency measures the time overhead introduced in transmission and is defined as [7]

$$\eta_t = \frac{D_L}{D_L + T_{\text{OH}}} \tag{2}$$

where D_L is the number of samples on transmitted signal dedicated to data transmission and T_{OH} is the overhead sample due to cyclic prefix, filter tails and zero padding. For all multicarrier modulations, $D_L = \beta N$ where β denotes the number of transmitted multicarrier symbols in a burst and N is the FFT size.

In OFDM, there is an overhead due to cyclic prefix. Whereas in UFMC there is an overhead caused by filtering and zero padding. The overhead in FBMC is introduced by long tail filters in each subcarrier which is independent from the length of the burst [1,5,7]. Thus, the overhead sample for each modulation technique is expressed as

$$T_{\text{OH}} = \begin{cases} \beta L_{\text{CP}} & \text{OFDM} \\ \beta(L_{\text{ZP}} + L_f - 1) & \text{UFMC} \\ N(K - \frac{1}{2}) & \text{FBMC} \end{cases} \tag{3}$$

where K is the overlapping factor of the filters, L_{CP} is the length of cyclic prefix, L_{ZP} is the length of zero padding and L_f is the filter length. By using (2) and (3), the time efficiency of each candidate waveform is given by

$$\eta_t = \begin{cases} \frac{N}{N+L_{\text{CP}}} & \text{OFDM} \\ \frac{N}{N+L_{\text{ZP}}+L_f-1} & \text{UFMC} \\ \frac{\beta}{\beta+(K-\frac{1}{2})} & \text{FBMC.} \end{cases} \tag{4}$$

Finally, the spectral efficiency of the proposed multicarrier modulation techniques is given by

$$\text{SE}_{\text{MC}} = \begin{cases} \frac{mN}{N+L_{\text{CP}}} & \text{OFDM} \\ \frac{Nm}{N+L_{\text{ZP}}+L_f-1} & \text{UFMC} \\ \frac{\beta m}{\beta+(K-\frac{1}{2})} & \text{FBMC} \end{cases} \tag{5}$$

where m is number of loaded bits in each subcarrier.

3.4 Computational Complexity

The computational complexity is evaluated in terms of the number of real valued multiplications and additions. To formulate the computational complexity of the proposed multicarrier modulation techniques, we assume the transmitter and the receiver are perfectly synchronized and there are N subcarriers from which N_0 is occupied with symbols. We only consider the signal generation, reception and equalization operation for the multicarrier signal. Whereas we do not consider the operation involved to channel encoder, decoder and channel estimation. Complex multiplication can be done with three real valued multiplication and complex addition requires two real valued multiplication. Thus, for N-point FFT the number of real valued additions and multiplications are given by [21]

$$
\begin{aligned}
A_{\text{FFT}} &= 3N \log_2 N - 3N + 4 \qquad \text{Addition} \\
M_{\text{FFT}} &= N \log_2 N - 3N + 4 \qquad \text{Mulitiplication.}
\end{aligned}
\tag{6}
$$

Based on the above assumptions, we calculate the complexity of the proposed multicarrier modulation techniques as follows.

Computational Complexity of CP-OFDM: The basic blocks in OFDM is the IFFT at the transmitter, the FFT and equalizers at the receiver. OFDM divides the total bandwidth into N-point IFFT/FFT, so the channel equalizer has single-tap coefficient per subcarrier. After some mathematical analysis, the total number of real valued multiplications and additions for OFDM with N-point FFT/IFFT using split-radix algorithm is summarized in Table 1 [21].

Table 1. Computational complexity of OFDM.

	Number of addition operation	Number of multiplication operation
Transmitter side	$3N \log_2 N - N + 2L_{\text{CP}} + 4$	$N(\log_2 N + 1) + 4L_{\text{CP}} + 4$
Receiver side	$3N \log_2 N - N + 2L_{\text{CP}} + 2N_0 + 4$	$N \log_2 N - 3N + 4N_0 + 4$

Computational Complexity of FBMC: The transmitter and receiver in FBMC systems are composed of filtering operation with N-parallel polyphase components working twice the symbol rate. The basic blocks which perform multiplication and addition are polyphase filter networks, OQAM pre/post-processing, and IFFT/FFT operation. The OQAM processing is considered to have only simple multiplication by ± 1 and $\pm j$ [5]. As shown in [2], the transmitter consists of N-point IFFT, N-branch polyphase filters with length of $L_p = KN$ and frequency shifting or phase rotation to get polyphase filters from the prototype. At the receiver side, the same operation is performed in reverse order. Thus, the total number of real valued multiplications and additions for FMBC systems with N-point FFT/IFFT using split-radix algorithm is summarized in Table 2.

Table 2. Computational complexity of FBMC with OQAM.

	Number of addition operation	Number of multiplication operation
Transmitter side	$2(3N(\log_2 N - 1) + 4) + 4N(K - 1) + 2N_0$	$2(N \log_2 N - 3N + 4) + 4NK + 4N_0$
Receiver side	$4N(K - 1) + 2(3N(\log_2 N - 1) + 4) + (4L_{eq} - 2)N_0$	$4NK + 4L_{eq}N_0 + 2(N \log_2 N - 3N + 4)$

Computational Complexity of UFMC: If we have B data blocks obtained by dividing N subcarriers, each block will have N/B subcarriers. The transmitter modulates each of the B-subbands as follows; first frequency domain symbols are brought to time domain using an N_{SB}-point IFFT where N_{SB} is the IFFT size on each subband. Then, filtering is performed in the frequency domain and all subbands are summed and transmitted. At the receiver side, windowing, $2N$-point FFT, equalization and signal recovery operation are performed. B number of IFFT with N_{SB} subbands results $M_{FFT}(N_{SB})$ complexity and to convert into frequency domain it results $M_{FFT}(2N_{SB})$ complexity at the receiver. Filtering each blocks with L-length filters result to $2N_{SB}$ complexity. Thus, the total number of real valued multiplications and additions for UFMC systems with N-point FFT/IFFT using split-radix algorithm is summarized in Table 3.

Table 3. Computational complexity of UFMC.

	Number of addition operation	Number of multiplication operation
Transmitter side	$B[A_{FFT}(N_{SB}) + A_{FFT}(2N_{SB})] + 4N_{SB}(B - 1) + A_{FFT}(2N)$	$B[M_{FFT}(N_{SB}) + M_{FFT}(2N_{SB}) + 8N_{SB}] + M_{FFT}(2N)$
Receiver side	$A_{FFT}(2N) + 2N_0$	$M_{FFT}(2N) + 4N_0$

Finally, the total computational complexity of each multicarrier modulation technique is calculated by adding the number of additions and multiplications on both the transmitter and receiver side.

4   Simulation Results and Analysis

4.1   Simulation Setup and Parameters

To compare the performances of the proposed multicarrier modulation techniques, we consider a single cell system with single antenna base station and a user with single receiving antenna. We also assume perfect channel state information both at the transmitter and receiver. Furthermore, we assume OFDM and UFMC waveforms employ guard intervals to mitigate inter symbol interference. Part of the simulation parameters considered in this work is shown in Table 4. The simulation parameters may vary in accordance with each comparison metrics.

Table 4. Parts of simulation parameters.

Parameters	Value	Remark
FFT size	64/1024	Vary as required
Subcarrier spacing	15 kHz	Same as LTE
Symbol mapping	16 QAM	Efficient scheme
OFDM parameters		
Length of CP	72	As in LTE
UFMC parameters		
Filter length	73	Assumed as $L_{cp} + 1$
Subband size	12	Proposed in [7]
Guard interval	72	Equal with CP
Size of FFT (N_{SB})	64	Consider to minimize computational complexity
FBMC parameters		
Overlapping	$K = 4$	Gives better sidelobe [2]
Prototype Filter	PHYDYAS filter	Proposed in [2]

4.2   Power Spectral Density (PSD) Comparison

Here, we analyze the normalized power spectral density of OFDM, FBMC and UFMC systems with respect to the normalized frequency. We consider 64-subcarriers with 15 kHz spacing and overlapping factor of 4. For UFMC, we use subband size of 12, Dolph-Chebyshev filter with stop-band attenuation of 40 dB [2]. The length of the filter is assumed to be the length of cyclic prefix plus one. The prototype filter for FBMC is PHYDYAS filter with length $L = NK$ at $K = 4$ [2]. Figure 1 shows the power spectral density of CP-OFDM, FBMC and UFMC.

The result shows that the proposed multicarrier modulation techniques have different side-lobe radiations. Having low out-of-band (OOB) emission is advantageous to support asynchronous transmission. It is shown that FBMC and UFMC achieve lower out-of-band emission compared to CP-OFDM. Due to the block filtering, UFMC achieves lower OOB leakage compared to OFDM but it is outperformed by FBMC. As shown in the figure, UFMC attains −60dB OOB emission around 33 normalized frequency. Whereas, OOB emission for FBMC decays completely before a normalized frequency of 20. FBMC can attain −60dB interference level easily which is sufficient to meet the regulatory constraints for many applications. Besides, low side-lobe level in FBMC allows advanced utilization of the allotted spectrum and this helps to improve the spectral efficiency.

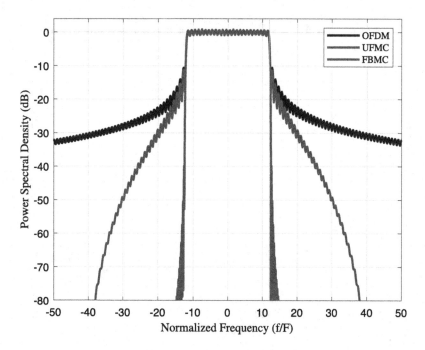

Fig. 1. Power spectral density of OFDM, UFMC, FBMC.

4.3 Spectral Efficiency Comparison

To evaluate the spectral efficiency, we consider the parameter based on LTE network with 10 MHz, QAM symbol mapping and an FFT size of 1024. For OFDM, size of CP is 72 samples. For UFMC, we use Dolph-Chebyshev filter of length 73 and length of padding is $L_{ZP} = 72$ with block size of 12. As discussed before, for CP-OFDM and UFMC the spectral efficiency is a function of the FFT size and modulation order but it is independent on the burst duration. Whereas in FBMC, it depends on the frame duration. To compare the proposed multicarrier modulation techniques, we calculate the number of bits that can be transmitted under given modulation efficiency and transmission time of 0.1-300 ms. The result in Fig. 2 shows that UFMC without guard interval gives nearly the same spectral efficiency to that of OFDM. But, in frequency selective fading channel the removal of guard interval results in degradation of the BER. So, we also include UFMC with zero padding (ZP) that help to mitigate ISI. This results lower spectral efficiency in UFMC. The spectral efficiency of FBMC is independent on type of propagation channel, because unlike UFMC and OFDM there is no extra guard interval insertion to mitigate the frequency selectivity of the channel.

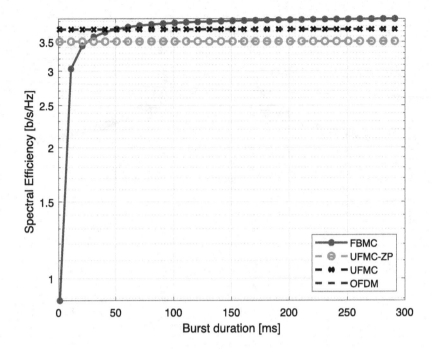

Fig. 2. Spectral efficiency of candidate multicarrier waveforms. We assume FFT size of $N = 1024$.

In Fig. 3, we plot the spectral efficiency by increasing the number of loaded bits in each subcarrier. The results shows that FBMC is not convenient at short transmission time. Whereas, the spectral efficiency of CP-OFDM and UFMC is independent on the burst duration. But, it is a function of FFT size and modulation parameters.

4.4   Bit Error Rate (BER) Comparison

To evaluate the BER performances of the candidate waveforms, we consider a carrier frequency of 2.5 GHz and an ITU-R Vehicular-A channel model with main parameters proposed in [19]. We use a Rayleigh fading propagation channel model with channel length and delay profile given in Table 5. The channel fading is assumed to be static for the duration of the symbol and perfect channel state information and synchronization are assumed. Besides, we use $N = 64$ subcarriers with 15 kHz subcarrier spacing for all waveforms. The measurements for the BER performance is taken with 300 channel realizations and 3 symbols for each channel realizations.

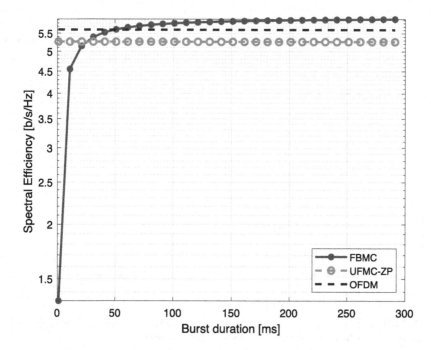

Fig. 3. Spectral efficiency of candidate multicarrier waveforms. We assume FFT size of $N = 1024$ and six bits are loaded on each subcarrier.

Table 5. Considered ITU-R vehicular A channel power delay profile [19].

Relative tap delay (ns)	Average power (dB)
0	0.0
310	−1
710	−9
1090	−10
1730	−15
2510	−20

Figure 4(a) shows the BER performances of the proposed waveforms when the Doppler frequency is zero ($f_d = 0$ Hz). Since, ISI caused by multipath has been completely canceled by the insertion of CP, OFDM has better performance at low Doppler frequency. Also, the UFMC curve is almost aligned with CP-OFDM. Which is achieved by zero padding with length of CP. While for FBMC, since the bandwidth of each subcarrier is small enough to make the channel approximately flat, the ISI introduced by pulse shaping is nearly imaginary. Therefore, FBMC is approximately orthogonal in the real domain and this gives good BER performance. But, compared to UFMC and OFDM, additional 1.4 dB is required to achieve a BER of 10^{-3}. We also show the result by increasing the Doppler frequency (f_d = 300 Hz). Since the delay spread become longer and channel become more frequency selective which is difficult to estimate and tracked accurately, the performances of all the waveforms degrade significantly as shown in Fig. 4(b).

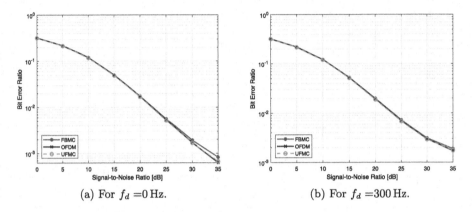

(a) For f_d =0 Hz.   (b) For f_d =300 Hz.

Fig. 4. BER performance of candidate waveforms in ITU-R Vehicular A channel model. The number of subcarrier is 64 with 6 bits in each subcarrier.

4.5   Computational Complexity Comparison

To compare the computational complexity of the candidate multicarrier modulation techniques, we consider a downlink system with single antenna configuration both at the user and the BS. The results are obtained by considering low complex equivalent implementations of the transceivers presented in Sect. 3. Figure 5 shows the number of real valued multiplications for the proposed multicarrier modulation techniques with respect to the length of the transmitted symbols. The result shows that when the number of transmitted symbol increases, the number of real valued multiplication is also increased.

We also evaluate the computational complexity by assessing the numerical overhead of the candidate waveforms under two different scenarios. For this evaluation, we assume an FFT size of $N = 1024$ with subcarrier spacing of 15kHz, transmission bandwidth of 10 MHz and maximum number of subcarrier fitting to given bandwidth is 665. To minimize the interface in asynchronous transmission, we use the number of guard subcarriers proposed in [17]. Accordingly, the number of subcarriers that actually carry data symbols is assumed to be $N_0 = 664$ for FBMC, $N_0 = 586$ for CP-OFDM and $N_0 = 658$ for UFMC. We consider the complexity due to data symbol processing only. Hence, the complexity due to channel estimation, channel encoding/decoding, synchronization and pilot symbol generation are neglected here.

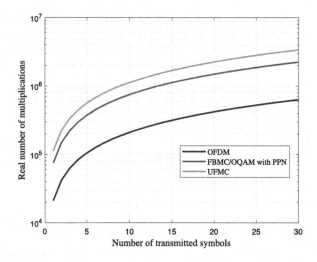

Fig. 5. Computational complexity of considered multicarrier modulation techniques.

We assume two deferent propagation scenarios. In the first case, ITU-R Vehicular-A channel model with medium delay spread is considered. As discussed in [20], with Vehicular-A channel model, assuming that the receiver is well synchronized both in time and frequency, it is sufficient to use one tap equalizer for FBMC. Longer equalizers may require to compensate synchronization imperfections but it adds the complexity. In OFDM, the CP length is assumed to be $L_{cp} = 1/14$ of useful symbol duration. In the second case, we assume high frequency-selective Vehicular-B channel model that is considered in 3GPP-LTE system development [20]. Here, we use longer sub-channel equalizer in FBMC with $L_{eq} = 5$ and the guard intervals in OFDM is increased to $L_{cp} = 1/8$ of the useful symbol. The zero prefix of UFMC is assumed to have the same length to the cyclic prefix of OFDM.

Table 6 summarizes the computational complexity of each waveforms under the proposed system setups. The results show that both UFMC and FBMC have higher computational complexity than OFDM. With optimized implementation, FBMC requires 3.6× more real number of multiplications than OFDM to transmit the same amount of symbols. This is due to addition of filtering operation and increase on length of equalizer to mitigate the frequency selectivity of the channel. Efficient implementation of UFMC results around 5.5× more complexity than OFDM.

Table 6. Number of multiplications and additions at two different scenarios.

Multicarrier techniques	Real number of	Case I	Case II
OFDM	Multiplications	21,800	22,024
	Additions	59,032	59,144
UFMC	Multiplications	122,376	122,376
	Additions	354,052	354,052
FBMC	Multiplications	67,600	79,888
	Additions	138,256	150,544

5   Conclusion

In this work, we evaluate the performances of FBMC and UFMC in terms of power spectral density, BER, spectral efficiency and computational complexity. The result shows that FBMC has lower OOB emission due to pulse-shaping filters instead of rectangular windows employed in OFDM systems. Besides, FBMC is almost insensitive to multiuser interference. Due to block filtering, UFMC achieves lower OOB leakage compared to OFDM but it is outperformed by FBMC. It is also shown that, when the transmission time gets longer, the spectral efficiency of FBMC is outperforming that of OFDM and UFMC. But, during short burst transmission, FBMC suffers from long filter tails and the spectral efficiency is lower than UFMC and OFDM. The spectral efficiency of UFMC is lower than OFDM due to its filter tails in addition to the guard interval.

We also show that under high fading environment, waveforms with sufficient guard interval has the best performance. However, addition of guard interval costs the spectral efficiency. Besides, the computational complexity of the proposed waveforms at the propagation channel with medium to high delay spread is provided. The result shows that the complexity of FBMC and UFMC is higher than OFDM. This is mainly due to filtering operation and multi-tap equalizers to mitigate channel interference.

References

1. Luo, F.-L., Zhang, C.: Signal Processing for 5G: Algorithms and Implementations. Wiley, Hoboken (2016)
2. Bellanger, M., et al.: FBMC physical layer: a primer. PHYDYAS **25**, 7–10 (2010)
3. Farhang-Boroujeny, B.: Filter bank multicarrier modulation: a waveform candidate for 5G and beyond. Hindawi Adv. Electr. Eng. (2014)
4. IMT vision: Framework and overall objectives of the future development of IMT for 2020 and beyond. International Telecommunication Union, Geneva, Switzerland, Recommendation ITU-R M.2083, September 2015
5. Farhang-Boroujeny, B.: OFDM versus filter bank multicarrier. IEEE Signal Process. Mag. **28**(3), 92–112 (2011)
6. Banelli, P., et al.: Modulation formats and waveforms for the physical layer of 5G wireless networks: who will be the heir of OFDM? arXiv:1407.5947, July 2014

7. Schaich, F., Wild, T., Chen, Y.: Waveform contenders for 5G-suitability for short packet and low latency transmissions. In: IEEE Vehicular Technology Conference (VTC-Spring), pp. 1–5 (2014)
8. Cai, Y., Qin, Z., Cui, F., Li, G.Y., McCann, J.A.: Modulation and multiple access for 5G networks. IEEE Commun. Surv. Tutor. **20**(1), 629–646 (2018)
9. Gerzaguet, R., Ktenas, D., Cassiau, N., Dore, J.B.: Comparative study of 5G waveform candidates for below 6 GHz air interface. In: Proceedings of the ETSI Workshop Future Radio Technology Focusing Air Interface (2016)
10. Liu, Y.., et al.: Waveform candidates for 5G networks: analysis and Comparison. arXiv:1609.02427v1 (2016)
11. Fazel, K., Kaiser, S.: Multicarrier and Spread Spectrum Systems: From OFDM and MC-CDMA to LTE and WiMAX, 2nd edn. Wiley, Hoboken (2008)
12. Prasad, R., Hara, S.: Multicarrier Techniques for 4G Mobile Communications. Artech House (2013)
13. Bellanger, M.: FS-FBMC: an alternative scheme for filter bank multicarrier transmission. In: 5th International Symposium on Communications, Control and Signal Processing, pp. 1–4 (2012)
14. Doré, J.B., Gerzaguet, R., Cassiau, N., Kténas, D.: Waveform contenders for 5G: description, analysis and comparison. Phys. Commun. **42**, 46–61 (2017)
15. Vakilian, V., Wild, T., Schaich, F., Ten-Brink, S., Frigon, J.-F.: Universal-filtered multicarrier technique for wireless systems beyond LTE. In: IEEE Globecom Workshop, pp. 223–228 (2013)
16. Knopp, R., Kaltenberger, F., Vitiello, C., Luis, M.: Universal filtered multicarrier for machine type communication in 5G. In: European Conference on Networks and Communications (2016)
17. Van Eeckhaute, M., et al.: Performance of emerging multicarrier waveforms for 5G asynchronous communications. EURASIP J. Wirel. Commun. Netw. **29**, 1–15 (2017)
18. Zhang, X., Chen, L., Qiu, J., Abdoli, J.: On the waveform for 5G. IEEE Commun. Mag. **54**(11), 74–80 (2016)
19. Zhang, X., Chen, L., Qiu, J., Abdoli, J.: Guidelines for evaluation of radio interface technologies for IMT-advanced. Report ITU-R M.2135-1 (2009)
20. European project ICT-211887 PHYDYAS, Deliverable D3.1: Transmit/receive processing (single antenna), Technical report, July 2008
21. Gerzaguet, R., et al.: The 5G candidate waveform race: a comparison of complexity and performance. EURASIP J. Wirel. Commun. Netw. (2017)
22. Taher, M.A., Kutheir, K.H.: FBMC as 5G candidate for high speed mobility. In: IOP Conference Series: Materials Science and Engineering, vol. 557, pp. 12–40 (2019)
23. Demir, A.F., Elkourdi, M., Ibrahim, M., Arslan, H.: Waveform Design for 5G and Beyond. arXiv:1902.05999 [eess.SP] (2019)
24. Shaiek, H., Zayani, R., Medjahdi, Y., Roviras, D.: Analytical analysis of SER for beyond 5G post-OFDM waveforms in presence of high power amplifiers. IEEE Access **7**, 29441–29452 (2019)

Synchronous Generator Excitation Loss Detection Based on Reactive Power Flow Limit

Alganesh Ygzaw[✉], Habtemariam Aberie, Kassaye Gizaw, and Belachew Bantyirga

Bahir Dar Institute of Technology, Bahir Dar University, Bahir, Ethiopia

Abstract. The direct current from the excitation system sustains the stator and rotor magnetically coupled with spawning reactive power in the generator. Though, any excitation system failure grades to generator loss of excitation and suspend power transmission from the generating unit to the grid. This paper presents a new excitation loss protection scheme based on the study of field voltage, quadrature axis voltage, and reactive power under specified system voltage. The proposed algorithm limits the reactive power consumption of the faulted generator to the ability of the system to feed the faulted generator without system loss of stability. In this paper, the IEEE-9 bus system is used to study the proposed approach to various excitation loss events. And the results showed that the new algorithm not only overwhelmed the mal-operation of the excitation loss relay but also detects all possible excitation failures without system collapse in a short time.

Keywords: Excitation loss protection · Reactive power limit · Synchronous generator

1 Introduction

Ever since discovered, electrical energy has gradually transformed life activities into easy and labor-intensive systems. On the other hand, the unprotected and unsecured transmission of electrical energy can cause serious damage to living things and their properties. So, a modern power system concern must be consistency and security on all parts of the power system (generation unit, transmission unit, and distribution unit) [1]. First and foremost, the efficacy of energy transmission mainly depends on synchronous generating machines as they are the source of energy. In a normal state, generators can produce and deliver active power due to the mechanical input and reactive power due to the field voltage from the excitation system [1]. However, any failure in the excitation system grades excitation loss in the generator and suddenly the machine will start to consume reactive power from the grid-connected with it to stay excited [2]. This results in voltage and current instability, generator over speed, and if it continues to a blackout of the whole system [3, 4]. This instability after excitation failure may lead to complete or partial excitation loss of the synchronous generator. Complete loss of excitation occurs when field winding open circuit, short circuit or sudden opening of the field supply breaker happen whereas partial loss of excitation can occur when suddenly

M. A. Delele et al. (Eds.): ICAST 2020, LNICST 384, pp. 200–214, 2021.
https://doi.org/10.1007/978-3-030-80621-7_15

field voltage drop or short-circuiting in a section of the field winding happens [2]. No matter how it is caused, loss of excitation represents huge damage to the generator and the whole system if early protection is apprehended. In 1949, Mason [5] suggested an impedance protection method using generator terminal voltage and current to protect Loss of Excitation (LOE). This method uses a negative off-set mho-type distance relay to sense the generator impedance variation in excitation loss condition. If the impedance of the generator falls under a predefined protective zone in the R-X plane, the relay detects loss of excitation and sends a trip signal to the field breaker. In 1975, Berdy [6] presented a method based on the addition of another mho unit to Mason's protection scheme aimed to protect lightly loaded generators. This type of protection is the most common method of LOE protection which detects the generator terminal parameter variation at any cause of excitation failures and it is the actual technique used in most power system industries until now. Later on, the impedance protection scheme was modified using modern computational methods such as neural networks [7, 8], decision tree [9], and fuzzy [10] algorithms which comparatively present good results. However, these methods require a considerable amount of training and their protection scheme mainly consists of a complex simulation scenario. With the help of digital relays, quadrangular lay which uses the rate of change of the reactance seen in the terminals of the machine was proposed in 2005, by S. R. Tambay and Y. G. Paithankar [11]. Similarly, another method based on the Space Vector Machine (SVM) technique to discriminate between Loss of Field (LOF) and stable power swing (SPS) is presented in [12]. However, both of the above-mentioned schemes need a significant amount of data for training. In 2016, Behnam M. and Jian Guo Zhu, [13] presented a setting free approach using resistance variation at the generator terminal as an excitation loss detector where the derivation of the resistance will become and remain negative a short period after the LOE event occurred. Though, the algorithm may reset for loss of excitation events with high slip frequency due to an oscillatory nature of resistance in variable speed associated with slip frequency.

M. Abedini et al. [14] proposed an analytical method using the rate of decay of the generator internal voltage with the field flux linkage variation. An adaptive and threshold loss of excitation index is introduced depend on terminal voltage to discriminate system disturbance from excitation failure such if the generator achieves a greater excitation loss index for a given sample, the loss of excitation will be detected. This method has accurate sensing results since it uses the capability curve of the generator, however, the setpoints identification is a difficult task and may involve extensive simulation processes that make it unpractical. Those authors modify the mentioned criterion in 2017 [15], which uses the Fast Fourier Transform (FFT) coefficient of three-phase active power to prevent the mentioned algorithm from mal-operation in the face of Stable Power Swig (SPS). Excitation loss detection through generator internal parameters can be evaluated also using flux interaction of the stator and rotor windings, internal voltage, or internal current measurements. A flux-based method is presented in [16], which uses the installed search coils in stator slots to measure the air-gap flux. This scheme, however, should normally be implemented by the generator manufacturer. In this paper, a new excitation loss protection scheme is proposed based on the variation of reactive power, quadrature axis voltage, and field voltage which are the parameters noticeably reduce in the excitation loss event. After calculating the minimum possible value of quadrature axis voltage using the generator measurable signals, the total amount of reactive power that the system can afford to feed faulted generator without system instability will be evaluated with low computational complications.

1.1 Generator Characteristics in Excitation Loss Event

Any synchronous generator has two inputs, torque input from a turbine coupled to its rotor and an excitation current coupled to the field winding of a rotor [1, 17]. Thus, the mathematical model of a synchronous machine is given by a set of differential equations representing the dynamics of the machine, exciters, and other controls and algebraic equations representing the network relation [18]. In this paper, a fourth-order (two-axis) generator model which neglects sub-transient effects is used as presented in [17] in the following equations.

$$T_e = E_d' i_d + E_q' i_q + (X_d' - X_q') i_q i_d \tag{1}$$

$$\omega_m' = \frac{1}{2H} [P_m - P_e - D(\omega - \omega_s)] \tag{2}$$

Where ωs is the synchronous speed, $\Delta \omega$ speed deviation, ω generator speed, Pm is mechanical power and Pe is electrical power. The d-axis and q-axis voltages and field voltage of the synchronous generator are also given as the following equations.

$$\frac{d}{dt} E_q' = \frac{1}{T_{d0}'} [(-E_q' + (X_d - X_d') i_d) + E_{fd}] \tag{3}$$

$$\frac{d}{dt} E_d' = \frac{1}{T_{q0}'} [(-E_d' - (X_q - X_q') i_q)] \tag{4}$$

Also the generator terminal parameters are given as the following equations.

$$V_t = V_d + j V_q \tag{5}$$

$$I_t = i_d + j i_q \tag{6}$$

Where the d-axis and q-axis currents are given as:

$$i_d = \frac{E_q' - V_q}{X_d'} \text{ And } i_q = \frac{V_d - E_d'}{X_q'}$$

$$P_t = V_d i_d + V_q i_q \tag{7}$$

$$Q_t = V_q i_d - V_d i_q \tag{8}$$

The main electrical and mechanical quantities of the generator including voltage, current, and rotation speed will deviate from the related steady-state values during the

LOE event. In the loss of excitation, the apparent power of a synchronous generator falls off to zero within a short time [1, 2] which causes a mismatch between the mechanical power input and the electrical power output. Generator speed rises exponentially and eventually reaches asynchronous conditions. At this point, the mechanical power produced by the turbine equates with the asynchronously developed electrical power [9].

To study the excitation loss event on a synchronous generator, the IEEE 9-bus test system has been modeled on MATLAB/SIMULINK as shown in the following figure. Also, the parameters of the generator under study are given in Table 1.

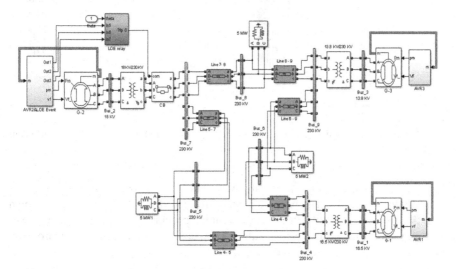

Fig. 1. SIMULINK model of IEEE 9-bus system

Table 1. Parameters of generators under study

Generator	MVA	kV	X_d	X'_d	T'_{do}
G-2	192	18	1.72	0.23	8

$$V_t = V_d + jV_q = \frac{X'_d - X_q}{1 + sT'_{q0}} i_q - R_a i_d - X'_d i_q + j(\frac{X'_d - X_d}{1 + sT'_{d0}} i_d + \frac{E_{fd}}{1 + sT'_{d0}} - R_a i_q + X'_d i_d)$$

(9)

$$e_i = E'_d + jE'_q = \frac{X'_d - X_q}{1 + sT'_{q0}} i_q + j(\frac{X'_d - X_d}{1 + sT'_{d0}} i_d + \frac{E_{fd}}{1 + sT'_{d0}})$$ (10)

As can be seen from Eqs. (9 and 10) and Fig. 2a, the terminal and internal voltage of the synchronous generator varies with generator field voltage reduction. Comparatively, the q-axis voltage diminishes faster than the other parameters as shown in Fig. 1b and

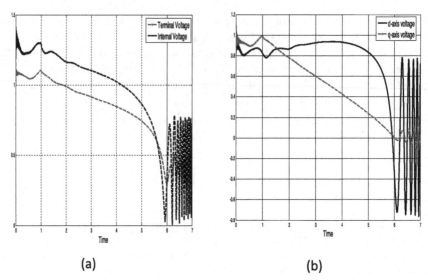

(a)   (b)

Fig. 2. Generator (a) Terminal and internal voltage (b) q-axis and d-axis voltage in LOE event created at 1 s

Eq. (3). This indicates that the terminal parameters of the generator are composted by the condition of the gird. The reactive power will indeed reduce to negative as shown in Fig. 3a. So does the reality, in the LOE event the generator consumes reactive power from the system. And the active power almost remains constant till loss of synchronism.

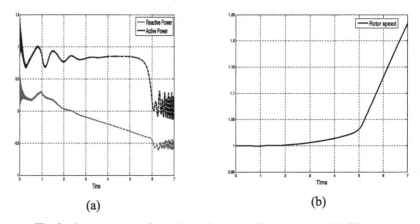

(a)   (b)

Fig. 3. Generator (a) active and reactive power (b) rotor speed in LOE event

If the system can feed the excitation system a reactive power, the generator parameters remains in synchronism. However, the moment the system stops reactive power feeding to a generator, the whole system loses synchronism. In this simulation, as can be shown in Fig. 3, LOE event is created in 1s and the generator loses synchronism after 4.23 s.

$$\omega = \frac{R_a i_d + V_d}{\Psi_q} = \frac{R_a i_d + V_d}{-E'_d - X'_q i_q} \tag{11}$$

Where the d-axis and q-axis induced stator flux linkages are given as:

$$\Psi_q = -E'_d - X'_q i_q \ \text{And} \ \Psi_d = E'_q - X'_d i_d$$

The speed of the generator rises under the loss of excitation event as shown in Fig. 3b. When the speed of the generator increases above the synchronous speed, the machine will act like an induction generator which induces rotor surface slip currents. This is because the speed of a rotating magnetic field is proportional to the frequency of excitation current. Voltage in excitation loss depresses to such extent under-voltage relays may sense it. This reduces the terminal impedance of a generator which can be expressed in terms of terminal voltage and current as of the following equation.

$$Z = \frac{V}{I} = R + jX = \frac{V^2 P_t}{P_t^2 + Q_t^2} + j\frac{V^2 Q_t}{P_t^2 + Q_t^2} \tag{12}$$

In excitation loss event, the resistance of the generator declines to zero gradually proportional to terminal voltage decay, and terminal reactance decreases to a negative value proportional to reactive power decline as can be shown in Fig. 4a. This results in terminal impedance reduction in the excitation loss event.

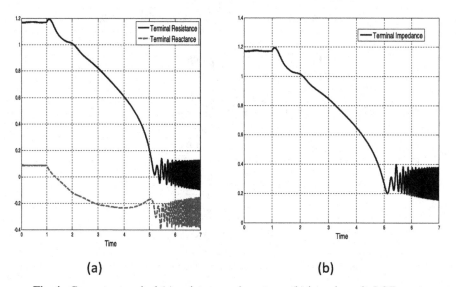

(a)   (b)

Fig. 4. Generator terminal (a) resistance and reactance (b) impedance in LOE event

2 Proposed Excitation Loss Detection Scheme

The main factors that affect the operation range of synchronous generator are armature current, terminal voltage, the limit of stability, field current, initial loading capacity, and minimum possible excitation. Thus, any variations of these parameters jeopardize the stability of the machine and the system as a whole.

In any LOE event, the field voltage noticeably decreases from the initial value and so the reactive power. Here, the reactive power keeps reducing to negative value until the generator loses synchronism if any action is not taken. In some conditions of system disturbances, the reactive power also reduces to negative but the field voltage raise in value to pay off the terminal voltage reduction. In this section, the stability of the system in loss of excitation will be studied to calculate the reactive power margin of a generator at a specified field voltage using the q-axis voltage decay in the excitation loss event. The general scheme of the proposed algorithm can be sum up as Fig. 5 flow chart. The q-axis voltage is highly dependent on field components and it is reasonable that its response really fasts for field failures than other parameters of the generator.

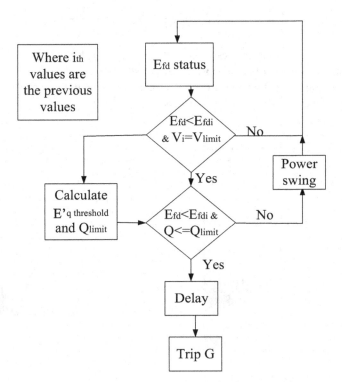

Fig. 5. Flow chart of proposed excitation loss protection

The minimum quadrature axis voltage reduction that leads to voltage collapse of the system will be calculated from the terminal voltage and field voltage of the generator. And this will be the threshold and minimum q-axis voltage that keep the system instability at any moment.

$$E'_q = i_d X'_d + v_q = \frac{X'_d}{\frac{X'_d - X_d}{1 + sT'_{d0}} + X'_d}(V_q + R_a i_q - \frac{E_{fd}}{1 + sT'_{d0}}) + V_t \sin(\delta) \qquad (13)$$

At the specified margin of terminal voltage, the q-axis voltage can be calculated from Eq. (13) above. The threshold q-axis voltage is also used to identify the minimum possible value of reactive power the system can feed the faulted generator without system collapse. Limiting the reactive power consumption of the generator will be the main concern of this proposed algorithm since the actual excitation loss relay mal-operation is due to the algorithm fails to limit the possible capability reactive power to the generator in excitation loss condition. In some kinds of literature, this concept has been used to detect excitation loss [19] but the unpredictable behavior of power systems in light load conditions, partial loss of field, and system outages have been threatening them. So, in this algorithm limiting the reactive power consumption with the internal field component will increase the sensitivity of the method for excitation loss event than system disturbances. Synchronous generator reactive power consumption ability in a given field voltage is highly dependent on the initial MW output of the machine. To understand the algorithm in different loading conditions, active power status is also one factor to identify the reactive power consumed by the generator. Thus, the reactive power of the synchronous generator in Eq. (8) can be re-formulated in terms of q-axis voltage and active power as the following equation.

$$Q_t = E'_{qthre} i_d - X'_d i_d^2 - (\frac{P_t - V_q i_q}{i_d}) i_q \qquad (14)$$

Where e'qthre is the threshold q-axis voltage and Pt the output active power of the synchronous generator. This reactive power identifies the ability of the system to recover the reactive power loss due to the excitation loss generator at the same time it is the amount of reactive power consumed by the faulted generator without voltage collapse. If the synchronous generator model considers sub-transient components, the generator parameters swing in the normal state should be counted through a reasonable time delay for tripping the generator. In this work, the two-axis generator model has been used so the transient characteristics of the generator have been considered with a time delay of 0.81 s.

The conventional method of excitation loss protection is based on the calculation of the impedance at the generator terminal. It has two circle zones plotted in the negative reactance coordinate of the R-X plane with offset value X'd/2 and with circle zones of 1pu and Xd for zone-1 and zone-2 respectively [6]. If the R-X value of the generator entered the protection zones of the relay, a trip signal will be sent after a pre-determined time delay. The relay has good performance in the full loss of excitation but it mal-operates in some partial loss excitation and power system disturbances. Figure 6 expresses the reactive power-voltage (Q-V) curve of LOE relay and the proposed algorithm in full and partial loss of excitation. In full loss of excitation, the generator consumes reactive power until the terminal voltage of the generator diminish to 0.289 pu before excitation loss relay detect the event. However, in the proposed scheme the generator was able to consume reactive power until the terminal voltage reduce to 0.86pu. Similarly in partial loss of excitation, the back-up protection have response faster than LOE relay as given in Fig. 6b. At the same loading condition, generator reactive power consumption is the same despite the type of excitation loss.

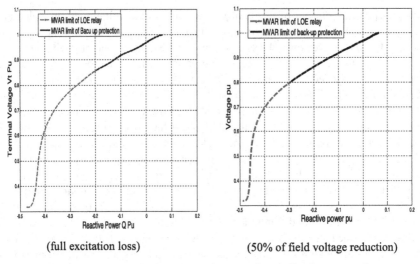

(full excitation loss)　　　　　　　　　(50% of field voltage reduction)

Fig. 6. Q-V curve of LOE relay and proposed excitation loss protection

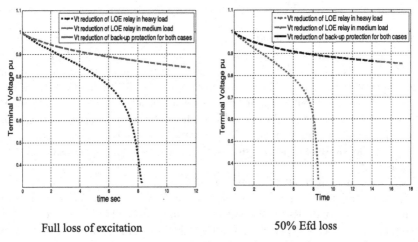

Full loss of excitation　　　　　　　　　50% Efd loss

Fig. 7. Terminal voltage reduction in LOE relay and back-up protection

On the other hand on the same type of excitation loss type, power consumption differs for various initial loading conditions. Thus, for 50% field voltage loss, the generator was able to consume reactive power until 0.289 pu terminal voltage reduction before detected through the LOE relay in heavy load condition which is similar to a full loss of excitation. As shown in Fig. 7, limiting reactive power consumption of faulted generator have maintained the system from voltage collapse and system loss of stability. In the proposed algorithm, the terminal voltage of the generator is kept at 0.86 pu for both full and partial loss of excitation. However, in the conventional relay, the terminal voltage reduced 0.28 pu before the relay detects the failure which may further jeopardize system stability in addition to generator excitation loss.

2.1 Results and Discussions

Full Loss of Excitation

The generator loses its excitation completely when the field voltage or field current supplied to the synchronous generator from the excitation system is lost and the excitation system fails to excite the synchronous generator completely. In this condition, the synchronous generator can produce active power due to the mechanical input but it completely stops producing reactive power. Full loss of excitation is initiated either due to field winding failure, main circuit breaker between the excitation system and generator failure, or sudden AC voltage loss to the exciter. Table 2 shows the comparison of excitation loss relay and the proposed back-up protection in the full loss of excitation. The back-up protection has improved the time elapsed to detect excitation loss and reactive power consumption limit of the generator. In field winding short circuit case, the proposed algorithm detects full loss of excitation 1.857 s after fault happen which is 2.303 s before the LOE relay. Similarly, for medium and light loaded generators the detection length has improved to about 16% of excitation loss relay. The excitation loss relay (impedance protection) have also detected full loss of excitation in less than 6.5 s in all loading conditions.

Table 2. Comparison of actual and proposed excitation loss detection in field winding short circuit

Initial loading (pu)	Tripping duration (sec)		Possible MVAR consumed by G-2 before fault detected (pu)	
	LOE relay	Proposed	LOE relay	Proposed
Heavy load	4.16	1.857	−0.431	−0.194
Medium load	5.804	4.537	−0.321	−0.2688
Light load	6.286	4.104	−0.231	−0.2055

Partial Loss of Excitation

Partial loss of excitation happens when the field winding voltage of the generator decrease in value for any reason. In heavily loaded generators it may cause severe damages as much as a full loss of excitation.

In PLOE, the filed voltage does not subject to null, so there will be some reactive power generation but not enough to feed the system so the generator still consumes

Table 3. Comparison of actual and proposed excitation loss detection in partial field voltage loss

%Efd loss	Initial loading (in pu)	Tripping status Y (sec)/N		Possible MVAR consumed by G-2 before fault detected (pu)	
		LOE relay	Proposed	LOE relay	Proposed
20%	H	26.46	12.86	−0.4897	−0.204
	M	N	N	−0.2720 (in 30 s)	−0.116 (in 30 s)
	L	N	N	−0.1906 (in 30 s)	−0.05 (in 30 s)
30%	H	15.21	7.24	−0.4882	−0.2021
	M	N	29.017	−0.2735 (in 30 s)	−0.19
	L	N	N	−0.1909 (in 30 s)	−0.101 (in 30 s)
40%	H	10.94	5.075	−0.4883	−0.198
	M	N	28.72	−0.2805 (in 30 s)	−0.264
	L	N	29.803	−0.1909 (in 30 s)	−0.1802
50%	H	8.563	3.935	−0.4887	−0.1957
	M	17.19	14.33	−0.2837	−0.2645
	L	N	15.37	−0.191	−0.1907
60%	H	6.99	3.22	−0.4858	−0.1945
	M	11.96	9.948	−0.2885	−0.266
	L	9.673	9.402	−0.198	−0.1965
70%	H	5.913	2.724	−0.482	−0.1938
	M	9.242	7.648	−0.2919	−0.2669
	L	7.332	7.11	−0.2076	−0.2045
80%	H	5.153	2.359	−0.4792	−0.1929
	M	7.632	6.216	−0.296	−0.265
	L	6.143	5.697	−0.216	−0.206
90%	H	4.592	2.079	−0.4768	−0.1939
	M	6.569	5.241	−0.3669	−0.268
	L	5.383	4.773	−0.2236	−0.2056

reactive power from the system even if that is slower than a full loss of excitation. To verify the reliability of the protection schemes in different LOE events, the method has been tested in all possible partial loss of field voltage in three different loading conditions as shown in Table 3. Similarly to a full loss of excitation, the proposed algorithm detects partial loss of excitation in heavily loaded generators twice less time than LOE relay in all possible field voltage reduction. LOE relay is not able to detect field voltage reduction until half of the rated value in medium and light loaded generators, and the proposed method has improved this.

LOE relay and also the proposed back-up protection have found not detecting 20% field voltage for medium and light load conditions and 30%Efd loss for light load condition. However, from the parameter variation of the generator and the whole system as shown in Fig. 8, the terminal voltage of the generator remains above 0.93pu. And this voltage value is a stable voltage range. So, the generator should not be tripped for the stable case since the un-necessary eliminating of synchronous generators will further jeopardize system stability despite its economic issue.

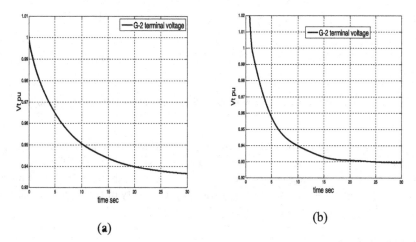

(a)

(b)

Fig. 8. Generator terminal voltage in partial loss of excitation (a) medium load 20%Efd loss (b) light load 30%Efd loss

Power Swing

Power swing is the oscillation of the machine rotor angle due to power system disturbances like a fault, generator, or line outages and load propagation that alters the mechanical equilibrium of one or more machines. LOE relay has mal-operate for severe power swings as having shown in Table 3. SPS and out of step conditions are simulated by three-phase to ground fault at G-2 terminal with pre-fault initial condition of 0.8485 + j0.06307 pu. In Out of Step (OOS) condition the generator becomes unstable and should be isolated from the remaining system but LOE protection should not give any response for this condition. LOE relay had actually detected a loss of synchronism which was caused by prolonged fault clearing times even in a short period of time than LOE event as shown in Fig. 9.

From the simulation results summarized in Table 4, all the mal-operation of LOE relay in system disturbance have overcome through the proposed excitation loss protection. In LOE and SPS event created at 1s, the LOE relay send a trip signal after 0.15 s SPS happened which is before the LOE event detected through the relay but the proposed algorithm sends a trip signal after 1.857 s which is the duration LOE event should be detected.

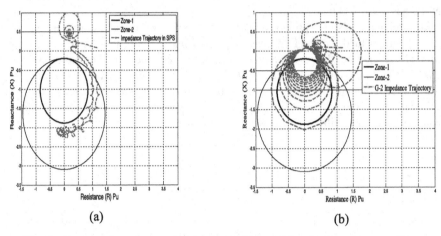

        (a)   (b)

Fig. 9. Generator impedance trajectory in (a) SPS condition (b) Out of step condition

From the simulation results, the proposed algorithm has differentiated any excitation loss event from any system disturbance such no trip signal is issued for any power swings. And while detecting the excitation failure, system stability is held by limiting the reactive power consumption of the generator to the ability of the system to feed the faulted machine without system collapse.

Table 4. Comparison of actual and proposed excitation loss detection in system disturbances

System disturbances	Fault clearing time (ms)	Tripping status Y (sec)/N	
		LOE relay	Proposed
SPS	100	N	N
	150	N	N
	200	Y (1.15 s)	N
OOS	250	Y (0.856)	N
	350	Y (0.420)	N

(continued)

Table 4. (*continued*)

System disturbances	Fault clearing time (ms)	Tripping status Y (sec)/N	
		LOE relay	Proposed
G3 outage and 100MW load addition in bus-2	–	N	N
G2-outage	–	N	N
G2&G3 outage	–	N	N
L5–7 outage	–	N	N
Load rejection at bus-6	–	N	N
Load rejection at bus-5 and short circuit fault at L8–9	100	N	N
SPS and LOE at 1s	200	Y (1.15 s)	Y (1.857)

3 Conclusion

Excitation loss not only imperils the faulted generator but also the whole system's stability due to electrical and mechanical power imbalance on the generator. Strictly limiting reactive power flow from the system to the generator using quadrature axis voltage has kept the system in stable condition even in the excitation loss event. Thus, the proposed algorithm has improved the detection time elapse to twice less for heavily loaded generators and almost 16% less for lightly loaded generators than LOE relay, detects the failure before system collapse, differentiates all system failures and excitation loss events, and have detected all the possible partial loss of excitation that can lead to system instabilities.

References

1. Kundur, P.: Power System Stability and Control. McGraw-Hill, New York (1994)
2. Me'ster, M., Kri'stof, V.: Loss of excitation of synchronous generator. J. Electr. Eng. **68**, 54–60 (2017)
3. Hasani, A., Haghjoo, F.: A secure and setting free technique to detect loss of field in synchronus generators. IEEE Trans. Energy Convers. **32**, 1512–1522 (2017)
4. Naser, N., et al.: Analytical technique for synchronous generators loss of excitation protection. The Institution of Engineering and technology, March 2017
5. Mason, C.R.: New loss-of-excitation relay for synchronous generators. Trans. Am. Inst. Electr. Eng. **68**(2), 1240–1245 (1949)
6. Berdy, J.: Loss of excitation protection for modern synchronous generators. IEEE Trans. Power Appar. Syst. **94**(5), 1457–1463 (1975)
7. Sharaf, A.M., Lie, T.T.: ANN based pattern classification of synchronous generator stability and loss of excitation. IEEE Trans. Energy Convers. **9**(4), 753–759 (1994)
8. Fan, B., et al.: The research UL-P of loss-of- excitation protection for generator based on the artificial neural networks. In: Asia-Pacific Power and Energy, pp. 1–4 (2009)

9. Amraee, T.: Loss of field detection in synchronous generators using decision tree technique. IET Gener. Transm. Distrib. **7**(9), 943–954 (2013)
10. de Morais, A.P., et al.: An innovative loss-of- excitation protection based on the fuzzy inference mechanism. IEEE Trans. Power Delivery **25**(4), 2197–2204 (2010)
11. Tambay, S.R., Paithankar, Y.G.: A new adaptive loss of excitation relay augmented by rate of change of reactance. In: IEEE Power Engineering Society General Meeting, vol. 2, pp. 1831–1835 (20050
12. Gokaraju, R., Sachdey, M.S., Ajuelo, E.: identification of generator loss-of-excitation from power-swing conditions using a fast pattern classification method. IET Gener. Transm. Distrib. **7**(1), 24–36 (2013)
13. Zhu, J.G., Mahamedi, B.: A setting-free approach to detecting loss of excitation in synchronous generators (2016)
14. Pasand, M.S., Abedini, M.: An analytical approach to detect generator loss of excitation based on internal voltage calculation. IEEE Trans. Power Deliv. **32**, 2329–2338 (2017)
15. Pasand, M.S., Abedini, M.: Flux linkage estimation based loss of excitation relay for synchronous generator. IET Gener. Transm. Distrib. **11**(1), 280–288 (2017)
16. Yaghobi, H., et al.: Study on application of flux linkage of synchronous generator for loss of excitation detection. Int. Trans. Electr. Energy Syst. **23**(6), 802–817 (2013)
17. Sauer, P.W., Pai, M.A.: Power System Dynamics and Stability. Prentice Hall, Hoboken (1998)
18. Padiyar, K.R.: Power System Dynamics: Stability & Control (2004)
19. Mozina, C.J., Reichard, M., et al.: Coordination of generator protection with generator excitation control and generator capability. In: IEEE Power Engineering Society General Meeting, pp. 1-4244-1298-6/07 (2007)

Estimation of Synchrophasor Parameters in the Presence of 3rd & 5th Harmonics and White Gaussian Noise

Kassaye Gizaw$^{(\boxtimes)}$, Alganesh Ygzaw, Belachew Bantyirga, and Habtemariam Aberie

Bahir Dar Institute of Technology, Bahir Dar, Ethiopia

Abstract. Nowadays, power systems, particularly distribution networks, often operate close to their stability limit due to the rapid growth of new customers and inauguration of industrial sectors. Though the advancement of renewable energy sources (RESs) and Flexible Alternating Current Transmission (FACT) devices are the right solutions to meet these demands, they increase the network's complexity and dynamic behavior. To solve these complexities, introducing advanced controllers that are fast, accurate, and have a reliable synchronization method is the most effective solution. On this basis, one of the foremost promising technologies that constitute the backbone of wide-area and local monitoring systems in real-time is the Phasor Measurement Units (PMU) device. Thus, in this paper, the synchrophasor estimation (SE) algorithm, which is the main component to build up a PMU, is developed using the iterative interpolated DFT technique. Even if the analyzed interferences are two harmonics (3rd and 5th), the developed algorithm can work for any type and number of interferences. Based on the simulation result demonstration, the algorithm can effectively estimate the amplitude, phase, and frequency within the maximum error of 0.039, 0.002, and 0.0001.

This research work can solve various interrelated problems of electrical utilities for those lacking a tool that can trace the system at proper time snapshot like in our country Ethiopia.

Keywords: Discrete Fourier transform (DFT) · SE algorithm

1 Introduction

Nowadays power systems often operate close to their stability limit due to the rapid growth of new customers and inauguration of industrial sectors in the existing distribution networks. Even if the advancement of RESs and FACT devices are the best solutions to meet these demands, they increase the complexity and dynamic behavior of the system [1].

Also, to enhance the efficiency of power system networks, they require the successful coordination of real-time processes such as real-time power flows and demand-side response along with the requirement of advanced technologies like grid control devices, smart meters, and agent-based distributed controls [2, 3].

© ICST Institute for Computer Sciences, Social Informatics and Telecommunications Engineering 2021
Published by Springer Nature Switzerland AG 2021. All Rights Reserved
M. A. Delele et al. (Eds.): ICAST 2020, LNICST 384, pp. 215–230, 2021.
https://doi.org/10.1007/978-3-030-80621-7_16

To solve these problems, investing in grid reinforcement can be the first viable option. However, this mechanism does not enable the control of flexible resources available in active distribution networks (ADNs). On top of that, it also involves a significant increase in capital expenditure. Another option that considerably reduces the required investments compared to the previous one is introducing advanced controllers that are fast, accurate, and have reliable synchronization methods [1]. These infrastructures are better than present solutions such as Supervisory Control and Data Acquisition (SCADA) and the distribution automation system (DAS). Within this context, one of the foremost promising technologies that constitute the backbone of wide-area and local monitoring systems in real-time is the Phasor Measurement Units (PMU) device.

The scientific literature in the field of synchrophasor is relatively recent. Based on the adopted signal model, its estimation algorithm can be a static or dynamic model [4].

Static signal model-based SE algorithms are the most common because of their low computational complexity and estimation accuracies. The majority of these methods are based on the direct implementation of the DFT due to its relatively low computational complexity, the capability to reject close by harmonics, and its ability to separate and identify the fundamental parameters of the signal [5–7]. Some methods have good performance in SE like a phase-locked loop (PLL) but they are poor in parameter selection [8]. Even though the method proposed in [7] tries to compensate for the long-range spectral leakage of the negative image of the main tone, it does not account for the spectral interference produced by tones other than the fundamental tone. The method presented in [9] satisfies the IEEE P- and M-Class Compliant test of PMUs.

Nevertheless, it doesn't consider the effects of odd harmonics like third and fifth-order harmonics, in which its analysis is vital for developing countries like Ethiopia. Some window-based methods may require an integral sample in each window [10]. However, non-integer samples in a window are common in reality because of some off-nominal components which can result in errors in the DFT. Some algorithms may have good harmonic rejection capability, but they are computationally complex and susceptible to noise [11, 12].

1.1 Phasor, Synchrophasor, and Phase Measurement Unit

During normal operation of a power system, voltage and current waveforms are usually modeled as follows.

$$x(t) = A_o . \cos(\omega_o t + \varphi_o), \ ==> \ \omega_o = 2\pi f_o t \tag{1}$$

Phasor Definition: The electrical systems in a sinusoidal steady-state are simplified by the adoption of a phasor transformation.

It allows representing a sinusoidal function of time like the one expressed by an Eq. (1) with a single complex constant and vice versa. Therefore, the above time-domain signal can be represented in the phasor form by transforming it into a complex exponential via Euler's formula [13].

$$x(t) = A . \cos(\omega t + \varphi) = \mathrm{Re}\left\{A \left/ \sqrt{2} e^{j(\omega t + \varphi)}\right.\right\} = \mathrm{Re}\left\{A \left/ \sqrt{2} e^{j\omega t} e^{\varphi}\right.\right\} \tag{2}$$

By assuming everything in the circuit remains at a steady sinusoid of the same frequency, it is rational to associate the sinusoid $x(t)$ to the complex number X and call it phasor.

$$X = |X|.e^{\varphi} \quad \text{(in a polar form)}.$$

Where $|X| = A\big/\sqrt{2}$, is the RMS value.

$$x(t) \rightleftarrows X = |X|.e^{\varphi} = |X|[\cos\varphi + j\sin\varphi]$$

$|X|.e^{\varphi} = X_r + jX_i$ (in a rectangular form) and $\arg(X) = \varphi = \tan^{-1}(X_i/X_r)$.

Synchro Phasor: the signal $x(t)$ in the above Eq. (1) can be represented as a synchrophasor using the complex function $X(t)$ with amplitude $A(t)$ and phase $\psi(t)$ of the main tone respectively, being t the UTC time-reference.

$$\begin{aligned}
x(t) \rightleftarrows X(t) &\triangleq A(t).e^{j\psi(t)} \\
&= A(t).e^{j(2\pi f(t)+\varphi)} \\
&= A(t)[\cos(\omega t + \varphi) + j\sin(\omega t + \varphi)]
\end{aligned} \tag{3}$$

where $A(t)$ and $\psi(t) = 2\pi f(t) + \varphi$ are the instantaneous peak amplitude and phase of the main tone of $x(t)$. The representation of this function on the complex plane is a complex number that describes a circular trajectory with an angular radius ω, amplitude A, and its initial phase φ.

1.2 PMU Technology in Distributions System

The prototypes of the modern synchronized "phasor measurement units" (PMUs) using GPS were built at Virginia Tech in the early 1980s, and it was commercial manufacture in1991 [14, 15].

According to the IEEE Standard. C37.118.1-2011, PMU is a device that estimates the synchro phasors such as frequency and rate of change of frequency (ROCOF) of the voltage/current waveforms depending on a common UTC reference [5] (Fig. 1).

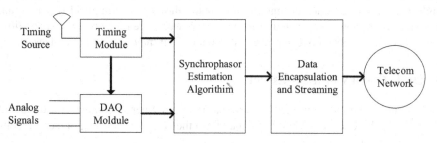

Fig. 1. Basic block diagrams of PMUs [8]

PMU technology has been initially developed to estimate transmission network parameters. Eventually, it has emerged as a potential control of ADNs and microgrids and a candidate for real-time monitoring [15].

By using synchrophasor technology, operators can monitor grid dynamics and reliability metrics. Also, they can identify and diagnose system problems, system stresses, oscillations, and other abnormal situations.

These enable them to take proactive actions to prevent or to reduce the footprint of blackouts and enable faster recovery after events [16].

The following Fig. 2 shows the performance comparison of PMU and SCADA when a voltage disturbance occurred on the Oklahoma power grid on April 5, 2011 [17].

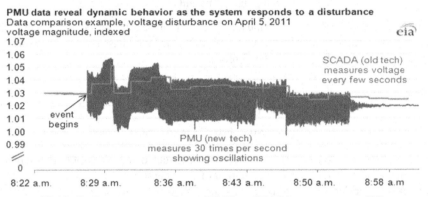

Fig. 2. Performance comparison of PMU vs. SCADA measurements [17]

In the above figure, it is clearly depicted that PMU measurements are very precise to captures the dynamic conditions. In contrast, SCADA measurement is not able to observe the dynamic characteristics of the power system as it relies on steady-state power flow analysis. As a result, it is not possible to take proper control action to alleviate the oscillation.

The other problem is that SCADA technology only gives the magnitude of different electrical quantities like voltages and currents. In the AC network, there is one essential parameter apart from the magnitude that is the angle which is a key indicator of the system stress. If we rely only on the magnitude of information without including the angle, we might lose some information and monitor the system wrongly [13]. These can, in turn, cause serious interrelated problems in a power system like relay misoperation, incorrect coordination between power equipment and it may also lead to a blackout.

2   DFT Theory and Its Effects

DFT is one of the most efficient tools to extract the frequency content of a finite and discrete signal sequence, which is obtained from the periodic sampling of a continuous time-domain signal.

PMU is nothing, but it is a name of a device where a robust algorithm can estimate the phasors of electrical quantities deployed on in its microcontroller unit, which makes it very smart and expensive [7]. A direct implementation DF-based SE algorithm is proposed in almost all of the previously reviewed literature due to low computational complexity, capable to isolate and identify the main tone parameters, good rejection of near harmonics, and accurate in steady-state and dynamic conditions [18]. Nevertheless, these qualities come with non-negligible drawbacks mainly caused by DFT computation, such as aliasing and spectral leakage.

Aliasing: is a problem that is related to the finite BW of the data acquisition system concerning the signal that we are interested to track. To be able to correctly reconstruct the signal $x(t)$ from $x[n]$, it must be sampled at a sampling rate F_s that must be at least two times higher than the maximum frequency component contained in the original spectrum $X(f)$ (Nyquist–Shannon theorem) [7]. It is usually corrected by using an anti-aliasing filter, but this may introduce a phase shift all over the spectrum that has to be compensated. The second mechanism to get rid of the problem is to select a higher sampling frequency (F_s) than F_m (maximum frequency component of our signal) which is unknown in the real signal. So, in the power system of such type applications, it is usually set the sampling frequency at the value of 10th of kHz because, at this frequency, typically don't have any other interfering components except transient. In the power system, the highest harmonic we can get is 25th harmonics, which is 1.25 kHz for 50 Hz fundamental frequency [19]. So, if the sampling frequency is set to 10 kHz, 15 kHz, or 100 kHz this hypothesis seems good than the first case (Fig. 3).

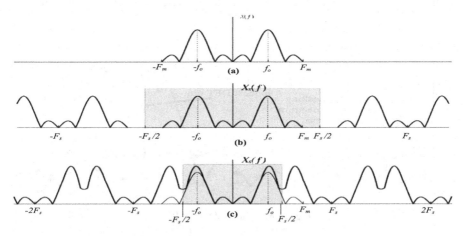

Fig. 3. Effects of aliasing [5]

Spectral Leakage: After the sampling of the original signal $x(t)$, it must be grouped in portions to be analyzed by the DFT. If the fundamental frequency (f_o) is not an integer multiple of frequency resolution (incoherent sampling), the zero crossings of the translated *sinc* functions will not happen exactly at multiples of $1/T$ and all the DFT indexes will not be an integer. As a result, we start to see several bins as they exhibit non-zero projection on the entire basis set due to the smearing frequency components as shown in Fig. 4. Even though most of the spectrum energy (bins that are adjacent to

f_o) will still be concentrated around, the highest frequency bin is not located precisely at the f_o. Spectral leakage can be short term or long term.

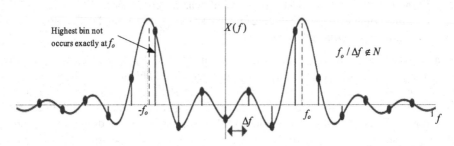

Fig. 4. Graphical representation of spectral leakage [5]

Short-term arise from the effects of the main lobe width of the FT of the adopted window which in turn makes very difficult in identifying the "true" maximum of a specific portion of the DFT spectrum.

Whereas the effect caused by the side-lobes (i.e., the "tails") of the FT of the adopted window is referred to as *long-term*. If it is not properly compensated by windowing, an additional source of error is associated with the presence of cross interaction between spectrum tones that are very close to each other, the so-called spectral interference occurs (Fig. 5).

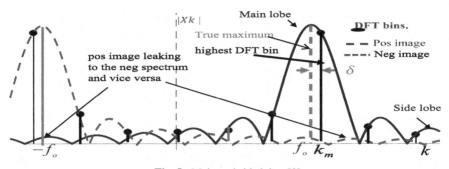

Fig. 5. Main and side lobes [9]

2.1 DFT Based SE Algorithms

Classical DFT-based SE. A trivial DFT-based SE algorithm approach estimates the parameters of the main DFT tone directly from the position of a local DFT maximum within a specific frequency range. It is based on the assumption that the maximum DFT bin lies precisely at the fundamental frequency. But if the window does not contain an integer number of periods of the signal $x[n]$, leakage occurs, and the main tone of the signal is located between two consecutive DFT bins as shown in Fig. 6.

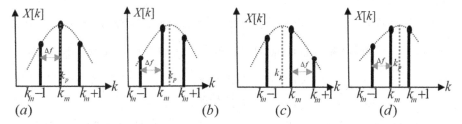

Fig. 6. Possible location of the three highest DFT bins

The pseudo-code of a trivial DFT-based synchrophasor estimation algorithm.

1. Sample the input signal x (t) → x[n]at sampling rate Fs.
2. Apply the rectangular window w_r *(n)* to *x[n]*;
3. Compute the DFT of w_r *(n)* · *x[n]*;
4. Apply a maximum search technique to find the DFT bin with the highest amplitude $|X(k_m)|$; being k_m is the index of the highest DFT bin of the spectrum.
5. Return estimated value of amplitude, phase, and frequency of $X(k_m)$;

$$f = k_m \Delta f, \quad A = |X(k_m)|, \quad \varphi = \angle X(k_m)$$

6. End procedure

The Interpolated-DFT Technique is a technique that allows estimating the main tone spectrum location by calculating the abscissa of the maximum of an interpolation curve of the DFT spectrum under the fulfillment of some essential assumptions. These assumptions are sufficiently higher sampling frequency than F_m, time-invariant parameters characterize the input signal, and the bins that are going to interpolated are only generated by the positive image of the tone.

Thus, to satisfy the first two assumptions, the window length containing a few periods of a fundamental tone and the sampling rates selected in a few kilohertz, respectively. Nevertheless, if the window includes few periods only, the DFT spectrum's energy will be concentrated in the lower frequency range; thereby, the positive and negative images of the main tone of the spectrum become relatively very close to each other. During this condition, the third assumption may not be fulfilled. Because in the case of incoherent sampling, the negative image tails of the main tone leaks into its positive spectrum, thereby bias the DFT bins used to perform the interpolation.

Thus, to solve this problem, the IpDFT starts its analytical analysis from the following four equations describing Hanning (Hann) window in the continuous-time domain, discrete-time domain, Fourier transforms and its DFT, respectively.

$$w_h(t) = 0.5(1 + \cos(2\pi t/T)) \tag{4}$$

$$w_H(n) = 0.5(1 - \cos(2\pi n/N)), \ n \in [0, N - 1] \tag{5}$$

$$W_H(\omega) = -0.25 \cdot D_N(\omega - 2\pi/N) + 0.5 \cdot D_N(\omega) - 0.25 \cdot D_N(\omega + 2\pi/N) \tag{6}$$

$$W_H(k) = -0.25D_N(k-1) + 0.5D_N(k) - 0.25D_N(K+1) \tag{7}$$

Where $D_N(\omega)$ the Dirichlet kernel (FT of the rectangular window) and its DFT is:

$$D_N(k) = e^{-j\pi k(N-1)/N} \frac{\sin(\pi k)}{\sin(\pi k/N)}, \quad k \in [0, N-1] \tag{8}$$

Let's consider the finite sequence (9) obtained by sampling with a sampling rate of a continuous waveform $x(t)$ characterized by a single frequency component at frequency:

$$x(n) = A\cos(2\pi f_o n T_s + \varphi), \quad 0 \le n \le N-1 \tag{9}$$

Where A is signal's amplitude, f_o is the signal's frequency in Hertz. Then its spectrum can be expressed in terms of its positive and negative image as follows.

$$\begin{aligned} X(f) &= X^+(f) + X^-(f) \\ &= \frac{A}{2} e^{j\psi} W_H(f - f_o) + \frac{A}{2} e^{-j\psi} W_H(f + f_o) \end{aligned} \tag{10}$$

Being $W_H(f)$ the Fourier transform of the Hanning window, A and ψ the amplitude and instantaneous phase of the signal $x(t)$ respectively.

By letting the effects of leakage are properly compensated by windowing, it is reasonable to neglect the long-range spectral leakage produced by the negative spectrum image on the positive frequency range thereby assumption three satisfies which is approximated mathematically as:

$$X(k) \approx X^+(k), \quad 0 \le k \le N/2 \tag{11}$$

These for the Hanning window, the fractional term δ can be estimated starting from the ratio between the two highest bins $X(km)$ and $X(km + \varepsilon)$ that, can be approximated as follows [62].

$$\frac{X(k_m + \varepsilon)}{X(k_m)} \approx \frac{W_H\big((\varepsilon - \delta) \cdot 2\pi/N\big)}{W_H(-\delta \cdot 2\pi/N)} \tag{12}$$

Where $W_H(\cdot)$ is the FT of the Hanning window, which is approximated as:

$$|W_H(\omega)| \approx \left|\sin(\frac{\omega N}{2})\right| \cdot \left|\frac{-0.25}{\sin(\frac{\omega}{2} - \frac{\pi}{N})} + \frac{0.5}{\sin(\frac{\omega}{2})} + \frac{-0.25}{\sin(\frac{\omega}{2} + \frac{\pi}{N})}\right| \tag{13}$$

$$\varepsilon = \begin{cases} 1 & \text{if} |X(k_m+1)| > |X(k_m-1)| \\ -1 & \text{if} |X(k_m+1)| < |X(k_m-1)| \end{cases} \tag{14}$$

By replacing (14) in (12) and recalling that $\lim\limits_{x \to 0} \sin(x) = x$, after simplification we get:

$$\frac{X(k_m + \varepsilon)}{X(k_m)} = \left|\frac{0.5}{\delta(\delta - \varepsilon)(\delta - 2\varepsilon)}\right| \left|\frac{\delta(\delta + 1)(\delta - 1)}{-0.5}\right| \Leftrightarrow = \left|\frac{\delta + \varepsilon}{\delta - \varepsilon}\right|$$

Therefore, the frequency correction δ becomes:

$$\delta = \varepsilon \frac{2|X(k_m + \varepsilon)| - |X(k_m)|}{|X(k_m)| + |X(k_m + \varepsilon)|} \tag{15}$$

Then IpDFT technique computes the initial waveform parameters (i.e., its frequency, amplitude, and phase) as follows:

$$f = (k_m + \delta)\Delta f$$
$$A = |X(k_m)| \left| \frac{\pi \delta}{\sin(\pi \delta)} \right| \left| \delta^2 - 1 \right| \tag{16}$$
$$\varphi = \angle X(k_m) - \pi \delta$$

2.2 The Iterative IpDFT Technique

IpDFT technique tries to compute the main tone parameters by letting the DFT bins are only generated from the positive image of the spectrum. Nevertheless, this assumption is not always the case and the bins may influence by the negative image of the main tone itself and other interfering tones like harmonics. Thus, the i-IpDFT technique tries to eliminate any interferences iteratively, and finally, it estimates the fundamental tone parameters.

So, to start the mathematical analysis of the i-IpDFT, let us consider a 3rd harmonic is added in the signal described by the Eq. (9). Hence, the highest and second-highest DFT bins, are used to estimate δ according to (15), they can be expressed as:

$$X(k_m) = \frac{1}{B}\left[\frac{A}{2}e^{j\varphi} \cdot W(-\delta) + \frac{A}{2}e^{-j\varphi} \cdot W(2k_m + \delta) \right] + X(K_{m,3}) \tag{17}$$

$$X(k_m + \varepsilon) = \frac{1}{B}\left[\frac{A}{2}e^{j\varphi} \cdot W(\varepsilon - \delta) + \frac{A}{2}e^{-j\varphi} \cdot W(2k_m + \varepsilon + \delta) \right] + X(K_{m,3} + \varepsilon) \tag{18}$$

Where $X(K_{m,3})$ and $X(K_{m,3} + \varepsilon)$ are the contribution of third harmonics for the first and second highest DFT bins respectively.

$$X(K_{m,3}) = \frac{A_3}{2B}\left(e^{j\varphi_3} \cdot W(-\delta_3) \right) + \frac{A_3}{2B}\left(e^{-j\varphi_3} \cdot W(2k_{m,3} + \delta_3) \right) \tag{19}$$

$$X(K_{m,3} + \varepsilon) = \frac{A_3}{2B}\left(e^{j\varphi_3} \cdot W(\varepsilon - \delta_3) \right) + \frac{A_3}{2B}\left(e^{-j\varphi_3} \cdot W(2k_{m,3} + \varepsilon + \delta_3) \right) \tag{20}$$

The second terms after the addition sign in the Eqs. (17) to (20) are spectral interference coming from the negative spectrum image of the corresponding tones. Then, these estimations can be subtracted from the original DFT bins to reduce the spectral interference so that the positive image of the spectrum mostly generates the compensated DFT bins. These compensated DFT bins are used to update the value of delta in the Eq. (15) and which again updates the tone parameters which is iterated for defined number iterations or performed until a given convergence criterion is achieved. Additionally, this process can be similarly used to eliminate any near harmonic components.

As a procedure, the effect of the main tone's negative image has to be compensated first iteratively, which affects highly before we analyze the contribution of harmonic components. Then the effects of harmonics can be analyzed one by one starting from the first harmonic which is closer to f_o. The estimated frequency can be expressed as;

$$f_o = k_{peak} \Delta f. \tag{21}$$

Where k_{peak} can be expressed as:

$$k_{peak} = k_{max} + \delta, \quad -0.5 \leq \delta \leq 0.5 \Rightarrow \begin{cases} k_{peak} = k_{max}, (\delta = 0), \rightarrow \text{coherent, no leakage} \\ k_{peak} \neq k_{max}, (\delta \neq 0) \rightarrow \text{incoherent, leakage} \end{cases}$$

Being k_m the index of the DFT bin characterized by the highest amplitude and δ is a fractional correction term.

Incoherent sampling, the highest DFT bin of the signal's spectrum is located at the maximum of the window lobe that can be used to estimate the frequency of the signal.

Figure 7 shows the general flow chart of the work. The first step is acquiring the input signal through current and potential transformers. Once the signal is received it has to be sampled at the desired sampling rate Fs and then it must be clustered in portions to be analyzed by the DFT which is called windowing. After the windowing, the first three DFT maximums has to be computed based on the trivial and IpDFT approach. Then after the errors in finding DFT maximums can be minimized by eliminating the effect of negative image spectral interference of the corresponding tone by using a technique called e-IpDFT. Once the effect of negative image interferences is eliminated to endurable value the spectral energy is computed which is vital to quantify the effect of other interferences. If the spectral energy is above some threshold value, the true parameters of all interferences are going to be estimated and subtracted from the original DFT spectrum iteratively to increase the accuracy of estimated fundamental tone parameters.

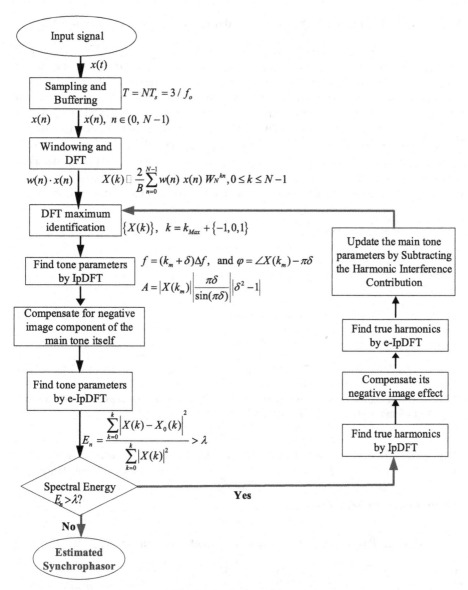

Fig. 7. General flow chart

3 Simulation Results and Discussion

For all scenarios, the fundamental phase is taken as 1.0471975511966 rad and the amplitude of the 3rd and the 5th harmonics are taken as 10% & 1% of the corresponding fundamental amplitude. The white Gaussian noise is considered as 60 dB.

3.1 Estimated Parameters When the Fundamental Frequency is Below 50 Hz

For frequency below 50 Hz, A_o & f_o, are randomly generated as 9.64310742178912 and 48.7340275 Hz respectively whereas the phase of the 3rd and 5th harmonics are assumed to be 0.130855503942357 rad and 0.00727912525993756 rad respectively.

The Frequency domain format of the windowed signal is shown in Fig. 8 (a). From this figure, the three signals of the spectrum which are the fundamental, 3rd, and 5th harmonics are shown. The classical DFT algorithm estimates the frequency exactly the index corresponding to the highest DFT bin which is 50 Hz in this case. Thus, to estimate the exact fundamental frequency the interference and the leakages need to be considered in Fig. 8 (b). The interferences around the fundamental tone from Fig. 8 (b) are occurred due to the trivial difference between the actual amplitude and the estimated one.

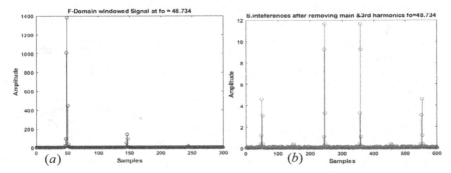

Fig. 8. (a) Frequency domain of windowed signal, and (b) interference spectrum after subtracting the main tone and 3rd harmonics, $fo = 48.7340275031078$

Lambda λ in Fig. 7 is set to 0.0001 for all scenarios where it is used to activate the algorithm to compensate for the interferences when their effect is significant. The errors in Fig. 9 are obtained after an elven iteration and the value of En at this iteration is found to be 0.000013454306809327.

3.2 Estimated Parameters When the Fundamental Frequency is 50 Hz

At a frequency of 50 Hz, A_o is taken as 10 whereas the phase of the 3rd and 5th harmonics are assumed to be 0.466031331142832 rad and 1.2263488297847 rad respectively as they are generated dynamically for each scenario.

It is already discussed that when the time domain signal is an integer multiple of the sampling frequency there will be coherent sampling thereby the maximum DFT bin is located almost in the middle of the other two bins which are nearly equal in amplitude as shown in Fig. 10 (a). As a result; the smearing frequency components reduced and the algorithm able to estimate the fundamental parameters in small iterations (Table 1).

Figure 10 (b) depicts the negative image leakages of the main tone for all DFT bins that have to be compensated for each positive image bins.

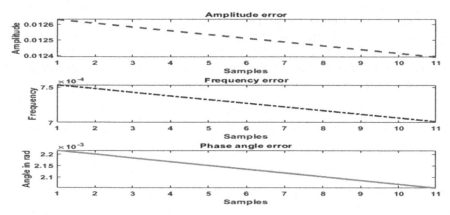

Fig. 9. Error in amplitude, phase, and frequency, $fo = 48.7340275031078$ Hz

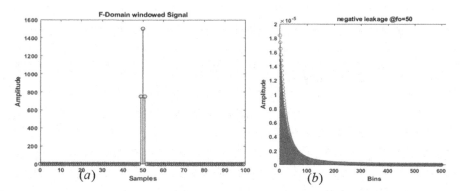

Fig. 10. (a) Frequency domain of windowed signal, and (b) magnitude of negative leakage of the main tone, $fo = 50$Hz

Table 1. Errors in amplitude, frequency, and phase $fo = 50\ Hz$

Iteration	1	2
Amplitude error	0.03914	0.03914
Frequency error	0.000142	0.000141
Phase angle error	0.002917	0.002915

3.3 Estimated Parameters When the Fundamental Frequency is Above 50 Hz

The algorithm is also tested when the real frequency is above the nominal value which is 50 Hz. The amplitude and the real frequency are assumed to be 9.48665553956213 and 51.6415849459746 Hz respectively. Similarly, the phase angle of the harmonics is randomly generated and their instant values for this scenario are 1.05155216148873 rad and 2.03957598834408 rad for 3rd and 5th harmonics respectively.

The classical DFT estimates the frequency 52 Hz which is the index of the highest DFT bin from Fig. 11 (a) but it is not the fundamental or the real frequency. Figure 11 (b) presents the interference after removing the main tone and 3rd harmonics and it is shown that there is an interference around the fundamental component other than the 5th harmonics which is due to the difference between true and estimated amplitude..

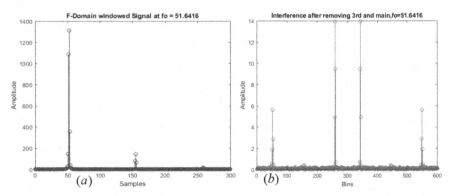

Fig. 11. (a) the spectrum of the windowed signal and (b) interferes spectrum after subtracting the main tone and 3rd harmonics (Fig. 12).

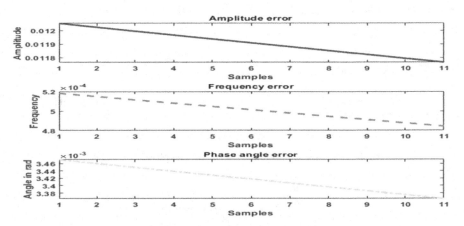

Fig. 12. Errors in amplitude, frequency, and phase, $fo = 51.6415849459746$ Hz

4   Conclusion

In this research work, an efficient method called the i-IpDFT technique has been anticipated to estimate the phasor parameters of the fundamental tone at three different instant of input signal parameters. The simulation results show that the i-IpDFT SE technique is robust and solves the limits of the IpDFT technique when estimating the parameters of a signal corrupted by interference signals and leakage generated by them and by the main ton itself. The errors in all scenarios are within the limit and acceptable for further applications of the power system, especially for distribution systems where most of its operations are not going on a nominal value as they are typically corrupted by non-linear loads and other factors.

Thus, considering the effects of noise and odd harmonics like third and fifth-order harmonics to know the real or fundamental parameters of the power system is vital for developing countries like Ethiopia.

References

1. Frigo, G., Derviskadic, A., Zuo, Y., Paolone, M.: PMU-based rocof measurements: uncertainty limits and metrological significance in power system applications. IEEE Trans. Instrum. Meas. **68**, 3810–3822 (2019). https://doi.org/10.1109/TIM.2019.2907756
2. Alzaareer, K., Saad, M.: Real-time voltage stability monitoring in smart distribution grids. IEEE Int. Conf. Renew. Energy Pow. Eng. REPE **2018**, 13–17 (2018). https://doi.org/10.1109/REPE.2018.8657671
3. Romano, P., Paolone, M., Arnold, J., Piacentini, R.: An interpolated-DFT synchrophasor estimation algorithm and its implementation in an FPGA-based PMU prototype. IEEE Pow. Energy Soc. Gen. Meet. (2013). https://doi.org/10.1109/PESMG.2013.6672906
4. Castello, P., Lixia, M., Muscas, C., Pegoraro, P.A.: Impact of the model on the accuracy of synchrophasor measurement. IEEE Trans. Instrum. Meas. **61**, 2179–2188 (2012). https://doi.org/10.1109/TIM.2012.2193699
5. Milano, F.: Advances in Power System Modelling, Control, and Stability Analysis (2016)
6. Thilakarathne, C., Meegahapola, L., Fernando, N.: Static performance comparison of prominent synchrophasor algorithms. In: 2017 IEEE Innovative Smart Grid Technologies - Asia Smart Grid Smart Community, ISGT-Asia 2017, pp. 1–6 (2018). https://doi.org/10.1109/ISGT-Asia.2017.8378392
7. Romano, P., Paolone, M.: Enhanced interpolated-DFT for synchrophasor estimation in FPGAs: theory, implementation, and validation of a PMU prototype. IEEE Trans. Instrum. Meas. **63**, 2824–2836 (2014). https://doi.org/10.1109/TIM.2014.2321463
8. Cai, X., Wang, C., Kennel, R.: A fast and precise grid synchronization method based on fixed-gain filter. IEEE Trans. Ind. Electron. **65**, 7119–7128 (2018). https://doi.org/10.1109/TIE.2018.2798600
9. Derviskadic, A., Romano, P., Paolone, M.: Iterative-interpolated DFT for synchrophasor estimation: a single algorithm for P- and M-class compliant PMUs. IEEE Trans. Instrum. Meas. **67**, 547–558 (2018). https://doi.org/10.1109/TIM.2017.2779378
10. Li, H.: Frequency estimation and tracking by two-layered iterative DFT with re-sampling in non-steady states of power system. EURASIP J. Wirel. Commun. Netw. **2019**(1), 1–19 (2019). https://doi.org/10.1186/s13638-018-1320-1
11. Kim, D.I., Chun, T.Y., Yoon, S.H., Lee, G., Shin, Y.J.: Wavelet-based event detection method using PMU data. IEEE Trans. Smart Grid. **8**, 1154–1162 (2017). https://doi.org/10.1109/TSG.2015.2478421
12. Maharjan, S., Peng, J.C.H., Martinez, J.E., Xiao, W., Huang, P.H., Kirtley, J.L.: Improved sample value adjustment for synchrophasor estimation at off-nominal power system conditions. IEEE Trans. Pow. Deliv. **32**, 33–44 (2017). https://doi.org/10.1109/TPWRD.2016.2586946
13. Palsodkar, S.S., Date, T.N.: Comparison of DFT and space vector method for synchrophasor measurement. In: Proc - 2018 4th International Conference on Computing Communication Control and Automation, ICCUBEA 2018, pp. 1–6 (2018). https://doi.org/10.1109/ICCUBEA.2018.8697374

14. Nuthalapati, S.(N.D.R.) (ed.): Power System Grid Operation Using Synchrophasor Technology. PEPS, Springer, Cham (2019). https://doi.org/10.1007/978-3-319-89378-5

15. Penshanwar, M.K., Gavande, M., Satarkar, M.F.A.R.: Phasor measurement unit technology and its applications-a review. In: International Conference on Energy Systems and Applications, ICESA 2015, vol. 17, pp. 318–323 (2016). https://doi.org/10.1109/ICESA.2015.750 3363

16. Bennett, J.M.: Towards ethnorelativism: a developmental model of intercultural competence. Springer, Heidelberg (1986)

17. EIA: U.{S}. {Energy} {Information} {Administration} ({EIA}) (2015). http://www.eia.gov/. Accessed 22 July 2019

18. Affijulla, S., Tripathy, P.: Development of phasor estimation algorithm for P-class PMU suitable in protection applications. IEEE Trans. Smart Grid 9, 1250–1260 (2018). https://doi.org/10.1109/TSG.2016.2582342

19. Soni, M.K., Soni, N.: Review of causes and effect of harmonics on power system. Int. J. Sci. Eng. Technol. Res. 3, 214–220 (2014)

Performance Analysis of Vertical Sectorization in Sub-6-GHz Frequency Bands for 4G Mobile Network Under Realistic Deployment Scenario

Seifu Girma Zeleke[(✉)], Beneyam B. Haile, and Ephrem Teshale Bekele

Addis Ababa Institute of Technology, Addis Ababa University, Addis Ababa, Ethiopia
{seifu.girma,beneyamb.haile,ephrem.bekele}@aait.edu.et

Abstract. Demand for enhanced mobile broadband has been significantly increasing due to increasing penetration of data-intensive mobile services. For accommodating this demand, various network capacity enhancing technologies including cell densification and applying more frequency bands have been investigated and incorporated in the fourth generation (4G) and fifth generation (5G) mobile technologies. Network densification can be performed by either deploying new small cells or further sectoring horizontally and vertically existing network sites. Performance benefits of vertical sectorization have been investigated but mostly for theoretical network environment and user demand distribution that significantly affect the benefits. In this paper, we present performance analysis for vertical sectorization under realistic network environment and user distribution for selected urban area of Addis Ababa, Ethiopia. The analysis is performed for sub-6-GHz bands including those identified for 5G. Network simulation is performed using MATLAB while network modeling and assumptions are developed based on data collected for target area of Addis Ababa from network management system of the Addis Ababa network. Propagation is computed using deterministic 3D ray tracing method based on building map for the target area. Performance results show that considerable performance benefits are achieved by applying vertical sectorization for both cell edge and cell center users. For instance, we observe that 3×2 configuration presents 236.6%, 504% and 821.5% user throughput gains compared to 3×1 configuration at 10%-ile, 50%-ile and 90%-ile.

Keywords: Vertical sectorization · Sub-6-GHz bands · 4G · 5G · 3D ray tracing

1 Introduction

Demand for enhanced mobile broadband has been increasing and is predicted to increase significantly [1, 2]. According to ITU [2], mobile traffic will grow at an annual rate of around 55% in 2020–2030 and global mobile traffic per month is estimated to reach to 607 EB in 2025 and 5016 EB in 2030. The traffic growth is not only because of rise of subscriptions for mobile services but also grow in traffic volume consumed per user. The monthly average consumed traffic per user is predicted to be 39.4 GB and 257 GB in 2025

© ICST Institute for Computer Sciences, Social Informatics and Telecommunications Engineering 2021
Published by Springer Nature Switzerland AG 2021. All Rights Reserved
M. A. Delele et al. (Eds.): ICAST 2020, LNICST 384, pp. 231–243, 2021.
https://doi.org/10.1007/978-3-030-80621-7_17

and 2030, respectively [2]. Likewise, mobile traffic growth has also been observed in rising market like Ethiopia as a result of growth of mobile internet penetration and other multimedia service usage, particularly in the major cities like Addis Ababa, Ethiopia [3, 4].

Various capacity enhancing technological advancements are introduced aiming to support these continuous increasing mobile data demands [5]. The low, mid and high frequency bands have been exploited in addition to technological innovations to support the rising data demands [6–9]. Mobile network operators need to fulfill the data demand by upgrading their network via with these new technologies and frequency bands. Among the innovated technologies, network densification enhances system capacity by reusing frequency spectrum and limiting the coverage area [10]. Densification can be either macro with vertical sectorization or small cell densification. Small cell densification requires additional sites and associated network elements. Macro densification with vertical sectorization does not require additional sites; it requires antenna capability that splits the cells in to inner and outer cells (see Fig. 1). This reduces cost of sites and associated network elements.

However before deploying and using these enhanced mobile broadband their performance impacts in realistic network environment need to be investigated more.

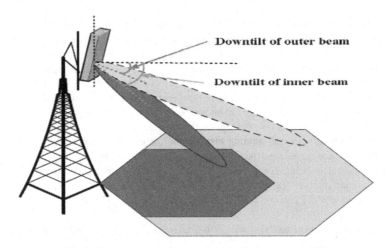

Fig. 1. Sector layout of vertical sectorization system [10].

A number of research works have been published regarding on vertical sectorization (VS). Early works mainly focus on study capacity impact of this technology for varying antenna configuration under synthetic simulation environments: propagation model, network layout, antenna pattern and demand nodes are simplified 3GPP cases [10–14]. The results showed promising gains can be obtained from this technique even if splitting the cell can introduce worse performance for cell edge users. Later optimization works which optimize network parameters with respect to antenna tilt angle, half power beam width and transmitted power of the method using different optimization techniques are conducted [15–19]. These later works also conducted simulation under synthetic environments. There are also some field trial experimental works that study and characterize the actual performance of vertical sectorization [20, 21]. Synthetic environment for simulation cases results in neglecting the influence of realistic network environments. However, there are very few works investigate the performance impact of this technology in realistic network environment [22–24] and work with the new operating frequency bands defined by 3GPP specification group [24].

The authors in [14] analyze the performance of different elevation beamforming scenarios: vertical sectorization with same carrier frequency, vertical sectorization with different carrier frequency based on CA and user-specific elevation beamforming. However, the paper conducted the research under legacy 2 GHz frequency band. Moreover, it works on the 3GPP simulation environments. Reference in [22] analyzed and compared performance impact of VS with super cell deployment and higher order horizontal sectorization in a real-world suburban environment. Reference in [23] examine performance impact of VS for various vertical HBPW and electrical tilt angles to observe the optimization space between two vertical sectors and the gain in terms of CDF of SINR and cell capacity. However, both references [22] and [23] do not consider the new operating bands. The author in [24] compare the performance of a cellular network using higher order sectorization in a horizontal domain, vertical sectorization, and super cell configuration under 28 GHz frequency as the operation band. However, it does not consider the sub 6 GHz frequency band. Moreover, it doesn't work on various combination of different inner and outer cell configuration. For best benefits of the technologies, their performances impact need to be investigated more under realistic network environments.

This research work addresses the aforementioned gaps stated above. Particularly, it investigates the performance impact of macro densification via vertical sectorization with the new operating subs-6 GHz frequency bands. These frequency bands are recommended to be used by both 4G and 5G network in addition to millimeter waves. Simulation is performed for various deployment scenarios focused to Addis Ababa use case. Realistic network environments imply: network topology of real building and terrain maps of Addis Ababa, Propagation is computed using deterministic 3D ray tracing and user distribution or demand nodes are located based on real network traffics collected from Ethio telecom.

The rest of paper is organized as follows: the next section presents system model and deployment scenarios. Studied scenarios, description of demand node distributions and parameters and assumptions used in simulation are described in Sect. 3. Section 4 provides simulation results and discussion. Finally, concluding discussions and potential research directions are given in Sect. 5.

2 System Model and Deployment Scenarios

2.1 System Model

This research work considers a downlink LTE mobile network with 18 numbers of macro sites in selected studied area as shown in Fig. 2. The notation c_m^i is used to refer macro LTE site having 3 sectors; each sector is identified by sector index i and m is used to show whether VS is applied or not at the i_{th} macro sector. For LTE macro sector, the value of m will be zero, but if VS is applied, m takes the value 1 and 2 to differentiate the inner and the outer sectors [25].

Without vertical sectorization, $SINR$ of a user located at u is given by [25],

$$SINR = \frac{p(u, c_0^z)}{\sum_{i \neq z} p(u, c_0^i) + N} \quad (1)$$

Where, $p(u, c_0^z)$ is the received power of a user from serving sector c_0^z.

And the throughput (TP) performance, using Shannon formula is given by [26],

$$TP = BW_{eff} N_{PRB} B_{PRB} \, \log_2 \left(1 + \frac{SINR}{SINR_{eff}} \right) \quad (2)$$

When VS is applied, $SINR$ of a user located at u is given by,

$$SINR' = \begin{cases} \frac{p(u, c_1^z)}{\sum_{i \neq z} (\sum_{m=1}^{2} p(u, c_m^i)) + N}, & \text{when user is associated with outer sector} \\ \frac{p(u, c_2^z)}{\sum_{i \neq z} (\sum_{m=1}^{2} p(u, c_m^i)) + N}, & \text{when user is associated with inner sector} \end{cases} \quad (3)$$

Where, $p(u, c_1^z)$ and $p(u, c_2^z)$ are received signal powers of the user located at u from outer and inner sectors respectively.

And, the TP performance is given by,

$$TP' = BW_{eff} N_{PRB} B_{PRB} \, \log_2 \left(1 + \frac{SINR'}{SINR_{eff}} \right) \quad (4)$$

Where, N_{PRB} is the number of Physical Resource Block (PRBs), B_{PRB} is the bandwidth per PRB, BW_{eff} is the adjusted bandwidth to fit with LTE system bandwidth efficiency and $SINR_{eff}$ is the adjusted SINR implementation efficiency.

The TP performance gain is then given by,

$$\eta = \frac{TP' - TP}{TP} \quad (5)$$

Antenna Models: In this paper, Huawei antenna patterns of the following models are used. For the existing 3 × 1 macro cells ADU451819 is used. In addition, AMAN software is used to create the required vertical and horizontal antenna pattern.

2.2 Deployment Scenarios

The analysis of vertical sectorization is performed for subs 6-GHz operating frequency bands specified by 3GPP specification groups and a down link LTE mobile network. The studied area is located in Addis Ababa Ethiopia that illustrates an urban scenario. The area is found around bole and covers an area of 2.82 km × 1.94 km. It has buildings of heights up to 80 m, terrain with different topography and latitude and longitudes of 38.745976 and 9.017116 respectively. The area consists of 18 macro cells; each site has 3 sectors in the existing Addis Ababa LTE network. The location of macro sites are shown below (see Fig. 2).

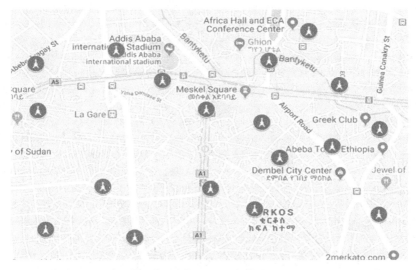

Fig. 2. Performance studied area.

3   User Distribution, Studied Scenarios and Simulation Setup

3.1   User Distribution

Demand nodes or user locations are one of the important parameters that has an impact on the performance of mobile network. Hence in this work, demand nodes are located using the real pick hour data collected from Ethio telecom.

To locate demand nodes, we did the following procedures. First, the studied area is divided in to several pixels. This is because the data are recorded pixel wise. The divided area has 10 rows and 14 columns. Then, for each pixel, we obtained the corresponding traffic density (g) and number of nodes (N). The traffic density is obtained dividing the collected traffic data of each pixel by the area of each pixel (a).

The number of demand nodes of each pixel is calculated as follows [27].

$$N_{m,n} = \frac{a * g_{m,n}}{r} \tag{6}$$

Where, a is the area of each pixel, $g_{m,n}$ is the traffic density of each pixel and r is the individual data requirement which is assume equal for all and less than the minimum traffic density. The Generated user distribution is shown in Fig. 3 below.

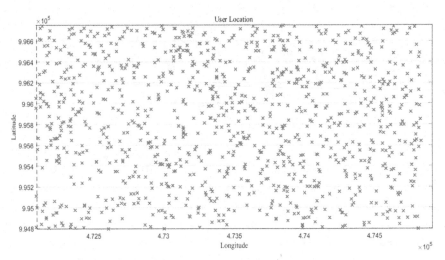

Fig. 3. Generated user demand nodes based on the above model.

3.2 Studied Scenarios and Simulation Parameters

Different scenarios are considered in this research work and they can be grouped in to two parts. The first group comprises scenarios 1 up to 4; both sectors use the same operating band. That means both inner and outer sectors configured with the same carrier frequency. The second group comprises scenarios 5 up to 7, different carrier frequencies are assigned to the inner and the outer sectors. Sectors configurations and simulation parameters and assumptions are shown in Table 1 and 2 below.

Table 1. Inner and outer sectors assigned frequency band.

Scenarios	Inner sector (MHz)	Outer sector (MHz)	Bandwidth (MHz)
Scenario 1	1800	1800	20
Scenario 2	2600	2600	80
Scenario 3	3600	3600	100
Scenario 4	5000	5000	100
Scenario 5	1800/2600	2600/1800	20/20
Scenario 6	1800/3600	3600/1800	(20/100)/20
Scenario 7	1800/5000	5000/1800	20/20

Table 2. Simulation parameters and assumptions.

Parameters	Values/Assumptions
Downlink transmit power	46 dBm
Frequency reuse factor	1
Base station height	40 m
Horizontal HPBW	64°
UE height	1.5 m
UE number in service area	1037
Simulation area	2.82×1.94 km^2
Receive antenna gain	0 dBi
BW$_{eff}$	0.5
SINR$_{eff}$	0.85
Thermal floor	−174 dBm/Hz
Noise figure	9 dB
Traffic distribution	Non-Uniform
Cell association	RSRP
Traffic model	Full buffer

4   Results and Discussions

This section presented performance of VS for LTE downlink mobile network with the new operating frequency bands defined by 3GPP group. Simulations are carried out to observe CDF of UE SINR and throughput performance of VS for different inner and outer band configuration stated in Sect. 3.2. All simulations are performed as follows: For each snapshot

- Pathloss of each user is calculated using proman
- Users are associated with their respective serving cell based on their signal level
- Assuming full load system, all available resource blocks are scheduled. Number of resource blocks for each user in a cell is the same.
- Calculate the down link SINR and throughput using Eq. (1), (2), (3) and (4) for all users.

Repeat this a number of times (400 times our case) and collect the statics.

Figure 4, 5 and 6 are plotted to see performance of UE SINR for network configuration categorized under group 1 and 2 which are listed in Table 1. What Fig. 4 makes different from Fig. 5 and 6 is that, the former use the same operating bands, whereas the latter uses different operating bands for inner and outer sectors. Figure 5 is plotted for the case which all the outer sectors use the legacy 1800 MHz bands and inner sectors are configured with the new frequency bands mentioned in Sect. 3.2. On the other hand,

Fig. 6 is plotted for the same inner carrier frequency 1800 MHz and different outer carrier frequency. For comparisons purpose the existing macro only (MO) 3 × 1 networks is used as a reference configuration.

As it can be seen in Fig. 4, applying vertical sectorization degrades CDF of UE SINR in all cases. This is because as a new cell incorporated, additional co-channel interferences also introduced. It can also be observed as the operating bands become higher CDF of UE SINR degrades more besides the more bandwidth we obtained. Among the studied cases, scenario 1 out performs the other studied configurations. But, as we move the lower operating bands, we get lower bandwidth as indicated in Table 1.

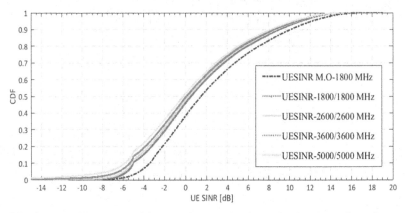

Fig. 4. CDF of UE SINR of the same inner and outer sectors bands configurations.

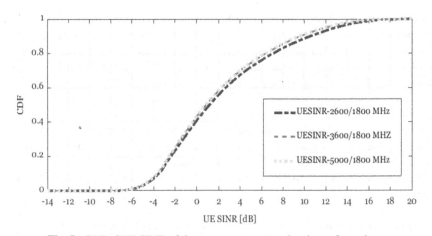

Fig. 5. CDF of UE SINR of the same outer sectors bands configurations.

Figure 5 and 6 are plotted to observe performance impact of configuring sectors with different operating frequency bands. As it can be seen in both figures such configuration has a better performance compared with sectors with same operating band. In Fig. 6, performance of the existing 3 × 1 configuration and group 2 cases are compared with respect to CDF of UE SINR under equal band width. As it can be observed from the figure, all configuration out performs the existing 3 × 1 MO configuration at 10%-ile, 50%-ile and 90%-ile of UE SINR (see Fig. 6).

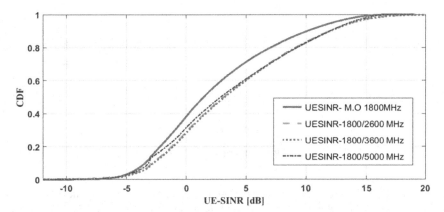

Fig. 6. CDF of UE SINR of the same inner sectors bands configurations.

Figure 7 is plotted to compare UE SINR of the existing MO network, VS 1800/1800 MHz and VS 1800/3600 MHz. Their UE SINR at 10%-ile: −3.44 dB, −5.04 dB and −2.76 dB, at 50%-ile: 1.46 dB, 0.51 dB and 3.24 dB and at 90%-ile: 10.12 dB, 8.96 dB and 11.99 dB respectively. The values show that scenario 6 out performs the other configuration at all percentile.

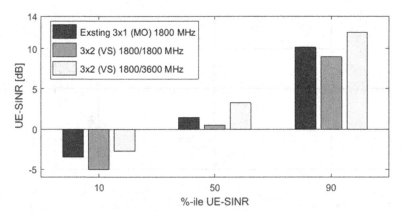

Fig. 7. Comparison of CDF of UE-SINR at 10%-ile, 50%-ile and 90%-ile.

Figure 8 and 9 show performance of UE throughputs which are plotted with antenna configuration listed under Table 1. The results are compared with the existing 3 × 1 network. As it can be observed in the figure, the entire identified configuration outperforms the existing 3 × 1 macro configuration. Specifically, scenario 6 significantly improves the performance of UE throughput in all percentiles.

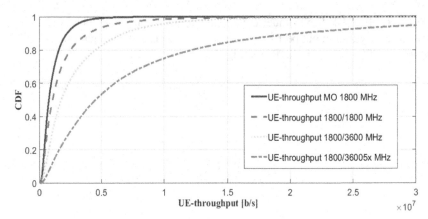

Fig. 8. CDF of UE throughput.

At 10%-ile UE throughput of the existing 3 × 1 configuration is about 0.273 Mbps where as scenario 6 with the same bandwidth is about 0.296 Mbps and scenario 6 with different band width is about 0.478 Mbps. At 50%-ile UE throughput of the existing 3 × 1 configuration is about 0.75 Mbps where as scenario 6 with the same bandwidth is about 1.06 Mbps and scenario 6 with different bandwidth is about 1.76 Mbps. At 90%-ile UE throughput of the existing network is about 2.23 Mbps whereas scenario 6 with same band width is about 3.96 Mbps and scenario 6 with the different bandwidth is about 6.83 Mbps (see Fig. 8 and 9).

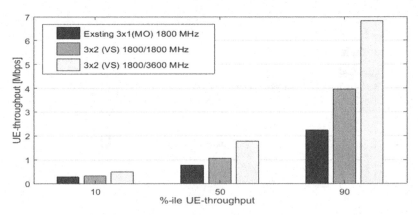

Fig. 9. Comparison of CDF of UE throughput at 10%-ile, 50%-ile and 90%-ile.

UE throughput gain at 10%-ile, 50%-ile and 90%-ile, for 3 × 2 1800/3600 MHz and 3 × 2, 1800/36005x MHz cases are compared to the existing 3 × 1 macro only configuration as depicted in Fig. 10. For equal bandwidth case, a relative gain of about 75.1%, 134.6% and 206.3 at 10%-ile, 50%-ile and 90%-ile respectively are obtained. For the case of 1800/36005x a gain of 236.6%, 504% and 821.5.7% at 10%-ile, 50%-ile and 90%-ile respectively are obtained compared with the existing macro only configuration (see Fig. 10). Therefore, applying vertical sectorization with different operating bands significantly improves both CDF of UE SINR and throughput at all percentile.

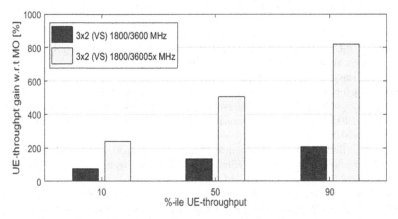

Fig. 10. UE-throughput percentile gain.

5   Conclusion

In this paper, we have analyzed performance impact of vertical sectorization in realistic network environment of Addis Ababa city for sub-6-GHz bands including the new 5G bands defined by 3GPP specification groups. CDF of UE SINR and throughput performances are used as a performance metrics. After analyzing the studied scenarios, throughput performance of the selected scenario is compared with the existing 3 × 1 LTE network. Based on the results, configuring VS with different operating bands results in a better performance compared to configuring both inner and outer sectors with the same carrier frequency. We also observed that, when the operating frequency become higher and higher UE SINR degrades. The identified configuration enhances system performance of user throughput up to 236.6%, 504% and 821.5% at 10%-ile, 50%-ile and 90%-ile respectively compared to the existing 3 × 1 configuration. This performance gain is obtained due to the introduction of additional resource elements and the improved UE SINR. Effect of vertical sectorization in high rise building, higher order vertical sectorization, multi objective optimization and cell association in vertical sectorization can be an important future work.

References

1. Cisco white paper, Cisco Visual Networking Index: Forecast and Methodology, 2016–2021. Cisco public (2017)
2. Report, IMT Traffic estimates for the years 2020 to 2030, ITU-R M.2370-0 (2015)
3. Adam, L.: Understanding what is happening in ICT in Ethiopia. A supply and demand side analysis of the ICT sector, Evidence for ICT Policy, Action Policy Paper (2012)

4. Haile, B.B., Aga, D., Mulu, B.: On the relevance of capacity enhancing 5G technologies for Ethiopia. In: 10th Ethiopian ICT Annual Conference, Addis Ababa, Ethiopia (2017)
5. Whitepaper, 5G vision and requirements, IMT-2020 (5G) Promotion Group (2015)
6. GSMA, 5G Spectrum: GSMA public policy position (2018)
7. Busari, S., Mumtaz, S., Al-Rubaye, S., Rodriguez, J.: 5G millimeter-wave mobile broadband: performance and challenges. IEEE Commun. Mag. **56**, 137–143 (2018)
8. 3GPP, 5G NR User Equipment (UE) radio transmission and reception, TS 38.101-1, Technical Specification, version 15.3.0 Release 15 (2018)
9. Sanad, M., Hassan, N.: A Sub-6 GHz multi-beam base station antenna for 5G with an arbitrary beam-tilting for each beam. In: Radio and Wireless Symposium (RWS), Orlando. IEEE (2019)
10. Fangchao, Z., et al.: A system level evaluation of vertical sectorization for active antenna system. In: 2015 IEEE/CIC International Conference on Communications, China, pp. 126–131. IEEE (2015)
11. Osman, N., Yilmaz, S., Jyri, H.: System level analysis of vertical sectorization for 3GPP LTE. In: 6th International Symposium on Wireless Communication Systems, Tuscany, pp. 453–457. IEEE (2009)
12. Youqi, F., Jian, W., Zhuyan, Z., Liyun, D., Hongwen, Y.: Analysis of vertical sectorization for HSPA on a system level: capacity and coverage. In: IEEE Vehicular Technology Conference (VTC Fall), Quebec, pp. 1–5. IEEE (2012)
13. Caretti, M., Crozzoli, M., Del, G., Orlando, A.: Cell splitting based on active antennas: performance assessment for LTE system. In: WAMICON 2012 IEEE Wireless & Microwave Technology Conference, Florida, pp. 1–5. IEEE (2012)
14. Song, Y., Yun, X., Nagata, S., Chen, L.: Investigation on elevation beamforming for future LTE-advanced. In: IEEE International Conference on Communications Workshop (ICC), Hungary (2013)
15. Wei, Z., Wang, Y., Lin, W.: Optimization of down tilts adjustment combining joint transmission and 3D beamforming in 3D MIMO. In: IEEE/CIC ICCC 2014 Symposium on Wireless Communications Systems, Shanghai, pp. 728–732. IEEE (2015)
16. Siew, N., Zhong, L., Sai, W., Yong, C.: Optimizing radio network parameters for vertical sectorization via Taguchi's method. IEEE Trans. Veh. Technol. **65**, 860–869 (2015)
17. Joydeep, A., Salam, A.: Optimizing vertical sectorization for high-rises. In: International Conference on Computing, Networking and Communications (ICNC), Garden Grove, pp. 1–5. IEEE (2015)
18. Jinping, N., Geoffrey, Y., Li, F., Wei, W., Weike, N., Xun, L.: Downtilts optimization and power allocation for vertical sectorization in AAS-based LTE-a downlink systems. In: IEEE 86th Vehicular Technology Conference (VTC-Fall), Toronto, pp. 1–5. IEEE (2017)
19. Fan, J., Li, W., Zhang, Y., Deng, J.: Fractional pilot reuse with vertical sectorization in massive MIMO systems. In: 2017 IEEE 85th Vehicular Technology Conference (VTC Spring), Sydney, pp. 4–7. IEEE (2017)
20. Fengyi, Y., Jianmin, Z., Weiliang, X., Xuetian, Z.: Field trial results for vertical sectorization in LTE network using active antenna system. In: IEEE International Conference on Communications (ICC), Sydney, pp. 2508–2512. IEEE (2014)
21. Weiliang, X., Qimei, C., Fengyi, Y., Qi, B., Yifei, Y.: Experimental investigation on a vertical sectorization system with active antenna. IEEE Commun. Mag. **54**, 89–97 (2016)
22. Muhammad, H., Usman, S., Jukka, L.: Analysis of vertical and horizontal sectorization in suburban environment using 3D ray tracing. In: 23rd International Conference on Telecommunications (ICT), Thessaloniki, pp. 1–6. IEEE (2016)
23. Zeleke, S., Haile, B.: Performance analysis of vertical sectorization for LTE realistic deployment scenario. In: Mekuria, F., Nigussie, E., Tegegne, T. (eds.) ICT4DA 2019. CCIS, vol. 1026, pp. 154–163. Springer, Cham (2019). https://doi.org/10.1007/978-3-030-26630-1_13

24. Usman, M., Ruttik, K., Jäntti, R.: Performance analysis of vertical and higher order sectorization in urban environment at 28 GHz. In: 26th International Conference on Telecommunications (ICT), Hanoi, pp. 8–10. IEEE (2019)
25. Derege, K., Wegmann, B., Viering, I., Klein, A.: Mathematical model for vertical sectorization (VS) in AAS based LTE deployment. In: 11th International Symposium Wireless Communication Systems, Barcelona, pp. 100–105. IEEE (2014)
26. Preben, M., et al.: LTE system capacity compared to Shannon bounds. In: IEEE VTC Spring 2007, Dublin, pp. 1234–1238. IEEE (2007)
27. Dongheon, L., Sheng, S., Xiaofeng, Z., Zhisheng, N.: Spatial modeling of the traffic density in cellular networks. IEEE Wirel. Commun. 21, 80–88 (2014)

Power Loss Reduction and Voltage Profile Improvement of Radial Distribution System Through Simultaneous Network Reconfiguration and Distributed Generation Integration

Habtemariam Aberie[(⊠)], Kassaye Gizaw, Belachew Banteyirga, and Alganesh Ygzaw

Bahir Dar University, Bahir Dar, Ethiopia

Abstract. In this paper Particle Swarm Optimization (PSO) based simultaneous distribution network reconfiguration and optimal Distributed Generation (DG) integration is conducted to significantly minimize the power losses and enhance the voltage profile of an electric power distribution network. The resource feasibility of solar and wind energy in Bahir Dar town was also assessed and the results revealed that solar energy production is more preferable. Backward/forward load flow analysis is deployed so as to determine the power losses and the voltage profile of each buses in the system. The proposed method is tested using MATLAB software in one of Bahir Dar distribution feeders called Bata feeder, and the objective function is evaluated by considering numerous constraints such as radiality, voltage profile, DG output limit and branch current limit. The simulation results obtained using simultaneous distribution network reconfiguration and DG insertion are encouraging. The voltage magnitude of all nodes is above the minimum threshold value and the minimum voltage is enhanced from 0.9150 pu to 0.9600 pu. In addition to this, the active and reactive power loss reduction are 54.42% and 46.37%, respectively. The cost effectiveness of the required DG size is also scrutinized and the payback period has become five years.

Keywords: Distributed generation · Network reconfiguration · Power loss · Voltage profile

1 Introduction

In an electric power distribution system, not only a substantial amount of power is lost but also the voltage profile of distant nodes from the main supplying substation are frequently below the minimum threshold value (0.95 pu) especially during heavy load conditions. This in turn exposes the end consumers to continuously suffer from under-voltage problem. G. Sasi Kumar, Dr. S. Sarat Kumar and Dr. S.V. Jayaram Kumar [9] in 2017 proposed the reconfiguration of an electrical distribution network for power loss

© ICST Institute for Computer Sciences, Social Informatics and Telecommunications Engineering 2021
Published by Springer Nature Switzerland AG 2021. All Rights Reserved
M. A. Delele et al. (Eds.): ICAST 2020, LNICST 384, pp. 244–258, 2021.
https://doi.org/10.1007/978-3-030-80621-7_18

reduction and voltage improvement. A new technique for reconfiguration of the network based on loss sensitivity factor to decide the switching combination and to achieve the best combination of switches for minimum active power loss and voltage profile enhancement which in turn improves the voltage stability in a radial distribution system is clearly presented. Only the active power loss is considered but the reactive power loss minimization has also been given equal emphasis especially when the feeder is connected to industries that large MVA inductive type of loads exist. I.J. Hasan, *M.R.Ab. Ghani and C.K. Gan* [1] in 2014 proposed optimum distributed generation allocation in a distribution system for power loss minimization and voltage profile enhancement using particle swarm optimization. The method had been tested on IEEE 33-bus radial distribution system and the results show that the stated method is effective in its performance. However, the feasibility study and the cost-effectiveness of distributed generation integration and reactive power loss reduction were not considered. Shreya Mahajan and Shelly Vadhera [2] in 2016 also presented optimal sizing and deploying of distributed generation unit by a modified multi-objective particle swarm optimization technique. The proposed method reduced the active power loss by 71.67% and maintained all node voltage magnitudes between the permissible limit but the real power loss can be significantly further minimized if the network topology is reconfigured optimally. R. Srinivassa Rao and others [7] in 2013 stated power loss minimization in distribution system using simultaneous network reconfiguration and distributed generation installation. Metaheuristic harmony search algorithm and sensitivity analysis are used for network reconfiguration and optimal DG location identification with an objective of real power loss minimization and voltage profile enhancement. The proposed method has been implemented on the IEEE 33-bus test system and the results obtained are encouraging. However, reactive power reduction has not been incorporated in the objective function besides any recent and effective optimization technique was not used.

From the literature reviewed, it is observed that all of the previous works focused on only active power loss minimization and voltage profile improvement in a radial distribution network. In this research, reactive power loss reduction, resource feasibility study of solar and wind type DG, possible location of tie-switches and cost-effectiveness of DG penetration on Bahir Dar power distribution network are also considered.

2   Resource Feasibility Study for Wind and Solar Energy

The solar and wind power plant energy outputs are strongly dependent on the sun radiation and the wind speed respectively which are stochastic in nature [10]. Therefore, the feasibility of resources for either solar and/or wind type DG installation at Bahir Dar town are first investigated before the study of their optimal size and appropriate bus location. The Ethiopian national metrology agency has recorded the sunshine hour of Bahir Dar city for ten consecutive years and these values are converted to solar irradiance. The results are depicted in Fig. 1 below.

Similarly, the wind speed at two meter above the ground for Bahir Dar town are collected from the metrology agency and these data are evaluated at forty meter as shown below (Fig. 2).

The solar irradiance of Bahir Dar city is from 4.0–5.5 kwh/m^2/day throughout the year whereas the cut-in wind speed is 2.71 m/s at 40 m height. Based on the resource

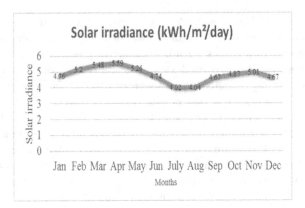

Fig. 1. Monthly average solar irradiance

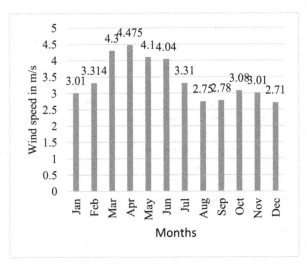

Fig. 2. Monthly wind speed at 40 m

data which are presented above, solar type DG is more preferable whereas the wind type DG is not feasible. Furthermore, solar type DG is more acceptable since it does not require any reactive power to inject electric power to the system to which it is connected whereas the wind type DG needs reactive power supply for its operation. On top of that, the wind speed continuously varies from hour to hour which in turn affects the stability of the power system and may not be able to cover the base load demand [15].

In general, considering the resource abundance of sunshine hour and wind speed in Bahir Dar city and considering the comparative benefits of PV versus wind, type I DG which injects only active power to the system is considered in this research for power loss minimization and voltage profile enhancement of a distribution network.

3   Optimal Tie-Switches Placement

Tie switches are normally open and are closed during reconfiguration to change topology of the network. Bahir Dar Distribution network consists of some sectionalize switches and two tie-switches. But only these two tie-switches are not sufficient enough to successfully reconfigure the network and it is a must to add at least two extra tie-switches. The best possible locations of these additional tie-switches are identified based on the following constraints.

i.   Line length between non-consecutive nodes
     The tie-line shall connect two non-consecutive nodes whose separation distance is smaller so that the tie-line impedance will be minimum possible.
ii. Geographical constraints
     Even if the distance between two non-consecutive nodes is the smallest as compared to others, they can't be taken as a sending node and a receiving node for the tie-line provided that if it is geographically impossible for the over-head line installation. In other words, the overhead tie-line should be installed following the edge of the street road so that there will be ease of maintenance.
iii. Voltage profile
     The voltage profile of the sending end voltage has to be relatively better than the sending end voltage.

Considering the above-mentioned criteria for tie-switches placement, the new single line diagram of the network equipped with four tie-switches, in which the two tie-switches (36 and 37) are added in this research whereas tie-switches (34 and 35) already exist before, is presented below in Fig. 3.

Based on the tie-lines (34, 35, 36 and 37) location, the following four loops are constructed.

$$L_1 = [3 \ 4 \ 5 \ 10 \ 14 \ 15 \ 16 \ 17 \ 34]$$
$$L_2 = [11 \ 12 \ 13 \ 23 \ 24 \ 25 \ 26 \ 35]$$
$$L_3 = [8 \ 18 \ 19 \ 20 \ 21 \ 29 \ 30 \ 36]$$
$$L_4 = [22 \ 27 \ 28 \ 31 \ 37]$$

Now, the main target of optimal network reconfiguration is that, which sectionalize line in each loop has to be opened so that an optimal and radial network structure with minimum possible power loss and better voltage profile can be obtained. The sectionalize lines to be opened are determined with PSO optimization as discussed in the coming sections.

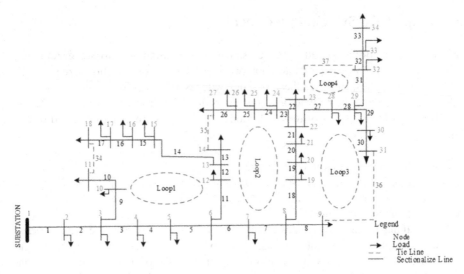

Fig. 3. Single line diagram of BATA feeder with tie-switches

4 Problem Formulation

4.1 Load Flow Analysis in Distribution System

The network shown in Fig. 4 is considered for optimization problem formulation of network reconfiguration. A set of recursive equations can be derived from this single line diagram so as to get the load flow equations of a radial distribution network.

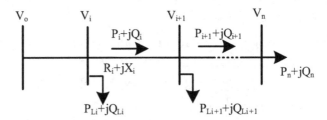

Fig. 4. Single line diagram of a radial distribution system

Active and reactive power losses between node i and $i + 1$ before network reconfiguration are formulated as follows [7].

$$P_{i+1} = P_i - P_{Loss,i} - P_{Li+1}$$

$$= P_i - \frac{R_i}{V_i^2}\left(P_i^2 + Q_i^2\right) - P_{Li+1} \tag{1}$$

$$Q_{i+1} = Q_i - Q_{Loss,i} - Q_{Li+1}$$

$$= Q_i - \frac{X_i}{V_i^2}\left(P_i^2 + Q_i^2\right) - Q_{Li+1} \tag{2}$$

Now, the power losses equation in the line connecting bus i and bus i + 1 can be derived as:

$$P_{loss}(i, i+1) = \frac{R_i}{V_i^2}\left(P_i^2 + Q_i^2\right) \tag{3}$$

$$Q_{loss}(i, i+1) = \frac{X_i}{V_i^2}\left(P_i^2 + Q_i^2\right) \tag{4}$$

The total power losses of the feeder are therefore calculated by summing up the losses of the line sections as shown below.

$$f_1 = P_{T,loss} = \sum_{i=1}^{N} \frac{R_i}{V_i^2}\left(P_i^2 + Q_i^2\right) \tag{5}$$

$$f_2 = Q_{T,loss} = \sum_{i=1}^{N} \frac{X_i}{V_i^2}\left(P_i^2 + Q_i^2\right) \tag{6}$$

4.2 Distribution Network Reconfiguration

Let the apparent power flow from bus i to $i + 1$ after network reconfiguration be $P_i' + jQ_i'$.

The power losses between these buses after the network topology is altered can be formulated following similar procedures shown above.

$$P_{loss}'(i, i+1) = R_{i,i+1}\left(\frac{P_i'^2 + Q_i'^2}{V_i^2}\right) \tag{7}$$

$$Q_{loss}'(i, i+1) = X_{i,i+1}\left(\frac{P_i'^2 + Q_i'^2}{V_i^2}\right) \tag{8}$$

Total power losses of the system after network reconfiguration are:

$$f_3 = \sum_{i=1}^{N} P_{loss}'(i, i+1) \tag{9}$$

$$f_4 = \sum_{i=1}^{N} Q_{loss}'(i, i+1) \tag{10}$$

Now, the change in active power loss and reactive power loss before and after network reconfiguration which are the first objective functions in this scenario are determined as shown in Eqs. 13 and 14.

$$F_1 = \Delta P^R = \left(\sum_{i=1}^{N} P_{loss}(i, i+1) - \sum_{i=1}^{N} P_{loss}'(i, i+1)\right) \tag{11}$$

$$F_2 = \Delta Q^R = \left(\sum_{i=1}^{N} Q_{loss}(i, i+1) - \sum_{i=1}^{N} Q'_{loss}(i, i+1) \right) \qquad (12)$$

Bus voltage is one of the most significant security and power quality indices. As a result, minimization of bus voltage deviation is chosen as the second objective. This objective function can be described as follows [5]:

$$F_3 = \sum_{i=1}^{N} (1 - V_i)^2 \qquad (13)$$

Lastly, thus three individual objective functions [F_1, F_2 and F_3] are combined together to get one multi-objective (MOF) optimization problem as shown below. However, the power loss objective function is formulated as maximization problem whereas the voltage deviation objective function is minimization problem. Therefore, the third objective function is changed to maximization problem by multiplying negative.

There are numerous system constraints that must be considered and fulfilled in the process distribution network reconfiguration. These constraints are listed and explained below.

Voltage Constraint: According to the IEEE standard, voltage magnitudes should be maintained between 0.95 pu and 1.05 pu.

$$0.95 \leq V_i \leq 1.05$$

Current Constraint: Current at each branch must be less than or equal to its maximum capacity. This constraint can be described as:

$$I_{ij} \leq I_{ij}^{max} \qquad (14)$$

Radiality Constraint: The distribution network is supposed to remain radial after network reconfiguration is applied since protection schemes implementation will be relatively easier. In other words, the number of branches in a certain loop before reconfiguration must greater than the number of branches after the reconfiguration at least by one unit.

$$\sum_{i=1}^{M_i} (|S_i|) \leq M_i - 1 \qquad (15)$$

Where M_i is the amount branches in the ith loop
S_i is the branch after reconfiguration

In general, the network reconfiguration problem formulation for power losses reduction and voltage profile improvement is as shown below.

Maximize

$$F = W_1 * \Delta P^R + W_2 * \Delta Q^R - W_3 * \sum_{i=1}^{N} ((1 - V_i)^2)$$

Subjected to

$$\begin{cases} 0.95 \leq V_i \leq 1.05 \\ I_{ij} \leq I_g^{max} \\ \sum_{i=1}^{M_i} (|S_i|) \leq M_i - 1 \\ W_1 + W_2 + W_3 = 1 \end{cases}$$

Where: W_1 and W_2 are the weighting factors given priority to reduction of real and reactive power losses, respectively.

W_3 is the weighting factor given priority to voltage profile improvement.

4.3 DG Sizing and Placement

DG insertion to a distribution system has numerous advantages viz. reduction of line losses, improvement of voltage profile, peak demand shaving, reduced environmental effects, and so on. However, it may lead to poor voltage profile and high-power loss if the DG size and location is not optimally determined. In this paper, PSO is used to allocate and select the optimal size of DG, and the objective function formulation along with system constraints and system modeling (depicted in Fig. 5) are shown below.

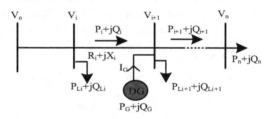

Fig. 5. Distribution network with DG

When DG is integrated to the distribution system as depicted in Fig. 6, the power loss equations derived above can be modified as:

$$P_{DG,Loss}(i, i+1) = \frac{R_i}{V_i^2} \left(P_i^2 + Q_i^2 \right) + \frac{R_i}{V_i^2} \left(P_G^2 + Q_G^2 - 2P_i P_G - 2Q_i Q_G \right) \quad (16)$$

$$Q_{DG,Loss}(i, i+1) = \frac{X_i}{V_i^2} \left(P_i^2 + Q_i^2 \right) + \frac{X_i}{V_i^2} \left(P_G^2 + Q_G^2 - 2P_i P_G - 2Q_i Q_G \right) \quad (17)$$

Net power losses reduction in the system is:

$$\Delta P_{loss}^{DG} = \frac{R_i}{V_i^2} \left(P_G^2 + Q_G^2 - 2P_i P_G - 2Q_i Q_G \right) \quad (18)$$

$$\Delta Q_{loss}^{DG} = \frac{X_i}{V_i^2} \left(P_G^2 + Q_G^2 - 2P_i P_G - 2Q_i Q_G \right) \quad (19)$$

As a result, the objective function can be formulated as shown below:

Maximize

$$F = W_1 * \Delta P_{loss}{}^{DG} + W_2 * \Delta Q_{loss}{}^{DG} - W_3 * \sum_{i=1}^{N}(1-V_i)^2$$

Subjected to
$$\begin{cases} 0.95 \leq V_i \leq 1.05 \\ I_{ij} \leq I_{ij}{}^{max} \\ P_G \leq P_G{}^{max} \\ Q_G \leq Q_G{}^{max} \\ W_1 + W_2 + W_3 = 1 \end{cases}$$

However, in this research type I DG is used since wind resource is not sufficient enough to generate the required power which is 1.25 MVA (50% of the total peak load). As a result, the reactive power constraint is not considered in this research because the power output from type I DG is only active power.

5 Simultaneous Network Reconfiguration and DG Allocation

In this scenario, the objective functions and constraints obtained before are merged together in order that the power loss reduction and bus voltage profile improvement will be significantly enhanced. Different weighting factors are also considered for active power loss reduction, reactive power minimization and voltage enhancement. More priority is given for active power loss reduction next to voltage profile upgrading.

Maximize

$$F = \sum_{i=1}^{N} W_i * \left(\Delta P_{bss}{}^{R}(i, i+1) + \Delta P_{loss}{}^{DG}(i, i+1) \right) - \sum_{i=1}^{N} W_3 * (1-V_i)^2$$

Subjected to
$$\begin{cases} 0.95 \leq V_i \leq 1.05 \\ I_{ij} \leq I_{ij}{}^{max} \\ P_G \leq P_G{}^{max} \\ \sum_{i=1}^{M_i}(|S_i|) \leq M_i - 1 \\ W_1 + W_2 + W_3 = 1 \end{cases}$$

6 Results and Discussion

Four separated scenarios are considered to test the effectiveness of the proposed method on power loss minimization and voltage profile enhancement. The total number of particles/populations for the simulation result are fifty while the minimum and maximum voltage magnitude are fixed to be 0.95 pu and 1.05 pu, respectively.

Scenario I: The existing system (base case) is simulated and the resulting voltage profile and power losses are depicted in Figs. 6 and 7, respectively.

Scenario II: The network topology is optimally reconfigured with the help the available sectionalize and tie-switches using PSO optimization without considering DG.
Scenario III: Type I DG is integrated with the network.
Scenario IV: The network is reconfigured simultaneous with DG installation.

The network reconfiguration simulation results reveal that the voltage profile of the system is significantly improved after the network is optimally altered as shown in Fig. 6 below (blue color). The minimum voltage before network reconfiguration was 0.9150 pu, and it is improved to 0.9467 pu after the topology is reconfigured using PSO optimization.

However, the voltage profile of some buses (6 7 8 9 and 11) is decreased after network reconfiguration is applied. This problem may happen most of the time since the topology of the network is changed. But the voltage profile of these buses is still above the minimum threshold value. Therefore, even if some buses voltage profile is affected when the network is altered, network reconfiguration results in remarkable voltage profile improvement.

Optimal distribution network reconfiguration not only enhances the voltage profile of the system but also it reduces the power losses substantially as shown in Fig. 7 below. The active power loss is reduced to 196.48 kW from 307.12 kW (base-case) whereas the reactive power loss is reduced to 194.16 kVAr from 258.70 kVAr (base-case). In other words, the active and reactive power loss reduction due to optimal network reconfiguration alone are 36.13% and 24.45%, respectively.

As shown in Fig. 6 (green color), the voltage profile of all buses except the first bus are moderately improved after 0.01pu DG size is connected at the end bus. The minimum voltage before the installation of DG was 0.9150pu but it is enhanced to 0.9369pu due to the integration of this DG.

Similarly, the power losses reduction when DG is connected to bus 34 is presented in Fig. 7 (scenario III). The active and reactive power losses are considerably minimized. In other words, the active power loss reduction is 34.06% whereas the reactive power loss reduction is 32.13%.

The power losses minimization and voltage profile enhancement of a distribution network using network reconfiguration and DG installation separately, are clearly discussed before. Both these methods can't achieve appreciable results in loss reduction and voltage improvement when they are considered individually. The network reconfiguration technique in parallel with DG installation was conducted using PSO algorithm in order that the voltage profile and loss minimization can be significantly enhanced.

As it can be observed all bus voltages after the network is reconfigured in parallel with DG installation are maintained above the minimum nominal value. For instance, the minimum voltage profile of the network before applying any techniques (base case) was 0.9150 pu and it is substantially upgraded to (0.9600 pu) when the proposed method is applied.

Likewise, Fig. 7 presents the network percentage total active and reactive power loss reduction when the afro-mentioned distribution network performance enhancement methods are considered. The results from this scenario, as it can be noted in Figs. 6 and 7 below, are very encouraging as compared with the results from when these methods are used exclusively. The active and reactive power loss reduction are 54.42% and 46.37%,

Table 1. Result summary of the proposed method

Scenarios	Performance measurements	
Scenario I	Switches Opened	33, 34, 35 & 36
	Active power loss (kW)	307.12
	Reactive power loss (kVAr)	258.70
	Minimum voltage (pu)	0.9150
	Maximum voltage deviation	8.5000%
	Average computing time (ms)	65
Scenario II	Switches opened	14, 23, 31 & 36
	Active power loss (kW)	196.48
	Reactive power loss (kVAr)	194.16
	Active power loss reduction	36.02%
	Reactive power loss reduction	24.95%
	Minimum voltage (pu)	0.9467
	Maximum voltage deviation	5.3300%
	Average computing time (ms)	130
Scenario III	Switches opened	33, 34, 35 & 36
	Size of the DG (MW)	1
	Bus location of the DG	34
	Active power loss (kW)	202.51
	Reactive power loss (kVAr)	175.59
	Active power loss reduction	34.06%
	Reactive power loss reduction	32.13%
	Minimum voltage (pu)	0.9369
	Maximum voltage deviation	6.3100%
	Average computing time (ms)	95
Scenario IV	Switches opened	14, 23, 31 & 36
	Size of the DG (MW)	1
	Bus location of the DG	31
	Active power loss (kW)	139.89
	Reactive power loss (kVAr)	138.74
	Active power loss reduction	54.42%
	Reactive power loss reduction	46.37%
	Minimum voltage (pu)	0.960
	Maximum voltage deviation	4.000%
	Average computing time (ms)	215

respectively. The convergence for network reconfiguration suppresses DG integration this due to the time required for each particle to try all available sectionalize and tie-switches combination for better performance.

In general, the results from all the scenarios are summarized and presented in Table 1. The results show that each method plays an important role, when they are applied independently, in the total active and reactive power losses minimization and system voltage profile improvement.

However, it can be noted that the last scenario which is simultaneous network reconfiguration and DG allocation has a paramount importance for loss minimization and voltage profile enhancement.

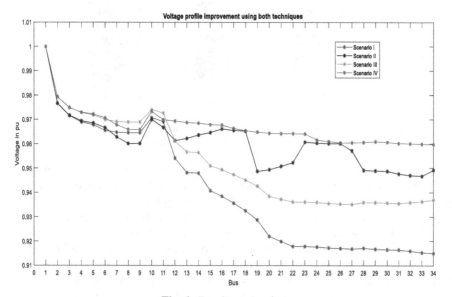

Fig. 6. Results comparison

7   Cost Analysis and Payback Period

The cost effectiveness of DG integration on the existing network is determined from the saving cost which is the difference of the losses in dollar before and after applying the proposed techniques. The existing network total power loss was 307.12 kW. In other words, 0.1098 million $/year is lost. After the proposed method is used, the power loss is reduced to 139.98 Kw that means 0.0500 million $/year is lost. This indicates that 0.0598 million $/year can be saved when 1 MW solar power plant is installed in conjunction with re-structuring the network topology.

The payback period is the ration of the capital cost to the saving cost as shown in Eq. (20) below.

$$Payback\ period = \frac{Capital\ cost(dollar)}{Saving\ cost(dollar/year)} \tag{20}$$

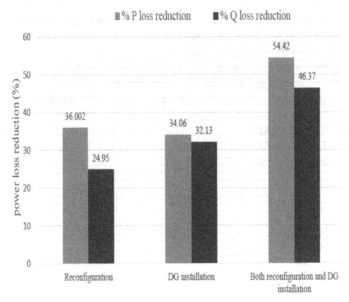

Fig. 7. Power loss reduction

The saving cost is already determined before whereas the capital cost is calculated by summing the cost for solar panel, inverters, battery, installation cost and maintenance cost. The initial capital cost for solar panel, inverters and batteries is 0.2093 million$, 0.0857 million$ and 0.00738 million$, respectively. The installation cost and maintenance cost are assumed to be no more than 0.00341 and 0.0003451 million $/year, respectively. Summing all these costs yields to total capital cost of 0.306 million$.

When the capital cost and the saving cost are substituted in Eq. (20) above, the payback period becomes around five years. This means that 0.05941 million $/year can be saved after five years from when the solar power plant is installed to the system.

8   Conclusion

In this research work, an effective method has been anticipated to reconfigure distribution networks simultaneous with optimal DG units' installation. In addition, various loss reduction methods (only network reconfiguration, only DG installation, DG installation simultaneous with network reconfiguration) are also simulated to confirm the superiority of the proposed method. One of the proficient meta-heuristic optimization techniques called PSO is used to simultaneously reconfigure and allocate DG units. The proposed method is tried on Bahir Dar distribution network specifically on BATA feeder at heavy load condition.

The simulation results show that 167.14 kW active power can be saved by applying the proposed method and also the entire buses voltage profile are maintained within the IEEE acceptable range. In other words, the active and reactive percentage power losses reduction due to this method are 54.42% and 46.37%, respectively and the minimum voltage profile is 0.9600 pu which confirms that simultaneous network reconfiguration and DG installation method is most effective in reducing power losses and improving the voltage profile compared to other methods.

The cost effectiveness and payback period are also assessed in detail. The results showed that 0.05941 million dollars can be saved in each year after five years from when the DG unit is integrated to the system.

References

1. Hasan, I.J., Ghani, M.Ab., Gan, C.K.: Optimum distributed generation allocation using PSO in order to reduce losses and voltage improvement (2014)
2. Vita, V.: Electricity distribution networks' analysis with particular references to distributed generation and protection. City University London (2016)
3. Minyou, H., Yuan, C.: Simulated annealing algorithm of optimal reconstruction in distribution system. Autom. Electr. Pow. Syst. **2** (1994)
4. Raut, U., Mishra, S.: Power distribution network reconfiguration for loss minimization using a new graph theory based genetic algorithm. In: 2017 IEEE Calcutta Conference (CALCON), pp. 1–5. IEEE (2017)
5. Biswas, S., Goswami, S.K., Chatterjee, A.: Optimum distributed generation placement with voltage sag effect minimization. Energy Convers. Manag. **53**(1), 163–174 (2012)
6. Kaur, N., Jain, S.K.: Placement of distributed generators for loss minimization and voltage improvement using particle swarm optimization. In: 2016 7th India International Conference on Power Electronics (IICPE), pp. 1–5. IEEE (2016)
7. Rao, R.S., Ravindra, K., Satish, K., Narasimham, S.: Power loss minimization in distribution system using network reconfiguration in the presence of distributed generation. IEEE Trans. Pow. Syst. **28**(1), 317–325 (2013)
8. El-Zonkoly, A.M.: Optimal placement of multi-distributed generation units including different load models using particle swarm optimization. IET Gener. Transm. Distrib. **5**(7), 760–771 (2011)
9. Kouzou, A., Mohammedi, R.: Optimal reconfiguration of a radial power distribution network based on Meta-heuristic optimization algorithms. In: 2015 4th International Conference on Electric Power and Energy Conversion Systems (EPECS), pp. 1–6. IEEE (2015)
10. Rezaei, P., Vakilian, M.: Distribution system efficiency improvement by reconfiguration and capacitor placement using a modified particle swarm optimization algorithm. In: 2010 IEEE Electrical Power and Energy Conference, pp. 1–6. IEEE (2010)
11. Esmaeilian, H.R., Fadaeinedjad, R.: Energy loss minimization in distribution systems utilizing an enhanced reconfiguration method integrating distributed generation. IEEE Syst. J. **9**(4), 1430–1439 (2015)
12. Niazi, G., Lalwani, M.: PSO based optimal distributed generation placement and sizing in power distribution networks: a comprehensive review. In: 2017 International Conference on Computer, Communications and Electronics (Comptelix), pp. 305–311. IEEE (2017)
13. Carpinelli, G., Celli, G., Pilo, F., Russo, A.: Distributed generation siting and sizing under uncertainty. In: 2001 IEEE Porto Power Tech Proceedings (Cat. No. 01EX502), vol. 4, p. 7. IEEE (2001)
14. Vallem, M.R., Mitra, J.: Siting and sizing of distributed generation for optimal microgrid architecture. In: 2005 Proceedings of the 37th Annual North American Power Symposium, pp. 611–616. IEEE (2005)

15. Sookananta, B., Kuanprab, W., Hanak, S.: Determination of the optimal location and sizing of distributed generation using particle swarm optimization. In: ECTI-CON2010: The 2010 ECTI International Confernce on Electrical Engineering/Electronics, Computer, Telecommunications and Information Technology, pp. 818–822. IEEE (2010)
16. Juma, S., Ngoo, L., Muriithi, C.: A review on optimal network reconfiguration in the radial distribution system using optimization techniques. In: Proceedings of Sustainable Research and Innovation Conference, pp. 34–40 (2018)
17. Saleh, O.A., Elshahed, M., Elsayed, M.: Enhancement of radial distribution network with distributed generation and system reconfiguration. J. Electr. Syst. 14(3) (2018)

A Comprehensive Review and Evaluation of Classical MPPT Techniques for a Photovoltaic System

Tefera T. Yetayew[1]([⊠]) and Tewodros G. Workineh[2]

[1] Department of Electrical Power and Control Engineering, Adama Science and Technology University, Adama, Ethiopia
[2] Electrical Power and Energy Program, Bahirdar Institute of Technology, Bahirdar, Ethiopia

Abstract. Extracting available maximum power is an important component of solar photovoltaic system which can be achieved by an efficient maximum power point tracking algorithm. Up to date review of related works summarized available MPPT algorithms as classical and modern optimization techniques. Among classical algorithms the incremental conductance (InCond) and perturb & observe (P&O) based tracking algorithms with duty ratio control are widely used due to relatively accurate MPP tracking capability and less implementation complexity under uniform radiation. However; steady-state oscillation, wrong perturbation direction for rapid climate change and failure to track the global peak under partial shade/mismatching operating conditions of the photovoltaic system are some of the limitations of these algorithms. Thus, in this work, a succinct review, formulations and evaluations of widely used classical techniques along with a proposed classical improved perturb and observe (IPO) to improve drawbacks of steady state oscillation has been done. The performance evaluation results of widely used classical perturbation based algorithms (InCond, P&O, IPO) using MATLAB/Simulink revealed improved performances of the improved perturbation based algorithm over the widely used classical (InCond, P&O) algorithms in reducing steady-state oscillations of step-change in irradiance without any partial shading condition of the photovoltaic (PV) of the PV system.

Keywords: Photovoltaic system · InCond · P&O · IPO · Steady-state oscillations

1 Introduction

Rapid growth of energy demand is a common phonon all over the world mainly due to population growth, industrialization and rapid growth of urbanization. Rapid exploitation of conventional energy sources such as coal, petroleum and natural gas is depleting the reserve all over the world and also resulted in global warming challenge to the planet earth. To solve or reduce these global challenges, efficient extraction and utilization of alternative and environmental friendly energy sources is the current research area where experts have been participating [1–3]. Among alternative sources of energy, solar energy

© ICST Institute for Computer Sciences, Social Informatics and Telecommunications Engineering 2021
Published by Springer Nature Switzerland AG 2021. All Rights Reserved
M. A. Delele et al. (Eds.): ICAST 2020, LNICST 384, pp. 259–272, 2021.
https://doi.org/10.1007/978-3-030-80621-7_19

utilization as a source of electricity is increasing at an alarming rate in the last two/three decades mainly due to clean source of energy, wide distribution of solar energy in many parts of the world, the conversion process has no moving parts, it can be generated at the point of use by which transmission cost/losses will be reduced, and abundant availability of the resource to manufacture photovoltaic cells. However, apart from poor conversion efficiency, solar photovoltaic system has also non-linear feature where its performance is highly affected by climatic conditions solar radiation and operating temperature, and requires high initial investment. These challenges call researchers in the area to look for efficient extraction algorithms of the available maximum power from the photovoltaic system [3–8].

Among different classical MPPT techniques proposed so far, fractional open/short circuit voltage/current methods can locate the maximum power point, however; the periodic short/open circuiting of the photovoltaic system for measurement purposes requires additional switch and this may result in complexity and losses. Perturbation based algorithms such as incremental conductance, perturb and observe, and hill-climbing algorithms share common shortcomings of oscillations during steady state condition, unable to locate the maximum power whenever there is partial shade and wrong tracking directions during fast change is atmospheric conditions [9–11]. Among widely used classical techniques, incremental conductance based maximum power extractions has been proposed to solve the limitation of perturb and observe based algorithm. Incremental conductance based method is based on the idea that slope of power versus voltage curve is zero at maximum power point and proposed to improve the tracking accuracy and dynamic performances for rapidly change in operating conditions. Theoretically, oscillation during steady state operation will be zero because. However; noise and digital resolution errors may create oscillations [10–12]. Thus, this paper provided a concise summary, the corresponding formulations of some of classical MPPT techniques for photovoltaic system and performance evaluations of widely used MPPT techniques along with the proposed voltage controlled classical improved P&O algorithm to improve steady-state oscillation problems of classical techniques.

The contents of this research are organized: the photovoltaic models and characteristics is presented in section two of the research, a concise review of related works and principle of maximum power extraction is presented in the third section of this research, a concise summary and formulations of common classical perturbation based algorithms is presented in the fourth section of the paper, implementations and results discussion for evaluation of some of widely used classical MPPT techniques and the improved perturbation based technique is presented in the fifth section of the research and the basic findings as concluding remarks are presented the sixth section of the research.

2 Photovoltaic Modules and Characteristics

Usually, photovoltaic modules are represented using equivalent circuit diagram of a current source connected parallel to a diode. Further improvement in accuracy of simulation of the simple model is done by adding a series resistor to consider connection losses and a shunt resistance considering leakage current. Summary of related works in the equivalent circuit models identified the available circuit models as, ideal diode, Rs, Rp and two diode Rp models having unknown parameters of three, four, and five respectively with improved accuracy of simulation. However, estimating unknown parameters is another challenge. Out of these models, Rp model with five unknown parameters is widely used due to relative accuracy and simplicity [13–15]. Environmental factors like operating temperature, speed of wind, surrounding humidity and radiation affect the performance of the photovoltaic module. Solar radiation has direct impact on the performance of the photovoltaic module, however; operating temperature has logarithmic and negative impact the performance of the photovoltaic module [13–17]. The corresponding equivalent circuit models and current-voltage (I-V)/power-voltage (P-V) characteristic plots and the corresponding effects irradiance and operating temperature on the performance of the module for a typical photovoltaic module (KC200GT) is presented in Fig. 1.

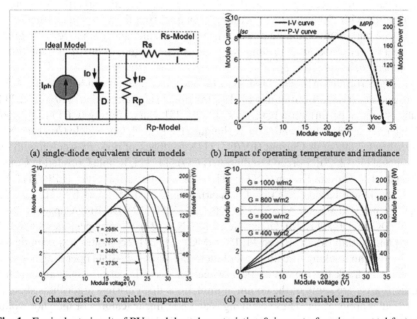

(a) single-diode equivalent circuit models

(b) Impact of operating temperature and irradiance

(c) characteristics for variable temperature

(d) characteristics for variable irradiance

Fig. 1. Equivalent circuit of PV modules, characteristics & impact of environmental factors

Mathematically, the current/voltage relations for the corresponding equivalent circuit models of single diode are presented in Eqs. (1)–(3) [13–17].

(i) Rs-Model:

$$I = I_{ph} - I_0\left[\exp\left(\frac{V + IRs}{vT}\right) - 1\right] \tag{1}$$

(ii) Rp-model:

$$I = I_{ph} - I_0\left[\exp\left(\frac{V + IR_S}{vT}\right) - 1\right] - \frac{V + IR_S}{R_P} \tag{2}$$

(iii) Ideal (simple-diode):

$$I = I_{ph} - I_o\left[\exp\left(\frac{V}{vT}\right) - 1\right] \tag{3}$$

where the dark saturation current is, I_o and modified ideality factor is vT.

3 Maximum Power Extraction of Photovoltaic Systems

An important component of photovoltaic system is maximum power point tracking where it main task is to operate the converter at the maximum available power of the photovoltaic system. Review of related works in the area verified availability of a number of algorithms with differences in operating principle, simplicity, cost and efficiency in tracking the maximum available power. The review result can summarize the available maximum power tracking algorithms for photovoltaic system in broad as evolutionary and classical technique [6–12].

Among perturbation based classical techniques, incremental conductance [3, 4, 11], perturb and observe, hill-climbing [11, 19], fractional short circuit current/voltage [11], variable step size perturbation based [11, 12, 20, 25], Curve-Fitting (CFT) [11], Look-up Table (LUT) [11], Differentiation Technique (DFT) [11], One-Cycle Control (OCC) [1], Feedback Voltage or Current (FV/FC) [11], feedback of power variation with current/voltage[11, 12, 20], Forced Oscillation (FCO) [11, 12], Ripple Correlation Control (RCC) [11, 12], Current Sweep (CST) [11], Estimated-Perturb-Perturb (EPP) [11], Parasitic Capacitance based (PCT) [11], Linearization-Based MPPT (LBT) [11, 20, 25], Load Current/Load Voltage Maximization (LCM/LVM) [12], DC Link Capacitor Droop Control (DC-LCDC) [11, 20], Gauss-Newton (GNT) [23, 24], Steepest-Descent (SDT) [24, 25] and Sliding-Mode-Based MPPT (SMC) [11, 24] techniques has been discovered. But, wrong tracking direction, oscillations during steady-state operating condition and unable to track the maximum peak whenever, there is partial shade/mismatching conditions arise are some of the common limitations that classical algorithms share for the particular application. These challenges and non-linear features of the photovoltaic module need algorithms to solve the problems [9–12, 18–24]. The operating points and the corresponding control action of a maximum power tracking algorithm for a particular photovoltaic module (KC200GT) are presented in Fig. 2.

Once the maximum power operating points is achieve, it is supposed to operate at that point unless there is a change in input/output parameter that shifts the MPP. Figure 2(b) shows the current/power locus plot to the maximum operating point. When the derivative of power with respecte to voltage is zero, that point is the maximum power point (in the graph, it is point C), PV voltage (V_{pv}) needs to be regulated either increasing or decreasing to/from MPP using some control action. For positive slope $(dP_{pv}/dV_{pv} > 0)$, V_{pv} increases and for negative slope $(dP_{pv}/dV_{pv} < 0)$, V_{pv} should decrease. Table in Fig. 2(c) shows the corresponding control action of the operating regions indicated. The current-voltage and power-voltage plots are indicated by the broken line trajectory [9, 11].

4 Concise Summary of Classical MPPT Techniques

Among perturbation based classical techniques, incremental conductance, perturb and observe, and hill-climbing algorithms are commonly used due to simplicity. These methods are efficient for uniform distribution of irradiance and they are simple to implement and inexpensive. However, they all share drawbacks of steady state oscillation, missing the right direction of perturbation for sudden change in atmospheric conditions like radiation, and unable to track the maximum power during partial-shade/mismatch operating conditions of the photovoltaic system [6–12, 22–24]. Descriptions to show the basic difference among classical techniques and the corresponding formulations are presented in the following sub-sections.

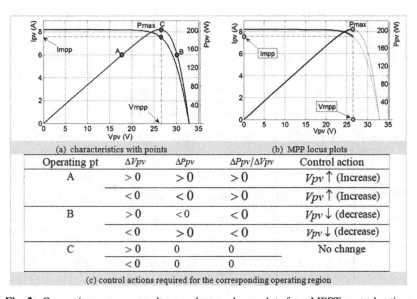

Operating pt	ΔV_{pv}	ΔP_{pv}	$\Delta P_{pv}/\Delta V_{pv}$	Control action
A	> 0	> 0	> 0	$V_{pv} \uparrow$ (Increase)
	< 0	< 0	> 0	$V_{pv} \uparrow$ (Increase)
B	> 0	< 0	< 0	$V_{pv} \downarrow$ (decrease)
	< 0	> 0	< 0	$V_{pv} \downarrow$ (decrease)
C	> 0	0	0	No change
	< 0	0	0	

(c) control actions required for the corresponding operating region

Fig. 2. Current/power versus voltage and power locus plots for a MPPT control actions

4.1 Perturb and Observe Algorithm

It is one of classical MPPT techniques characterized by perturbation of operating point and observe. The PV operating point is perturbed periodically by changing the voltage at PV source terminals, and after each perturbation, the control algorithm compares the values of the power fed by the PV source before and after the perturbation. For positive change in PV power, the direction of perturbation will be in the same direction otherwise direction of perturbation will be reversed [11, 18, 19, 25]. The mathematical representation of P&O algorithm is given in Eq. (4).

$$x_{k+1} = x_k \pm \Delta x = x_k + (x_k - x_{k-1})sign\,(p_k - p_{k-1}) \tag{4}$$

where x represents the variable of perturb, Δx is the perturbation size; and p is the available power from the photovoltaic system. In general, the algorithm can be described in Fig. 3.

4.2 Incremental Conductance Algorithm

Incremental conductance algorithm is among commonly used classical techniques where the principle of operation is based on the slope of power versus voltage curve. In principle, it is supposed to improve the drawbacks of steady-state oscillation and wrong direction of perturbation during fast climate changes. However, practically sampling, quantization error and noise results in oscillation with reduced amplitude [3, 4, 11, 26]. The direction of perturbation is based on comparison result of conductance and incremental conductance until the operating points reach at the MPP ($dP_{pv}/dV_{pv} = 0$). The principle can be described mathematically using Eq. (5).

$$\begin{aligned} \frac{dP_{pv}}{dV_{pv}} &= \frac{d(V_{pv}I_{pv})}{dV_{pv}} = I_{pv} + V_{pv}\frac{dI_{pv}}{dV_{pv}} \\ &= \frac{1}{V_{pv}} \cdot \frac{dP_{pv}}{dV_{pv}} = \frac{I_{pv}}{V_{pv}} + \frac{dI_{pv}}{dV_{pv}} \end{aligned} \tag{5}$$

Expressions in Eq. (6) show signs of conductance and incremental conductance relative to MPP [11, 25, 26].

$$\begin{cases} \dfrac{dP_{pv}}{dV_{pv}} = 0, & \dfrac{I_{pv}}{V_{pv}} = -\dfrac{dI_{pv}}{dV_{pv}} & G = \Delta G,\ at\ MPP \\[3mm] \dfrac{dP_{pv}}{dV_{pv}} > 0, & \dfrac{I_{pv}}{V_{pv}} > -\dfrac{dI_{pv}}{dV_{pv}} & G > \Delta G,\ left\ of\ MPP \\[3mm] \dfrac{dP_{pv}}{dV_{pv}} < 0, & \dfrac{I_{pv}}{V_{pv}} < -\dfrac{dI_{pv}}{dV_{pv}} & G < \Delta G,\ right\ of\ MPP \end{cases} \tag{6}$$

The procedures for implementation of InCond MPPT technique can be described using the flow chart in Fig. 4. $I(k)$, $V(k)$ and V_{ref} in the algorithm shows the photovoltaic current, the photovoltaic voltage and reference voltage to the voltage controller of the boost converter respectively.

4.3 Variable Step-Size Perturbation

MPPT techniques (P&O, hill-climbing and InCond) discussed in sections above use fixed step-size perturbation. Variable step-size perturbation based MPPT techniques can solve

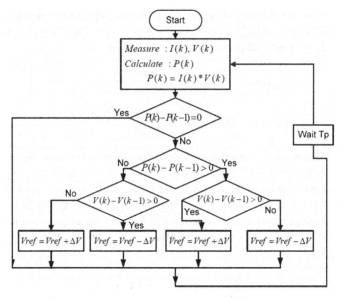

Fig. 3. Flowchart to implement P&O MPT technique

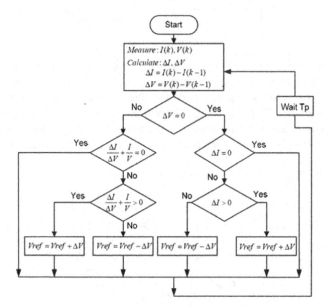

Fig. 4. Incremental conductance algorithm

limitations of oscillation during steady-state operation and missing the right direction of perturbation for rapid change in climatic conditions [12, 20, 27]. The expression in Eq. (7) shows the principle of perturbation with different size.

$$
\begin{cases}
d(k) = d(k-1) \pm N \left| \dfrac{\Delta P}{\Delta V} \right| \\
d(k) = d(k-1) \pm N \left| \dfrac{P(k) - P(k-1)}{V(k) - V(k-1)} \right|
\end{cases}
\tag{7}
$$

where coefficient N is factor toe scale to be determined during step size selection and the duty cycle is given by $d(k)$. Variable scaling factor can be determined by choosing large step size, Δd, initially. The derivative of power with voltage can be determined under constant step condition with Δd_{max} that can be selected as the maximum limit for the variable size operation [20]. Around MPP, derivative of power with voltage is the lowest value and for convergence of MPPT, variable step size rule should fulfill the relation in Eq. (8).

$$
\begin{cases}
N \left| \dfrac{\Delta P}{\Delta V} \right|_{fixed\ step = \Delta D\ max} < \Delta d_{max} \\
N < \Delta d_{max} / \left| \dfrac{\Delta P}{\Delta V} \right|_{fixed\ step = \Delta d\ max}
\end{cases}
\tag{8}
$$

where $\left| \frac{\Delta P}{\Delta V} \right|_{fixed\ step = \Delta d\ max}$ is the $\left| \frac{\Delta P}{\Delta V} \right|$ at fixed step size operation of Δd_{max}.

If N is determined by satisfying the relation in Eq. (8), a fast dynamic response can be achieved. If the relation is not satisfied, the MPP tracking will continue working with fixed step size [20]. The principle of variable perturbation size can be explained using P-V characteristic curve in Fig. 5. The initial operating point (P) is assumed to be P_1 with the assumption of perturbation size to be one. Imposing perturbation with size proportional to the photovoltaic power change, we can have the sequence P_1–P_7 [12, 20].

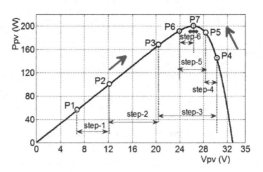

Fig. 5. P-V characteristic showing variable step-size perturbations

4.4 Reference Voltage Constant

Maximum power extraction based on the principle of constant reference voltage is based on the assumption that the corresponding voltage for the maximum power point is constant whenever there is change is radiation as shown in Fig. 6(a) and assumed that there is no change in operating temperature. Figure 6(b) shows the impact of operating temperature on the reference voltage [11, 19].

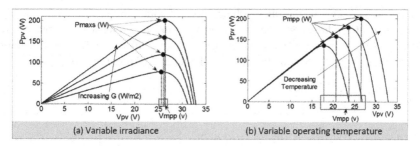

Fig. 6. Power versus voltage plots for variable radiation and operating temperature

4.5 Perturbation Based Improved MPPT Algorithm

Different techniques have been proposed to solve drawbacks of classical techniques. The research in [27] proposed a maximum power tracking algorithm to solve the failure to perturb the right direction whenever there is a rapid change in irradiance by taking measurements at half of sampling time in between sampling instants without any perturbation as shown in Fig. 7 (a). Power change between P_x and P_k is caused by MPPT perturbation and change in operating conditions. The basic concept behind can be described by Eq. (9) having the idea of constant radiation within one sampling instant.

$$\begin{cases} \Delta P = \Delta P_1 - \Delta P_2 = (P_x - P_k) - (P_{k+1} - P_x) \\ \quad = 2P_x - P_{k+1} - P_k \end{cases} \tag{9}$$

After calculating the change in power (ΔP), the process follows the principle of perturbation based technique approach. This method has drawbacks of increased complexity and also the probability missing right direction of perturbation when there is a rapid change in irradiance after a period of half sample time. To solve the drawbacks of perturbation based classical techniques, an improved perturbation based algorithm is formulated based on the idea described in [27]. Unlike the technique described above, additional measurement will be done close to P_{k+1} point ($\geq 80\%$ of one sample time). The basic procedures for implementation of the proposed algorithm can be explained using the flowchart in Fig. 7 (b). The parameters Ix and Vx are the measured PV current and voltages respectively.

5 Evaluation of Classical MPPT Techniques

Performance evaluation of widely used classical techniques (P&O and InCond) and the proposed technique has been done for variation of solar radiation keeping other factor at standard test conditions.

5.1 Architecture for Implementation

The basic components of the photovoltaic system include the maximum power point tracking algorithm, the boost converter and the controller along with the pulse width modulating signal generator. The architecture of the over all system for implementation is given in Fig. 8. In this schematic diagram, the letter "D" represents the diode.

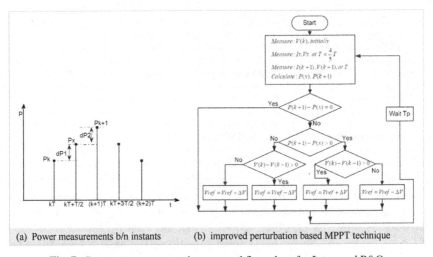

(a) Power measurements b/n instants   (b) improved perturbation based MPPT technique

Fig. 7. Power measurements instants and flow-chart for Improved P&O

Tables in Fig. 9(a) and (b) give the converter component values and manufacturer data sheet specifications of the commercial PV module selected for implementation respectively.

5.2 Discussions of Results

The performance evaluation of the corresponding algorithm has been done for variable input of radiation while keeping other factors at standard test condition. Figure 10 shows the MPP trajectories tracked (solid and colored lines) for the corresponding MPPT technique and P-V characteristic curves with circled dots indicating theoretical maximum power points.

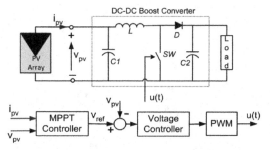

Fig. 8. Implementation diagram

Parameter	Value
Input voltage (V_{in})	$V_{in} = 26V$
Output voltage (V_{out})	$V_{out} = 100V$
Switching frequency (f_s)	$f_s = 25kHz$
Output voltage ripple ($\Delta V_o/V_o$)	1%
Load (R_L)	$R_L = 50\ \Omega$
Inductance (L)	$L = 75\mu H$
Input Capacitance (C_1)	$C_1 = 100\mu F$
Output capacitance (C_2)	$C_2 = 592\mu F$
(a) specifications of the Boost converter	

Parameter	Value
Voltage at MPP	Vmpp = 26.3V
Current at M P	Imp = 7.61A
Open Circuit Voltage	Voc = 32.9V
Short Circuit Current	Isc = 8.21A
Temp. Coeff. Isc, α_{Isc}	+3.18 mA/°C
Temp.Coeff. V_{OC}, β_{Voc}	−123 mV/°C
N0 of cells in series (Ns)	54
(b) specifications PV modules at STC	

Fig. 9. Specifications for Boost converter and KC200GT PV module

The plots in Fig. 10 (a) are for the step increase in irradiance, solid lines indicate the MPP trajectories and Fig. 10 (b) show the results for step decrease with the same step as in (a) and solid lines are for traced MPP paths for the corresponding MPPT technique. Maximum power points on the I-V plot in Fig. 10 look close to each other. To see clearly the differences, absolute value deviations from theoretically computed and plotted in Fig. 11. Small deviations are observed for the proposed and InCond techniques than P&O. This shows improved performances of the proposed MPPT technique apart from easy implementation reduced complexity compared to InCond technique.

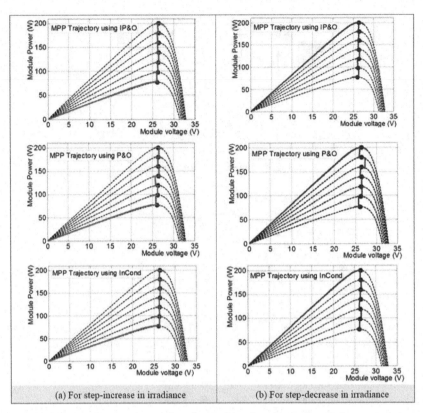

Fig. 10. MPP locus plots for the given test input of radiation

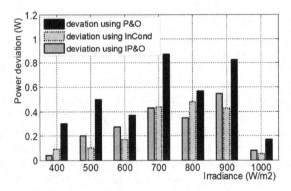

Fig. 11. Deviation of MPPs from theoretical values

6 Conclusions

As part of objective of the research paper, a concise summary of literatures on global energy demand growth, fast depletion of conventional source of energy and the corresponding challenges is presented in the introduction part of the research paper. In the same unit, rapid growth of utilization of photovoltaic power system, promising benefits and challenges of photovoltaic systems due to the non-linear characteristic, strong impact of atmospheric conditions, high initial installation cost requirement and the need for efficient extraction techniques is presented. The broad classification of available MPPT techniques, advantages, drawbacks and formulations for PV-systems application of classical techniques is presented concisely in the paper.

Performance evaluation of the widely used classical techniques of perturbation based (InCond, P&O) and improved perturbation based (IPO) with the criterion of capability in tracking maximum power point trajectory, oscillation reduction during steady state operating condition and maximum power tracking efficiency improvements for test conditions of step increase and decrease radiation is done. The proposed improved P&O MPPT technique showed significant improvements over P&O technique for the prescribed measurement criterion apart from the advantages of simple to implement and less complexity.

In summary, this paper can help to develop clear image of the concepts and operating principles of classical maximum power point techniques and identify the drawbacks of wrong perturbations during fast change in radiation, oscillation during steady-state and unable to track the maximum power point when the photovoltaic system is operating in partial-shade or mismatching conditions.

References

1. Singh, G.K.: Solar power generation by PV (photovoltaic) technology: a review, pp. 1–13 (2013). Elsevier
2. Salam, Z., Ishaque, K., Taheri, H.: An improved two-diode photovoltaic (PV) model for PV system. In: Proceedings of Joint International Conference, pp. 1–5 (2010)
3. Paz, F., Ordonez, M.: Zero oscillation and irradiance slope tracking for photovoltaic MPPT. IEEE Trans. Industr. Electron. **61**(11), 6138–6147 (2014)
4. Kai, C., Shulin, T., Yuhua, C., Libing, B.: An improved MPPT controller for photovoltaic system under partial shading condition. IEEE Trans. Sustain. Energy **5**(3), 978–985 (2014)
5. Gupta, S., Tiwari, H., Fozdar, M., Chandna, V.: Development of a two diode model for photovoltaic modules suitable for use in simulation studies. In: Proceedings of Power and Energy Engineering Conferencs (APPEEC), pp 1–4 (2012)
6. Femia, N., Lisi, G., Petrone, G., Spagnuolo, G., Vitelli, M.: Distributed maximum power point tracking of photovoltaic arrays: novel approach and system analysis. IEEE Trans. Industr. Electron. **55**(7), 2610–2621 (2008)
7. Liu, F., Duan, S., Liu, F., Liu, B., Kang, Y.: A Variable step size INC MPPT method for PV systems. IEEE Trans. Industr. Electron. **55**(7), 2622–2628 (2008)
8. Weddell, A.S., Merrett, G.V., Al-Hashimi, B.M.: Photovoltaic sample-and-hold circuit enabling MPPT indoors for low-power systems. IEEE Trans. Circuits Syst. **59**(6), 1196–1204 (2012)

9. Mei, Q., Shan, M., Liu, L., Guerrero, J.M.: A novel improved variable step-size incremental-resistance MPPT method for PV systems. IEEE Trans. Industr. Electron. **58**(6), 2427–2434 (2011)

10. Gomes, M.A., Galotto Jr., L., Sampaio, L.P., de Azevedo, G., Canesin, C.A.: Evaluation of the main MPPT techniques for photovoltaic applications. IEEE Trans. Industr. Electron. **60**(3), 1156–1167 (2013)

11. Esram, T., Chapman, P.L.: Comparison of photovoltaic array maximum power point tracking techniques. IEEE Trans. Energy Convers. **22**(2), 439–449 (2007)

12. Kollimalla, S.K., Mishra, M.K.: Variable perturbation size adaptive P&O MPPT algorithm for sudden changes in irradiance. IEEE Trans. Sustain. Energy **5**(3), 718–728 (2014)

13. Xiao, W., Edwin, F.F., Spagnuolo, G., Jatskevich, J.: Efficient approaches for modeling and simulating photovoltaic power systems. IEEE J. Photovoltaic **3**(1), 500–508 (2013)

14. Cristaldi, L., Faifer, M., Rossi, M., Ponci, F.: A simple photovoltaic panel model: characterization procedure and evaluation of the role of environmental measurements. IEEE Trans. Instrum. Meas. **61**(10), 2632–2641 (2012)

15. Ismail, M.S., Moghavvemi, M., Mahlia, T.M.I.: Characterization of PV panel cells and global optimization of its model parameters using genetic algorithm. Energy Convers. Manag. **73**, 10–25 (2010)

16. Ishaque, K., Salam, Z.: An improved modeling method to determine the model parameters of photovoltaic (PV) modules using differential evolution (DE). Sol. Energy **85**(9), 2349–2359 (2011)

17. Rekioua, D., Matagne, E.: Optimization of Photovoltaic Power Systems: Modelization. Simulation and Control. Springer, New York (2012). https://doi.org/10.1007/978-1-4471-2403-0_7

18. Femian, N., Petrone, G., Spagnuolo, G., Vitelli, M.: Power Electronics and Control Techniques for Maximum Energy Harvesting in Photovoltaic Systems. Taylor & Francis Group (2013)

19. Xiao, W., Dunford, W.G.: A modified adaptive hill climbing MPPT method for photovoltaic power systems. In: Proceedings of 35th Annual IEEE Power Electronics Specialists Conference, pp. 1957–1963 (2004)

20. Piegari, L., Rizzo, R.: Adaptive perturb and observe algorithm for photovoltaic maximum power point tracking. IET Renew. Power Gener. **4**(4), 317–328 (2010)

21. Syafaruddin, E.K., Hiyama, T.: Artificial neural network-polar coordinated fuzzy controller based maximum power point tracking control under partially shaded conditions. IET Renew. Pow. Gener. **3**(2), 239–253 (2009). https://doi.org/10.1049/iet-rpg:20080065

22. Alajmi, B.N., Ahmed, K.H., Finney, S.J.: Fuzzy-logic-control approach of a modified hill-climbing method for maximum power point in microgrid standalone photovoltaic system. IEEE Trans. Pow. Electron. **26**(4), 1022–1030 (2011)

23. Liu, Y., Huang, S., Huang, J., Liang, W.: A particle swarm optimization-based maximum power point tracking algorithm for PV systems operating under partially shaded conditions. IEEE Trans. Energy Convers. **27**(4), 1027–1035 (2012)

24. Sundareswaran, K., Sankar, P., Nayak, P.S.R., Simon, S.P., Palani, S.: Enhanced energy output from a PV system under partial shaded conditions through artificial bee colony. IEEE Trans. Sustain. Energy **6**(1), 198–209 (2015)

25. Femia, N., Petrone, G., Spagnuolo, G., Vitelli, M.: Optimization of perturb and observe maximum power point tracking method. IEEE Trans. Pow. Electron. **20**(4), 963–973 (2005)

26. Jain, S., Agarwal, V.: A new algorithm for rapid tracking of approximate maximum power point in photovoltaic systems. IEEE Pow. Electron. Lett. **2**(1), 16–19 (2004)

27. Sharma, P., Duttagupta, S.P., Agarwal, V.: A novel approach for maximum power tracking from curved thin-film solar photovoltaic arrays under changing environmental conditions. IEEE Trans. Ind. Appl. **50**(6), 4142–4151 (2014)

Dynamic Performance Evaluation of Type-3 Compensator for Switch-Mode Dc-Dc Converter

Tefera T. Yetayew[1(✉)] and Tigist D. Wudmatas[2]

[1] Adama Science and Technology University, P.O 1888 Adama, Ethiopia
[2] Bahirdar Polytechnic College, Bahirdar, Ethiopia

Abstract. This paper describes application of type-3 compensated error amplifier for switch-mode dc-dc converter using OrCad/Pspice simulation tool. For several decades power supply design has been showing a gradual movement away from the use of linear power supplies to the more practical switched mode power supply. The linear power supply contains a mains transformer and a dissipative series regulator that increase the size extremely and heavy 50/60 Hz transformers, and also very poor power conversion efficiencies approximated below 50%. These drawbacks are improved using switch mode power supplies that incorporates fast switching devices having estimated efficiency of above 80%, compact size and light in weight. These features are mainly due to the controller as a basic building block apart from the Dc-Dc converter, which is the heart of switch mode Dc power supply. Thus, in this paper application of type-3 compensated error amplifier for switch-mode dc-dc converter has been proposed and implemented using OrCAD/Pspice tool. Accordingly, dynamic and steady-state performance/evaluations have been performed for step changes input/output (load) side. The results revealed that the system has fast dynamic response and reduced steady-state error for input and output side disturbances.

Keywords: Switch mode dc-dc converter · Type-3 compensator · Dynamic response

1 Introduction

The ever increasing advancement in modern electronic systems needs high quality, efficient, portable size, light weight and reliable power supplies. Linear regulated power supplies are operating at low frequency, need large size transformer, large size inductors and have low efficiency. Thus, utilization of switch mode power supplies of ac or dc types are also growing at a faster rate to satisfy the need of modern electronic system [1–6]. Switch mode Dc power supplies comprises of basic blocks of the feedback controller and Dc-Dc converter along with PWM generation and gate driver circuit. The feedback control action also controls the Dc-Dc converter. The converters can be of isolated or non-isolated. The non-isolated converters include buck, boost and buck-boost converters [1, 7–9]. This papered focused on modeling and simulation of switch mode Dc-Dc buck converter suing OrCad/Pspice software tool. The tasks involved include

M. A. Delele et al. (Eds.): ICAST 2020, LNICST 384, pp. 273–283, 2021.
https://doi.org/10.1007/978-3-030-80621-7_20

design of Dc-Dc buck converter for a preset specification, design of the feedback loop controller/compensator, developing Pspice model of the whole system and perform simulations to see the steady state and dynamic performance of the system for disturbance of input and output side.

The contents of this paper are organized into six sections. Section 2 presented concise description of switch mode Dc-Dc converters, schematic representations and relations non-isolated switch-mode Dc-Dc converters. The third section presented specifications, design of the power converter and the feedback controller. The forth section presented OrCad/Pspice circuit model of the feedback loop Dc-Dc buck converter considered in this paper. Simulation results and discussions of dynamic and steady-state responses when the system is subjected to step changes in reference input voltage and step changes in external load are presented in Sect. 5 of the paper. Finally, summary of findings are presented in Sect. 6 of the paper.

2 Switch Mode Dc-Dc Converters

Switch mode converters use fast switching power electronic devices of the on and off states of the switches (the feature that makes switch mode converters achieve high efficiency). The high frequency operation of power electronic switches use high frequency and lighter weight transformers, filter capacitors and inductors. And operating at high frequency can achieve fast dynamic response to changes in load and reference voltage. The heart of switch mode Dc power supply is Dc-Dc converter circuit. The basic functions of dc–dc converters may be convert a dc input voltage to a dc output voltage, regulate the dc output voltage against load and line voltage changes, reduce the ac voltage ripple on the dc output voltage, provide isolation between the input and the load and protect the supplied system and the input source from electromagnetic interference [1, 9].

Availability of a large variety of Dc-Dc converters is presented in literatures. Among them, converters with isolation and without are some of them [1, 6–9]. Dc-Dc converters with no transformer coupling/isolation can be classified as step-down (buck) converter, step-up (boost) converter and step-down/step-up (buck-boost) converter. Analysis of the these converters for continuous conduction conditions is based on the assumptions that the circuit is operating in the steady state, the inductor current is continuous (always positive), the capacitor is very large, and the output voltage is held constant at voltage Vo, the switching period is T; the switch is closed for time DT and open for time $(1 - D)$ T and ideal components [6, 10]. The schematic diagrams, input/output characteristic and relations of Dc-Dc converters with not transformer coupling for continuous conduction mode are given in Fig. 1.

To achieve stable performance of the switch mode Dc-Dc converters, feedback loop controller to adjust the duty ratio of switches is usually applied. The variation in the duty ratio is in response to disturbances from input/output side to keep the output parameter same as the reference value. Usually, voltage and current mode feedback loop controls are used. In voltage mode control, the output voltage is sensed and input to the error amplifier. The difference between the output and reference voltage is feed to the voltage controller. The voltage controller comprises of the controller, comparator having inputs

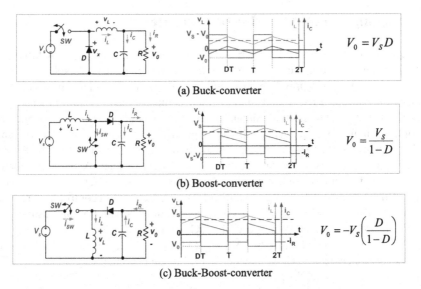

(a) Buck-converter

(b) Boost-converter

(c) Buck-Boost-converter

Fig. 1. Switch-mode non-isolated Dc-Dc Converters, characteristics and relations

of control signal and saw tooth waveform generator to produce PWM signal which is fed to drivers of controllable switches in the dc-dc converter. This mode of control has an advantage of simple and flexible in implementation, however, this mode has delayed line voltage regulation. The schematic diagram in Fig. 2(a) shows basic components of voltage mode control [6, 11, 12]. In current mode control, an additional inner current loop to feedback the inductor current is used. This signal is converted to voltage and replaces the saw tooth waveform. This mode of control has better dynamic performance relative to voltage mode control. However, large number of components and implementation complexity are major disadvantages of this mode of control. Figure 2(b) shows schematic representation of current mode of control [1, 6].

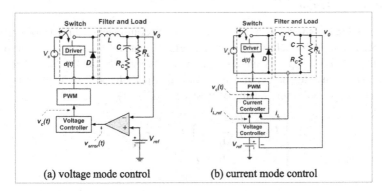

(a) voltage mode control   (b) current mode control

Fig. 2. Schematic diagrams of common control modes for a buck converter

3 Designing Switch-Mode Dc-Dc Converter

The Dc-Dc converter circuit is the heart of a Dc switch mode power supply. In this paper, buck converter operating in continuous-current conduction mode is considered as main part of the switch mode supply. The basic building blocks of the regulated buck converter includes the switch, drive circuit, output filter, compensator (error amplifier), and a pulse-width modulating circuit. Voltage mode control is designed and implemented. The output voltages of dc power supplies are regulated to be within a specified tolerance band in response to changes in the output load and the input line voltages by modulating the duty ratio to compensate for variations in the input or load. A feedback control system for power supply control compares output voltage to a reference and converts the error to a duty ratio. The design specifications, parameters, and control requirements are given in Table 1. Selection of converter specifications is based on the assumptions that for electronics laboratory purpose, the DC voltage is usually ± 5 V or ± 12 V or ± 15 V. Thus, assuming tolerance of 5 V, output voltage may vary up to 20 V. Switching frequency is selected above 20 kHz which is the human hearing threshold.

Table 1. Design specifications

Input voltage	50 [V] to 200 [V] dc
Output voltage	Maximum 20 [V] dc
Load current	5 [A]
Switching frequency	200 [kHz]
Ripple voltage	<0.5
Change inductor current (Δi_L)	<0.8 [A]

3.1 Converter Design

The design of buck converter considers only selecting component values according to the design specifications. Switch selection and thermal (heat sink) design is not considered because the scope of paper is modeling and simulation regulated switch mode buck converter. The values for inductance for a specified peak-to-peak inductor current and capacitance can be determined using expressions in Eq. (1).

$$\begin{cases} L = \left(\dfrac{V_S - V_0}{\Delta i_L f} \right) D = \dfrac{V_0(1 - D)}{\Delta i_L f} \\ C = \dfrac{1 - D}{8L(\Delta V_0/V_0)f^2} \end{cases} \tag{1}$$

Substituting the given values, L = 75 uH. For continuous conduction add 25% of L and then L = 93.75 uH and the capacitance, C = 46.66 uF. The value of internal resistance of capacitor, RESR = 0.3 and for the inductor, very small value is considered.

The feedback controller to regulate the output voltage must be designed to meet the objectives of zero steady state error, good dynamic response and low noise susceptibility [13, 14].

3.2 Compensator Design

The controller/compensator can be realized using PID controller, lead-lag compensators or using compensated error amplifiers of different types, sliding mode control, etc. [15–17]. In this paper, compensated error amplifier of type-3 is considered because the frequency response can provide sufficient phase angle difference to meet the stability criterion of a minimum phase margin of 45° [6]. The schematic diagram of type-3 compensated error amplifier is given in Fig. 3.

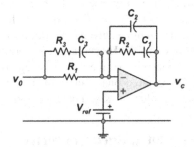

Fig. 3. Compensated error amplifier.

The small-signal transfer function given in Eq. (2) is expressed in terms of input and feedback impedances Zi and Zf.

$$G(s) = \frac{\tilde{v}c(s)}{\tilde{v}o(s)} = -\frac{Zf}{Zi} = -\frac{\left(R_2 + \frac{1}{sC_1}\right) || \frac{1}{sC_2}}{R_1 || \left(R_3 + \frac{1}{sC_3}\right)} \tag{2}$$

Rearranging the expression in Eq. (2) can be expressed as Eq. (3).

$$G(s) = -\frac{R_1 + R_3}{R_1 R_3 C_3} \frac{\left(s + \frac{1}{R_2 C_1}\right)\left(s + \frac{1}{(R_1 + R_3)C_3}\right)}{s\left(s + \frac{C_1 + C_2}{R_2 C_1 C_2}\right)\left(s + \frac{1}{R_3 C_3}\right)} \tag{3}$$

Assuming C2 << C1 and R3 << R1, expression in Eq. (3) can be simplified to Eq. (4)

$$G(s) \approx -\frac{1}{R_3 C_2} \frac{\left(s + \frac{1}{R_2 C_1}\right)\left(s + \frac{1}{R_1 C_3}\right)}{s\left(s + \frac{1}{R_2 C_2}\right)\left(s + \frac{1}{R_3 C_3}\right)} \tag{4}$$

In the design of the compensated error amplifier, first choose R1 and Table 2 gives expressions to compute other component values [6].

Table 2. Expressions to determine component values

R_1 choose first	$C_1 = \dfrac{\sqrt{K}}{\omega_{co}R_2}$
$R_2 = \dfrac{\lvert G(j\omega_{co}\rvert R_1}{\sqrt{k}}$	$C_2 = \dfrac{1}{\omega_{co}R_2\sqrt{K}}$
$R_3 = \dfrac{1}{\omega_{co}\sqrt{K}C_3}$	$C_3 = \dfrac{\sqrt{K}}{\omega_{co}R_1}$

Controller is designed in frequency domain using OrCAD Pspice tool. For the controller to have stable response a phase margin of at least 45° is a commonly used criterion for stability [6, 18]. The crossover frequency of 8 kHz and a phase margin of 60° is considered. Accordingly, the frequency response of the buck converter to see the phase and gain margins is given in Fig. 4. Figure 4(b) shows the frequency response of the buck converter ac equivalent circuit model given Fig. 4(a). From the frequency response plot, at the crossover frequency of 8.0 kHz and a phase margin of approximately 65°, the Pspice ac frequency sweep shows that the output voltage is 14.5 dB and the phase angle is −131.98°. Thus, the required phase angle of the amplifier will be 191.980. Accordingly, the corresponding values of K and other component values are computed.

4   Pspice Model of Regulated Buck Converter

Pspice circuit models used for simulation purpose may vary according to the goal of simulation. To evaluate the current and voltage waveforms with detail variations such as peak-to-peak values needs a circuit model with a switching device or model of the switch with basic characteristic of actual switching device.

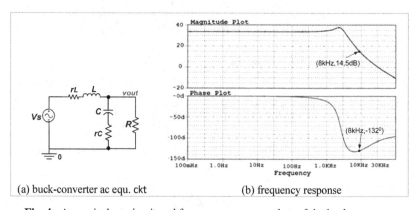

(a) buck-converter ac equ. ckt   (b) frequency response

Fig. 4. Ac equivalent circuit and frequency response plots of the buck converter

The simulation model that considers switches has the transient time for the overall system large than switching period that increase execution time of the program. The most widely used simulation goals to predict the dynamic behavior of converters consider average values of switching waveforms. The transient behaviors of the system can analyzed by considering linear circuit that the responses will be averaged values of switching waveforms [19, 20]. Figure 5 shows averaged Pspice models of closed loop dc-dc buck converter considered in this paper. RL1+ and RL2+ are external loads added to see step responses when the regulated converter is subjected to step changes in load.

5   Results and Discussions

To evaluate the dynamic and steady-state performances of the system a number of simulation tasks have been performed. The simulation tasks and different cases considered include (i) step-response of averaged and switched models, (ii) response of step change in input reference and (iii) response to step change in external loads.

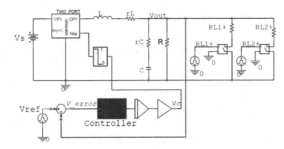

Fig. 5. Averaged Pspice models of regulated buck converter

5.1   Step-Responses of Averaged and Switched Models

Step response of both switched and averaged models for step input reference voltage of 20 V is recorded in Fig. 6. Switched model response is considered to see the detail transient responses of peak-to-peak change in inductor current ac ripple voltage of capacitor. The switched averaged model has output voltage ripple and inductor current changes from average value. The simulation result of steady-state response in Fig. 6(c) show that the peak to peak ripple voltage (output voltage) is (20.161 − 19.872 = 0.289 V). This magnitude is very much less than peak-to-peak voltage value (<5 V) set at the specifications table during design stage. And for the inductor current, peak-to-peak inductor current is, 7.0757 − 6.2541 = 0.8216 A which within the specification given at designed stage (<0.8 A). The simulation results in sections below consider only.

5.2   Responses for Step-Change in Reference Input

Step change in reference input voltage at time t = 1 ms (from 10 V to 20 V) is applied. The responses in Fig. 7 show very small overshoot and short settling to the reference input for the averaged Pspice model in Fig. 5. The result shows that whenever there is change in reference input voltage, the controller tries to keep the output voltage the same as the reference input with fast dynamic response.

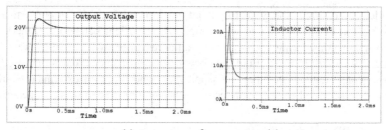

(a) step response for average model

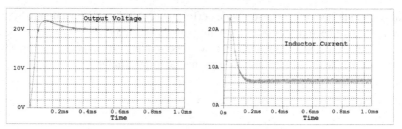

(b) step response for switched model

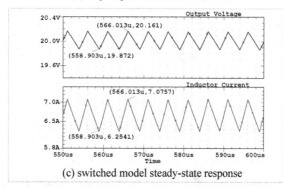

(c) switched model steady-state response

Fig. 6. Pspice Probe outputs of averaged and switched models of the system

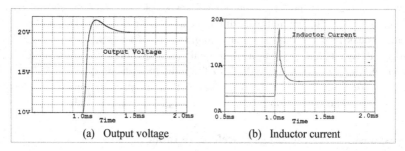

(a) Output voltage   (b) Inductor current

Fig. 7. Transient responses

5.3 Responses for Step Change in External Loads

Case-1: A step change in external load of RL+ = 3 Ω is connected in parallel with the existing 3 Ω at time t = 2 ms during the simulation period of 3 ms for the averaged Pspice model in Fig. 5. The transient responses given in Fig. 8 shows responses for output voltage and inductor current for step-change in external load. The results show fast dynamic responses to achieve the specified output for the reference input of 20 V. The inductor current shows an increase from 6.66 A to ≈11.7 A in response to added external load.

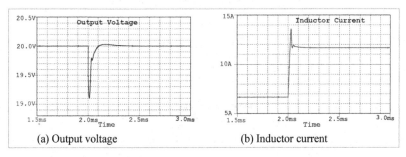

       (a) Output voltage   (b) Inductor current

Fig. 8. Pspice model Probe outputs for a step change in load

The output is to be regulated at 20 V for the reference input voltage of 20 V. The phase margin of this circuit is 60° when the load is 3 Ω and slightly greater than 60° when the load changes to 3∥3 Ω. A step change in load occurs at t = 2 ms. If the circuit were unregulated, the output voltage would change as the load current changed because of the inductor resistance. The control circuit adjusts the duty ratio to compensate for changes in operating conditions. The simulation results show that the system considered kept stable for step changes in external loads.

Case-2: The second case considered step-change in external loads to be connected in parallel to the 3 Ω load at different time instances of the simulation period. Accordingly, RL1+ = 2 Ω and RL2+ = 3 Ω are connected at time instances of 1ms and 2 ms respectively. The switching periods and pulses of external loads is given in Fig. 9(a). For the indicated four periods, the output voltage shows fast move to achieve the reference input voltage, 20 V. The inductor current shows step increase from 6.66 A to ≈12.7 A again to ≈18 A for the simulation period up to 3 ms in response to addition of external loads and again back to ≈11.8 A and again reduced to 6.66 A for simulation periods of 2 ms in response to step removal of external loads.

For all input reference input voltage values, the output voltage is nearly the same as input. In this paper, since the voltage levels considered is small level and averaged model is considered, the output and input reference are approximately equal. Actually, if switched model is considered, switching and conduction losses may contribute losses even though not as such significant. This shows, the conversion efficiency of switch mode power electronic converters is above 95%.

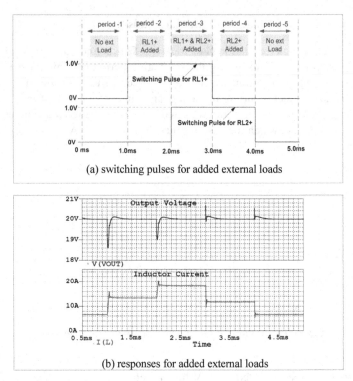

(a) switching pulses for added external loads

(b) responses for added external loads

Fig. 9. Pspice Probe outputs for a step change in external loads

6 Conclusions

The major tasks completed this paper include design, modeling, simulation and performance evaluation of type-3 error amplifier compensated switch mode dc-dc buck converter. The system considered is tested for input reference and external load step changes at various times of the simulation period. The dynamic and steady state responses revealed that performances of switch mode dc power supply has efficiency of greater than 95%, fast dynamic response, reduced overshoot and very small steady-state error using type-3 compensator proposed.

References

1. Mohan, N., Undeland, T.M., Robbins, W.P.: Power Electronics: Converter, Applications and Design. Wiley and Sons
2. Liao, W.-H., Wang, S.-C., Liu, Y.-H.: Generalized simulation model for a switched-mode power supply design course using MATLAB/SIMULINK. IEEE Tran. Educ. **55**(1), 36–47 (2011)
3. Rashid, M.H., Introduction to Pspice Using OrCAD for Circuits and Electronics, 3rd edn. Pearson Educ. Inc., USA (2004)

4. Singh, S., Bhim Singh, G., Bhuvaneswari, V.B.: Improved power quality switched-mode power supply using buck–boost converter. IEEE Trans. Indus. Appl. **52**(6), 5194–5202 (2016). https://doi.org/10.1109/TIA.2016.2600675
5. Rehman, Z., Al-Bahadly, I., Mukhopadhyay, S.: Multi input DC–DC converters in renewable energy applications – an overview. Renew. Sustain. Energy Rev. **41**, 521–539 (2015)
6. Mohan, N.: First Course on Power Electronics and Drives. MNPERE, USA (2003)
7. Sivakumar, S., Jagabar Sathik, M., Manoj, P.S., Sundararajan, G.: An assessment on performance of DC–DC converters for renewable energy applications. Renew. Sustain. Energy Rev. **58**, 1475–1485 (2016). https://doi.org/10.1016/j.rser.2015.12.057
8. Zhang, N., Sutanto, D., Muttaqi, K.M.: A review of topologies of three-port DC–DC converters for the integration of renewable energy and energy storage. Renew. Sustain. Energy Rev. **56**, 388–401 (2016)
9. Schilling, M., Schwalbe, U., Reimann, T.: Practical control loop design and verification in switch mode power supply applications. In: IEEE International Exhibition and Conference for Power Electronics, Intelligent Motion, Renewable Energy and Energy Management, pp. 1–8 (2014)
10. Taghvaee, M.H., Radzi, M.A.M., Moosavain, S.M., Hizam, H., Marhaban, M.H.: A current and future study on non-isolated DC–DC converters for photovoltaic applications. Renew. Sustain. Energy Rev. **17**, 216–227 (2013)
11. Bensaada, M., Stambouli, A.B.: A practical design sliding mode controller for DC–DC converter based on control parameters optimization using assigned poles associate to genetic algorithm. Electr. Power Energy Syst. **53**, 761–773 (2013)
12. Taddy, E., Lazarescu, V.: Modeling and simulation of a switch-mode synchronous buck converter. In: Proceedings of the 2014 6th International Conference on Electronics, Computers and Artificial Intelligence (ECAI), pp. 43–48 (2014)
13. Mahery, H.M., Babaei, E.: Mathematical modeling of buck–boost dc–dc converter and investigation of converter elements on transient and steady state responses. Electr. Power Energy Syst. **44**, 949–963 (2013)
14. Singh, B., Shrivastava, A.: Buck converter-based power supply design for low power light emitting diode lamp lighting. IET Power Electr. **7**(4), 946–956 (2014)
15. Navarro-Lopeza, E.M., Cortes, D., Castroc, C.: Design of practical sliding-mode controllers with constant switching frequency for power converters. Electric Power Syst. Res. **79**, 796–802 (2009)
16. Muhamad, N.D., Aziz, J.A.: Simulation of power electronic converters with sliding mode control using PSpice. In: 2008 IEEE 2nd International Power and Energy Conference, pp. 231–236 (2008)
17. Benadero, L., Giral, R., El Aroudi, A., Calvente, J.: Stability analysis of a single inductor dual switching dc–dc converter. Math. Comput. Simul. **71**, 256–269 (2006)
18. Shireen, W., Nene, H.: Control and design aspects of power electronic converters using Pspice. Adv. Technol. Learn. **3**(1) (2006)
19. Naik, M.V., Samuel, P.: Analysis of ripple current, power losses and high efficiency of DC–DC converters for fuel cell power generating systems. Renew. Sustain. Energy Rev. **59**, 1080–1088 (2016)
20. Diallo, D., Belkacem, F., Berthelot, E.: Design and control of a low power DC-DC Converter fed by a photovoltaic array. In: 2007 IEEE International Electric Machines and Drives Conference, vol. 2, p. 1288–1293 (2007)

Inset-Feed Rectangular Microstrip Patch Antenna Array Performance Enhancement for 5G Mobile Applications

Mulugeta T. Gemeda[✉] and Kinde A. Fante

Faculty of Electrical and Computer Engineering, Jimma Institutes of Technology, Jimma University, Jimma, Ethiopia
{mulugeta.geneda,kinde.anlay}@ju.edu.et

Abstract. The advancements in wireless communication systems need a low cost, minimal weight, and low-profile antenna arrays that are capable of providing high performance over a wide frequency band. In this regard, the patch antenna is considered as a candidate antenna type for 5G communication systems. However, the bandwidth of microstrip patch antenna (MSPA) is narrow; its directivity, gain, and radiation efficiency are low. Moreover, attempting to improve the performance of the MSPA by integrating a large number of patch antenna in the array leads to increased mutual coupling and reduced radiation efficiency, and directivity of the antenna. Therefore, to address these challenges, this paper presents the performance enhancement of MSPA array for 5G mobile applications. To achieve this, inset-feed impedance matching techniques, quarter-wavelength impedance transformer, and optimization of the parameters of different MSPA array structures have been simultaneously used. All the studied antenna structures are designed using FR-4 substrate with a dielectric constant of 4.4 to operate at 28 GHz and the performances have been analyzed using a CST antenna simulator. The simulation results show that directivity of the proposed single element, 2×1, 4×1, 4×4, and 8×8 rectangular MSPA arrays are 7.41 dBi, 9.451 dBi, 11.2 dBi, 15.8 dBi, 19.31 dBi; the bandwidths are 572 MHz, 575 MHz, 1394 MHz, 332 MHz, 368 MHz; the radiation efficiency is more than 95% for one-dimensional MSPA arrays and more than 80% for the two-dimensional MSPA arrays. As compared to designs reported in the literature, the proposed antennas show significantly improved performance.

Keywords: Beam-gain · Fifth-generation · MSPA · Millimeter-wave · 28 GHz

1 Introduction

Over the past few decades, the continual development of new generations of wireless communication technology brought a significant impact on the daily

M. A. Delele et al. (Eds.): ICAST 2020, LNICST 384, pp. 284–303, 2021.
https://doi.org/10.1007/978-3-030-80621-7_21

lives of human beings. Therefore, nowadays more and more users have gotten their devices connected to the networks which are causing a constant increase in data traffic and hastening the need for enormous capacity in the upcoming years. However, the allowable frequency ranges of the existing wireless network generations are too congested. Consequently, this cannot handle the present rapid growth in wireless data and network traffic. Hence, in the near future, the use of the currently unused spectrum is, therefore, being highly encouraged and thus the subsequent next network generation is on emerging stage which is claimed to be fifth-generation of the wireless network [1–3].

The fifth-generation (5G) wireless communication systems are expected to highly enhance communication capacity by exploiting enormous unlicensed bandwidth specifically, in the mm-wave band. It is also expected to be ready to provide and support very high data rates, the maximum amount as 100 times of 4G capacity which results in a replacement challenge on network requirements as well as in the antenna designs to satisfy the expected data rate and capacity [4–7]. The working frequency for the 5G communication systems continues to be being debated but 6 GHz, 10 GHz, 15 GHz, 28 GHz, and 38 GHz bands are among the expected ones. However, the federal communication commission (FCC) approved the allocation of huge bandwidths at 28 GHz, 37 GHz, and 39 GHz [8].

In wireless communication systems, antennas are widely used to transmit or receive electromagnetic energy over the specified frequency ranges. However, the new advancements in wireless communication technology require antennas with a lightweight, and low profile. In this regard, the microstrip patch antennas represent a lucid choice for wireless devices due to their low fabrication cost, lightweight and volume, and a low-profile configuration as compared to the other bulky types of antennas. The microstrip patch antenna (MSPA) is easy and versatile in terms of resonant frequency, polarization, pattern, and input impedance. The patch antennas may be mounted on the surface of high-performance aircraft, spacecraft, rockets, satellites, missiles, cars, and even hand-held mobile telephones. Therefore, the MSPA plays a significant role within the fastest-growing wireless communications industry. But, the thickness of the substrate material deteriorates the MSPA bandwidth and radiation efficiency, by increasing surface wave and spurious feed radiation along with the feeding line. Consequently, undesired cross-polarized radiation is led by feed radiation effects. Moreover, the MSPA suffers from losses such as conductor, dielectric, and radiation which results in narrowing the bandwidth and lowering the gain [9–13]. Because of this performance limitation, the bandwidth of MSPA is narrow; its directivity, gain, and radiation efficiency are low for the emerging 5G communication systems.

Therefore, attempting to extend the performance of MSPA for 5G communication systems, several designs of single element MSPA has been demonstrated in [8,13–18] using a patch with substrate integrated wave-guide, multi-layer, and multi-patch designs, by incorporating multiple slots on the patch, by employing different impedance matching techniques and a defected ground plane, tuning dimension of the antenna. However, it has been revealed that the radiation pattern of the single antenna is relatively wide and also, its beam gain and directivity are low for futuristic 5G communications. Therefore, to increase the performance of the single-element patch antenna, different sizes of linear MSPA array are demonstrated in [3,10,14–17] by increasing the number of the array element, using proper impedance matching technique, serial microstrip feeding techniques, and tuning the substrate thickness. The proposed linear MSPA improves the performance of single MSPA in terms of beam directivity and gain. But, it produces high side-lobe levels which reduce overall radiation efficiency of the antenna and also, linear antenna array is capable to scan only one-dimensional plane i.e., either the elevation plane or azimuth plane.

Generally, the previous demonstrated works tried to achieve better performance in terms of one or two specific performance metrics, and also the main intention of the studies was only for linear MSPA array. Therefore, in this study, we are motivated to design both linear and planar rectangular MSPA array and enhance the performance in terms of all key performance metrics for 5G communication systems at 28 GHz. To achieve these objectives, we have used inset-feed impedance matching, quarter-wavelength impedance transformer, and design parameters optimization techniques as methodology.

The rest of the paper is organized as follows. Section 2 describes the design concept of; single element, 2×1, 4×1, 4×4, and 8×8 rectangular MSPA array. Section 3 presents the simulation results and discussion of all studied antenna. Finally, Sect. 4 summarizes our concluding remarks.

2   Design of Linear and Planar MSPA Arrays

In this section, we present the design concept of five different structures of MSPA arrays. The first three antenna arrays are one-dimensional and the remaining two antennas are two-dimensional arrays. We start the design concept with a single element MSPA.

2.1   Single Element Inset-Feed Rectangular MSPA

The physical structure of a single element MSPA is shown in Fig. 1. This antenna is designed using the FR-4 substrate with a dielectric constant (ε_r) of 4.4 and a loss tangent of 0.0025. The width of the patch is 3.3 mm and excited using 50 Ω microstrip feed-line with width of 0.4783 mm. The over all dimension of this 8.5 mm × 8.5 mm × 0.244 mm and this structures is employed as building block for other MSPA arrays. The performance of the antenna depends on the selection of its design parameters. In this work, our aim is not to show the effect of each parameter of the antenna on its performance. The detail discussion about the effect of the parameters of the antenna on its performance can be found in [12]. The optimized design parameters of this antenna structure are summarized in Table 5 in the Annex. The design parameters are optimized to boost the performance of this patch antenna in terms of beam gain, directivity, bandwidth, and radiation efficiency.

Fig. 1. Proposed single inset-feed rectangular MSPA.

2.2   2×1 Inset-Feed Rectangular MSP Array

The structure of a 2×1 inset-feed rectangular MSPA array is indicated in Fig. 2. The proposed antenna array is designed using 2 rectangular patches arranged in 2×1 formation. In this particular design, a microstrip transmission line of 1:2 power divider is used to feed the two antenna elements. Which is linked with a serial 50Ω microstrip transmission line feed of width 0.4738 mm and later divided into two 100Ω lines having a width of 0.23915 mm. The length of the transmission line is 1.27696 mm and the line widths are adjusted accordingly to optimize the performance trade-offs. The chosen separation distance between the array elements is 5.4 mm and the substrate height is similar to that of single element MSPA. This antenna structure is designed to enhance the performance of the single element rectangular MSPA in terms of its beam gain, directivity, bandwidth, return loss, and VSWR. The optimized design parameters of the proposed 2×1 inset-feed rectangular MSPA array model are reported in Table 6 within the Annex.

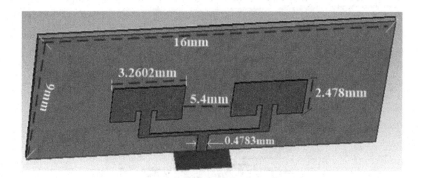

Fig. 2. Proposed 2×1 inset-feed rectangular MSPA array.

2.3   4×1 Inset-Feed Rectangular MSPA Array

A 4×1 inset-feed rectangular MSPA array is designed by connecting two 2×1 arrays as shown in Fig. 3. In the design, successive branching of corporate feed with equal path length to each element has been used to feed all the elements. The last feeder is normalized to 50Ω having a width of 0.4783 mm which is later branched to two 100Ω microstrip lines to feed two antenna elements. Besides, quarter-wave transformers are used for proper impedance matching to connect the patch to the transmission line. The separation distance between the patch is 5.4 mm. The optimized design parameters of the proposed 4×1 inset-feed MSPA array model are listed in Table 7 within the Annex.

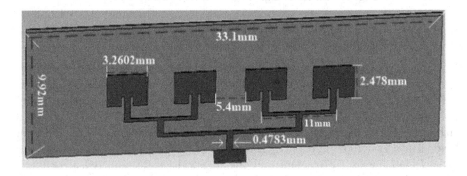

Fig. 3. Proposed 4×1 inset-feed rectangular MSPA array.

2.4   4×4 Inset-Feed Rectangular MSPA Array

The proposed design of 4×4 inset-feed rectangular MSPA array is depicted in Fig. 4. To reduce the return loss of the antenna, a quarter-wave impedance trans-

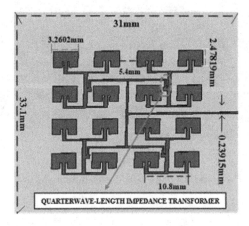

Fig. 4. Proposed 4×4 inset-feed rectangular MSPA array.

former is used. The quarter-wave impedance transformer improves the matching quality of the radiating element and the feeder line. This is the unique feature of our design. The optimized parameters of the proposed 4×4 inset-feed MSPA array are listed in Table 8 in the Annex.

2.5   8×8 Inset-Feed Rectangular MSPA Array

The physical structure of 8×8 inset-feed rectangular MSPA array is indicated in Fig. 5. It is designed to enhance the performance of the above proposed linear MSPA arrays and 4×4 inset-feed MSPA array in terms of their gain, directivity, bandwidth, and scanning dimensions. The structure has 100Ω feeder line impedance. Similar to the 4×4 MSPA array described in the above section, the impedance matching network uses a quarter-wave impedance transformer for better impedance matching. The optimized parameters are width of the patch and microstrip feeder, inset length and width, and ground plane dimension.

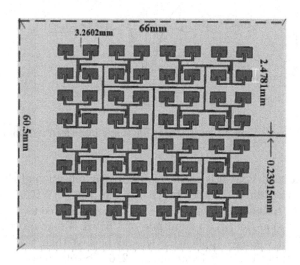

Fig. 5. Proposed 8×8 inset-feed rectangular MSPA array.

3   Simulation Results and Discussion

In this section, we present the simulation result and discussion of five different structures of antenna arrays. We first optimize the performance of a single element MSPA by selecting the suitable parameters and then increase the elements of the antenna array to enhance certain performance parameters. The optimized design parameters that are used for the simulations are listed in the Annex. To analyze the performance of the designed antenna, we simulated the proposed design of MSPA using CST software.

3.1   Single Inset-Feed Rectangular MSPA

The performance characteristics of an antenna is usually described by using different performance metrics like the return loss, bandwidth, VSWR, and beam gain. The return loss is a parameter which is used to indicate the amount of power that is lost to the load and does return as a reflection. Also, it indicates how well the matching between the transmitter and antenna has taken place [13]. For optimum working conditions, the return loss curve must show a dip at the operating frequency with minimum dB value and a flat line throughout other frequency scales. The return loss plot of the studied MSPA is indicated in Fig. 6. From the plot, we observed that at 28 GHz, the return loss of the antenna is 20.24 dB and also, −10 dB impedance bandwidth of the antenna is 572 MHz.

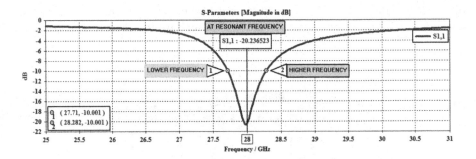

Fig. 6. Return loss versus frequency plot for single inset-feed rectangular MSPA.

The magnitude of VSWR is used to quantify the reflection of the power from the antenna to the source. Therefore, the smaller the VSWR is the better the antenna matched to the transmission line and power delivered to the antenna. For an ideal transmission line, the magnitude of VSWR is one and the acceptable level for practical wireless application should be less than two [12,13]. From Fig. 7, the VSWR of the studied antenna is 1.216. The obtained VSWR indicates that the impedance between the microstrip feeder line and the patch edge of the proposed antenna is well matched to the characteristic impedance by using properly selected dimension of the inset length and width.

Another interesting parameter that characterizes the radiation properties of an antenna and distinguishes one antenna from the other is the radiation pattern [13]. From Table 1, we observe that the designed antenna has a directional radiation pattern with a directivity of 7.404 dBi, a gain of 7.19 dBi, and radiation efficiency of 94.95% and 94.27% respectively. Besides, the side lobe level of the antenna is −12.1 dB and half-power beam width occurred at 72.3 degrees as shown in Fig. 8. The key implication of this result is that the proposed antenna radiates highly towards the desired direction and less in other directions.

The performance comparison of the proposed single radiating element antenna with designs reported in the literature is shown in Table 1. From the

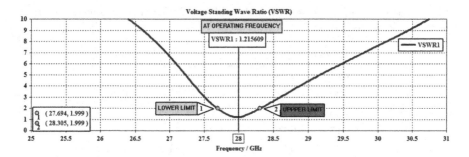

Fig. 7. VSWR versus frequency plot for single inset-feed rectangular MSPA.

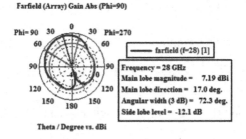

Fig. 8. 2D radiation pattern of single inset-feed rectangular MSPA

table, it is evident that the examined antenna show minimum return losses and VSWR as compared to designs reported in [7,13,18,22], but it is large as seen with antenna presented in [20–24]. In terms of the beam-gain, the proposed design outperforms the designs reported in [10,18–24]. Similarly, in terms of radiation efficiency, the designed antenna shows better performance than the designs presented in [10,13,19,20,24]. Finally, the proposed antenna achieves wider bandwidth compared to the design presented in [10,24], but it is narrow as compared to designs reported in [7,19–21]. Therefore, the proposed patch antenna gives a highly competitive performance as compared to other similar antenna reported in the literature.

Where, η_{rad} denotes radiation efficiency, S_{11} denotes return losses, and BW denotes bandwidth.

3.2 2×1 Inset-Feed Rectangular MSPA Array

As indicated in Fig. 9, the return loss of the proposed 2×1 MSPA array is less than −10 dB between 27.755 GHz and 28.33 GHz, and exactly at the resonant frequency, it is −19.886 dB. The obtained return loss is low since the impedance at the last feeding structure of 1:2 microstrip power divider with equal path length is well matched to the characteristic impedance of the feed point through the designed width of the last microstrip feeder line. The −10 dB return loss bandwidth of the antenna is about 575 MHz. The bandwidth of the 2×1 antenna

Table 1. Performance comparison of single MSPA at 28 GHz.Performance comparison of single MSPA at 28 GHz.

Ref.	S_{11} (dB)	GAIN (dBi)	VSWR	η_{rad} (%)	BW (GHz)
[7]	13.48	4.48	1.538	78.9	0.847
[10]	−20.53	6.21	1.02	65.6	0.4
[13]	−15.35	-	1.79	87.8	-
[18]	−17.4	6.72	1.28	-	-
[19]	−23.67	6.7	-	81.2	1.15
[20]	−39.37	6.37	1.022	86.73	2.48
[21]	−39.7	5.23	-	-	4.1
[22]	−14.151	6.06	1.488	-	0.8
[23]	−22.2	6.85	1.34	-	-
[24]	−27.7	6.72	1.22	75.875	0.463
This work	−20.24	7.19	1.22	94.95	0.572

array is 3 MHz higher than that of the single element MSPA described in the previous section.

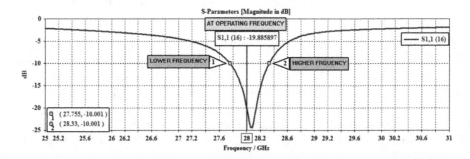

Fig. 9. Return loss versus frequency plot for 2×1 inset-feed rectangular MSPA array.

The VSWR versus frequency plot for 2×1 rectangular MSPA array is shown in Fig. 10. At 28 GHz, the VSWR of the antenna is 1.344 for the optimized design parameters of the antenna. Besides, from Fig. 11, we observe that the side lobe level of the studied array is −16.8 dB, and a half-power beam width of the radiation pattern occurs at 78.9 degrees. The radiation efficiency of the antenna is 96.56%, the directivity is 9.451 dBi, and gain is 9.3 dBi as indicated in Table 2. Generally, the overall performance of 2×1 rectangular MSPA array shows superior performance than the single element antenna described in the previous section.

The summarized comparative analysis of 2×1 antenna array designs reported in the literature is shown in Table 2. From the table, it is evident that the

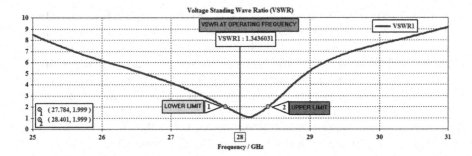

Fig. 10. VSWR versus frequency plot for 2×1 inset-feed rectangular MSPA array.

Farfield Gain Abs (Phi=90)

Phi= 90   30   0   30   Phi=270

farfield (f=28) [1]

Frequency = 28 GHz
Main lobe magnitude =   9.3 dBi
Main lobe direction =   11.0 deg.
Angular width (3 dB) =   78.9 deg.
Side lobe level = -16.8 dB

Theta / Degree vs. dBi

Fig. 11. 2D radiation pattern of 2×1 inset-feed rectangular MSPA array.

proposed antenna has minimum return losses and VSWR as compared to the designs reported in [9,13,22]. The proposed design achieves better radiation efficiency and total radiation efficiency than the design reported in [13,22].

Table 2. Performances comparison of the existing and proposed 2×1 MSPA array.

Ref	Subs. type	F_O (GHz)	S_{11} (dB)	DIR (dBi)	GAIN (dBi)	VSWR	η_{rad} (%)	η_{tot} (%)	BW (MHz)
[9]	ROG	28	−16.65	12	12.4	-	-	-	-
[13]	FR-4	28	−14.7	9.853	-	1.624	92.7	87.77	-
[22]	FR-4	28	−14.8	6.74	6.15	-	86.28	-	-
This work	FR-4	28	−19.886	9.451	9.3	1.344	96.56	92.53	575

Where, η_{rad} denotes radiation efficiency, η_{tot} denotes total radiation efficiency, S_{11} denotes return losses, and BW denotes bandwidth.

3.3   4×1 Inset-Feed Rectangular MSPA Array

The return loss plot of 4×1 inset-feed rectangular MSPA array is shown in Fig. 12. At the resonant frequency, the magnitude of the return loss of the array is about −27.4218 dB, and also, the −10 dB impedance bandwidth of the proposed antenna is 1.394 GHz. As shown in Fig. 13, at 28 GHz, the VSWR of the antenna is 1.1059 which is very close to the ideal values. From the achieved results, it can be observed that the 4×1 inset-feed MSPA array achieved wider bandwidth and minimum VSWR than that of the single patch antenna and 2×1 MSPA array.

The simulated 2D radiation pattern of the 4×1 MSPA array model is shown in Fig. 14. The side lobe level of this antenna is −11.8 dB and the half-power beam width occurred at 72.3 degrees. The designed antenna has the beam gain, directivity, radiation efficiency, and total radiation of 11.06 dBi, 11.2 dBi, 97.41%, and 96.56% respectively as depicted in Table 3. The beam gain and directivity are improved because the number of the array elements has increased from two to four and the radiating array inter-element space has been properly selected in such a way that, the radiation from each array element is added together constructively in the desired direction.

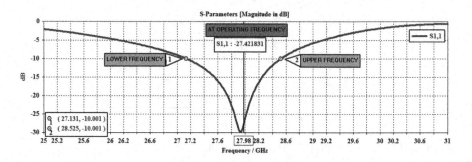

Fig. 12. Return loss versus frequency plot for 4×1 inset-feed rectangular MSPA array.

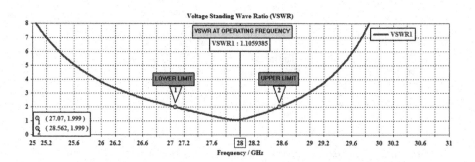

Fig. 13. VSWR versus frequency plot for 4×1 inset-feed rectangular MSPA array.

The performance of the proposed 4×1 MSPA array is compared with the antenna of the same structure reported in the literature. As shown in Table 3, in terms of the return loss, VSWR, and radiation efficiency, the proposed design

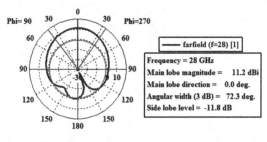

Fig. 14. 2D radiation pattern of 4×1 inset-feed rectangular MSPA array.

Table 3. Performance comparison of the existing and proposed 4×1 MSPA array.

Ref	Subs. type	F_O (GHz)	S_{11}(dB)	DIR (dBi)	GAIN (dBi)	VSWR	η_{rad} (%)	η_{tot} (%)	BW (GHz)
[13]	FR-4	28	−21.4476	11.99	-	1.6502	83.95	78.9	-
[16]	FR-4	28	−17.6	-	-	-	79.9	-	0.540
This work	FR-4	28	−27.4218	11.2	11.06	1.1059	97.41	96.56	1.394

outperforms the design reported in [13,16]. But, in terms of gain and directivity, the design reported in [13] outperforms the proposed antenna.

Where, η_{rad} denotes radiation efficiency, η_{tot} denotes total radiation efficiency, S_{11}, and BW denotes bandwidth.

3.4   4×4 Inset-Feed Rectangular MSPA Array

Fig. 15 shows the return loss plot of the 4×4 inset-feed rectangular MSPA array model. The return loss of the antenna is less than −10 dB between 27.819 GHz and 28.151 GHz. However, at 28 GHz, it is −33.149 dB and the −10 dB working bandwidth of the designed antenna is about 332 MHz. From Fig. 16, it is observed that, at the resonant frequency, the VSWR of the antenna is 1.045 which is very close to the ideal value. Generally, both inset feed and quarter-wave impedance matching techniques with the tuned width of the microstrip transmission line have been used to minimize the impedance mismatch of the proposed antenna at the feed networks and the edge of the patch. As a result, the minimum value of VSWR has been achieved at 28 GHz.

The simulated 2D radiation pattern of the 4×4 MSPA array is shown in Fig. 17. Half-power beam width of the antenna occurred at 25.8 degrees and the side lobe level of 11.1 dB has been achieved from the designed antenna. From Table 4, we can observe that the studied 4×4 rectangular MSPA array shows the radiation efficiency of 86.543%, directivity of 15.8 dBi, and gain of 15.17 dBi.

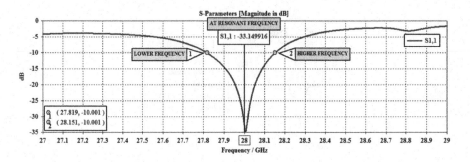

Fig. 15. Return loss versus frequency plot for 4×4 inset-feed rectangular MSPA array.

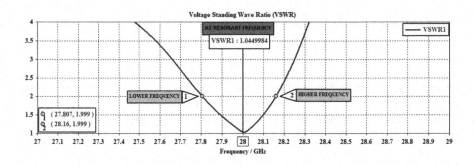

Fig. 16. VSWR versus frequency plot for 4×4 inset-feed rectangular MSPA array.

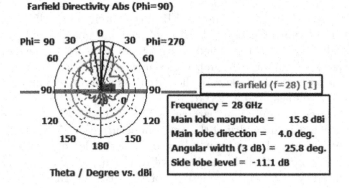

Fig. 17. 2D radiation pattern of 4×4 inset-feed rectangular MSPA array.

3.5 8×8 Inset-Feed Rectangular MSPA Array

The simulated return loss of the proposed 8×8 inset-feed rectangular MSPA array is given in Fig. 18. At the resonant frequency, the return loss of the antenna is −17.749 dB. The −10 dB return loss bandwidth of this antenna is 368 MHz. As compared to the 4×4 antenna array structure, the 8×8 inset-feed rectangular MSPA array achieves wider bandwidth.

Figure 19 shows the VSWR plot of examined 8×8 rectangular MSPA array. From the plot, at the resonant frequency, the VSWR of the antenna is 1.298. On the other side, the side lobe level of this antenna is −10 dB, and the half-power beam width occurs at 12.8 degrees as shown in Fig. 20. As indicated in Table 4, the designed antenna array has radiation efficiency, beam directivity, and gain of 79.73%, 19.31 dBi, and 18.33 dBi respectively. The 8×8 inset-feed MSPA array improves the directivity and gain of 4×4 inset-feed MSPA array by 3.51 dBi and 3.16 dBi.

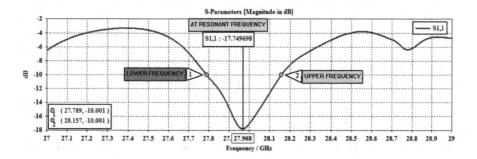

Fig. 18. Return loss versus frequency plot of 8×8 inset-feed rectangular MSPA array.

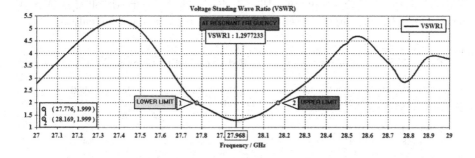

Fig. 19. VSWR versus frequency plot for 8×8 inset-feed rectangular MSPA array.

Generally, from simulation results of all the studied antenna arrays summarized in Table 4, the performance of the linear antenna arrays improved as

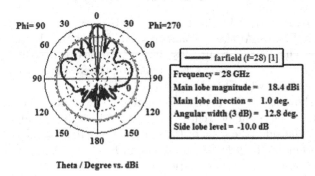

Fig. 20. 2D radiation pattern of 8×8 inset-feed rectangular MSPA array.

the number of radiating elements increases from one to four. However, we have observed that the trend does not continue further. For instance, the performance of a linear antenna array of 8×1 is significantly lower than that of 4×1 in terms of return loss, mutual coupling, and VSWR, and they are out of the acceptable range. In addition to this, a linear increment of the antenna array size reduces the compactness of the structure which is not desired in many applications. The 4×4 antenna array structure achieves the lowest values of the return loss and VSWR due to the introduction of a quarter-wave impedance transformer in the matching network design. The planar structures (4×4 and 8×8) have lower radiation efficiency as compared to the linear antenna array structures (1×1, 2×1, and 4×1). This is due to the increased loss and mutual coupling between the elements in the planar antenna array structures. However, their directivity and gain are significantly above that of the linear structures as can be depicted from Table 4. Overall, our extensive study of different antenna array structures using simulation shows that there is no single best design in terms of all the performance parameters of the antenna. Hence, there is a design trade-off that should be considered depending on the requirements of a particular application.

Table 4. Simulation results of all studied inset-feed rectangular MSPA array.

Type	F_0 (GHz)	S_{11} (dB)	DIR (dBi)	GAIN (dBi)	VSWR	η_{rad} (%)	η_{tot} (%)	SLL (dB)	BW (MHz)
1×1	28	−20.24	7.404	7.18	1.216	94.95	94.2	−12.1	572
2×1	28	−19.88	9.451	9.299	1.344	96.56	92.53	−16.8	575
4×1	28	−27.42	11.2	11.06	1.106	97.41	96.56	11.8	1394
4×4	28	−33.15	15.8	15.17	1.045	86.54	85.08	−11.1	332
8×8	28	−17.75	19.31	18.33	1.298	79.73	74.28	−10	368

Where, η_{rad} denotes radiation efficiency, η_{tot} denotes total radiation efficiency, S_{11}, SLL denotes side lobe level ,and BW denotes bandwidth.

4   Conclusions

In this paper, the performance of single element, 2×1, 4×1, 4×4, and 8×8 inset-feed rectangular MSPA arrays have been meticulously optimized for 5G mobile applications. At the resonant frequency, the simulation result shows that, the return loss and bandwidth of the proposed single, 2×1, and 4×1 inset-feed rectangular MSPA arrays are $-20.234\,$dB, $-19.89\,$dB, $-27.42\,$dB, and 572 MHz, 575 MHz, 1394 MHz; also, their directivity are 7.41 dBi, 9.451 dBi, 11.2 dBi respectively. The radiation efficiency of all one-dimensional antenna arrays is above 95%. Similarly, the return loss of the designed 4×4 and 8×8 MSPA arrays are $-33.15\,$dB, $-17.75\,$dB and the bandwidth are 332 MHz and 368 MHz. Moreover, the directivity and radiation efficiency are 15.8 dBi, 19.31 dBi and 86.54%, 79.7% respectively.

From the simulated result analysis of the linear MSPA array structures, it has been observed that increasing the array element from one to four, the antenna shows the improvement in directivity, gain, radiation efficiency, and bandwidth. However, the magnitude of the side lobe has increased which is unwanted. Similarly, in planar MSPA array structures, as the array element is increased from sixty to sixty-four the improvement is obtained in terms of directivity, gain, and bandwidth. But, in terms of the magnitude of return loss, VSWR, and radiation efficiency, MSPA array with sixty elements outperforms the one with sixty-four radiating elements. Generally, as compared to existing antenna array designs reported in the scientific literature, the proposed antenna arrays show significantly improved performance. Therefore, all optimized MSPA array structures proposed in this paper have suitable performance characteristics for the emerging 5G mobile applications.

Annex

Optimized Design Parameters of Proposed MSPA

Table 5. Optimized design parameters of single inset-feed MSPA.

Optimized design parameters	Symbols	Values
Width of the patch	PW	3.3 mm
Length of the patch	PL	2.47 mm
Width of the ground plane	GW	8.5 mm
Length of the ground plane	GL	8.5 mm
Length of inset-feed	YO	0.9054 mm
Length of inset-gap	Gp	0.23915 mm
Substrate thickness	SH	0.244 mm
Length of microstrip feeder line	LMFL	2.55 mm
Width of microstrip feeder line	WMFL	0.4783 mm

Table 6. Optimized design parameters of 2×1 inset-feed MSPA array.

Design parameters	Symbols	Values
Width of the patch	PW	3.2602 mm
Length of the patch	PL	2.478 mm
Width of the ground plane	GW	16 mm
Length of the ground plane	GL	9 mm
Substrate thickness	SH	0.244 mm
Gap of inset-feed	Gp	0.23917 mm
Length of inset feed	YO	0.745 mm
Distance between the patch	D	5.4 mm
Length of microstrip feeder line	LMFL	2.0219 mm
Width of microstrip feeder line	WMFL	0.4784 mm
Length of 1:2 microstrip power divider	LFMPD	0.23915 mm
Width of 1:2 microstrip power divider	WFMPD	11 mm

Table 7. Optimized design parameters of 4×1 inset-feed MSPA array.

Design parameters	Symbols	Values
Width of the patch	PW	3.2602 mm
Length of the patch	PL	2.478 mm
Width of the ground plane	GW	33.1 mm
Length of the ground plane	GL	9.92 mm
Length of inset-feed	YO	0.744 mm
Gap of inset-feed	Gp	0.2392 mm
Substrate thickness	SH	0.244 mm
Length of microstrip patch feeder	LMFL	2.0209 mm
Width of microstrip patch feeder	WMFL	0.4783 mm
Length of 1:2 microstrip power divider	LFMPD	0.23915 mm
Width of 1:2 microstrip power divider	WFMPD	11 mm
Length of 1:4 microstrip power divider	LSMPD	0.23915 mm
Width of 1:4 microstrip power divider	WSMPD	22 mm

Table 8. Optimized design parameters of 4×4 inset-feed MSPA array.

Design parameters	Symbols	Values
Width of the patch	PW	3.261 mm
Length of the patch	PL	2.47819 mm
Width of the ground plane	GW	31 mm
Length of the ground plane	GL	33.1 mm
Length of inset-feed	YO	0.9054 mm
Gap of inset-feed	GP	0.23916 mm
Length of microstrip feeder line	LMFL	2.55 mm
Width of microstrip feeder line	WMFL	0.4783 mm
Length of 1:2 microstrip power divider	LFMPD	0.23915 mm
Width of 1:2 microstrip power divider	WFMPD	10.8 mm
Length of last microstrip feeder line	LLMFL	0.23915 mm
Width of last microstrip feeder line	WLMFL	15.38 mm
First quarter transform width	FQTW	0.3 mm
First-quarter transform Length	FQTL	0.47831 mm
Second quarter transform length	SQTL	0.338 mm
Third-quarter transform width	TQTW	0.23915 mm

Table 9. Optimized design parameters of 8×8 inset-feed MSPA array.

Design parameters	Symbols	Values
Width of the patch	PW	3.2602 mm
Length of the patch	PL	2.4781 mm
Width of the ground plane	GW	66 mm
Length of the ground plane	GL	60.5 mm
Gap of inset-feed	GP	0.23916 mm
Length of inset-feed	YO	0.95 mm
Distance between the patch	D	5.4025 mm
Length of microstrip feeder line	LMFL	2.227 mm
Width of microstrip patch feeder	WMFL	0.4783 mm
Length of 1:2 microstrip power divider	LFPD	0.23915 mm
Width of 1:2 microstrip power divider	WFPD	10.8 mm
Length of last microstrip feeder line	LLMFL	0.23915 mm
Width of last microstrip feeder line	WLMFL	32.9726 mm
First quarter transform width	FQTW	0.3 mm
First-quarter transform Length	FQTL	0.47831 mm
Second quarter transform width	SQTW	0.4783 mm
Second quarter transform length	SQTL	0.338 mm
Third-quarter transform width	TQTW	0.23915 mm
Third-quarter transform length	TQTW	1.2769 mm

References

1. Dahlman, M.G., Parkvall, S., Peisa, J.: 5G wireless access: Requirements and realization. IEEE Commun. Mag. **52**(12), 42–47 (2014)
2. Gu, X., Liu, D., Baks, C.: A multilayer organic package with 64 dual-polarized antennas for 28GHz 5G communication. In: Proceedings of the IEEE International Microwave Symposium, pp. 1899–1901 (2017)
3. Dheeraj, M., Shankar, D.: Microstrip patch antenna at 28GHz for 5G applications. J. Sci. Technol. Eng. Manage. Adv. Res. Innov. **1**(1), 20–23 (2018)
4. Marcus, M.J.: 5G and IMT for 2020 and beyond. In IEEE Wireless Communication (2015)
5. Annalakshmi, E., Prabakaran, D.: A Patch array antenna for 5G mobile phone applications. Asian Jo. Appl. Sci. Technol. **1**(3), 48–51 (2017)
6. Zhang, J., Guizani, M., Zhang, Y.: 5G Millimeter wave antenna array: design and challenges. In: IEEE Wireless Communication, pp. 106–112 (2017)
7. Omar, D., Dominic, B., Franklin, M.: A 28GHz rectangular microstrip patch antenna for 5G applications. Int. J. Eng. Res. Technol. **12**(6), 854–857 (2019)
8. Hakanoglu, B., Sen, O., Turkmen, M.: A square microstrip patch antenna with enhanced return loss through defected ground plane for 5G wireless networks. In: Second URSI Atlantic Radio Science Conference, pp. 1–4 (2018)

9. Pranathi, G.V., Rani, N.D., Satyanarayana, M.: Patch antenna parameters variation with ground plane dimensions. Int. J. Adv. Res. Elect. Electron. Instrum. Eng. **4**(8), 7344–7350 (2015)
10. Safpbri, J., Muhammad, A.J., Shaifol, I.I.: 28GHz microstrip patch antennas for future 5G. J. Eng. Sci. Res. **2**(4), 01–06 (2018)
11. Priya, K.N., Sravanthi, S.G., Narmada, K.: A microstrip patch antenna design at 28GHz for 5G mobile phone applications. Int. J. Electron. Elect. Comput. Syst. **7**(3), 204–208 (2018)
12. Balanis, C.A.: Antenna Theory: Analysis and Design, 3rd edn. John Wiley and Sons, Inc., Hoboken (2005)
13. Mohamed, B., Hegazy, E.A.: Design and analysis of 28GHz rectangular microstrip antenna. WSEAS Trans. Commun. **17**, 2224–2864 (2018)
14. Abubakar, S., Mahabub, H., Dulal, H.: Design and radiation characterization of rectangular microstrip. Am. J. Eng. Res. **8**(1), 273–281 (2019)
15. Kukunuri, S., Neelaveni, A.M.: Design and development of microstrip patch antenna at 2.4GHz for wireless applications. Indian J. Sci. Technol. **11**(23), 1–5 (2018)
16. Dheeraj, M., Shankar, D.: Design and analysis of 28GHz millimeter-wave antenna array for 5G communication systems. J. Sci. Technol. Eng. Manage. Adv. Res. Innov. **1**(3), 1–9 (2018)
17. Neha, K., Sunil, S.: A 28GHz U-slot microstrip patch antenna for 5G applications. Int. J. Electromag. Develop. Res. **6**(1), 363–368 (2018)
18. Ravi, K., Uma, S.: A compact microstrip patch antenna at 28GHz for 5G wireless applications. In: IEEE Conference Second, Third International Conference and Workshops on Recent Advances and Innovations in Engineering, November 2018
19. Misbah, A., Abdalla, M., Essam, H.: Design and analysis of millimeter wave microstrip patch antenna for 5G applications. In: International Conference on Technical Sciences, pp. 137–142 (2019)
20. Kaeib, A.F., Shebani, N.M., Zarek, A.R.: Design and analysis of a slotted microstrip antenna for 5G communication networks at 28GHz. In: 19th International Conference on Sciences and Techniques of Automatic Control and Computer Engineering (STA), 24–26 March 2019
21. Ghazaoui, Y., El Alami, A., El Ghzaoui, M., Das, S., Barad, D., Mohapatra, S.: Millimeter-wave antenna with enhanced bandwidth for 5G wireless application. J. Instrum. (JINST) **15**, T01003 (2020)
22. Kavitha, M., Dinesh Kumar, T., Gayathri, A., Koushick, V.: 28GHz printed antenna for 5G communication with improved gain using array. Int. J. Sci. Technol. Res. **9**(3), 1–7 (2020)
23. Sivabalan, A., Pavithra, S., Selvarani, R., Vinitha, K.M.: Design of microstrip patch antenna for 5G. Int. J. Control Autom. **13**, 546–552 (2020)
24. Darsono, M., Wijaya, A.R.: Design and simulation of a rectangular patch microstrip antenna for the frequency of 28GHz in 5G technology. In: International Conference on Innovation in Research (2020)

Blockchain Based Green Coffee Supply Chain Management to Improve Traceability and Transparency (Case Study on Sidama Coffee)

Temesgen Mihiretu Abebe[1]([✉]) and Alehegn Melesse Semegn[2]

[1] Faculty of Electrical and Computer Engineering, Bahir Dar Institute of Technology, Bahir Dar University, Bahir Dar, Ethiopia
[2] Faculty of Mechanical and Industrial Engineering, Bahir Dar Institute of Technology, Bahir Dar University, Bahir Dar, Ethiopia

Abstract. Ethiopia is one of coffee producing countries in the world, especially it is known for coffee Arabica. The coffee supply chain includes different participating organizations from its production place up to its consumption in the international market. Ethiopian coffee suffers from the two most prominent supply chain problems which are provenance traceability and transaction transparency for the participating parties. In this paper, we tried to implement blockchain technology for the Ethiopian green coffee supply chain to improve traceability and transparency by using Sidama coffee as case study. Distributed ledger technology was proposed to solve those problems by distributing a record of coffee transactions throughout the network participants. Among available blockchain technologies, we choose Hyperledger blockchain technology because it is suitable for business to business (B2B) model. We were able to design and implement a number of smart contracts using Hyperledger composer modeling language based on our field study and deploy them in the underlying Hyperledger Fabric blockchain network. The prototype system was able to create a traceable route for the coffee by recording every transaction in an immutable and untampered way and the transactions were transparent for participating parties since they get an exact copy of ordered transaction as a block. We also were able to solve confidentiality issues in the network by implementing multiple channels in the network.

Keywords: Supply chain · Traceability · Transparency · Distributed ledger technology · Blockchain · Hyperledger fabric · Hyperledger composer · Coffee · Peers · Smart Contract

1 Introduction

1.1 Background

A supply chain is the network of all the individuals, organizations, resources, activities, and technologies involved in the production of a commodity and Marketing of produced

M. A. Delele et al. (Eds.): ICAST 2020, LNICST 384, pp. 304–318, 2021.
https://doi.org/10.1007/978-3-030-80621-7_22

commodity to the different market places [1]. This involves multiple processes, from the procurement of raw materials, to design and fabrication of products by manufacturers, delivery of the resulting product to consumers, and can even include post-sales logistics support. Supply chain management (SCM) integrates all of these steps and orchestrates the people, input materials, processes, and technologies required to ensure a smooth flow. Given the complexity of most supply chain networks, there are many challenges associated with managing supply chains.

Coffee is the main source of the economy and culture of different countries throughout the world. Among those countries, Ethiopia is well-known as the origin of Arabica coffee that produces largely in the country [2]. Ethiopia's coffee has its own peculiar quality produced in the different parts of the country. Ethiopia produces coffee in different production systems like forest, semi-forest, garden, and plantation that made the country unique from other coffee producing countries. Although coffee is a traditionally worldwide traded cash crop with new markets emerging, many agricultural dependent developing countries like Ethiopia are struggling with the production and marketing of their coffee [3]. Coffee is the most important crop in Ethiopia even it is the most influential commodity to the national economy and it is also the leading export commodity. It plays a crucial role in generating foreign currency to the country at a large level. Coffee supply chains are often complex, with beans sometimes changing hands of times on the journey from producer to consumer. Small farmers typically sell their coffee beans to local traders, often agents for big coffee millers and exporters, who transport the coffee to the processing plant.

Blockchain technology is a distributed ledger that can record transactions among different participants as a cryptographical chain of blocks in a verifiable and permanent way [4]. It is a relatively early-stage technology when compared with the most prominent implementation current cryptocurrency like Bitcoin and Ethereum. Blockchain is a replicated distributed ledger technology (DLT) that verifies and stores transactions occurring in a peer-to-peer network [5, 6]. At its core, blockchain is a distributed ledger technology that leverages the resources of a large peer-to-peer network to verify and approve transactions [2]. These transactions are recorded chronologically in blocks and the blocks are linked together cryptographically and stored permanently on the blockchain which creates an immutable chain. The blockchain data structure is a timestamped list of blocks. Blocks are containers aggregating transactions. Every block is identifiable and linked to the previous block in the chain through cryptographic hashes.

Smart contracts [7] are semi-autonomous programs running on the blockchain. They can store and update variables and instantiate and invoke other smart contracts. It is a computer code running on top of a blockchain containing a set of rules under which the parties to that smart contract agree to interact with each other [8]. It is a computer protocol that facilities the transfer of digital assets between parties under the agreed-upon conditions. It is similar to a traditional contract in most ways including the definition of rules and penalties around the agreement except for the fact that it can also enforce the agreed-upon obligations automatically [9]. If and when the pre-defined rules are met, the agreement is automatically enforced. The smart contract code facilitates, verifies, and enforces the negotiation or performance of an agreement or transaction. Once launched, smart contracts are fully autonomous; when contract conditions are met, pre-specified and agreed actions occur automatically.

Blockchain has been employed for a number of use cases starting from its first implementation [10] for peer to peer Bitcoin transaction management. Even though Bitcoin was the first double-spending free peer to peer transaction, after that a number of cryptocurrencies platforms have been innovated like Ethereum [11], Corda [12], and Hyperledger Fabric [13]. Ethereum was the first blockchain infrastructure with smart contract implementation in addition to Ether cryptocurrency with a solidity programming language for business implementation.

Based on the participation of peers in the consensus process, blockchain platforms can be divided into two [14]. The first form of blockchain platform is known as a public blockchain platform. It means that the network is available for the public and any interested peer can be part of the network and participate in the consensus process. Among a large number of platforms, Bitcoin and Ethereum are the two most common digital currency platforms of public blockchain. Ethereum platform is not only a digital currency but also able to execute programmable smart contracts which can automate digital world contracts and process [9]. Ethereum is the most popular platform for smart contract development on the public blockchain infrastructure. The second form of blockchain is known as permissioned blockchain platform. In this type of platform, each participating party should have a digital credential and need permission to participate in the network consensus process. The main purpose of permissioned blockchain platform is to create confidentiality on transaction execution and ledger distribution and increase throughput [14]. Hyperledger fabric is the most dominant type of permissioned blockchain which is developed by Linux foundation.

Blockchain technology can potentially be applied to a wide variety of industries, including energy, supply chain, food safety, education, finance, insurance, medical, etc. IBM uses Hyperledger Fabric to implement a diamond supply chain [15]. The implications for supply chain management are promising, as it could provide a solution to the current challenges faced and help the overall supply chain become more efficient. By using a decentralized database to provide a shared reality across non-trusting entities such as suppliers, manufacturers and even consumers [7], a blockchain can improve transparency and traceability in the supply chain process. In the research work [16] the researchers use blockchain technology for school information management to create an immutable school record. As pertinent information regarding the physical goods and other relevant events are securely and reliably recorded on the blockchain, smart contracts can also be used to automatically execute when specific conditions are met [7, 14]. This provides flexibility and can help to simplify the complex multi-party systems that a supply chain typically consists of. Although the use case is clear, actual implementations of blockchain technology in SCM are yet to proliferate widely. Hence, more research is required to investigate the possibility and practicality of such an application. In our knowledge, there is no implementation of blockchain for coffee supply chain management especially in developing countries like Ethiopia use case which is saturated more than enough bureaucracy and unstable traditional system.

1.2 Problem Statement

As discussed above, the Ethiopian coffee supply chain encompasses all of the activities starting from the earliest stage of coffee plantation and collection up to the final stages of end-users or consumers. With the impact of globalization, supply chains typically cross the boundaries of both organizations and countries. Through all this stage there are a number of direct participants including the farmers (growers), collectors, exporters, primary coffee processors, secondary coffee processors, coffee roasters, and international coffee buyers. All the above participants (stakeholders) are direct participants; meaning they are the one that transacts the coffee supply chain business. Also, there are indirect participants like, Ethiopian Tea and Coffee Authority (EthioCTA), Ethiopia Commodity Exchange (ECX), regional organs, certification institutions, etc. on the chain to manage and control the market activities.

In between every transaction point, there is at list one contract paper that needs the third party for approval and including the contract paper, there is an enormous amount of data flows. So, throughout the coffee supply chain network, there are a number of processes and relationships across the stakeholders. All of those processes and relationships need proper management mechanisms in order to ensure the smooth operation of the Ethiopian coffee supply chain.

Having all the above participants, asset, business relation, and communication between them; there are different issues which need more attention for a better outcome in the coffee supply chain. The issues include involvement of third parties in the transaction, being difficult to trace coffee provenance and history in a digitized way, transactions are not transparent within the specified chain line for its participants, and trust between participating parties are impossible to build trust through reputation in the current supply chain system. Now a day Ethiopia's coffee is losing its price in the international market due to one or more of the above problems. Specifically, the international market complains about the coffee traceability including its production process and origin and purity. Also, through time, the existing market becoming more unfair especially for coffee farmers due to none transparency in the market. In addition, the system is vulnerable to black-market, which make the country lose lots of foreign currency.

In this paper, we propose a blockchain-based smart contract system to solve traceability and transparency issues in Sidama green coffee supply chain. What we believe is through a distributed ledger system it is possible to trace the provenance of coffee in the supply chain and it going to be easy to make transactions transparent among the participating parties while keeping the confidentiality of private data's in the supply chain network.

2 Methodology

2.1 Data Collection and Requirement Formulation

The data collection was undertaken in two phases. The first one is a visit to different stakeholders at Addis Ababa including EthioCTA, ECX, and Sidama Coffee Farmers' Cooperative Union (SCFCU). The second phase was the visit and data collection at Hawassa and nearby coffee growing and processing towns.

The collected data from different sources were analyzed in a way that suitable for blockchain-based system design and implementation. Other than the scientific literature, we used Federal democratic Republic of Ethiopia (FDRE) proclamation No.1051/2017 "Coffee Marketing and Quality Control proclamation" proclamation page 9657, FDRE Regulation No. 433/2018 "The Coffee Marketing and Quality Control Council of Ministers" Regulation page 10568, and "Coffee Marketing and Quality Control Directive" Directive page 002/2018.

Existing Supply Chain Model for Sidama Coffee. In our field study what we found is that, there are a number of participants in the Sidama coffee supply chain. Participants include growers, investors (commercial producers), suppliers, exporters, and coopera-tives/union. According to [15], the Ethiopian government establishes six coopera-tives/unions and SCFCU is one of those cooperative unions.

Sidama zone has 12 coffee-producing districts and throughout those districts SCFCU has 57 cooperatives unions with a total member of 86,658 farmers. Also, there are 112 direct exporter growers, each of them has more than 2hectare farms for coffee production, and coffee suppliers, who collect coffee from growers and sell their supply coffee product to ECX. In general, the total area to be cultivated by coffee in Sidama zone is about 80,592.24 hectares, among this amount of area 43,120.44 hectares cultivated with organic coffee in those 12 districts.

Then based on the above finding we tried to put a picture of the Sidama coffee supply chain as shown in Fig. 1. As clearly shown in the diagram, there are four main routes of the Sidama coffee supply chain. The first and the most common way are done through the ECX market including farmers, suppliers, and exporters as the main participant. The second path is through cooperative union in which at the lower level near to farmers there are farmers' cooperatives of coffee grower and primary processor and in the upper level as exporter there is one cooperative union. The third path is direct exporter investors who have legality in coffee farming, processing, and exporting from the government. The last one is coffee growers who have the power to export directly to the international market and have such legality from the government.

Related to our research parameters, which are traceability and transparency, we found the following point from the data collection process.

- There has been a pilot physical project by ECX for coffee traceability before around three years ago. But it fails due to management problems like sorting, leveling, loading and unloading by man power. But still, there was no support from ICT based traceability implementation in the market.
- As we expected while starting this study, what we found is that transaction transparency is the main problem in the system.
- Also, black market is another main problem in the market process which makes the country loses lots of foreign currency.

2.2 System Setup

For the design and development of a prototype system to undertake an experiment on the proposed system local blockchain environment was established using the following hardware and software resources.

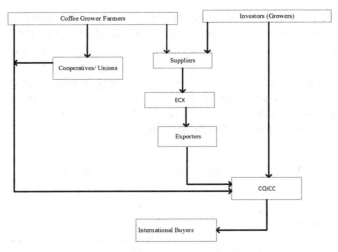

Fig. 1. Coffee marketing supply chain of Sidama coffee

Hardware Setup. For the deployment of Hyperledger Fabric blockchain node network local area network was established using six computers with the following specifica-tions.

- Five of them were HP computers with single socket 3.5 GHz speed, six core, 8 GB primary memory, and 1 TB HDD
- One Dell with single socket 3.6 GHz four core, 16 GB primary memory, and 5 TB HDD
- **Software Setup.** On top of the above hardware setup, different software setups were approached. Since the numbers of participants are much greater than six nodes, vagrant is used to design the virtual machines for the blockchain participant node. To orchestrate and configure the fabric peer network Ansible orchestration tool was used.

For the blockchain network infrastructure design and deployment Hyperledger fabric peer docker image was used. The process of selecting a blockchain platform should be derived from understanding the application area use case. In our research, the use case has B2B nature based on participants, interactions and asset transactions. So, we choose Hyperledger Fabric blockchain platform for our system blockchain implementation.

So, having Hyperledger Fabric there are different platforms and tool which makes application implementation and development easy enough. Among the list of tools we choose to use Hyperledger Composer for business network (Smart contract) development using object-oriented modeling language.

3 Design and Implementation

Almost all businesses are involved in exchanging some form of values. They exchange those values from one firm to the other in the business process through their agents or workers. While exchanging value they try to keep their own book of records which is the ledger of value exchanges by the respective business firms. In the context of Hyperledger fabric blockchain; there is a concept of an asset, which can be tangible or intangible, to represent values [18]. Value exchanges are formulated to a transaction which transfers the asset in the business process. The participants of the network commit the asset transaction in the network. So, in Hyperledger fabric, blockchain means it is a distributed chain of blocks throughout the network peers, where each block is a committed transaction to transfer assets from one firm to other by participants.

Table 1. Green coffee export supply chain participants

No	Participants	Role in the business network
1	Coffee grower	The main grower of coffee in the region including farmers and small-scale growers
2	Coffee supplier	The one who collect coffee from grower, process it to supply coffee and sell to exporters in ECX market
3	Coffee exporters	They buy supply coffee from coffee suppliers, process it to export coffee, create a contract with foreign buyers to sell export coffee, and sell their coffee based on their contracts
4	Commercial producers	They are coffee grower supplier coffee processor and event exporters
5	Union/Cooperative	They collect RCCP only from their members, they process supply and export coffee in their industry and they sell coffee for external buyers
6	EthioCTA	They control coffee production, processing and export process in general. They give export license for potential traders, they support farmers for better productivity
7	ECX	It creates a market system for supply coffee in the country
8	Coffee quality inspection and certification center (CQICC)	They inspect export coffee and certify its quality
9	Regional Organ	They follow RCCP and supply coffee production and primary markets
10	ECX warehouses	They give coffee quality inspection, grading service, and warehouse service for supply coffee

So, based on the data collected from our field study, we identity the participants and assets of the green coffee export supply chain in Sidama coffee as list in Table 1 and Table 2 respectively.

From the above list of participants from 1–5 are traders, means direct participants of the business, and from 6–10 are governmental regulatory and controlling indirect participants.

Table 2. Green coffee export supply chain assets

No	Assets	Description
1	Coffee	It is the main asset in the supply chain. It has different forms in different market places like at primary market red cherry coffee or coffee with pulp, at ECX market supply coffee and at international market export coffee
2	Contract	It is an agreement between two or more traders in the network like export coffee contract, contract between exporter and grower, etc.

Among a number of transactions in the Sidama coffee supply chain we tried to aggregate those transactions in some group and we select the following three transactions for this system implementation and testing purpose. The first transactions as shown in Algorithm 1 is simple coffee sell and buy between two parties which transfer the ownership of some amount of coffee with some amount of price. It is the most common transaction in different levels of the coffee supply chain, especially in the ECX market line. The second and the third transaction as shown in Algorithm 2 and Algorithm 1 are contract-based coffee transactions in the supply chain network.

Algorithm 1. Coffee transaction pseudocode

```
Input: coffeeSeller, coffeeBuyer, coffee[], transaction Centeer,
coffeeType, unitPrice, transactionStatus, physicalAddres
Output: tx
if coffeeSeller is valid id or coffeeBuyer is not valid id then
   throw error
else
   tx.coffeeBuyer.coffee[] <- coffeeSeller.coffee[]
   tx.coffeeSeller.price <- coffeeBuy
   er.coffee[]*coffeeSeller.unitprice
   tx.transactionCenteer <- transactionCenteer
   tx.date <-current system date
   tx. physicalAddres <- physicalAddres
   tx.transactionStatus <- transactionStatus
   tx.timestamp <- current system datedate
return tx
```

Algorithm 2. Contract agreement transaction pseudocode

```
Input: coffeeSeller, coffeeBuyer, coffeeType, quantity, unit-
Price, SellerRight, SellerObligation, buyerRight, buyerObliga-
tion, deliveryPlace, expiryDate, contractType
Output: contract
   if coffeeSeller is valid id or coffeeBuyer is not valid id
   then
      throw error
   if coffeeSeller or coffeeBuyer dicard then
      throw error
   if ethioCTA not approved the contract then
      throw error
   if ECX not register the cotnract then
      throw error
   contract.coffeeBuyer <- coffeeBuyer
   contract.coffeeSeller <- coffeeSeller
   contract.SellerObligation <- SellerObligation
   contract.SellerRight <- SellerRight
   contract.buyerObligation <- buyerObligation
   contract.buyerRight <- buyerRight
   contract.deliveryPlace <- deliveryPlace
   contract.contractType <- contractType
   contract.quantity <- quantity
   contract.unitPrice <-unitPrice
   contract.expiryDate <-expiryDate
   contract.contractDate <- current system date
return contract
```

Algorithm 3. Contract delivery pseudocode

```
Input: contract, coffeeSeller, coffeeBuyer, coffee [], quantity,
deliveryPlace,
Output: tx, contract
    if coffeeSeller is valid id or coffeeBuyer is not valid id
    then
        throw error
    if contract is expired then
        throw error
    if contract.quantity greater than zero then
        throw error
    tx.coffeeBuyer.coffee[] <- coffeeSeller.coffee[]
    contract.quantity <- contract.quantity - quantity
    tx.coffeeSeller.price <-
    coffeeBuyer.coffee[]*contract.unitprice
    tx.deliveryPlace <-deliveryPlace
    tx.date <-current system date
return tx, contract
```

3.1 Hyperledger Fabric Elements and Our Design Perspective

As stated in the introduction section, Hyperledger is the project under the Linux Foundation for the incubation of blockchain technology for business. It contains two categories of technology which are DLT frameworks with four initiative including Hyperledger fabric and tools including Hyperledger composer [19]. As mentioned above, for the proposed blockchain green coffee supply chain system we used Hyperledger Fabric, which is production ready framework, as a blockchain framework and Hyperledger composer as a business network development tool. Fabric is a framework that means it is not a platform like database management systems and web servers rather fabric is a set of infrastructure and application building blocks with practices and guidelines for creating blockchain applications [18]. So out of this framework based on the specific blockchain application requirements, it is possible to create infrastructure design that would use in the blockchain building block. So, in application development (chain code/smart contract/business network), we can access the underline infrastructure using standard components, API's, and functions. Hyperledger fabric basically has the following infrastructure elements.

Peers are primary concepts in Hyperledger Fabric since they are the backbone of the network. A peer is a Fabric application component that runs in a Docker container and is responsible for maintaining a copy of the ledger and providing programmatic access to the information on the ledger via the world state database [20]. An organization will typically have more than one peer, primarily for high availability. There are three types of peers which are

- Committing Peer: maintain leger and state. Commit transaction, may hold smart contract/chain code

- Endorsing Peer: Specialized committing peer that receives a transaction proposal for endorsement, response granting or denying endorsement, must hold a smart contract

Orderer node (Part of ordering service), approves the inclusion of transaction blocks into the ledger and communicates with committing and endorsing peer nodes. It does not hold either a smart contract or a ledger. Ordering Service is the network-level service responsible for determining the order in which transactions coming from any participant in the business network should be committed to the ledger which is the consensus process in literal blockchain definition.

Since Hyperledger Fabric is a private, permissioned blockchain, identity plays a critical role. Identity of individuals as well as Fabric Components such as peers and orderers are defined by their certificates from a pluggable Membership Service Provider (MSP). Any certificate authority can be (and often is) used, but Fabric also includes one in the box, called the Hyperledger Fabric Certificate Authority (CA).

Channel is a means of creating one-to-one private communication between channel participating peers. Each channel has its own private ledger record. So, channel in Hyperledger fabric is meant for the implementation of data and transaction confidentiality.

Based on the requirements we formulated above and the nature of the selected blockchain framework, regarding Hyperledger fabric infrastructure we suggested the following combination of elements as a design specification for the proposed system.

In business, organizations own the business values and they transact those values between them. In Hyperledger fabric network those organizations can be transformed as potential security domains and units of identity and can participate in the network through their peers [21]. They use their MSP to issue identities and certificates for their peers as well as clients for smart contract access privileges. The ordering service should be implemented as a separate organization with ordering peer only.

So, what we suggest is that every legally identified organization should be participated at least as a commuting peer to hold ledger. Governmental organizations should provide commuting peers since they act as legal regulators in most transactions. Growers and personal participants can be a member of authority organs and get their credential from them. Each organization, who contributes peer to the network should contain MSP-CA for network credential management. Every endorsing peer from any organization should contain the chain code. So, as shown in Table 1 while the system implemented it needs a minimum of ten organizational peer nodes.

As shown in Fig. 1, the Sidama green coffee supply chain has a number of vertical routs between different coffee traders which are independent of each other. Governmental organs are almost part of every rout of the network. The data and transaction in each rout should be confidential and transparent for their respective routes. So, in Hyperledger fabric infrastructure, we suggested transferring every rout to channels in the network. Regarding ordering service, we used a solo orderer for prototype testing but for real-world application design, we suggest Apache Kafka for stability and availability [22].

3.2 System Implementation

In the proposed system implementation process the first task was creating the local network by assembling the physical devices. The six computers were connected locally based on the universities network through data link-layer switch and each of them run Ubuntu 16.04LT Linux distribution. Since six nodes are not enough to host the proposed system organizational peers, we create a virtual environment on each computer with the following specification using virtual box software and vagrant tool.

- 2GB primary memory, storage expandable up to 50GB HDD, bento/ubuntu-16.04 vagrant box,

Then the Hyperledger Fabric infrastructures were orchestrated in the established network using Ansible automation tool based on each experimental setup. The smart contract was developed using Hyperledger Composer model language and deployed the network using composer CLI commands.

4   Result and Discussion

The system was implemented step by step starting from the blockchain infrastructure up to smart contract development and deployment. We implemented a smart contract for two types of asset moments in the supply chain using Hyperledger composer and deploy the resulting chain code on our design and implementation of Hyperledger Fabric blockchain infrastructure. A number end to end of tests were undertaken in the implemented system. In the system clients of a respective organization can submit transactions to the blockchain network and after the execution of those transactions; blocks are created and added to the chain as shown in Fig. 2.

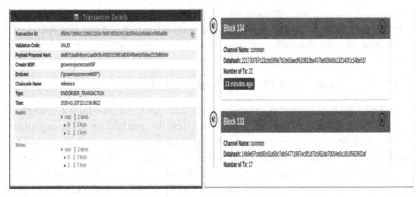

Fig. 2. Sample transaction detail after execution and added to a block and two consecutive blocks

4.1 Single Channel Configuration

First, we implement the system with a single common channel throughout the network in which all the participant organizations were part of the one common channel. What we found in this experiment is that whenever any transaction made in the business network all participants will be notified and get a copy of the block to add to their ledger then the transaction become transparent enough throughout the network.

The main problem within this configuration is each participating organization are part of every transaction processing which potentially slow down the network especially in transaction pick time because the ordering service operation is done is sequential. Since every commuting peers of the participating organization get the copy of the block in its ledger, confidentiality of transactions has a possibility of being compromised in the business process. The worst case is if the endorsement polity is vulnerable for error or mistake in the deployment process of smart contracts to the underlying blockchain chain infrastructure the endorsement process in system is may fail totally.

4.2 Multiple Channel Configurations

Then we configured the network from single channel infrastructure in to four channels to resolve the above problems in the first experimental result. Based on the existing market route as shown in Fig. 1, the first channel two channels were exemplary channels based on the business interaction between SCFCU and their member cooperatives, the third channel is an exemplary channel for direct growers and investors and the last channel is an exemplary for the normal supply chain route through the ECX market. EthioCTA, CQIC, and SNNPR have commonly participated in all four channels since they are a regulatory and controlling organization in the Ethiopia coffee supply chain network.

What we found in this experiment is that transactions are endorsed only by those endorsing peers of organizations who are responsible for the operation held by the specified transactions and the members of the channel get the copy of the block to be chained in their ledger. So, transactions are transparent within the channel and it is confidential from outside on the specified channel. Also is improves the speed of the system because all four channels can commit and order transaction in parallel.

4.3 The Effect of Number of Peers Per Organization

Within multiple channel setups, two experiments were undertaken which are single peer per organization and two peers per organization to test the availability of the organization on the network if one of its peer crashes. Then in both setup, we try to kill randomly the peer container of an organization in the network. In single peer node case availability is compromised in such peer shutdown cases since it only has one anchor peer. But when a node has two or more than two peers in the network if one of them fails even the anchor peer itself the rest of the peer will continue their participation in the network. Since the crypto operations in the peers are resource intensive while we increase the number of participating peers per organization it slows down the system as shown in Fig. 3.

The system was able to record every transfer of coffee in the network and create a chain of blocks that could be used as a single source for the history of the coffee

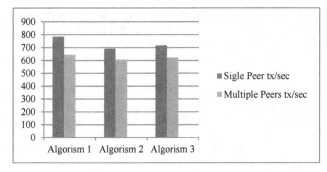

Fig. 3. Transaction throughput over single peer setup and two peer setups

rout in the supply chain. At any point in the network, we were able to trance where the coffee comes from with its detailed information. Also, the system was able to create a business contract between participating parties without the involvement of third and transact coffee based on the agreed-upon contract.

5 Conclusion and Recommendation

This paper tried to investigate the existing Ethiopia green coffee supply chain using Sidama coffee as a case study and it design and develop a blockchain-based solution to improve the most prominent problems which are traceability and transparency. The implemented prototype system was able to implement the most critical transactions which are the exchange of coffee products and a contract between participating parties. We were able to implement the blockchain network architecture for thirteen organizations based on the available resources. In the implemented system every transfer of the coffee was well recorded in the system with full information and the executed transaction were shared among participating parties which gives a single truth about coffee history in the supply chain. So, the resulting system makes coffee traceable throughout its journey from its source up to its destination. Since every participating organization gets its own copy of the ledger transparency was confirmed in the system. A Single network implementation architected had a problem of confidentiality but is solved using a multichannel system.

In the near feature, we plan to work on more detailed experiments like implementing more crash tolerance consensus mechanisms, incorporating more transactions in the system, and assessing mare scalable network architecture.

References

1. Buurman, J.: Supply Chain Logistics Management. McGraw-Hill (2002)
2. Duguma, T.F.: Value Chain Analysis of Ethiopian Coffee (Coffea arabica)
3. Jena, P.R., et al.: The impact of coffee certification on small-scale producers' livelihoods: a case study from the Jimma Zone, Ethiopia. Agric. Econ. **43.4**, 429–440 (2012)
4. Lansiti, M., Lakhani, K.R.: The Truth about Blockchain. Harvard Business Review, 01- Jan-2017. https://hbr.org/2017/01/the-truth-about-blockchain. Accessed on 14 July 2019

5. Swan, M.: Blockchain: Blueprint for a New Economy. O'Reilly, US (2015)
6. Tschorsch, F., Scheuermann, B.: Bitcoin and beyond: a technical survey on decentralized digital currencies. IEEE Commun. Surv. Tutor. **18**(3), 2084–2123 (2016)
7. Omohundro, S.: Cryptocurrencies, smart contracts, and artificial intelligence. AI Matt. **1**(2), 19–21 (2014)
8. Smart Contracts. https://blockchainhub.net/blog/infographics/smart-contracts-explained. Accessed on 27 July 2019
9. Cong, L.W., Zhiguo, H.: Blockchain disruption and smart contracts. No. w24399. National Bureau of Economic Research (2018)
10. Satoshi, N.: Bitcoin: A peer-to-peer electronic cash system(2008). https://bitcoin.org/bitcoin.pdf
11. Vitalik, B.: Ethereum: A next-generation smart contract and decentralized application platform. https://github.com/ethereum/wiki/wiki White-Paper. Accessed on 4 Aug 2019
12. https://docs.corda.net/_static/corda-introductory-whitepaper.pdf. Accessed on 13 August 2019
13. https://hyperledger-fabric.readthedocs.io/en/latest/chaincode.html. Accessed on 18 August 2019
14. Pongnumkul, S., Chaiyaphum, S., Suttipong, T.: Per-formance analysis of private blockchain platforms in varying workloads. In: 2017 26th Inter-national Conference on Computer Communication and Networks (ICCCN). IEEE (2017)
15. https://www.ibm.com/blogs/think/2018/04/global-jewelry-ibm-blockchain. Accessed on 10 Sept 2019
16. Bore, N., et al.: Towards blockchain-enabled school information hub. In: Proceedings of the Ninth International Conference on Information and Communication Technologies and Development. ACM (2017)
17. Kodama, Y.: New role of cooperatives in Ethiopia: the case of Ethiopian coffee farmers cooperatives (2007)
18. Gaur, N., et al.: Hands-on Blockchain with Hyperledger: Building Decentralized Applications with Hyperledger Fabric and Composer. Packt Publishing Ltd. (2018)
19. Hyperledger. https://www.hyperledger.org/. Accessed on 21 June 2019
20. Androulaki, E., et al.: Hyperledger fabric: a distributed operating system for permissioned blockchains. In: Proceedings of the Thirteenth EuroSys Conference. ACM (2018)
21. Designing a Hyperledger Fabric Network: https://medium.com/coinmonks/designing-a-hyperledger-fabric-network-7adcd78dabc3. Accessed on 2 Nov 2019
22. Apache Kafka. http://kafka.apache.org. Accessed on 15 Oct 2019

Wireless Local Area Network Intrusion Detection System Using Deep Belief Networks

Temesgen Mihiretu Abebe[1](✉) and Menore Tekeba Mengistu[2]

[1] Faculty of Electrical and Computer Engineering, Bahir Dar Institute of Technology, Bahir Dar University, Bahir Dar, Ethiopia
[2] School of Electrical and Computer Engineering, Addis Ababa Institute of Technology, Addis Ababa University, Addis Ababa, Ethiopia
menore.tekeba@aait.edu.et

Abstract. In computer security Intrusion Detection System (IDS) is a mechanism of detecting an intruder in the system and notifying malicious activities for system administrators. The IDS researches on wireless Local Area Network (LAN) started recently. Until now there are some researches like publishing Aegean Wi-Fi Intrusion Dataset (AWID) dataset publically for the research community and evaluating the dataset using different machine learning algorithms. In this paper, we propose Deep Belief Network (DBN) to evaluate AWID dataset for intrusion detection analysis. Since AWID dataset contains different data types which are numeric, string, and hexadecimals; before training the model and evaluation of its performance the dataset is preprocessed and finally 102 attributes are used for system training. Also, two-stage feature selection is implemented to reduce the training cost and improve system performance. The first stage is removing duplicated attributes which reduced the dataset size to 68 attributes. The second stage is done by applying Weka implemented Information Gain Ratio (IGR). Using three thresholds three datasets are prepared with 41 attributes, 34 attributes, and 25 attributes. The system was able to achieve 98.55% accuracy with 102 attributes and it was able to improve this result to 98.97% with selected 34 attributes set evaluation.

Keywords: Wireless Intrusion Detection System (WIDS) · AWID dataset · Deep Belief Networks (DBN) · Feature selection

1 Introduction

In the history of computing, there are different security threats. Most of the security measure to protect computers and networks from threats can be classified as protection and detection mechanisms. Protection mechanisms are the way of protecting a system from threats by taking different actions even though it is not enough to secure the system. That is why detection and monitoring mechanisms are as necessary as protection mechanisms to alert the system administrators about security threats by tracking the system activities and network traffic. An IDS is a security system that monitors computer systems

© ICST Institute for Computer Sciences, Social Informatics and Telecommunications Engineering 2021
Published by Springer Nature Switzerland AG 2021. All Rights Reserved
M. A. Delele et al. (Eds.): ICAST 2020, LNICST 384, pp. 319–334, 2021.
https://doi.org/10.1007/978-3-030-80621-7_23

and network traffic and analyzes that traffic for possible hostile attacks originating from outside the organization and furthermore for system misuse or attacks beginning from inside the organization [1]. In general, IDS can be classified into two broad categories that are Host-based IDS (HIDS) and Network based IDS (NIDS). Host-based IDS look after the host system activities and in other way NIDS monitors the network traffics.

Based on the methods of intrusion detection mechanism they used to detect malicious traffic NIDS can be classified as a signature (misuse) based NIDS (SNIDS) and anomaly detection-based NIDS (ADNIDS) [2]. In the case SNIDS rules for the specific type of attack are pre-installed in the network environment, then the IDS based on the specified rule detects the signature of the traffic for the specified attack. In the case of ADNIDS whenever deviation from the normal traffic is observed it will be classified as intruders.

In a computer network, Wireless Fidelity (Wi-Fi) is a wireless connection type other than wired local area network. Wi-Fi is a recently growing technology for local area connections because it is easy and less expensive to implement than wired LAN. But it is vulnerable to various attacks and intruders because of its security vulnerable features [3–6]. So, studying IDS for wireless network independently from the wired network gives a better advantage for wireless network security.

Anomaly detection could be done using different mechanisms such as using different artificial intelligence (AI) algorithms, statistical methods, data-miming based, etc. and there are different researches and implementation using such methodologies. Artificial intelligence is one of the modern computing mechanism with a dream of achieving human level intelligence. Deep learning is one of the most recent studies of AI under the machine learning field to reach the promise of AI. Deep learning is the way of multi-layer network machine learning architecture. It includes different algorithms, among them DBN is recently proved to be very effective for a variety of machine learning problems [7].

There are different tool and researches regarding IDS based on different approach like rule-based, data mining techniques, machine learning algorithms, support vector machines, etc. But most of the researches are done for LAN [1, 8–10]. Since the vulnerability and attack type of wireless network is different from that of wired network [11–14], there should be an independent equivalent research practice for wireless network IDS. On wireless IDS after AWID dataset [3] there are some work using different machine learning techniques [3, 15–17]. The main problem is still the performance of the classification of attacks and normal traffic in not satisfactory and need to be improved as much as possible. So, since DBN is proven to be the best deep learning classifier in some recent works like [1], evaluating AWID dataset using DBN and also studying the effect of feature selection on the performance of the implemented system is a very important and challenging task as the wireless domain IDS.

The rest of the paper is organized as follows. In Sect. 2, related researches on wireless LAN IDS are discussed in detail. The system design and implementation is discussed in Sect. 3 and the dataset and dataset preprocessing techniques will discuss in Sect. 4. Then the result is discussed in Sect. 5. Finally, in the conclusion is goes in Sect. 6.

2   Literature Review on Related Works

Intrusion detection system in computer network was the active research field for a long period of time. Based on the nature of LAN IDS can be classified as wired LAN and wireless LAN. Since this research work focused on wireless IDS in this section literature on wireless IDS will discuss.

An intrusion detection system in a computer network was the active research field for a long period of time. Based on the nature of LAN IDS can be classified as wired LAN and wireless LAN. Since this research work focused on wireless IDS in this section literature on wireless IDS will discuss.

For wireless LAN IDS, the researchers in [3] publish AWID dataset by collecting from 802.11 Wi-Fi networks which contain normal and different attack traffics in 2015. Even though the dataset is collected from WEP protected network, the researcher states that the dataset can be used for WPA/WPA2 protected network IDS researches [3]. Their work can be seen in two perspectives. The first one is the publication of publicly available labeled dataset for the Wi-Fi network IDS research community. The second one is, they were able to evaluate the most known attack from 802.11 WEP protected Wi-Fi network standard using different machine learning techniques, which are Adaboost, J48, ZeroR, OneR, Random Tree, Random Forest, Nave Bayes and Hyperpipes [3]. For both feature sets J48 outperform the other classification algorithms and the reduced 20 attributes dataset performs better than the 156 featured datasets [3]. They also showed that feature selection and avoiding feature redundancy have great significance on the detection performance of IDSs [3].

The research in [16] works on the evaluation of AWID dataset using machine learning algorithms with Information Gain (GI) and Chi-Squared statistics (CH) filter-based feature selection techniques. Their main aim was to show the effect of feature selection on the performance of IDS attack detection [16]. Through their experimental result, they were able to show that feature reduction can improve detection accuracy and classification speed. But when they further reduce the number of features, the performance of the system decreases [16]. The machine learning technique they used for evaluation was OneR, J48, Random Forest, Random Tree, and Ada Boost. From their experimental result, Random Tree performs better for high-level class distribution and Random forest performs better for finer grain class distribution [16].

The research in [17] implements a majority voting technique for wireless IDS with a data mining technique for feature selection which was able to reduce the feature set to 20. The majority voting is a combination of Extra Trees of 20 trees, Random Forests of 20 trees, and the Bagging classifier of 10 Decision Trees as base estimator [17]. They implement Decision Trees, Extra Trees, and Random Forests for all feature sets and reduced feature set and they found that none of them performed better than J48 which is the best performer in [3]. Then they implement a bagging classifier for all feature sets and reduced feature set and it gives slightly better performance with better timing [17]. Finally, they implement their proposed system for all feature sets and reduced feature set and they found that it has better performance and the reduced dataset was able to achieve similar performance with minimal execution time [17].

The work in [15] focused on improving the detection level of impersonation attack which was insignificance in [1]. They use Artificial Neural Network (ANN) for feature selection and Stacked Auto Encoder (SAE) for classification and they evaluate their proposed system using AWID-CLSR for both training and testing [15]. Also, they prepare the balanced version of the dataset in their preprocessing step for training purpose since the dataset contains a huge number of normal instances compared to attack instances, especially impersonation Attack [15].

3 System Design and Implementation

The proposed system architecture is shown in Fig. 1. It starts by selecting a specific dataset for training and testing from the AWID dataset collection. Then the next step is preprocessing of both the training and testing dataset which results a normalized version of both training and testing datasets. The preprocessed dataset is able to use for training and testing purposes on the system. Then feature selection process was applied to select the most discriminant features of the datasets. Finally, from the above steps, there are two datasets that are full featured and selected feature version dataset version.

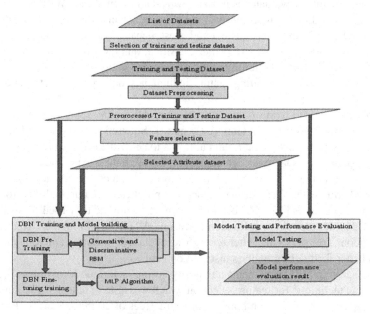

Fig. 1. System workflow

Then the next step is the training of DBN using each version of the datasets. The training process contains two steps. The first one is unsupervised pre-training using greedy layer-wise training through stacked Restricted Boltzmann Machine (RBM) and the second is fine-tuning the weight parameter of pre-trained DBN using back propagation neural network (BPNN) algorithm. Then the results of the above two training process will be trained DBN classifier which is the intended wireless IDS model.

3.1 Deep Belief Network Training

Deep Belief Network (DBN) is a probabilistic generative model made of multiple layers of latent stochastic variables [18]. It is a graphical model as depicted in Fig. 2, which learns to extract a deep hierarchical representation of training data. The top two layers give an undirected bipartite Boltzmann Machines (BMs) while the lower layers form a directed sigmoid belief network.

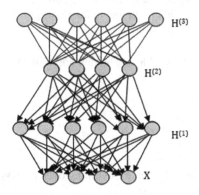

Fig. 2. Deep belief network

The training process consists of two steps [1, 18]. The first one is unsupervised pre training and the second one is supervised fine-tuning. The unsupervised pre-training method is used to initialize the hidden layer weights while building a deeper model. In the pre-training step of DBN each layer of the network will train using RBM in a greedy layer-wise manner. The trained RBM will be used to construct the pre-trained layer of DBN. Starting from the first up to the last layer they will modeled as generative RBM but the last layer of DBN with the classifier layer will be modeled as discriminative RBM [19]. The training process will continue from the input layer up to the last layer in a greedy layer-wise manner for unsupervised pre-training of DBN. After unsupervised pre-training, the next part of the system training is supervised fine-tuning. The purpose of fine-tuning is to more refine the hidden layer weight value using supervised algorithms. In this research BPNN [19–21] is used for fine tuning the pre-trained DBN.

3.2 Restricted Boltzmann Machine

An RBM is a bipartite graph in which visible units that represent observations are connected to binary stochastic hidden units using undirected weighted connections [22]. They are restricted in a sense that there are no visible-visible or hidden-hidden connections [23].

RBM has an efficient training procedure that makes it suitable for building blocks for DBN. The training set can be modeled using two layers RBM in which the visible unit connected to the input vector and the feature extractor corresponds to the hidden units of RBM. The energy of joint configuration (v, h) of visible and hidden units expressed as follow in Eq. (1)

$$E(v,\ h,\ \theta) = \sum_{i=1}^{V} \sum_{j=1}^{H} W_{ij}v_ih_i - \sum_{i=1}^{V} b_iv_i - \sum_{j=1}^{H} a_jh_j \qquad (1)$$

Where

- v_i and h_j are the state of visible unit i and hidden unit j.
- b_i and a_j are the bias of visible unit i and hidden unit j.
- W_{ij} is the weight on the connection between visible unit i and hidden unit j.

The joint probability of the visible and hidden unit of RBM is a function of the above energy function and given as in Eq. (2).

$$p(v, h) = \frac{1}{Z} e^{-E(v,h)} \qquad (2)$$

Where:

- Z is the partition function and given by summing over all possible pairs of visible and hidden vectors as shown in Eq. (3).

$$Z = \sum_{v,\ h} e^{-E(v,h)} \qquad (3)$$

The probability that the network assigns to a visible vector, v, is given by summing over all possible hidden vectors is given by as follows in (4).

$$p(v) = \frac{1}{Z} \sum_{h} e^{-E(v,h)} \qquad (4)$$

Gibbs Markov chain of the visible and hidden unit pair of variables used to estimate the gradient on the log-likelihood of RBM. It is the process of consecutive sampling h given v then v given h until the end of the chain. The chain starts from t = 0 meaning from the input vector then proceed to (v_t, h_t) where 't' is the number of sampling iteration. The derivative of the log-probability of a training vector with respect to a weight is given in Eq. (5).

$$\frac{\partial \log p(v)}{\partial w_{ij}} = \langle vihj \rangle data - \langle vihj \rangle model \qquad (5)$$

The angle brackets are used to denote expectations under the distribution specified by the subscript that follows. This leads to a very simple learning rule for performing stochastic steepest ascent in the log probability of the training data:

$$\Delta w_{ij} = \varepsilon \left(\langle v_ih_j \rangle data - \langle v_ih_j \rangle model \right) \qquad (6)$$

Where ε is learning rate of the weight update.

The above equation state that the weight updates is the difference of expectation of visible and hidden unit udder data and model distribution.

Since there is no direct connection between hidden units of RBM, getting the unbiased sample $\varepsilon\langle v_i h_j \rangle data$ is easy from the training vector. State of each hidden unit hj of the hidden layer set to 1 given the training vector can computed in the following probability Eq. (7).

$$p\left(h_j = 1|v\right) = \sigma\left(b_j + \sum_i v_i w_{ij}\right) \tag{7}$$

Also, to get the sample of each visible unit vi of the visible layer given the hidden layer can computed in the following probability Eq. (8).

$$p(v_i = 1|h) = \sigma\left(a_i + \sum_j v_i w_{ij}\right) \tag{8}$$

But getting an unbiased sample of $\langle v_i h_j \rangle model$ is not as simple as the data distribution. It could calculate using Constructive Divergence (CD) which is approximation of the gradient through alternative Gibbs sampling starting from visible layer units for some specified time. It is denoted as CD n where n denotes number of full alternative Gibbs sampling [24]. A single iteration of alternating Gibbs sampling consists of updating all of the hidden units in parallel using Eq. (7) followed by updating all of the visible units in parallel using Eq. (8).

The fast way of training as proposed by [22, 25] include setting the state of the visible units to the training vector, then sample the hidden units in parallel form the visible units using Eq. (7). The final step is the reconstruction process which is sampling the visible units in parallel from the hidden unit using Eq. (8). Then the above weight update equation can be simplified as shown in Eq. (9), (10), and (11).

$$\Delta w_{ij} = \varepsilon\left(\langle v_i h_j \rangle data - \langle v_i h_j \rangle model\right) \tag{9}$$

$$\Delta a = \varepsilon(\langle v_i \rangle data - \langle v_i \rangle model) \tag{10}$$

$$\Delta b = \varepsilon\left(\langle h_j \rangle data - \langle h_j \rangle model\right) \tag{11}$$

4 Dataset

Aegean Wi-Fi Intrusion Dataset (AWID) is a collection of different wireless LAN datasets [3] for research purpose. Based on the attack class labeling there are two categories, which are high label (AWID-CLS) and finer grained (AWIDATK) [26]. The high level contains four classes namely normal, injection, impersonation and flooding in both training testing dataset. The finer grain version contains 16 classes based on the actual attack types. Then based on their size both high label and finer grained contain full dataset which is tagged as 'F' namely AWID-CLS-F and AWID-ATK-F and reduced dataset which is tagged as 'R' namely AWID-CLSR and AWID-ATK-R respectively. Each of them has separate training and testing datasets.

AWID dataset contains 156 attributes including the attack class [3]. They are composed of mainly from MAC layer information like source and destination address, initialization vector, ESSID, etc. The rest of attributes contain Radio tap information, general frame information, and frame number.

While the researchers of [3] preparing the dataset, they tested and study around 24 wireless LAN attacks based on their conceptual similarities. First, they study those attacks by grouping them using their attack purposes in to key retrieving attack, Key stream Retrieving Attacks, availability attacks, and Man-in-the-Middle Attacks. Key retrieving attacks tries to crack the Secret Key offline by monitoring specific packets.

It is passive type of attack; so, it is untraceable unless the attacker tries to execute the active version of the attack by injecting a large number of packets in the network. Key stream Retrieving Attacks focuses on retrieving key stream that can be used to create other attacks through injection. Availability attacks are commonly known as denial of service (DoS) attack since the attacks try to deny the system service by consuming or blocking the resource in the network. But since IDS system try to infer common patterns among the attack of the same class, they categorize the attacks according to the attack methodologies of execution. So, the new groups of attack are injection, flooding, impersonation and passive attack. All the attacks they studied are grouped under this list of attacks especially in the fine-gray (CLS) version of the dataset as shown in the Table 1.

Table 1. Wireless LAN Attacks and their classification

Attack class	Attack	Purpose	Target
Injection	ARP Injection, ChopChop, Fragmentation	Key Cracking	Network
Flooding	Deauthentication, Disassociation, Disassociation, Deauthentication broadcast, Disassociation broadcast, Block Acknowledge, Authentication Request, Fake Power Saving, CTS, RTS, Beacon, Probe Request, Probe Response	DoS	Client
Impersonation	Caffe Latte, Hirte, Honeypot, Evil Twin	Keystream, M-i-M	Network, client
Passive	FMS, Korek, PTW, Dictionary	Key Cracking	Network

4.1 Dataset Preprocessing

The purpose of the preprocessing step is to prepare the dataset in the way that comfortable for proposed DBN machine learning classification algorithms. The preprocessing mechanism has the following steps.

- In the dataset there are some values which are unassigned or missing values which are represented as question mark (?), and it is assigning '0' as value for those not available values.
- The SSID nominal value attack is encoded to numeric value based on their frequency in the specified attribute of the dataset. The other string valued attribute in the dataset is the attack classes. They are encoded as Normal to '1', Flooding to '2', Injection to '3' and Impersonation to '4' numeric value.
- The third step is type casting of hexadecimal values to their decimal equivalent. This involves converting hexadecimal values to their respective numeric value.
- The fourth step is scaling all the attributes between zero and one using Eq. (12).

$$Z_i = \frac{x_i - \min(x)}{\max(x) - \min(x)} \tag{12}$$

Where:

- Z_i is scaled value.
- x_i is current attribute value from the dataset.
- min(x) is minimum value in the given attribute and
- max(x) maximum value in the given attribute
- Since DBN work on only real number valued attributes, the final step is removing NaN valued attributes from the dataset.

After the above preprocessing step out of the total attributes 52 of them have NaN. So, the resulting dataset of the preprocessing experiment has 103 attributes including the class labeling which is numeric valued and normalized between zero and one it is called version one dataset[1].

The next step in preprocessing is the attribute selection process which is implemented in two stages. The first one is removing the redundant attributes from the version one dataset by keeping single one of each attribute and its results version two of the dataset with 68 unique attributes without the class labeling. The second stage is feature selection using the entropy of each attribute for the class labeling. It is done using Weka implemented information gain feature selection algorithm. Based on their information gain value, attributes are ranked and by setting up some threshold values the most discriminant attributes are selected. To show the relationship between the number of attributes in the dataset and the performance of the system, three thresholds are used that result three different new versions of datasets as shown in Table 2.

The first version is using 0.015 threshold value and the resulting dataset has 41 attributes, the second version is using 0.05 and the resulting dataset has 34 attributes, and the last is results 25 attribute dataset version with 0.2 thresholds. So, the three new datasets are called as version three, four, and five respectively.

---

[1] Dataset version means nothing but it is the ways of identifying different datasets resulted from preprocessing and attribute selection procedures.

Table 2. Attributes information gain ratio value

No.	IG Threshold	Number of attributes
1	0.2	25
2	0.05	34
3	0.015	41

5 Experimental Result and Discussion

We use Dell OptiPlex 7020 desktop with the following specification and tools for system implementation and testing.

- Intel(R) Core (TM) i5-5500U CPU @ 3.70 GHz
- 8.0 GB DDR3 memory (RAM)
- Matlab R2016a
- Weka version 3.8

The first experiment is done using 102 attribute training and testing dataset for training and testing respectively. The system was able to achieve 98.55% accuracy with 100% of the training dataset. But accuracy is not the only way to measure the performance of a model especially in the case of unbalanced multiclass dataset as mentioned in [27–30] so let's discuss various performance metrics starting from the confusion matrix in Table 3.

Table 3. Confusion matrix for 100% 102 attributes training dataset

	Normal	Injection	Flooding	Impersonation
Normal	99.9717	0.0539	24.8240	30.7436
Injection	0.0034	99.9460	0	0
Flooding	0.0243	0	75.17599	0.0199
Impersonation	0.0006	0	0	69.2365

It shows that the classification accuracy of the normal and injection target classes is close to 100% which is 99.97% and 99.94% respectively, flooding is classified 75.17%, and impersonation is classified 69.23%. Based on the above confusion matrix other performance metrics are computed as shown in Table 4.

Precision or sensitivity is the number of true positive prediction of the specified class out of total positive prediction. As shown in the table based on their precision value the attack classes descending order is Impersonation, Injection, Normal, and Flooding. So, Impersonation class is the most precise than the other class and Flooding is less precise.

Table 4. Performance measure for 102 attribute model

Classes	Precision	Specificity	Recall	F-Measure
Normal	98.479	81.736	99.971	99.22
Injection	99.8925	99.996	99.946	99.919
Flooding	97.861	99.976	75.175	85.031
Impersonation	99.978	99.999	69.236	81.814

In another way, specificity is the measure of true negative prediction of the class out of the total negative prediction. Impersonation has higher specificity, Injection has the second, Flooding has the third, and Normal has the fourth and last specificity value.

Recall is the measure of the specified class true positive prediction out of that class actual true positive. From the four-class domain their recall value order is Normal, Injection, Flooding, and Impersonation. It means that in the case Normal and Injection classes, the model was able to predict truly above 99.9% to their respective class out of the given true class data and in the case of Flooding and Impersonation it is around 75.17% and 69.23% respectively.

F-Measure is the way of combining the class precision and recall using weighted harmonic mean. Injection has the highest F-measure value 99.91% and then normal with 99.22%, flooding with 85.03% and impersonation with 81.81% value follows.

5.1 Experiment of the Effect of Attribute Selection on the Performance of the System

As discussed in Sect. 4-A, there are four versions of datasets that are a result of the pre-processing and feature selection process. The system is trained independently and its performance is evaluated as shown in Fig. 3.

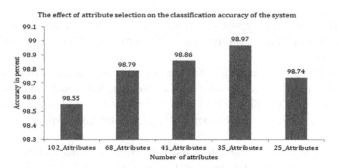

Fig. 3. Classification accuracy for different datasets

The classification accuracy of the system increases up to some point while we reduce the number of attributes by selecting the most discriminating attribute but it decreases when it decreases farther. The first accuracy improvement is from 98.55% to 98.79%

as a result of removing duplicated attributes from the dataset. Then next consecutive experiments are based on the feature selection using their IGR values. The system was able to achieve the best performance with 35 attribute set and those attributes are listed in Table 5.

Table 5. The most discriminative attributes based on classification accuracy

No	Attribute	No	Attribute
1	frame.time_epoch	18	wlan.duration
2	frame.time_delta	19	wlan.ra
3	frame.time_relative	20	wlan.da
4	frame.cap_len	21	wlan.ta
5	radiotap.flags.fcs	22	wlan.sa
6	radiotap.channel.freq	23	wlan.bssid
7	radiotap.channel.type.ofdm	24	wlan.frag
8	radiotap.channel.type.2ghz	25	wlan.seq
9	radiotap.antenna	26	wlan_mgt.fixed.timestamp
10	wlan.fc.type	27	wlan_mgt.fixed.beacon
11	wlan.fc.subtype	28	wlan_mgt.fixed.reason_code
12	wlan.fc.ds	29	wlan_mgt.ssid
13	wlan.fc.frag	30	wlan_mgt.tim.dtim_period
14	wlan.fc.retry	31	wlan.wep.iv
15	wlan.fc.pwrmgt	32	wlan.wep.icv
16	wlan.fc.moredata	33	wlan.qos.priority
17	wlan.fc.order	34	data.len

With feature reduction while the system achieves better classification accuracy decreases the training time from five hours and thirty-four minutes to three hours and thirty-five minutes.

As discussed above, accuracy is not the only measure for the performance of the system and it is clearly described that it is a good practice to make analysis on other performance metrics. The discussion is on the result of the 34-attribute set dataset. So as usual first let's see the confusion matrix of the classification result as shown in Table 6.

It shows that the system is able to classify the Normal class above 99.8%, Injection class 99.98%, Flooding class 93.49%, and Impersonation class 78.45% correctly. When compared to the previous 102 attribute result, in the case of Normal and Injection classes classification accuracy is almost similar but in the case of Flooding and Impersonation classes, there is a great improvement in their classification accuracy. Also, precision, specificity, recall, and F-measure performance metrics are computed for each class based on this confusion matrix as shown in Table 7.

Table 6. Confusion matrix for 34 attributes dataset

	Normal	Injection	Flooding	Impersonation
Normal	99.8046	0.0119	6.5042	21.4951
Injection	0.0038	99.988	0	0
Flooding	0.1650	0	93.4957	0.0548
Impersonation	0.0265	0	0	78.45012

Table 7. Performance measure of 34 attribute model

Classes	Precision	Specificity	Recall	F-Measure
Normal	98.479	81.736	99.971	99.22
Injection	99.8925	99.996	99.946	99.919
Flooding	97.861	99.976	75.175	85.031
Impersonation	99.978	99.999	69.236	81.814

As shown in the table Injection is the most precise one and followed by Impersonation, Normal, and flooding classes. In the case of specificity Injection is the most specific than the other class. The second specifically classified class is Impersonation followed by Flooding and the last specifically classified class is Normal class. Regarding recall Injection comes first and followed by Normal, Flooding and Impersonation. Also, in the case of F-measure value, which is the combination of precision and recall, Injection class has the highest value and followed by Normal, Flooding and Impersonation.

5.2 Result Comparison with Previous Works on Wireless Intrusion Detection Systems

The first research that evaluates AWID dataset using different machine learning algorithms is the research work by [3] and they were able to achieve 96.19% classification accuracy with J48 algorithm. They also select twenty attributes manually and they were able to improve the classification accuracy to 96.25%. The research work in [16] was able to achieve 95.12% using Random Tree with 41 attributes. Also, the research in [17] was able to achieve 96.32% in both full attribute set and 20 attribute set datasets. The research [15] was able to achieve 65% classification accuracy on impersonation attack with selected 35 attributes.

In this research, it was able to achieve 98.55% with 102 attributes and was able to improve this result to 98.97% with thirty-four selected attributes. When we see the individual class classification accuracy Normal and Injection was able to classify above 99.9% in both full feature and thirty-four attributes. In the case of Flooding, it was able to achieve 75.17% in 102 attribute dataset and it was able to improve to 93.45% using 34 attributes. Also, Impersonation is able to detect 69.23% while using 102 attribute and it was able to improve to 78.45% using 34 attributes. So, the above result discussion clearly shows that the approach followed by this research is able to achieve better classification accuracy than similar previous works. The other strength of this research is, it uses only DBN to evaluate AWID dataset as a single efficient system. But in most of the researches, they use different machine learning algorithms and each algorithm has different classification accuracy in each class.

6 Conclusion

In this research wireless network IDS using DBN deep learning algorithm was proposed. For model building and performance evaluation, AWID dataset was used. The dataset was pre-reprocessed and feature selection was implemented to get the most discriminating features. Then a number of experiments have done on the implementation of the proposed system. In the first experiment, the system was able to achieve 98.55% while using 100% of the training dataset. The second Experiment is on the effect of the attribute selection on the performance of the system. Each of the four versions of datasets are evaluated and the result shows that the classification accuracy increases until 34 attributes and it falls down when the attribute set farther reduced to 25. So, using attribute selection it was able to improve the classification accuracy to 98.97%. Finally, when the proposed system is compared with similar previous works it was able to achieve better performance especially in the case of flooding and impersonation class detection. In the future, we plan to work on other versions of the dataset.

References

1. Alom, M.Z., Bontupalli, V., Taha, T.M.: Intrusion detection using deep belief networks. In: 2015 National Aerospace and Electronics Conference (NAECON), pp. 339–344. IEEE (2015)
2. Javaid, A., Niyaz, Q., Sun, W., Alam, M.: A deep learning approach for network intrusion detection system. In: Proceedings of the 9th EAI International Conference on Bio-inspired Information and Communications Technologies (formerly BIONETICS). ICST (Institute for Computer Sciences, Social-Informatics and . . , pp. 21–26 (2016)
3. Kolias, C., Kambourakis, G., Stavrou, A., Gritzalis, S.: Intrusion detection in 802.11 networks: empirical evaluation of threats and a public dataset. IEEE Commun. Surv. Tutorials 18(1), 184–208 (2015)
4. Waliullah, M., Gan, D.: Wireless lan security threats & vulnerabilities. Int. J. Adv. Comput. Sci. Appl. 5(1) (2014)
5. Feng, P.: Wireless lan security issues and solutions. In: 2012 IEEE symposium on robotics and applications (ISRA), pp. 921–924. IEEE (2012)
6. Parte, S., Pandya, S.: A deep learning approach for network intrusion detection system. In: Wireless LAN: Security Issues and Solutions. International Conference on Innovation and Research in Technology for Sustainable Development 2012, pp. 104–107 (2012)
7. Salakhutdinov, R.: Learning deep generative models. Ann. Rev. Statist. Appl. 2, 361–385 (2015)
8. Jha, J., Ragha, L.: Intrusion detection system using support vector machine. Int. J. Appl. Inf. Syst. 3, 25–30 (2013)
9. Lakshmi, D.G.P.: Intrusion detection system using modified support vector machine. Network. Commun. Eng. 10, 430–434 (2015)

10. Salama, M.A., Eid, H.F., Ramadan, R.A., Darwish, A., Hassanien, A.E.: Hybrid intelligent intrusion detection scheme. In: Gaspar-Cunha, A., Takahashi, R., Schaefer, G., Costa, L. (eds.) Soft computing in industrial applications, pp. 293–303. Springer Berlin Heidelberg, Berlin, Heidelberg (2011). https://doi.org/10.1007/978-3-642-20505-7_26
11. Kaur, N., Monga, S.: Comparisons of wired and wireless networks: a review. Int. J. Adv. Eng. Technol. **5**(2), 34–35 (2014)
12. Sheldon, F.T., Weber, J.M., Yoo, S.-M., Pan, W.D.: The insecurity of wireless networks. IEEE Secur. Priv. **10**(4), 54–61 (2012)
13. Stimpson, T., Liu, L., Zhang, J., Hill, R., Liu, W., Zhan, Y.: Assessment of security and vulnerability of home wireless networks. In: 2012 9th International Conference on Fuzzy Systems and Knowledge Discovery, pp. 2133–2137. IEEE (2012)
14. Vibhuti, S.: Ieee 802.11 wep (wired equivalent privacy) Concepts And Vulnerability. San Jose State University, CA, USA, CS265 Spring (2005)
15. Aminanto, M.E., Kim, K.: Detecting impersonation attack in wifi networks using deep learning approach. In: Choi, D., Guilley, S. (eds.) Information Security Applications, pp. 136–147. Springer International Publishing, Cham (2016). https://doi.org/10.1007/978-3-319-56549-1_12
16. Thanthrige, U.S.K.P.M., Samarabandu, J., Wang, X.: Machine learning techniques for intrusion detection on public dataset. In: 2016 IEEE Canadian Conference on Electrical and Computer Engineering (CCECE), pp. 1–4. IEEE (2016)
17. Alotaibi, B., Elleithy, K.: A majority voting technique for wireless intrusion detection systems. In: 2016 IEEE Long Island Systems, Applications and Technology Conference (LISAT), pp. 1–6. IEEE (2016)
18. Hinton, G.E., Osindero, S., Teh, Y.-W.: A fast learning algorithm for deep belief nets. Neural Comput. **18**(7), 1527–1554 (2006)
19. Schalkoff, R.J.: Artificial Neural Networks. McGraw-Hill Higher Education (1997)
20. Rojas, R.: The backpropagation algorithm. In: Rojas, R. (ed.) Neural networks, pp. 149–182. Springer Berlin Heidelberg, Berlin, Heidelberg (1996). https://doi.org/10.1007/978-3-642-61068-4_7
21. Yam, Y., Chow, T.: Extended backpropagation algorithm. Electron. Lett. **29**(19), 1701–1702 (1993)
22. Hinton, G.E.: A practical guide to training restricted Boltzmann machines. In: Montavon, G., Orr, G.B., Müller, K.-R. (eds.) Neural Networks: Tricks of the Trade: Second Edition, pp. 599–619. Springer Berlin Heidelberg, Berlin, Heidelberg (2012). https://doi.org/10.1007/978-3-642-35289-8_32
23. Fischer, A., Igel, C.: An introduction to restricted boltzmann machines. In: Alvarez, L., Mejail, M., Gomez, L., Jacobo, J. (eds.) Progress in Pattern Recognition, Image Analysis, Computer Vision, and Applications, pp. 14–36. Springer Berlin Heidelberg, Berlin, Heidelberg (2012). https://doi.org/10.1007/978-3-642-33275-3_2
24. Cote, M.-A., Larochelle, H.: An infinite restricted boltzmann machine. Neural Comput. **28**(7), 1265–1288 (2016)
25. Marlin, B., Swersky, K., Chen, B., Freitas, N.: Inductive principles for restricted boltzmann machine learning. In: Proceedings of the Thirteenth International Conference on Artificial Intelligence and Statistics, pp. 509–516 (2010)
26. Kolias, C., Kambourakis, G., Stavrou, A., Gritzalis, S.: AWID attributes, http://icsdweb.aeg ean.gr/awid/attributes.html. Accessed on 10 Sept 2017
27. Wang, S., Yao, X.: Relationships between diversity of classification ensembles and single-class performance measures. IEEE Trans. Knowl. Data Eng. **25**(1), 206–219 (2011)
28. Sokolova, M., Lapalme, G.: A systematic analysis of performance measures for classification tasks. Inf. Process. Manage. **45**(4), 427–437 (2009)

29. Nguyen, G.H., Bouzerdoum, A., Phung, S.L.: Learning pattern classification tasks with imbalanced data sets. In: Pattern Recognition. IntechOpen (2009)
30. Ferri, C., Hernandez-Orallo, J., Modroiu, R.: An experimental comparison of performance measures for classification. Pattern Recogn. Lett. **30**(1), 27–38 (2009)

Trajectory Tracking Control of Quadrotor Unmanned Aerial Vehicle Using Sliding Mode Controller with the Presence of Gaussian Disturbance

Biruk Tadesse Nadew$^{(\boxtimes)}$ ⓘ, Asrat Mulatu Beyene ⓘ, Beza Nekatibeb, and Mulugeta Debebe

Addis Ababa Science and Technology University, Addis Ababa, Ethiopia
{biruk.tadesse,asrat.mulatu,beza.nekatibeb,
mulugeta.debebe}@aastu.edu.et

Abstract. In this research paper, trajectory following control of the quadrotor unmanned aerial vehicle (UAV) is carried out using the sliding mode controller (SMC) to control the position and attitude of the quadrotor, including the impact of disturbances. Due to their low cost, simplicity configuration of the structure, ability to hover, maneuverability, vertical take-off, and landing (VTOL) capability, and the ability to accomplished a variety of tasks, Quadrotor UAV has become an increasingly common research subject in recent years. The complex model of the quadrotor, including aerodynamic effects, was derived using Newton-Euler formalization. Here, SMC controllers were designed to track reference trajectories for the nonlinear model. The robustness and reliability of the controller are checked by applying external random disturbances to the quadrotor's position and attitude. Finally, by using MATLAB /Simulink, the action of the quadrotor/quadcopter under the suggested control scheme has been implemented. The results show that all control system becomes stable and robust in terms of disturbance rejection.

Keywords: UAV · Quadrotor · SMC · Dynamic modeling

1 Introduction

The maneuverability, low cost, structural simplicity, ability to flying and hovering, vertical take-off and landing capability, and ability to perform a different type of tasks in aerospace and control engineering, quadcopter UAV has become a popular research subject in recent years [1]. The various uses, such as video production, inspection, monitoring, law enforcement, rescue and search, and many others, inspire this study. UAV flights can be operated either fully autonomously by the onboard computers or by a certain degree of remote control by an operator on the ground or in a separate vehicle [2, 3].

© ICST Institute for Computer Sciences, Social Informatics and Telecommunications Engineering 2021
Published by Springer Nature Switzerland AG 2021. All Rights Reserved
M. A. Delele et al. (Eds.): ICAST 2020, LNICST 384, pp. 335–350, 2021.
https://doi.org/10.1007/978-3-030-80621-7_24

The analysis of the control design and simulation of autonomous drones has been approached in numerous ways by various literary works. The first dynamic quadrotor model was adopted via the Lagrangian approach. It was a partial differential equation for the quadcopter dynamic systems, that had been derived from the Lagrangian equation of the model [3, 4].

As discussed in [5, 6], it has been shown that it is possible to use linear control techniques to control the quadrotor UAV by linearizing the dynamics around the operating stage, commonly selected to be the hover. In this case, several unmodeled dynamics were overlooked and left out of the system during linearization, leading to a lack of controller efficiency. Backstepping [7, 8], sliding mode controller (SMC) [8, 9], and the feedback linearization [10, 11] were shown to be efficient for quadrotor control under these nonlinear control methods. Nevertheless, without understanding aerodynamic drag torque and force, gyroscopic torque, and unexpended environmental distributions, several of those experiments were investigated.

In [12], Wang et al. for a quadrotor developed a hierarchical system of time - varying adaptive control to follows 3D reference trajectory influenced by payload and time-varying disruption of wind raft variance. The concern was that the researcher had poorer control efficiency because of the neglect of the gyroscopic effect of a quadrotor and its rotors. [13], Bouzid et al. experimented with online disruption compensation using the model-free control (MFC) concept to deal with the uncertain component of the device (i.e., unmodelled dynamics, disruptions, etc.) on "trajectory tracking control of quadrotor UAV". The result obtained was fine, but rotor and quadrotor moment impacts were not taken into account in the work. The established nonlinear and complex dynamic model of the quadcopter is on the basis of a model of torque and thrust obtained from static thrust experiments with constant thrust and torque coefficients. As the vehicle undertakes complex maneuvers requiring substantial displacement and speeds [4–8]. Such a model is no longer true. In addition to excluding the disruption effect, the other issue is that most studies ignore the aerodynamic impact, the gyroscopic moment that exists because of the quadrotor body and its rotors [5, 6]. This affects the efficiency of trajectory tracking being decreased.

This paper discusses a thrust model that integrates the mediated momentum effects associated with the rotor and quadrotor body. Also, the aerodynamic drag force and torque are considered in the model. And Gaussian disturbance is added to the system angular and translational position and then, by using a sliding mode controller achieved better trajectory performance and fast disturbance rejection capability.

2   Mathematical Modelling of Quadrotor UAV

The system has all body frames, and inertial or earth frames F_b (x^b; y^b; z^b) and F_i (x^i; y^i; z^i) respectively. And the model split into rotational and translational coordinates, naturally [14].

$$\xi = (x; \ y; \ z) \in R^3, \quad \eta = (\phi; \ \theta; \ \psi) \in R^3 \tag{1}$$

Where x, y, and z are translational position for x, y, and z, dynamics respectively; and ϕ, θ, ψ, are the angular position of the roll, pitch, and yaw dynamics respectively. Using

Newton-Euler formalism, the following model equation rotational (Euler dynamics) and translational dynamics have been derived.

$$
\begin{aligned}
\ddot{\phi} &= \tfrac{1}{I_x}\left(U_2 - k_4\dot{\phi}^2 - J_r\Omega_r\dot{\theta} + (Iy - Iz)\dot{\theta}\dot{\psi}\right) \\
\ddot{\theta} &= \tfrac{1}{I_y}\left(U_3 - k_5\dot{\theta}^2 + J_r\Omega_r\dot{\phi} + (Iz - Ix)\dot{\phi}\dot{\psi}\right) \\
\ddot{\psi} &= \tfrac{1}{I_z}\left(U_4 - k_6\dot{\psi}^2 + (Ix - Iy)\dot{\theta}\dot{\phi}\right) \\
\ddot{x} &= \tfrac{1}{m}\left((c_\phi s_\theta c_\psi + s_\phi s_\psi)U_1 - k_1\dot{x}\right) \\
\ddot{y} &= \tfrac{1}{m}\left((c_\phi s_\theta s_\psi - s_\phi c_\psi)U_1 - k_2\dot{y}\right) \\
\ddot{z} &= \tfrac{1}{m}\left((c_\phi c_\theta)U_1 - k_3\dot{z}\right) - g
\end{aligned}
\right\} \tag{2}
$$

$$
\dot{X} = f(X, U) \tag{3}
$$

Where $\ddot{\phi}, \ddot{\theta}, \ddot{\psi}$ are the angular acceleration; $\dot{\phi}, \dot{\theta}, \dot{\psi}$, angular speed for translational roll, pitch, and yaw dynamics respectively. And $\ddot{x}, \ddot{y}, \ddot{z}$ are acceleration; $\dot{x}, \dot{y}, \dot{z}$ are velocity/speed vector for translational x, y, and z, dynamics respectively; m is mass quadrotor, g is gravitational acceleration; $[U_1, U_2, U_3, U_4]^T$ are the lift force, tilt (roll) torque, pitch torque, and yaw torque, and these are called control input vector for altitude, roll, pitch, and yaw, dynamics respectively. $I_x, I_y,$ and I_z denote the moment of inertia of a quadrotor's x-axis, y-axis, and z-axis dynamics, respectively. Jr denotes the vertical or z-axis inertia of the rotors. $[k_1, k_2, k_3, k_4, k_5, k_6]$ are aerodynamic drag torque and force coefficients. The control inputs are assigned as follows:

$$
\begin{aligned}
U1 &= F_i = \sum_{i=1}^{4} F_i = b\sum_{i=1}^{4} w_i^2 = F_1 + F_2 + F_3 + F_4 = F \\
U2 &= \tau_\phi = \mathcal{L}(F_4 - F_2) = \mathcal{L}b(w_4^2 - w_2^2) \\
U3 &= \tau_\theta = \mathcal{L}(F_3 - F_1) = \mathcal{L}b(w_3^2 - w_1^2) \\
U4 &= \tau_\psi = c(F_1 - F_2 + F_3 - F_4) = d(w_1^2 - w_2^2 + w_3^2 - w_4^2);
\end{aligned} \tag{4}
$$

Where Fi is the thrust force generated by the ith rotors, w_i is the speed of the ith rotors; d, b, $\mathcal{L}$ are thrust factor, drag factor, and length of quadrotor arm respectively.

X is the State vector, is

$$
X = \left[\phi, \dot{\phi}, \theta, \dot{\theta}, \psi, \dot{\psi}, x, \dot{x}, y, \dot{y}, z, \dot{z}\right]^T \in R^{12} \tag{5}
$$

And it can be written as

$$
X = [x_1, x_2, x_3, x_4, x_5, x_6, x_7, x_8, x_9, x_{10}, x_{11}, x_{12}]^T \in R^{12} \tag{6}
$$

$$
U = [U_1, U_2, U_3, U_4]^T \tag{7}
$$

The interaction between dynamics of positions (x, y), altitude (z) and rotational (ϕ, θ, ψ) are represented by the state-space model of the studied quadrotor is obtained as follows:

$$\begin{aligned}
\dot{x}_1 &= x_2, \dot{x}_2 = c_1 x_4 x_6 + c_2 x_2^2 + c_3 \Omega_r x_4 + b_1 U_2 \\
\dot{x}_3 &= x_4, \dot{x}_4 = c_4 x_2 x_6 + c_5 x_4^2 + c_6 \Omega_r x_2 + b_2 U_3 \\
\dot{x}_5 &= x_6, \dot{x}_6 = c_7 x_2 x_4 + c_8 x_6^2 + b_3 U_4 \\
\dot{x}_7 &= x_8, \dot{x}_8 = c_9 x_8 + \frac{1}{m}(c_\phi s_\theta s_\psi + s_\phi s_\psi) U_1 \\
\dot{x}_9 &= x_{10}, \dot{x}_{10} = c_{10} x_{10} + \frac{1}{m}(c_\phi s_\theta s_\psi - s_\phi s_\psi) U_1 \\
\dot{x}_{11} &= x_{12}, \dot{x}_{12} = c_{11} x_{12} + \frac{1}{m}(c_\phi c_\theta) U_1 - g
\end{aligned} \tag{8}$$

$$U_x = \left(c_\phi s_\theta c_\psi + s_\phi s_\psi\right) = c_{x_1} s_{x_3} c_{x_5} + s_{x_1} s_{x_5}$$

$$U_y = \left(c_\phi s_\theta c_\psi - s_\phi s_\psi\right) = c_{x_1} s_{x_3} s_{x_5} - s_{x_1} c_{x_5} \tag{9}$$

Where,

$$c_1 = \frac{I_y - I_z}{I_x}; \ c_2 = -\frac{k_4}{I_x}; \ c_3 = -\frac{J_r}{I_x}; \ c_4 = \frac{I_z - I_x}{I_y}; \ c_5 = -\frac{k_5}{I_y}; \ c_6 = \frac{J_r}{I_y}; \ c_7 = \frac{I_x - I_y}{I_z}$$

$$c_8 = -\frac{k_6}{I_z}; \ c_9 = -\frac{k_1}{m}; \ c_{10} = -\frac{k_2}{m}; \ c_{11} = -\frac{k_3}{m}; \ b_1 = \frac{1}{I_x}; \ b_2 = \frac{1}{I_y}; \ b_3 = \frac{1}{I_z}$$

and Uy are used to derive the reference trajectory for phi and theta (ϕ_d, θ_d) from the simulated loop (x and y dynamics). Therefore, the desired roll and pitch paths are derived from the position controllers from Eq. (9).

$$U_x = \left(c_{\phi_d} s_{\theta_d} c_\psi - s_{\phi_d} c_\psi\right) \text{ and } U_y = \left(c_{\phi_d} s_{\theta_d} s_\psi - s_{\phi_d} c_\psi\right) \tag{10}$$

$$\begin{bmatrix} \phi_d \\ \theta_d \end{bmatrix} = \begin{bmatrix} \arcsin\left(U_x s_\psi - U_y c_\psi\right) \\ \arcsin\left(\left(U_x c_\psi - U_y s_\psi\right)/c_{\phi_d}\right) \end{bmatrix} \tag{11}$$

3 SMC Design for the Nonlinear Dynamic Model

Sliding mode control (SMC) is a form of Variable Structure Control (VSC) which is performed by pulling the trajectories of the system state to the set-point surface called a sliding surface. The nature of the path of the state is separated into two parts [21]. This is named "the reaching stage" from the initial state until the intersection with the sliding surface. This direction is called "the sliding process" from the intersection with the sliding surface until the origin. Slotine and Li suggested the universal form of the equation in [15–20, 22].

$$S(x) = \left(\lambda_x + \frac{d}{dt}\right)^{f-1} e(x) \tag{12}$$

Where x is the control state or variable vector, e(x) is tracking deviation expressed as $x_d - x$, λ_x is a constant greater than zero that describes the surface dynamics and f is the relative degree of the sliding mode controller Entry conditions to the sliding surface were used for the Lyapunov-based method. This makes a positive scalar function, referred to below in Eq. (13), called the Lyapunov chosen function. The control rule that fulfills this function was selected for the dynamic state variables and selected [22]:

$$\dot{V} < 0, \text{ where } V > 0 \tag{13}$$

For selecting the Lyapunov stable function there is no universal principle. In this case the positive Lyapunov candidate function for each single dynamics systems the suitable function is chosen as:

$$V = \frac{1}{2}s^2 \tag{14}$$

Clearly seen that it is a positive definite, and its derivative $\dot{V} < 0$ (i.e., $\dot{V} = s\dot{s} < 0$). The aim is to attract the paths of the machine state to hit the sliding or switching surface and, considering the existence of ambiguity, remain on it. Tracking error is the deviation between the desired result and the state's exact expected values, defined as follows:

$$e_{i+1} = \dot{e}_1; e_i = x_{id} - x_i, (i = 1, 2 \ldots 6) \tag{15}$$

Based on the reaching low, "constant reaching low" the derivative of the sliding surface meets that $\dot{V} = s\dot{s} < 0$ condition given by [23] as

$$\dot{s}_i = -K_i \text{sgn}(s_i) \tag{16}$$

Thus $K_i > 0$, represents a constant rate.

$$\text{sgn}(s_i) = \begin{cases} 1, & s_i > 0 \\ 0, & s_i = 0 \\ -1, & s_i < 0 \end{cases} \tag{17}$$

K_i's value is too little; it will take too long to hit the period. On the other hand, too much Ki value will produce extreme chattering, so the success of SMC will determine the option of K_i value. Equation (14) is used to choose the SMC sliding surface feature so that the sliding surface can be chosen on the basis of tracking deviation, as seen below:

$$s_1 = \lambda_1 \phi_e + \dot{\phi}_e, \quad \phi_e = \phi_d - \phi = e_1 \tag{18}$$

$$s_2 = \lambda_2 \theta_e + \dot{\theta}_e, \quad \theta_e = \theta_d - \theta = e_2 \tag{19}$$

$$s_3 = \lambda_3 \psi_e + \dot{\psi}_e, \quad \psi_e = \psi_d - \psi = e_3 \tag{20}$$

$$s_6 = \lambda_6 z_e + \dot{z}_e, \quad z_e = z_d - z = e_6 \tag{21}$$

$$s_x = \lambda_4 x_e + \dot{x}_e, \quad x_e = x_d - x = e_4 \tag{22}$$

$$s_y = \lambda_5 y_e + \dot{y}_e, \quad y_e = y_d - y = e_5 \tag{23}$$

Where, $\lambda_{1...6}$ must satisfy the Hurwitz stability condition or greater than zero.

Equation (18), (19), (20), (21), (22), and (23), are the sliding surface & its tracking deviation for roll dynamics; for the pitch dynamics; for the yaw dynamics; for altitude dynamics, for x-dynamics, for y-dynamics respectively. The nonlinear dynamic model is split into subsystems called internal and external dynamics. The position dynamics of the internal system (X and Y) produces the optimal angular position called roll and pitch (ϕ_d and Θ_d). The rest subsystem is the altitude, roll, pitch, and yaw dynamics of the external system (z, ϕ, Θ, ψ) [14, 16–18].

In the case of internal dynamics, it influences the rotation of the quadcopter. However, external interference is made, which in turn affects the movement of the quadcopter. So, to stabilize this problem, the SMC is used.

3.1 SMC Design for the Dynamics of Quadrotor

The tracking deviation or error, and the switching surface for tilt (roll) angle determined in Eq. (18) the 1st derivative of the sliding surface is

$$\dot{s}_1 = \lambda_1 \dot{e}_1 + \ddot{e}_1 = \lambda_1 \dot{\phi}_e + \ddot{\phi}_e = \lambda_1(\dot{\phi}_d - \dot{\phi}) + \ddot{\phi}_d - \ddot{\phi}; \tag{24}$$

From Eq. (16) $\dot{s}_1 = -K_1 sgn(s_1)$ & Eq. (2): $\ddot{\phi} = \dot{x}_2 = c_1 x_4 x_6 + c_2 x_2^2 + c_3 \Omega_r x_4 + b_1 U_2$ equating with Eq. (24 c) and then, U_2 an be calculated as follows:

$$U_2 = \frac{1}{b_1}\left[\ddot{\phi}_d - c_1 x_4 x_6 + c_2 x_2^2 + c_3 \Omega_r x_4 + \lambda_1(\dot{\phi}_d - \dot{\phi}) - \dot{s}_1\right], \quad or$$

$$U_2 = \frac{1}{b_1}\left[\ddot{x}_{1d} - c_1 x_4 x_6 - c_2 x_2^2 - c_3 \Omega_r x_4 + \lambda_1 \dot{e}_1 + K_1 sgn(s_1)\right] \tag{25}$$

Where, $\dot{e}_1 = (\dot{\phi}_d - \dot{\phi}) = \dot{\phi}_e$. This design approach is repeating for all later systems. The controller becomes:

$$U_3 = \frac{1}{b_2}\left[\ddot{x}_{3d} - c_4 x_2 x_6 - c_5 x_4^2 - c_6 \Omega_r x_2 + \lambda_2 \dot{e}_2 + K_2 sgn(s_2)\right] \tag{26}$$

$$U_4 = \frac{1}{b_3}\left[\ddot{x}_{5d} - c_7 x_2 x_4 - c_8 x_6^2 + \lambda_3 \dot{e}_3 + K_3 sgn(s_3)\right] \tag{27}$$

$$U_1 = \frac{m}{c_{x1}c_{x3}}\left[\ddot{z}_d - c_{11}x_{12} + g + \lambda_6 \dot{e}_6 + K_6 sgn(s_6)\right] \tag{28}$$

The same algorism is used to drive the control laws for U_x and U_y to stabilize the positions X and Y dynamics of the Quadcopter, respectively. 1st derivative of sliding surface for x-dynamics is calculated as:

$$\dot{s}_4 = \lambda_4 \dot{e}_4 + \ddot{e}_4 = \lambda_4 \dot{x}_e + \ddot{x}_e = \lambda_4(\dot{x}_d - \dot{x}) + \ddot{x}_d - \ddot{x}, \quad \dot{s}_4 = -K_4 sgn(s_4) \tag{29}$$

The nonlinear dynamic modeling in Eq. (1) for the translational X dynamics are

$$\ddot{x} = \dot{x}_8 = \ddot{x}_7 = c_9 x_8 + \frac{1}{m}(c_\phi s_\theta c_\psi + s_\phi s_\psi)U_1$$

Where, $u_x = (c_\phi s_\theta c_\psi + s_\phi s_\psi) = c_{x_1} s_{x_3} c_{x_5} + s_{x_1} s_{x_5}$

Therefore, the x-dynamics acceleration became $\ddot{x} = c_9 x_8 + \frac{1}{m} U_x U_1$, Equating from Eq. (29), the SM control input U_x for desired X position can be obtained as:

Therefore, the x-dynamics acceleration became $\ddot{x} = c_9 x_8 + \frac{1}{m} U_x U_1$, Equating from Eq. (28), the SM control input U_x for desired X position can be obtained as:

$$U_x = \left\{ \frac{m}{U_1} [\ddot{x}_{7d} - c_9 x_8 + \lambda_4 \dot{e}_4 + K_4 \text{sgn}(s_4)] \right\} \tag{30}$$

The same approaches for y-dynamics the controller becomes

$$U_y = \frac{m}{U_1} [\ddot{x}_{9d} - c_{10} x_{10} + \lambda_5 \dot{e}_5 + K_5 \text{sgn}(s_5)] \tag{31}$$

Figure 1 shows the overall system's SIMULINK block diagram. It includes controller of altitude (Z-dynamics), X-position, Y-position, heading (yaw), attitude roll, and attitude pitch dynamics control sub-system blocks. The parameter used for simulation are listed in Tables 1 and 2.

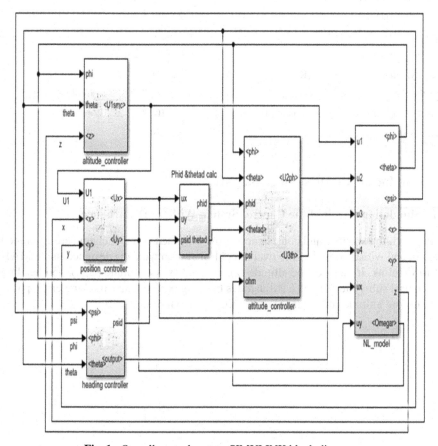

Fig. 1. Overall control system SIMULINK block diagram

Table 1. Parameters used for SMC simulation purpose

Dynamics	K_i (accepted constant)	λ_i	ρ (boundary)
Roll-attitude	224.5	25.05	0.00099
Pitch-attitude	224.5	25.05	0.00099
Yaw-heading	223	15.05	0.00099
X - position	334	15.05	0.00099
Y - position	334	15.05	0.00099
Z - altitude	224.5	15.05	0.00099

Table 2. Parameters used for the quadrotor model simulation

Parameter	Value and unit
Coefficient of lift (b)	$29.8*10^{-4}$ Ns^2 rad^{-2}
Coefficient of drag (d)	$33*10^{-6}$ Nms^2 rad^{-2}
Total mass (m)	$8.23*10^{-1}$ kg
Length of arm (l)	0.350 m
Inertia for motor (J_r)	$28.4*10^{-4}$ kg m^2
Aerodynamic friction coeffs ($K_{1,2,3}$)	$37.29*10^{-2}$
Inertia moment for quadrotor (Ix,y,z)	$10^{-2}*\{0.5, 0.5, 0.1\}$ in (kg m^2) resp.
aerodynamic drag coeffs for translational ($K_{4,5,6}$)	$55.6*10^{-3}$
Gravity (g)	9.81 m/s^2

4   Simulation Results and Analysis

4.1   Simulation Result of the Control System Without Disturbance

In this part, the stability and consistency of the proposed control scheme are examined without and with disruption. The overall control system which is designed using MAT-LAB/Simulink. It includes the altitude (z), position (x, y), attitude (ϕ, θ), and heading (ψ) control sub-system. Figure 2 illustrates tracking performance, tracking error, phase portrait, and altitude control input of the altitude dynamics.

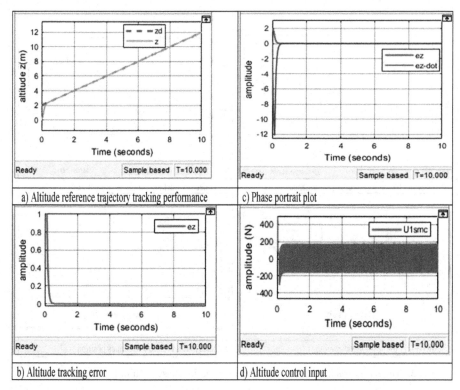

Fig. 2. a) Altitude reference trajectory tracking controller performance b) tracking error c) phase-plot d) control input of altitude SMC

Clearly seen from Fig. 2, the set-point path starts from two (m) after 0.35 s the real path tracks the set-point (desired) zd = (2 + t) and starts from 0.45 s, the tracking error is very small nearly 0.002 s. The phase plot shows that the control system error change is going to zero within 0.3 s. This implies the control system is stable.

Figure 3 shows the simulation result of the SM controller to track the directions X and Y in the comparison trajectories. The real path (x) tracks the specified path (xd = 4*sin(t)) at 0 s. In the cases of Y position, the real trajectory is the optimal one (yd = 5*cos(t)) after 0.4 s. The result reveals that the suggested controller has accomplished its monitoring targets in both positions.

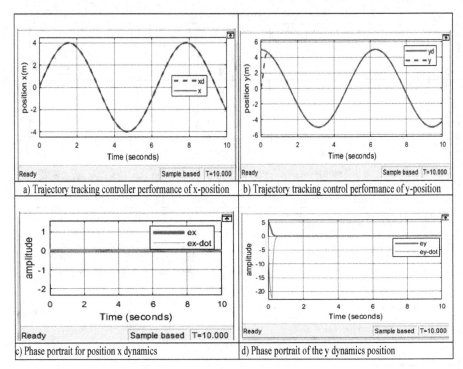

a) Trajectory tracking controller performance of x-position

b) Trajectory tracking control performance of y-position

c) Phase portrait for position x dynamics

d) Phase portrait of the y dynamics position

Fig. 3. Trajectory tracking abilities of position and its phase portrait for x, y dynamics

Figure 4 shows the trajectory tracking performance and their SMC control input for roll, for pitch and, for yaw trajectory tracking. The roll and pitch dynamics are called the attitude of the quadrotor. Its dynamics are generated from the X and Y position dynamics. The controller performance objectives are achieved for the three rotational dynamics (i.e., Roll, Pitch, and Yaw) of the quadrotor.

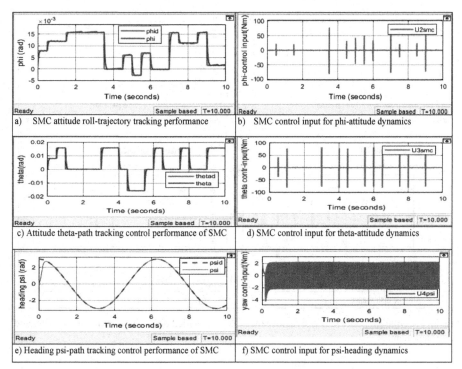

Fig. 4. Trajectory tracking performance and its SMC control input for rotational roll, pitch, and yaw dynamic

4.2 Simulation Results of the Proposed Control System with Gaussian Disturbance

Here the designed control system is tested by adding external disturbance (it is called Gaussian disturbance) on the system. The simulation results in Fig. 5; illustrate the output of the Gaussian (normal) spontaneous disruption signal. Particularly, this disruption involves the variation of the air, the wind, and the rain effects that occur in the quadrotor's actual world.

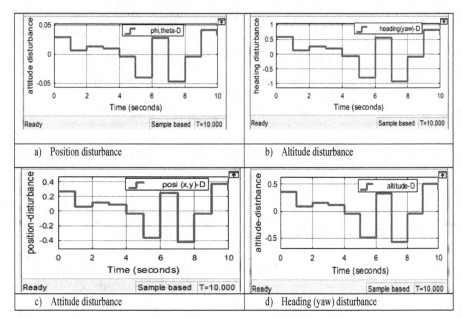

Fig. 5. External random Gaussian disturbances that are added on position, altitude, attitude, and heading dynamics

Figure 6 demonstrate that the unknown disruptions enter the system unexpectedly, the proposed SM controller immediately takes the necessary action to change the system to be stable and refuse the effects of the added disturbance. The time taken by the controller to eliminate the Gaussian type of disturbance is less than 0.2 s for all the dynamics. The overall simulation results depict that in the cases of disturbance avoidance, the proposed SM controller scheme is robust and versatile.

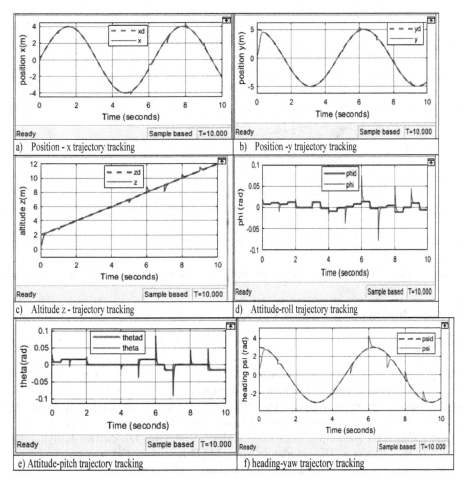

Fig. 6. Trajectory tracking performance of a) position-x, b) position-y, c) altitude, d) roll, e) pitch, and f) yaw controller with disturbance

4.3   3D-Helical Trajectory Tracking Performance

Here for translational (X, Y, and, Z) dynamics in space, the designed SMC approaches for three-dimensional helical trajectory following controllers were applied. It is visible from Fig. 7; effective tracking of the 3D-helical track was achieved. This shows a 3D-helical reference trajectory produced when the quadrotor initially flies from point (0, 0, 0) m after trajectories (4sin(t), 5cos(t), 2 + t) m in the directions of X, Y, and Z, respectively. This 3D-helical pathway simulation result illustrates the reliability of the controller and its robustness. That means the controller manages any type of motion of the quadrotor.

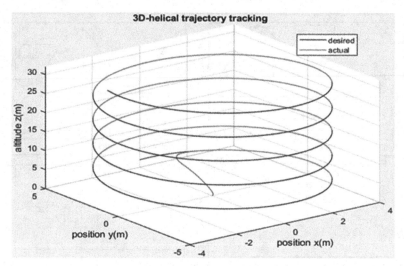

Fig. 7. SMC 3D-helical trajectory tracking for (4sin (t), 5cos (t), 2 + t) m

5 Conclusions and Future Works

5.1 Conclusion

The quadrotor (quadcopter) nonlinear dynamic model is obtained by using the Newton-Euler force-torque equation. Here there are translational and rotational (Euler) dynamics in the nonlinear quadcopter model. The effect of gyroscopic moment resulting from the quadcopter body and its rotor blade takes into account and the model also integrates aerodynamic drag force and torque. The sliding mode controller was designed for the dynamic model of the quadrotor. The simulation using MATLAB / Simulink was performed to verify the validity and performance of the proposed controller here.

The sliding mode controllers are used for monitoring the angular dynamics (attitude and heading) translational dynamics (position and altitude) of the quadcopter. The position (x, y), and altitude control system contains three states. The control inputs are strongly coupled and nonlinear for both input and output. Therefore, SMC is used to stabilize this type of nonlinear coupled systems. The result shows SMC makes the actual path to track the reference one within 0.5 s in the average of the overall system. And it performs better tracking ability with a minimum error. Many unknown and unmodelled disruptions influence its motion and the quadrotor's stability while the quadcopter is operating. To validate the robustness of the controller by guessing the nonlinear external disturbance within a certain range and adding it to the quadrotor output terminal. This impact of disruption was controlled effectively by the suggested controller. That means that the controller changes (takes a swift action) immediately and makes a stable track. Thus, in case of disturbance rejection, the planned control method is robust.

5.2 Future Works

In the dynamic model of the quadrotor, the controllers are derived by considering certain assumptions (such as the quadcopter configuration is rigid and symmetrical, the propeller blades are rigid, and the rotational system dynamics are bound in range to prevent singularities). The dynamic model and design control system without these considerations were obtained for further investigation. Unmodeled noise (chattering) effects may be minimized. However, another study might adjust the controller scheme to optimize using particle swarm (PSO) or generic algorithm (GA) or fuzzy logic tuning techniques. And the other direction of research is the higher-order and integral (HISMC) instead of SMC. This could increase its tracking efficiency for different trajectories.

References

1. Jategaonkar, R.: Flight Vehicle System Identification a Time Domain Methodology. American Institute of Aeronautics and Astronautics Inc., Reston (2015)
2. Norris, D.: Build Your Own Quadcopter. McGraw-Hill Education, New York (2014)
3. Vachtsevanos, K.P., Valavanis, G.J.: Handbook UAV. Springer, New York (2015). https://doi.org/10.1007/978-90-481-9707-1
4. Quan, Q.: Introduction to Multicopter Design and Control. Springer, Beijing (2017). https://doi.org/10.1007/978-981-10-3382-7
5. Bouabdallah, S., Noth, A., Siegwart, R.: PID vs LQ control techniques applied to an indoor micro quadrotor. In: International Conference on Intelligent Robots and Systems (2004)
6. Pounds, P., Mahony, R., Corke, P.: Modelling and control of a quadrotor. In: Australasian Conference on Robotics and Automation, Auckland, NZ (2006)
7. Madani, T., Benallegue, A.: Backstepping control for a quadrotor helicopter. In: IEEE/RSJ International Conference on Intelligent Robots and Systems (2006)
8. Bouabdallah, S., Siegwart, R.: Backstepping and sliding-mode techniques applied to an indoor micro quadrotor. In: IEEE International Conference on Robotics and Automation, Barcelona, Spain (2005)
9. Xu, R., Ozguner, U.: Sliding mode control of a quadrotor helicopter. In: Proceedings of the 45th IEEE Conference on Decision and Control, San Diego, CA, USA (2006)
10. Lee, D., Kim, H.J., Sastry, S.: Feedback linearization vs. adaptive sliding mode control for a quadrotor helicopter. Int. J. Control Autom. Syst. 3(7), 419–428 (2009)
11. Tengis, Ts., Batmunkh, A.: State feedback control simulation of quadcopter model. In: IEEE 2016 11th International Forum on Strategic Technology, Novosibirsk, Russia (2016)
12. Wang, C., Song, B., Huang, P., Tang, C.: Trajectory tracking control for quadrotor robot subject to payload variation and wind gust disturbance. J. Intell. Robot. Syst. (2016)
13. Bouzid, Y., Siguerdidjane, H., Bestaoui, Y., 3D trajectory tracking control of quadrotor UAV with on-line disturbance compensation. In: IEEE Conference on Control Technology and Applications, Kohala Coast, Hawaii, USA, August 2017
14. Rezoug, A., Hamerlain, M., Achour, Z., Tadjine, M.: Applied of an adaptive higher order sliding mode controller to quadrotor trajectory tracking. In: IEEE International Conference on Control System, Computing and Engineering, Penang, Malaysia, November 2015
15. Shtessel, Y., Edwards, C., Fridman, L., Levant, A.: Sliding Mode Control and Observation. Springler, Birkhäuser (2014). https://doi.org/10.1007/978-0-8176-4893-0
16. Johan From, P., Tommy Gravdahl, J., Ytterstad Pettersen, K.: Vehicle-Manipulator System. Springer, London (2014). https://doi.org/10.1007/978-1-4471-5463-1

17. Ghazbi, S.N., Aghli, Y., Alimohammadi, M.: Quadrotors unmanned aerial vehicles: a review. Int. J. Smart Sens. Intell. Syst. **9**(1) (2016)
18. Villanueva, A., Castillo-Toledo, B., Bayro-Corrochano, E.: Multi-mode flight sliding mode control system for a quadrotor. In: 2015 International Conference on Unmanned Aircraft Systems (ICUAS), Denver, Colorado, USA, June 2015
19. Yi, K., Gu, F., Yang, L., He, Y., Han, J.: Sliding mode control for a quadrotor slung load system. In: Proceedings of the 36th Chinese Control Conference, Dalian, China, 26–28 July 2017
20. Gherouat, O., Matouk, D., Hassam, A., Abdessemed, F.: Modeling and sliding mode control of a quadrotor unmanned aerial vehicle. J. Autom. Syst. Eng. **10**(3), 150–157 (2016)
21. Jiukin, L.: Sliding Mode Control Using MATLAB. Elsevier Inc., Beijing (2017)
22. Liu, J., Wang, X.: Advanced Sliding Mode Control for Mechanical Systems. Springer, Dordrecht (2014). https://doi.org/10.1007/978-3-642-20907-9
23. Derbel, N., Ghommam, J., Zhu, Q. (eds.): Applications of Sliding Mode Control. SSDC, vol. 79. Springer, Singapore (2017). https://doi.org/10.1007/978-981-10-2374-3

Direct Adaptive Fuzzy PI Strategy for a Smooth MPPT of Variable Speed Wind Turbines

Abrham Tadesse[1]([✉]), Endalew Ayenew[2], and L. N. K. Venkata[2]

[1] Faculty of Electrical and Computer Engineering, Bahir Dar Institute of Technology,
Bahir Dar University, Bahir Dar, Ethiopia
[2] College of Electrical and Mechanical Engineering, Addis Ababa Science and Technology
University, Addis Ababa, Ethiopia

Abstract. For this generation, life is too complex without sufficient energy. Due to the increase demand of energy from time to time, several researchers are too eager on renewable energy sources to have good enough, clean and greenhouse effect free energy. Thanks to its cost effectiveness, wind power is the primary focus of professionals on energy area and it is the fastest rising energy source. Adaptive fuzzy proportional integral (AFPI) is proposed here to keep a maximum power of a wind turbine (WT). From various methods of maximum power point tracking (MPPT), tip speed ratio (TSR) is selected here. TSR has the ability to retrieve the optimum desired speed of the generator for every wind speed value. For a WTs, a 1.5 MW permanent magnet synchronous generator (PMSG) is chosen because of its self-excitation property that enables high power factor and efficiency operation. The system efficiency is verified by MATLAB software. After all, the final result with proposed strategy display better performance than the outcome with conventional controller.

Keywords: Wind turbine · Permanent magnet synchronous generator · MPPT · Direct adaptive fuzzy proportional integral

1 Introduction

In order to produce electrical power, the desire to use renewable energy as a sustainable and readily accessible alternative to fossil fuels is growing dramatically [1]. Increasing energy requirements and the adverse environmental impact of fossil fuels made renewables a very important option, preferable and market competent. Because the world has immense wind energy resources, it is easy to understand wind energy is the world's growing technology with respect to power generation. As per experts, taking around 10–15% of the available wind could supply the world's entire electricity needs [2, 3]. The WTs speed has been set fixed for the past few years. However, the optimum performance of fixed speed turbines is too difficult to achieve the final goal. While it is simple to determine the optimum torque, it is difficult to monitor and achieve instantaneous tracking because of the inertia of the mechanical system, as the wind velocity changes

© ICST Institute for Computer Sciences, Social Informatics and Telecommunications Engineering 2021
Published by Springer Nature Switzerland AG 2021. All Rights Reserved
M. A. Delele et al. (Eds.): ICAST 2020, LNICST 384, pp. 351–360, 2021.
https://doi.org/10.1007/978-3-030-80621-7_25

rapidly. If the established TSR is adopted, this condition becomes too bad when the wind speed is below rated value while the acceleration or deceleration torque is very low. As a consequence, the energy produced is actually slightly less than the full energy available [1, 4, 8, 9]. Therefore, here, a variable speed WT with TSR based MPPT is proposed to solve the above problem.

In this paper, an adaptive fuzzy PI controller is proposed to get maximum energy as well as in order to achieve both economic and technological efficiency. For a wind speed below the rated value, TSR method works to obtain the optimum desired speed of the generator while a pitch angle controller is activated with a speed of a wind greater than the rated value [5–7, 10]. As a WT generator, PMSG is chosen to be beneficial in which its self-excitation as well as high efficiency and power factor activity [1, 3].

Low performance nature is the main weakness of WECS. MPPT algorithm should therefore be used in the partial load field. In [8], proportional derivative (PD) controller dependent maximum power tracking is studied. However, there have been some short-comings. The way of finding parameters P, I, and D (mostly trial and error) offers an incentive for improperly calibrated control gains, decreasing the precision and daynamic efficiency of the entire system [1]. MPPT via fuzzy is proposed in [4] and [11]. The good side of this works is that they used a fuzzy strategy that can easily eliminate the need for accurate system model. But since one of the controllers fills the void between each other, a blend of the two, that is fuzzy with traditional controller, is better than each alone. In [1], for a maximum power extraction, a phase lag compensator controller is presented. However, for the first min times, the system has highly oscillatory responses and the science is not yet well established.

2 System Modelling

2.1 Wind Turbine Modelling

Conditions like speed of wind, density of air, blade diameter, altitude and such should be considered strictly to have efficient wind power.

With a speed of a wind, V_w the kinetic energy, KE, is given as

$$\text{KE} = \frac{1}{2}mV_w^2 \tag{1}$$

$$K_E = \frac{1}{2}\rho\pi R^2 dV_w^2 \tag{2}$$

Where K_E is kinetic energy, m is mass of wind, v is speed of wind, A is the rotor area, R is the blade length, and d is the thickness of the air disk. Finally the overall mechanical power P_w, of wind can be expressed as follows

$$P_w = \frac{Energy}{Time} = \frac{K_E}{t}$$

$$P_w = \frac{1}{2}\rho\pi R^2\left(\frac{d}{t}\right)V_w^2 = \frac{1}{2}\pi R^2 V_w^3 \tag{3}$$

This means that the energy gained from the actual speed of wind is varied with a cube degree [3]. As per Betz law, it is impossible to extract all the available power from wind. So the maximum possible mechanical power that can be gained is given in [12].

$$P_m = \frac{1}{2}\rho C_p(\lambda, \beta)\pi R^2 V_w^3 \tag{4}$$

Where p_m, is the mechanical power, ρ is density of air (kg/m^3), R is radius of the blade in meter, Vw is speed of wind in meter per second, C_p is the power coefficient.
In [13], the power coefficient, C_p is given as

$$Cp(\lambda, \beta) = 0.5176\left(\frac{116}{i} - 0.4\beta - 5\right)e^{-\frac{21}{i}} + 0.0068 \tag{5}$$

Where:

$$\frac{1}{\lambda i} = \frac{1}{(\lambda\lambda + 0.08\beta)} - \frac{0.035}{\beta^3 + 1} \quad and \quad \lambda = \frac{\omega_m * R}{V_w}$$

2.2 PMSG Model

For a WTs application PMSG is very powerful and suitable [1]. Now a day's, due to its benefits such as high energy density, easy control technique, high reliability, low maintenance costs, and its self-excitation nature, PMSG is competent and preferable over DFIG. In this paper, 1.5 MW rated power, 23.5 rpm rated speed, and 26 number of pole pair of PMSG is used. But it is too costly to manufacture permanent magnets and this is the main drawbacks of synchronous permanent magnet generators [14]. In d-q axis the proposed generator is modelled as follows [3]. Diode rectifiers and a multichannel boost converters are the power electronic converters used in this paper.

$$V_d = R_s i_d - \omega_e L_q i_q + \frac{d}{dt}L_d i_d \tag{6}$$

$$V_q = R_s I_q + \omega_e L_d i_d + \omega_e \lambda_r + \frac{d}{dt}L_q i_q \tag{7}$$

3 Proposed Adaptive Fuzzy PI Controller

Both MPPT and pitch angle of a WT has different control methods. Modern control techniques based on artificial intelligence have now been established. The proposed controller, AFPI is one of these modern controllers. In this work, both MPPT and pitch angles are controlled via adaptive fuzzy PI (AFPI) and offers attractive features such as quick response and excellent smooth power [16].

3.1 Tip Speed Ratio (TSR) Based MPPT Control

In order to preserve the tip speed ratio to the optimum value at which maximum power can be gained, the tip speed ratio (TSR) control method controls the generator's rotational speed. In addition to the knowledge of the optimum tip speed ratio of a WT, this approach needs the wind speed to be calculated to extract all possible power [15]. As stated previously, this work proposes an adaptive fuzzy proportional integral strategy for a TSR control. As a fuzzy logic input, both change in error and error of the speed of the generator from its TSR calculated desired speed are given. The fuzzy logic output directly tunes K_p and K_i constants of the proportional integral controller. Which in turn the K_P and K_i constants are taken as an inductance current reference, i_L* of the boost converter. The reference, i_L* is then compared with the actual current of the inductor in boost converter. The difference of the currents above feeds to the discrete proportional integral and eventually the discrete conventional controller produces a duty cycle for a PWM which in turn the PWM helps to switch the boost converter IGBT.

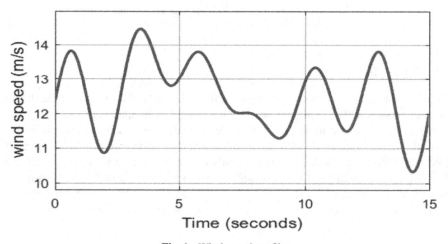

Fig. 1. Wind speed profile

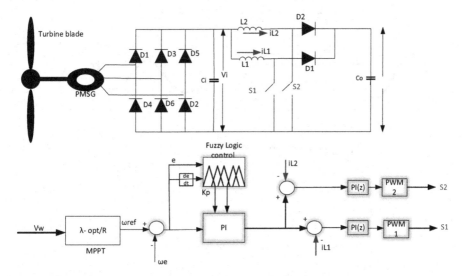

Fig. 2. Block diagram of TSR based MPPT control of an interleaved boost converter.

4 Results and Discussions

The system proposed here is a 1.5 MW large scale WT. To show the effectiveness of the proposed system the software tool taken here is MATLAB. With an input of speed of wind in Fig. 1, the outcomes of the speed of generator in both adaptive fuzzy PI and proportional integral alone has a result of shown in Fig. 3. The desire generator speed is calculated through the TSR energy maximization method. For this particular paper, the optimum TSR is selected as $\lambda\text{opt} = 6$. It is seen from Fig. 3 the reaction with proposed controller has a quick and smooth result than traditional one. Besides to this, the outcome of the proposed one well tracks the speed of the generator as compared to the conventional results. In Fig. 4 the power coefficient c_p response of the conventional controller is highly oscillatory and the outcome of the proposed controller is more stable and smooth compared to the c_p reaction of conventional PI controller. We may infer from this that the proposed systems solution is better since the ultimate objective is to obtain maximum smooth electrical power. As it is seen in Fig. 5, one can understand easily the result with proposed system has a fast and an average of maximum power is gained relative to the conventional proportional integral controller. As stated in Eq. 4, the power coefficient variation mainly affects the mechanical power. The variation of the mechanical power is in proportion with the change in power coefficient as expected. In addition to that, it is easy to notice the proposed and PI controller based mechanical power outputs are below the rated value,1.5 MW.

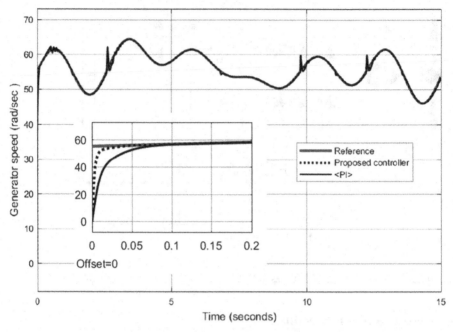

Fig. 3. Generator Speed

However, in the proposed method, an average of maximum smooth power is gained in relative to traditional proportional integral controllers. As the wind speed changes at each instant the output voltage of a WT generator changes in proportion. That is, when a wind speed gets high for a certain instant, the output voltage of the three phase generator also gets high simultaneously. For example, for a time instant 3 to 4 s in Fig. 1, the speed of a wind gets high. With this time interval, the generator output voltage increases directly in proportion. The diode rectifier proposed for this paper gets its input from a PMSG. The uncontrolled diode rectifier then rectifies the output voltage of the generator as such like in Fig. 7. Then, the result of the rectifier is magnified via DC/DC booster circuit after passing through DC link capacitor. To sum up, the proposed interleaved boost converter boosts the rectified voltage and gives an acceptable outcome as shown in Fig. 8.

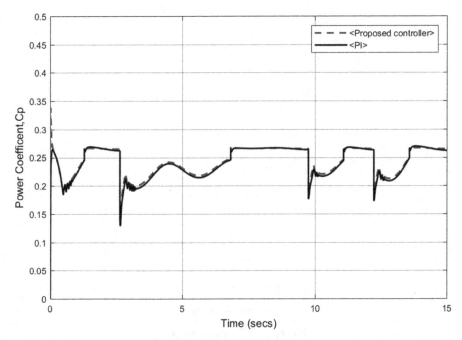

Fig. 4. Power coefficient, Cp

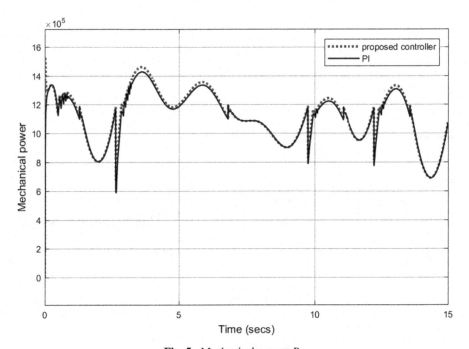

Fig. 5. Mechanical power, P_m

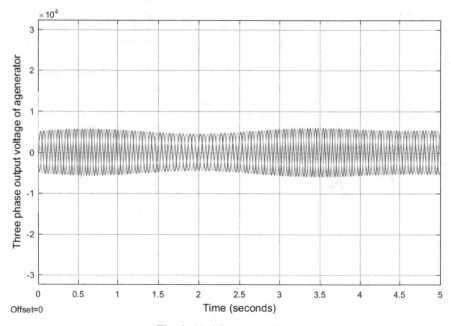

Fig. 6. PMSG output voltage

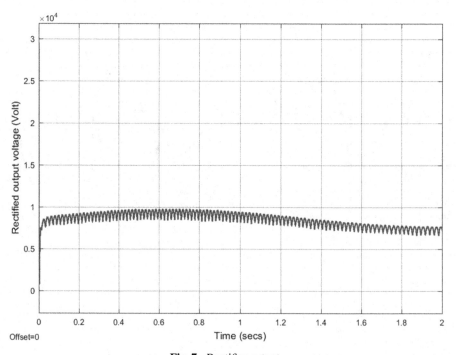

Fig. 7. Rectifier output.

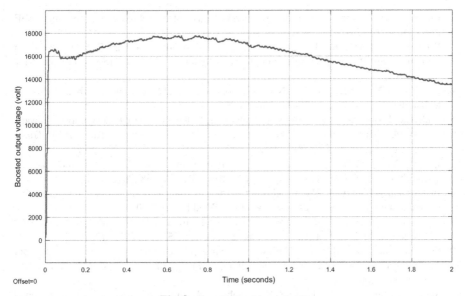

Fig. 8. Boost converter output.

5 Conclusion

For a WECS proposed here a MATLAB software tool has been taken out to check the performance of the proposed controller and evaluate the efficiency of the overall system. In this work, a design of adaptive fuzzy proportional integral controller for a maximum power extraction strategy has been applied. By using the proposed strategy, where the proportional K_p, and integral K_i, gains are find out automatically through fuzzy logic concepts, the outcome of the system shows that the proposed design can have the ability to control the TSR based generator speed tracking effectively. The outcome of proposed system and the result with PI controller alone are compared and the effectiveness of the proposed one is shown. Finally, it is possible to infer from the study that adaptive fuzzy PI strategy provides a reasonably fast, smooth and less oscillatory outcome for the given input. By Keeping the rotor as well as generator from injury the proposed strategy provides attractive feature with respect to the goal of the paper compared to the traditional one, which again implies the efficacy of the proposed method. To sum up, the strategy used in this paper gives the expected outcomes and shows better result over PI controller alone.

Acknowledgment. The authors would like to acknowledge Mr. Dejenie Fikir for his valuable comments.

References

1. Hamatwi, E., Davidson, I.E., Gitau, M.N.: Rotor speed control of a direct driven permanent magnet synchronous generator-based wind turbine using phase-lag compensators to optimize wind power extraction. J. Control Sci. Eng. 10 (2017)

2. Bin, S.K., Wu, Y., Lang, N.Z.: Power Conversion and Control of Wind Energy Systems. IEEE Press, Hoboken (2011)
3. Khaligh, A., Onar, O.G.: Energy Harvesting: Solar, Wind, and Ocean Energy Conversion System Energy, Power Electronics and Machines Series, p. 368. CRC Press, Ali Emadi, New York (2010)
4. Liu, J., Gao, Y., Geng, S., Wu, L.: Nonlinear control of variable speed wind turbines via fuzzy techniques. IEEE Access **5**, 27–34 (2017)
5. Muhando, E.B., Senjyu, T., Uehara, A., Funabashi, T., Kim, C.H.: LQG design for megawatt-class WECS with DFIG based on functional models' fidelity prerequisites. IEEE Trans. Energy Convers. **24**(4), 893–904 (2009)
6. Uehara, A., et al.: A coordinated control method to smooth wind power fluctuations of a PMSG-based WECS. IEEE Trans. Energy Convers. **26**, 550–558 (2011)
7. Ben Smida, M., Sakly, A.: Pitch angle control for grid-connected variable-speed wind turbine system using fuzzy logic : a comparative study. Wind Eng. **12** (2016)
8. Power, H.M.W.: A novel sensorless MPPT controller for a high-efficiency microscale wind power generation system. IEEE Trans. Energy Convers. **25**(1), 207–216 (2010)
9. Qiao, W., Zhou, W., Aller, J.M., Harley, R.G.: Wind speed estimation based sensorless output maximization control for a wind turbine driving a DFIG. IEEE Trans. Power Electron. **23**(3), 1156–1169 (2008)
10. Senjyu, T., Sakamoto, R., Urasaki, N., Funabashi, T., Fujita, H., Sekine, H.: Output power leveling of wind turbine generator for all operating regions by pitch angle control. IEEE Trans. Energy Convers. **21**(2), 467–475 (2006)
11. Elmas, C., Deperlioglu, O., Sayn, H.H.: Aptive Fuzzy Logic Control for DC-DC Converters. Expert Syst. App. **36**, 1540–1548 (2009)
12. Muyeen, S.M.: Wind Energy Conversion Systems: Green Energy and Technology, p. 552. Springer, Abu Dhabi U.A.E. (2012)
13. Koutroulis, E., Kalaitzakis, K.: Design of a maximum power tracking system for wind-energy-conversion applications. IEEE Trans. Indust. Electron. **53**(2) (2006)
14. Bracke, X.: Maximum Power Point Tracking of Small Wind Turbines with a Full Active Rectifier. Dep. Electr. Energy, Syst. Autom. Gent Univ., p. 172 (2014)
15. Sumathi, S., Ashok Kumar, L., Surekha, P.: Solar PV and Wind Energy Conversion Systems. Springer International Publishing, Cham (2015)
16. Patcharaprakiti, N., Premrudeepreechacharn, S., Sriuthaisiriwong, Y.: Maximum power point tracking using adaptive fuzzy logic control for grid-connected photovoltaic system. Power Eng. Soc. Winter Meet. 2002, p. 18. IEEE (2002)

Security Constrained Economic Dispatch
of Renewable Energy Systems

Shewit Tsegaye[1(✉)], Fekadu Shewarega[2], and Getachew Bekele[3]

[1] Jimma University, 378, Jimma, Ethiopia
[2] University of Duisburg-Essen, 47057 Duisburg, Germany
[3] Addis Ababa University, 385, Addis Ababa, Ethiopia
getachew.bekele@aait.edu.et

Abstract. This paper presents Security Constrained Economic Dispatch (SCED) of renewable energy systems (RES). Reformulation of SCED for RES comprising biomass, large and micro-hydro plants, solar PV, solar thermal, waste to energy plant, wind farm and geothermal has been carried out. This enables RES prime-moved power systems provide secure and reliable service. Each of these sources requires problem formulation and constraint handling mechanism that take into account security limits and credible contingencies. Modified IEEE 118 bus system (NREL-118 test system), Ethiopian renewable energy system, and modified New England 39-bus system with high RES penetration features were used as case studies. Modeling and simulation was conducted on MATLAB, MATLAB/MATPOER, and DIGSILENT power factory simulation platforms. According to the simulation results obtained, it is deduced that the economic dispatch of RES is a promising step in connection to developments needed in the adoption and realization of smarter grids.

Keywords: Security constraints · Economic dispatch · Power system operation · Integrated Renewable energy sources

1 Introduction

When a sudden interruption or blackout occurs, we notice the importance of electricity in our daily lives. Moreover, a sudden and uncontrolled power outage can cause a highly regarded threat to social and economic endeavors of energy-addicted society. Considering the Ethiopian electric power network, a power-system of integrated renewable energy sources, the supply of power interrupts every time it rains. These interruptions can impose considerable damage to production plants, service centers, and home appliances [1].

Blackout report data of Ethiopian electric power network (2013–2016), reported 15 major blackouts. Production plants and service centers were down for an average of four months a year. Natural incidents, equipment failure, and supply-demand mismatch, collectively called contingencies cause most of these blackouts [1, 2]. The first challenging aspect of power system operation is that electrical energy, unlike other commodities;

M. A. Delele et al. (Eds.): ICAST 2020, LNICST 384, pp. 361–375, 2021.
https://doi.org/10.1007/978-3-030-80621-7_26

is difficult to store in significant amounts. Implying that electrical power must be consumed at same time it is generated. For reliable supply of power, it is therefore essential to maintain the balance between generation and demand.

This aspect requires a method of balancing generation and demand considering generation limits, transmission security constraints, contingencies, and uncertainties i.e. Security-constrained economic dispatch (SCED). SCED is allocating generation levels to the generating units in a power system so that the system load can be supplied entirely and most economically while satisfying different security constraints [3, 4]. In the energy market context, the main objective of SCED is to minimize the operation cost while continuously respecting the operational constraints of the power system network. This means minimizing the cost function subject to generation limits, transmission constraints, and security level limits.

Several authors used different methods to solve this problem, for example, iterative method, gradient-based techniques, interior point method, linear programming and dynamic programming [5]. A substantial number of articles reported SCED in the perspective of artificial intelligence [6], integrated renewable energy source [7, 8], and post-disturbance corrective actions [9]. Stephen Frank et al. [10, 11] examines the recent trends towards stochastic, or non-deterministic, search techniques and hybrid methods for OPF.

The other challenging aspect is the intermittency and variability of renewable energy sources. With increasing emphasis on using renewables to mitigate climate change effects, many new challenges hinder the power industry from advancement [12]. A small change in a variable renewable source can cause a large surplus or lack of power output and subsequently affect the security of power system networks with a limited flexibility.

In this paper, it has been put the choice firmly on:

- Reformulating SCED problem including security constraints and credible contingencies.
- Identifying challenges posed to SCED due to intermittent RES penetration.
- Recommending a hybrid computational intelligence-based optimization method for SCED of RES.

Articulation of challenging aspects of economic dispatch with security constraints and uncertainty of renewable energy systems, identification of further challenging developments needed in the adoption of smarter grids, and indicating ways to address them is also the novelty of this study.

Nomenclature

ai = constant coefficient measure of losses

bi= constant coefficient representing fuel cost

Bij= active power loss coefficients

c = Weibull probability distribution factor

Ch = Hydropower generation cost

Ci = constant coefficient of salary and wages

f (x) = function to be minimized

FBth= biomass generation cost

FGth= Geothermal power generation cost

fpw= wind power probability function

Fsth= solar thermal power generation cost

Fth= thermal power generation cost

g l (x) = Inequality constraints

G= solar irradiance

Gstd= standard solar irradiance

h k(x) = Equality constraints

Hi= average head

K = Number of equality constraints

k= Weibull probability distribution factor

L= Number of inequality constraints

Ncc= Number of Credible contingencies

NG= Number of generating units

NL = Number of security levels

Npoz = Number of prohibited zones

ϕ = Credible contingencies

Ph r= Hydropower output

PBth= biomass power output

PD= Power demand

Cs= solar power generation cost

Csp= solar power penalty cost

Csr= solar power reserve cost

Cw= wind power generation cost

Cwp= wind power penality cost

Cwr= wind power reserve cost

DR I = ramp rate limit

PGth= geothermal power output

Phgi = Hydropower unit output

Pi max= maximum power generation limit

Pi min= minimum power generation limit

PL = Power loss

Psg = solar power output

Psr= rated solar power output

Psth= solar thermal power output

Pth= thermal power output

Pwr= wind power output

Qi= discharge outflow

Rca= certain irradiance point set at 150 w/m2

Sl = Security level

Sl max = maximum Security level

SRi= spinning reserve limit

SSR= maximum spinning reserve limit

Vi= cut in wind speed

Vo= cut out wind speed

Vr= rated wind speed

Vwt= forecasted wind speed

x i (1)= Security constraint

2   Renewable Energy Systems

The contribution of renewable resources to the energy portfolio globally has been steadily increasing over the past few years [4]. RES are systems that harness two or more forms of locally available renewable energy resources to supply a variety of energy demand in an efficient, cost- effective and practical way. Such systems can operate well in both off-grid/stand-alone mode and when connected to a centralized grid.

RESs are highly site-specific, stochastic in, and unevenly distributed around the world with little or no costs. They depend on the climatic conditions, geographical factors and seasons of the site under consideration [9]. Due to the increasing level of uncertainties introduced by renewable energy sources (RESs), traditional deterministic decision making in the electric power industry is gradually shifting towards stochastic decision making which explicitly considers the uncertainty in the power output of RES generators.

The most widely used renewable resources as inputs to RES are biomass, hydro, solar, wind, and geothermal. The prime significance of RES is its focus to energize and electrify remote rural areas as promoted by hybrid systems, in order to achieve sustainable development and improve the basic living environment of communities [13, 14] (Fig. 1).

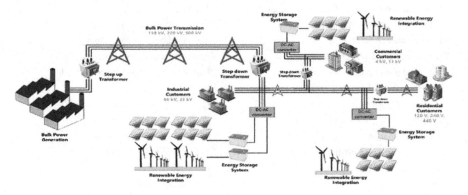

Fig. 1. Possible schematic diagram of RES [11]

Several number of renewable integration studies have focused on optimization requirements of power system with high renewable penetration such as wind [7, 15] gas [12] natural gas [16] and photovoltaic (PV) [17]. In this seminar paper RES comprising biomass, large and micro-hydro plants, solar PV, solar thermal, waste to energy plant, wind farm, and geothermal with their problem formulation and constraint handling mechanisms are discussed.

3   SCED Problem Formulation

3.1   Problem Formulation

Relations between the cost of generating power and the operating cost that rely on power flow output and forecasted values for the load demand are determined for each dispatch interval [18, 19]. The general form of SCED problem is:

$$optimize f(x), x \in R^n \tag{1}$$

Subject to

$$h_k(x) = 0 \forall 1, 2 \ldots m \tag{2}$$

$$g_l(x) \leq 0 \forall 1, 2 \ldots L \tag{3}$$

In a practical power system, the SCED problem is non-linear and multi-objective due to operation constraints. The non-detailed formulation of SCED problem due to the necessary assumptions can lead to a limitation in the modelling of a large-scale power system. General form of multi objective optimization is:

$$Optimize f(x) = (f_1(x), f_2(x), f_{Nobj}(x) \tag{4}$$

Subject to

$$g_l(x) = 0 \forall i = 1, 2 \ldots m$$

$$h_k(x) \leq 0 \forall k = 1, 2, \ldots K$$

$$x_i(1) \leq x_i \leq x_i(0) \tag{5}$$

Multi-objective optimization approach in SCED context refers to minimizing generation cost and maximizing the security level of the operating system while considering a variable and intermittent generation [9]. The main objective of power systems operation is to supply consumers with electric power in a reliable way i.e. optimal loading is required to alleviate this mismatch. This paper uses renewable resources as inputs to RES such as biomass, hydro, solar, wind, and geothermal. Each of these sources requires problem formulation, and constraint handling mechanisms.

Hydro: f1(x) represents objective function of hydro power generation plants [20]

$$\min f_1(x) = C_h \sum_{i=1}^{N_{hg}} P_{hgj}(t) \tag{6}$$

Where

$$P_{hgj}(t) = \sum_{t=1}^{24} \sum_{i=1}^{N_G} 0.00981 \eta_i H_{ij} Q_{ij} \tag{7}$$

Wind: the power for assumed wind speed is given by [7, 21]:

$$P_{wr} = \begin{cases} 0, for v_{wt} \leq v_i \text{ and } v_{out} \geq 0 \\ P_{wr}(\dfrac{v_{wt} - v_i}{v_r - v_i}), for v_i \leq v_{wr} \leq v_{out} \\ P_{wr}, for v_r \leq v_{wt} \leq v_{out} \end{cases} \tag{8}$$

In addition, its corresponding objective function is f₂(x)

$$f_2(x) = C_w \sum_{i=1}^{N_{WG}} P_{wgj}(t) + \sum_{t=1}^{24} \sum_{i=1}^{N_{WG}} C_R + C_P \tag{9}$$

C_R and C_P defined by $C_{Rw} + P_w j(t) - (P_{wr} j(t) - \alpha V)$, $C_{Pw} + ((P_w j(t) - \alpha V) - P_{wr} j(t))$ represent the reserve cost function and penalty cost function of wind power generation respectively. Reserve cost function helps to determine the debit that can be produced from the probability distribution function of variable wind speed [8, 21]. The probability distribution function for the power output of variable wind in the range of ($v_i \leq v \leq v_r$) can be determined by:

$$f_{pw} = \frac{K_{rvi}}{P_{wc}} \left[\frac{1 + \frac{h_{Pw}(v_t)}{P_{wr}}}{C} \right]^{K-1} x e^{\left[\frac{h_{Pw}(v_t)}{P_{wr}} \right]_K} \tag{10}$$

Where K and C are Weibull probability distribution factors.

$$K = \left(\frac{\sigma}{v_m}\right)^{-1.086} \tag{11}$$

$$C = \frac{V_m}{T(1 + \frac{1}{K})} \tag{12}$$

Solar PV: the solar power output that can be extracted from a given solar irradiance G is [14, 22]:

$$P_{sg}j(t) = P_{sg}(G) = P_{sr}j\left(\frac{G^2}{G_{std} + R_{ca}}\right) \tag{13}$$

And its corresponding objective function is represented by $f_3(x)$

$$f_3(x) = C_s \sum_{i=1}^{N_{sg}} P_{sg}j(t) + \sum_{t=1}^{24} \sum_{i=1}^{N_{sg}} C_R + C_P \tag{14}$$

Where for $0 < G < R$ ca:

$$P_{sg}j(t) = \sum_{t=1}^{24} \sum_{i=1}^{N_{sg}} (C_R + C_P) \tag{15}$$

C_R and C_P defined by $C_{RS} + P_S j(t) - (P_{Sr}j(t) - \alpha V)$, $C_{PS} + ((P_S j(t) - \alpha V) - P_{Sr}j(t))$ represent the reserve cost function and penalty cost function of solar PV generation respectively. Reserve cost function helps to determine the debit produced from the probability distribution function of variable solar radiation. The probability distribution function for the power output of variable solar irradiance can also be determined using Weibull probability distribution function [23, 24].

Thermal: Despite the difference in their constraints, renewable energy sources adapted from thermal power plants have similar objective function [24, 25]. REs adapted from thermal power plant considered in this study include geothermal power plants, solar thermal power plants, biomass and waste to energy plants.

$$f_4(x) = C_{th} \sum_{i=1}^{N_{th}} P_{th}j(t) \left[\alpha_1 \sum_{i=1}^{N_{Gth}} F_{Gth} P_{Gth} + \alpha_2 \sum_{i=1}^{N_{Sth}} F_{Sth} P_{Sth} + \alpha_3 \sum_{i=1}^{N_{Bth}} F_{Bth} P_{Bth} \right] \tag{16}$$

Where

$$F_{th} = a_i P_{th}^2 + b_i P_{th} + c_i \tag{17}$$

$$F_{Gth} = a_i P_{Gth}^2 + b_i P_{Gth} + c_i \tag{18}$$

$$F_{Sth} = a_i P_{Sth}^2 + b_i P_{Sth} + c_i \tag{19}$$

$$F_{Bth} = a_i P_{Bth}^2 + b_i P_{Bth} + c_i \tag{20}$$

3.2 Constraint Formulation

In power systems, continuously respected operation constraints and limits ensure a reliable and secure operation of the system.

1. Demand and generation balance

$$P_D + P_L = \sum_{i=1}^{N_{hgg}} P_{hg} + \sum_{i=1}^{N_{wg}} P_{wg} + \sum_{i=1}^{N_{sg}} P_{sg} + \sum_{i=1}^{N_{th}} P_{th} \tag{21}$$

2. Generation limits

$$P_i^{\min} \leq P_i \leq P_i^{\max} \tag{22}$$

$$P_{\min} \leq 0.00981 \eta_i H_{ij} Q_{ij} \leq P_{\max} \tag{23}$$

$$0 \leq P_w j(t) \leq P_{wr} \tag{24}$$

$$0 \leq P_s j(t) \leq P_{sr} \tag{25}$$

$$0 \leq P_h j(t) \leq P_{hr} \tag{26}$$

3. Prohibited operating zones

$$P_i^{\min} \leq P_i \leq P_i^{Lj} \forall j = 1, 2 \ldots N_{Poz} \tag{27}$$

$$P_i^{V_j - 1} \leq P_i \leq P_i^{lj} \tag{28}$$

$$P_i^{V_J - 1} \leq P_i \leq P_i^{\max} \tag{29}$$

4. Transmission constraints: For transmission constraints Kron's loss equation is considered

$$P_L = \sum_{i=1}^{n} \sum_{j=1}^{m} P_{gi} B_{ij} P_{gj} = B_{oo} + \sum_{i=1}^{n} B_{io} P_{gi} + \sum_{i=1}^{n} \sum_{j=1}^{m} P_{gi} B_{ij} P_{gj} \tag{30}$$

Where

$$B_{ij} = \frac{\cos(\theta_i - \theta_j) R_{ij}}{\cos \phi_i \cos \phi_j V_i V_J} \tag{31}$$

$$B_{oo} = \sum_{i=1}^{n} \sum_{j=1}^{m} P_{Di} B_{ij} P_{Dj} \tag{32}$$

$$B_{ij} = -\sum_{j=1}^{m} \left(B_{ij} + B_{ji} \right) \tag{33}$$

5. Security limits

$$S_1 \leq S_1^{\max} \forall l = 1, 2 \ldots N_L \tag{34}$$

$$\phi_j P(t) > o \forall j = 1, 2 \ldots N_C \tag{35}$$

6. Generator ramp rate limits

$$\max(P_i^{\min}, P_i^{t-1} - DR_i) \leq P_i(t) \leq \min(P_i^{\max}, P_i^{t-1} + DR_i) \tag{36}$$

7. Spinning reserve limits

$$\sum_{i=1}^{N_G} S_{Ri} \geq S_{Sr} \tag{37}$$

8. Water discharge and reservoir limits:

$$X_i^{\min} \leq X_i \leq X_i^{\max} \tag{38}$$

$$V_i^{\min} \leq V_i \leq V_i^{\max} \tag{39}$$

$$Q_i^{\min} \leq Q_{ij} \leq Q_j^{\max} \tag{40}$$

$$V_i^{\min} \leq V_{ij} \leq V_j^{\max} \tag{41}$$

$$V_{i,j+1} = V_{ij} - (Q_{ij} - q_i + S_{ij})\Delta t + \sum_{K \in K_j} \left(Q_{ij} + S_{kij} + I_j \right)\Delta t \tag{42}$$

9. Renewable energy penetration rate constraints

$$P_w j(t) + P_s j(t) + P_h j(t) + P_{th} j(t) \leq \Psi P_D \tag{43}$$

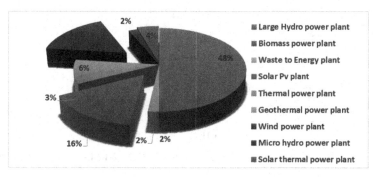

Fig. 2. Considered energy share of RES adopted from modified IEEE 118 bus system zone 2&3

Constraint (9) considers thermal (biomass, solar-thermal, geothermal), hydro, wind, and solar PV penetration ratios, ψ. And their energy share adopted from Ethiopian energy system according to editing and adopting features of NREL IEEE 118 bus system zones is given in the figure below [13, 26] (Fig. 2).

Hasnae Bilil et al. [27] formulated a multi-objective problem that allows optimization of both the annualized renewable energy cost and the system reliability defined as the renewable energy load disparity (RELD) considering the lack of energy as well as the exceed weighted by a penalty factor. The instability created by the integration of variable renewable energy sources made SCED a complex optimization problem [28]. Regarding wind energy penetration, several methods have been used to solve this problem [29]. Stephen Frank et al. [11] generally gives state of the art, recent developments and future trends of power flow and examines the recent trend towards stochastic, or non-deterministic, search techniques and hybrid methods for OPF.

4   Case Studies and Solution Methods

Many researchers use case study/test system databases for a number of important areas of power systems operations and planning, including unit commitment, economic dispatch, optimized allocation of distributed generation, fault detection [26]. However, there are a number of fundamental limitations associated with many current test systems, such as considering only very brief periods, having generally smaller systems than those seen in practice, and other aspects that make many practitioners view them as unrealistic [26]. For this limitations research facilities are intensively improving, updating and deploying state of the art test systems including modified IEEE 118 bus system and modified New England 39 Bus system (Fig. 3, Table 1).

NREL-118 test system, using the transmission representation of the IEEE 118-bus test system best suits for high penetration of renewable energy sources. NREL-118 system includes information, which is currently not included in other public IEEE bus test systems. These are detailed generation constraints(upward/downward ramping, minimum generation level, minimum up/downtimes, heat rate and fuel use at different load levels, start and shutdown costs) and time-synchronous yearlong actual and day-ahead forecast time series for wind and solar power as well as regional electricity load [26].

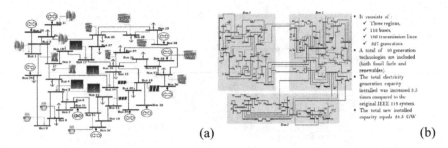

Fig. 3. (a) Modified New England 39 Bus system [13] (b). NREL-118test system [26]

Table 1. Data sources and usage

Test system	Data source	Ref	Details
Modified New England 39-Bus System	• Illinois center for a smarter electric grid(ICSEG), • Dynamic IEEE test systems, • Eelectric grid test repository,	[13]	• https://icseg.iti.illinois.edu/ieee-39-bus-system/, • https://www.kios.ucy.ac.cy/testsystems/index.php/dynamic-ieee-test-systems/ieee-39-bus-modified-test-system, • https://electricgrids.engr.tamu.edu/electric-grid-test-cases/new-england-ieee-39-bus-system/
NREL IEEE-118 bus system	• NREL: transforming energy • Electric grid test repository • U.S. Department of Energy Office of Scientific Technical Information	[26]	• https://www.nrel.gov/news/program/2016/21643.html • https://electricgrids.engr.tamu.edu/electric-grid-test-cases/ieee-118-bus-system/ • https://www.osti.gov/biblio/1416258-extended-ieee-bus-test-system-high-renewable-penetration
Ethiopian renewable energy system[1]	• Energypedia • Export gov	[1]	• https://energypedia.info/wiki/Ethiop_Energy_Situation • https://www.export.gov/article?id=Ethiopia-Energy

Ethiopian renewable energy system is not a complete test system. It has been adopted in this study so that its economic dispatch can be tested within zones that exhibit full and complete dispatch data set.

In this study, the modified IEEE 118 bus system modified New England 39 Bus system and Ethiopian renewable energy systems were selected case studies with high renewables penetration features to consider security levels and credible contingencies. The solution method employed to solve this optimization problem emanates from its problem formulation and it is multi-objective multivariable optimization method. DIGSILENT Power factory and MATLAB/MATPOWER 6.0 simulation tools were used.

5   Results and Discussions

The results of SCED for RES obtained from DIGSILENT power factory and MATLAB are presented below.

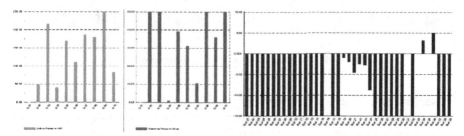

Fig. 4. Active and reactive power dispatch, voltage and power angle deviation of New England 39 Bus system with no RES

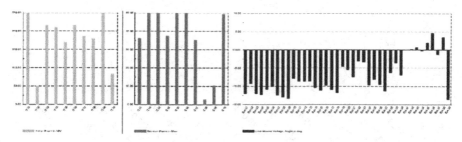

Fig. 5. Active /reactive power dispatch, voltage & power angle deviation of modified New England 39 Bus system with RES

Figures 4 and 5present the effect of RES penetration to a conventional New England 39 bus system. Dig silent for identifying the challenges posed to power grid due to

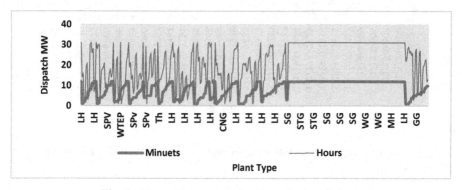

Fig. 6. Generation cost in an hourly and minutely basis

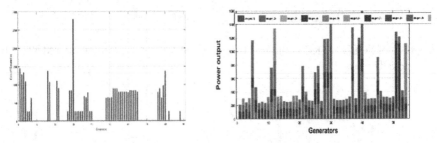

Fig. 7. Power generation dispatch of the involved RES

renewables entry is used. It clearly shows the effect of demand –supply affecting the power angle and voltage. This part of the study is challenging to carry out on MATLAB.

Figures 6 and 7 depict the energy share of RES including which type of energy address which dispatch and time it takes to complete the task. The power dispatch challenges such as duck curve can be overcome using RES.

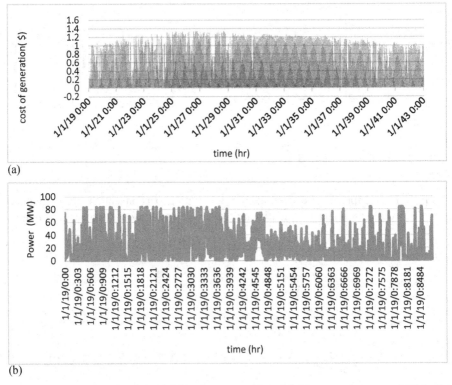

Fig. 8. (a).Generation dispatch of Ethiopian renewables and (b) generation cost of Ethiopian energy systems

Figure 8 presents Cost of energy generation per kWh in properly regulated energy markets and power dispatch of Ethiopian power system of selected renewable energy conversion technologies.

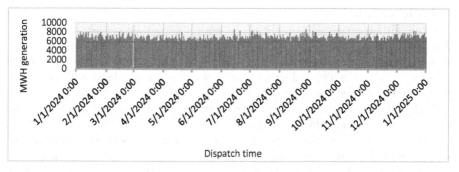

Fig. 9. Daily MWh generation dispatch

Figure 9 presents the total MWH dispatch of the RESs for NREL 118 bus system.

Table 2. Multi-variable multi-objective simulation results

Gen	Plant Type	MVMO solution	Gen	Plan Type	MVMO solution
	Hydro	12.65	34	Solar	12.16
4	Hydro	11.28	36	wind	10.3
6	Hydro	17.84	40	wind	14.18
8	Hydro	21.38	42	wind	15
10	Hydro	258.86	46	Geothermal	75
12	Hydro	95.76	49	Hydro	110
15	Solar	15	54	Solar	40.82
18	Solar	15	55	wind	13.14
19	Wind	12.5	56	Geothermal	14.52
24	Wind	10	59	Hydro	157.26
25	Hydro	289.98	61	Thermal	41.92
26	Hydro	421.8	62	wind	11.82
27	Waste	13.7	65	Hydro	400
31	Thermal	43.1	66	Hydro	120
32	Biomass	11.02	69	Hydro	525
Cost		1279.17		Cost ($/hr)	1601.26
P_L		14.382		P_L	19.605

Table 2 Presents the results of selected generating units comprising different types of plants. Indicating where the RES are situated, it also shows the economic cost and power transmission loss considering credible contingencies and uncertainties.

6 Conclusions

This paper presents Security Constrained Economic Dispatch (SCED) of renewable energy systems (RES). Reformulation of SCED for RES comprising biomass, large and small hydro, solar PV, and solar thermal, waste to energy plant, wind farm, and geothermal was carried out.

Each of these sources requires problem formulation and constraint handling mechanisms that consider credible contingencies. Modified IEEE 118 bus system (NREL-118test system), modified New England 39-Bus system and Ethiopian renewable energy systems with high penetration of RES were used as case studies. Modeling and simulation was conducted on MATLAB/MATPOER, and DIGSILENT power factory simulation platforms.

According to the simulation results, it can be deduced that economic dispatch of RES with their security constraints is a promising step towards the realization of smart and modern grid operation. As part of future work, it is recommend a hybrid computational intelligence based optimization method for SCED of integrated renewable energy sources.

References

1. Tikuneh, M.A., Worku, G.B.: Identification of system vulnerabilities in the Ethiopian electric power system. Glob. Energy Interconnect **1**(3), 358–365 (2018)
2. Mondal, M.A.H., Bryan, E., Ringler, C., Mekonnen, D., Rosegrant, M.: Ethiopian energy status and demand scenarios: prospects to improve energy efficiency and mitigate GHG emissions. Energy **149**, 161–172 (2018)
3. Santhosh, A., Farid, A.M., Youcef-Toumi, K.: Real-time economic dispatch for the supply side of the energy-water nexus. Appl. Energy **122**, 42–52 (2014)
4. Wang, Q.: "Risk-based security-constrained optimal power flow: mathematical fundamentals, computational strategies, validation, and use within electricity markets by Qin Wang A dissertation submitted to the graduate faculty in partial fulfillment of the requirem" (2013)
5. Zhu, D., Hug-Glanzmann, G.: "Decomposition methods for stochastic optimal coordination of energy storage and generation". In: IEEE Power & Energy Society General Meeting, vol. 2014-Octob, no. October, pp. 1–5 (2014)
6. Goos, G., et al.: LNCS 6145 - Advances in Swarm Intelligence.
7. Jihane, K., Cherkaoui, M.: Economic dispatch optimization for system integrating renewable energy sources. In: AIP Conference Proceedings, vol. 1968 (2018)
8. Biswas, P.P., Suganthan, P.N., Qu, B.Y., Amaratunga, G.A.J.: Multiobjective economic-environmental power dispatch with stochastic wind-solar-small hydro power. Energy **150**(April), 1039–1057 (2018)
9. Jin, X., et al.: Security-constrained economic dispatch for integrated natural gas and electricity systems. Energy Procedia **88**, 330–335 (2016)
10. Frank, S., Steponavice, I., Rebennack, S.: Optimal power flow : a bibliographic survey i formulations and deterministic methods. Energy Syst. **3**, pp. 221–258 (2012)

11. Frank, S., Steponavice, I., Rebennack, S.: Optimal power flow: a bibliographic survey II: non-deterministic and hybrid methods. Energy Syst. **3**(3), 259–289 (2012). https://doi.org/10.1007/s12667-012-0057-x

12. Chamanbaz, M., Dabbene, F., Lagoa, C.: AC optimal power flow in the presence of renewable sources and uncertain loads, February, 2017

13. Ciornei, I.: Novel Hybrid Optimization Methods for the Solution of the Economic Dispatch of Generation in Power Systems (2011)

14. ElDesouky, A.A.: Security and stochastic economic dispatch of power system including wind and solar resources with environmental consideration. Int. J. Renew. Energy Res. **3**(4), 951–958 (2013)

15. Augustine, N., Suresh, S., Moghe, P., Sheikh, K.: Economic dispatch for a microgrid considering renewable energy cost functions. In: 2012 IEEE PES Innovative Smart Grid Technologies ISGT 2012, pp. 1–7 (2012)

16. Murali, M., Sailaja Kumari, M., Sydulu, M.: A genetic algorithm based security constrained economic dispatch approach for LMP calculation. Int. J. Energy Sci. **3**(2), 116–126 (2013). www.ijesci.org

17. Salcedo-Sanz, S., Yao, X.: A hybrid Hopfield network-genetic algorithm approach for the terminal assignment problem. IEEE Trans. Syst. Man Cybern. Part B Cybern. **34**(6), 2343–2353 (2004)

18. Mumtaz, F., Bayram, I.S.: Planning, operation, and protection of microgrids: an overview. Energy Procedia **107**(June), 94–100 (2017)

19. Weibezahn, J., Kendziorski, M.: Illustrating the benefits of openness: a large-scale spatial economic dispatch model using the Julia language. Energies **12**(6), 1153 (2019). https://doi.org/10.3390/en12061153

20. Moreno, S.R., Kaviski, E.: Daily scheduling of small hydro power plants dispatch with modified particles swarm optimization. Pesqui. Oper. **35**(1), 25–37 (2015)

21. Cheng, W., Zhang, H.: A dynamic economic dispatch model incorporating wind power based on chance constrained programming. Energies **8**(1), 233–256 (2015)

22. Suresh, V., Sreejith, S.: Economic dispatch and cost analysis on a power system network interconnected with solar farm. Int. J. Renew. Energy Res. **5**(4), 1098–1105 (2015)

23. Ferris, M.: "Modeling and Computation of Security-constrained Economic Dispatch with Multi-stage Rescheduling Power generation, transmission and distribution Determine generators' output to reliably meet the load," pp. 1–31 (2014)

24. Brini, S., Abdallah, H.H., Ouali, A.: Economic dispatch for power system included wind and solar thermal energy. Leonardo J. Sci. **8**(14), 204–220 (2009)

25. E. T. H. No, D. O. F. Sciences, E. T. H. Zurich, and E. T. H. Zurich, "ii c 2013 Maria Vrakopoulou All Rights Reserved," vol. 6, no. 237 (2013)

26. Pena, I., Brancucci, C., Hodge, B.M.: An extended IEEE 118-bus test system with high renewable penetration. IEEE Trans. Power Syst. **8950**, 281–289 (2017)

27. Bilil, H., Aniba, G., Maaroufi, M.: Multiobjective optimization of renewable energy penetration rate in power systems. Energy Procedia **50**, 368–375 (2014)

28. Xia, X., Elaiw, A.M.: Optimal dynamic economic dispatch of generation: a review. Electr. Power Syst. Res. **80**(8), 975–986 (2010)

29. Natsheh, E.M.: "Hybrid Power Systems Energy Management Based on Artificial Intelligence," PHD Thesis, vol. PHD Thesis, no. July, 2013

Wind Power Potential Estimation by Using the Statistical Models-Adama, Ethiopia

Endalew Ayenew[1]([✉]) [iD], Getachew Biru[2] [iD], Asrat Mulatu[1] [iD],
and Santoshkumar Hampannavar[3] [iD]

[1] Center of Excellence for Sustainable Energy, College of Electrical and Mechanical Engineering, Addis Ababa Science and Technology University, Addis Ababa, Ethiopia
asrat.mulat@aastu.edu.et

[2] Electrical Power and Control Engineering, School of Electrical Engineering and Computing, Adama Science and Technology University, Adama, Ethiopia

[3] School of Electrical and Electronics Engineering, REVA University, Bangalore, India

Abstract. This paper is aimed to statistically estimate wind power that can be converted to electrical power. It is important to have an inclusive fact of wind phenomena to efficiently plan the generation of power from the wind. To estimate wind power potential, this paper includes daily average wind speeds, monthly average wind speeds, and related wind power density, and frequency distribution based on wind speed probability frequency, Weibull and Rayleigh distributions. The two parameters for Weibull distribution were found out using data from the Adama wind farm site. The yearly average wind power densities for wind velocity frequency distribution, the Weibull distribution, and the Rayleigh distribution models 412 W/m^2, 370 W/m^2, and 532 W/m^2 respectively were estimated using wind speed statistics of the 2018 year at the ADAMA wind farm site. The value of estimated wind power density by Rayleigh distribution models is equivalent to maximum power density of the site. The result of this study shows that the selected site has utility-scale potential wind power.

Keywords: Rayleigh probability distribution · Weibull probability distribution · Wind power estimation

1 Introduction

The wind is a global recognized potential source of energy. It is important to have comprehensive facts of the wind phenomenon to efficiently plan the generation of power from the wind plants. This study is aimed to statistically evaluate wind power potential at the Adama wind farm site in Ethiopia. In Ethiopia due to a quick increment in the demand for energy utilization for development, there is a fast decline of natural energy sources like biomass. It needs to give attention to wind energy assessment and then capture utilizable energy from it. According to the statistics that were mentioned [1]; Ethiopia has a wind energy potential capacity of about 18.7 GW at the wind velocity of 7.5 to 8.8 m/s at 50 m height above the ground. Wind power potential capacity of

M. A. Delele et al. (Eds.): ICAST 2020, LNICST 384, pp. 376–388, 2021.
https://doi.org/10.1007/978-3-030-80621-7_27

Ethiopia is also indicated by [2]. That is the total national wind energy potential for grid connectable electricity from wind is about 100 GW. This can be captured from 20,000 square kilometers estimated land part of the country. Therefore, based on this information and energy needs, Ethiopia plans to generate 7 GW electricity from wind farms by 2030. Globally the wind energy contribution was reached 600 GW in 2018 [3].

Wind resources assessments are the basis for identifying and realizing the potential site of qualified wind energy and mitigating related risks. This was depicted by Premono B. S et al. [4] focusing on the recital of wind turbines. Power in the wind is related to the cube of the wind velocity. A 10% variation in wind velocity creates about 33% changes in wind power. Such fact is one of the main motivations to carry out wind resource appraisal. The other reason is variation in wind speed; wind shears causes great unpredictable loads that creating fatigue on the wind turbine blades since the blades run in regions of variant wind velocity. Turbulence causes dynamic loads on wind turbines. This paper focused to address the first point using resource assessments such as daily mean wind velocities, monthly average wind velocities, and related wind power density using wind pace frequency model, and Weibull and Rayleigh models. To evaluate a specific site's wind power capacity, wind speed occurrence has to be used as a scaling factor of an envoy wind turbine power curve. Wind class of the selected place is categorized using wind power density with average wind speed [2, 5] of a considered wind site. Theoretically expected wind power to be harvested from the selected site and related parameters were formulated by Altunkaynak et al. [6] considering variations in wind speed. More emphases have been carried on wind power estimation using mixture distribution [7–9].

The next parts of this paper are comprised of four sections; Theoretical Background of Statistical Models for Wind Data Analysis, method, Result and Discussion, and Conclusion.

2 Theoretical Background of Statistical Models for Wind Estimation

In the implementation of wind energy assessment and harvesting, the selected wind farm site is characterized by many statistical models. Wind energy resource potential site and estimation of its power generation capacity can be carried out using different statistical models. In the execution of the selected statistical model, the availability of varying measured wind velocity data at a specific height of that site is required. Using this data, the commonly accepted statistical models such as wind speed incidence distribution, the Weibull distribution, and the Rayleigh distribution were implemented and analyzed the data. The probability (likelihood) density and cumulative distribution functions of these models with their plots were employed. The wind power density at any wind speed in the selected site over the sampling period is stated by the expression [10]

$$\frac{p}{A} = p(v) = \frac{1}{2}\rho.v^3 f(v) \tag{1}$$

For ρ is the density of air in kg/m^3, P/A is in W/m^2 for A is swept area; an average wind power density $\overline{P}$ in the selected site is

$$\overline{p} = \int_0^\infty p(v).dv \tag{2}$$

For f(v) in Eq. (1) describes frequency appearance of random wind velocity (v), this can be wind speed frequency likelihood density, Weibull's probability density, or Rayleigh's probability density.

2.1 Weibull Distribution and Rayleigh Distribution Functions for Wind Power Estimation

To carry out wind energy resource capacity appraisal, two parameters Weibull probability density function which has been widely used in documents [7, 11] is described by (3) for v, b and a are wind velocity, scale factor in m/s and unit less shape factor respectively, and are greater than zero.

$$f(v) = \frac{a}{b}\left(\frac{v}{b}\right)^{a-1} \exp\left(-\left(\frac{v}{b}\right)^a\right) \tag{3}$$

The Weibull cumulative distribution function is also described in [11, 12] is

$$F(v) = \int_0^v f(v)dv = 1 - \exp\left(-\left(\frac{v}{b}\right)^a\right) \tag{4}$$

Based on a value of shape parameter, Weibull distribution is related to different other probability distribution functions; particularly for $a = 2$, it becomes Rayleigh distribution for the scale parameter can be set equal to average wind speed.

The Rayleigh distribution model is the easiest wind speed probability distribution function to represent the wind energy potential or possible resource. To describe this function the mean wind pace is considered as a scaling factor. Rayleigh probability density and its cumulative distribution functions are respectively described [11, 13] as shown below.

$$f(v) = \frac{\pi}{2}\left(\frac{v}{v_{mn}^2}\right) \exp\left(-\frac{\pi}{4}\left(\frac{v}{v_{mn}}\right)^2\right) \tag{5}$$

For v_{mn} is a statistical mean wind speed of sample data.

$$F(v) = 1 - \exp\left(-\frac{\pi}{4}\left(\frac{v}{v_{mn}}\right)^2\right) \tag{6}$$

Weibull Distribution Parameters Determination. There are several techniques to evaluate the shape factor and scale factor in Weibull distribution using real-time wind data. The frequently used techniques are the graphical, moment, maximum likelihood, the least square regression, energy pattern factor, and the standard deviation methods [11, 13–16]. For this study, the energy pattern factor technique (EPF) was used in finding the Weibull distribution parameters. EPF is described as the average of the cube of each wind pace measured at considered height and site divided by the cube of the average speed of wind of the whole data [17, 18]. That is the division of power density exists in the wind to the power associated with the cube of average wind speed. EPF is formulated using per month mean wind power density (MMWPD) as follows. Per month mean power available in aerodynamic is

$$P = 0.5A\rho \sum_{i=0}^{n} \frac{v_i^3}{n} \tag{7}$$

$$MMWPD = \frac{P}{A} = 0.5\rho \sum_{i=0}^{n} \frac{v_i^3}{n} \tag{8}$$

For v_i is daily mean wind speed in the sample measured at instant i day, and n is total days in the month. The cube of statistical mean wind speed (V_{mn}) is

$$v_{mn}^3 = \left[\sum_{i=1}^{n} v_{\frac{i}{n}} \right]^3 \tag{9}$$

Then the energy pattern factor is

$$EPF = \frac{\sum_1^n \frac{v_i^3}{n}}{\left[\sum_1^n v_{\frac{i}{n}} \right]^3} = \frac{MMWPD/0.5\rho}{v_{mn}^3} \tag{10}$$

According to [19, 20] the shape and scaling factors of Weibull distribution are described as

$$\alpha = 1 + \frac{3.69}{EPF^2} \tag{11}$$

$$b = \frac{v_{mn}}{\Gamma(1 + 1/a)} \tag{12}$$

Where the gamma function was expressed as

$$\Gamma(a) = \int_0^\infty x^{a-1} e^{-x} dx \tag{13a}$$

$$\Gamma(1 + a) = a\Gamma(a) \tag{13b}$$

The Weibull scale parameter can be calculated by applying the following relation [21].

$$b = \frac{v_{mn}.a^{2.6674}}{0.184 + 0.816.a^{2.78855}} \tag{14}$$

Available Wind Power Density Estimation by Weibull and Rayleigh Models. Using the Weibull parameters those were already found, meaningful powers available in the wind such as most likely wind power and highest wind power at the selected site and height are estimated. These two powers associated with the most likely wind speed and the wind speed that carrying maximum power respectively. The most likely wind speed (V_{mps}) is a most repeated wind speed used in selected the probability distribution and its expression [11, 21] was given as

$$V_{mps} = b\left(\frac{a-1}{a}\right)^{\frac{1}{a}} \tag{15}$$

The expression for wind speed that carries the highest power (V_{maxp}) is

$$V_{maxp} = b\left(\frac{a+2}{a}\right)^{\frac{1}{a}} \tag{16}$$

The unit of V_{mps} and V_{maxp} is m/s. The most frequent power density (P_{fpd}) and maximum power density (P_{mpd}) are good indications of the amount of power available on the site. These power densities can be manipulated by substituting Eq. (15) and Eq. (16) in to Eq. (17) for v is V_{mps} or V_{maxp}.

$$P_{fpd} = 0.5\rho V_{mps}^3 \tag{17}$$

$$P_{mpd} = 0.5\rho V_{maxp}^3 \tag{18}$$

Applying the Weibull and Rayleigh model, the average power density available at the selected site can be manipulated by substituting Eq. (12) in to Eq. (17) for V_{mps} equal to V_{mn} and in m/s. The mean power density for the Weibull model (P_{we}/A) is described as

$$\frac{P_{we}}{A} = 0.5\rho V_{mn}^3 = 0.5\rho b^3 \Gamma\left(1 + \frac{3}{a}\right) \tag{19}$$

In the case of Rayleigh model, the Weibull shape parameter was set to 2 with scale parameter is equal with V_{mn}, average power density in the wind (P_R/A) was described as

$$\frac{P_R}{A} = \frac{3}{\pi}\rho V_{mn}^3 = \frac{3}{\pi}\rho b^3 \tag{20}$$

2.2 Wind Power Density Estimation Based on the Wind Speed Frequency Distribution

The wind pace frequency distribution likelihood density function was derived as follows.

$$f(v_i) = \frac{freq_i}{\sum_{i=1}^{n} freq_i} \tag{21}$$

For *freq$_i$* is the number of wind pace occurrences in each bin and i = 1, 2,..., n is bin number. Monthly mean wind speed is

$$V_{mn} = \sum_{i=1}^{n} v_{mni} \cdot f(v_i) \qquad (22)$$

V$_{mni}$ is the average wind speed of each bin. Monthly mean power density (P_{fd}/A) based on wind speed probability distribution is formulated by

$$\frac{P_{fd}}{A} = \sum_{i=1}^{n} [\frac{1}{2}\rho \cdot (v_{mni})^3 \cdot f(v_i)] \qquad (23)$$

3   Method

Real wind speed data measurement was gathered for a year at the ADAMA farm site. The real-time series data was obtained from Ethiopia Electric Power. This site is geographically located at the latitude of 8° 18′ 35.5″N, the longitude of the 38° 53′ 4.2″E and elevation of 1712 m above sea level in Ethiopia about 95 km far away to the south of Addis Ababa. Data were collected at 10 m above ground. At this site, a steady atmosphere density of 1.2 kg/m³ was considered. Wind speed samples were collected using a WICOM-32 data logger (wind computer). Data is logged every 600 s or 10 min. In 24 h or a day WICOM-32 data logger stores 144 samples of average wind speed, highest wind speed, lowest wind, and standard deviance in m/s and wind direction in degree. One sample measurement is 7.2, 11.6, 3.5, 1.6, 85°. The statically daily mean wind speeds for twelvemonth were processed using Microsoft Excel and Matlab. All other wind speed statistics and statistical estimation of wind power were done using daily mean wind speeds.

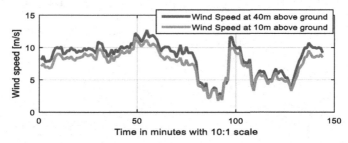

Fig. 1. Real-time wind speed profiles on January 1st, 2018 every 10-min wind pattern.

Real time-series wind speed data on the first day of January 2018 has been indicated in Fig. 1. The data was gathered at 10 m and 40 m height which fluctuates in the range of 6–14 m/s, and 12–17 m/s correspondingly. This indicates a variation of wind pace in space and time. Daily fluctuating wind speed in January, March, and September of the 2018 year was shown in Fig. 2. This gives information about daily wind patterns. In most of the durations in these months wind speed exceeds 4 m/s. From Fig. 2 it is clear that in January about 20–25% of the month, the wind velocity is varying between 7 and 10 m/s.

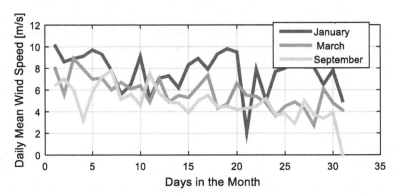

Fig. 2. Real-time wind speed profiles in January, March, and September of 2018 daily wind pattern

The wind pace direction was presented in Fig. 3 for wind incidence at a 10-m height above the ground at the Adama Wind Farm Station. In this Figure, WS, N, E, S, and W are represented wind speed (m/s), North (reference), East, South, and West directions respectively. Figure 3 indicated that yearly dominant wind was coming from ENE and West directions with a magnitude greater than 5 m/s.

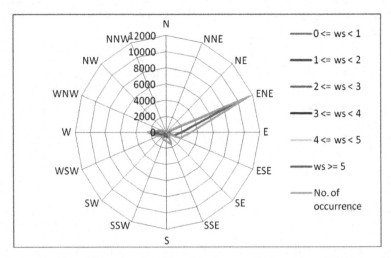

Fig. 3. Wind Speed Direction (wind Rose) in the year 2018 at Adama Wind Farm Site

4 Result and Discussion

The statistical mean wind speeds for twelvemonths and Weibull distribution parameters were calculated. Their values were tabulated in Table 1. In all cases mean speed exceeds 5.5 m/s. The standard wind turbine hub height is 50 m.

Table 1. Per month mean wind speed at 10-m height, two parameters of Weibull distribution function and gamma function value at Weibull distribution Shape factor for months in 2018

Month	Parameters						
	V_{mn}	EPF	a	b	V_{mps}	V_{maxp}	$\Gamma(1 + 3/a)$
January	7.7200	1.14	3.84	7.99	7.3900	8.9200	0.9300
February	7.2700	1.08	4.19	7.45	6.9800	8.1800	0.9100
March	5.7700	1.18	3.67	5.96	5.4700	6.7100	0.9400
April	5.5500	1.17	3.71	5.78	5.3100	6.4900	0.9300
May	5.7800	1.10	4.07	5.97	5.5700	6.5900	0.9200
June	6.8000	1.12	3.97	7.10	6.5300	7.7800	0.9200
July	7.1900	1.09	4.10	7.39	6.9000	8.1400	0.9100
August	6.8300	1.15	3.79	7.09	6.5400	7.9300	0.9300
September	5.0000	1.20	3.56	5.20	4.7400	5.9000	0.9400
October	5.7500	1.19	3.63	5.99	5.4800	6.7600	0.9400
November	7.8200	1.04	4.42	7.99	7.5300	8.6800	0.9100
December	7.6900	1.08	4.15	7.90	7.3900	8.6800	0.9200

The wind speed profile at this tallness can be approximately evaluated using the wind speed profile at 10 m height by applying power-law with a 0.2 shear factor. Because the ADAMA farm site is a terrain with small trees and crops. Hence, the mean wind speed will be 7.60 m/s. Other important results in Table 1 Weibull distribution parameters are manipulated by using the energy pattern factor method. In each month the size (scale) factor is greater than the shape (appearance) factor. Its value is near the value of average speed. The most likely wind speed, as well as the wind speed carrying the highest power, was found using the manipulated Weibull parameters. From Table 1 it was seen that most likely wind pace is less than mean wind pace whereas the wind pace that transports the highest power is greater than mean wind pace in all months. This indicates there is an opportunity to capture wind power greater than the mean value. These parameters in combination with the required gamma function value are used to find the power densities corresponding to most probable, maximum, Weibull, and Rayleigh models as the results are tabulated in Table 3.

For numerical examination of the selected site wind power capacity, real-time wind paces, which are presented in Fig. 1 and Fig. 2 were arranged in the frequency distribution as in Table 2. The January month wind speed (v_i) is clustered into bin classes as indicated

Table 2. January real-time wind pace in occurrence packet and probability density distributions based on wind speed probability density ($f(v_i)$), Weibull ($f_{we}(v_i)$), wind speed frequency distribution power density (P_{fd}/A) and Rayleigh ($f_{Ra}(v_i)$) functions.

Bin	Speed Range	V_{mni} (m/s)	$freq_i$	$f_{We}(v_i)$	$f_{Ra}(v_i)$	$f(v_i)$	V_{mn} (m/s)	P_{fd}/A (W/m^2)
1	0–1	0	0	0	0	0	0	0
2	1–2	2	1	0.0108	0.0614	0.0323	0.0677	0.35849
3	2–3	0	0	0	0	0	0	0
4	3–4	0	0	0	0	0	0	0
5	4–5	0	0	0	0	0	0	0
6	5–6	5.20	4	0.1170	0.1066	0.1290	0.6710	21.77156
7	6–7	6.40	3	0.1669	0.1055	0.0968	0.6194	30.44253
8	7–8	7.64	7	0.1822	0.0959	0.2258	1.7252	120.8364
9	8–9	8.45	8	0.1630	0.0865	0.2580	2.1807	186.8442
10	9–10	9.40	7	0.1180	0.0738	0.2258	2.1226	225.0615
11	10–11	10.2	1	0.0749	0.0627	0.0323	0.3290	41.07902
Sum			31	0.8328	0.5924	1	7.7155	626.40

in Table 2 second column. The average wind speed (V_{mni}) in each bin is in the third column. Observations or frequencies (freq) of each speed and corresponding probability distribution are listed in the fourth and seventh columns respectively. The fifth and sixth columns represent the values of Weibull and Rayleigh probability density at each speed. The highest monthly power density is found for the wind speed is flanked by 8 and 10 m/s. Considering the wind speed likelihood density ($f(v_i)$) function, the total monthly power density is 313.2 W/m^2. In this month, if a single unit wind turbine generator with a blade length of 37 m and 70 m hub height will be installed, 11.7 MW power can be obtained using the vertically extrapolated data which was measured at 10 m into the height of turbine hub applying power-law with the shear factor of 0.2. This is a good indication for Ethiopian to expand wind farm plants around the ADAMA wind farm site and hence conserve forest that is used for biomass to meet energy demand.

Figure 4 and Fig. 6 represent the likelihood density function of the Weibull model and the Rayleigh model respectively. From these statistical figures, it is clear that in all twelvemonths the means speed for the Weibull probability density distribution is shifted to the right side from statistical mean speed whereas in the case of the Rayleigh probability density distribution the means from the plot are around the statistical mean speed of each month wind speed. Figure 5 as well as Fig. 7, represents the cumulative distribution function of the Weibull model and the Rayleigh model respectively. In these figures, some of the plots were overlapped since the data in different months are closely the same. From the Weibull cumulative distribution plot and evaluating Eq. (4) with parameters in Table 1; it can be concluded that 60% of the data in the sample is more than the statistical mean wind speed for January month.

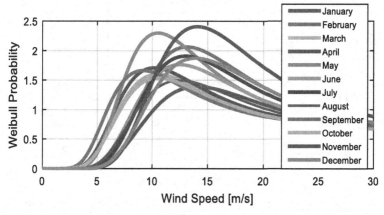

Fig. 4. ADAMA wind speed characteristic in 2018 by Weibull Probability Density function

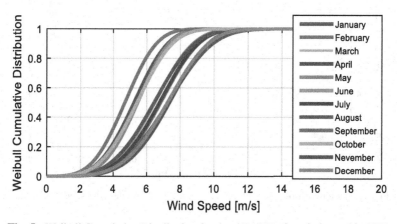

Fig. 5. Weibull Cumulative Distribution for the ADAMA site wind speed in 2018.

Similarly, from the Rayleigh cumulative distribution curve and evaluating Eq. (6) with parameters in the same Table, in January and February 54% of data is greater than the statistical mean wind speed. These hold for the whole data in the considered year.

Using available wind speed data with the implementation of the selected models, the values of mean wind power densities were evaluated. The results are tabulated in Table 3. These are the majority significant results that used in deciding whether the selected site wind power capacity is permissible or not. At this site in January, November, and December the power density was very large. In September, April, and October it was relatively lower than the power densities of other months. As indicated in Table 3, ADAMA wind farm site has 850 W/m^2, 814 W/m^2, 629 W/m^2, and 568 W/m^2 power densities for utmost extractable, by Rayleigh distribution model, wind pace frequency distribution model, and Weibull distribution model respectively in January 2018 at 10 m above the ground. The Rayleigh model provides relatively more power than the other models.

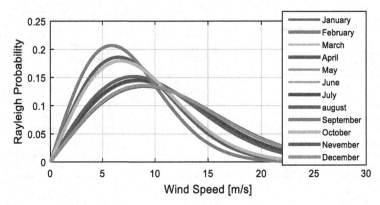

Fig. 6. ADAMA wind speed characteristic in 2018 by Rayleigh Probability Density function

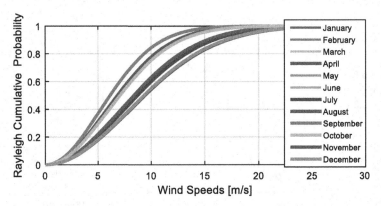

Fig. 7. Rayleigh Cumulative Distribution for ADAMA site wind speed in 2018.

For the results in Table 3, the annual average estimated power densities were calculated for most probable power density method, utmost power density approach, Rayleigh model, wind speed frequency distribution model, and Weibull model and the obtained values are $322 \, W/m^2$, $545 \, W/m^2$, $532 \, W/m^2$, $412 \, W/m^2$, and $370 \, W/m^2$ correspondingly. The estimated mean wind power density using the Rayleigh model is almost equivalent to this maximum power density for the Adama wind farm. The application of the Weibull model and wind speed frequency distribution model to estimate power in the selected wind farm site gave good results. As it was seen in Table 3 the results obtained by these three statistical models were between most probable power density and maximum power density which confirms and validates the adequacy of the result. It needs to compare the mean wind speeds in Table 1 and the power densities in Table 3 with wind class data as it was documented in [2, 5]. Hence, the Adama wind farm site is in an excellent wind class and suitable for wind energy harvesting.

Table 3. The average wind power densities, wind speed probability, Weibull and Rayleigh distributions; and corresponding most probable and maximum power densities for the twelve month at Adama wind farm site at 10 m above the ground in the year of 2018.

Month	Power densities (W/m^2)				
	P_{fd}/A	P_{we}/A	P_R/A	P_{fpd}	P_{mpd}
January	629.0000	568.0000	814.0000	484.0000	850.0000
February	494.4000	453.1000	660.4000	408.1000	656.6000
March	264.9000	238.1000	337.7600	195.9000	362.2000
April	240.5000	216.3000	304.1200	179.7000	328.1000
May	257.0000	234.0000	340.0000	207.0000	344.0000
June	420.0000	381.0000	552.0000	333.0000	564.0000
July	486.0000	442.0000	644.0000	394.0000	648.0000
August	438.8100	396.4100	568.1200	338.2100	598.4300
September	177.2600	159.2300	224.4300	128.5600	246.6600
October	268.0000	242.0000	342.0000	198.0000	370.0000
November	594.8100	551.4600	810.2100	512.3200	784.4000
December	584.54	546.3400	786.120	484.3000	784.760

5 Conclusion

The wind resource assessment includes daily average wind speeds, per month average wind speeds, wind power density, and frequency distribution based on wind speed probability frequency, Weibull and Rayleigh distributions. The wind paces were collected using the WICOM-32 data logger at the ADAMA wind farm site at 10 m above the ground. The two parameters for Weibull distribution were determined. The annual mean wind power densities, as a result, wind pace frequency distribution, Weibull distribution, and Rayleigh distribution models 412 W/m^2, 370 W/m^2, and 532 W/m^2 respectively were estimated in the year 2018. The estimated mean wind power density using the Rayleigh model is almost equivalent to this maximum power density for the Adama wind farm. For sthis site, the annual maximum harvestable power density is 545 W/m^2. Based on the collected data and its analysis the selected site is in the excellent wind class. It has utility-scale potential wind power. This is a good indication for Ethiopian to expand wind farm plants around the ADAMA wind farm site and hence conserve natural resources like biomass that most of the countryside communities use to meet energy demand.

References

1. Getechaw, B., Abdulfetah, A.: Investigation of wind farm interaction with Ethiopian electric power corporation's grid. Energy Procedia **14**, 1766–1773 (2012)
2. Ethiopian Rural Energy Development and Promotion Centre, Final Report- Solar and Wind Energy Utilization and project Development Scenarios 3–8 (2007)

3. Arthouros, Z.: Renewables 2019 Global Status Report, pp. 84–90 (2019)
4. Premono, B.S., Tjahjana, D.D.D.P., Hadi, S.: Wind energy potential assessment to estimate the performance of selected wind turbine in the northern coastal region of Semarang-Indonesia. In: ICESNANO AIP Conference Proceedings, vol. 1788, p. 030026 (2016). 030026-1–030026-10
5. Abdüsselam, A., Tarkan, E., Ismail, D., Zekai, S.: Theoretical derivation of wind power probability distribution function and applications. Appl. Energy **92**, 809–814 (2012)
6. Kwgdh, R., Kanthi, P.: Wind speed analysis and energy calculation based on mixture distribution in narakkalliya, Sir Lanka. J. Nat. Sci. Foundation Sri Lanka **44**(4), 409–416 (2016)
7. Carta, J.A., Ramírez, P.: Use of finite mixture distribution models in the analysis of wind energy in the Canarian Archipelago. Energy Convers. Manag. **48**(1), 281–291 (2007). https://doi.org/10.1016/j.enconman.2006.04.004
8. Kollu, R., Rayapudi, S.R., Narasimham, S.V.L., Pakkurthi, K.M.: Mixture probability distribution functions to model wind speed distributions. Int. J. Energy Environ. Eng. **3**(1), 1–10 (2012). https://doi.org/10.1186/2251-6832-3-27
9. Vaughn, N.: WIND ENERGY Renewable Energy and the Environment, 2nd ed., Taylor & Francis Group, LLC 67 (2014)
10. Dahmouni, A.W., Ben Salah, M., Askri F.F., Aloui, S., Ben, N.: Wind energy potential in the site of Borj-Cedria in Tunisia, CICME 08, pp. 101–108 (2008)
11. Sathyajith, M.: Wind Energy: Fundamentals Resource Analysis and Economics, pp. 68–84. Springer-Verlag, Berlin, Heidelberg (2006)
12. Chang, T.P.: Estimation of wind energy potential using different probability density functions. Appl. Energy **88**, 1848–1856 (2011)
13. Manwell, J.F., Mcgowan, J.G., Rogers, A.L.: Wind energy explained: Theory, Design and Application, pp. 55–65, 2nd edition. John Wiley & Sons Ltd., Hoboken (2009)
14. Chang, T.P.: Performance comparison of six numerical methods in estimating Weibull parameters for wind energy application. Appl. Energy **88**, 272–282 (2011)
15. John, T., Tony, W.: Renewable Energy Resources, 2nd edition, Taylor & Francis (2006)
16. Li, X.: Green Energy, Basic Concepts and Fundamentals, Springer-Verlag London Limited, Heidelberg (2011)
17. Seyit, A.A., Ali, D.: A new method to estimate Weibull parameters for wind energy applications. Energy Convers. Manage. **50**, 1761–1766 (2009)
18. Centre for Wind Energy Technology, Course material: Seventh international training course on wind turbine technology and applications, Chennai C-WET 3–26 (2011)
19. Rocha, P.A.C., de Sousa, R.C., de Andrade, C.F., da Silva, M.E.V.: Comparison of seven numerical methods for determining Weibull parameters for wind energy generation in the northeast region of Brazil. Appl. Energy **89**(1), 395–400 (2012). https://doi.org/10.1016/j.apenergy.2011.08.003
20. Anastasios, B., Dimitrios, C., Thodoris, D.K.: A nomogram method for estimating the energy produced by wind turbine generators. Sol. Energy **72**, 251–259 (2002)
21. Ahmed, S.A., Mahammed, H.O.: A Statistical Analysis of Wind Power Density Based on the Weibull and Rayleigh models of "Penjwen Region" Sulaimani/ Iraq, JJMIE, pp. 135–140 (2012)

Assessment of Solar Resource Potential for Photovoltaic Applications in East Gojjam Zone, Ethiopia

Engidaw Abel Hailu[1]($\boxtimes$), Amache Jara Godebo[1], Ghantasala Lakshmi Srinivasa Rao[1],
Ayodeji Olalekan Salau[2], Takele Ferede Agajie[1], Yayehyirad Ayalew Awoke[1],
and Tesfaye Mebrate Anteneh[1]

[1] Debre Markos University, P.O. Box 269, Debre Markos, Ethiopia
[2] Afe Babalola University, Ado Ekiti, Nigeria

Abstract. The primary challenge in choosing the right electrification approach across the globe is understanding the local energy resource potential. In this paper, the result of solar resource potential assessment of East Gojjam (EG) Zone, Ethiopia is presented. The solar insolation, an important parameter in designing and planning solar photovoltaic systems, at four meteorological stations of EG (viz. Debre Markos, Debrewerq, Mota and Yetnora) is estimated from sunshine hour and extraterrestrial radiation. The hour of bright sunshine data which covered eleven years has been collected from National Meteorological Agency Bahir Dar Branch. This data is prepared and used to estimate the solar insolation using a well-known linear Ångström-Prescott (A-P) model. The site-specific A-P model is adopted by using regression coefficients, 'a' and 'b', which are obtained from well-known empirical formulas. The empirical formulas were validated using the measured data from other sites in the region. The annual mean daily solar insolation (kWh/m^2/day) for Debre Markos, Debrewerq, Mota, and Yetnora is estimated to be 5.47, 7.05, 6.11, and 6.16, respectively. According to the monthly solar insolation profile, EG receives the highest and lowest solar insolation in April at Debrewerq and July at Debre Markos, respectively. The solar insolation profile at Debre Markos demonstrates a significant inconsistency while Debrewerq receives more uniform solar radiation throughout the year; and therefore, the later site is the most suitable for solar photovoltaic energy investments with a highest and more uniform clearness index profile throughout the year.

Keywords: Solar energy potential · East Gojjam · Sunshine hour · Solar insolation

1 Introduction

The energy supply of Ethiopia is mainly based on biomass while the rate of access to electricity services is one of the lowest in the world. Waste and biomass took a share of 91% of Ethiopia's energy supply, followed by petroleum (7%) and electric energy (2%).

M. A. Delele et al. (Eds.): ICAST 2020, LNICST 384, pp. 389–403, 2021.
https://doi.org/10.1007/978-3-030-80621-7_28

Electric energy is still enjoyed only by urban households and industries [1]. Meanwhile, with an average economic growth rate of 10.8%, the economy is one of the fastest-growing in the world. Moreover, the country has planned to achieve climate-friendly economic development until 2025 [2]. Ethiopia produces about 9TWh of electricity per year, 96% of which is from hydroelectric power plants and the remaining 4% is from wind and geothermal power plants [2]. About 83% of the country's citizens are living in remote rural areas which are either inaccessible to the central electricity grid system or not covered by grid extension to date. More than 95% of rural areas do not have access to electricity [1]. The rural residents still depend on firewood for cooking and heating and imported kerosene and solar lanterns for lighting uses. As a result, with a growing population, the consumption of firewood is rising with a consequence of deforestation leading to global warming and health-related problems. About 70% of health clinics and 76% of primary schools do not have access to electricity [3] which negatively affects health and education services. Nevertheless, to support rural development, rural households and institutions need to be supplied with adequate and reliable electric power [4].

By considering the socio-economic and environmental aspects, rural electrification policies should be formulated linking the efforts of the government and private sector. Data-driven policies and regulations need to be formulated to implement rural electrification approaches. Among the rural electrification approaches are grid extension, renewable or diesel generator based mini-grids, or solar home systems [4]. The choice of electrification approach depends on available energy resource potential and the feasibility of the technology [5, 6]. Planning and formulating sustainable energy policy which supports a sustainable economy by prioritizing the use of local resources and promoting energy independence requires high-quality renewable energy (RE) resource and other geographic information data [7–23]. Without detailed knowledge of the spatial and temporal distribution of RE data, it is hardly possible to make informed decisions ranging from policymaking, investment decisions, and power sector planning.

Determination of the RE potential like solar energy of a region requires that extensive measurements of high quality be made at a large number of stations covering the major climatic zones of the region [14]. The solar energy potential of any location expressed in the form of global horizontal solar radiation (also known as solar insolation or peak sun hours) in kWh/m^2 is the sun's radiant energy from all directions incident on a horizontal surface on earth of unit area. It is typically expressed daily for a given month. The solar insolation is an essential parameter for sizing solar energy and irrigation systems [24, 25]. The amount of solar insolation received at any location on earth depends on the time of the day, time of the year, the local latitude, weather conditions, and the orientation of the receiving surface [13, 14, 16, 21, 22].

Four techniques can be used to estimate the solar insolation of any location across the globe. These are direct in-situ measurements using pyranometer, satellite image data processing [16, 24], derivation of solar insolation from some other measured meteorological data, and extrapolation from nearby stations. In-situ measurement, though it is more expensive than any other method [5, 13, 16, 26, 27], provides the most reliable data. However, in Ethiopia, there are only a few meteorological stations in major cities (Addis Ababa, Dire Dawa, Gonder, Bahir Dar, Jimma and Wonji) that are equipped to measure solar radiation directly on the site [28, 37, 40]. Solar radiation data for any location in the world can be found from Surface Meteorology and Solar Energy (SSE/NASA), Solar and Wind Resource Assessment (SWERA), Photovoltaic Geographical Information System (PVGIS), SOLCAST data sets [31]. However, the data obtained from these datasets cannot be used reliably for detailed feasibility study and design as the data is interpolated or extrapolated from other regions of the world or evaluated from satellite image processing [23, 24]. Solar radiation can be obtained by conversion of readily available meteorological data such as sunshine hours, relative humidity, temperature, soil temperature, number of rainy days, altitude, latitude, total precipitable water, albedo, cloudiness, and evaporation. Authors in [11, 13, 16–19, 21, 26, 32, 33] have stated that conversion of sunshine hours into solar radiation is the most common method which has been utilized around the world where there are no solar radiation measurement facilities [14–17, 19–22, 24].

Varieties of empirical models has been developed to obtain solar radiation from other climatic parameters [13–17, 26, 33–35]. The linear Ångström-Prescott model is the most suitable and commonly utilized model to estimate solar insolation for any location from the extraterrestrial solar radiation, and the ratio of actual sunshine duration to the length of the day [17, 19, 22, 24, 28, 29, 33, 34, 36–43]. In the research work presented in [37], with the use of measured solar radiation data, it is proved that it is possible to use Ångström models to estimate solar radiation with minimal error. Authors in [38, 39] estimated the solar radiation from sunshine duration for rural areas in Southern and Northern Ethiopia by using the Ångström model. Regression coefficients of a = 0.33 and b = 0.43 are utilized for both regions. In another paper in [28], authors calculated regression coefficients from measured solar radiation and sunshine duration data for major cities and towns in Ethiopia where solar radiation measurement instruments are available, and showed different locations have different regression coefficients. Authors in [40] showed that regression constant 'a' is a cosine function of latitude while 'b' is more or less constant and proposed the use of location-specific regression constants to obtain reliable results. However, latitude, sunshine duration, and maximum day length are found important factors that determine constants 'a' and 'b' [14, 15, 19, 36, 41]. All these parameters are site-dependent [22]. However, if none of these data is available for estimation, it is possible to use values from nearby locations with similar climatological conditions [28, 32].

In this paper, monthly mean solar insolation for the four meteorological stations in East Gojjam is estimated from the relative sunshine duration and daily average extraterrestrial radiation by using regression constants, 'a' and 'b', derived from empirical formulas proposed by Samuel [16]. Sunshine duration also is known as hours of bright sunshine is the sum of all periods (in hours) during the day when the direct solar irradiance equals or exceeds 120 Wm^{-2} [19, 44]. Extraterrestrial radiation is the amount of solar radiation incident on a horizontal surface outside the earth's atmosphere; and it is obtained theoretically considering the seasonal variation of the distance between the earth and the sun [17–23, 32–34].

2 Study Area

East Gojjam Zone is one of the eleven political administrations in the Amhara Region, Ethiopia. It lies between 9.84°–11.24° North (N) latitudes and 37.05°–38.53° East (E) longitudes. Figure 1(a) shows the location of East Gojjam Zone in Ethiopia. With four town administrations and sixteen rural districts, East Gojjam Zone has twenty administrative regions. The population of East Gojjam Zone is estimated to reach 3.8 million. According to government reports, only 8% of the inhabitants of East Gojjam have access to electricity [45] which is far less than the country's average electricity access of 28% [2]. The primary sources of energy in the region are fuelwood for cooking and kerosene for lighting. In East Gojjam Zone, there are only four meteorological data measurement stations located at Debre Markos (10.33°N, 37.73°E), Debrewerq (10.66°N, 38.17°E), Mota (11.08°N, 37.88°E), and Yetnora (10.17°N, 38.12°E). Black dots in Fig. 1 indicate the location of the meteorological stations in East Gojjam. These stations are administered by National Metrological Agency (NMA) Bahir Dar Branch Office. The stations gather meteorological data like temperature, rainfall, wind speed and direction, sunshine duration, etc. and none of these stations can measure solar radiation as there are no measuring instruments. The estimation of solar insolation will be done for these meteorological stations.

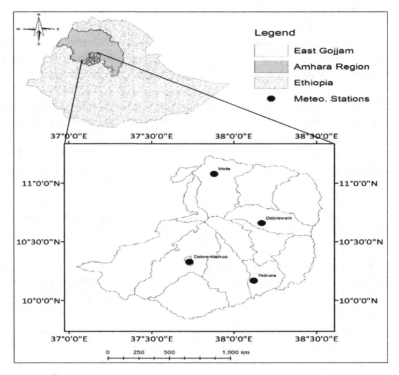

Fig. 1. Location of meteorological stations in East Gojjam Zone

3 Data and Methods

3.1 Data Collection and Preparation

The hours of bright sunshine data which covered eleven years (2008–2018) for the four meteorological stations have been obtained from National Meteorological Agency, Bahir Dar Branch. The daily hours of sunshine data are processed to obtain the monthly mean daily hours of bright sunshine for each year. The eleven years' monthly mean daily hours of bright sunshine data is processed for the second time using a simple spreadsheet to find the long term monthly average of daily hours of sunshine of the sites and the result is presented in Table 1. This data will be used subsequently to estimate the daily solar insolation and other important information for respective stations.

Table 1. Monthly average daily hours of bright sunshine for meteorological stations.

Month	Debre Markos	Debrewerq	Mota	Yetnora
Jan	8.38	10.16	9.48	10.01
Feb	9.09	9.99	10.21	9.56
Mar	7.91	10.04	8.97	9.47
Apr	7.54	10.36	9.21	8.56
May	6.57	10.28	8.99	8.28
Jun	5.16	9.60	7.01	7.39
Jul	3.13	9.07	5.50	6.29
Aug	3.70	8.58	4.76	5.64
Sep	5.36	9.90	8.46	7.14
Oct	7.98	10.25	8.29	8.94
Nov	8.51	10.20	9.30	9.60
Dec	9.35	9.93	9.73	9.95
Av.	6.89	9.84	8.33	8.40

3.2 Estimation of Solar Insolation

The monthly mean daily hours of bright sunshine data are used to estimate monthly mean daily solar insolation using the most convenient and widely used Ångström-Prescott model as given by Eq. (1) [9, 12, 14, 15, 19, 42, 43]:

$$H = H_0(a + b\,(S/S_0))\tag{1}$$

where H = monthly mean daily solar insolation (kWh/m^2/day), S = monthly mean daily hours of bright sunshine, S_0 = monthly mean length of the day in hours which can be obtained by using Eq. (5), 'a' and 'b' are empirical constants determined for a particular site, H_0 = monthly mean daily extraterrestrial radiation (kWh/m^2/day) on a horizontal surface which can be computed by [7, 12, 19, 25, 42, 43]:

$$H_0 = 24G_{sc}/(1000\pi)[(1 + 0.033\cos(360d/365)]\ [\cos\varphi\cos\delta\sin\omega + (\pi\omega/180)\sin\varphi\sin\delta] \qquad (2)$$

where G_{sc} is solar constant with a value of 1367Wm^{-2}, d: is the number of the day of the year starting from 1st of January as 1 and continues to December 31as 365(366), φ (degrees): latitude of the location, δ (degrees): is sun declination angle obtained by using Eq. (4), ω (degrees): is monthly mean sunset hour angle given by [12, 25]:

$$\omega = \cos^{-1}(-\tan\varphi.\tan\delta) \qquad (3)$$

$$\delta = 23.45\sin(360(284 + d)/365) \qquad (4)$$

The monthly mean length of the day, S_0 (hours) is given by [12, 25]:

$$S_0 = 2\omega/15 \qquad (5)$$

Parameters d, δ, ω, S_0 and H_0 are estimated for the mean day of each month.

The physical significance of empirical constants 'a' and 'b' is that 'a' is a measure of the overall atmospheric transmission for total cloud conditions and is a function of the type and the thickness of the cloud cover, while 'b' is the rate of increase of H/H$_0$ with S/S$_0$. Different empirical formulas have been utilized in different regions of the world to obtain 'a' and 'b' from site-specific parameters, S and S$_0$. Some of the most familiar expressions for 'a' and 'b' [12, 14–16, 24, 25, 32, 42] are tested with 4–9 years measured annual mean solar insolation and sunshine hour data at Gondar, Addis Ababa and Bahir Dar [28]. The results obtained using Eqs. (6) and (7) [16], were found to be better than others.

$$a = -0.27 + 1.75(S/S_0) - 1.34(S/S_0)^2 \qquad (6)$$

$$b = 1.32 - 2.93(S/S_0) + 2.30(S/S_0)^2 \qquad (7)$$

These expressions are adjusted until the percentage deviation of the calculated solar insolation from the measured value is less than 2% for the three test sites.

Finally, expressions presented in Eq. (8) and (9) are obtained to estimate 'a' and 'b':

$$a = -0.27 + 1.74(S/S_0) - 1.15(S/S_0)^2 \qquad (8)$$

$$b = 1.32 - 2.99(S/S_0) + 2.29(S/S_0)^2 \qquad (9)$$

3.3 Estimation of Clearness Index

The clearness index (K) is a measure of the clearness of the atmosphere. It is the fraction of the solar radiation that is transmitted through the atmosphere to strike the surface of the Earth. It is a dimensionless number between 0 and 1 [30]. The value 0 signifies that a total cloud cover occurs and no irradiance is to be received on the ground. Conversely, a value of 1 signifies that the maximum theoretical amount will be received on the ground i.e. clear, sunny conditions and the solar radiation reaches the earth's surface with a more direct (beam) component. Knowledge of clearness index distribution for a particular site helps in deciding whether the site is suitable for concentrating solar thermal applications or not and to estimate its thermal output [46]. The monthly mean daily clearness index K is obtained from the monthly mean daily solar insolation, H and monthly mean daily extraterrestrial solar radiation, H_0 with the following expression [23, 27, 30]:

$$K = H/H_o \tag{10}$$

4 Results and Discussion

4.1 Monthly Mean Daily Solar Insolation for East Gojjam

The monthly mean hours of bright sunshine data are first converted into the monthly mean relative sunshine duration, S/S_0, by dividing the observed monthly sunshine data, S, (Table 1) by the corresponding monthly mean maximum possible sunshine S_0 obtained from Eq. (5) for mid of each month. Then the monthly mean hours of bright sunshine S/S_0 for each site is used in Eq. (8), (9), (2), and (1) to obtain the monthly mean values of empirical coefficients, 'a' and 'b', extraterrestrial radiation, H_0 and solar insolation, H for all sites. H and H_0 are both in kWh/m^2/day. The detailed results are presented in Table 2.

The monthly mean daily hours of bright sunshine S in the region is in the range of 3.13 h at Debre Markos in July and 10.36 h at Debrewerq in April. The relative sunshine duration (S/S_0) as shown in Fig. 2 is between 0.25 at Debre Markos in July and 0.89 at Debrewerq in November and January. In general terms, the relative sunshine duration for all sites lowers from May to September and gets deeper in rainy months (June to August). Debrewerq has a more uniform profile of relative sunshine duration (between 0.69 in August and 0.89 in November and January) than any other station with an annual mean value of 0.82. In the meantime, Debre Markos has a less uniform sunshine duration (between 0.25 in July and 0.82 in December) with its annual mean value of 0.57.

As it is stated earlier, empirical coefficients 'a' and 'b' are calculated from relative sunshine duration for respective months. The monthly profile of empirical coefficients 'a' and 'b' for the four meteorological stations is shown in Fig. 3 and Fig. 4 in respective order.

As shown in Fig. 3, 'a' and 'b' are highly dependent the cloud conditions. In the rainy months of June to September, 'a' gets smaller while 'b' gets bigger. This effect is more significant for Debre Markos station while Debrewerq has more uniform 'a' and 'b' profiles.

Table 2. Monthly mean H, H_o, a, b and K for study sites

Site	Month	H_o	S/S_o	a	b	H	K
Debre Markos	Jan	8.83	0.73	0.39	0.36	5.72	0.65
	Feb	9.55	0.78	0.39	0.38	6.52	0.68
	Mar	10.23	0.66	0.38	0.34	6.20	0.61
	Apr	10.54	0.62	0.37	0.35	6.11	0.58
	May	10.45	0.53	0.33	0.38	5.51	0.53
	Jun	10.30	0.41	0.25	0.48	4.59	0.45
	Jul	10.33	0.25	0.10	0.72	2.80	0.27
	Aug	10.44	0.30	0.15	0.63	3.52	0.34
	Sep	10.30	0.44	0.28	0.44	4.87	0.47
	Oct	9.71	0.68	0.38	0.35	5.97	0.62
	Nov	8.98	0.74	0.39	0.36	5.87	0.65
	Dec	8.57	0.82	0.38	0.41	6.15	0.72
	Annual mean	9.85	0.57	0.35	0.36	5.48	0.56
Debrewerq	Jan	8.78	0.89	0.37	0.47	6.89	0.79
	Feb	9.55	0.86	0.38	0.44	7.16	0.75
	Mar	10.23	0.84	0.38	0.42	7.53	0.74
	Apr	10.54	0.85	0.38	0.43	7.83	0.74
	May	10.45	0.82	0.38	0.41	7.54	0.72
	Jun	10.30	0.76	0.39	0.37	6.91	0.67
	Jul	10.33	0.72	0.39	0.35	6.65	0.64
	Aug	10.44	0.69	0.38	0.35	6.54	0.63
	Sep	10.30	0.82	0.38	0.41	7.39	0.72
	Oct	9.71	0.87	0.36	0.49	7.83	0.81
	Nov	8.98	0.89	0.33	0.60	8.24	0.92
	Dec	8.57	0.87	0.37	0.45	6.55	0.77
	Annual mean	9.85	0.82	0.38	0.42	7.19	0.73
Mota	Jan	8.73	0.83	y0.38	0.42	6.34	0.73
	Feb	9.48	0.88	0.37	0.46	7.33	0.77
	Mar	10.20	0.75	0.39	0.37	6.76	0.66
	Apr	10.55	0.75	0.39	0.37	7.00	0.66
	May	10.50	0.72	0.39	0.35	6.72	0.64

(*continued*)

Table 2. (*continued*)

Site	Month	H_o	S/S_o	a	b	H	K
	Jun	10.36	0.55	0.34	0.37	5.63	0.54
	Jul	10.38	0.44	0.27	0.45	4.86	0.47
	Aug	10.47	0.38	0.23	0.51	4.45	0.43
	Sep	10.28	0.70	0.38	0.35	6.47	0.63
	Oct	9.65	0.71	0.39	0.35	6.10	0.63
	Nov	8.88	0.81	0.38	0.40	6.30	0.71
	Dec	8.46	0.86	0.38	0.44	6.37	0.75
	Annual mean	9.83	0.70	0.38	0.35	6.15	0.63
Yetnora	Jan	8.85	0.87	0.37	0.45	6.80	0.77
	Feb	9.56	0.82	0.38	0.41	6.86	0.72
	Mar	10.24	0.79	0.39	0.39	7.12	0.69
	Apr	10.54	0.70	0.38	0.35	6.63	0.63
	May	10.44	0.66	0.38	0.34	6.33	0.61
	Jun	10.28	0.59	0.36	0.35	5.79	0.56
	Jul	10.31	0.50	0.31	0.40	5.28	0.51
	Aug	10.44	0.46	0.29	0.43	5.03	0.48
	Sep	10.30	0.59	0.36	0.35	5.83	0.57
	Oct	9.72	0.76	0.39	0.37	6.51	0.67
	Nov	9.00	0.83	0.38	0.42	6.56	0.73
	Dec	8.59	0.87	0.37	0.45	6.60	0.77
	Annual mean	9.86	0.70	0.38	0.35	6.21	0.63

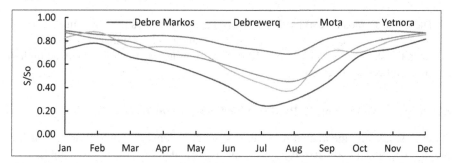

Fig. 2. Monthly profile of relative sunshine duration for meteorological stations

Using respective values of 'a', b, S/S_o, and extraterrestrial radiation H_o, the solar insolation profile as shown in Fig. 5 is obtained. As it is shown in the figure, the solar

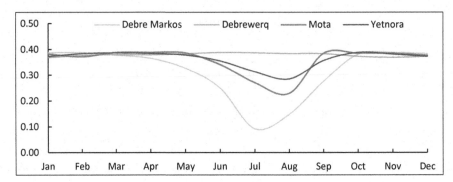

Fig. 3. Monthly profile of 'a'

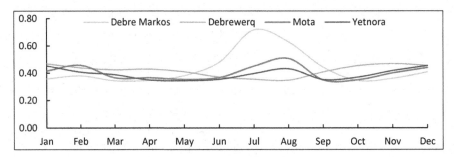

Fig. 4. Monthly profile of 'b'

insolation for the meteorological stations from October to February is close to each other. However, for the rainy months of June to September, the values are significantly different from each other. The solar insolation profile at Debre Markos site shows significant variability from month to month being the lowest in July and the highest in February while Debrewerq receives the highest and more uniform solar radiation throughout the year.

The monthly mean clearness index, K for the study sites is as shown in Fig. 6. The clearness index gets deeper in the rainy months (June to September) because of thick clouds in the sky. Debre Markos and Debrewerq demonstrate the lowest and the highest clearness indices, respectively.

4.2 Ångeström-Prescott(A-P) Model for East Gojjam Zone

For each study site, the annual mean values of coefficients, 'a' and 'b' are calculated; and the A-P model was derived for each site as presented in Table 3. From Table 3, the average values of 'a' and 'b' for East Gojjam are both 0.37.

From the annual mean values of a, b, S/S_0 and H_0, the annual mean solar insolation for the meteorological stations is obtained; and the result is presented in Table 4.

As presented in Table 4, Debrewerq receives the highest annual mean daily solar insolation (7.05 kWh/m^2/day) followed by Yetnora (6.16 kWh/m^2/day) and Mota

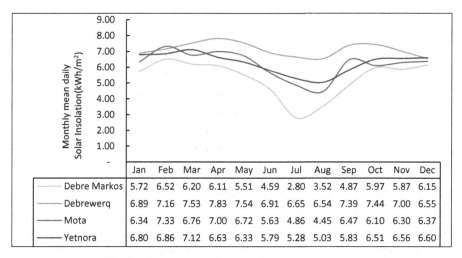

Fig. 5. Monthly mean insolation values for study sites

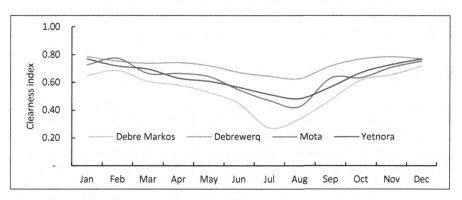

Fig. 6. Monthly mean clearness index profile of the study sites

Table 3. Angstrom-Prescott model for study sites

Site	a	b	Å-P Model
Debre Markos	0.35	0.36	$H/H_0 = 0.35 + 0.36 S/S_0$
Debrewerq	0.38	0.41	$H/H_0 = 0.38 + 0.42 S/S_0$
Mota	0.38	0.35	$H/H_0 = 0.38 + 0.35 S/S_0$
Yetnora	0.38	0.35	$H/H_0 = 0.38 + 035 S/S_0$
Average (East Gojjam)	0.37	0.37	$H/H_0 = 0.37(1 + S/S_0)$

(6.151 kWh/m²/day) in descending order. However, even though, Debre Markos and Debrewerq receive the same magnitude of extraterrestrial radiation (9.85 kWh/m²/day),

Table 4. Annual mean values of S/S_0, a,b, H_0 and H

Site	S/S_0	a	b	H_0	H
Debre Markos	0.57	0.35	0.36	9.85	5.47
Debrewerq	0.82	0.38	0.41	9.85	7.05
Mota	0.69	0.38	0.35	9.83	6.11
Yetnora	0.70	0.38	0.35	9.86	6.16
Average	0.70	0.37	0.37	9.85	6.20

Debre Markos receives the lowest annual mean solar insolation among the four study sites because of its lowest clearness index (as shown in Fig. 4) and sunshine duration resulted from mostly cloudy days throughout the year. In general, the mean global horizontal radiation for East Gojjam Zone is 6.20 kWh/m^2/day which actually tells that the region has a very good solar energy potential. Taking the results in Fig. 2 and Table 4 in mind, Debrewerq is the best site in the study area for solar energy projects with 82% of annual mean relative sunshine duration and uniform solar radiation profile throughout the year.

5   Conclusion

Knowledge of energy resource potential helps in making policies, investment decisions and power sector planning. In this paper, the result of the assessment of solar energy potential for East Gojjam Zone is presented. The solar energy potential expressed in the form of solar insolation was obtained from sun-shine hour data which was collected from NMA Bahir Dar Branch. Ångeström-Prescott Model has been adopted and utilized to calculate solar insolation from extraterrestrial radiation and the ratio of hours of bright sunshine to length of the day. The adopted A-P model is $H = 0.37(1 + S/S_0)$. The solar insolation profile at Debre Markos and Debrewerq demonstrates the maximum and the minimum variability during the year, respectively. East Gojjam Zone receives the highest solar radiation (7.83 kWh/m^2/day at Debrewerq) in April and the lowest solar radiation (2.82 kWh/m^2/day at Debre Markos) in July with an annual mean value of 6.20 kWh/m^2/day which is considered as a very good solar resource potential. Comparing meteorological stations in terms of uniformity of solar insolation profile, clearness index, and annual mean solar insolation, Debrewerq, and Debre Markos are being the best and worst sites, respectively for solar photovoltaic energy generation investments.

Acknowledgment. The authors would like to pass their sincere gratitude to Debre Markos University for funding the research work presented in this paper. A very great appreciation would like to go to the National Meteorological Agency, Bahir Dar Branch Office for the support provided during data gathering.

References

1. Mondal, H., Bryan, E.: Ringler, C., Mekonnen, D., Rosegrant, M.: Ethiopian energy status and demand scenarios: prospects to improve energy efficiency and mitigate GHG emissions. Energy **149**, 161–172 (2018)
2. Energy situation in Ethiopia. https://energypedia.info/wiki/Ethiopia_Energy_Situation.last. Accessed 2 August 2019
3. Ethiopia's transformational approach to universal electrification. https://www.worldbank.org/en/news/feature/2018/03/08/ethiopias-transformational-approach-to-universal-electrification. Accessed 3 August 2018
4. Rizzo, F. Mandelli, S., Ledda, M., Dell'Orto, G., Merlo, M.: A tool for pre-feasibility techno-economic comparison of rural electrification options: grid extension and off-grid systems. In: 8th Southern Africa Regional Conference 2017, Cape Town (2017)
5. Morcillo-Herrera, C., Hernández-Sánchez, F., Flota-Bañuelos, M.: Practical method to estimate energy potential generated by photovoltaic cells: practice case at Merida City. Energy Procedia **57**, 245–254 (2014)
6. Jacobson, M., Draxl, C., Jimenez, T., O'Neill, B.: Assessing the wind energy potential in Bangladesh. Technical Report, National Renewable Energy Laboratory (2018)
7. Tapiador, F.J.: Assessment of renewable energy potential through satellite data and numerical models. Energy Environ. Sci. **2**(11), 1142–1161 (2009)
8. Castro, C., Mediavilla, M., Miguel, L., Frechoso, F.: Global solar electric potential: a review of their technical and sustainable limits. Renew. Sustain. Energy Rev. **28**, 824–835 (2013)
9. David, A., Ngwa, N.R.: Global solar radiation of some regions of Cameroon using the linear angstrom and non-linear polynomial relations (Part I) model development. Int. J. Renew. Energy Res. **3**(4), 984–992 (2013)
10. Marzo, A., et al.: Daily global solar radiation estimation in desert areas using daily extreme temperatures and extraterrestrial radiation. Renew. Energy **113**, 303–311 (2013)
11. Ramachandra, T.V.: Solar energy potential assessment using GIS. Energ. Educ. Sci. Technol. **18**(2), 101–114 (2007)
12. Razmjool, A., Heibati, M., Ghadimi, M., Qolipour, M., Nasa, J.: Using angstrom-prescott (a-p) method for estimating monthly global solar radiation in kashan. J. Fundam. Renew. Energy Appl. **6**(5), 1–4 (2016)
13. Manzano, A., Martín, M.L., Valero, F., Armenta, C.: A single method to estimate the daily global solar radiation from monthly data. Atmos. Res. **166**, 70–82 (2015)
14. Ertekin, C., Yaldiz, O.: Comparison of some existing models for estimating global solar radiation for Antalya (Turkey). Energy Convers. Manage. **41**, 311–330 (2000)
15. Samuel, C.N.: A comprehensive review of empirical models for estimating global solar radiation in Africa. Renew. Sustain. Energy Rev. **78**, 955–995 (2017)
16. Samuel, T.D.M.A.: Estimation of global radiation for Sri Lanka. Sol. Energy **47**(5), 333–337 (1991)
17. Mubiru, J., Banda, E.J.K.B., D'Ujanga, F., Senyonga, T.: Assessing the performance of global solar radiation empirical formulations in Kampala, Uganda. Theor. Appl. Climatol. **87**(1–4), 179–184 (2007). https://doi.org/10.1007/s00704-005-0196-2
18. Zabra, K.: Estimation of global solar radiation in Greece. Sol. Wind Technol. **3**(4), 267–272 (1986)
19. Bahel, V., Srinivasan, R., Bakhsh, H.: Solar radiation for Dhahran. Saudi Arabia. Energy **11**(10), 985–989 (1986)
20. Tadros, M.T.Y.: Uses of sunshine duration to estimate the global solar radiation over eight meteorological stations in Egypt. Renew. Energy **21**, 231–246 (2000)

21. Trnka, M., Zalud, Z., Eitzinger, J., Dubrovsky, M.: Global solar radiation in Central European lowlands estimated by various empirical formulae. Agric. For. Meteorol. **131**, 54–76 (2005)

22. Jin, Z., Yezheng, W., Gang, Y.: General formula for estimation of monthly average daily global solar radiation in China. Energy Convers. Manage. **46**, 257–268 (2005)

23. Page, J.: McEvoy's Handbook of Photovoltaics.3rd edn. Academic Press, Cambridge (2018)

24. Soulouknga, M.H., Coulibaly, O., Doka, S.Y., Kofane, T.C.: Evaluation of global solar radiation from meteorological data in the Sahelian zone of Chad. Renew. Wind Water Solar **4**(1), 1–10 (2017). https://doi.org/10.1186/s40807-017-0041-0

25. Soulouknga, M.H., Falama, R.Z., Ajayi, O.O., Doka, S.Y., Kofane, T.C.: Determination of a suitable solar radiation model for the sites of Chad. Energy Power Eng. **9**, 703–722 (2017)

26. Chen, J., et al.: Empirical models for estimating monthly global solar radiation: a most comprehensive review and comparative case study in China. Renew. Sustain. Energy Rev. **108**, 91–111 (2019)

27. Okogbue, E.C., Adedokunb, J.A., Holmgren, B.: Hourly and daily clearness index and diffuse fraction at a tropical station, Ile-Ife, Nigeria. Int. J. Climatol. **29**, 1035–1047 (2009)

28. Drake, F., Mulugetta, Y.: Assessment of solar and wind energy resources in Ethiopia. I. solar energy. Sol. Energy **57**(3), 205–217 (1996). https://doi.org/10.1016/S0038-092X(96)00094-1

29. Sarkar, M.N.I.: Estimation of solar radiation from cloud cover data. Renew. Wind Water Solar **3**(11), 1–15(2016)

30. Namrata, K., Saksena, S., Sharma, S.P.: Comparison of different models for estimation of global solar radiation for Jharkhand (India) region. Smart Grid Renew. Energy **4**, 348–352 (2012)

31. Vignola, F.E.: Solar Energy Forecasting and Resource Assessment Book title. 1st edn. Elsevier Inc. (2013)

32. Rietveld, M.R.: A new method for estimating the regression coefficients in the formula relating solar radiation to sunshine. Agric. Meteorol. **19**, 243–252 (1978)

33. Supit, I., Kappel, R.R.: A simple method to estimate global radiation. Sol. Energy **63**(3), 147–160 (1998)

34. Kamel, M.A., Shalaby, S.A., Mostafa, S.S.: Solar radiation over Egypt: comparison of predicted and measured meteorological data. Sol. Energy **50**(6), 463–467 (1993)

35. Mahmud, A., et al.: Solar energy resource assessment of the Geba Catchment, Northern Ethiopia. Energy Procedia **57**, 1266–1274 (2014)

36. Nage, G.D.: Estimation of monthly average daily solar radiation from meteorological parameters: sunshine hours and measured temperature in Tepi, Ethiopia. Int. J. Energy Environ. Sci. **3**(1), 19–26 (2018)

37. Argaw, N.: Estimation of solar radiation energy of Ethiopia from sunshine data. Int. J. Solar Energy **18**(2), 103–113 (1996)

38. Bekele, G., Boneya, G.: Design of a photovoltaic-wind hybrid power generation system for Ethiopian remote area. Energy Procedia **14**, 1760–1765 (2012)

39. Bekele, G., Tadesse, G.: Feasibility study of small hydro/PV/wind hybrid system for off-grid rural electrification in Ethiopia. Appl. Energy **97**, 5–15 (2012)

40. Bayou, T., Assefa, A.: Solar radiation maps for Ethiopia. J. EAEA **8**, 7–16 (1989)

41. Nnabuenyi, H.O., Okoli, L.N., Nwosu, F.C., Ibe, G.: Estimation of global solar radiation using sunshine and temperature based models for Oko Town in Anambra State, Nigeria. Am. J. Renew. Sustain. Energy **3**(2), 8–14 (2017)

42. Srivastava, R.C., Pandey, H.: Estimating Angstrom-Prescott coefficients for India and developing a correlation between sunshine hours and global solar radiation for India. Hindawi Publ. Corp. **2013**, 1–7 (2013)

43. Tessema, S., Bekele, G.: Resource assessment and optimization study of efficient type hybrid power system for electrification of Rural District in Ethiopia. Int. J. Energy Power Eng. **3**(6), 331–340 (2014)

44. NMA Dataset and Information Resource. http://www.ethiomet.gov.et/data_access/inform ation. Accessed 2 September 2019
45. East Gojjam Zone. https://en.wikipedia.org/wiki/East_Gojjam_Zone. Accessed 3 August 2019
46. Lai, C.S., Li, X., Lai, L.L., McCulloch, M.D.: Daily clearness index profiles and weather condition studies for photovoltaic systems. In: 9th International Conference on Applied Energy, ICAE2017, pp.21–24, Cardiff, UK (2017)

IT, Computer Science and Software Engineering

Amharic Information Retrieval Based on Query Expansion Using Semantic Vocabulary

Berihun Getnet[1(✉)] and Yaregal Assabie[2]

[1] Department of Computer Science, Wolkite University, Wolkite, Ethiopia
`berihun.getnet@wku.edu.et`
[2] Department of Computer Science, Addis Ababa University, Addis Ababa, Ethiopia
`yaregal.assabie@aau.edu.et`

Abstract. The increase in large scale data available from different sources has demanded advancement in information retrieval. As a result, information retrieval based on learning from high dimensional vectors based on the words adjacent to other words or surrounding terms has become more attractive in recent times. The meaning is extracted from the context of words but not using the actual sense of words. The system responds to relevant results for the users by expanding the original queries from semantic lexical resources constructed automatically from a text corpus using neural word embedding. In this study, we propose query expansion for Amharic information retrieval using semantic vocabulary. The semantic vocabulary is automatically constructed from a text corpus using neural word embedding. The user's query is expanded based on the word analog prediction. Information retrieval using semantic vocabulary based on ranked and unranked retrieval increases by a recall of 24 and 15%, respectively albeit at the expense of some precision.

Keywords: Query expansion · Semantic vocabulary · Word embedding · Amharic information retrieval

1 Introduction

Due to a growing need of users to search for relevant documents, much attention has been given over the years to improve the performance of information retrieval systems. Query expansion has been one of the core issues considered for improvement of information retrieval systems. It is the process of reformulating the original query into a set of additional multiple similar terms to retrieve more relevant documents from data sources [1]. Query expansion is traditionally implemented by making use of manually constructed linguistic resources such as thesaurus, dictionary and WordNet [2]. Query expansion based on semantics has recently become more popular due to the understanding that meaning is subjective [1, 3]. However, manual construction of such resources is difficult as the task is labor-intensive and time consuming. On the other hand, the availability of large corpora and high-speed processing power of computers has brought an opportunity

M. A. Delele et al. (Eds.): ICAST 2020, LNICST 384, pp. 407–416, 2021.
https://doi.org/10.1007/978-3-030-80621-7_29

for automatic construction of linguistic resources. Thus, there has been a growing interest among researchers and developers in automation and data-driven linguistic analysis where lexical resources like semantic vocabulary, thesaurus, dictionary, and WordNet can be constructed either automatically from natural language texts [3–5].

One of the theories effectively applied for analyzing linguistic data is distributional semantics. Distributional semantics assumes that the meaning is extracted from word contexts and its distributions across a vector space [6–8]. In this case, the meaning of words is extracted from the text considering that words occurring in similar contexts are semantically similar. Thus, semantic vocabulary can be constructed automatically from a corpus based on the assumption that words distributed across a multidimensional vector space could have the similar meaning. The multidimensional vector space is created using word embedding technique [2, 9]. Then, semantically related words are organized into semantic vocabulary using word clustering technique. Words are clustered based on the similarity of words. Various information retrieval systems employed semantic vocabulary for query expansion [1–3]. In this work, we present Amharic information retrieval system with query expansion. Query expansion relies on the semantic vocabulary constructed automatically from a text corpus using word embedding technique followed by clustering of word senses.

The remaining part of this paper is organized as follows. Section 2 presents linguistic characteristics of Amharic. In Sect. 3, we present the proposed Amharic information retrieval system. Experimental results are discussed in Sect. 4 our conclusion is presented in Sect. 5.

2 The Amharic Language

2.1 Amharic Writing System

Amharic is the working language of Ethiopia. Although many languages are spoken in Ethiopia, it is serving as the *lingua franca* of the country. Amharic is written using Ethiopic script which has 34 characters with 7 vowels. The seven vowels are አ /äl/, ኡ /u/, ኢ /i/, አ /a/, ኤ /e/, እ /ə/ and አ /o/. Each character is modified with the vowels yielding seven orders. For example, the character ከ /kä/ is modified using vowels as ኩ /ku/, ኪ /ki/, ካ /ka/, ኬ /ke/, ክ /kə/ and ኮ /ko/. In addition, there are also labialized characters like ኳ /kua/, ሷ /sua/, ሏ /lua/, ሟ /mua/, etc. Ethiopic script uses punctuation marks such as comma (፣), semicolon (፤), full stop (።), colon (፥) and preface colon (፦). The script has its own characters for numbers as well.

2.2 Characteristics of Amharic Language

Amharic exhibits complex morphological processes through derivation and inflection that apply mainly on word classes such as verbs, nouns and adjectives [10, 11]. Typically, Amharic verbs are generated through a two-step process from verbal roots: *stem formation* and *verb formation*. Amharic verbal stems, from which various forms of verbs are formed, can be derived from verbal roots by affixing vowels. For example, the verbal stem ሰበር- /säbär-/ is derived from the verbal root

ስ-በ-ር /s-b-r/. The process of Amharic verb formation is usually completed by marking stems for any combination of person, gender, number, case, tense/aspect and mood. Accordingly, the following verbs can be generated from the verbal stem: ሰበርኩ /säbärku 'I broke'/, ሰበርኩህ /säbärkuh 'I broke you'/, ሰበርን /säbärn 'we broke'/, ተሰበርኩ /täsäbärku 'I was broken'/, ሰበረች /säbäräc 'she broke'/, etc. The characteristic feature that a single instance of a verb can be marked for a combination of person, case, gender, number, tense, aspect, mood and others leads to the possibility of generating tens of thousands of verbs from a single verbal root through the processes of derivation and infection.

From the perspective of morphological structure, Amharic nouns can be derived and non-derived [10, 11]. Derived nouns are formed though morphological processes applied on various word origins. Words like ቤት /bet 'house'/, ሃገር /hagär 'country'/ and ሰው /säw 'human'/ are non-derived nouns. On the other hand, words like መልስ /mäls 'response'/ and ደግነት /dägənät 'generosity'/ are nouns derived from the verbal root ም-ል-ስ /m-l-s 'to respond'/ and the adjective ደግ /däg 'generous'/, respectively. Similar to nouns, Amharic adjectives can be derived and non-derived [10, 11] where derived adjectives can be formed from verbal roots by infixing vowels between consonants (e.g. ድ-ር-ቅ /d-r-q 'to dry'/ → ደረቅ /däräq 'dry'/), nouns by suffixing bound morphemes (e.g. ተራራ /tärara 'mountain'/ → ተራራማ /tärarama 'mountainous') and stems by prefixing or suffixing bound morphemes (e.g. ደካም- /däkam-/ → ደካማ /däkama 'weak'/). Amharic nouns and adjectives are inflected for number commonly by suffixing -ኦች /- oc/ or -ዎች /-woc/, definiteness by suffixing -ኡ /-u/ or -ዉ /-wu/, objective case by suffixing -ን /-n/, possessive case by suffixing different morphemes depending on the subject, and gender by suffixing -ኢት /-it/. These inflections can appear alone or in combination at the same time, along with prepositions and negation markers which leads to the generation of thousands of word forms from a single noun or adjective. For example, ያለባለቤቶቹ /yaläbaläbetocu 'without the owners of the house'/ is generated from the morphemes yä-ʔalä-balä-bet-oc-u (yä- 'preposition- of/with', ʔalä- 'nega- 'negation marker- not/without', balä- 'possessive 'possessive marker- owner of', bet 'house', -oc 'plural marker', and –u 'definite marker - the') where the core morpheme is the noun ቤት /bet 'house'/.

3 The Proposed Solution

The proposed Amharic information retrieval system performs query expansion using semantic vocabulary. The semantic vocabulary is automatically generated from a collection of Amharic documents by applying text processing. The processed text is used for neural word embedding from which clustering is made based on the similarity of word senses. Then, the semantic vocabulary is constructed from clusters of related words. On the other hand, the processed text is used for generating index terms representing Amharic documents. From the users side, the same text processing task is performed on the queries. Then, query expansion is made using the semantic vocabulary. Finally, the search of relevant documents is made by matching expanded query terms against index terms. Figure 1 shows system architecture of the proposed Amharic information retrieval system.

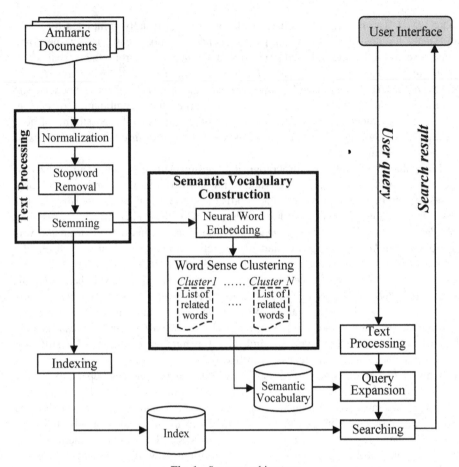

Fig. 1. System architecture

3.1 Text Processing

In general, information retrieval systems undergo text processing for a better document representation. However, the specific tasks may vary due to differences in the characteristics of languages. In our work, text processing involves character normalization, stopword removal and stemming. Text processing is performed on Amharic document collection during indexing and construction of semantic vocabulary. Similarly, it is also applied on user query.

Text Normalization. Text normalization is an essential step in Amharic text processing. Amharic is known to have a few set characters with similar pronunciation but different symbols. The base characters having such properties are: {ሀ /häl/, ሐ /häl/, ኀ /häl/, and ኸ /häl/}, {ሰ /säl/ and ሠ /säl/}, {አ /ʔäl/ and ዐ /ʔäl/}, and {ጸ /ṣäl/ and ፀ /ṣäl/}. Furthermore, the fourth orders of {ሀ /häl/, ሐ /häl/, ኀ /häl/, and ኸ /häl/} and {አ /ʔäl/ and ዐ /ʔäl/} have similar pronunciation with the respective base forms. As there are no standards established on how to use characters, a single word may be written differently. For example, ፀሐይ /ṣähäy/ 'sun'/ may also be written as ጸሐይ /ṣähäy/, ፀሀይ /ṣähäy/, ፀኀይ /ṣähay/, ፀሐይ /ṣähayl/, ጸሃይ /ṣähayl/, etc. where all of them are considered as the same word (and pronounced the same). Thus, to avoid such variations in a word, we applied character normalization where ሀ /häl/, ሰ /säl/, ኧ /ʔäl/ and ፀ /ṣäl/ are used to represent the respective characters with similar pronunciation. We also use the first orders of characters to represent the respective fourth orders having similar pronunciation.

Stopword Removal. Stopword removal is a typical step in information retrieval. The objective is to remove non-content-bearing terms from documents and queries. Although standard stopwords are available for various languages, there are no standard and ready-made stopwords for the purpose of Amharic information retrieval. In our work, we identified stopwords from the document collection by considering frequently occurring words across each document. We used a total of 1200 terms are identified as stopwords. Examples include ነው, ነበር, ሆኖም, እና, ገለፁ, ዘገበዋል, አስታወቀ, ተናገረዋል, ብለዋል, ወይ, etc. A list of stopwords is created and stored in a file to filter out non-content-bearing terms during document and query processing.

Stemming. Stemming is required for conflating terms to a common form so as to avoid term variations arising as a result of morphological process. In our work, we modified the Amharic stemmer developed by Alemayehu and Willet [12] for stemming words.

3.2 Semantic Vocabulary Construction

The semantic vocabulary is used as a resource for query expansion. It is constructed automatically from the processed text. To this effect, we apply neural word embedding followed by clustering based on word senses. Neural word embedding vectorizes words on a multidimensional space using Word2vec based on the notion that words surrounding another word can be contextually similar. Word sense clustering automatically clusters vectors of similar terms across the n-dimensional spaces. The dimension of the word-space model is determined by the number of words to be plotted across the n-dimensional space. Dimension reduction is performed to get the most important features of the document.

Neural Word Embedding. The preprocessed and stemmed words are feed into the word-space modeling which embeds the words across a multidimensional space via the contexts of the words. The word embedding is implemented using Word2vec based on the continuous bag of words (CBOW) model. The CBOW model learns the embedding by predicting the current word based on its context. The idea behind CBOW architecture is that meaning can be inferred from a word surrounding another word. The Word2vec takes a text corpus as input and produces the word vectors as output. To vectorize the words, we consider the parameters like context window size, minimum occurrence count of words, dimension size, workers, architecture, mean value, hierarchical softmax, and negative sampling. To improve the overall performance of the system, we reduce the vector size to 300. The maximum distance between the target and the context word is considered to be 10. Training is carried out using parallel processing. Then, we apply vector normalization for better performances and memory use. It implies computing the semantic distances between vectors by forgetting the previously learned vectors. Figure 2 shows sample word vector visualized using *t*-distributed stochastic neighbor embedding (*t*-SNE).

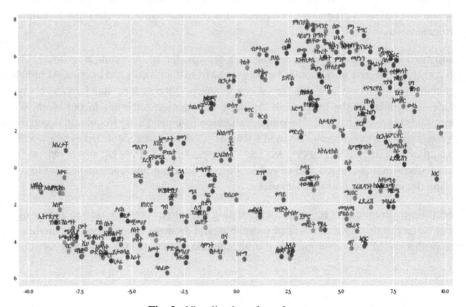

Fig. 2. Visualization of word vector

Word Sense Clustering. In order to construct the semantic vocabulary, semantically related words are clustered based on their similarity. The similarity of words is computed based on the cosine values which are implemented with vector orientation. Higher cosine values (approaching 1) indicate higher word relatedness. Based on their orientation words close to each other are grouped into a certain semantic cluster across the *n*-dimensional spaces without predefined labels or categories. An example of clusters of words in technology domain is shown in Fig. 3.

3.3 Searching

Searching of relevant documents is performed by matching index terms with expanded query terms. Index terms represent Amharic documents whereas expanded query terms represent users' needs. During the process of indexing, text processing activities of normalization, stopword removal and stemming are applied to Amharic documents. We also apply similar text processing on the queries. When the user provides the queries, the system expands the original query automatically from the semantic vocabulary. The queries are reformulated and words are matched against the indexed data which will return more relevant documents for the user based on the score for query terms and document ranks.

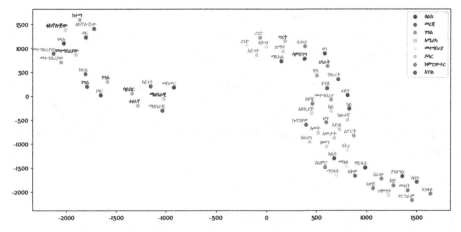

Fig. 3. Cluster of semantically related words in technology domain

4 Experiment

4.1 Corpus Collection and Implementation

Amharic text documents are collected from various sources covering 9 domains and another general domain. A total of 8,540 Amharic documents are used for training and testing purpose. Table 1 shows the domains long with the corresponding number of documents.The proposed information retrieval system is implemented using Python. We have constructed a total of 44,497 lists of semantically related vocabulary from all domains. Indexing and searching are implemented using Whoosh library.

Table 1. Amharic corpus used for training and testing.

Domain	Number of documents
Religion	1,189
Business	1,317
Sport	900
Politics	1,002
Law	1,037
Art	1,016
Health	272
Technology	978
Health	529
General	300
Total	**8,540**

4.2   Test Result and Discussion

For testing purpose, we use 9 queries and a total of 90 relevant and 518 indexed documents expanded with the top 5 number of similar words. When increasing the number of expanded words, the probability of returning the relevant documents increases. As a result, the recall increasing while precision is decreasing. This is expected due to the increasing number of retrieved documents. Relevance is measured using both ranked and unranked sets of retrieval. Table 2 presents mean average recall and precision for ranked and unranked retrieval sets evaluated with and without the use of semantic vocabulary for query expansion.

Table 2. Evaluation of the proposed system

Retrieval Set	Without semantic vocabulary		With semantic vocabulary	
	Recall (%)	Precision (%)	Recall (%)	Precision (%)
Unranked	69	44	84	24
Ranked	45	81	69	77

Generally, our system is better for recall-oriented applications as recall increases with the use of semantic vocabulary. The use of semantic vocabulary for query expansion helps the system perform better with the top five most similar terms. Figure 4 shows a comparison of retrieval effectiveness for unranked retrieval set with and without the use of semantic vocabulary for query expansion. The values in each test case show recall with semantic vocabulary (Rwsv), precision with semantic vocabulary (Pwsv), recall without semantic vocabulary (Rwosv), and precision without semantic vocabulary (Pwosv).

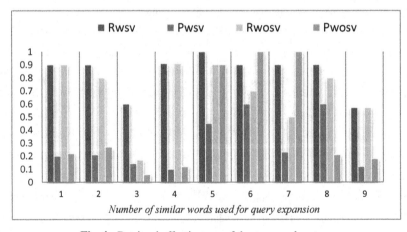

Fig. 4. Retrieval effectiveness of the proposed system

We show that ranked retrieval is generally better than unranked retrieval. Using ranked retrieval many relevant documents are retrieved in their priority relevance based on the ranks in descending order. When the indexed documents are too huge ranked retrieval could save searching time than an unranked retrieval system. For ranked retrieval, we compare the performance of three ranking functions: *TF-IDF*, *BM25F* and *frequency*. Experimental results show that the BM25F ranking function outperforms better than other ranking functions.

5   Conclusion

The need to use and access lexical resources to enhance information retrieval using query expansion has become more fundamental in natural languages including Amharic. The resources made available for query expansion may be either manually built or automatically created from large document collections. Contextual meaning extraction also becomes more essential these days. Creating resources manually is labor-intensive, and time-consuming when the dataset is huge. Thus, we proposed an automatic way of creating Amharic semantic vocabulary using neural word embedding which helps to extract contextual meaning. The semantic vocabulary is used for query expansion where experimental results show significant improvement in recall albeit at the expense of some precision. Thus, future work is directed at employing additional techniques for improving precision. Moreover, we also recommend to deal further with the morphological characteristics of Amharic language.

References

1. Raza, M.A., Mokhtar, R., Ahmad, N., Pasha, M., Pasha, U.: A taxonomy and survey of semantic approaches for query expansion. IEEE Access **7**, 17823–17833 (2019)
2. Carpineto, C., Romano, G.: A survey of automatic query expansion in information retrieval. ACM Comput. Surv. **44**(1), 1–50 (2012)
3. Rivas, A.R., Iglesias, E.L., Borrajo, L.: Study of Query Expansion Techniques and Their Application in the Biomedical Information Retrieval, Sci. World J. (2014)
4. Aklouche, B., Bounhas, I., Slimani, Y.: Query expansion based on NLP and word embeddings. In: Proceedings of the Twenty-Seventh Text Retrieval Conference (TREC 2018), Gaithersburg, Maryland, USA (2018)
5. Kuzi, S., Shtok, A., Kurland, O.: Query Expansion Using Word Embeddings. In: Proceedings of the 25th ACM International on Conference on Information and Knowledge Management, pp. 1929–1932, (2016)
6. Venelin, K., Maria, S., Martí, M.: Comparing distributional semantics models for identifying groups of semantically related words. Procesamiento del Lenguaje Natural **57**, 109–116 (2016)
7. Alessandro, L.: Will Distributional Semantics Ever Become Semantic? In: Proceedings of the 7th International Global WordNet Conference, Tartu, (2014)
8. Claveau, V., Ewa, K.: Distributional Thesauri for Information Retrieval and vice versa, in Language and Resource Conference, LREC (2016)
9. Azzopardi, L., Stein, B., Fuhr, N., Mayr, P., Hauff, C., Hiemstra, D. (eds.): ECIR 2019. LNCS, vol. 11437. Springer, Cham (2019). https://doi.org/10.1007/978-3-030-15712-8
10. Assabie, Y.: Development of amharic morphological analyzer using a hybrid approach. Technical Report, Ethiopian Ministry of Communication and Information Technology, Addis Ababa, Ethiopia (2017)

11. Abate, M., Assabie, Y.: Development of amharic morphological analyzer using memory-based learning. In: Przepiórkowski, A., Ogrodniczuk, M. (eds.) NLP 2014. LNCS (LNAI), vol. 8686, pp. 1–13. Springer, Cham (2014). https://doi.org/10.1007/978-3-319-10888-9_1
12. Alemayehu, N., Willett, P.: Stemming of Amharic words for information retrieval. Literary Linguist. Comput. **17**(1), 1–17 (2002)

Improving the QoS of Fog Nodes Using Delay Sensitive Task Offloading

Asrat Mulatu Beyene[(⊠)] [ID]

BDA and HPC Center of Excellence, Addis Ababa Science and Technology University, Addis Ababa, Ethiopia
`asrat.mulatu@aastu.edu.et`

Abstract. Fog computing is an extension of cloud computing where services are provided at the edge of a network. With the growth of the Internet of Things (IoTs) different applications are emerging. Many of these applications are delay sensitive that demand better reliability. Different task scheduling algorithms were proposed to manage such applications under fog computing environments. Still, it is difficult to meet the required latency requirements of applications with existing algorithms. Therefore, in this paper, a delay sensitive offloading algorithm is proposed that considers two different criteria during scheduling – the expected deadline of a given task and the computational capability of nodes. The effectiveness of the proposed algorithm is evaluated by using two typical working scenarios of fog nodes where comparative analysis with two popular task offloading algorithms have been made. The overall result shows that the proposed algorithm can provide as much as 37% improvement in the average response time of tasks in IoT applications.

Keywords: Fog computing · Task scheduling · Internet of Things · Delay sensitive · QoS requirements

1 Introduction

In the emerging 5G technology, ultra-low latency and high reliability are demanded from IoT applications [1]. Many research works tried to explore the possibility of fog computing by having the fog layer between the cloud and IoT devices [2]. And others modified some aspect of IoT architectures to minimize delay [3]. Fog computing tried to achieve such requirements by making computations at the edge of the network. But, due to resource constraint, uneven distribution of IoT devices in the domain, and natural variety of tasks it demanded extra effort to fulfill it. Minimizing delay of services, utilizing resources effectively, and minimizing power consumption are still existing challenges [4].

For many applications, another entity executes tasks on behalf of IoT devices and return results to those devices [5]. Some tasks demanding high computing devices and others resource-constrained ones in fog computing environment. To solve this contradiction a technique called offloading is used. It is used to outsource tasks and entities that

M. A. Delele et al. (Eds.): ICAST 2020, LNICST 384, pp. 417–431, 2021.
https://doi.org/10.1007/978-3-030-80621-7_30

work together to achieve the final computational goal of applications [5]. Task offloading is attractive for emerging IoT and cloud computing applications in that it can occur among IoT devices, edge devices, and fog nodes.

Many mobile services have been introduced with the emergence of different smart devices in the market. Mobile devices are resource-constrained. And, due to their mobility it is, usually, essential to offload part of their tasks to the cloud. Furthermore, integration of machine learning algorithms is needed to attain the required smartness of many services such as image processing and online gaming [6]. Efficient task execution is necessary, especially, when intelligence and sophistication of tasks become higher. But, the capability of IoT devices usually can fulfill the resource requirements of tasks. In these cases, the tasks are offloaded to the middleware [7]. This middleware is the fog layer that contains computing resources such as fog devices, fog servers, and gateways. In some situations, it might be required to offload some tasks to the cloud server [5]. However, tasks are offloaded to fog nodes for storage in addition to computation [5, 8].

2 Related Works

As presented in Table 1 there are many research efforts in the area of fog computing [9, 12, 14, 16, 19, 20, 22, 23, 28], edge computing [1, 21, 24, 25, 30, 31, 34], cloud computing [4, 10, 11, 15], of their combinations among them like fog-cloud [17, 18, 37], fog-cloud-edge [29], or of with IoT [5, 6, 13, 26, 33, 35, 36]. Some these proposed scheduling algorithms [1, 10, 11, 21, 34], analytical models [13, 14], heuristic algorithms [12, 16, 19, 20, 25, 28], optimizations [17, 18, 24, 28, 33, 35], architectures/frameworks [9, 23, 29, 36, 37], intelligent algorithms [6, 30, 31, 33], dynamic [1, 9, 10, 21, 33] and on-demand algorithms [16, 23, 24, 26]. Many worked on task offloading [1, 5, 6, 9–11, 13, 16–21, 23–26, 28, 29, 31–37], few included data [24, 30], and yet very few worked only on data [22]. Many of the research works involve optimizing computational ressources [1, 4, 6, 9–11, 13, 16–26, 28–31], and some considered both computational network resources [22, 32–37]. From the works considered in this review one can understand that the area is a hot research area where scenario based improvement on existing task offloading algorithms is demanded [4, 5, 12, 15, 27].

In this work, task offloading algorithm is proposed among fog nodes to enable tasks to meet their deadline requirements based on delay requirements of the tasks and computational capabilities of nodes.

3 Selected System Architecture

The system architecture considered in this work has four layers with IoT devices in the first, lower-level fog nodes in the second, aggregate fog nodes and cloud servers in the third and fourth layers, respectively.

3.1 IoT Devices

Data sources, from which various forms of data are generated, like Wi-Fi sensors, actuators, and smart devices, lay in this layer. This layer consists of physical and virtual sensors, where any data generation device could fall into any of these groups.

Table 1. Summary of related works

Author	System considered	Algorithm name/type	Improvement focus	Offloading type
Sladana Josilo et al. [16]	Fog Computing	Game theoretic analysis based Decentralization Algorithm	Task	Computation
Christine Fricker et al. [14]	Fog computing	Analytical model	-	Load Balancing
Tongxiang Wang et al. [10]	Mobile cloud computing	Cooperative Multi-tasks Scheduling on ACO algorithm (CMSACO)	Task	Computation
Mika Jia et al. [11]	Distributed Cloud computing	Scheduling algorithm	Task	Computation
Ashkan Yousefpour et al. [13]	IoT-Fog-Cloud Scenario	Analytical model	Task	Computation
Xiaohui Zhao et al. [17]	Fog-cloud computing	Optimal energy consumption algorithm	Task	Computation
Jianbo Du et al. [18]	Fog-cloud computing	Low-complexity suboptimal algorithm	Task	Computation offloading and resource allocation
Qiliang Zhu et al. [19]	Fog computing	Task offloading policy	Task	Computation
Te-Yi Kan et al. [20]	Fog computing	Heuristic load distribution algorithm	Task	Computation
Lingfang Gao [21]	Mobile edge computing	Task offloading strategy & priority-based task scheduling algorithm	Task	Computation
Mohammed Al-khafajiy et al. [36]	Fog-IoT Computing	Generic IoT-Fog based architecture	Task	Computation & network
Tomislav Shuminoski et al. [37]	Mobile cloud-fog computing	5G-based Fog-Cloud Computing Framework	Task	Computation & network
Quang Duy La et al. [6]	Fog computing & IoT apps	AI based algorithm	Task	Computation

(*continued*)

Table 1. (*continued*)

Author	System considered	Algorithm name/type	Improvement focus	Offloading type
Mithun Mukherjee et al. [22]	Fog computing	Quadratic-ally constraint quadratic programming (QCQP)	Data	Computation & network
Yeonjin Jin et al. [23]	Fog computing	On-demand offloading architecture	Task	Computation
Ibrahim Alghamdi et al. [24]	Mobile edge computing	Optimal offloading rule	Task & data	Computation
Jiuyun Xu et al. [25]	Mobile edge computing	Branch-and-Bound Algorithm	Task	Computation
Huaiying Sun et al. [26]	Generic IoT-Fog-Cloud system	Energy & time efficient computation offloading and resource allocation(ETCORA) algorithm	Task	Computation
Hyame Assem Alameddine et al. [1]	Edge Computing	Dynamic Task Offloading and Scheduling	Task	Computation
Ashkan Yousefpour et al.[9]	Fog Computing	QoS-aware Dynamic Fog Service Provisioning (QDFSP) Framework	Task	Computation
Yijin Pan et al. [29]	Hierarchical Fog-Cloud-Edge Computing System	Hierarchical Fog-Cloud-Edge Radio Access Networks (C-RANs) Architecture	Task	Computation
Jieun Kang et al. [30]	Edge computing	Intelligent offloading model	Task & data	.Computation
Md Delowar Hossain et al.' [31]	Densely Deployed Small-Cell Networks with Multi-Access Edge Computing	Fuzzy Based Collaborative Offloading (FCTO) Scheme	Task	Computation

(*continued*)

Table 1. (*continued*)

Author	System considered	Algorithm name/type	Improvement focus	Offloading type
Sudip Misra et al. [33]	Cloud- Software Defined Fog-IoT	Detour - Dynamic Task Offloading	Task	Computation & network
Sladana Josilo [34]	Edge Computing	Resource allocation & scheduling scheme	Task	Computation & network
Mohamed K. Hussein et al. [35]	Fog-IoT Computing	Ant Colony Optimization	Task	Computation & network

3.2 Lower-Level Fog Nodes Layer

This layer contains fog nodes that are capable of performing computation and storage. It accepts requests generated form IoT devices that need better computational power.

3.3 Aggregate Fog Nodes Layer

This layer is composed of servers and gateways which control fog nodes located at the lower layer. These devices have more computational capability and storage capacity when compared to lower-level fog nodes. Those tasks that are deadline insensitive and computation-intensive are executed in this layer.

3.4 Cloud Layer

This layer contains cloud servers and data centers that provide networking, computational, and storage services. This layer executes or stores tasks received in two ways. The first is directly from IoT devices while the other is from aggregate fog nodes.

4 Proposed Task Offloading Algorithm

4.1 System Model

The proposed task offloading algorithm functions as follows. First, tasks generated from various IoT devices are sent to the nearest fog node for computation. Since tasks generated from IoT devices are heterogenous and fog node resources are limited (computation power, battery life and storage), all incoming tasks may not be served in that nearest fog node. So, the tasks are evaluated to choose the best place for execution. In the system model depicted in Fig. 2, task's deadline time is the first criterion used in scheduling. Based on the type of task and data transfer requirements, expected network delay is computed. The result is then used for driving the expected service time. By combining the two (task deadline and type), it is possible to get a better QoS and minimum overall response time. Referring to Fig. 1, tasks can be executed at one of the upper three layers.

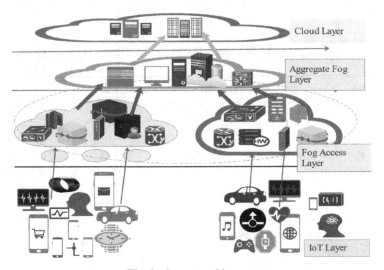

Fig. 1. System architecture

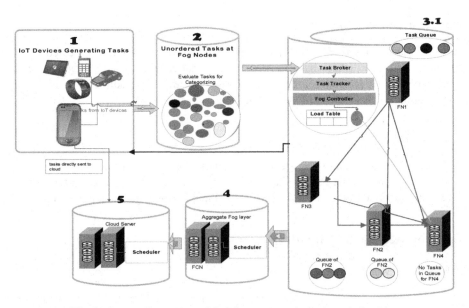

Fig. 2. Proposed system model to demonstrate the proposed algorithm

So, tasks that are not executed at the Fog Access (or lower-level fog nodes) layer can be executed at the aggregate or cloud layers. The aggregate layer stores or executes task when it gets a request from lower-level fog nodes. But, the cloud layer may get requests directly from the IoT devices or via the aggregate nodes.

4.2 Discerption of the Proposed Algorithm

Figure 3 and Fig. 4 show both the pseudocode and flowchart of the proposed task offloading algorithm. As it is depicted in the figures, tasks sent from IoT devices arrive at the nearest fog node in a Poisson rate. The tasks are classified according to the nature of the device that has generated the task. Then, the status of each fog node is checked whethe it fulfils the deadline or not. Based on which the task is offloaded to the best possible fog node in the cloud system.

5 Evaluation of the Proposed Offloading Algorithm

5.1 Simulation Parameters and Settings

For simulation purposes, the parameters of the processing capabilities of the fog nodes, aggregate fog nodes, and the cloud server are shown in Table 2 and 3. The CloudAnalyst tool is configured to generate periodic rapid simultaneous requests to create traffic based on 1) the number of online users at a given time, 2) the input data size of requests, 3) the instantaneous network characteristics, and 4) the hardware behavior of the fog nodes, aggregate fog nodes, and cloud servers. Twenty different IoT devices are used to generate different tasks. These includes, among others, smart speakers, smart watches, smartphones, TV sets, smart cane, lighting sets, refrigerators, smart clothes, and biosensors. Five fog nodes are used that have different computational power since fog nodes are heterogeneous in the real world. One aggregate fog node and one cloud server both with ten virtual machines are also considered.

IoT devices initiate requests, send it to the cloud server directly or to the nearest fog node. Based on the proposed algorithm, if it sends the request to a fog node the task would be processed at the receiver fog node or offloaded either to the best neighboring fog node (with minimal response time) or to the aggregate fog node. Since, transmission delay has a huge impact on response time; the bandwidth has been appropriately set between IoT devices and fog nodes, and among fog nodes themselves. Consequently, the link between IoT devices and fog nodes is subdivided into three categories. The bandwidth between IoT devices, that generates simple tasks (S), is assumed to be 250 Kbps. Those IoT devices that generate medium tasks (M) have 25 Mbps and those devices that generate large tasks (L) have a 54 Mbps bandwidth. The transmission rate among fog nodes is set to 100 Mbps as explained in [2, 9]. Depending on the above parameters, the proposed algorithm was compared with FCFS and Dynamic task offloading algorithms as they are put in [10] and [11], respectively.

Even though there are many recently proposed task offloading algorithms in cloud and fog computing systems the two algorithms are selected based on their popularity and regarding as the basic ones in area as discussed in [5] and [12].

First Come First Served Task Offloading Algorithm (FCFS): This algorithm works based on the arrival time of tasks. For time-sensitive applications it is less efficient. The reason behind this is the waiting time for tasks is higher. Large tasks that arrive early need much time for execution and force time-sensitive tasks to wait much longer.

Algorithm - 1: Offloading a Task

Input: Task, the deadline of a task, type of task and candidate nodes n, and data size
Output: Target fog node, Response time
  1. Request received from IoT device
  2. Identify task type (S-small, M-medium, L-large)
  3. If Fog node j is free
  4.   Assign request to the node for execution
  5. End if
  6. Else
  7. If (Deadline > 100ms)
  8.   Offload task to the cloud server
  9. End if
  10. If (Deadline > 80 & Deadline < 100)
  11.   Offload task to the Aggregate fog node
  12. End if
  13. Else
  14. Calculate execution time E_t of the task at node j
  15. Calculate waiting time W_t of the task in the queue
  16. Calculate transmission delay D_t for the task
  17. Calculate Service time (Sojourn time) $S_t = W_t + E_t + D_t$
  18. If (Deadline > S_t)
  19.   Assign task in the queue of node j
  20. End if
  21. Else
  22.   min = S_t
  23. for each candidate node, k = 1 to n do
  24.   calculate transmission delay $D_t(j,k)$
  25.   calculate the execution time of task i at node k
  26.   calculate service time S_{tk} of task i at node k
  27.   if S_{tk} < min
  28.   min = S_{tk}
  29.   End if
  30. End for
  31. If Deadline < min
  32.   Offload task to that node k with min service delay
  33. End if
  34. Else
  35. If Deadline < S_t < min
  36.   Assign the task to node j
  37. End if
  38. Else
  39. Assign the task to the node k with min service time
  40. End

Fig. 3. Pseudocode of the proposed algorithm

Dynamic Task Offloading Algorithm: This algorithm operates based on the queue size of fog nodes. It offloads tasks to neighboring fog node if the queue size exceeds

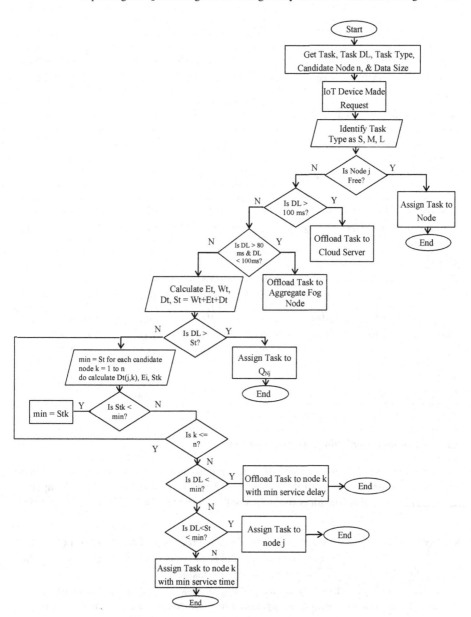

Fig. 4. Flowchart of the proposed algorithm

the threshold value of the fog node. Even though it treats all incoming tasks in the same way, it works better than the FCFS algorithm. Since it only considers the queue size of fog nodes to offload tasks it results in reduced overall response time. However, the requirements of individual tasks are not achieved, oftentimes [12].

Table 2. Processing capability of nodes

Parameter	FN1	FN2	FN3	FN4	FN5	AFN	Cloud Server
Storage (MB)	1000000	500000	500000	700000	1000000	10000000	1000000000
No. of Processors	2	2	2	2	2	4	4

Table 3. Network bandwidth parameters

Node/Node	FN1	FN2	FN3	FN4	FN5	AFN	Cloud
IoT Devices (Kbps/Mbps/ Mbps)	250/25/54	250/25/54	250/25/54	250/25/54	250/25/54	-	250/25/54
FN1	100	100	100	100	100	300	-
FN2	100	100	100	100	100	300	-
FN3	100	100	100	100	100	300	-
FN4	100	100	100	100	100	300	-
FN5	100	100	100	100	100	300	-
AFN	300	300	300	300	300	-	1000
Cloud server	1000	1000	1000	1000	1000	1000	-

5.2 Scenario-Based Comparative Analysis

Experimentation has been done with two different scenarios. These scenarios are aimed to evaluate the effectiveness of the proposed algorithm with nodes processing capabilities. The first scenario considers fog nodes with identical and the second with those with varying processing capabilities.

Scenario 1: Average Delay of Tasks with Similar Processing Capability of Fog Nodes.
Table 4 and Fig. 5 presents the average delay of tasks in the three algorithms when Fog Nodes of identical processing capability is considered.

Table 4 and Fig. 5 shows the average delay of tasks executed on similar fog nodes. The result shows that the proposed algorithm has improved response times that go up to 34% and 22% when compared with FCFS and Dynamic task offloading algorithms.

Scenario 2: Response Time of Tasks with Different Processing Capability of Fog Nodes.
Table 5 and Fig. 6 shows the average delay of tasks in each algorithm by deploying fog nodes with different computational capabilities.

The result shows that the proposed algorithm has up to 37% and 25% improvements of response times when compared with FCFS and Dynamic task offloading algorithms.

The idea behind assigning different computation capability for fog nodes come from real-world scenarios. It tests the proposed algorithm to be useful for resource-constrained

Table 4. Summarized average delay of tasks with similar capability of fog nodes

Tasks	Algorithms		
	FCFS	Dynamic	Proposed
1	50.041	50.043	50.002
2	110.375	107.612	86.395
3	60.238	63.249	51.82
4	64.52	62.249	50.054
5	67.745	61.296	50.818
6	70.172	61.85	50.001
7	73.992	69.968	58.748
8	185.121	155.773	121.648
9	61.893	61.901	50.892
10	65.495	61.536	50.804
11	60.903	56.905	67.882
12	56.043	62.21	50.114
13	130.549	112.874	120.114
14	65.096	50.906	44.811
15	60.94	49.826	46.799
16	49.637	50.829	48.922
17	65.701	57.729	60.194
18	139.754	115.33	125.395
19	59.871	50.493	42.482
20	50.027	54.705	49.709

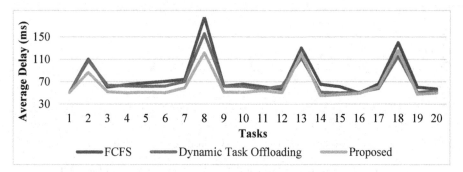

Fig. 5. Average delay of tasks with a similar processing capability of fog nodes

devices and nodes. Moreover, its ability to find and assign tasks to the most appropriate nodes during offloading is exhibited by the results obtained in Table 4 and Fig. 6.

Table 5. Summarized average delay of tasks with different capability of fog nodes

Tasks	Algorithms		
	FCFS	Dynamic	Proposed
1	50.041	50.043	50.03
2	110.375	107.612	83.68
3	60.238	63.249	51.765
4	64.52	62.249	49.935
5	67.745	61.296	50.818
6	70.172	61.85	60.703
7	73.992	69.968	57.33
8	185.121	155.773	116.213
9	61.893	61.901	50.79
10	65.495	61.536	58.712
11	60.903	56.905	46.951
12	56.043	62.21	50.791
13	130.549	112.874	125.536
14	65.096	50.906	43.837
15	60.94	53.826	47.797
16	49.637	50.829	41.861
17	65.701	61.729	54.698
18	139.754	115.33	121.523
19	59.871	50.493	41.473
20	50.027	54.705	45.906

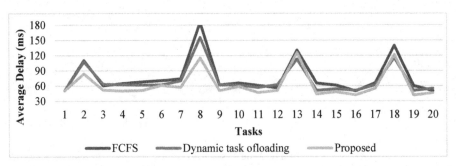

Fig. 6. Average delay of tasks with different processing capability of fog nodes

6   Conclusions

The growth of the Internet of Things (IoT) opens up new challenges and opportunities. Different task scheduling algorithms are proposed to serve those IoT applications. Existing task scheduling algorithms have gaps in treating delay-sensitive tasks arrived at fog nodes. In this paper, deadline-based offloading algorithm has been proposed that can reduce the average delay of tasks. It solves the problem in two ways, one, by prioritizing tasks based on their deadline and offload those tasks that are delay sensitive to neighboring fog nodes that can achieve the delay requirements. The proposed algorithm is evaluated with two other common task-offloading algorithms and using two different scenarios based on varying computational capacities. The results confirmed that it is possible to get up to 37% improvement of average response time of delay sensitive tasks.

Although this work improved the response time of tasks, some critical questions need to be assessed to further understand and improve the effectiveness of the proposed algorithm. The additional energy consumption of the proposed algorithm needs to be investigated to apply it on resource-constrained IoT devices. Moreover, the observed improvements in average response times are not consistent with varying number of tasks which deserve further investigations to know the underlying reasons.

References

1. Alameddine, H.A., Sharafeddine, S., Sebbah, S., Ayoubi, S., Assi, C.: Dynamic task offloading and scheduling for low-latency IoT services in multi-access edge computing. IEEE J. Sel. Areas Commun. **37**(3), 668–682 (2019)
2. Saurabh, S., Hassan, M.F., Khan, M.K., Jung, L.T., Awang, A.: An analytical model to minimize the latency in healthcare internet-of-things in fog computing environment. PLoS ONE **14**(11), e0224934 (2019)
3. Fricker, C., Guillemin, F., Robert, P., Thompson, G.: Analysis of an offloading scheme for data centers in the framework of fog computing. ACM Trans. Model. Perform. Eval. Comput. Syst. (TOMPECS). **1**(4), 1–8 (2016)
4. Ma, X., Zhao, Y., Zhang, L., Wang, H., Peng, L.: When mobile terminals meet the cloud: computation offloading as the bridge. IEEE Network **27**(5), 28–33 (2013)
5. Aazam, M., Zeadally, S., Harras, K.A.: Offloading in fog computing for IoT: review, enabling technologies, and research opportunities. Futur. Gener. Comput. Syst. **87**, 278–289 (2018)
6. La, Q.D., Ngo, M.V., Dinh, T.Q., Quek, T.Q., Shin, H.: Enabling intelligence in fog computing to achieve energy and latency reduction. Digit. Commun. Networks. **5**(1), 3–9 (2019)
7. Wang, S., et al.: Adaptive federated learning in resource constrained edge computing systems. IEEE J. Sel. Areas Commun. **37**(6), 1205–1221 (2019)
8. Elgazar, A., Harras, K., Aazam, M., Mtibaa, A.: Towards intelligent edge storage management: determining and predicting mobile file popularity. In: 2018 6th IEEE International Conference on Mobile Cloud Computing, Services, and Engineering (MobileCloud), pp. 23–28. IEEE, Bamberg, Germany (2018)
9. Yousefpour, A., et al.: FogPlan: a lightweight QoS-aware dynamic fog service provisioning framework. IEEE Internet Things J. **6**(3), 5080–5096 (2019)
10. Wang, T., Wei, X., Tang, C., Fan, J.: Efficient multi-tasks scheduling algorithm in mobile cloud computing with time constraints. Peer-to-Peer Networking Appl. **11**(4), 793–807 (2017). https://doi.org/10.1007/s12083-017-0561-9

11. Jia, M., Liang, W., Xu, Z.: QoS-aware task offloading in distributed cloudlets with virtual network function services. In: Proceedings of the 20th ACM International Conference on Modelling, Analysis and Simulation of Wireless and Mobile Systems, pp. 109–116. Florida, USA (2017)

12. Ghobaei-Arani, M., Souri, A., Rahmanian, A.A.: Resource management approaches in fog computing: a comprehensive review. J. Grid Comput. **18**(1), 1–42 (2019). https://doi.org/10. 1007/s10723-019-09491-1

13. Yousefpour, A., Ishigaki, G., Jue, J.P.: Fog computing: towards minimizing delay in the internet of things. In: 2017 IEEE International Conference on Edge Computing (EDGE), pp. 17–24. IEEE, Honolulu, USA (2017)

14. Kim, S.: New application task offloading algorithms for edge, fog, and cloud computing paradigms. Wirel. Commun. Mobile Comput. (2020)

15. Akherfi, K., Gerndt, M., Harroud, H.: Mobile cloud computing for computation offloading: issues and challenges. Appl. Comput. Inform. **14**(1), 1–6 (2018)

16. Jošilo, S., Dán, G.: Decentralized algorithm for randomized task allocation in fog computing systems. IEEE/ACM Trans. Networking **27**(1), 85–97 (2018)

17. Zhao, X., Zhao, L., Liang, K.: An energy consumption oriented offloading algorithm for fog computing. In: Lee, J.-H., Pack, S. (eds.) QShine 2016. LNICSSITE, vol. 199, pp. 293–301. Springer, Cham (2017). https://doi.org/10.1007/978-3-319-60717-7_29

18. Du, J., Zhao, L., Feng, J., Chu, X.: Computation offloading and resource allocation in mixed fog/cloud computing systems with min-max fairness guarantee. IEEE Trans. Commun. **66**(4), 1594–1608 (2018)

19. Zhu, Q., Si, B., Yang, F., Ma, Y.: Task offloading decision in fog computing system. China Commun. **14**(11), 59–68 (2017)

20. Kan, T.Y., Chiang, Y., Wei, H.Y.: QoS-aware mobile edge computing system: multi-server multi-user scenario. In: 2018 IEEE Globecom Workshops (GC Wokshops), pp. 1–6. IEEE, Abu Dhabi, UAE (2018)

21. Gao, L., Moh, M.: Joint computation offloading and prioritized scheduling in mobile edge computing. In: 2018 International Conference on High Performance Computing and Simulation (HPCS), pp. 1000–1007. IEEE, Orléans, France (2018)

22. Mukherjee, M., et al.: Task data offloading and resource allocation in fog computing with multi-task delay guarantee. IEEE Access. **7**, 152911–152918 (2019)

23. Jin, Y., Lee, H.: On-demand computation offloading architecture in fog networks. Electronics **8**(10), 1076 (2019)

24. Alghamdi, I., Anagnostopoulos, C., Pezaros, D.P.: Delay-tolerant sequential decision making for task offloading in mobile edge computing environments. Information **10**(10), 312 (2019)

25. Xu, J., Hao, Z., Sun, X.: Optimal offloading decision strategies and their influence analysis of mobile edge computing. Sensors. **19**(14), 3231 (2019)

26. Sun, H., Yu, H., Fan, G., Chen, L.: Energy and time efficient task offloading and resource allocation on the generic IoT-fog-cloud architecture. Peer-to-Peer Networking Appl. **13**(2), 548–563 (2019). https://doi.org/10.1007/s12083-019-00783-7

27. Lin, L., Liao, X., Jin, H., Li, P.: Computation offloading toward edge computing. Proc. IEEE **107**(8), 1584–1607 (2019)

28. Vu, T.T., Nguyen, D.N., Hoang, D.T., Dutkiewicz, E., Nguyen, T.V.: Optimal Energy Efficiency with Delay Constraints for Multi-layer Cooperative Fog Computing Networks. arXiv preprint arXiv:1906.03567 (2019)

29. Pan, Y., Jiang, H., Zhu, H., Wang, J.: Latency Minimization for Task Offloading in Hierarchical Fog-Computing C-RAN Networks. arXiv preprint arXiv:2003.11685 (2020)

30. Kang, J., Kim, S., Kim, J., Sung, N., Yoon, Y.: Dynamic offloading model for distributed collaboration in edge computing: a use case on forest fires management. Appl. Sci. **10**(7), 2334 (2020)

31. Hossain, M.D., Sultana, T., Nguyen, V., Nguyen, T.D., Huynh, L.N., Huh, E.N.: Fuzzy based collaborative task offloading scheme in the densely deployed small-cell networks with multi-access edge computing. Appl. Sci. **10**(9), 3115 (2020)

32. Bala, M.I., Chishti, M.A.: Optimizing the computational offloading decision in cloud-fog environment. In: 2020 International Conference on Innovative Trends in Information Technology (ICITIIT), pp. 1–5. IEEE, Kottayam, India (2020)

33. Misra, S., Saha, N.: Detour: dynamic task offloading in software-defined fog for IoT applications. IEEE J. Sel. Areas Commun. **37**(5), 1159–1166 (2019)

34. Josilo, S.: Task placement and resource allocation in edge computing systems. Ph.D. diss., KTH Royal Institute of Technology (2020)

35. Hussein, M.K., Mousa, M.H.: Efficient task offloading for IoT-based applications in fog computing using ant colony optimization. IEEE Access. **8**, 37191–37201 (2020)

36. Al-Khafajiy, M., Baker, T., Waraich, A., Al-Jumeily, D., Hussain, A.: IoT-fog optimal workload via fog offloading. In: 2018 IEEE/ACM International Conference on Utility and Cloud Computing Companion (UCC Companion), pp. 359–364. IEEE, Zurich, Switzerland (2018)

37. Shuminoski, T., Kitanov, S., Janevski, T.: Advanced QoS provisioning and mobile fog computing for 5G. Wirel. Commun. Mobile Comput. 2018 (2018)

Demystifying Predictive Analytics with Data Mining to Optimize Fraud Detection in the Insurance Industry

Betelhem Zewdu[1]([✉]) and Gebeyehu Belay[2]

[1] School of Computing and Informatics, Department of Information Technology, Wachemo University, Hosaena, Ethiopia
[2] Institute of Technology, Computing Faculty, Bahir Dar University, Poly Main Campus, Agri Building 71 First Floor, Bahir Dar, Ethiopia

Abstract. The insurance industry is a company that renders risk management in the form of finance, humans, etc. ensuring contracts. Fraud is one risk, which does for self benefits or interest. In workmen's compensation, insurance fraud is intentional deception for gaining some interest in the form of health expenditures, which is challenging to handle manually. In this study, we proposed and introduced a novel approach to demystifying a predictive analytics approach using data mining techniques. The model can detect and predict fraud suspicious insurance claims with a particular emphasis on Insurance Corporation in the case of Workmen's Compensation. We use ensemble clustering followed by classification techniques for developing the predictive model. The predictive analytics applied to build an analytical model of the known variables' value to build a model that can predict the value of the variable of the unknown value. K-Means clustering algorithm is employed to find the natural grouping of the different insurance claims as fraud and non-fraud. The resulting cluster is employed to develop the classification model. The classification performed using the J48 and JRip algorithm to create the model of classifying fraud suspicious insurance claims using the AdaBoost method JRip as a base classifier, and it scored an accuracy of 98.26% on an 80% split CLAIM_REPORT_LENGTH_DATE is the determinant factor for predict fraud suspicious.

Keywords: Fraud · Detection · Data mining · Optimization · Predictive analytics · Determinant factor

1 Introduction

The insurance industry is a growing industry, which plays a vital role in ensuring the economic aspects of a county. In the encyclopedia, insurance is a sector of protection or risk management from losses. Risk management to hedge against the problem of accidental or uncertain circumstances. Fraud protection is a problem and a concern for many organizations. Fraud in workmen's compensation insurance is an intentional

M. A. Delele et al. (Eds.): ICAST 2020, LNICST 384, pp. 432–442, 2021.
https://doi.org/10.1007/978-3-030-80621-7_31

deception to gain benefits in the form of health expenditures. A false representation of facts in words or conduct, misleading claims, or concealment of what should have been disclosed that cheats and is intended to deceive. It is an illegal action of the individual will act upon someone else or institutes to theft or injury [1]. For example, a dishonest person may be called a fraud. Therefore, the data towards such practices are challenging and huge. The data is sensitive and also sophisticated, which is growing in a multi-dimension.

There are two most common types of claimant workmen's compensation fraud occurring in the insurance company [2]. (i) Abusers fraud: employees might not injure at work, or that can happen elsewhere and claim the injury occurred at work. Some of these may not document fraudulent workers' compensation claims but also file fraudulent automobile or general liability claims. (ii) Opportunists fraud: these employees are injured at work but then take advantage of more benefits than they should. They work to extend their interest beyond a reasonable period; exaggerate their symptoms; are uncooperative with treatment plans, and use delaying techniques when medical providers or employers take positive actions for the claims management process. Claims by opportunists can also become very costly, again deflecting payments from the parties who deserve them. The most common form of workmen's compensation insurance fraud is the exaggeration of claims; this refers to as Opportunistic Fraud.

Insurance companies are collected a large amount of data in their day to day activities. As the company's services and works become more advanced in technology, insurance companies store a large amount of data from their customers every day in a claim process. A very large amount of data is generated from a different database like underwriting and claim departments. These data are invaluable information about their customers' behavior, service, and preferences. The huge amount of data stored by a company it must be further manipulated to get useful information. However, to extract valuable information from this enormous data it takes time and effort for companies in hand. Knowledge extracted from the data can be used to develop new products and services to meet customers' needs. The need to provide more effective and customer-centric service becomes necessary to succeed in the business. Due to their protective regulations, extracting information from the database caused a lot of time. In this situation, the potential applicability of data mining is, therefore, to extract useful knowledge, pattern, and prediction ability from this data.

The fraud problem is the fact of a fraudulent claim, which is a concern of financial burden on insurers and result in the overall insurance costs. The estimated cost of property and casualty fraud each year is billion dollars losses [3]. According to IBM Corporation, insurance companies lose millions of dollars each year through fraudulent claims because they do not have a way to detect which claims are legitimate and which may be fraudulent.

Furthermore, fraud is a major problem for the insurance industry. Although the true cost of fraud for the industry, and subsequently for insurance policyholders who bear this cost through higher premiums cannot be known. The FBI estimates the total cost of insurance fraud is estimated to be more than $40 billion per year [4]. Another research indicates the annual insurance fraud cost for the property and casualty insurance industry is over 25 billion dollars. From this Workers' compensation insurance alone accounts for a sizable portion of this total cost [5]. To explore such complex data, an advanced analytic tool is pertinent, which is proposed in this study, predictive analytics with data mining techniques and algorithms.

2   Related Works

There are also researches conducted to investigate the application of data mining in the insurance industry. As [6] has tried to apply Data Mining Techniques in Health Fraud Detection, and [7] worked on Detection of Automobile Insurance Fraud [5]. The conducted research is also on Predicting Workers' Compensation insurance fraud use SAS Enterprise Miner 5.1 and SAS Text Miner. The author focused on building predictive models to score an open claim for a propensity to be fraudulent [8]. It also worked Mining Insurance Data for Fraud Detection in the area of motor insurance at Africa Insurance Share Company. The author tried to do the applicability of the data mining technique in developing models that can detect and predict fraud suspicious insurance claims. The same work also has been done [9] An Integration of Prediction Model with Knowledge Base System for Motor Insurance Fraud Detection in the case of Awash Insurance Company S.C. The author tried to integrate the predictive model with a knowledge base system to detect insurance fraud.

Moreover, [10] studied the identification algorithm and model construction of Automobile Insurance Fraud by using data mining technology, which depends on an outlier's data [11]. Also studied in fraud detection in health insurance using data mining techniques. And this paper explores predictive analytics in insurance fraud detection using data mining technique. In addition to this, [12] also researched Data Mining Techniques in Fraud Detection. He focused on present some classification and prediction data mining techniques which is important to handle fraud detection [13]. Works on Modeling Insurance Fraud Detection Using Ensemble Combining Classification. He tried to solve the imbalance dataset problem by applying a proposed novel partitioning-under sampling technique using base-classifiers for insurance fraud detection.

3   Methodology

In this research work, we use the rule to identify red flag variables to scores the claims, which indicates fraud or not. In addition to this, the data analytics approach employs to discover hidden patterns in the data, which support fraud prediction. The predictive model is the one in data analytics, and it needs categorized data about fraud and non-fraud suspicious from the historical data. However, the data, we get from the insurance is not organized. So, to conduct this experimental research first, it needs to develop clustering techniques followed by classification. Unsupervised Clustering technique classifies the data into clusters having similar characteristics using the right set of variables that are indicative of fraudulent claims that should be able to cluster the fraudulent claims and non-fraudulent claims in different clusters. K-mean clustering is one of the algorithms we use for this research work. And the second technique develops a classification model, which helps to predict insurance fraud suspicious claims. For this purpose, the J48 decision tree and JRip rule-based algorithm are applied, as it is shown in Fig. 1.

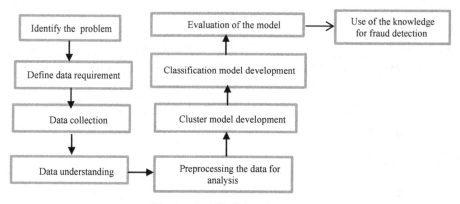

Fig. 1. Model building flowchart

For this thesis work, secondary data are used from the database of the EIC main branch in Addis Ababa. There are different insurances offered by the company, from this, the study is considered in workmen's compensation daily claim registration/process form to be filled by the experts of the insurance company. We use WEKA data mining tool for analysis purpose because it is java based open-source data mining tool which has a collection of data mining algorithms such as lazy, rules-based, decision trees, and so on. The original dataset which gets from the INSIS database is 17296 records, 27 attributes and the file size is a 6.56MB from the year 2011–2015 G.C. The whole dataset, which is gotten from the insurance database, is not important to the data mining task. We took a long time to preprocess the data i.e. the irrelevant or inappropriate data fields/records are removed first discuss with the domain experts in the insurance because they have not any influence on fraud detection. For this study, the object type column missed value filled by WEKA ReplaceMissingValues nearest records mean value (the most common class). CLAIM_REPORT_LENGTH_DATE (this refers to the length of the accident report date since its occurrence) is derived from the EVENT DATE and NOTIFICATION DATE columns of the data set. CLAIM_REPORT_LENGTH_DATE = EVENT_DATE-NOTIFICATION_DATE.

After discarding the irrelevant data, the total records account in the study is 1.92 MB with 17275 records and 10 attributes are prepared for further computational analysis listed in the following table, Table 1.

4 Experiment and Discussion

For the proposed predictive model, we use 17275 records and 10 attributes dataset for clustering and classification algorithms. K-Means clustering-based model use as an input for classification techniques using the J48 decision tree and JRip rules algorithm. Thre experiments using a clustering algorithm to change the default parameter of the K-Means algorithm for labeled the claim as fraud and non-fraud and select. The categories of features as their similarities to the segment of the claim within a cluster. For validating the clustering result, which is the initial model of the empirical analysis of the given instance, the researcher would use the number of iteration within a cluster sum of squared

Table 1. Final selected attribute for the study

No	Attribute name	Data type	Description	Remark
1	CLAIM_REPORT_LENGTH_DATE	Varchar2	The length of the accident report date since the occurrence of an accident	Derived
2	CLAIM_OFFICE	Varchar2	Branch service unit. The data type of this attribute is initially Number	
3	RISK_TYPE	Varchar2	The type of risk has occurred in the accident	
4	CLAIM_STATE	Varchar2	Refers to the status of the claim. The data type of this attribute is initially Number	
5	COVER_TYPE	Varchar2	The type of policy/coverage the insured buy from the insurance	
6	NOTIFICATION_DATE	Varchar2	The event/ accident that has been notified in the insurance. The data type of this attribute is initially date	
7	EVENT_PLACE	Varchar2	The place where the accident has occurred	
8	OBJECT_TYPE	Varchar2	Whether the insurance was bought as an individual or group. The data type of this attribute is initially Number	
9	PROFESSION	Varchar2	The type of job of the insured	
10	CLAIM_AMOUNT	Varchar2	The amount of recovered money	

error and domain expert judgment. For clustering algorithms, we set a threshold value to determine what patterns discover for each subsequent cluster model, which supports to identify and label the cluster based on given data. We set the value of k as 2 for identity fraud and non-fraud from the given data sets. In addition to this, the 10-folds cross-validation and percentage split test options are used for training and testing the classification model. These are the experimental setups that we follow to do the analysis.

4.1 Clustering-Based Model Development

Before experimenting, the threshold value set for numeric attributes, which use build, the clustering model. The threshold value for each attributes determined using Weka's minimum, maximum, and mean values displayed for the attribute shows in Table 2.

Table 2. Threshold values used for a cluster

CLAIM_REPORT_LENGTH_DATE		CLAIM_AMOUNT				
		DEATH	PTD	TTD	MHFO	Threshold
0–5	Fast	<10,000	<2000	≤1500	<500	Low
6–15	Moderate	≤20,000	≤3500	≤1750	<1000	Medium
>15	Slow	>20,000	>3500	>1750	>1000	High

In Table 2, the field annotated as PTD is permanent total disablement. TTD is temporary total disablement. MHFO is Medical, Pharmaceutical, Hospital, Funeral, and Other. The number of clusters chosen based on data sets and its clear visualization towards fraud detection. Among the experiments we did, we selected the last ones. For validating the clustering result that the intracluster similarity measure (within-cluster sum of squared error) is the number of iteration of the experiments for the converge as possible [14]. In addition to this, the domain expert's objectiveness evaluation, which considering the claim notification period, document submission formats, length of the claim report date, and other information. The following table shows the selected cluster experiment for the study in Table 3.

Table 3. Training of the 2nd experiment with seed value 10 to 100 and default distance function

Clustering result of the Second Experiment						
Distance function	K-value	Seed Value	Cluster Distribution		Number of Iteration	Within cluster sum of squared errors
			C1	C2	5	82869.74
Euclidean distance	2	100	4242 (25%)	13033 (75%)		

The second experiment presents for each segment of the cluster, as it shows in Table 4. The ranking is determined based on the fraudulence nature of the insurance claims.

Table 4. The 2nd experiment clustering result and rank of clusters

Cluster	Description	Rank
1	Slow claim reported date, Northern Addis branch, WC_MHFO risk type, Annulled claim state, WRKMEN_CMG cover type, Notification date Friday, event place Others, object type Group, High claim amount, and All Other Estates: Machinists and Drivers Profession	1 (this means this cluster is considered as fraud suspicious)
2	Fast claim reported date, South Addis branch, WC_MHFO risk type, paid claim state, WRKMEN_CMG cover type, Notification date Tuesday, event place Others, object type Group and Low claim amount and Daily Laborers Profession	2 (this means this cluster is considered as non-fraud)

From three experiments that were done in the clustering technique, the one is select with a smaller cluster sum square error and a minimum number of iteration depicts in the following figure, Fig. 2.

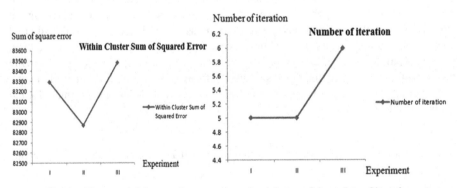

Fig. 2. Cluster model sum of square error clustering model number of iteration

4.2 Classification Based Model Development

After we developed a clustering model, we developed a predictive model using the classification techniques to define the fraud parameters. The predictive model developed using the J48 decision tree, JRip rule algorithm, and the ensemble method. From the ensemble method, the Meta classifier of Adaboost and Bagging with J48 and JRip has as the base learners, whereas stacking to mix two algorithms J48 and JRip in the classifier of the J48 algorithm. The records are classified based on their values for the given cluster index, and the model is trained by employing the 10-fold cross-validation and the percentage split classification modes (Table 5).

Table 5. 80% split of ensemble method with JRip as base learner

Method	Algorithm	Correctly classified		Incorrectly classified		Time taken/s
		In %	Instance	In %	Instance	
AdaBoost	JRip	98.26	3395	1.73	60	355.43 s
Bagging		95.97	3316	4.02	139	987.45 s
Stacking	JRip & J48	96.23	3325	3.76	130	1181.87 s
80% training and 20% testing percentage split						

From the above table, in an 80% split, the Adaboost Meta classifier for the JRip algorithm scored an accuracy of 98.26%. From total testing datasets of 3455 records, 3395 records are correctly classified, while 60 records are incorrectly classified. On the other hand, bagging classifier scores the accuracy of 95.97% and 3316 records are classified correctly while 139 records are classified incorrectly from a total number of the testing set. Besides this, the stacking method classifier scored 96.23% accuracy and from the total testing set, 3325 records are correctly classified whereas 130 records are incorrectly classified from the total testing set.

4.3 Comparative Analysis

For this study, a number of the experiment was done but we present only the finally selected ones in the above table. However, these are some experiments done for the classification model in the single and ensemble method mention in Table 6 to select the final one.

Figure 3 shows the comparison of ensemble method classifiers in an 80% percentage split.

As the experiment result showed, the pattern that characterizes the length of the claim report date is slow, the claim state is annulled, the notification date is either Monday or Friday and the claim amount is high, a given claim is fraud suspicious. On the other hand, the length of the claim report date is fast, the claim state is paid, the notification date is neither Monday nor Friday, and the claim amount is low, a given claim is a non-fraud suspicious claim. Plus, the proposed work is demystifying the predictive analytics for workmen's insurance fraud suspicious claims by using an ensemble method and defining the determinant factors, which produces higher performance classification accuracy. Therefore, it is conceivable to conclude that the Adaboost ensemble method JRip algorithm as a base classifier is more appropriate to this particular case.

Table 6. Model comparison

Method	Algorithm	Accuracy of Models in %
Single	J48	96.19
	JRip	96.30
AdaBoost	J48	96.29
	JRip	97.74
Bagging	J48	96.59
	JRip	96.61
Stacking	JRip &J48	96.75
10 folds cross-validation		
Single	J48	95.83
	JRip	95.89
AdaBoost	J48	96.43
	JRip	**98.26**
Bagging	J48	96.09
	JRip	95.97
Stacking	JRip & J48	96.23
80% training and 20% testing percentage split		

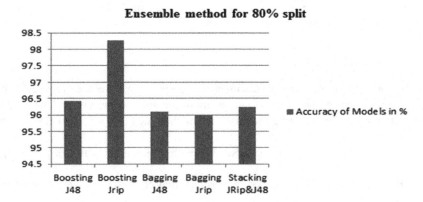

Fig. 3. Ensemble methods for comparison in 80% split

In addition to this, as we see a determinant factor in gain ratio the CLAIM_REPORT _LENGTH _DATE is the most determinant factor that causes predict fraud suspicious claim. Besides claim state and the claim amount is also the determinant factor. Here are some rules that gain from the JRip rule-based classifier algorithm.

Rule1: (CLAIM_REPORT_LENGTH_DATE = Slow) and (CLAIM_STATE = Annulled) and (NOTIFICATION_DATE = Friday) => Cluster = cluster0 (Fraud Suspicious)

If claim report length date = Slow AND claim state = Annulled AND notification date = Friday THEN the probability is to suspect fraud.

Rule2: (CLAIM_AMOUNT = High) and (CLAIM_REPORT_LENGTH_DATE = Slow) and (CLAIM_STATE = Annulled) => Cluster = cluster0 (Fraud Suspicious)

If claim amount = High AND claim report length date = Slow AND claim state = Annulled THEN predicts to suspect fraud.

Rule3: (CLAIM_STATE = Paid) and (OBJECT_TYPE = Individual) and (NOTIFICA-TION_DATE = Tuesday) => Cluster = cluster1 (Non- Fraud Suspicious)

If claim state = Paid AND object type = Individual AND notification date = Tuesday the probability is non-fraud.

5 Conclusion

In conclusion, insurance companies lose millions of dollars each year through fraudulent claims. And predictive analytics ways used to minimize fraud by detecting the cases. The data we used obtained from the insurance company database. It did not indicate a given claim is whether fraudulent or not, use a clustering technique to find out the natural grouping of data. The data set clustered and used as an input for the classification technique to predict fraud. We use the K-Means clustering algorithm for segmenting the data into the target classes of fraud and non-fraud. By changing the default parameters of the data, the experiments are done to generate a conceptual model that can create different cluster groups of insurance claims. Among the three models, the one with K = 2, Seed value = 100, and Euclidean distance function revealed better segmentation of the insurance claims.

The clustering outputs used for input for the classification model for model building using the J48 decision tree, JRip rule algorithm, and ensemble method. The model developed with the 10-fold cross-validation and 80% percentage split. From this model boosting ensemble method, particularly Adaboost Meta classifier JRip rule as a base classifier scored accuracy 98.26%, which better than the other and the final selected algorithm for this study. And, CLAIM_REPORT_LENGHT_DATE is the determinant factor that predicts fraud.

Acknowledgments. We would like to thanks the anonymous reviewers for their detailed review, valuable comments, and constructive suggestions. This research did not receive any specific grant from funding agencies in the public, commercial, or not-for-profit sectors.

References

1. FBI Insurance Fraud. https://www.fbi.gov/stats-services/publications/insurance-fraud. Accessed 24 Aug 2020

2. Woodfield, T.J.: Predicting Workers' Compensation Insurance Fraud Using SAS® Enterprise Miner™ 5.1 and SAS® Text Miner (2005)
3. Yan, C., Li, Y.: The identification algorithm and model construction of automobile insurance fraud based on data mining. In: Fifth International Conference on Instrumentation & Measurement, Computer, Communication and Control (IMCCC) (2015)
4. Rawte, V., Anuradha, G.: Fraud detection in health insurance using data mining techniques. In: International Conference on Communication, Information & Computing Technology (ICCICT) (2015)
5. Bhowmik, R.: Data mining techniques in fraud detection. J. Digit. Forensics Secur. Law **3** (2015)
6. Hassan, A.K.I., Abraham, A.: Modeling insurance fraud detection using ensemble combining classification. Int. J. Comput. Inf. Syst. Ind. Manag. Appl. **8**, 257–265 (2016)
7. Farlex Inc. Fraud (2013). http://legaldictionary.thefreedictionary.com/fraud. Accessed 3 Sept 2016
8. Jennings, G.: The three most common types of workers' comp fraud, and how to prevent them, 11 November 2014. http://www.propertycasualty360.com/2014/11/11/here-are-the-3-most-common-types-of-workers-comp-f. Accessed 31 Mar 2017
9. IBM Financial Crimes Insight for Claims Fraud (2020)
10. Pal, R., Pal, S.: Application of data mining techniques in health fraud detection. Int. J. Eng. Res. Gener. Sci. **3**(5), 129–137 (2015)
11. Subudhi, S., Panigrahi, S.: Detection of automobile insurance fraud using feature selection and data mining techniques. Int. J. Rough Sets Data Anal. **5**(3), 1–20 (2018). https://doi.org/10.4018/IJRSDA.2018070101
12. Tariku, A.: Mining insurance data for fraud detection: the case of Africa insurance share company. Master thesis Addis Abeba University, June 2011
13. Abdi, C.: An integration of prediction model with knowledge base system for motorinsurance fraud detection: the case of awash insurance company S.C. Master thesis Addis Abeba University, February 2016
14. Jain, S., Aalam, M.A., Doja, M.N.: K-means clustering using WEKA interface. In: Computing For Nation Development (2010)

Efficient Image Processing Technique for Solid Waste Bin Detection

Bereket Simon Balcha$^{(\boxtimes)}$

Department of Information Technology, Wolkite University, Wolkite, Ethiopia
bereket.simon@wku.edu.et

Abstract. The main challenge in the technology of image processing is designing of efficient technique for a suitable application area, because the technology is application dependent. Therefore, great attention must be given to designing of the efficient technique and utilizing of the efficient one for the right application. The main aim of this paper is proposed to design image processing techniques by applying Canny edge detection method for extraction of edges. Next, Hough Transform (HT) for getting strong and thin lines from extracted edges. Eventually, orthogonality checking for corner detection and cropped corner parts of image for similarity matching to detect solid waste bin (SWB). To detect corner of the image correctly, two orthogonal lines whose length and coordinate points are thoroughly considered. These orthogonal lines are extracted from detected corners. A 20-by-20pixel width of the detected corner part is cropped. Similarity matching of template image with original image by using cross correlation is done for the correctly detected corner part of the images. Eventually, performance evaluation of the designed technique with existing techniques is done which shows the proposed technique is efficient in detection of SWB.

Keywords: Canny · Hough transform · Orthogonality checking · Corner detection · Cross correlation · Solid waste bin

1 Introduction

Image processing is a way of performing operations such as preprocessing, segmentation, feature extractions and classifications of digital images on digital computer using computer vision algorithms. Image processing technique is a method or an algorithm used to perform these operations. The digital image processing technology has been widely used in many scopes such as solid waste management, food engineering, environment and medical care and so on [1].

The secret of selecting image processing in this work rather than another related technology like machine learning, deep learning is since the input image, SWB, should not be labeled and no need of layering the image. This is because it is possible to identify the image having captured it correctly from its dumping area.

© ICST Institute for Computer Sciences, Social Informatics and Telecommunications Engineering 2021
Published by Springer Nature Switzerland AG 2021. All Rights Reserved
M. A. Delele et al. (Eds.): ICAST 2020, LNICST 384, pp. 443–456, 2021.
https://doi.org/10.1007/978-3-030-80621-7_32

In digital image processing, image preprocessing, edge detection, feature extraction and classification are particularly the major stages [2, 3]. Techniques for each phase are different even if the whole phases are applied to one specific application. Researches are also undertaken separately for these stages as well. Image preprocessing is a way of removing unwanted information from the image before submitting it to the next image processing stages. It is the method used to prepare images for the further analysis like segmentation and feature extraction [3].

Image segmentation is the most important and challenging task in image processing. It is a process of partitioning an image into meaningful parts which have similar properties and features [4].

The main reason [4] for segmentation in image processing is to extract some features from the image for further analysis. One type of this segmentation is edge detection which is the way of extracting available edges from the images.

One of the most important application areas of the image processing technology is SWB detection. The SWB is a container that contains rubbish until it is collected and disposed. The solid waste is daily outcome of human activities, which can never stop [1]. There are various sources of solid waste which generates large and diverse nature of waste in urban cities. The SWB detection using image processing is a way of detecting the bin by using different image processing techniques [1, 5].

In here, author designed efficient method for SWB detection using image processing techniques such as edge detection, line detection, corner detection and similarity matching. The SWB image data is used by capturing the bin directly from the waste dumping area in Addis Ababa city.

2   Related Work

2.1   Edge Detection Technique

An edge is the most significant feature in the image to analyze the image. And edge detection is the most important and hot research field in the computer vision. There are many edge detection techniques in the image processing.

The works in [6, 7] surveyed the common and classical edge detection algorithms under image segmentation in image processing. The author of this paper concluded that Canny edge detection algorithm is an optimal algorithm among the recommended edge detection algorithms like Sobel, Laplacian of Gaussian and Prewitt edge detectors. Other than Canny edge detection technique, these three techniques have performance problems. Some of these problems are resulting in high error rate which means there are a response for non-edge during edge extraction, high distance of edge pixels in actual and testing images, and there is also a probability of occurrence of noisy pixels in extracted edges [6, 7]. The main secret of famousness of this algorithm is it has three special good characteristics. As authors [6–8] illustrated three good criteria of this algorithm are: first-low error rate this means that edge occurring in the image should not be missed and there should be no response for non-edge. Second-good localization this means the distance between the edge pixels as found by the detector and the actual edge is to be minimum and the third criteria is single response this means that to have one response for a single edge. These three criteria made the Canny edge detection algorithm the leading-edge detection algorithm in the field of image processing.

2.2 Applications of Image Processing in SWB Detection

As the application areas of image processing is not limited to specific discipline, there are many more contributions of the technology to many domains. One of the applications which is selected by respective researcher of this work is SWB detection and monitoring. Then, the respective author focused on designing an efficient image processing and detection technique for the SWB. Contribution of image processing to effective SWB detection is that, firstly, data acquisition is done, then the color image is converted to grayscale image. Then the grayscale image is resized accordingly and given to edge detection method.

Having detected available edges from the SWB, an edge connection and line formation method is applied. After extracting strong straight lines, the target area should be identified. Eventually, similarity matching is computed to identify true images and match a template image with image in database images [9, 10].

Shafiqul et al. [5] developed the system for SWB detection and classification using image processing. The work tried to bring good solution for SWB detection having used embedded system. However, the system used inefficient image processing techniques such as Dynamic Time Warping (DTW) which detects the bin of solid waste. The drawback of this work is that the work did not consider what will happen if there is noise in the image which means there is no image smoothing method used. The work is also computationally too expensive during calculating whole parts of template with original image for similarity matching.

Hannan et al. [11] developed the system to extract features from the SWB to detect and classify the SWB level using image processing. The work solves the urgent problem by extracting features which is easy and fast to decide the waste level. However, the work did not use efficient image processing technique to extract features and computationally expensive because it considers whole image pixels during matching for true images. There is no described technique for corner detection of the bin as well. The work extracts features using HT only which is not the right way in image processing. Because firstly, the image should be detected correctly having done the right edge detection techniques, then line should have been detected using HT. And also, mechanism to detect the corner of the SWB should be clearly done then, suitable similarity matching techniques should be used. The work missed these main techniques.

3 Proposed Solution

3.1 Introduction

The main objective of this paper is to design efficient image processing technique which effectively detects the SWB. The new technique results:

- effective in edge detection
- effective in line detection
- effective in corner detection
- effective in similarity matching

3.2 Edge Detection Method

In this paper, author selected Canny edge detection to extract and detect the edges from the grayscale image of SWB effectively. The reason for the selection of this technique is already said by previous researchers that the method is effective in resulting in response to single edge, low error rate and good localization.

Therefore, based on this evidence the method is chosen for this paper and details of working principle for this Canny edge detection technique is clearly depicted in the methodology part in the following Fig. 1.

3.3 Line Detection Technique

In this paper HT technique is used and which is an efficient method for detecting lines in binary images. The idea of the Hough algorithm is to transform the shape of interest into its parameter space. For instance, a line in a Cartesian coordinate system (x, y) can be represented as [12],

$$y = mx + b \tag{1}$$

where m is slope of the line and b is interception with y. Each line is characterized uniquely by pair of constants m and b. Consequently, any line can be represented by a point in a coordinate system m and b. In another word, any point (x, y) is associated with a set of values for m and b which satisfy Eq. 1, and can be rewritten as [12],

$$m = \frac{y}{x} - \frac{1}{x}b \tag{2}$$

Therefore, each point (x, y) is represented by a line in a (m, n) space. Algorithmic steps for slope-intercept parametrization of HT looks like the following ones [12, 13]:

- Build a parameter space with suitable quantization level for line slope m and intercept b,
- Create an accumulator array A (m, b),
- Set A (m, b) = 0 ∀ (m, b),
- Extract image edge using Canny edge detector,
- For each pixel on image edges (xi, yi) ∀ (mk, bl), verify equation: $b = x_i mk + y_j$, Increment A (mk, bl) = A (mk, bl) + 1,
- Find the local maxima in the A (mk, bl) which indicates the lines in the parameter space.

Moreover, the slope intercept parameterization is quite acceptable. But there is a problem when vertical lines are close to vertical. In this situation, the slope approaches to infinity. To avoid this problem [13], polar coordinates should be used, which are expressed as:

$$\rho = x \cos\theta + y \sin\theta \tag{3}$$

Where ρ is the minimum distance to the origin and θ is the angle of the line with the horizontal axis, both are related to m and b through

$$m = -\frac{\cos\theta}{\sin\theta} \tag{4}$$

$$b = \frac{\rho}{\sin\theta} \tag{5}$$

3.4 Designing of Corner Detection Technique

Having detected strong lines from HT technique, it is needed to detect corners of the SWB correctly and efficiently. Corner detection is a method of detecting intersecting of two orthogonal lines for the SWB [14, 15]. In here, the main thing to extract lines which could be corners are identified by using orthogonality of two lines.

In addition to this, lengths and angles of lines are also considered. However, to identify the two orthogonal lines, the author of this research work used intersection points for these two orthogonal lines.

To test that two lines are orthogonal, it is necessary to use the following equations [16].

$$\rho 1 = \cos\theta 1 x + \sin\theta 1 y \tag{6}$$

$$\rho 2 = \cos\theta 2 x + \sin\theta 2 y \tag{7}$$

$$(\cos\theta 1 * \cos\theta 2) + (\sin\theta 1 * \sin\theta 2) = 0 \tag{8}$$

$$x = ((\rho 1 \sin\theta 2) - (\rho 2 \sin\theta 1)) / ((\cos\theta 1 * \sin\theta 2) - (\cos\theta 2 * \sin\theta 1)) \tag{9}$$

$$y = ((\rho 1 \cos \theta 2) - (\rho 2 \cos \theta 1)) / ((\cos \theta 2 * \sin \theta 1) - (\cos \theta 1 * \sin \theta 2)) \qquad (10)$$

If Eq. 8 is true, then the two lines are orthogonal unless two lines are not orthogonal. And Eqs. 9 and 10 show that the intersection coordinate for two orthogonal lines. If these equations satisfy, then it is possible to find corners by using intersection point for only two orthogonal lines. In this case, it must be noted that to get corners for SWB image, the above equations should be satisfied. Therefore, from top lines extracted from HT technique, lines which are orthogonal are considered to detect corners for SWB image. However, there are many lines may be orthogonal to each other, but to detect corners from these many orthogonal lines, the lengths and intersection points for those particular orthogonal lines are considered to efficiently detect true corners from those of unnecessary lines among top lines.

3.5 Similarity Matching Method

In this paper cross correlation is technique is used and which is a way of performing similarity matching between template and actual images. The equation for correlation coefficient to do similarity matching is as follows [4, 17]:

$$c(I, T) = \frac{\sum m \sum n(I_{mn} - \mu_I)(T - \mu_T)}{\sqrt{\left(\sum m \sum n(I_{mn} - \mu_I)^2\right)\left(\sum m \sum n(T_{mn} - \mu_T)^2\right)}} \qquad (11)$$

Where I is the candidate corner area in the image, T is the SWB template, m and n are indices to each pixel in I and μI and μT are means of pixel values of I and T respectively. The location of the template superimposed on the actual image with the highest correlation value is considered as true image.

To do similarity matching, rather than checking whole part of image which will be computationally too cost, author used the following method to do it. First, the orthogonality of the two intersecting lines is checked, then the coordinate for these lines is computed and considered as corner of the image as well as it is checked with the coordinate of the template image. Then, 20-by-20pixel width of the detected corner is cropped. Finally, by using cross correlation, this cropped image is checked with all respective cropped images of original with the same pixel width as template image, 20-by-20. The correlation coefficient whose coefficient is highest is considered as true corner and in turn true image SWB.

3.6 Architecture of the Methodology

In this paper, author designed the efficient image processing technique by using the following methodology.

- Description for above Methodology

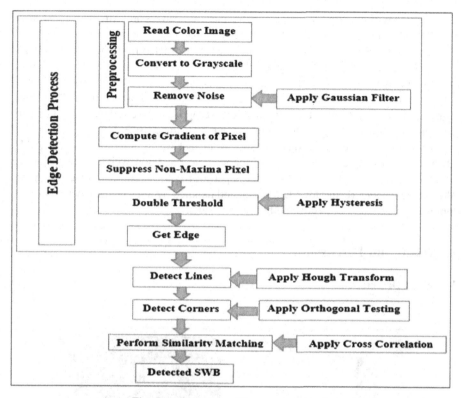

Fig. 1. Architecture of the proposed work

This above Fig. 1 shows firstly, the color image whose pixel value is around 2^{24} is given as input to the system, then the system converts it to grayscale image whose pixel value is around 256 to reduce the computation cost. The color image is captured from real waste dumping place from Addis Ababa city around sub-city of Akaki-Kality in area of Alembank, and Akaki.

The design methodology used here is probable simple sample method. The reason is because the shape of SWB is rectangular shape and it is the same in all cities of Addis Ababa. And the image is captured by smartphone of TECNO mobile with selfie camera stick. During capturing, the distance between the camera man and the bin is around 2 m away and from surface of the bin to top of camera selfie stick is 3-m-long. Because to effectively capture four corners of the bin, the distance should be thoroughly determined.

Then, an image preprocessing technique which is Gaussian filter is applied to smooth the image and remove random noise occurs during image capturing. Having removed the noise, computation of gradient for a pixel is done to extract the edges with its direction from the image. Next to this, Non-Maxima Suppression (NMS) which ignores weak edges and reserves strong edges based on fixed high and low threshold value T.

Then again, applying double threshold to finalize the edge extraction process. This is the process of removing thick edges and reserving thin and strong edges which could be actual edges of the original image. Finally, the strong edges are extracted. These steps show the edge detection process as it has been depicted in the figure.

Next to edge extraction process, strong lines are extracted from the extracted edges using HT. Then, from extracted available lines, the system detects corner by considering the length and intersection point of these two orthogonal or intersecting lines. From detected corner, the system computes an angle from these orthogonal lines. Then after, 20-by-20pixel width from detected corner part is cropped to do effectively the similarity matching of template image with original image by using cross correlation.

For this paper, the image data is taken from real waste dumping place in Addis Ababa city by using selfie stick and smartphone to test that how well the new technique works. The reason is that since this work is part of research-project initiated by Addis Ababa Science and Technology University and handled by a team in the department of computer science and respective author of this paper.

4 Result and Discussion

4.1 Edge Detection

a) Grayscale image   b) extracted edge

Fig. 2. Edge extraction process

Above Fig. 2 shows extraction of edges by using Canny edge technique. As it is said Canny technique is optimal edge techniques by previous researchers resulting in single edge, low error rate and good localization. Based on this information, author of this paper applied the technique to grayscale image because the technique is only applicable for grayscale image and the result is shown in Fig. 2 in b.

And the technique also smooths the random noise and results in preprocessed result by involving Gaussian filter with in it.

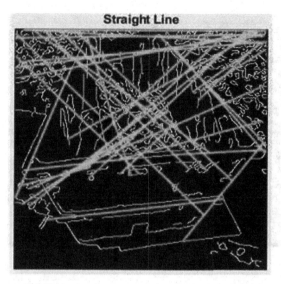

Fig. 3. Strong lines extracted from detected edges

4.2 Line Detection

Figure 3 shows that extracted strong lines by using HT from extracted edges of Fig. 2b. In this result there are 35 lines are extracted from the MATLAB tool by considering a line that when the length of a line is more than 81 and merging two-line segments when a gap between them is less than 31.

4.3 Corner Detection

In the above Fig. 4, corner is detected from strong extracted lines by orthogonality checking. As it has been proved that in order to detect corner in the SWB image, the orthogonality of two lines should be preserved. This means that two longest lines whose coordinates are checked and validated by the actual coordinates of image should be intersecting each other.

As it seen in Fig. 3, there are many lines at most 35 lines are extracted and among those lines there are again many lines which are intersecting one other. From these lines, lines which could be corner/s are validated particularly by their coordinate points. And in Fig. 4, the two lines are orthogonal and their coordinate as it is circled in the figure are validated to detect the corner correctly. The detected corner shows that since the author of this paper used camera stick to capture the SWB image, it was challenging to perfectly capture all four sides which create four respective corners for the SWB image. So, if the one corner which is intersecting of two longest is correctly detected, it is considered as true SWB image and in Fig. 4 shows that correct corner of the image.

4.4 Similarity Matching

As it said, to do similarity matching, checking whole part of image which will be computationally too cost. So, author used orthogonality of the two intersecting lines, then

Fig. 4. Corner detection of corner

the coordinate for these lines is computed and considered as corner of the image. And then, it is checked with the coordinate of the template image. Eventually, 20-by-20pixel width of the detected corner is cropped.

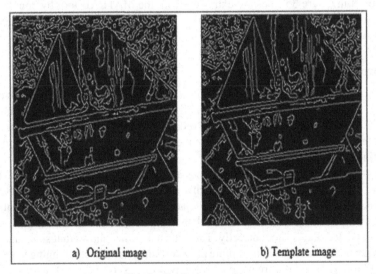

a) Original image   b) Template image

Fig. 5. Similarity matching

The above Fig. 5, shows that similarity matching using cross correlation for only detected corner part (Fig. 6).

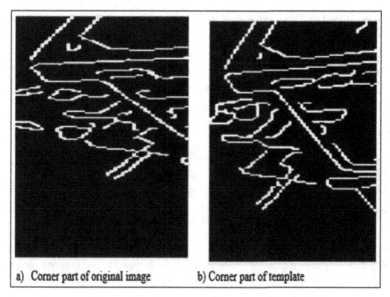

| a) Corner part of original image | b) Corner part of template |

Fig. 6. Similarity matching using cropped parts of images

4.5 Performance Testing

To show that how far the technique is good, the author evaluated the performance testing based on edge detection and similarity matching technique. For edge detection techniques, Structural Similarity Index Metric (SSIM) and Signal to Noise Ratio (SNR) parameters are used for four different edge detection techniques. For similarity matching, cross correlation coefficient is used.

Table 1. Comparisons of different edge detection techniques

Parameter	Sobel	LoG	Prewitt	Canny
SSIM	0.0046	0.0047	0.0046	0.0048
SNR	−56.96	−54.17	−56.95	−52.38

The Table 1 shows that there are four different edge detection techniques like Sobel, Laplacian of Gaussian (LoG), Prewitt and Canny. Performance evaluation for these different edge detection techniques is based on detection of true edge, low error ratio and single response. These qualities are measured by SSIM which is used to measure the structural similarity between two images and Signal to Noise Ratio (SNR) measures that image quality based on the pixel difference between two images.

When there is high numerical value for both SSIM [18] and SNR [19], the method is better to detect available edges on the image. Therefore, from above Table 1, Canny edge detection has high values in both metrics so that the method is optimal method to detect edges. Based on this evidence, it makes the technique efficient in edge detection from SWB image.

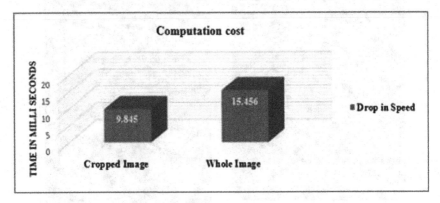

Fig. 7. Computation time for similarity matching for specific and cropped corner

Computing similarity matching for whole image of template with actual image is not cost effective. Therefore, it is necessary to do the computation only for correctly detected part of corner of the images. If the template of corner is detected effectively by using corner detection method, then it is possible to detect whole image of template correctly as well. Because corners are the main target area of the rectangular SWB image. Then, 20-20pixels width of edges of template image along the intersecting lines in the corner is cropped and superimposed on actual image to do similarity matching efficiently.

This is cost effective in reducing computation time than superimposing on whole part of the image and also detects shifted image within domain of the detected corner part. The comparative testing for running time of both whole image and cropped corner part is shown in the above Fig. 7. This is also another parameter which makes the designed new method is efficient in performing similarity matching only for specific part of images.

5   Contribution to New Knowledge

The efficiencies of the method are consideration of length and coordinating point of two intersecting lines from detected lines during corner detection, cropping of specific part for corner and finally, performing similarity matching of template image with original image by using only both cropped part of the images as well.

The technique has shown its better performance in edge detection technique by comparing with common existing edge detection techniques. And it is applied to SWB image to extract strong and weak edges of the image. It also has shown that similarity matching is efficient in performing for only detected and cropped part of the image rather than considering whole image. This results in reducing computation cost. Eventually, the designed method is not only applicable to SWB detection but also, to other application areas based on the structure and type of the application.

6 Conclusion

Designing of efficient image processing technique for SWB has been achieved successfully with the following components. These are edge extraction using optimal technique, Canny. Performance of the evidence of confidence for this optimality of the Canny technique has been tested and verified with quality assessment parameters such as SSIM and SNR. Having effectively extracted, next step is extracting lines by connecting extracted strong and thin edges using HT. Then, to detect the SWB image correctly and effectively, corner detection using orthogonal lines are detected.

During corner detection, length and coordinating point of these two intersecting lines are particularly considered. Then after, the specific part of detected corner part is cropped. Eventually, similarity matching of template image with original image is performed by using only both cropped part of the images. This is particularly to reduce running time during similarity matching of template with original image. This similarity matching is done by using cross correlation and the coefficient whose value is the largest considered as similar image.

The performance testing for used techniques is done with existing techniques in edge detection and cross correlation in order to show that the designed technique by respective author is efficient in detecting the SWB effectively. Therefore, our proposed technique is robust in identifying true position of SWB from other objects by using corner detection and orthogonality checking. It is also computationally cost effective in performing similarity matching by considering only cropped corner part which is correctly detected corner part as well.

The future work which should extended from this work is since the work here is part of the research-project already initiated and under construction by sponsor of Addis Ababa Science and Technology, it should include feature extraction and classification for the detected image to show the status of SWB like empty, medium and full.

After completion of the work, it will be good input for municipals of the city, Addis Ababa, to effectively monitor and manage solid wastes.

References

1. Zailah, W., Hannan, M.A., Al Mamun, A.: Image acquisition for solid waste bin level classification and grading. J. Appl. Sci. Res. **8**(6), 3092–3096 (2012)
2. Shukla, V.S., Vala, J.: A survey on image mining, its techniques and application. Int. J. Comput. Appl. (0975–8887) **133**, 4 (2016)
3. Khedaskar, S.V., Rokade, M.A., Patil, B.R., Tatwadarshi, P.N.: A survey of image processing and identification techniques. VIVA-Tech Int. J. Rese. Innov. **1**(1), 10 (2018)
4. Kaur, D., Kaur, Y.: Various image segmentation techniques: review. Int. J. Comput. Sci. Mob. Comput. **3**(5), 809–814 (2014)
5. Shafiqul Islam, Md., Hannan, M.A., Basri, H., Hussain, A., Arebey, M.: Solid waste bin detection and classification using Dynamic Time Warping and MLP classifier. Waste Manag. **34**(2), 281–290 (2014). https://doi.org/10.1016/j.wasman.2013.10.030
6. Kabade, A.L., Sangam, V.G.: Canny edge detection algorithm. Int. J. Adv. Res. Electron. Commun. Eng. (IJARECE) **5**(5), 4 (2016)
7. Canny edge detection algorithm application for analysis of the potential field map. ResearchGate, p. 10 (2016)

8. Öztürka, S., Akdemira, B.: Comparison of edge detection algorithms for texture analysis on glass production. In: World Conference on Technology, Innovation and Entrepreneurship, Istanbul (2015)

9. Gunasegaran s/o Madasamy, Razali, Z.B.: An application of image processing for automated mixed household waste sorting system. In: International Conference on Man Machine Systems (ICoMMS2012), Malaysia (2012)

10. Arebey, M., Elfituri, A., Hannan, M.A.: Content-based image retrieval system for solid waste bin level classification and recognition. J. Hum. Appl. Sci. (JHAS) **27**, 17 (2015)

11. Hannan, M.A., Zaila, W.A., Arebey, M., Begum, R.A., Basri, H.: Feature extraction using Hough transform for solid waste bin level detection and classification. Environ. Monit. Assess. **186**(9), 5381–5391 (2014). https://doi.org/10.1007/s10661-014-3786-6

12. Murillo-Bracamontes, E., Martinez-Rosas, M., Miranda-Velasco, M., Martinez-Reyes, H., Martinez-Sandoval, J., Cervantes-de-Avila, H.: Implementation of Hough transform for fruit image segmentation. Procedia Eng. **35**, 230–239 (2012). https://doi.org/10.1016/j.proeng.2012.04.185

13. Rahmdel, P.S., Comley, R., Shi, D., McElduff, S.: A review of Hough transform and line segment detection approaches. In: International Conference on Computer Vision Theory and Applications (2015)

14. Subban, R., Prabakaran: Corner detection methods. Middle-East J. Sci. Res. **23**(10), 2521–2532 (2015)

15. Kang, S.K., Choung, Y.C., Park, J.A.: Image corner detection using Hough transform. In: Marques, J.S., Pérez, N., de la Blanca, P., Pina, P. (eds.) Pattern Recognition and Image Analysis: IbPRIA 2005, pp. 279–286. Springer, Heidelberg (2005). https://doi.org/10.1007/11492542_35

16. Aziz, F., Arof, H., Mokhtar, N., Mubin, M., Talip, M.: Rotation invariant bin detection and solid waste level classification. Measurement **65**, 19–28 (2015). https://doi.org/10.1016/j.measurement.2014.12.027

17. Filev, P., Hadjiiski, L., Sahiner, B., Chan, H.-P., Helvie, M.A.: Comparison of similarity measures for the task of template matching of masses on serial mammograms. American Association of Physicists in Medicine, Michigan (2005)

18. Mohammadi, P., Ebrahimi-Moghadam, A., Shirani, S.: Subjective and objective quality assessment of image: a survey (2014)

19. George, A.G., Prabavathy, A.: A survey on different approaches used in image quality assessment. Int. J. Emerg. Technol. Adv. Eng. **3**(2), 7 (2013)

Amharic Open Information Extraction with Syntactic Sentence Simplification

Seble Girma$^{(\boxtimes)}$ and Yaregal Assabie

Department of Computer Science, Addis Ababa University, Addis Ababa, Ethiopia
yaregal.assabie@aau.edu.et

Abstract. Open Information Extraction (OIE) is the process of discovering domain-independent relations from natural language text. It has recently received increased attention and been applied extensively to various downstream applications, such as text summarization, question answering, and informational retrieval. In this paper, we propose a method of OIE for Amharic language. To improve the performance of relation extraction, the proposed OIE method implements a sentence simplification technique that breaks down complex and compound sentences into simple sentences. Linguistic rules are utilized to extract domain-independent and unanticipated relation instances with their arguments from simple sentences. The proposed method and algorithms are implemented and evaluated with a dataset from different domains. Test results show that the system achieved an overall precision of 0.88.

Keywords: Open Information Extraction · Chunking · Sentence Simplification · Relation Extraction

1 Introduction

Information Extraction (IE) is the task of automatically extracting structured information from text. The core task of IE systems is to identify entities and relationships expressed using natural languages. However, the traditional paradigm of IE requires either hand-tagged training examples for each target relation or pre-specified relations along with hand-crafted extraction rules as input. As such inputs are specific to the target domain, shifting to a new domain requires extensive human involvement in creating new extraction patterns [1]. Thus, traditional IE systems are not portable across domains and do not scale to massive and heterogeneous corpora like the Web where the relations are unanticipated [2]. To overcome these limitations, Open Information Extraction (OIE) has become more strongly suggested. OIE has made possible to process massive text corpora without restriction to extract a certain type of relations and attributes, and without having to require much human effort [3].

The OIE paradigm was introduced by Banko *et al.* [1] aiming to develop domain-independent extractors of information by providing ways to extract unrestricted relational information from text. OIE has several advantages over traditional IE approaches [4, 5].

© ICST Institute for Computer Sciences, Social Informatics and Telecommunications Engineering 2021
Published by Springer Nature Switzerland AG 2021. All Rights Reserved
M. A. Delele et al. (Eds.): ICAST 2020, LNICST 384, pp. 457–469, 2021.
https://doi.org/10.1007/978-3-030-80621-7_33

It made easier to extract many kinds of relations without requiring manual labor to build extraction rules and hand-tagged training examples. Because of its ability to extract information for all relations at once without having them named explicitly, it also has a significant scalability advantage over previous IE architectures. Traditional IE systems usually search for entities that are associated with the type of relation which the system was configured to extract whereas an OIE system tries to find relations as well as the entities taking part in those relations which are not predefined. Traditional IE systems require a specific pattern for each relation. On the other hand, OIE systems need a set of patterns that are not related to any specific relation, and these features are useful to extract relations of any nature.

In recent years, a variety of OIE systems have been developed. However, most systems have been designed, implemented and evaluated predominantly for English language. Amharic language, in a variety of respects, has different linguistic structures from other languages like English. To the best of our knowledge, no research works have been done on Amharic OIE yet. This paper presents an OIE for Amharic text which extracts domain-independent relations from Amharic text.

The remaining part of this paper is organized as follows. Section 2 presents research and development works in OIE. The proposed solution is presented in Sect. 3 and experimental results are discussed in Sect. 4. Finally, we make our conclusion in Sect. 5.

2 Related Work

OIE is the task of extracting relations with their corresponding arguments from natural language text. Some of OIE systems which are developed for different natural language are reviewed below.

Etzioni *et al.* [1] introduced TextRunner, an OIE system that trained a Naïve Bayes classifier with POS and NP-chunk features to extract relationships between entities. The system has used a small set of handwritten rules to heuristically label training examples from the Penn Treebank. TextRunner was evaluated using a test corpus of 9 million Web documents and it obtained 7.8 million tuples. A set of 400 randomly selected tuples were evaluated by human reviewers and 80.4% were considered correct.

Wu and Weld [6] presented an OIE system called WOE which used Wikipedia as a source of training data. The WOE system generates relation-specific training examples by matching Wikipedia Infobox content with corresponding patterns. WOE can learn two kinds of extractor: *WOEparse* and *WOEpos*. WOEparse learns from dependency path patterns, and WOEpos is trained with shallow features like POS tags. Comparing with TextRunner, WOEpos runs at the same speed, but achieves an F-measure which is between 18% and 34% greater. WOEparse achieves an F-measure which is between 72% and 91% higher than that of TextRunner but runs about thirty times slower due to the time required for parsing.

Etzoni *et al.* [7] presented ReVerb, which aimed to prevent incoherent and uninformative extractions errors from TextRunner. To eliminate incoherent extractions and to reduce uninformative extractions, the system is designed to capture relation phrases expressed by a Verb-Noun combination that satisfies their pre-defined syntactic and lexical constraint. It is reported that ReVerb achieves an AUC (area under Precision-Recall curve) twice as big as TextRunner and WOEpos, and 38% greater than WOEparse.

Aiming to improve OIE by covering a larger number of relation expressions and expanding OIE representation to allow additional context information such as attribution and clause modifiers, Mausam *et al.* [8] presented the system OLLIE. OLLIE uses the output of OIE systems to bootstrap learning of the relation patterns and then additionally applies lexical and semantic patterns to extract relations that are not expressed through verb phrases. It is reported that OLLIE extracts up to 146 times as many extractions than ReVerb and it obtains 1.9 to 2.7 times more area under precision yield curves compared to ReVerb.

Del Corro and Gemulla [9] presented a clause-based approach implemented in ClausIE. For each input sentence, ClausIE first computes the dependency parsing of the sentence and then determines a set of clauses using the dependency parsing. Next, for each clause, it determines the set of coherent derived clauses based on the dependency parsing and finally it generates propositions from the coherent clauses. Hand-crafted rules utilizing the dependency structure of a sentence are used. It is reported that ClausIE achieves better precision than Reverb. ClauseIE's accuracy relies on the dependency parser used for parsing.

OIE systems for languages other than English also have been implemented. Gamallo *et al.* [10] presented a multilingual system, named DepOE that uses the heuristic strategy to perform unsupervised extraction of triples using a rule-based analyzer and dependency parser to extract relations represented in English, Spanish, Portuguese, and Galician. The authors reported that accuracy of 68% is reached, while ReVerb reaches 52% accuracy for the same dataset.

Tseng *et al.* [11] presented a Chinese OIE called CORE that adopt existing Chinese text analyzing approaches to identify the main relation in a given sentence. It is reported that CORE yields relatively promising F1 scores than Reverb.

Nam *et al.* [3] presented a Korean OIE system called SRDF. The SRDF system is designed to extract triples from Korean natural language text based on the use of singleton property and other NLP techniques such as part-of-speech tagging and chunking. SRDF enables extracting multiple numbers of triples from a single sentence via reification. It is reported that the system achieves 81% precision, 86% recall, and 83% F-score for detecting relation and 66% precision, 65% recall and 65% F-score for generating triples.

In summary, according to the experiment results reported thus far, the rule-based systems achieve better accuracy than data-based systems. The results also show that systems that are based on dependency analysis achieved significantly higher precision and recall than those relying on shallow syntax. However, the shallow feature-based approach is very promising in terms of speed, ease of implementation, and portability to other languages. On the other hand, deep syntactic parsing methods are prone to slow performance and their implementation is not easily available for many languages [8].

Moreover, because of heavy reliance on linguistic tools such as part-of-speech taggers and dependency information as well as immediate lexical information to define patterns or constraints for relations, it is difficult to directly apply the aforementioned methods and techniques to low-resourced languages like Amharic. Moreover, the morphological complexity of Amharic poses unique challenges in the development of NLP applications in general and OIE in particular. Thus, in this work, we propose a design for Amharic that takes the characteristics of the language into consideration.

3 The Proposed Solution

The proposed method for Amharic OIE consists of two main tasks: *Sentence Simplification* and *Relation Extraction*. Sentence Simplification breaks complex and compound sentences down into simple sentences from which relation instances are extracted. Initially, the input sentence is divided into non-overlapping phrases using phrasal chunking which relies on POS and morphological tags of words. Then, the Sentence Simplification component segments the sentence into a number of self-contained simple sentences that are easier to process. Finally, relation instances are extracted in N-ary format from those simplified sentences.

3.1 Sentence Simplification

The structure of senetences affects the effectiveness of relation extraction in texts. Simple sentences have convenient structures for extracting relation instances. On the other hand, complex and compound sentences pose difficulties in the process of relation extraction. Thus, simplification of such sentences helps to improve the performance of OIE. In this work, We have developed a set of simplification rules that segment and paraphrase the input Amharic sentences and generate simpler sentences. Since the resulting sentences might need further simplification, the process of syntactic simplification is structured in a recursive loop. The syntactic simplification loop starts by checking if the input sentence is a simple sentence which is identified by counting the number of verb phrases. If the sentence contains exactly one verb phrase, the sentence will be classified as a simple sentence. If two or more verb phrases joined by coordinate conjunctions are detected, the sentence will be classified as a compound sentence. Otherwise, the sentence will be classified as a complex sentence. The overall process of sentence simplification involves *clause splitting* and *paraphrasing*.

Clause Splitting. Amharic clauses can be of two types: coordinate and subordinate. A compound sentence is composed of two or more independent clauses joined by a coordinating conjunction (i.e., አና/ʔana 'and'/, ወይም/wäyəm 'or'/, ግን/gən 'but'/, etc.,).. Semicolon ("፤") and comma ("፣") can also function as conjunctions. On the other hand, Amharic subordinate clauses contain both a subject and a verb, but do not express a complete thought. In Amharic, subordinate clauses are recognizable by affixes attached to the verb. Examples of Amharic subordinate clauses which are derived from the verb መጣ /mäṭa 'he came'/ are shown in Table 1. Thus, Amharic clause splitting comprises of *coordinate clause splitting* and *subordinate clause splitting*. A given sentence is iteratively split into clauses until all existing clauses are split.

Coordinate Clause Splitting. The coordinate conjunctions joining the clauses are required to be detected and then the sentence is split at the conjunctions. For instance, the following sentence contains three complete and independent clauses which are joined by semicolons.

[በኢትዮጵያ አና ኤርትራ መካከል የአየር ትራንስፖርት ተጀምሯል]clause1፤ [ሁለቱም አገራት ኤምባሲያኞቻቸውን ክፍተዋል]clause2፤ [በዚሁ ሳምንትም ሁለቱ ሀገራት ዝግ ሆነ የቆየውን ድንበራቸውን ክፍት በማድረግ በየብስ ትራንስፖርት መገናኘት ጀምረዋል]clause3፡፡

Table 1. Examples of Amharic subordinate clauses

Clause	Transliteration	Translation	Affixes
በመጣም	Bimäṭam	although he came	በ-...-ም /bi-...-m/
እንደመጣ	Ɂəndämäṭa	as he came	እንደ- /Ɂəndä-/
ካልመጣ	Kalmäṭa	unless he comes	ካል- /kal-/
ስለመጣ	Slämäṭa	because he came	ስለ- /slä-/
ከመጣ	Kämäṭa	if he comes	ከ- /kä-/
እስኪመጣ	Ɂəskimäṭa	until he comes	እስኪ- /Ɂəski-/
ሲመጣ	Simäṭa	when he came	ሲ- /si-/
እየመጣ	Ɂəyämäṭa	while he came	እየ- /Ɂəyä -/
የመጣ	Yämäṭa	who/that/which came	የ- /yä -/

Before splitting the sentence, it is necessary to check if both parts of the sentence are independent clauses. To be considered as an independent clause, they should at least have one verb. Custom created POS tags and morphological information is used for splitting into coordinate clauses. Table 2 shows tags that are created by combining POS and Morphological information.

Table 2. Custom created POS tags and morphological information.

Tags	POS	Morphology
ND	N	Definite or Accusive noun
NPD	NP	Definite or Accusive noun with prefixes
GV	V	Gerundive Verb
IV	V	Imperfective Verb
AV	V	Auxiliary Verb
PV	V	Perfective Verb
PAV	V	Passive Verb
PPV	V	Perfective Passive Verb
IRV	V	Imperfective Relative Verb
PRV	V	Perfective Relative Verb
PPRV	V	Perfective Relative Passive Verb
IRPV	V	Imperfective Relative Passive Verb
PGAV	V	Passive gerundive Auxiliary verb
GAV	V	Gerundive Auxilary verb
INF	N	Infinitive

Algorithm 1 shows how compound sentences are split into coordinate clauses. The algorithm accepts chunked compound sentences tagged with POS and morphological information and returns a list of clauses. The algorithm first looks for coordinate conjunction. If conjunction is detected, the sentence will be split there and the first part will be checked if it contains a verb. If it contains a verb, the first part will be added to the detected clause list and the remaining part of the sentence will be processed iteratively using a similar procedure.

```
Input:Chunked    sentences   tagged   with   POS   and   morphological
information(S)
Output: list of clauses (CLAUSE_LIST)
Begin
   Initialize INIT to Zero.
   For each token T in S which is tagged as "CONJ",
       Substring INIT to index of T and assign into a variable CLAUSE.
       Define a variable VERB_COUNT to the number of chunks in CLAUSE
       which contain a verb type of (IV, AV, PV PAV, PPV, PGAV, GAV).
       Set INIT to the index of T.
       If VERB_COUNT >= 1
           Add CLAUSE to CLAUSE_LIST
       End If
   End For
   Output CLAUSE_LIST
End
```

Algorithm 1. Coordinate clause splitting

Subordinate Clause Splitting. In order to simplify complex sentences, the main clause should be separated from the subordinate clause. Then, the main and the subordinate clauses are transformed into independent sentences. To this effect, we have developed an algorithm that takes chunked complex sentences tagged with POS and morphological information as an input and returns a list of clauses. Since the algorithm takes chunked sentences as input, the boundaries of chunks are used to identify subordinate clauses. Algorithm 2 shows how complex sentences are split into clauses. The algorithm iterates through all chunks of the sentence to look for a chunk containing a verb. If found, the phrase will be marked as a subordinate clause and it will be removed from the main clause. Both resulting clauses, i.e. main clause and subordinate clauses will be paraphrased to generate independent sentences.

```
Input:Chunked    sentences   tagged   with   POS   and   morphological
information(S)
Output: list of clauses (CLAUSE_LIST)
Begin
   For each Chunk C in S
     If C contain a verb of type of (PRV, IRV, PPRV, IPRV)
         Add C to CLAUSE_LIST
         Remove C from S
     End If
   End For
   Add S to CLAUSE_LIST
   Output CLAUSE_LIST
End
```

Algorithm 2. Subordinate clause splitting

Paraphrasing. In order to produce well-formed sentences from the individual clauses, they should be paraphrased. Sentence paraphrasing is a process of rewriting a sentence generated by clause splitting while preserving its meaning. The process includes rearranging the order of words in a sentence and changing the verb form by removing affixes of the verb. After splitting the subordinate clause from the main clause, affixes of the verb of the subordinate clause will be removed and then the order of the phrases will be rearranged based on the voice of the verb. For instance, to generate a simple sentence from a relative clause, the algorithm first checks if the voice of the verb is passive or active. If it is passive, the noun phrase found after the verb is a subject and a noun phrase found before the verb is an object. If the verb has an active voice, the noun phrase found before the verb will be a subject and a noun phrase found after the verb is an object. Finally, a sentence will be formed by removing affixes of the verb and combining the subject, object, and verb. Subordinate clauses might share the subject or object of the main clause. Thus, the main clause needs to be paraphrased. For example, the following sentence contains a relative clause where paraphrasing is made by taking the subject of the main clause.

Sentence: [ለዓመታት በውጣ ውረዶች የተፈተነው የኢትዮጵያ ትራንስፖርት አሠሪዎች ፌዴሬሽን] [ምሥረታ] [ተከናወነ] ::
Relative clause: ለዓመታት በውጣ ውረዶች የተፈተነው የኢትዮጵያ ትራንስፖርት አሠሪዎች ፌዴሬሽን
Main clause: የኢትዮጵያ ትራንስፖርት አሠሪዎች ፌዴሬሽን ምሥረታ ተከናወነ::
Paraphrased relative clause: የኢትዮጵያ ትራንስፖርት አሠሪዎች ለዓመታት በውጣ ውረዶች ተፈተነ::
Paraphrased main clause: የኢትዮጵያ ትራንስፖርት አሠሪዎች ፌዴሬሽን ምሥረታ ተከናወነ ::

Algorithm 3 shows the implementation of the paraphrasing algorithm. The algorithm takes a list of clauses as input and generates a list of well-formed sentences.

```
Input: List of POS and morphological tagged clauses (Cs )
Output: list of simple sentences (SENTENCE_LIST)
Begin
  For each Clause C in Cs
    If C is relative clause
        Replace C in main clause by a noun phrase found after the verb
        If C contain  active verb
            Set SUBJECT by a noun phrase found before the verb
            Set OBJECT by a noun phrase found after the verb
        End If
        If C contain passive verb
            Set SUBJECT by a noun phrase found before the verb
            Set OBJECT by a noun phrase found after the verb
        End If
        Remove affixes from the verb
        Concatenate SUBJECT, OBJECT and verb and add it to
        SENTENCE_LIST
    End If
    If C is not relative clause
        Remove affixes from the verb
        Concatenate C with all chunks found before C and add it to
        SENTENCE_LIST
    End If
  End For
      Add main clause to SENTENCE_LIST
      Output SENTENCE_LIST
End
```

Algorithm 3. Paraphrasing algorithm

3.2   Relation Extraction

The main goal of an OIE system is to extract arbitrary relations with their corresponding arguments from natural language text. In this work, we identify and extract four relation types from a give sentence: *verb-based relation*, *has-relation*, *is-a relation* and *noun-mediated relation*.

Verb-based Relation Extraction. Verb-based relations can be represented in predicate-argument structure as *Rel (Arg1, Arg2)* where *Rel* is the verb of the sentence, *Arg1* is the subject of the sentence and *Arg2* is indirect object, direct object, complement, or adverb. Since Amharic sentence has a subject-object-verb structure, verb-based relations can be detected by the presence of a verb at the end of the sentence. Algorithm 4 shows the verb-based relation extraction algorithm. Consider the following example.

[አበበ] [ትላንትና] [ከአዲስ አበባ] [መጣ]::

The first chunk is the first argument አበበ and the verb መጣ is the relation phrase and the other phrases are the second argument of the relation. Accordingly, the extracted relations are:

መጣ (አበበ , ከአዲስ አበባ).
መጣ (አበበ , ትላንትና).

```
INPUT:Chunked   sentences   tagged   with   POS   and   morphological
information(S)
OUTPUT: relation tuples in predicate argument structure
BEGIN
      For each chunk C in S.
            IF C contain a verb
                  Predicate = C
            End IF
            IF C is the first chunk and it is a noun phrase
                  Argument1 = C
            END IF
            IF C does not contain a verb
                  Add C to ArgumentList
            END IF
      END FOR
            output the relation in form of predicate (Argument1,
            ArgumentList))
END
```

Algorithm 4. Verb-based relation extraction

HAS Relation Extraction. HAS relation expresses possession or ownership in a sentencce. In Amharic sentence, HAS relation is implicitly expressed between two consecutive nouns when the first noun is in genitive case. The following examples show HAS relations in Amharic.

የአበባ ልጅ : HAS (አበባ ,ልጅ).
የአለም ጎደኛ: HAS (አለም, ጎደኛ).

Algorithm 5 shows the implementation of the HAS relation extraction. The algorithm takes noun phrases tagged with POS and morphological information. The algorithm checks if a noun in genitive case followed by another noun is found in the input noun phrase. If found, the word itself will be the first argument and words found after it is the second argument.

```
INPUT:Noun phrases tagged with POS and morphological information (NP)
OUTPUT: HAS relation tuple in predicate argument structure
BEGIN
      IF a noun in genitive case, followed by other noun is found.
            Argument1 = the noun itself
            Argument2 = the next noun
      END IF
      output the predicate in form of HAS (Argument1, Argument2))
END
```

Algorithm 5. HAS relation extraction

IS-A Relation Extraction. IS-A relation is an implicitly expressed relation between a proper noun and a common noun. In Amharic, this kind of relation is found when a proper noun comes after a common noun. The following example shows IS-A relation.

የኢትዮጲያ ራዕtoo ኃይሌ ገብረስላሴ: IS-A (ኃይሌ ገብረስላሴ , ራዕtoo).

The implementation of IS-A relation extraction is shown in Algorithm 6. The algorithm takes noun phrases tagged with POS and morphological information as an input and returns a list of IS-A relations. By iterating to each word in the text, it looks for an agent noun which is followed by another noun. If found, the words found after the agent noun is extracted as the first argument and the agent noun will be extracted as the second argument.

```
INPUT:Noun phrases tagged with POS and morphological information (NP)
OUTPUT: IS-A relation tuple in predicate argument structure
BEGIN
     If an agent noun followed by a noun is found
          Argument1 = noun phrase found after the agent noun
          Argument2 = the agent noun
     END If
     output the predicate in form of IS (Argument1, Argument2))
END
```

Algorithm 6. IS-A relation extraction

Noun-Mediated Relation Extraction. Noun-mediated relation expresses a binary relation between two nouns. In Amharic sentence, a common noun found between two proper nouns indicates the presence of a noun-mediated relation between two the proper nouns. For example, from a noun phrase የኢትዮጵያ ድሞ ሃይሌ ገብረስላሴ, a common noun ድሞ is a relation between ኢትዮጵያ and ሃይሌ ገብረስላሴ. It can be represented in predicate-argument structure as: ድሞ (ሃይሌ ገብረስላሴ, ኢትዮጵያ). Agent nouns are used to detect noun-mediated relations. The implementation of noun-mediated relation extraction is demonstrated in Algorithm 7. The algorithm takes noun phrases tagged with POS and morphological information as input. The algorithm first looks for an agent noun that is found between two nouns. If found, the noun found after the agent noun is extracted as the first argument, the noun found before the agent noun is extracted as the second argument, and the agent noun will be extracted as the predicate.

```
INPUT: Noun phrases tagged with POS and morphological information (NP)
OUTPUT: noun-medicated relation tuple in Predicate-Argument structure
BEGIN
     IF an agent noun is found between two nouns
          Predicate = agent noun
          Argument1 = noun phrase found after the agent noun
          Argument2 = noun phrase found before the agent noun
     END IF
     output the predicate in form of predicate (Argument1, Argument2)
END
```

Algorithm 7. Noun-mediated relation extraction algorithm

4   Experiment

4.1   Dataset Collection

To test the performance of the system, text corpus was collected from online Amharic news sources such as The Reporter Ethiopia[1] and Walta Media and Communication

---

[1] https://www.ethiopianreporter.com.

Corporate[2]. The corpus was collected randomly from different domain areas to study the sensitivity of the proposed system to variation in domain. In order to create an annotated dataset for extraction, each sentence is tagged with POS, morphological information and relation. A total of 215 tagged sentences are used for testing the system. From these sentences, we annotated 768 relations that consists of 414 verb-based relations, 207 HAS relations, 78 noun-mediated relations and 69 IS relations.

4.2 Test Result

A system implementing the algorithms was developed and used to evaluate the proposed approach, The collected corpus was used to test the performance of the system. Test results are shown in Table 3.

Table 3. Test result

Relation	Ground truth	Extraction result		
		Total extracted	Correctly extracted	Precision
Verb-Based	414	310	286	0.92
HAS	207	140	128	0.91
IS	69	50	39	0.78
Noun-Mediated	78	56	41	0.73
TOTAL	768	556	494	0.88

4.3 Discussion

Test results show that the proposed system has extracted 556 instances of relations from 215 sentences with a precision of 88%. Considering the errors made by the system, in general, we found that 56.5% of errors are due to complex and malformed sentences. Although the performance of AOIE can be significantly improved by simplifying complex sentences, the system achieves only 73% accuracy in sentence simplification. After a thorough analysis of each error returned by the sentence simplification component on the test dataset, most of the errors are due to failures in simplifying highly complex sentences. The sentence simplification algorithm has shortcomings in handling sentences that contain one or more clauses that share the subject or objects with the main clause, and/or contain other embedded clauses. This limitation often leads to incorrect and over-specified predicates and arguments, missed relation instances, and it also produces relation instances that are inconsistent with the information contained in the original sentence. For instance, consider the following sentence.

---

[2] http://www.waltainfo.com.

በሻኪሶ ከተማ አካባቢ ነዋሪዎች በተነሳ ተቃውሞ ምክንያት ሥራውን እንዲያቆርጥ በተደረገው የሚድርክ ወርቅ ኩባንያ ንብረት በሆነው የለገደንቢ ወርቅ ማምረቻ ላይ የከናዳ ከፍተኛ ባለሙያዎች ጥናት ሊያካሂዱ እንደሆነ ታወቀ::

The relation generated by the system is: ሥራውን እንዲያቆርጥ ጥናት ሊያካሂዱ እንደሆነ ታወቀ (Arg1: "በሻኪሶ ከተማ አካባቢ ነዋሪዎች", Arg2: "በተነሳ ተቃውሞ ምክንያት ")". The first argument of this extraction is incorrect, it should be "የከናዳ ከፍተኛ ባለሙያዎች". It also contains an over-specified predicate. There is also one missed relation: ነው (Arg1: "የለገደንቢ ወርቅ ማምረቻ", Arg2: "የሚድርኽ ወርቅ ኩባንያ", Arg3: "ንብረት"). Moreover, 32.7% of the errors are due to errors in morphological analysis and POS tagging. For instance, from the sentence "በዓድዋ ጦርነት የተሰው ጀግኖችን አፅም በክብር ለማሳረፍ ታሰበ:", two relation instances were expected from the system: ታሰበ (Arg1: "ጀግኖችን", Arg2: "አፅም", Arg3: "በክብር ለማሳረፍ") and ለማሳረፍ) and ተሰው ("ጀግኖች", "በዓድዋ ጦርነት"). However, since the morphological analyzer did not label the "የተሰው" as a relative verb, the relative clause is not detected and the sentence couldn't be simplified. As a result of this, only one instance of relation which contains an over-specified argument is extracted by the system: "ታሰበ (Arg1:"በዓድዋ ጦርነት የተሰው ጀግኖችን ", Arg2: "አፅም", Arg3: "በክብር ለማሳረፍ ").

The remaining types of errors made by the system are due to erroneously chunked phrases. Incorrectly chunking the sentence often leads to incorrect predicate or arguments. For instance, the sentence: "የኢትዮጵያ አየር መንገድ በረራዎች ለሁለት ሰዓታት ተቋረጡ" is chunked erroneously as: [የኢትዮጵያ አየር] [መንገድ በረራዎች] [ለሁለት ሰዓታት] [ተቋረጡ]. Thus, incorrect relation ተቋረጡ (Arg1:" የኢትዮጵያ አየር" Arg2: "መንገድ በረራዎች", Arg3:-"ለሁለት ሰዓታት") is extracted instead of: ተቋረጡ (Arg1: "የኢትዮጵያ አየር መንገድ በረራዎች", Arg2:-"ለሁለት ሰዓታት").

5   Conclusion

In this paper, we present Amharic OIE system. It is understood that rule-based approaches operating on deep parsed sentences yield the most promising results for OIE systems, as they enable higher precision. However, Amharic has limited tools and resources making it difficult to apply deep dependency parser. As a result, we have implemented a rule-based Amharic OIE system that operates on shallow parsed sentences. To minimize the difficulty of relation extraction from shallow parsed sentences, we introduced a sentence simplification component that converts complex and compound sentences into a list of simple sentences without losing the overall semantics of the original sentence. Our experimental results have shown that sentence simplification minimizes the reliance of relation extraction on deep parsed sentences. This indicates that the performance of system can be further improved by enhancing the capability of sentence simplification component.

References

1. Banko, M., Cafarella, M.J., Soderland, S., Broadhead, M., Etzioni, O.: Open information extraction from the web. IJCAI **2007**, 2670–2676 (2007)

2. Fader, A., Soderland, S., Etzioni, O.: Identifying relations for open information extraction. In: Proceedings of the Conference on EMNLP, pp. 1535–1545. Association for Computational Linguistics, Stroudsburg (2011)
3. Sangha, N., Younggyun, N., Sejin, N., Key-Sun, C.: SRDF: korean open information extraction using singleton property. In: Proceedings of the 14th International Semantic Web Conference (2015)
4. Mausam M.: Open information extraction systems and downstream applications. In: Proceedings of the Twenty-Fifth International Joint Conference on Artificial Intelligence, IJCAI 2016. AAAI Press: 2, pp. 4074–4077 (2016)
5. Abreu, S.C., Bonamigo, T.L., Vieira, R.: A review on relation extraction with an eye on portuguese. J. Braz. Comput. Soc. **19**, 553–571 (2013)
6. Wu, F., Weld, D.S.: Open Information Extraction using Wikipedia. In: The 48th Annual Meeting of the Association for Computational Linguistics, Uppsala, Sweden (2010)
7. Etzioni, O., Fader, A., Christensen, J., Soderland, S.: 2011. open information extraction: the second generation. In: Proceedings of the 22nd international joint conference on Artificial Intelligence IJCAI 2011, pp. 3–10, Barcelona, Catalonia, Spain, 16–22 July 2011
8. Mausam, S.M., Soderland, S., Bart, R., Etzioni, O.: Open language learning for information extraction. In: EMNLP-CoNLL, pp. 523–534 (2012)
9. Del Corro, L., Gemulla, R.: ClausIE: clause-based open information extraction. In: Proceedings of the 22nd International Conference on World Wide Web, WWW 2013, pp. 355–366. ACM, New York (2013)
10. Gamallo, P., Garcia, M., Fernández-Lanza, S.: Dependency-based open information extraction. In: ROBUS-UNSUP Workshop at EACL-2012, Avignon, France (2012)
11. Tseng, Y.-H., et al.: Chinese open relation extraction for knowledge acquisition. In: EACL, pp 12–16 (2014)

Evaluation of Corpora, Resources and Tools for Amharic Information Retrieval

Tilahun Yeshambel[1]([✉]), Josiane Mothe[2], and Yaregal Assabie[3]

[1] IT PhD Program, Addis Ababa University, Addis Ababa, Ethiopia
tilahun.yeshambel@uog.edu.et
[2] INSPE, Univ. de Toulouse, IRIT, UMR5505 CNRS, Toulouse, France
josiane.mothe@irit.fr
[3] Department of Computer Science, Addis Ababa University, Addis Ababa, Ethiopia
yaregal.assabie@aau.edu.et

Abstract. Amharic is the working language of Ethiopia. It is the second-most commonly spoken Semitic language in the world next to Arabic. Amharic is morphologically complex and under-resourced, which poses tremendous challenges for natural language processing. The development of fully functional Amharic text processing applications is a non-trivial task for researchers and developers. Despite attempts to develop some applications, lack of standards in corpus collection and resource development resulted in the problem of interoperability. The aim of this paper is to present and evaluate the accessibility of Amharic corpora, resources and tools with the purpose of highlighting the status of Amharic language processing applications. We present available resources and linguistic tools, assess their usability and effectiveness, investigate the implications of the morphological complexity and put the way forward in the development of Amharic text processing applications.

Keywords: Amharic language · Amharic NLP tools · Amharic resources · Challenges of Amharic language processing · Morphological complexity

1 Introduction

Digital information is available in different formats such as text, audio, image, or video. Powerful and sophisticated applications are mandatory in order to manage all these digital information. With the huge and continuously increasing amount of information available on the Web, languages for representing data and knowledge occupy a central place in managing this tremendous quantity of data (Mihalcea and Mihalcea 2001). For this purpose, Natural Language Processing (NLP) tools and resources play great roles to improve various automatic computational tasks. The effectiveness of NLP tools, the sizes and qualities of resources have significant impacts on the performance of Information Retrieval (IR), Information Extraction (IE), Sentiment Analysis (SA), Machine Translation (MT), Question-Answering (QA), Named Entity Recognition (NER), Relation Extraction (RE), and Text Classification (TC) and other applications (Jochim 2013).

M. A. Delele et al. (Eds.): ICAST 2020, LNICST 384, pp. 470–483, 2021.
https://doi.org/10.1007/978-3-030-80621-7_34

NLP tools are used for classification of sounds of a language at phonological level, analysis of word components such as suffix, prefix and root at morphological level, word analysis such as lexical meaning and part-of-speech at lexical level, sentence analysis at syntactic level, disambiguation of word in the context at semantic level, etc. (Jurafsky and James 2000). Developing NLP tools and resources for languages is not trivial especially for morphologically complex languages.

Amharic is the working language of Ethiopia currently having a population about 110 million (countrymeters 2020). It is the second-most commonly spoken Semitic language in the world next to Arabic. The growth of Amharic digital data accelerates the demand for technologies and NLP tools for on-line data processing. However, Amharic is still considered as under-resourced language since there are few attempts made to develop Amharic NLP tools, corpora and applications. Furthermore, the complex morphology of Amharic has hindered the development of NLP applications for the language. Although the number of resources has been increasing and the performance of the systems is improving since 2000, the existing tools and resources have not been reviewed, assessed, evaluated, compared and presented in a systematic way till now.

The purpose of this paper is to present state-of-art linguistic tools and resources on Amharic. Our contribution also relies on a first evaluation and comparison of these resources so that their quality and standard is better understood, which facilitates research and development in the field of Amharic NLP. More specifically, this paper explains characteristics of Amharic language and provides an extensive overview of state-of-the-art linguistic tools and resources. We present the key characteristics of Amharic morphology as it plays a central aspect for the development of many NLP applications. Tools and resources are also practically evaluated by conducting some preliminary experiments.

The rest of this paper is organized as follows. Section 2 provides background information about Amharic language and its specificities where we examine the orthography and morphology of the language. Section 3 discusses Amharic corpora and resources available digitally along with Amharic text processing tools. In Sect. 4, we present our evaluation on accessible corpora, resources and tools. Finally, we make our conclusion in Sect. 5.

2 Amharic Language

Amharic is the working language of Ethiopia and serves as a common communication language among different language speakers throughout the country. A wide variety of literature including religions, fictions, poetries, plays, newspapers, magazines, businesses, etc. are produced in Amharic. Amharic is the family of Semitic language[1] and the most widely used language in Ethiopia having a population of around 110 million (countrymeters 2020). It is also the second most spoken Semitic language in the world after Arabic (Gamback et al. 2006). The language has its own 34 base characters where each of them has 7 forms/orders making them total of 238 characters. In addition, there are also dozens of labialized characters, 10 unique punctuation marks and 20 unique digits (Yaqob 1997). Each Amharic character is grouped into either consonantal or syllabary writing system and its writing system is from left to right. There are no upper and

---

[1] Other Semitic languages are for example: Arabic, Tigrinya, Hebrew, Geez, etc.

lower case letter variations and no conventional cursive form words in Amharic writing system.

Amharic consonants which mostly carry the semantic core of a word can form the root of the word. The Amharic root is a series of base character while a word is a collection of phonemes. Word can be a single morpheme or contain several of them. Different types of prefixes and suffixes can be attached to the stem to form the inflected words. Words are formed by modifying the root itself internally and not simply by the concatenation of affixes to word roots (Shashirekha and Gashaw 2016). Amharic has a complex morphology. For instance, according to the experimental report of Assabie (2017), tens of thousands of words can be generated from a given Amharic verbal root. Phonemes, morphemes, roots, stems, and surface words are word units of Amharic. Its words formation involves affixation, reduplication, changing the form of character in a stem (Argaw *et al* 2004). Surface word can be formed by changing stem form or by adding affixes that are usually used for changing the tense, number, gender and case (subjective, objective, possessive) of a word. Amharic word classes undergo complex derivations and inflections. From a given word class, we can generate many words that have similar or different word classes. Assabie (2017) reported that Amharic nouns can be derived from verbal roots by in-fixing vowels between consonants, adjectives by suffixing bound morphemes, stems by prefixing or suffixing bound morphemes, stem-like verbs by suffixing bound morphemes, and nouns by suffixing bound morphemes and compound words. Amharic nouns can also be inflected with number, definiteness, gender, objective case, and possessive case. Amharic adjectives can be derived from verbal roots by in-fixing vowels, nouns by suffixing bound morphemes, stems by suffixing bound morphemes and compound words of nouns and adjectives by affixing vowels. Amharic adjectives can be inflected with number, definiteness, gender, and cases (objective, possessive, etc.). Amharic verbs have even more complex morphology than other word classes. They can be derived from verbal roots, verbal stems, compound words of stem and verbs, sub words and verbs. They can also be inflected for person, gender, number, case, tense, and mood. From a given Amharic root, it is possible to generate a number of stems out of which a large number of surface words can be derived. Furthermore, preposition and negative marker can be attached as affixes on different word classes to generate surface words (Assabie 2017).

3   Amharic Corpora, Resources and Tools

3.1   Corpora

Amharic corpora and resources are required for the evaluation purpose in different research fields such as MT, IR and text analysis in general. Some of the Amharic text corpora which are available digitally and utilized for the development of Amharic NLP tools, IR or other text-centered tasks by different researchers are presented below.

Walta Information Center (WIC) Corpus. this corpus is prepared by linguists at Addis Ababa University with the financial support of Walta Information Center. It is available both in Amharic characters and transcribed form called System for Ethiopic Representation in ASCII (SERA). It contains 1,065 Amharic news articles which have

200,863 words (33,408 unique words) organized in 4,035 sentences. Since the corpus contains news items, the domain of the corpus is much diversified. It includes topics like politics, economics, science, sport, religion, business, etc.

Ethiopian Language Research Center (ELRC) Corpus. this is the annotated version of WIC corpus. It has been annotated with Part-Of-Speech (POS) tags manually by the Ethiopian Language Research Center (ELRC) at Addis Ababa University (AAU). The corpus is tagged with 30 different POS tags (Demeke and Getachew 2006).

Amharic Bible Corpus. this corpus is prepared by students at AAU. It has 39 categories which contain different number of sections. It contains a total of 13,300 sentences organized into 924 documents (Bruck and Tilahun 2015).

AAU NLP Task Force Corpus. this corpus is prepared by language technology staff members from IT Doctorial Program at Addis Ababa University for Amharic, Afaan Oromo and Tigrigna languages with diverse content (Abate et al. 2018). The project is still on-going and the corpus is continuously being updated.

Amharic Wikipedia Corpus. the Amharic Wikipedia was established in 2004. Currently, it contains 13,657 articles and 15 main categories about various topics such as science, language, history, mathematics, engineering, philosophy, Ethiopia, geography, etc.

Amharic Corpus for Machine Learning (ACML). this corpus has been prepared by Gamback (2012). The data set consists of free texts collected from Ethiopian News Headlines (ENH), Walta Information Center (WIC) and Amharic fiction "Fikir Iske Meqabir" (FIM). It is a set of 10,000 ENH articles for a total of 3.1 million words, 1,503 words from the WIC corpus, and 470 words from FIM book. Some machine learning-based tagging experiments have been carried out on this corpus (Alemu 2006). The purpose of this corpus was to collect word frequency, prefix and suffix. This corpus is not publicly accessible.

Amharic Adhoc Information Retrieval Test Collection (2AIRTC). Yeshambel *et al.* (2020b) created Amharic IR test collection based on CranField and Text REtrieval Conference (TREC) format. The test collection has 12,538 domain independent documents collected from various sources, a topic set with 240 user information need, and the associated relevance *judgment*. The corpus is created to enhance researches in Amharic IR and is made publicly accessible to research community.

Amharic Morphologically Annotated Corpora (AMAC). Yeshambel *et al.* (2020c) created stem-based and root-based morphologically annotated corpora semi-automatically. The annotation segments surface words into affixes, stems and roots. The number of annotated documents is 6,069 full text documents which contain 72,814 sentences or 1,592,351 morphologically annotated words.

3.2 Resources

Dictionary. the Amharic machine readable dictionaries (MRDs) entries are represented by their citation forms. Some of the commonly used Amharic dictionaries are Aklilu (1987), Berhanu (2004) and Birhan (1993). Aklilu (1987) developed the Amharic–English dictionary which contains 15,000 Amharic words along with their English translations. Berhanu (2004) built the Amharic-French dictionary that contains 12,000 Amharic entries. Birhan (1993) developed Amharic-Amharic dictionary which contains 56,000 entries. This dictionary is used to handle synonyms.

Stopword List. Yeshambel *et al.* (2020a) built morpheme-based Amharic stopwords based on semantics and corpus statistics (frequency, mean, variance and entropy). The stopword list is created by considering the characteristics of the language from a large morphologically annotated corpus. As the root form conflates all variants of a term to a common representation, the stopword list contains roots of words. The applicability of the created stopword list was evaluated using Amharic IR system. Prior to this work, few stopword lists were created manually for a specific purpose. For example, Mindaye et al. (2010) built a stopword list of 77 entries while Eyassu and Gambäck (2005) created a stopword list with 745 entries for the purpose of stopword removal in IR system. However, the entries were selected without considering morphological characteristics and statistical information of the terms. Thus, their applicability is limited to the specific systems for which they are created.

3.3 Tools

NLP is used to analyze, understand, alter, or generate natural language. This can be achieved by using automated NLP tools. Few numbers of Amharic NLP tools were developed using rule-based and machine learning approaches for various purposes. Some of the important Amharic NLP tools are text preprocessing tools, stemmers, POS taggers, morphological analyzers, morphological synthesizers and parsers. Preprocessing is the primary task used to make the data ready or clean for further processing. Amharic words need to be preprocessed for further Amharic NLP application development. Text preprocessing is used to enhance IR and other text-based tasks. A stemmer aims at reducing inflectional and derivational written words form to their stem or base form. It removes prefixes, suffixes, in fixes, circumfixes and redundant character from a given word. POS taggers aim at marking words in a given text with relevant parts-of-speech and are used to understand a text in natural language. Morphological analysis helps to find the minimal units of word which holds linguistic information for further processing whereas morphological synthesis is the process of returning surface forms from a sequence of underlying (lexicon) forms. Parsing is the process of analyzing a given sentence by identifying its constituents. It identifies the subjects and objects of a sentence, different phrases such as noun phrases, adverbial phrases, and adjective phrases.

Text Preprocessing Tools. Relevant Amharic text preprocessing tools include tokenizer, normalizer, and transliterator. Tokenization is splitting a text into sentences and then into words. Normalization is the process of transforming texts into a single canonical form which then commonly used in various text-based tasks. Text normalization requires being aware of what type of text is to be normalized and how it is to be processed after wards. In Amharic writing system there are characters with the same pronunciation but different symbols which are called homophones. Amharic base characters having such property are {ኽ /ʔə/ and ዐ /ʔə/}, {ሠ /sə/ and ሰ /sə/}, {ሀ /hə/, ሐ /hə/, ኀ /hə/ and ኸ /hə/}, and {ጸ /ts'ə/ and ፀ /ts'ə/}. Amharic character normalization involves changing Amharic character with the same phone into one canonical orthographic form. Transliteration is required as Amharic texts are published using Ethiopic script and a variety of fonts. Some of which may not be Unicode compliant. In order to simplify the analysis and to have a unified representation of texts, Amharic texts are transliterated into American Standard Code for Information Interchange (ASCII) representation. Amharic Unicode representations such as UTF-8 become common and easy to analyze text. However, for NLP tasks, transliterated texts are preferable. In Amharic fonts, except Unicode supported ones, characters which have diacritic markings need more than one byte in their internal representation so as to use one byte for the basic character and additional one byte for the diacritic marking. For example, ሉ /lu/ needs two bytes to represent internally, one byte for ለ /lə/ and another byte for "-". This creates difficulty to use Amharic character/Fidel that has diacritic markings by considering it as a single unit. For this reason, first the Amharic texts need to be changed in to Unicode representation and then transliterated it into ASCII letters (Yaqob 1997). As for Latin languages, tokenization can be done by considering Amharic punctuations and space between words. Normalization is achieved my mapping each homophone character to a single orthographic canonical form. Due to such simplicity, researchers develop their own tokenizer and normalizer when a need arises. However, a standard canonical form is not yet set by linguists. As a result, researchers randomly choose one of the orthographic forms. Transliteration can also be done by mapping the Amharic characters into ASCII letters using a mapping table. ASCII representation of consonant and vowels for transliteration is not standardized and researchers develop their own transliteration rules. One of the most commonly used transliteration rule is SERA (Gasser 2011).

Stemmers. Alemayehu and Willett (2002) built a rule-based Amharic stemmer and evaluated the effectiveness of stemming for Amharic information retrieval (Alemayehu and Willett 2003). The prefixes and suffixes were removed and took into account letter inconsistency and reiterative verb forms. The stemmer was tested on 1,221 words and performs 95.9% accuracy. The compression rates of stem and root processing are 50.3% and 58.6%, respectively. The performance of word-based, stem-based, and root-based retrieval was compared using 40 Amharic queries against 548 Amharic documents, and it was reported better recall levels for stem and root-based retrieval over word-based. Alemu and Lars (2007) developed a rule-based stemmer. The aim was to solve the problem of stemming Amharic words and reducing them to their base/stem forms for Cross Lingual Information Retrieval (CLIR) applications. A total of 65 rules were constructed on the entire Amharic morphology. The experiment was conducted on ACML data set. The correctness of the stemmer was tested through Amharic-English, Amharic-French, and Amharic-Amharic dictionaries. An accuracy of 60% for the old fashioned fiction text and 75% for the news articles were achieved. Mengistu (2009) developed an Amharic stemmer using peak and plateau, entropy and complete word methods. A corpus containing 6, 270 words was prepared for training and testing the methods. The corpus was divided into 80:20 for training and testing, respectively. The experimental results indicate that the peak and plateau method performed 71.8% accuracy and the entropy and complete word methods performed 63.95% and 57.99% accuracy, respectively. Tekalign (2014) developed an Amharic text stemmer using the rule-based Longest-Match Method. The stemmer can remove affixes using Amharic Nyala font directly without transliteration. It removes prefix, infix and suffix from a given word to get the stem of each word. It was evaluated manually using stemmed 1,500 words, 310 prefixes and 611 suffixes and performed 85% accuracy.

POS Taggers. Getachew (2001) developed an Amharic POS tagger using Hidden Markov Model. The tag set was designed with words as the smallest units for tagging without splitting a word into its morphemes (prefixes, a stem and suffixes). The tagger was tested with one page of text using a set of 25 tags and scores accuracy at about 90%. Sisay (2005) used 10 of the tag sets along with Aklilu (1987) dictionary for verification purpose. The experiment was done on five news articles that had been annotated manually to evaluate the stochastic model based on conditional random fields using 5-fold cross-validation. The accuracy of the system was 74%. Gamback et al. (2009) developed a tagger using TnT, SVMTool and Mallet approaches with three different tag sets. Detailed experiment was carried out on ELRC dataset. Test results reported the accuracies of 85.56%, 88.30%, and 87.87% for TnT, SVM and MaxEnt, respectively. Gebrekidan (2010) developed a tagger using knowledge of Amharic morphology and machine learning algorithms with a set of 31 tags. The objective was to improve the performances of taggers developed by Getachew (2001), Sisay (2005), Demeke and Getachew (2006), and Gamback et al. (2009). CRF++ was used for segmenting data whereas LIB-SVM was used for classification and regression purpose. The experiment was done by CRF, SVM, and TnT and Brill machine learning algorithms and 10-fold cross validation using ELRC corpus which provided average accuracy of 90.95%, 90.43%, 87.41% and 87.09%, respectively. The tagging was improved compared previous works due to better preprocessing tasks and the use of vowel patterns and root as features, machine learning algorithms and parameter tuning. The error analysis of CRF and SVM was between 39% and 45% using confusion matrices. Yifru et al. (2011) conducted experimental research to investigate the best method for under-resourced and morphologically rich languages. Disambig, Moses, CRF++, SVMTool, MBT, and TnTwere the tagging strategies implemented in this research. The experiment was conducted using 31 tags on ELRC corpus which has been divided into training, development and evaluation test sets in the proportion of 90:5:5. Accuracies of 75.1% and 74.4% were obtained with SVM and Disambig, respectively. High gain is observed on TnT strategies. It was reported that HPR and hybrid combination methods were promising to improve POS tagging performance for under-resourced languages.

Morphological Analyzers. Tesfaye (2002) used unsupervised learning approach based on probabilistic models to extract stems, prefixes, and suffixes for building a morphological dictionary. On top of that, a modified version of Harris's algorithm of successor frequency was applied to detect plausible word break points. An experiment was carried out on the transcribed first 50 pages of Amharic text containing 5,736 words. A precision of 0.95 and a recall of 0.90 were obtained. Sisay and Haller (2003) investigated the morphology of Amharic verbs in the context of machine translation and presented the implementation of morphological analyzer for Amharic using Xerox Finite State Tools (XFST) method. The different classification schemes for Amharic verbs that have been forwarded are discussed followed by the implication. It was stated that morphological analysis for Amharic with XFST can handle most of the morphological phenomena except some derivation processes which involve simultaneous application of both stem inter-digitations and reduplication. The experiment was carried out on 3.1 million words of Amharic news text. They achieved 0.88–0.94 recall and 0.54–0.94 precision depending on the word-class. Sisay (2005) developed a morphological analyzer and tagger using conditional random. The work dealt with bound morphemes of prepositions, conjunctions, relative markers, auxiliary verbs, negation markers and coordinate conjunctions, but leaves out other bound morphemes such as definite articles, agreement features such as gender and numbers, case markers (objective, possessive), etc., and considered them to be part of the word. The best analyzing result (84%) was obtained by using character, morphological and lexical features. Amsalu and Gibbon (2006) developed Amharic analyzer using XFST. The experiment was conducted on a text of 1,620 words from an Amharic Bible corpus. The system provided precisions of 0.54, 0.94 and 0.81 for recall levels of 0.94, 0.85 and 0.88 for verbs, nouns and adjectives, respectively. Gasser (2011) developed a morphological analyzer and synthesizer using a rule-based approach and Akililu's (1987) dictionary. The analyzer marks-up the stems, roots, and POS. It uses lexical Finite State Transducer (FST). Prefix and suffix FSTs were concatenated onto the stem FST to create the full verb morph tactic FST. The remaining FSTs implemented alternation rules that apply to the word as a whole, including allomorphic rules and general phonological or orthographic rules. The analyzer was tested on 200 Amharic verbs, nouns and adjectives that were selected randomly. On this data set the analyzer performed 99% accuracy for Amharic verbs and 95.5% accuracy for Amharic nouns and adjectives. Mulugeta and Gasser (2012) developed a morphological analyzer for Amharic verbs using supervised machine learning approach. The training data used to formulate morphological rules was prepared manually from 216 romanized verbs. After training, 108 rules for affix extraction, 18 rules for root template extraction and 3 rules for internal stem alternation were used. CLOG learns rules as a first order predicate decision list. The approach was tested on 1,784 Amharic verbs and its accuracy is 86.99%. Abate and Assabie (2014) developed morphological analyzer using memory-based supervised machine learning approach. The goal was to extract stems from nouns and adjectives, and roots from verbal stems. Morphological analysis was used to classify the grammatical functions of morphemes and morphological structure of morphologically inflected words. The morphological analysis component comprises the feature extraction to deconstruct a given word, morpheme identification to split and extrapolate, stem and root extraction to label segmented inflected words with their morpheme functions. TiMBL was used as a learning tool. The experiment was conducted on 181 romanized verbs and 841 nouns. 8,075 instances were extracted from nouns and adjectives. Leave-one-out (LOO) cross-validation for IB1 algorithm and 10-fold cross-validation technique was used to test the performance of the system with IB1 and IGtree classifier engines algorithms. An average accuracy of 96.40% was achieved with IB1 algorithm on LOO method. On the other hand, the system provided 93.59% and 82.26% accuracy using IB1 and IGtree algorithms, respectively using 10-fold method on previously unseen verbs and nouns.

Parsers. Abiyot (2000) developed an Amharic parser for verbs and their derivations. A knowledge-based system that parses verbs, and nouns derived from verbs was designed. Root pattern and affixes were used to determine the lexical and inflectional category of the words. The parser was tested on 200 verbs and nouns; the accuracy was 86% for the verbs and 84% for the nouns.

Synthesizers. Lisanu (2002) developed word synthesizer for Amharic perfect verbs. A combination of rule based and neural network approaches were used. The experiment was conducted using 14 roots and some affixes which were selected by domain experts on type A, type B and type C perfective verb forms. The rule-based approach performed near to 100% accuracy whereas the accuracy of the neural network approach is 81.48%. The accuracy of the neural network system in predicting type A, B and C perfective verb forms is 80%, 25% and 100%, respectively. On the other hand, Gasser (2011) developed Amharic word synthesizer. FST and rule-based approaches were used for implementation. An experiment was run on major verb root classes to generate 10 to 25 verbs. The system performed 100% accuracy on 330 test data.

4   Evaluation of Corpora, Resources and Tools

We reviewed the aforementioned corpora, resources and tools where it was understood that there was no standard that governs the format and general characteristics that the resource should have. Each researcher was found to construct resources in line with the specific needs of the NLP tasks. Moreover, the reported performances of NLP tools were based solely on the non-standard resources. Accordingly, it was difficult to make fair comparisons among similar NLP tools. On the other hand, most of the developed NLP tools are not publicly available which hinders the evaluation process. Taking this scenario into consideration, we conducted the evaluation first by qualitative analysis and then using quantitative means. Thus, accessible tools are evaluated based on their performance, accessibility, usability, utility (plug into other system), portability and maintainability. These parameters are selected since they are some of the most common techniques to evaluate computational resources and tools.

4.1   Qualitative Evaluations

Corpora. the size of most of the existing corpora is not sufficient for applications such as IR, NLP tools and machine learning. Acceptable and reputable IR experiments are based on ten thousands and million number of various documents. On top of that, the corpora are not preprocessed. They are mainly collections of documents from which formatting tags are removed. Hence, both the quantity and the quality of many corpora are not sufficient for the development of NLP tools and applications. On the other hand, most of the corpora are not publicly accessible.

Resources. Amharic dictionaries are very limited in size compared to the richness of the language and also when compared to dictionaries in other languages. Amharic dictionaries are not sufficient to verify lemmatization, or to handle synonyms. Their usability is very limited as they are in the format of spreadsheet files. So far, they are used by very few researchers. Alemu and Asker (2006) used Berhanu's (2004) dictionary to evaluate the output of Amharic stemmers and for CLIR applications to reduce query terms in the source language to the exact corresponding citation form in the MRD. Aklilu (1987) dictionary has been used by Gasser (2011) and Sisay (2005) to develop Amharic morphological analyzer, POS tagger, stemmer and machine translator. Majority of the existing Amharic stopwords are not collected and organized scientifically (Mindaye et al. 2010; Eyassu and Gambäck (2005)). Researchers collected stopwords lists based on their language knowledge without validation by linguists, which is an important step considering the morphological complexity of Amharic.

Tools. the functionalities of the existing Amharic NLP tools are limited. Hence, it is very difficult to use them as a component in other applications like IR, question answering or text summarization. The existing tools are very often limited to certain types of words. For example, Mulugeta and Gasser (2012) developed morphological analyzer for Amharic verbs. On the other hand, Lisanu (2002) developed a morphological synthesizer for Amharic perfective verbs. Gasser's (2011) morphological analyzer is available freely on the web and in executable format. It has a command line interface, can be configured and run easily on different environment. However, this analyzer usually has not been much utilized in Amharic applications such as IR. The output of this analyzer is not suitable to integrate with IR system. The output contains more than one stems for variants. Furthermore, root and POS are represented by English while the stems are in Amharic. This by itself needs complicated preprocessing task. Taggers developed by Yifru et al. (2011) and Gebrekidan (2010) have command line interfaces. Furthermore, they are not publicly accessible and are not executable file. They are used by very few researchers (Sintayehu 2013). In general, most of the tools are not accessible which limits both the capability of evaluating them and their utility for other researchers.

Many of the existing corpora, resources and tools are not suitable for Amharic IR. IR experiments require large scientifically built corpora and resources. However, except Yeshambel *et al.* (2020b), all existing corpora are simply collections of small documents without topic set and relevant judgments. They are not used to test retrieval system automatically. As a result, in IR previous experiments (Mindaye et al. 2010; Wordofa 2013; Asefa 2013; Bruck and Tilahun 2015) the respective researchers created few user query topics relevant to the corpus they used for. However, acceptable IR experiments should be carried out by running 50+ queries on a large corpus. On the other hand, some stopword lists contain variants of stopwords rather than basic stems (Mindaye et al. 2010; Eyassu and Gambäck (2005)). However, there are many variants for a given Amharic stopword. Therefore, Amharic IR system is not able to remove stopwords from index terms and query terms using many of the existing lists. Furthermore, the existing Amharic dictionaries are designed based on citation form. The citation form of an Amharic word is different form its stem or root. Therefore, the existing dictionaries are not useful in IR such as CLIR system.

4.2 Quantitative Evaluations

Tools have been evaluated by the researchers who developed them but neither on the same collection nor the same task. Indeed, there is no reference collection as it is the case in other languages such as English or Arabic for example. Therefore, we started to develop an evaluation framework to be able to compare the various tools and resources. To evaluate preprocessing and NLP tools, we started with small dataset consisting of few words (verbs, nouns and adjective) with prefix, suffix and circumfix. Then, we continuously increased the dataset to evaluate how the system functions different scenarios. We observed that Gasser's (2011) morphological analyzer performs well if the word is available in Aklilu (1987) dictionary. However, if the word is not in the dictionary the performance decreases. Preliminary experiments on taggers developed by Yifru et al. (2011) and Gebrekidan (2010) were conducted using ELRC corpus as training and testing data set. They performed well on the test data set. However, when using any other dataset, their performances decrease drastically. This may be due to the size of the training corpus. The stemmer developed by Alemayehu and Willett (2002) is cited in some researches (Munye and Atnafu 2012; Wordofa 2013). However, the fully functioning system is not currently accessible. Only parts of the stemmer which are prefix and suffix removal are available. Table 1 shows a summary of evaluations on accessible tools. Since it is very difficult to make evaluation automatically and repeatable, the evaluations were made manually by building a small data set.

Table 1. Summary of evaluations on Amharic NLP tools

Tools	Developers	Accuracy (%)	Dataset (words)
Taggers	Gasser (2011)	64.91	200
	Yifru et al. (2011)	86.75	200,863
	Gebrekidan (2010)	87.30	200,863
Stemmer	Alemayehu and Willett (2002)	41.40	75
	Tekalign (2014)	25.40	75
Synthesizer	Lisanu (2002)	82.72	375

Morphological processing is one of the fundamental tasks of retrieval systems. The aim is to conflate variants to their common form. The retrieval effectiveness of IR system depends largely on the accuracy of linguistic processing tools such as stemmer and analyzer. However, as shown in Table 1, the performances of stemmers are low. Some of them over-stem (Tekalign 2014) and the others under-stem (Alemayehu and Willett 2002). In case of over-stemming, many non-related words are conflated to a common stem. On the contrary, many variants cannot be conflated to a common stem in case of under-stemming. These will significantly affect the precision and recall of Amharic IR system. The retrieval performance of some IR system based on the existing tools is low. For example, using the stemmer developed by Alemayehu and Willett

(2002), Amharic-English CLIR system (Munye and Atnafu 2012) achieve a retrieval performance of 0.74 whereas a retrieval system developed by Alemayehu and Willett (2003) performed recalls of 0.21, 0.35 and 0.64 at a cut of 5, 10 and 20, respectively. Moreover, identification of nouns in documents and user query is important in Amharic IR. However, the performance of the existing taggers on a corpus other than training data set is poor.

5   Conclusion

The morphological complexity of Amharic has brought challenges in developing useful IR resources, corpora, and tools. This paper presents efforts that have been attempted so far along with evaluations of the contributions. In comparison with other resourceful languages, few resources and tools have been developed for Amharic. However, even most of the existing resources and tools are not publicly accessible. Only few of the existing Amharic tools and resources are used in academia for research purposes. The major obstacles that hinder the progress on the development of Amharic IR are the complex morphology of the language, lack of sufficiently annotated corpus and lack of standards in resource construction and application development. Empirical evaluations conducted on accessible tools show that most of the tools are generally domain dependent and their performance drastically decreases when tested on out-of-domain scenarios.

References

Abate, M., Assabie, Y.: The development of Amharic morphological analyzer using memory based learning. In: Ethiopia Information Communication Technology Annual Conference 2014, pp. 11–18 (2014)

Abate, S.T., et al.: Parallel corpora for Bi-Lingual English-Ethiopian languages statistical machine translation. In: Proceedings of the 27th International Conference on Computational Linguistics, New Mexico, USA, pp. 3102–3111 (2018)

Abiyot, B.: Developing automatic word parser for Amharic verbs and their derivation. Master's thesis, Addis Ababa University, Addis Ababa (2000)

Aklilu, A.: Amharic-English dictionary, 1st edn. Kuraz Printing Press, Addis Ababa (1987)

Alemayehu, N., Willett, P.: Stemming of Amharic words for information retrieval. Lit. Linguist. Comput. 17(1), 1–17 (2002)

Alemayehu, N., Willett, P.: The effectiveness of stemming for information retrieval in Amharic. Program: Electron. Libr. Inf. Syst. 37(4), 254–259 (2003)

Alemu, A., Asker, L.: Amharic-English information retrieval. In: Peters, C. et al. (eds.) CLEF 2006. LNCS, vol. 4730, pp. 43–50. Springer, Heidelberg (2006). https://doi.org/10.1007/978-3-540-74999-8_5

Alemu, A., Asker, L.: An Amharic stemmer: Reducing words to their citation forms. In: Proceedings of the 2007 Workshop on Computational Approaches to Semitic Languages: Common Issues and Resources, pp. 104–110. Association for Computational Linguistics (2007)

Amsalu, S., Gibbon, D.: Finite state morphology of Amharic. In: 5th Recent Advances in Natural Language Processing, pp. 47–51 (2006)

Argaw, A.A., Asker, L., Cöster, R., Karlgren, J.: Dictionary-based Amharic – English information retrieval. In: Peters, C., Clough, P., Gonzalo, J., Jones, G.J.F., Kluck, M., Magnini, B. (eds.) CLEF 2004. LNCS, vol. 3491, pp. 143–149. Springer, Heidelberg (2005). https://doi.org/10.1007/11519645_14

Asefa, G.: Ontology-based semantic indexing for Amharic text in football domain. Master's thesis, Addis Ababa University, College of Natural Science, Ethiopia (2013)

Assabie, Y.: Development of Amharic morphological analyzer. Technical report, Ethiopia Ministry of Communication and Information Technology, Addis Ababa, Ethiopia (2017)

Berhanu, A.: Amharic-Français Dictionnaire, 1st edn. Shama Books, Addis Ababa (2004)

Birhan, K.: YeAmarinja Mezgebe Qalat. Ethiopian Languages Study and Research Center. 1st edn. Artistic publisher, Addis Ababa (1993)

Bruck, A., Tilahun, T.: Bi-gram based query expansion technique for Amharic information retrieval system. Int. J. Inf. Eng. Electron. Bus. 7(6), 1 (2015)

Countrymeters: Ethiopian Population. http://countrymeters.info/en/ethiopia. Accessed 11 Sept 2020

Demeke, G., Getachew, M.: Manual annotation of Amharic news items with part-of-speech tags and its challenges. In: Ethiopian Languages Research Center Working Papers, vol. 2, pp.1–16 (2006)

Eyassu, S., Gambäck, B.: Classifying Amharic news text using self-organizing maps. In: Association for Computational Linguistics, pp. 71–78. Ann Arbor, Michigan (2005)

Gamback, B.: Tagging and verifying an Amharic news corpus. Lang. Technol. Norm. Less-Resour. Lang. **79**, 79–84 (2012)

Gamback, B., Olsson, F., Atelach, A., Asker, L.: Methods for Amharic part-of-speech tagging. In: Proceedings of the first Workshop on Language Technologies for African languages, pp. 104–111. Association for Computational Linguistics (2009)

Gamback, B., Sahlgren, M., Atelach, A., Lars, A.: Applying machine learning to Amharic text classification. In: WOCAL 5: 5th World Congress of African Linguistics. Citeseer (2006)

Gasser, M.: Hornmorpho: A System for morphological processing of Amharic, Afaan Oromo, and Tigrinya. In: Conference on Human Language Technology for Development, Alexandria, Egypt (2011)

Gebrekidan, B.: Part of speech tagging for Amharic. Master's thesis, University of Wolverhampton, School of Law, Social Science and Communication, United Kingdom (2010)

Getachew, M.: Automatic part of speech tagging for Amharic: an experiment using Stochastic Hidden Markov Model (HMM) approach. Master's thesis, Addis Ababa University, Addis Ababa (2001)

Jochim, C.: Natural language processing and information retrieval methods for Intellectual Property Analysis. Ph.D. thesis, University of Stuttgart, Germany (2013)

Jurafsky, D., James, H.: Speech and Language Processing: An Introduction to Natural Language Processing, Computational Linguistics, and Speech, 1st edn. Prentice Hall, USA (2000)

Lisanu, K.: Design and development of automatic morphological synthesizer for Amharic perfective verb forms. Master's thesis, school of Information Studies for Africa, Addis Ababa University, Addis Ababa (2002)

Mengistu, G.: Automatic stemming for Amharic text: an experiment using successor variety approach. Master's thesis, Addis Ababa University, Addis Ababa (2009)

Mihalcea, F., Mihalcea, I.: Word semantics for information retrieval: moving one step closer to the semantic web. In: Tools with Artificial Intelligence, Proceedings of the 13th International Conference on Tools with Artificial Intelligence, pp. 280–287. IEEE (2001)

Mindaye, T., Atnafu, S., Redwan, H.: Searching the web for Amharic content. Int. J. Multimed. Process. Technol. (JMPT) **1**(1), 318–325 (2010)

Mulugeta, W., Gasser, M.: Learning morphological rules for Amharic verbs using inductive logic programming. In: Workshop on Language Technology for Normalization of Less-Resourced Languages (SALTMIL8/AfLaT2012), pp.7–12 (2012)

Munye, M., Atnafu, S.: Amharic-English bilingual Web search engine. In: Proceedings of the International Conference on Management of Emergent Digital EcoSystems, MEDES 2012, pp. 32–39 (2012)

Shashirekha, H., Ibrahim, G.: Dictionary based Amharic-Arabic cross language information retrieval. ASCTY, pp.49–60. NATP (2016)

Sintayehu, H.: Designing an information extraction system for Amharic vacancy announcement text. Master's thesis, Informatics faculty, Addis Ababa University, Addis Ababa (2013)

Sisay, F.: Part-of-speech tagging for Amharic using conditional random fields. In: Proceedings of ACL-2005 Workshop on Computational Approaches to Semitic Languages, Ann Arbor, Mich, pp. 47–54 (2005).

Sisay, F., Haller, J.: Application of corpus-based techniques to Amharic texts. In: Proceedings of MT Summit IX Workshop on Machine Translation for Semitic Languages (2003)

Tekalign, B.: Developing stemmer for Amharic text using longest-match method. Master's thesis, Arba Minch University, Arba Minch (2014)

Tesfaye, B.: Automatic morphological analyzer for Amharic an experiment employing unsupervised learning and auto segmental analysis approaches. Master's thesis, informatics faculty, Addis Ababa University, Addis Ababa (2002)

Wordofa, M.: Semantic indexing and document clustering for Amharic information retrieval. Master's thesis, Informatics faculty, Addis Ababa University, Addis Ababa (2013)

Yaqob, D.: Transliteration on the internet: the case of Ethiopic. In: Proceedings of the International Symposium on Multilingual Information Processing, Tsukuba, Japan (1997)

Yeshambel, T., Mothe, J., Assabie, Y.: Construction of morpheme-based Amharic stopword list for information retrieval system. In: the 8th EAI International Conference on Advancements of Science and Technology, Bahir Dar (2020a)

Yeshambel, T., Mothe, J., Assabie, Y.: 2AIRTC: the amharic adhoc information retrieval test collection. In: Arampatzis, A., et al. (eds.) CLEF 2020. LNCS, vol. 12260, pp. 55–66. Springer, Cham (2020b). https://doi.org/10.1007/978-3-030-58219-7_5

Yeshambel, T., Mothe, J., Assabie, Y.: Morphologically annotated Amharic text corpora. In: Proceedings of 44th ACM SIGIR Conference on Research and Development in Information Retrieval, Canada (2020c). https://doi.org/10.1145/3404835.3463237

Yifru, M., Tefera, S., Besacier, L.: Part-of-speech tagging for under-resourced and morphologically rich languages: the case of Amharic. In: HLTD 2011, pp. 50–55 (2011)

Construction of Morpheme-Based Amharic Stopword List for Information Retrieval System

Tilahun Yeshambel[1]([⊠]), Josiane Mothe[2], and Yaregal Assabie[3]

[1] IT PhD Program, Addis Ababa University, Addis Ababa, Ethiopia
tilahun.yeshambel@uog.edu.et
[2] INSPE, Univ. de Toulouse, IRIT, UMR5505 CNRS, Toulouse, France
josiane.mothe@irit.fr
[3] Department of Computer Science, Addis Ababa University, Addis Ababa, Ethiopia
yaregal.assabie@aau.edu.et

Abstract. One of the major forms of pre-processing in information retrieval and many other text processing applications is filtering out stopwords. They are ignored by many retrieval systems during indexing and retrieval in order to enhance retrieval effectiveness and efficiency. The aim of this paper is to present the construction of morpheme-based Amharic stopwords and investigate their effect on information retrieval tasks. The stopword list is constructed based on the semantics of Amharic words and corpus statistics: frequency, mean, variance, and entropy parameters. The stopword list is evaluated using Lemur on Amharic information retrieval test collection. Removal of stopwords has shown significant impact on retrieval effectiveness, size of index and term weighting of non-stopwords. On the other hand, their presence in index and query negatively affects the retrieval effectiveness of Amharic retrieval system. The average precisions of retrieving with and without stopwords using language modeling on root-based approach are 0.24 and 0.70, respectively.

Keywords: Morphological analysis · Corpus statistics · Semantics · Complex-language · Amharic · Stopword

1 Introduction

Stopword identification is one of the important tasks of text processing applications such as text classification, Information Retrieval (IR), text summarization, etc. [1]. In many languages, stopwords are functional and general words with low discriminatory power to differentiate between text documents, and affect efficiency [2]. They include articles, conjunctions, personal pronouns, prepositions, etc. These are frequently occurring words in a natural language and evenly distributed words across documents in corpus. They make up large portion of the text. They are considered as unimportant in many applications and thus, many text preprocessing applications remove them before processing documents and queries to improve system performance, save memory space and processing time [1, 3]. The two commonly used stopword removal techniques are the

M. A. Delele et al. (Eds.): ICAST 2020, LNICST 384, pp. 484–498, 2021.
https://doi.org/10.1007/978-3-030-80621-7_35

use of stopword list and inverse document frequency (IDF) value. For example, natural language toolkit (NLTK) has lists of stopwords for 16 different languages[1], and [4] removes stopwords using their IDF values.

IR is the process of finding relevant documents for users' query. Stopwords are ignored by many IR systems during indexing and query processing [2, 5]. In IR, stopword list contains frequent words that are ineffective to distinguish one document from others. Elimination of these words from the index reduces the space requirement and increases retrieval effectiveness in different languages. Depending on the complexity of the language, they can be removed before or after text processing such as stemming. The retrieval systems such as Okapi [6], Terrier [7], Lemur[2] and Lucene4IR[3] use stopword list to improve retrieval effectiveness.

Stopword lists can be constructed either manually or automatically. Manual construction involves the analysis of the semantics of words in a given language whereas automatic construction of stopword lists is using statistics information from large corpus. For example, Feng *et al.* [3] built a Chinese stopword list using TREC (Text Retrieval Conference) Chinese corpora. The list was constructed automatically based on the combination of the mean of probability, variance of statistical model and entropy of information model. On the other hand, Hindi text stopword list was constructed based on term weighting and relevance of words with respect to corpus [8]. The final generic stopword list was compiled based on the aggregation of term weight and entropy value. The Persian stopword list was generated based on terms' frequency, normalized IDF and information model [9]. Words with high-frequency, low IDF value, and with high entropy values are considered as stopwords, which belong to adverbs, prepositions, interjections and auxiliary parts-of-speech. As reported in this research, removal of stopwords minimizes the number of index terms by 27%. A standard stopword list for Malay language was built using word's frequency, variance, and entropy from a corpus that has 7,363,578 tokens [5]. Words with highest frequency, variance and entropy values were considered as stopwords. The intersection of the top n words from term frequency, variance and entropy were used to generate the final stopword list that contains 339 words. There are also other stopword lists for various languages such as Chinese, English, French, German, Arabic, Portuguese and Spanish languages[4].

Few attempts were made to create Amharic stopwords [10]. Mindaye et al . [11] created manually a stopword list which contains 77 words. However, this list has problems. First, the list contains small number of stopwords. From the actual number of stopwords available in the language, this list ignores many stopwords. Second, the list contains variants of a stopword rather than basic stems. Therefore, in one side it is difficult to list all variants of each stopword. On the other hand, using all variants of stopwords increases the length of the list. This creates unnecessary computational time specially on online processing of texts such as query processing. Samuel and Bjorn [12] create news specific stopword list which contains 745 words automatically. Like Mindaye et al. [11], this list contains variants of stopwords. Since this list is domain specific, it

---

could not be applicable in other domains. Alemayehu and Willett create corpus based stopword list which contains 148 stems [13]. In addition to the non-content bearing words, numerals are included in this list. The list contains the basic stems and citation forms of stopwords. However, there are more than one stems for variants of some stopwords, {ነበር, ነበር}, {ደግሞ, ዳግም}, {ሁን, ሆን}, e.g. etc. Generally, it can be observed that the construction of stopwords for Amharic IR system attempted so far has not followed the scientific methods used to create a list of stopwords and cannot be used as a generic resource for Amharic IR. As a result, some research and development works on Amharic IR do not remove stopwords [14–17] while others remove based on non-standard stopword list created manually [11, 18] or automatically [4]. The manually created stopword lists are compiled for a specific purpose and are randomly handpicked without proper consideration of the techniques employed to identify stopwords. Furthermore, the lists include only few stopwords as samples. On the other hand, the automatically constructed stopword list considered only IDF values and does not take into account stopword distribution in Amharic texts and the characteristics of the language.

The morphological characteristics of languages play a significant role in the identification of stopwords. Words generated from the same root in morphologically simple languages have one common stem. For such languages, a stemmer can conflate variants to one common form and thus, the frequency information about each term can be computed after applying stemming. As a result, terms which are distributed across many documents in the corpus can be identified by their IDF values. In such cases, IR systems developed based on term frequency are performing well. However, morphologically complex languages like Amharic have multiple stems for words generated from the same root. For instance, words such as ሰበረ /səbərə 'he broke'/, ተሰባሪ /təsəbari 'that can be broken'/, and አስበረ /ʔəsəbərə 'he helped to break'/ have the basic stems ሰበር- /səbər-/, ሰባር- /səbar-/ and ሰበር- /səbər-/, respectively. Hence, the use of stems provides distorted frequency since each stem is considered as different. Thus, Amharic stems need one more reduction analysis to extract their common form which is the root. In the aforementioned example, the three stems have one common root represented as ስ-ብ-ር /s-b-r/. Hence, collection statistics can be computed accurately based on root forms. This calls for the application of morphological analysis before the identification of stopwords in Amharic IR. However, to our best knowledge, there is no systematically constructed Amharic stopword list so far that considers term statistics and morphological characteristics of the language. Therefore, the aim of this paper is to generate Amharic stopword list using frequency, mean, variance and entropy values of root forms of words.

The rest of this paper is organized as follows. Section 2 briefly describes the characteristics of Amharic language. Section 3 presents the construction of Amharic stopword list. Experimental results and discussion are presented in Sect. 4. Section 5 highlights the effect of the constructed stopwords in Amharic IR. Finally, conclusion and future research directions are forwarded in Sect. 6.

2 Amharic Language

Amharic is the working language of the government of Ethiopia. It belongs to Semitic languages families. The language uses Ethiopic script for writing, which has 33 basic characters where each of them has 7 different forms representing consonant-vowel combination [4]. On top of basic characters there are labialized characters such as ሏ /lwa/, ሟ /mwa/, ሷ /swa/, ቋ /qwa/, ሯ /rwa/, etc. Their structure is consonant-vowel-vowel combinations [4, 19]. In addition, the script has its own punctuations and numbers. Its rich literary heritage has endowed the language with huge written resources.

Amharic is morphologically rich and complex language. The word formation process undergoes complex inflectional and derivational process [20]. Words can be formed directly from their roots by inserting vowels between radicals, from stems by attaching affixes, reduplication of one of the character of the stem or word itself, or compounding. Inflectional and derivational words change their forms for different purposes such as nouns, adjectives, adverbs, and verbs formation. Thousands of surface words can be generated from an Amharic root and its stems by changing the shape of characters in a stem or root, and by attaching affixes on stems [20]. In Amharic, verbal stems are derived from root's consonants by interdigitating vowel patterns. There are different templates/stem structures for the formation of words in various forms such as perfective, imperfective, jussive, imperative, etc. [21]. Amharic has many morphemes that play significant roles in morphology and syntax. Morphemes appear as affixes that have their own functions carrying different types of syntactic and semantic information. Amharic affixes are classified as prefix, suffix, infix, and circumfix, which might be added at the beginning, end, inside, or both at the beginning and end of the stems, respectively. They are attached to the base forms to mark for gender, number, case, person or others, and give additional functions to the roots or stems of words. More than one morpheme might exist on a given word. According to [22], an Amharic word might take up to four prefixes and five suffixes. For example, the word የሚያስመጣላቸውን /jəmijasmət'alatʃəwin/ is made from four prefixes (የ /jə preposition/, ም/m nominalizer/, ይ /ji third person singular subject marker for imperfect verb/, and አስ /ʔəs causative/); imperfect verb (መጥ /mət'/); and four suffixes (ኣ /ʔa third person singular subject marker for imperfect verb/, ል/li beneficative/, ኣቸው/ʔatʃəw object marker for third person plural/, ን /n accusative/). Due to such level of complexity, the morphological structure of Amharic is an important issue in the development of natural language processing applications.

3 Construction of Amharic Stopword List

Stopwords are generally useful for providing a good structure for a text. However, they contribute little meaning to the content. They can be identified using different techniques such as dictionary-based and automatic approaches. Dictionary-based approaches are inefficient and very expensive as stopwords are selected manually. On the other hand, automatic methods construct a list of stopwords based on statistical information such as term frequency, IDF, and variance from a large corpus. The characteristics of languages may play significant role in selecting the techniques employed for the construction of stopword lists. Considering the characteristics of Amharic, we built domain independent stopword list by combining two methods: *semantic-based* and *corpus-based*. Semantic-based identification of stopwords is carried out by analyzing the nature or semantics of words in the language whereas corpus-based method applied by considering the statistical information of words in a corpus.

3.1 Semantic-Based Identification of Stopwords

Based on the semantics of words, Amharic words can be classified into two as main and sub-word classes. The main word classes include verbs, nouns, adjectives and adverbs whereas sub-words include exclamation, conjunction, preposition, etc. Main word classes provide meaning by their own. On the other hand, sub-words are functional words used mainly for the formation of phrases, sentences and paragraphs. They occur commonly in many descriptions of different events. However, they contribute little to the description of the topics covered by the text, and they have structural function rather than meaning. According to [23], Amharic sub-word classes are characterized by lack of meaning by their own, inability to undergo morphological derivation and inflection, lack of morphemes for various parameters, and they have small word size. Amharic stopwords which satisfy these characteristics are collected from an Amharic book "Yamarigna Sewasiw" [23]. It includes words such as ወደ /wədə 'towards'/, እንደ /ʔində 'like'/, ስለ /silə 'about'/, እስከ /ʔiskə 'up to'/, ወዘተ /wəzətə 'and so on' /, ጎፍ /goʃ 'bravo'/, እ. /ʔu 'oh'/, ዋ /wa 'warning'/, ይልቅ /jilik 'instead'/, etc.

3.2 Corpus-Based Identification of Stopwords

Corpus-based identification of Amharic stopwords is made by analyzing the frequency, mean, variance and entropy of words in Amharic text corpus. Non-content-bearing words in Amharic are usually used to structure sentences and paragraphs. They are used for keeping the coherence of a text rather than describing the subject matter. Non-content-bearing words are also used as morphemes in Amharic word formation. Accordingly, morphological analysis needs to be done before identification of stopwords. Thus, statistics of terms is computed on morphologically analyzed text corpus. The process of corpus-based stopword identification is presented in Fig. 1.

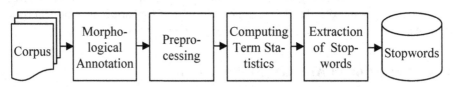

Fig. 1. The process of corpus-based Amharic stopword identification

Corpus Collection: Identification of many non-content-bearing Amharic words is carried out using statistics of terms computed from a representative corpus. To this effect, we collect documents from Amharic Wikipedia[5], religious books, blogs[6], and news sources[7] to create a corpus. Thus, the corpus has 5,737 documents which contain 64,637 sentences and 1,315,371 words. The corpus is built for the general purpose of Amharic IR test collection as well.

---

[5] https://am.wikipedia.org.

[6] http://www.danielkibret.com/.

[7] http://www.waltainfo.com/.

Morphological Annotation: All words in the corpus are annotated with morphological segments. The annotations segment surface words into their constituent parts called morphemes based on stems and root forms. The morphemes can be preposition, stem, root, person marker, tense marker, conjunction, plural marker, etc. As the corpus is built for general purpose, all morphemes in each word are tagged with morphological information. The general structure of a morphologically annotated word W is:

$$[p\_]^* w [\_s]^*$$

where p is a prefix morpheme, "_" is a morphological segment marker, w is the root or stem of W, s is a suffix morpheme, [...] denotes optionality, and * denotes the possibility of multiple occurrence. For example, the word የሚያስመጣላቸውን /jəmijasmət'alatʃəwn/ is annotated as follows.

የ_ም_ይ_አስ_መጥ_አ_ል_አቸው_ን
jə_mi_ji_as_mət'_ʔa_li_ʔatʃəw_n
p p p p w s s   s   s

Preprocessing: Preprocessing of the annotated corpus involves character normalization and removal punctuation marks and. A major task of preprocessing task in Amharic corpus is normalization. The process is required due to the fact that some characters have similar phonemes but different graphemes. Base characters having such property are {ሀ /hə/, ሐ /hə/, ኀ /hə/ and ኸ /hə/}, {ሠ /sə/ and ሰ /sə/}, {ጸ /ts'ə/ and ፀ /ts'ə/}, and {አ /ʔə/ and ዐ /ʔə/}. Thus, ሰላጸሀፃ can also be written as ሥለሀሐፃ,ሰላጸሐፃ, ሥለጸኀፃ, ሥለጸሀፃ,ሰላጸኀፃ, ሥለጸሐፃ, etc. although some of them rarely appear in a text. As there is no standard established for character normalization, we used the rules shown in Table 1 to normalize characters. Furthermore, due to similarity in phonemes, the fourth orders ሃ /ha/, ሓ /ha/, ኃ /ha/ and ኻ /ha/ are normalized to ሀ/hə/ whereas ኣ /ʔa/ and ዓ /ʔa/ are normalized to አ /ʔə/.

Table 1. Character normalization

Base character	Normalized form	Example Original word	Normalized word
ሐ		ሐረግ	ሀረግ
ኀ	ሀ	ኀይል	ሀይል
ኸ		ኸለት	ሁለት
ሠ	ሰ	ሠያዪ	ሰዳይ
ዐ	አ	ዓለም	አለም
ፀ	ጸ	ፀሁፍ	ጸሁፍ

Computing Term Statistics: In the development of IR systems, term statistics has been widely used to identify stopwords. However, the notion of terms depends on the characteristics of languages. For morphologically simple languages, stems can be considered as terms. However, this is not the case with morphologically complex languages like Amharic. We hypothesize that morphemes used to form Amharic words could be used as a basis for computing term statistics. Thus, in this work, we consider morphemes as terms. Accordingly, for the entire corpus that we collected, we compute morphemes frequency, mean, variance and entropy as described below.

Document and Collection Frequency: The document frequency of a morpheme indicates the number of documents the morpheme exists whereas collection frequency is the total morpheme frequency throughout the corpus. In this case, all morphemes from all documents are ranked according to their document frequency and collection frequency. Then, a threshold value was set to determine stopwords from ranked morpheme. Furthermore, morphemes that are evenly distributed throughout the collection and satisfy the threshold value are considered as stopwords [24]. Document frequency *df* computed as:

$$df(M_i) = \sum_{i=1}^{N} \textbf{morpheme\_ status}(D_i) \tag{1}$$

where M_i is the ith morpheme in the corpus, D_i is the ith document in the corpus, N is the total number of morphemes in the collection. If a morpheme appears in a given document, its status is 1 otherwise 0. Collection frequency *cf* is computed as:

$$cf(M_i) = \sum_{i=1}^{N} MFD_i \tag{2}$$

where MFD_i is the morpheme frequency in each document, N is total number of documents in the corpus. In this paper, a morpheme frequency is un-normalized total number of times a morpheme occurs in a document.

Mean: This is another way to measure the overall distribution of morphemes in the whole corpus. The mean probability *mp* of each unique morpheme in the whole corpus is computed as:

$$p(M_i) = \frac{MF}{TM} \tag{3}$$

where $p(M_i)$ is morpheme probability, *MF* is morpheme frequency in each document and *TM* is the total number of morphemes in the document. Then, the mean probability of each morpheme, *mp* (M_i), in all documents is computed using as:

$$mp(M_i) = \frac{\sum_{i=1}^{N} p(M_i)}{N} \tag{4}$$

where N is total number of documents.

Variance: This is the other way to check the distribution of morphemes throughout the documents in the corpus. Variance *v* is computed as:

$$v(M_i) = \frac{\sum_{i=1}^{n} (n(Mi) - m(M_i))^2}{N} \tag{5}$$

where $v(M_i)$ is the ith morpheme variance, $n(M_i)$ is normalized morpheme frequency in a document, $m(M_i)$ is mean value, and N is the total number of distinct morphemes in the document.

$$m(M_i) = \frac{\sum_{i=1}^{n} MF}{N} \tag{6}$$

where MF is morpheme frequency and N is the number of words in a document.

Entropy: This is used to measure the information value e of each morpheme in the corpus. This method is based on the amount of information a morpheme carries. Stopwords are known to have low explanatory values [3]. If the entropy value of a word is high, then the information value of the word is low. The entropy value of each morpheme in the corpus is calculated as:

$$e(M_i) = \sum_{i=1}^{n} p(M_i).\log \frac{1}{p(M_i)} \tag{7}$$

where $p(M_i)$ is the probability of morpheme frequency and is calculated by dividing the morpheme frequency via the total number of morphemes in the document.

Extraction of Stopwords: The frequency, mean, variance and entropy values of each morpheme in the corpus are compared against other morphemes in the corpus to select stopwords. The intersection of the top n words from these statistical information are selected as stopwords. Finally, the stopword list contains stem-based and root-based stopwords. The top 250 morphemes from the four stopwords lists (Table 2, Table 3, Table 4 and Table 5) are merged together to generate the aggregated corpus based stopword list. These morphemes make up a large fraction (more than 60%) of the Amharic text documents. However, the amount of information carried by these morphemes is negligible. The final Amharic stopword list is generated from the intersection of the frequency, mean, variance and entropy stopword lists with few linguistics experts' analyzed words. The list contains 222 words. Variants of a stopwords are not included in the constructed stopwords list. Their length is from one to five characters. They occur much more frequently than other morphemes. They include prepositions (e.g. ወደ /wədə 'to'/, እንደ /ʔinidə 'such as'/, ስለ /silə 'about'/, እስከ /ʔisikə 'up to'/, በ /bə 'by'/, ከ /kə 'from'/, etc.), conjunctions (e.g. እና /ʔina 'and'/, ወይም /wəyim\xE2 \x80\x98or'/, ይሁን እንጅ /yihun ʔinidʒ 'however'/, ምክንያት /miknijat 'because'/, እዚህ /ʔizih 'this'/, ይልቅ /jilik 'instead'/, etc.), negative markers አል /ʔəl 'not'/, ም /mə/), indefinite articles (እንድ /ʔənid 'an'/), auxiliary verbs ኢ-ል /ʔ-l 'say'/, ን-በ-ር /n-b-r 'was'/, etc.), ወዘተ /wəzətə 'and so on'/, etc. These and the like words are found at the top of the four lists (frequency, mean, variance, and entropy).

4 Result and Discussion

4.1 Result

The overall distributions of morphemes in the corpus are measured using frequency, mean, variance, and entropy values as presented as follows. From a statistical point of view, the intersection of top n morphemes across various measurements are considered as stopwords. Accordingly, a total of 222 stopwords are identified and included in our list of stopwords. The list of sample morphemes with highest morpheme and collection frequencies are shown in Table 2. The distribution of stopwords across many documents in the corpus is presented in Table 2. Their document and collection frequency are higher than non-stopwords. Stopwords are found in majority of the documents with high collection frequency. Morphemes that had low frequencies are excluded from stopwords.

Table 2. Top 10 morphemes with highest document and collection frequency

Morpheme	Document frequency	Collection frequency
ዩ /jə 'of'/	5,737	190,726
በ /bə 'by'/	5,733	139,870
ኡ /ʔu 'they'/	5,731	141,646
ኧ /ʔə 'he'/	5,727	105,751
ው /wɨ 'the'/	5,717	99,033
አል /ʔəl 'not'/	5,715	72,269
አ /ʔə 'he'/	5,709	73,261
መ /mə nominator/	5,708	91,533
ት /tə passivizer/	5,707	84,031
ን /nɨ accusative/	5,703	92,342

Amharic stopwords have high mean probability values compared to the majority of non-stopwords. Samples of stopwords with the highest mean probability are shown in Table 3.

Table 3. Top 20 morphemes with highest mean values

Morpheme	Mean	Morpheme	Mean
ዩ /jə 'of'/	0.05810	አት /ʔəti 'not'/	0.01434
በ /bə 'by'/	0.04196	አስ /ʔəs 'be the cause of'/	0.01011
ኡ /ʔu 'they'/	0.04079	ሁ-ን /h-n 'happen'/	0.00888
ኧ /ʔə 3pms/	0.02915	አቸው /ʔətʃəw 'are'/	0.00806
ው /wɨ 'the'/	0.02836	ድ-ር-ግ /d-r-g 'act'/	0.00738
መ /mə nominator/	0.02570	ዩ /jə 'that'/	0.00712
ን /nɨ accusative/	0.02554	እንደ /ʔɨndə 'like'/	0.00675
ት /tə passivizer/	0.02451	ላይ /laj 'on'/	0.00553
አል /ʔəl 'not'/	0.01565	እንዲ /ʔɨndi 'as'/	0.00329
አች /ʔotʃ 'many'/	0.01549	ነው /nəw 'is'/	0.00326

Stopwords have highest variance probability value than almost all content bearing morphemes. They are located at the top of the ranked list. Table 4 shows top 10 morphemes with highest variance values.

Table 4. Top 10 morphemes with highest variance values

Morpheme	Variance	Morpheme	Variance
? /jə 'of'/	0.00132	ው /wɨ 'the' /	0.00038
ቡ /bə 'by'/	0.00072	ን /ni 'we'/	0.00031
ኡ /ʔu 'the'/	0.00069	መ /mə Inf/	0.00031
አ /ʔə 3psm/	0.00055	ተ /tə pas/	0.00029
ኧ /ʔə 3psm/	0.00045	ኦች /ʔotʃi 'many'/	0.00018

Stopwords have highest entropy value than non-stopwords. The top *n* morphemes with the highest entropy value are extracted as candidate for stopwords. Table 5 shows top 10 morphemes with highest entropy values.

Table 5. Top 10 morphemes with highest entropy values

Morpheme	Entropy	Morpheme	Entropy
? /jə 'of'/	38.01462	ተ /tə pas/	20.68732
ቡ /bə 'by'/	31.38035	አ /ʔə 3psm/	20.17104
ኡ /ʔu 'the'/	30.22907	መ /mə Inf/	18.96849
ው /wɨ 'the'/	24.00580	አል /ʔəl 'not'/	16.54033
ን /ni 'we'/	22.48845	ለ /lə 'to'/	14.58708

4.2 Discussion

Based on their nature they can be classified into three. The first types of Amharic stopwords exist by themselves and can accept prefixes and suffixes. For instance, the stopword ሌላ /lela 'other'/ can take the prefix ? /jə 'of'/ and the suffix ኦች /ʔəotʃi 'many'/ become የሌሎች /jəlelotʃ 'any others'/. The second types of stopwords exist as standalone words but do not take affixes, e.g. ወዘተ /wəzəta 'and so on'/, ወይም /wəyɨm 'or'/, etc. The third types of stopwords exist as part of Amharic words and act as prefix or suffix. For instance, the words ከጎንደር /kəgondər 'from Gondar'/ and በመኪናው /bəməkinaw 'the car'/ contain the prepositions ቡ /bə 'by'/ and the suffix ው /wɨ 'the'/, respectively. As the meaning of stopwords indicated in Tables 2, 3, 4 and 5, they are similar to English language semantically and functionally except linguistic differences. Unlike morphologically simple languages, identification of Amharic stopwords is not an easy task. The challenges are the existence of many forms for a stopword. The majorities of stopwords undergo complex morphological process, and merge with each other or other words to form new words as shown in Table 6.

Table 6. Examples of morphological changes in stopwords

Word	Morpheme	Morphological information
በወስጥና	በ_ውስጥ_ና /bə_wist'_ʔina/	preposition-stem-conjunction
የእነዚህ	የ_እነ_እዚህ /jə_ʔina_əzih/	genitive-preposition- demonstrative
በመሆኑ	በ_መ_ሀ-ን_ኡ /ba_ma_h-n_ʔu/	preposition-nominalizer-root-definite
ከሰውና	ከ_ሰው_ና /kə_səw_ʔina/	preposition-stem-conjunction

As shown in Table 6, many of Amharic stopwords affix with other stopwords or non-stop words. They might change their forms depending on their context. Therefore, it is not possible to find and remove all Amharic stopwords directly before morphological analysis. Hence, to see their distribution and information content in the corpus, their frequency (document and collection), mean, variance and entropy need to be computed after morphological analysis. Previously created stopword lists contain simply small number of variants of stopwords. However, it is very difficult, if not impossible, to include all variants into a list of stopwords. The following examples show how various word forms can be formed from a single stopword.

ውስጥ: ውስጥና, ውስጥም, የውስጥ, ለውስጥ, በውስጥ, ከውስጥ, የውስጥና, ከውስጥም, ከውስጥና, ለውስጥና, በውስጥም, ውስጥን, በውስጥህ, በውስጥና, በውስጧ, የውስጥም, ውስጥህ, ውስጥስ, ከውስጣቸው, በውስጡ, ከውስጧ, etc.

መካከል: መካከልም, በመካከል, በመካከላቸው, ከመካከላቸው, በመካከሏ, መካልና, በመካከልሽም, ከመካከል, በመካከልም, የመካከለኛው, በመካከሉ, etc.

በኩል: በበኩላቸው, የበኩላቸውን, የበኩሉን, በበኩሉ, በኩልም, የበኩሏን, በበኩሏ, በየበኩላቸው, የበኩላችንን, በበኩላችሁ, የበኩላቸው, የበኩሌን, በበኩላቸው, በበኩሉ, የበኩላችሁን, በኩልና ,etc.

ላይ: በላይ, ላይም, ከላይ, ላይና, በላይም, ባላይ, የላይኛው, ወደላይ, በላይና, የላይኛውን, በላይዋ, በላይኛው, የላይ, ላይኛው, በበላይ, እላይ, ላይኛውን, ከበላይ, የላይኛውና , ለበላይ, etc.

ብቻ: ብቻውን, ብቻቸውን , ለብቻ, ለብቻው, ብቻም, ብቻየን, ለብቻቸው, ለየብቻ, ብቻዋን, ለብቻዋ, ብቻህን, ብቻችንን, ብቻውንም, ብቻቸሁን, ለብቻዋ, ለብቻቸን, etc.

ኃላ: በኃላ, በኃላም, ወደኃላ, ከኃላ, የኃላ, ከኃላው, በኃላና, ኃላም, ከኃላቸው, ከኃላየ, ኃላው , በኃላማ, በኃላው, ከኃላሁ, ከኃላየ, ከኃላችን, በኃላስ, ኃላየ, የኃላው, ኃላየ, ኃላውም, etc.

ሌላ: ሌሎች, በሌሎች , በሌላ , ከሌሎች, ሌላው, ሌላኛው, ለሌሎች, ሌሎችም, በሌሎችም, የሌላቸው, የሌሎች, ሌሎችንም, ከሌላው, ሌሎችን, ለሌሎችም, ከሌሎችም, የሌሎችን, እንደሌሎች, ለሌላ, ሌላውም, ለሌላው, በሌላው, በሌላም, ከሌላ, የሌላቸውን, ሌላም, የሌሎችንም, ወደሌሎች, የሌሎችም, በሌሎችም, ስለሌሎች, ከሌሎች, ሌላየ, የሌላ, የሌላውን, ለሌላቸው, በሌላው, በሌላኛው, etc.

እዚህ: በዚሁ, ከዚሁ , በዚሁም, እነዚሁ, ለዚሁ, ለዚሁም, ስለዚሁ, እነዚሁን, ከዚሁም, እዚሁ, የዚሁ, በእዚሁ, ከእዚሁ, ከዚሁ, እንደዚሁ, ስለዚሁም, ከእዚሁም, ወደዚሁ, በዚሁ, የእዚሁ, ለእዚሁ, የዚሁን , በዚሁች, የእዚሁን, etc.

In our work, such morphological variants of a stopword are represented by one common form that is stored in the stopword list. Some Amharic stopwords have both stem and root forms. However, only root-based approach can conflate all variants of a stopword to one common form. For example, the stopword ን-ብ-ር /n-b-r/ has two stem forms which are ነበር- /nəbər- 'was'/ and ነበር- /nəbar- 'was'/. Thus, we use root forms to represent Amharic stopwords. Analysis of the Amharic stopwords reveals that most of them are affixes without particular semantic information. They are rather used for syntactic purpose such as definite articles, prepositions, conjunctions, negative markers, etc. appearing mostly as prefixes and suffixes.

5   Evaluation of Stopwords

The constructed generic Amharic stopword list contains morphemes and may be used in various fields. The stopwords are evaluated based on their effect on term weighting and retrieval effectiveness. Experiments were conducted to test the impact of stopwords on term weighting and retrieval effectiveness as follows.

The Effect of Stopwords on Term Weighting: The effect of Amharic stopwords on term weighting is investigated and tested. Term weighting is used in IR field to extract the most relevant terms of documents. The Term Frequency-Inverse Document Frequency (TFIDF) of every word in each document was computed to evaluate the importance of each word to represent document content. The term weighting of stopwords and some non-stop words were evaluated using Amharic IR test collection [25]. The statistical analysis and the comparison between the existence and removal of stopwords on term weighting are presented in Table 6 as follows. Documents and terms are selected randomly in the corpus. It can be seen that the term weighting of non-stop words slightly increases after elimination of stopwords. This means that the importance of terms to represent the subject matter in each document increases. The TFIDF values of stopwords are zero or close to zero. For example, stopwords such as የ /jə/, በ /bə/, ኡ /ʔu/, እ /ə/, ው /wɨ/, አል /ʔəl/, አ /ʔə/, መ /mə/, ተ /tə/ and ን /ni/ have zero TFIDF values whereas stopwords such as እና /ʔina/, ኦች /ʔotʃ/, እት /ʔət/, አስ /ʔas/ , እንደ/ʔinidə/, አችው /ʔətʃəw/, እንዲ /ʔinidi/, ዎች /wotʃ/, ነው /nəw/ and ላይ /laj/ have values ranging from 0.01 to 0.07. This means that they are not significant to describe the content of documents.

The Impacts of Stopwords on Retrieval Effectiveness: The   effect   of   stopwords removal on Amharic IR retrieval effectiveness is tested on Amharic IR test collection [25]. The evaluation was done using Lemur and trec_eval tools on language modeling approach. Figure 2 shows retrieval effectiveness with and without stopwords on stem-based and root-based approaches. The top two graphs (labeled in red and blue) represent root-based and stem-based retrieval without stopwords while the bottom two graphs (green and yellow) represent root-based and stem-based retrieval with stopwords. The evaluation is made using the same Amharic IR test collection [25]. It can be seen that there is a significant difference between Amharic retrieval with and without stopwords on stem-based and root-based approaches. The bottom graph (in yellow) and the second top graph (in blue) indicate retrieval with and without stopwords on stem-based app-roach, respectively. The third top graph (in green) and top graph (in red) are retrieval with and without stopwords on root-based approach, respectively. Root-based retrieval is better than stem-based retrieval. This is because root-based approach is best to conflate all variants but not stem-based approach.

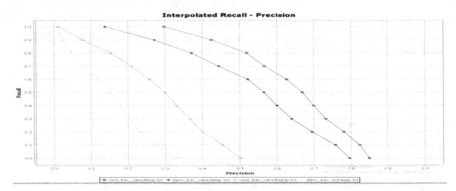

Fig. 2. Retrieval effectiveness with and without stopwords

In addition to retrieval effectiveness, the impact of stopwords on index size is evaluated. The number of morphemes decreases significantly after stopwords removal. The numbers of morphemes before and after stopwords removal are 3,399,172 and 1,316,504, respectively. The effect of stopwords on the size of index file is shown in Table 7. Removal of stopwords has reduced the size of index file, which minimizes the time of processing index file.

Table 7. Index size with and without stopwords on root-based corpus

Index type	Corpus size in MB	Index size
With stopwords	33.0 MB	25.1 MB
Without stopwords	24.1 MB	15.1 MB

The availability of standard stopword is a major factor in developing different Amharic applications. We believe that a resource developed for a research purpose should be easily available to researchers and developers. Hence, the developed stopword list in this research is made publicly accessible online for future researches. So it enables researchers and developers to build their systems at minimal cost.

6 Conclusion

Amharic is one of the under-resourced languages facing lack of NLP resources, tools and corpora. We present an Amharic stopword list created by considering the semantics and characteristics of stopwords in the language, and by analyzing their distribution in a corpus. The applicability of stopwords is systematically evaluated using Amharic

IR system. Thus, the stopword list is believed to be a generic resource for other NLP applications as well. The stopword list is made publicly available for the research community and can be accessed through a request made to the corresponding author at: tilahun.yeshambel@uog.edu.et.

References

1. Gerlach, M., Shi, H., Amaral, L.A.N.: A universal information theoretic approach to the identification of stopwords. Nat. Mach. Intell. (2019)
2. Antoine, B.: Understanding and customizing stopword lists for enhanced patent mapping, vol. 29, no. 4, pp. 308. Elsevier (2007)
3. Feng, Z., Lee, W., Xiaotie, D., Song, H., Sheng, W.: Automatic construction of Chinese stopword list. In: Proceedings of the 5th WSEAS International Conference on Applied Computer Science, pp. 1010–1015, Hangzhou (2006)
4. Alemu, A., Lars, A.: Amharic-English information retrieval. In: Workshop of the Cross-Language Evaluation Forum for European Languages, pp. 43–50. Springer (2006).
5. Khalifa, C., Rayner, A.: An Automatic construction of Malay stopwords based on aggregation method, Singapore, pp. 180–189. Springer Nature Pte Ltd. (2016)
6. Ibrahim, A.: Effects of stopwords elimination for Arabic information retrieval: a comparative paper. Int. J. Comput. Inf. Sci. 4(3), 119–133 (2006)
7. Ounis, I., Amati, G., Plachouras, V., Macdonald, C., Johnson, D.: Terrier: a high performance and scalable information retrieval platform. In: SIGIR Open Source Workshop 2006 Seattle, Washington (2005)
8. Rani, R., Lobiyal, D.: Automatic construction of generic stopwords list for Hindi text. Proc. Comput. Sci. 132(Iccids), 362–370 (2018)
9. Sadeghi, M., Vegas, J.: Automatic identification of light stopwords for Persian information retrieval systems. J. Inf. Sci. 40(4), 476–48 (2014)
10. Yeshambel, T., Mothe, J., Assabie, Y: Evaluation of corpora, resources and tools for Amharic information retrieval. In: ICAST2020. springer, Bahir Dar (2020a)
11. Mindaye, T., Redwan, H., Atnafu, S.: Searching the Web for Amharic content. Int. J. Multimed. Process. Technol. (JMPT) 1(1), 318–325 (2010)
12. Samuel, E., Bjorn, G.: Classifying Amharic news text using self-organizing maps, vol. 71 (2005)
13. Alemayehu, N., Willett, P.: Stemming of Amharic words for information retrieval. Literary Linguist. Comput. 17(1), 1–17 (2002)
14. Alemayehu, N., Willett, P.: The effectiveness of stemming for information retrieval in Amharic. Prog.: Electron. Libr. Inf. Syst. 37(4), 254–259 (2003)
15. Asefa, G.: Ontology-based semantic indexing for Amharic text in football domain. Master's thesis, Addis Ababa University, College of Natural Science, Ethiopia (2013)
16. Hirpa, A.: Probabilistic information retrieval system for Amharic language. Master's thesis, Addis Ababa University, School Of Information Science, Ethiopia (2012)
17. Mengistu, B.: N-gram-based automatic indexing for Amharic text. Master's thesis, Addis Ababa University, School Of Information Science, Ethiopia (2002)
18. Mengiste, B.: Automatic ontology learning from unstructured Amharic text. Master's Thesis, Addis Ababa University, College Of Natural Sciences, Department Of Computer Science, Ethiopia (2013)
19. Asker, L., Argaw, A., Gambäck, B.: Applying machine learning to Amharic text classification. WOCAL 5: 5th World Congress of African Linguistics, pp. 7–11. Addis Ababa University, Ethiopia (2006)

20. Assabie, Y.: Development of Amharic morphological analyzer. Technical report, Ministry of Communication and Information Technology, Addis Ababa (2017)
21. Yifru, M., Wolfgang, M.: Morphology-based language modeling for Amharic. Ph.D.'s thesis, University of Hamburg, departments of informatics, German (2010)
22. Mulugeta, W., Michael, G.: Learning morphological rules for Amharic verbs using inductive logic programming. Workshop on Language Technology for Normalisation of Less-Resourced Languages (SALTMIL8/AfLaT2012), pp. 7–12 (2012)
23. Yimam, B.: Yamarigna Sewasiw (Amharic Grammar). 2nd edn. CASE, Addis Ababa (2001).
24. Stefano, F., Floriana, E., Domenico, G.: Automatic learning of linguistic resources for stopword removal and stemming from text. Elsevier Proc. Comput. Sci. **38**, 116–123 (2014)
25. Yeshambel, T., Mothe, J., Assabie, Y.: 2AIRTC: the amharic adhoc information retrieval test collection. In: Arampatzis, A., et al. (eds.) CLEF 2020. LNCS, vol. 12260, pp. 55–66. Springer, Cham (2020b). https://doi.org/10.1007/978-3-030-58219-7_5

Ventilator Prototype Controlled and Monitored by an IoT Platform

Fabián García-Vázquez, Héctor Alonso Guerrero-Osuna[(⊠)],
José Manuel Ortiz Rodríguez, Ma. Del Rosario Martínez Blanco,
and A. del Rio-De Santiago

Posgrado en ingeniería y tecnología aplicada, Unidad Académica de Ingeniería Eléctrica,
Universidad Autónoma de Zacatecas, Ramon López Velarde 801,
9800 Zacatecas, Zacatecas, Mexico
hectorguerreroo@uaz.edu.mx

Abstract. The coronavirus pandemic caused a radical change in everyone's life, the number of infected persons increases each day, in some hospitals in Mexico, especially in rural areas, artificial respirators are not available to treat this disease, since they are costly devices high. The prototype presented in this paper is built in order to reduce costs in all aspects. The structure was built with economical but resistant materials and the IoT platform reuses the existing infrastructure such as computers and cell phones to create a graphical interface that minimizes the use of components, in addition, the electronic system uses inexpensive devices that are easy to find in the market and even recyclable. The prototype has three automatic modes of operation with certain frequencies, which are for children, adolescents and adults. As well, a manual configuration was added to modify the frequency from the operating system. The structure of the ventilator has a cam system that allows the pressure to be changed in a medical resuscitator AMBU, modifying the level of oxygen that can be supplied to a patient. The prototype approved its functioning in terms of the mechanism, the frequency is changes depending on the age of the patient with its respective pressure for oxygen supply, but it is important to mention that the ventilator is still in the testing phase and has not yet been evaluated with a patient, since, authorization is required from the health sector and this stage is under development.

Keywords: IoT · Artificial respirator · Ventilator · COVID-19

1   Introduction

Due to the coronavirus pandemic that occurred in early this year, as of June 2020, a total of 823 626 cases have already been confirmed and this caused the death of 40,598 deaths worldwide, for this reason, it was necessary to create technology that was capable of dealing with this disease [1, 2]. Professionals from around the world present their proposals to help reduce the number of infected in their countries, by bioengineering, medical devices are being created to help save the lives of infected patients. Artificial

M. A. Delele et al. (Eds.): ICAST 2020, LNICST 384, pp. 499–511, 2021.
https://doi.org/10.1007/978-3-030-80621-7_36

respirators or mechanical ventilators have become one of the protagonists of this pandemic due to the large number of infected who may be in intensive care, which is why more ventilation equipment is required in public and private hospitals in Mexico and whole world [3, 4]. Different countries around the world have focused their economic resources to obtain a greater number of these equipment's, due to their specific characteristics, they are not easy to produce and even companies that have never manufactured medical devices before have joined the task to develop ventilator to supply the high demand for appliances. This type of ventilators not only works against Covid-19, but they are essential to survive other lung pathologies. In 2009, they were of great help against the epidemic of influenza AH1N1 for the recovery of seriously ill patients [5].

In recent years, technological evolution has led to great advances both in ventilation modes and in the monitoring of respiratory variables. All this makes the study of mechanical ventilation has become somewhat complex, with abundant manuals and courses that delve into the subject in various ways. Mechanical ventilation is an artificial respiration procedure that uses a mechanical device to completely or partially re-place the ventilatory function [6]. A ventilator is a system capable of generating pressure on a gas so that a pressure gradient appears between it and the patient. It should not be forgotten that mechanical ventilation is not a treatment in itself, but rather a life support technique that allows respiratory function to be maintained while other curative treatments are in place. Within the treatment, the doctor determines the mode of ventilation by pressure, volume or flow, depending on the physiological conditions to the lungs so that they can absorb the oxygen that goes to the bloodstream [7, 8].

As soon as the pandemic started, an initiative was started by working groups around the world called "Covid-Makers", in order to propose ventilator prototypes to the hospital networks of their respective countries. Most of these prototypes focus on developments using 3D printers, which produce the parts needed to build the ventilators. On the other hand, the designs are shared among the community so that anyone can print the pieces from anywhere [9, 10]. These ventilators have structures that allow the frequency to be varied depending on the age of the patient, in addition to a feedback system to measure the amount of oxygen supplied [11].

Variations between these prototypes commonly occur in the materials and components used, particularly the proposal presented in this paper consists of a low-cost ventilator, but unlike 3D printing, it is proposed to use other more common types of materials [12]. However, the main difference is concentrated in the electronic system and the control and monitoring interface. Every ventilator has a control and monitoring interface, in professional equipment there are screens in which the operator can observe frequency and oxygen levels. Furthermore, if low-cost ventilators are required, it is important to economize on all aspects. The decision to use an IoT platform through a computer or cell phone is due to the accessibility to these devices and the internet, in this way the existing infrastructure is reused, and savings can be made in the construction of the system, avoiding using a physical control and monitoring screen. Nevertheless, it could be thought that the use of an IoT platform increases the cost of the system, but in the market, you can find low-cost devices that perform the control and wireless communication functions to achieve the IoT systems [13, 14].

2 Proposed System

This paper presents a proposal for the development of a low-cost ventilators, implemented one of the most widely used technologies at the moment, the Internet of Things (IoT). The IoT can be used to control and monitor various electronic devices, in order to carry the information on a smartphone or computer connected to the internet [15]. The implementation of this ventilator consists of a structure formed by a system of cams that press an Ambu medical device used in manual resuscitation, for the purpose to provide oxygen flow to the patient. A wiper motor is used to move the cam system, since, it has different speeds, modifying the frequency of oxygen supply. In addition, there is a circuit with a power and control interface for system operation.

The paper is organized as follows, the third section "Methodology" describes the design and development of the system. The fourth section "Results" shows the results obtained from the development and implementation of the system. Finally, the fifth section "Conclusions", reflects on the operating system, as well as the possibility of future work.

3 Methodology

3.1 Development of Ventilator Structure

Due to the idea of building a low-cost ventilator, materials that were inexpensive and easily accessible were used, because as a result of to the pandemic, many businesses closed and obtaining the corresponding material became a challenge. Initially, it was considered to use acrylic as the main material for the structure, but after evaluating the tools available for making cuts and perforations, it was decided to use wood. Thanks to the great cooperation of maker engineers around the world, it was possible to study different proposals for ventilators, one of which is based on the structure of our project is by the OxyGEN initiative. OxyGEN is a device that automates the manual ventilation process for patients in emergency situations where there are not enough ventilators available, developed by a group of professionals led by the company Protofy.xyz, with the scientific support of Hospital Clínic, Hospital Germans Trias i Pujol and the UB of Barcelona [16]. The structure built for this work is based on one of OxyGEN's projects, with the necessary adaptations to build it with our own tools. One of the reasons for choosing this structure, apart from its low cost, its designed can be made from common tools, without the need for extra machinery. The structure measures approximately 21 cm wide, 35 cm long and 35 cm high. Figure 1 shows a 3D design of the structure of the Ventilator.

The mechanism of the structure is based on a cam system, considering the pressure exerted on the Ambu can be modified by increasing or decreasing the size of the cam, this is important due to the pressure depends on various factors, some of them are the age and weight of the patient. Another important feature of the structure is the gear system, which is responsible for moving the cam shaft. The operation of the structure is based on a motor installed in the gear system, whereby the cam is moved by pushing a support that moves the Ambu, allowing contractions in the resuscitator depending on the frequency of the motor. Figure 2 presents the different parts that make up the structure.

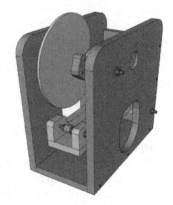

Fig. 1. 3D Design for the ventilator.

Fig. 2. 3D design of the different parts of the ventilator.

The construction of the structure was carried out from the available materials, some aesthetic changes were made with respect to the original design, without affecting the main operation of the system. The cam has an opening so that it is easy to install and avoid removing the shaft completely. Figure 3 shows the result obtained from the structure for the ventilator.

3.2 Development of the Electronic System

An electronic system capable of controlling the engine speed by pulse width modulation (PWM) was designed, which varies the frequency with which the Ambu is pressed on the ventilator. A direct current (DC) electric motor recycled from a windshield wiper was selected as it has a torque strong enough to perform the movement of the gear system. These types of engines are 12v and have several defined speeds, specifically, the one that uses this ventilator have two speeds. The ventilator can be used without hardware components, but this could only have two established frequencies, but it is required to control the speed at will to vary the frequency, for this reason the corresponding elements of both power and control are added.

In the power, an H bridge was used that allows the motor to rotate in both directions and control it with PWM. In the control part, there is a microcontroller and Wi-Fi

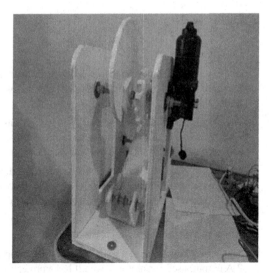

Fig. 3. Result of the structure for the ventilator.

NodeMCU module that is the main element of the IoT. Furthermore, using the NodeMCU it is possible to generate a control and monitoring system through a web page interface, which is used to select the required configuration, in this case, four modes are configured, which are for children, adolescents and adults, that work automatically due to they have established frequencies, the fourth configuration is manual and is carried out by means of a variable resistance (Potentiometer), in which the frequency can be modified in relation to the variable resistance.

3.3 Hardware

As discussed, different hardware modules are used to do IoT-enabled things. In this work, we have used different hardware modules to make the electronic system of the ventilator. Table 1 shows all the components used.

Once the components were selected, the corresponding peripherals were interconnected on the same structure. The general system is powered through the 12 v source, so it is necessary to supply the ventilator with the single-phase 110 v electrical network. Figures 4 and 5 shows the electrical connection of the hardware for ventilator operation.

3.4 Software

There are different platforms that allow programming the NodeMCU, for example, you can configure the standard Arduino IDE to be able to program the ESP8266 and the boards based on this popular SoC. For this, you need to add the corresponding packages to the Arduino IDE board manager. The IoT component used in the ventilator is the NodeMCU, its main advantage being the incorporation of a Wi-Fi module that allows creating IoT projects or wireless systems. Table 2 shows the main characteristics of the NodeMCU [17].

Table 1. Hardware elements for the ventilator.

Component	Description
NodeMCU ESP-12E	Open source IoT platform that includes firmware running on Espressif Systems' Wi-Fi ESP8266 SoC and hardware is based on the ESP-12 module
H Bridge BTS7960	This controller uses the Infineon BTS7960 Chips as an H bridge to allow the control of the motors, it has a protector against overheating and overcurrent, since this driver can generate a current of up to 43 A
Potentiometer 100k	Mechanical variable resistance, when manipulated, a fraction of the total potential difference is obtained between the central terminal and one of the ends, behaves like a voltage or voltage divider
DC Motor 12 v	Recycled 12 V windshield wiper motor, has a 4-point terminal, in which two different speeds can be obtained
Power supply 12 v 2 A	This power supply has a 110–220 v AC voltage input and a 12vDC at 2 A output, used for motor power. It has a protection system against overloads, short circuits and voltage changes

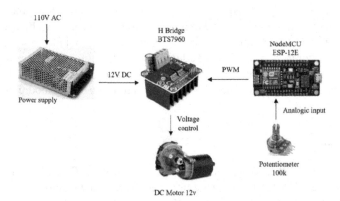

Fig. 4. Ventilator electrical connection diagram

In a first stage, the NodeMCU was configured only as a controller to test the hardware elements, mainly the mechanical system. In this programming, tests were carried out on the motor to determine the frequency based on PWM signals. The resolution of the PWM in the NodeMCU is 10 bits, there are 1024 levels of variation for the duty cycle. With this information, the following relationship was found regarding motor frequency and PWM. In Table 3 it can be seen that the motor remains motionless until it has a duty cycle at a level of 550, which corresponds to 53.7 percent of the total motor voltage, with a frequency of 19 revolutions per minute, but with this duty Cycle torque is too weak to move AMBU bracket. With a level of 700 a frequency of 23 rpm is reached, and the torque is sufficient to contract the AMBU. It is worth mentioning that these tests were performed with the lowest engine speed, the highest PWM level reached a speed of 31 rpm.

Fig. 5. Connecting the ventilator hardware.

Table 2. Main technical specifications of the NodeMCU.

Parameters	NodeMCU
Memory	32-bit
Processor	LX 106
Processor clock	80 MHz 160 MHz
Storage	16 MB
Built-in Wi-Fi	2.4 GHz supports 802.11b/g/n
ADC PIN	1 (10-bit resolution)
GPIO Pins	10
Operating voltage	3.3 V

Table 3. Relationship between the PWM of the NodeMCU and the frequency of the DC motor.

PWM Level	Frequency
0	0
150	0
300	0
450	0
550	9 rpm
700	15 rpm
850	23 rpm
1000	30 rpm

3.5 IoT Platform

In order to control and monitor the ventilator through a web page it was necessary to implement a web server that stores, processes and delivers pages to web clients, that is, that web browsing is allowed on our laptops and smartphones, sending certain parameters to the NodeMCU, to vary the frequency of the motor. Communication between the client and the server is done using the protocol called Hypertext Transfer Protocol (HTTP). In this protocol, a client initiates communication by making a request for a specific web page using HTTP, and the server responds with the content of that web page or an error message if it cannot. The pages delivered by a server are mainly HTML documents [18].

One of the best features that ESP8266 offers is that you can not only connect to an existing Wi-Fi network and act as a web server, but you can also configure your own network, allowing other devices to connect directly to it and access pages Web. For specific purposes of this work, a STA mode network was created where the NodeMCU connects to an existing Wi-Fi network (one created by a wireless router) and this assigns it an IP address, which can be accessed through a browser, see Fig. 6.

The IP address assigned to the NodeMCU, allows you to configure the web server and deliver web pages to all the devices connected under the existing Wi-Fi network. On the website, an interface was designed to interact with the ventilator operator, as mentioned above, there are 4 modes of operation, the frequency for each of the modes depends on many factors, in this case the age was only taken as a reference of the patient, see Table 4 [19].

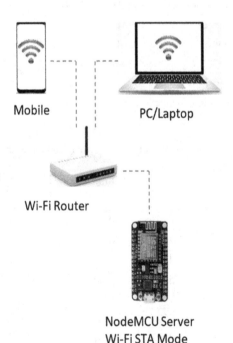

Mobile   PC/Laptop

Wi-Fi Router

NodeMCU Server
Wi-Fi STA Mode

Fig. 6. Wi-Fi STA configuration of the NodeMCU.

Table 4. Normal values of respiratory rate

Age	Breaths per minute
Newborn	30–80
Younger Infant	20–40
Older Infant	20–30
Children from 2 to 4 years old	20–30
Children from 6 to 8 years old	20–25
Adult	15–20

4 Results

Based on the previous information, certain frequencies were established for each mode of operation of the ventilator and they are available to configure from the IoT platform, Fig. 7 shows the control and monitoring panel.

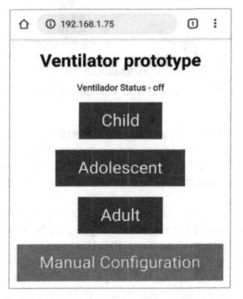

Fig. 7. IoT interface for ventilator control and monitoring

The ventilator is divided into 4 operations according to the selected configuration, to test each of the configurations, a neonatal medical Ambu was used as shown in Fig. 8. To access control and monitoring on the website, it is necessary to have the IP address assigned by the Router to the NodeMCU. The programming of the system was carried out in the Arduino IDE, where a program was created in which the SSID and password credentials are embedded in the program, so the NodeMCU establishes an internet connection and it is possible to access the interface of said page. It was verified that in each of the configurations, the frequency changed and even the size of the cam was varied to exert more or less pressure on the Ambu. Figure 9 show a diagram of the ventilator operation.

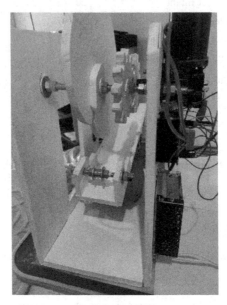

Fig. 8. Tests with the ventilator prototype

As can be seen in the diagram, to change the operating mode it is necessary to stop the respirator, mainly this is done for safety reasons, in order to avoid a change in the operating mode due to an inadvertent issue or due to an error, in this way it is avoided that the frequency can change from one moment to another without the authorization of the operator.

Each configuration resulted in positive results regarding the frequency variation, and the IoT platform responded efficiently and quickly. Figure 10 shows the response of the IoT interface for each of the configurations, Fig. 10(a) corresponds to the child configuration with a frequency of 30 rpm, Fig. 10(b) corresponds to the adolescent configuration with a frequency of 23 rpm, Fig. 10(c) corresponds to the adult con-figuration with a frequency of 15 rpm, Fig. 10(d) corresponds to the manual configuration, which can change from 12 rpm to 31 rpm.

The ventilator has not yet been tested with a patient, since they must comply with the regulations established by the local health department and must evaluate the performance of the ventilator for use, this stage is still in the development phase and could be reflected in a work future.

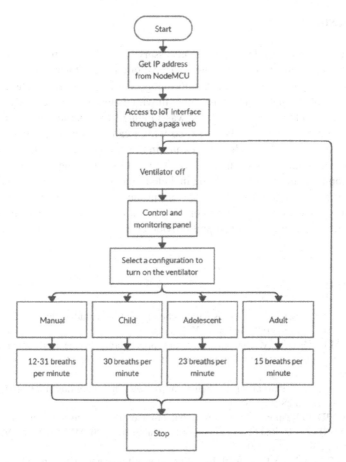

Fig. 9. Ventilator operation system

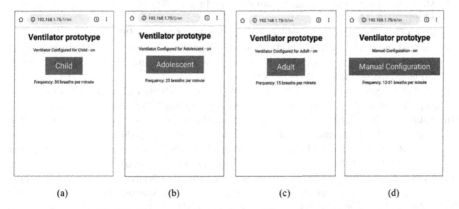

Fig. 10. Response of operating modes on the ventilator.

5 Conclusions

Due to the coronavirus pandemic, it was necessary to implement measures that would help critically ill patients through bioengineering. For our part, it was decided to develop a wireless autonomous control and monitoring system through the interface of a web page for a ventilator, which is low cost and built with materials that are easily accessible to obtain and recyclable. The ventilator was mounted on a structure that allows the pressure in a medical Ambu to be modified with a cam system, changing the size of the cam to demand a higher or lower pressure in the Ambu. The ventilator has not yet been tested with a patient since approval by the health sector is necessary, this stage is under development and will possibly be included in a work in the future, to finish this stage it is proposed to add a feedback system in the volume of oxygen, through flow sensors that will calculate the amount of oxygen supplied to the patient, in this way a better performance can be obtained and provide an improvement in the quality of the prototype.

References

1. World Health Organization. https://apps.who.int/iris/bitstream/handle/10665/331685/nCo Vsitrep01Apr2020-eng.pdf. Accessed 28 June 2020
2. Ranney, M.L., Griffeth, V., Jha, A.K.: Critical supply shortages—the need for ventilators and personal protective equipment during the Covid-19 pandemic. New England J. Med. **382**(18), e41 (2020)
3. The new england journal of medicine. https://www.nejm.org/doi/full/10.1056/NEJMp2 006141. Accessed 28 June 2020
4. CDC COVID-19 Response Team: Severe outcomes among patients with coronavirus disease 2019 (COVID-19) United States, February 12–March 16, 2020. MMWR Morb. Mortal Wkly Rep. **69**(12), 343–346 (2020)
5. White, D.B., Lo, B.: A framework for rationing ventilators and critical care beds during the COVID-19 pandemic. Jama **323**(18), 1773–1774 (2020)
6. Meng, L., et al.: Intubation and ventilation amid the COVID-19 outbreak. Anesthesiology **132**(6), 1317–1332 (2020)
7. De La Calle Reviriego, B.: Ventilación mecánica. Rev. Clin. Esp **197**(4), 13–24 (1997)
8. Santos-López, M., Jaque-Ulloa, D., Serrano-Aliste, S.: Métodos de desinfección y reutilización de mascarillas con filtro respirador durante la pandemia de SARS-CoV-2. Int. J. Odontostomatol. **14**(3), 310–315 (2020)
9. 3D-Printed Splitter for Use of a Single Ventilator on Multiple Patients During COVID-19. https://www.liebertpub.com/doi/full/10.1089/3dp.2020.0102. Accessed 05 Sept 2020
10. Smith, K.: Green Left Weekly - 3D printed ventilator parts save lives (humanities & social sciences collection) - informit. Green Left Weekly (1257), 19 (2020)
11. Farré, R., Puig-Domingo, M., Ricart, P., Nicolás, J.M.: Ventiladores mecánicos de emergencia para la COVID-19. Emerg. Mech. Ventilators Covid-19. 7–8 (2020)
12. Clarke, A.L.: 3D printed circuit splitter and flow restriction devices for multiple patient lung ventilation using one anaesthesia workstation or ventilator. Anaesthesia **75**, 819–820 (2020)
13. Tobin, M.J.: Basing respiratory management of COVID-19 on physiological principles. Am. J. Respir. Crit. Care Med. **201**(11), 1319–1320 (2020)
14. Pearce, J.M.: A review of open source ventilators for COVID-19 and future pandemics. F1000Research **9**, 218 (2020)

15. Stojmenovic, I.: Fog computing: a cloud to the ground support for smart things and machine-to-machine networks. In: 2014 Australasian Telecommunication Networks and Applications Conference (ATNAC), pp. 117–122 (2015)
16. OxyGEN Project. https://www.oxygen.protofy.xyz/community?lang=es. Accessed 24 June 2020
17. Singh, H., Pallagani, V., Khandelwal, V., Venkanna, U.: IoT based smart home automation system using sensor node. In: 2018 4th International Conference on Recent Advances in Information Technology (RAIT), pp. 1–5 (2018)
18. NodeMcu. https://www.nodemcu.com/index_en.html. Accessed 20 June 2020
19. Talamas Márquez, J.: Habilidades Básicas III Toma de signos vitales. Univ. Juarez del Estado Durango 1(1), 14 (2016)

Scrum LPC – A Value-Based Framework for Learning Process Coaching

Martina Müller-Amthor$^{(\boxtimes)}$ ⓘ and Georg Hagel ⓘ

University of Applied Sciences Kempten, Bahnhofstr. 61, 87435 Kempten, Germany
{martina.mueller-amthor,georg.hagel}@hs-kempten.de

Abstract. To foster students' agile process of learning in team and to pervade their own self-regulated and self-reflecting thriving process by value-based Scrum Learning Process Coaching is the motivation of the authors as researcher and practitioner in both software engineering and other STEM-education. This article describes the introduction the most famous Framework Scrum as an agile methodology, particular with regard to increase awareness of values. As a first step, it appears relevant to find out whether there exists a positive effect on the learning outcomes of participants in value-based scrum and what are the impacts of value-based support. The research question is as follows: Do team values in the frame of value-based Scrum Learning Process Coaching influence the performance of the students' team? In order to answer the question an experimental study was conducted with students in German higher education of Software Engineering (N = 78). The research is qualified by using mixed methods. The authors use both questionnaires of the Team Climate Inventory for value education in teamwork and semi-structured interviews. Therefore, we research the impacts of using value-based Scrum Learning Process Coaching as a framework of agile self-regulated and more self-motivated learning. The results show that groups with dedicated values benefit from their intensive teamwork with higher performance and better grades. This study consider many articles describing the use of scrum teaching in Software Engineering establishing a virtual or real capstone project. However, there is no awareness yet, that Scrum Framework could be a sustainable self-development tool for an agile thriving mindset.

Keywords: Agile learning · Scrum Learning Process Coaching · Higher education

1 Introduction

The link between innovative ideas developed in software and engineering industries and the new possibilities for digitalization and virtualization around the delivery of agile teaching and learning will become a major area of interest for educators and engineers.

This article will inspire broadly the awareness for agile learning at the level of higher education through the structured adaptation of Scrum. Such an agile framework is important due to the fact, that future challenges are characterized by complexity,

M. A. Delele et al. (Eds.): ICAST 2020, LNICST 384, pp. 512–533, 2021.
https://doi.org/10.1007/978-3-030-80621-7_37

interdisciplinary and holocracy. Currently, innovative research seems almost unsolvable, because an agile mindset is needed. In addition, valuable Scrum is based on profound values that team working considers to be central to value-driven behavior and action nowadays time [1, 2]. Since 2017, the establishment of the value-based version (commitment, focus, respect, openness and courage) was a remarkable improvement and the sentence of Jeff Sutherland, the inventor of Scrum: "Scrum is a tool to change the world" [1]. R. Chatley [3] describes how to bring agile methods from industry to the classroom and creates more opportunities to communicate with students and customers about their needs through adapted project-based teaching of software engineering. The framework *Valuable Scrum Learning Process Coaching* (LPC) could be the answer of helping students to plan and perform their work, especially by value-based teamwork in fulfilling project-, problem- or scenario-based curriculum. The introduction of *Scrum* into higher education is significant for the learning practice and specific to Science, Technology, Engineering, and Mathematics (STEM) in higher education. It could be an important contribution to acquiring self-responsible, self-regulated, self-organized and self-reflective processes preparing for lifelong learning and to achieving a holistic self-development and self-efficacy.

2   Valuable Scrum as Learning Process Coaching

The following section presents related work covering the elements of the concept.

2.1   What is Valuable?

Kluckhohn [4] describes a value that a person considers desirable for himself and others. In western societies, there have been discussions of a change in values since ca. 1980. This change in values must be taken into account in educational and leadership behaviour, if people are to be reached and motivated [5–7].

The values of a team influence behaviour and steer the perception et vice versa. In this way, they form an internal and thus also an external concept of compliance [8]. It is important to mention that the change in values considers more self-realization, more autonomy, more attention to feedback and appreciation - as well as the consideration of ethical issues such as sustainability. In the case of values from the domain of intellectual autonomy, on the other hand to affective autonomy on the other hand it is more favored that individuals develop and pursue their own ideas and thoughts. This includes Schwartz [9] curiosity, tolerance and creativity.

The order of modernity does not only rely on external observation, but also uses the self-observation of the team members to examine their values and conscience. The internalized values and expectations always motivate to critically examine and improve one's own self-efficacy. This is an important aspect for the own learning and development of new task solutions. In this context of the learning process, self-efficacy is defined as a value in itself [10]. It is the expectation that one will be successful in a certain matter. It is essential to the way things are approached. A high level of self-efficacy means that one has the confidence to do many things and is willing to face challenges often and with pleasure. A low self-efficacy means on the other hand, that challenges cannot be solved, so they are avoided [11].

In particular, the self-efficacy of one's own learning process can be promoted by continuous feedback and encouragement from the colleagues and teachers. A support of learning process coaches should always be designed to increase the self-efficacy of learners [12, 13].

2.2   Scrum as Practical Approach to Developing Agile Thrive Mindset

In the context of this value based agile concept for an agile teaching and learning arrangement called Scrum LPC, the most important roles, events and artifacts will be described here again in Fig. 1. The framework can support a holistic learning process for STEM in higher education. It shows the most important elements of Scrum LPC in the applied scenario of a value-based learning process coaching. This results from the analysis and key impacts of already published didactical approaches [14–19]. A detailed description is given in [16].

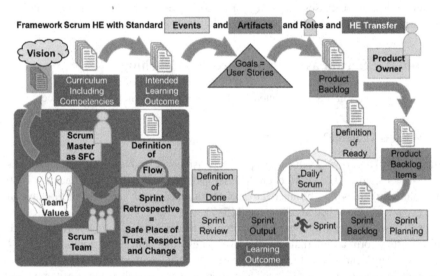

Fig. 1. Overview *Scrum-LPC* – process of learning with a Solution-Focused Coach [cf. 16]

As described in [1] and [16] in 2017, the five most important values are the following: Commitment, focus, respect, openness and courage. "Thus, these five values are obvious!" Therefore, we use the so-called five-finger feedback [21] as a reflection method. Each finger of a hand is supposed to stand for a value. In this way, each finger of a hand is given a specific meaning and represents therefore a concrete value. For this purpose, the students receive 140 value cards and can choose exactly five values from these cards, which are particularly important to themselves and which should also correspond to the size and significance of the finger, if possible. In this way, the student gets an overview of the values he or she wants to represent in the team from a wide range of values. Thinking about and discussing which values are important to him or her and how he or she will live them is an important cognitive and emotional process. The next important development step is to work out and define five team values together. These are to be binding for the team during the period of the collaboration. In this way, the students create their own value system for future teamwork. To confirm the commitment and possibly facilitate later intervention, they sign the "Five Fingers" with their first name, as shown in Fig. 2.

This commitment is the fundamental prerequisite that in the retrospective phase of the SFC, students can take responsibility for reflecting on these values both for themselves and once again for the team with the following questions: "Have you lived within your possibilities during your learning process? What are you doing in order to achieve the best possible outcome? Were you able to advocate team values?".

Fig. 2. Results of the Five-Finger-Method by transfer the Scrum values firstly to own values and secondly to team-values with the commitment by personal signature.

Considering the students' point-of-view, the didactical approach with the methodology of value-based Scrum LPC allows to improve their own learning process reflecting the learning cycle: Plan, Do, Check and Learn (PDCL). This PDCL cycle promotes a holistic learning process, as the concepts of the different experimental and didactic approaches of Scrum in the educational context already show [14–19].

The following elements of the Scrum PDCL cycle, Müller-Amthor describes in [16]:

- Curriculum Including Competencies with Intended Learning Outcomes
- Goals of the learning process as User Stories
- Artifacts like Product Backlog, Sprint Backlog, Definitions of Ready, Definition of Done, Definition of Flow
- Roles of the *Product Owner*, the student group as *Scrum Team*, supported by of the *Scrum Master* and
- Events of Sprint Planning, "Daily" Scrum as Stand-up, virtually or in physical presence, Sprint Review, Sprint Retrospective (Retro).

The *Scrum Team* had a shared understanding of what it means for work to be complete and the Sprint goal is pervaded. The phases of the events reflect Plan, Do, Check and Learn. Essentially, the *Retro* is the most significant section for the value-based learning objectives. They are "to inspect, understand and adapt the interactions between learning skills, strategies and knowledge in cognitive performance" [16, p. 2].

This challenge encourages the *Scrum Team* and the individual to formulate a path to enhance themselves and the teamwork with increased collaboration. By responding to the Quick Check of Flow questionnaire linked to the Team Climate Inventory Items, students acquire a mindset and a culture of agility. The agile methods of teamwork improve their collaborative skills. "Therefore, the definition of agility should be the ability to continuously adapt to their complex, future- and solution-focused needs" [16, p. 2]. A SFC that works in a value-based and sustainable way should power Scrum LPC. For both the lecturers themselves and support staff, it is necessary to have a sufficient understanding of basic psychological knowledge. Empathy is required for understanding interaction and attending to students' needs. Only from this, the student develops his or her intrinsic motivation and well-being according to self-determination theory from Ryan and Deci [22]. In this way, better self-regulated, creative team solutions can emerge. Thus, it is necessary to succeed in deciphering the psychological needs for student action. Well-directed questions from the SFC to the student should raise student's awareness of their own obstacles and challenges. Thus, it is necessary to succeed in deciphering the psychological needs for students' actions. It takes encouragement to discover old dogmas in a solution-focused way, not just to mask them. This creates a terrain for future thriving.

2.3 What is Learning Process?

Now the question arises what we understand as to the process of learning and how we structure the phases of this process. First, the column headings are described in short form of Table 1 to get an overview of the holistic learning process supported by Scrum LPC.

This alignment and comparison should demonstrate the transferability of a methodology from industry to educational institutions. Thus, an agile and lean framework can be used to achieve high quality learning experiences as shown in Fig. 3.

In detailed phases of lifelong learning phases, diverse profiling takes place. According to the retrospective phase, questions are designed in the subarea to stimulate the students to think about their versatile needs and the status of their self-efficacy. Finding suitable answers to these questions gives a good prerequisite for further growth. For this purpose, suggestions for methods and tools are available, which help to deepen and to document the thoughts on the questions posed. Finally, the elements of the Scrum Framework are assigned to demonstrate the holistic nature of the coaching learning process. Figure 3 describes the most important elements related to the *Scrum* events and artifacts and shows the core of the educational framework of Scrum LPC with the "PDCL-cycle as the real holistic process of learning" [16, p. 2].

In this publication, only the planning and the checking phase should be emphasized, because this is the entry into value-based Scrum. The analysis and the awareness of one's own values is an important basis for the recognition of the motives that are rooted in them. So is quite clear, that as the word "motives" from the word root already says, this is the base of motivation. If students know and name their own values, they can communicate about these values with others in the team.

If the team values are fixed for a certain period of cooperation, the motives and motivation become visible to everyone in the team.

If a discussion happens about values and students ask questions to themselves, then this can lead to further reflection, as follows:

Table 1. Overview of the process of learning in Fig. 3

Headings	Description	Scrum LPC
Learning-Cycle	*Plan, Do, Check, Learn (PDCL)*	
Process of Learning	*PLAN: Planning as a kind of advanced organizing* → *"Ante" Learning*	***Scrum Values*** *Sprint planning*
	DO: Execute and Exercise → *Learning in Action*	*Sprint with* *"Daily" Scrum*
	CHECK: Evaluate and Reflect → *Learning on Action*	*Sprint Review* *Sprint Retrospective, in particular* *to **Scrum Values***
	LEARN: Adapt and Thrive → *Learning new Action* → *change and continuous* *improvement* → *Thrive Mindset*	***Scrum Values***
LLL-Phases	*Lifelong-Learning* *– Self-reflexive Profiling (generally)* *– Competence balancing (specific study programm or task-based)* *– Individual development planning (specific task-related)* *– Experimenting, Gaining experience, Implementing solutions, Getting task done, Achievement* *– Subject, Learning Behaviour, Learning Success, Learning Strategy, Learning Emotion, Learning Context (Setting and Environment)* *– Self-Determination, Self-Motivation, Autonomy, Participation, Well-Being, Self-awareness*	***Scrum Values***
Catalogue	*Questions for the respective lifelong learning phase*	***Scrum Values***
Method/Tool	*Appropriate and suitable coaching tools*	*–*
Scrum LPC	*Scrum Learning Process Coaching events, artifacts*	*–*

Learning-Cycle	Process of Learning	LLL-Phases	Catalogue of Questions	Method/Tool	SCRUM LPC
P	- PLAN/Planning>>"Ante" Learning				Transparency in a Sprint Planning
		Self-reflexive Profiling (generally)			
			- Am I clear about the *value-based goals* of my life?	Human Needs, **Values, Attitudes** -->Motives -->Motivation	*Scrum Values* >> **Personal Values** >>>>*(Scrum)* **Team Values**
			- In which areas of life do I want to contribute even more to my own well-being and thrive in my life?	Wheel of Life	
				Talent-Empowerment-Strengths Questionnaire	Dialog about strength-oriented fields of development and action
				Personality Test in combination with Learning Style Test	Learning Strategy Development
		Competence Balancing (specific study programm or task-based)			
			"Should" - What is the expectation that I should fulfill?	STEM-functional and attention to non-technical skills	- *Curriculum Including Competencies* - *Intended Learning Outcome*
			Which specific, task-related vision could I formulate?	AS-IF-Frame	- *Vision* - *Epics*
			"Actual" -Am I clear about the *value-based self-motivation* of learning? - What do I do particularly well? - What do I want to engage in a self-determined way?	collaboration, communication, self-directed exploration, etc. --> multi-complex competences with a catalogue of questions for self-reflecting	*Definition of Flow*
			"Target-actual comparison" - What are my strengths and areas of development?	Competence balancing Strengthen strengths, weaken weaknesses	*Product/Sprint Backlog* with tasks for exercises and tests meeting the *Sprint Goal*
		Individual development planning (specific task-related)			
			"Targets" - Which learning goals/focused learning outcomes do I set myself?	Coverdale, ILO, GROW, Circle of Influence, SMART, etc.	- *User Stories* - *Product Backlog* - *Definition of Ready*
			What do I think, how clear are the value-based goals of my team?	Learning objectives agreement	- *Sprint* (>= one week or other fixed period of time) - *Sprint Planning* - *Sprint Backlog*
			"One Way" - How do I achieve my learning goals?	Flow channel - Learning strategies - Learning Tasks with estimation	*Sprint* - *Sprint Backlog Items* with *Scrum Board* under consideration *Definition of Flow*
D	- DO/Execute/Exercice>>Learning in Action				Transparency in a Sprint
		Experimenting			
		Gaining experience			
		Implementing solutions			
		Area of tension		Collegiate learning, Learning partnership, Individual dialogue for a learning process coaching, Innovative learning landscapes and platforms	"Daily" Scrum or "Stand-up" with three questions, which help the Team meeting the *Sprint Goal* ? 1) What did I achieved yesterday? 2) What will I do today? 3) Do I see any impediment that prevents me?
		Getting task done			*Learning outcomes:* using also social media by collaborative platform
		Achievement			*Definition of Done*

Fig. 3. Holistic process of learning performed by Scrum LPC (proprietary description)

Learning-Cycle	Process of Learning	LLL-Phases	Catalogue of Questions	Method/Tool	SCRUM LPC
C	- CHECK/Evaluate/Reflect >> Learning on Action				Inspect
		Subject	"What did I want to consider/try out in the concrete situation/...store in the brain in the long term?"	Task: practical, functional,...	Daily personal *Flow Check* *Review* after the Sprint
		Learning Behaviour	"What did I do and how?"	Quick-Check: Learning Behaviour (time scheduling, workload, effective learning methods)	*Retrospective* - Impediments - Learning requirements
		Learning Success	"What have I achieved?"	Learning outcomes related to - Tasks (test questions, exercises) - Competences - *Values*	*Review and Retrospective* Evaluation
		Learning Strategy	"What strategy worked/ What didn't work? Why?"	Success diary of key topics	Review and Retrospective
		Learning Emotion	"What was I thinking and feeling?" (values, emotions, impressions)	Quick-Check: Learning Emotion	*Review and Retrospective* Daily personal *Flow Check* incl. Impediments Backlog
		Learning Context (Setting and Environment)	"What place and context worked?/ What didn't work? Why?"	Success diary of key topics, Checklist of Yes/ButNotYet	Review and Retrospective
L	- LEARN/Adapt/Thrive>>Learning new Action>>Change, Continuous Improvement>>Thrive Mindset				Adapt
		Self-Determination	"What will I do differently next time?"		*Product/Sprint Backlog Refinement*
		Self-Motivation	What are my really motives? Am I intrinsically motivated? What can motivate me extrinsically?	Motivation - Cards, Videos or other Apps, etc.	Iteration with *value-based Scrum* or *Dialog about strength-oriented fields of development and action*
		Autonomy	"What does this mean to me?"	competence balancing and transfer to other competence areas	Iteration with new *Sprint Backlog Items*
		Participation	"Which values have I experienced as fostering?"	Five-Finger-Method	Iteration with *value-based Scrum*
		Well-Being	Do I really live joyfully and harmoniously?	Success diary of key topics	
		Self-awareness	"What's left to do?" "What do I want to document and what can I record / pass on as 'knowledge management' for myself or for others?"	Learning Diary/WIKI Preparation "Planning New" and transfer	*Product/Sprint Backlog Refinement* *Iteration with new Sprint Backlog Items*

Fig. 3. (*continued*)

- What was the purpose of my values selected from the list that I have so far "appreciated" through experience?
- What opportunities are there to try to experience the negotiated team values in the here and now?
- Which values are so important to me that I want to live them in the near future?
- When the analysis of the team values in relation to the team goals can provide us with information about what is important in our cooperation?
- How effective a values-based relationship can be with each other?

It is possible that better common understanding will result in improved cooperation. The analysis of the team values in relation to the team goals could provide an indication of the relationship and the effectiveness of working together.

2.4   What Are the Tasks of a Learning Process Coach?

The next import question is how we can support the learning process and manage the continuous improvement with an agile coach.

The *Scrum Master* advises as a service- and solution-focused coach, who clarifies the students' needs and works attentively on the change potential of each individual "Problem talk creates problems; solution talk creates solutions" [23]. This is the key sentence, which S. de Shazer used in 1985 to establish his special solution-oriented short therapy, which is now frequently practiced by school counselors. Through purposeful questioning techniques, empathy, emotional intelligence, and use of encouragement, students are nurtured in their needs and values. One of the most important tasks of the SFC is to facilitate the learner's search and discovery process for his or her own solution to the challenge and to create aspirations for a positive transformation in his or her own learning process. The SFC asks clear, direct, primarily open-ended questions, one at a time, at a pace that allows for thinking and reflection by the student. He or she allows the learner to complete speaking without interrupting unless there is a stated coaching purpose to do so. The SFC shares observations, intuitions, comments, thoughts and feelings to serve the student's learning and forward movement. The SFC assists students to identify their beliefs that they need to address or resolve in order to achieve what they want to reach. The approach of this methodology supports students to discover their resources themselves and to use them actively as well as beneficially. The main goal is to create and stimulate self-awareness and to train this ability. Another critical competency of the SFC is both attentive, mindful as well as active listening. This requires a high degree of self-control and a correspondingly reflective focus on value-oriented activities.

"The *Scrum Master* is the key actor who shapes the project and therefore the learning environment and whose main task includes motivating students to learn by using autonomy-supportive strategies instead of final controlling behaviors" [16, p. 2]. She or he is a professional who is called a facilitator. They primarily manage teamwork in an active and structured way by fostering collaboration, coordination, communication and collegiality. In addition, these people enjoy excellent moderation, visualization, and presentation skills. The distinctive value-based and solution-oriented coaching with simultaneous high conflict ability, in order to overcome or mitigate through obstacles and resistances, is their daily of life. He or she is responsible for the implementation and facilitation of lean and agile task as best practices of the students and methodologies across *Scrum Teams*.

More sustainable, effective and efficient is the joint development of possible solutions. It triggers valuable and esteemed processes of reflection and promotes the development of individually tailored strategies. Important learning processes can be triggered in this way, both in terms of teamwork and with regard to change management. The development of collegial relationships and open discussions about possible alternative development approaches are the result. By stopping to whine and to complain, a broad scope of expectation is created so that change is not only possible, but also inevitable [24, 25]. This allows the *Scrum Team* to achieve their shared learning goals sprint by sprint because they have a trusted leader as an SFC to call on when needed, who is committed to the spirit of agile teaching, and who exemplifies agility to the students through his or her own life [cf. 16, S. 2].

2.5   What Should Be the Effect of Learning Process-Coaching?

LPC should foster self-efficacy in a balance of four challenges to strengthen self-esteem or self-worth for an agile, sustainable and thrive mindset as the Fig. 4 shows.

Fig. 4. Self-Efficacy in a balance of four challenges to strengthen Self-esteem/Self-worth (proprietary description)

Based on the PCDL-cycle with the phases of Plan, Do, Check and Learn four perspectives are described. There are "I am", "I should", "I can" and "I will" as described by Fig. 4. The model involves four main components of self-efficacy thriving an agile mindset by fostering both self-esteem and self-worth.

Primarily, self-responsibility including awareness of values, needs, and attitudes is at the beginning of the cycle. This is the factor that the given research question answers: "Do team values in the context of values-based Scrum LPC influence student team performance?" Because if each team member knows what is a meaningful experience of self-responsibility, team responsibility will also emerge and vice versa. In this process, each individual in the team has the opportunity to present his/her motives and plan his/her learning objects that are specific, measurable, achievable, meaningful, and time-bound. This is also performed depending on her/his personality and learning type. The SFC must create opportunities to have these type specifics analyzed.

The next phase of "DO" uses the "to do," "doing," and "done" sections to formulate the competencies that students should develop in order to succeed in realizing, implementing, and accomplishing their target tasks. "I should" is the challenge and accomplishing it requires resilience, perseverance, self-control, and awareness.

The third phase of the "check" follows with the self-reflection of "I can". This includes knowledge of curriculum topics on the one hand and learning strategies, learning emotions, and learning context on the other. This "I can" perspective is described by the already mentioned Review and Retro in the Scrum Framework and explored with the design of the quantitative method of the questionnaire as well as the qualitative method of the semi-structured interview or the results and analysis of the Mixed Methods, discussed in the following Sect. 3 and 4.

The last phase includes volition, the "I will" perspective. It corresponds with the definition of Ryan and Deci [22], who characterize self-determination as a complicated and complex process for human development. The will to shape as a positive energy with self-motivation creates the best condition for the decision between autonomy and participation. Well-being arises only when it is accompanied by self-awareness, knowing what serves self-worth. This is the essence of human existence and creates the energy for the next, new PDCL cycle in a higher level of an agile, thriving mindset with healthy self-awareness and the appropriate self-esteem to expect and live improved self-efficacy.

3 Experimental Study

We aim to answer the following research question: Do the team values in the frame of value-based Scrum LPC influence the performance of the student-teams?

We conducted the research in the Bachelor degree program of computer sciences, business informatics and game engineering at the University of Applied Sciences Kempten in Germany during the academic year 2017–2019. It is important to provide the undergraduates with agile methods and their implementation in Software Engineering. Therefore, it is an obligatory module of five Credit Points. The 78 Bachelor's students originate from different study-programs and completed three or four semesters of their studies and should have developed a solid knowledge of programming and process models like *Scrum*.

In next section, the research methodology is presented followed in this study. The design of the quantitative method of the questionnaire and the qualitative method of the semi-structured interview, respectively the results and analysis of the mixed methods is then discussed.

3.1 Methodology - Quantitative Design

Müller-Amthor [16, pp. 9–13] investigated that the Team Climate Inventory (TCI) published by Anderson and West [26] can be used to gain validated insights into the metacognitive perception and reflection of teamwork [27]. This basic reference of the British original was adapted to cultural and linguistic needs [28].

In this respect, the results of the acceptance research conducted are certainly a significant part of this study. However, what will be decisive, it is the adaptation in relation to the presented research question: Does the didactical-agile approach of Scrum learning process coaching generate stronger teamwork when a *Scrum Master* intervenes as a value-oriented and solution-focused learning process coach?

This study now presents the findings of the two most significant and most frequently used factors, *Vision* and *Task Orientation*, with a total of seven detailed factors, but only four of them are contextualized to value-based interventions. Nevertheless and for completeness, the seven factor details shall be mentioned and are presented below. It is crucially important to highlight that for the most important phase of the retrospective, which serves for reflection on a meta-level, only four so-called factor components (*) are considered relevant.

- **Vision** with Clarity*, Value of team objective*, Sharedness and Attainability. Table 2 shows only the results in the *Vision* factor, which is defined as an idea of a valued outcome representing a higher goal and involve clarity (easy to understand), value of team objectives (valued outcome, visible to individuals in the group), because they are relevant for the value-oriented perspective. The sharedness (extension of the *Vision*) and attainability (achievable widespread acceptance) are published in [16].
- **Task-Orientation** with High Standards*, Reflection* and Synergy
  The so-called output orientation was included as an additional factor in the study by [27] of the German version. Apparently, this factor design shows a special affinity to solution-oriented approaches, the formulation and comprehensibility of common values and quality-related characteristics. Reflection could be actively cultivated, if this phase is continuously executed with high mindfulness as an attribute. Despite uncertainty, ambiguity and dissent in factual and technical questions, the team members nevertheless can find out their individual competences. The goal is to work with increasing transparency for their shared expert knowledge and to cultivate themselves in mindful reflection. For the next sprint, employees consequently plan the next steps on the path to more mindfulness, higher awareness, and improved autonomy. This development opportunity illustrates Table 3.

The quantitative evaluation is based on a questionnaire at the end of each semester. As described in [16], the scale was constructed as follows: The total sample size of 78 students was distributed among 14 teams that agreed to participate. This resulted in between four and seven members per participating group. The optimal size of the development team is small enough to stay agile and large enough to do significant work in a sprint. According to the Scrum Framework, a typical team includes both a learning assistant *Scrum Master* and an assistant *Product Owner*, as well as the learning *Scrum Team* members.

3.2 Result of the TCI-Evaluation of the Retrospective

In order to prepare the learning or adaptation phase of the PDCL cycle, as shown in Fig. 4 as self-determination, a structured *Sprint-Retrospective* is required in the check phase. The learning success is initiated by a real situation to solve a challenge and the team performance is measured by the evaluation of the TCI items. Only a minimal change in the *Scrum Master's* behavior results that all employees of the *Scrum Team* are able to perceive their common team goals in the appropriate depth and just in time. The *SFC* as *Scrum Master* follows the motto: "You should not force a team to follow assumed rules. Help them discover and adopt better ways of doing things their way - step by step

- implementing the next right thing during each iteration." The consequence is that it leads to better design results as planned, because profound and far-reaching behavioral changes of all people involved are the result. "Inversely, it seems that the higher the goal or the desired change, the harder it will be to establish a cooperative relationship between all roles, and the more likely that the team will fail. The students' action after PDCL represents the real learning process." [cf. 16, p. 3].

Thus, Table 3 describes how the cycle of repeating *Retro* as a formal framework condition creates opportunities - again and again - to recognize the improvements in a specific way and actually makes them available in a structured way for the new implementation phase, namely the next sprint. This is the actual main goal: Perceive the peak of the learning event! It helps to make participants aware of their reflective capacity based on their values, which is a necessary condition to customize and individualize the learning process.

By creating an environment for the best feasible team development, *Scrum Teams* can be pushed to peak performance. Through a structured agenda and the so-called "golden rules of *Retro*" as well as the tool-based "Quick Check of Flow" [29, 30], the *Scrum Master* supports both the learners themselves and the team in recognizing the need to adjust their behavior in the next sprint and to promote a continuous improvement process [16, p. 3]. The proof of a better team climate is provided by the measurement result. It shows the high total number of points and the percentage increase of the evaluation points after a *Retro* session in Table 2 and 3. This allows the conclusion that the *Scrum Master* as SFC has a significant influence, whereby the evaluation points of the so-called factor details give an impression of the distribution and frequency of the evaluated aspects.

Table 2. Results in the Factor "Vision" [cf. 16, p. 3]

Factor elements	Influence (I) of *Scrum Master* before/after *Retrospective(Retro)*			
	Question	*Points[a] before Retro*	*Points[a] after Retro*	*(I) in%*
Clarity	How clear are you about what your team objectives are?	504	561	11.3
Value of team objectives	To what extent do you think they are useful and appropriate objectives?	508	556	9.4
	How worthwhile do you think these objectives are to your team?	471	498	5.7

[a] Evaluation Points Sum of 78 students with a 9 point response ranging from 1 = not at all to 9 = completely.

This also suggests that the SFC ensured that the group keeps focusing on their shared value-based vision and thus individuals are more motivated to work together to explore new solution-oriented ways of working.

The author describes the results of the study [16]. Only the very important highlights should show the consequences for agile learning events:

- The analysis shows that the team goals were assessed 11.3% more clearly, after the *Scrum Team* has interacted with the *Scrum Master*, who moderates the *Retro*. In this case, the SFC motivates the team in the *Retro* to talk about the team goals again. In this way, the team is consciously committed and focused on the team objectives in its current situation and shapes its activities appropriately.
- The value of the team goals is 9.4% higher than before the retro. Thus, the participating students describe the fixed goals as "useful and appropriate".
- The question of how valuable the agreed goals are for your *Scrum Team* according to your personal opinion increases by 5.7%.

Target tasks are successfully completed in a timelier manner when the students become aware of the relevant resources in the important retro phase. Thus, they achieve better progress with a high level of responsibility and experience the self-efficacy that is so crucially important. In the new Sprint Planning process, they trust themselves to do more than they previously expected. The members influence each other interactively and the small groups work with a high level of commitment without having to work overtime.

Furthermore, the output orientation factor of the TCI correlates with the Scrum Framework even in the two sub-areas. "Highest standards" realize the *Definition of Ready*, the *Definition of Done* and the *Definition of Flow*. These recommendations enable each team to receive relevant and specific support at the time they need it. Thus, the solution-focused coaching model plays a role especially for students in STEM courses when designing skills are required.

- The factor detail "High Standards" increased by 9.6%. This improvement is certainly assigned to the flexible but however binding and committing application of the Scrum Framework. The team is encouraged to self-check continuously. Nevertheless, this can also trigger a certain psychological pressure and negative scenarios can arise. This is where the role of the experienced SFC, who provides valuable guidance for the further design process, becomes to be extremely important. In particular, the trainer's persuasiveness and willingness to design, help to eliminate the crises in the team in order to achieve the optimum as a whole team. An improvement of 6.8% is seen here as well. The question of what the optimum means has to be clarified for all members of the *Scrum Team* sufficiently.

- The factor detail "Reflection" is permuted twice in the phase "Self-Check". This most important phase in the process of learning includesthe *Review* and the *Retro*event in the Scrum Framework. First, the *Review* concerns the correct assessment of the

Table 3. Results in the Factor "Output-Orientation" [cf. 16, p. 4]

Factor details	Influence (I) of *Scrum Master* before/after *Retro*			
	Question	*Points*[b] *before Retro*	*Points*[b] *after Retro*	*(I) in %*
High standards	Is it really important to the team members that the team achieves the highest standards of planned performance?	558	612	9.6
	Are there clear criteria in the team, which are sought by the members in order to achieve the optimum as an entire team?	435	465	6.8
Reflection	Does the team continually monitor its own performance in order to achieve the highest standards?	486	511	5.1
	Are team members prepared to question the basis of what the team is doing?	531	546	2.8
	Does the team critically appraise potential weaknesses in what it is doing in order to achieve the best possible outcome?	549	612	11.4

[b] Evaluation Points Sum of 78 students with a 9 point response ranging from 1 = strongly disagree 9 = strongly agree.

expertise. In addition, there is also the question whether the self-regulated as well as self-organized approach is suitable and appropriate for the individual learning process of the functional tasks. Secondly, a very important point for the development of students' reflective ability is the framework-specific time of an event called *Retrospective*. This reserved time allows not only feedback but also another level of mindful reflection for the team and for each participant as a human being, trustworthy and just in time, as well as organized by the spirit of *Scrum Master* as SFC. [16, p. 4]

- As already mentioned in the factor detail "High Standards", some team members find the constant control between them uncomfortable. "Students frequently quoted the phrase from [1] that Scrum is easy and simple to understand, but difficult to master" [cf. 16, p. 5]. Developing self-discipline in the process of learning is the great challenge for both the students themselves and the self-organized team, which requires resilience, perseverance, self-control and consciousness, as shown by the improvement of 5.1% and 2.8%, respectively. Analysing the survey scores per group, the conclusion is, "that teams who really explore their common values in the beginning of their teamwork and use the five-finger-feedback method as a guide for the *Retro* are more willing to critically appraise their potential weaknesses. This is shown by the high level increase of 11.4% after a moderated *Retro*" [cf. 16, p. 5].

Value-Based Factor Vision

While in the previous two sections we presented the most significant factors of vision and output orientation out of a total of four factor statements, the next section describes the values-based research on how students really engage to live their chosen values as well. Thus, the research questions are as follows (Fig. 5):

1. Am I clear about the value-based goals of the project?
2. What do I think, how clear are the value-based goals of my team?

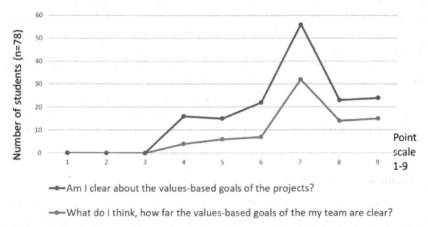

➡️ Am I clear about the values-based goals of the projects?

➡️ What do I think, how far the values-based goals of the my team are clear?

Fig. 5. Results in the Success Factor of value-based Scrum: "Clarity", Evaluation Points Sum of 78 students with a 9 point response ranging from $1 =$ not at all to $9 =$ completely.

78 students express the clarity of the value-based objectives quite clearly between 6 and 8 points, and no one gave less than three points. However, the next statement shows that the agreement with the other values of the team members is on average lower. The following qualitative factors could be designed based on this evaluation. Do the commitment and the trust of each individual in the group and the lived courageous exchange of the team members about their values play an important role? The identification rate with the group values is significantly lower. Could this be due to the fact that the tasks in the group were not formulated clearly enough? Was there not enough communication time provided in the limited online event? Should we offer more time in breakout sessions

to give more space for the discussion of values? It was remarkable in the observation of group processes that those with a shared values-based vision were more motivated to develop new solution-oriented working methods. Within this experimental study, a variety of effects could be identified that had an impact on the learning process and the learning success of the students. As described above, the quality of team performance is strongly related to strength-oriented relationship work, appreciative communication in the four phases of the PDCL cycle of the success-oriented learning process, and in the value-based actions of the *Scrum Master*. Becoming aware of one's own team performance as a team and seeing it as a product and not just as the sum of individual results is an important prerequisite not only for the success of the *Scrum Team*, but also for the learning process of the individual *Scrum Team* member.

3.3 Methodology - Qualitative Design

In the summer-semester 2020, we decided to interview the participants of the *Scrum Teams* for the efficacy of the new course design, after using the value-based Scrum LPC as the methodology with semi-structured interviews of five teams after the end of course and after the examination in August 2020. The interviews were semi-structured and a catalogue of possible supported interview questions, so that the researcher can refer to them when the questions arise in the individual interview session, thus enabling a deeper reflection on the learners personal learning behavior, learning strategy, learning emotion and learning context. Altogether 23 undergraduates participated in the course and 21 in the interviews. Each interview took 20 min. The author of this article conducted the interviews. She was not in a responsible teaching position in the course but as the *Scrum Master's* support; she could ensure that the students could reflect their experiences during the course openly and trustfully. So for example we were able to find out for example, when a student says that he or she has not improved the learning process, whether there is a reason for an learning obstacle or another impact factor that exists in addition to value-based trust.

3.4 Result of the Interviews

In the beginning of the teamwork, we could document the result of the second Scrum Retrospective fixing the values with the Five-Finger-Method per group. Figure 6 shows the overview of the agreed team-values and the transparency of some team performance indicator. First, this summary served as orientation for the interview in each group, and each team member discussed how they realized the values personally.

After the course and after obtaining the results of the written examination, we ask the students the following questions concerning the value-based strategy of the didactical approach in semi-structured interviews. Table 4 shows as we have received answers with of the same tenor and get meaningful insights by a response rate of 91% of the student participants. That is good enough to get started with the next step running the analysis.

3.5 Discussion

Following the evaluation, metacognitive awareness and reflection on teamwork using the Team Climate Inventory will be discussed and the qualitative answers given by the

Value 1 - Thumb	Value 2 – Pointer Finger
Commitment	**Focus**
Addis: Openness	Addis: Discipline
Bahir: Target achievement	Bahir: Teamwork
Chico: Honesty	Chico: Thoughtfulness
Adama: Accept task without resistance	Adama: Finish tasks on time and not be disturbed
Begi: Quality	Begi: Experience

Value 3 – Middle Finger	Value 4 – Ring Finger
Respect	**Openness**
Addis: Loyality	Addis: Flexibility
Bahir: Trust	Bahir: Honesty
Chico: Openness	Chico: Trust
Adama: Let others finish speaking	Adama: Accept new tasks
Begi: Diversity	Begi: Transparency

Value 5 - Pinkie
Courage
Addis: Autonomy
Bahir: Allowed to Make Mistakes
Chico: Solidarity
Adama: Have the courage to ask questions
Begi: Responsibility

Fig. 6. *Scrum Team* values sorted by Five-Finger-Method per group

Table 4. Value-based Questions and Responses of the Semi-structured Students' Interviews

Questions	Responses
Which competence could you intensify through value based Scrum LPC?	• Self-discipline (you had to complete a task by a fixed deadline so that you or the team members could complete tasks based on the solution of this task), but also generally working according to Scrum • Task distribution • My ability to communicate • Trust and confidence • Responsibility for the team performance increase my self-motivation • Perseverance with Sisyphus tasks
Which team competence did the project team jointly develop on a value-based approach?	• Focus on essentials • Working and solution finding together in a team • Sharing tasks • Helping each other when I did not know how to solve a task on my own
Were the jointly agreed team values decisive for your joint behavior?	• Sometimes we looked at our "Five-Finger-Hand" • Less fear to ask my mates, *Scrum Master* and *Product Owner* • "All for each and each for all"

students, which were used to find explanations of what was observed in the data of the TCI. This can prove the aggregation of the collected data by team name.

The advantages of a value-based Scrum LPC are that the approach provide an insight into the learning process of students. We succeeded in supporting the self-reflection process about their own functional competence and their soft skills. This is an important prerequisite for lifelong learning, because reflectiveness "includes the ability to deal with change, to learn from experience and to think and act critically" [cf. 29] as the German Qualification Guide defines. The documents of Retrospective reflect a special role in dealing with change and learning from experience. This emphasizes that students were not only guided by the SFC to reflect, but also became aware of their own self-reflection and learning processes. This is a central competence for experience-based learning, for further development and thus especially for innovative learning. Scrum LPC seems to offer the possibility to create a high level of trust. An increasing self-efficacy and a positive attitude could be a motivating factor leading to a good successful exam.

Sometimes it develops really a trustful talk about the missing motivation and even about the fear and human failure. The SFC states that the latter have to be analyzed for assessing one's abilities and interest in her or his obstacles. The question should be allowed, why students have this kind of learning and whether this inner beliefs prevents them from applying new learning strategies. Through Scrum LPC students get the opportunity to reflect on their own prerequisites and attitudes in comparison with other team members. This is of interest when it comes to designing their own learning process more effectively and efficiently. Self-determined learning to its greatest extent is a process in which the student can decide and influence significantly whether, when, for what, what and how he or she learns. Each *Sprint* after the appreciative *Retrospective* gives the student a new chance to thrive with an agile mindset.

4   Conclusion and Perspective

An evaluation of the most important TCI factors and conclusion at the end summarizes the research outcomes. We must put even more emphasis on value-based *Scrum Team* working as an instrument of integrated student advisory service by solution-focused coaching. We use the German words for "educational biplane", when we use the subject of study as a vehicle of a holistic self-development. It enables the increase of self-esteem and the implementation of self-effective learning arrangements for an agile mindset of students' thriving. They intensified their learning strategy, which is suited for the own personality. Furthermore, it produces a higher success rate as to pass examination for software engineers. A long-term study will determine, discuss and qualify how the value-based Framework Scrum LPC supports the value-aware SFC in noticing the difficulties and challenges related to the intended learning outcome and the missing motivation in students' learning procedures. The study proves that the use of values and their reflection by the Scrum LPC increase the team performance. This was diagnosed with the allocation of the TCI as a certain inventory of measuring the better capacity for teamwork. The evaluation also confirms that Scrum LPC with the specific procedure of asking and answering questions in the *Retro* improves the self-learning competencies in connection with self-regulated learning behavior in an agile and success-oriented way, self-emotion and self-motivation for the process of learning. Hence, based on the semi-structured interviews, this approach is expected to deliver valuable results on students' self-reflectiveness learning and its facilitation in the context Software Engineering education. However, Scrum LPC could also be an approach for preparing students for a successful career in the other fields of STEM-Engineering.

In summary, it is worth to mention that the self-determination and the focus of the mated values effect the students' workload, which does not seem to have increased, however functional results have improved and even we led to better grades. This is due to their shift in esteemed behavior towards the team during lectures, means *"Daily" Scrum* or rather *Stand-up* meetings, *Reviews*, *Retrospectives*. The responsibility of the Scrum roles causes more activity, e.g. discussing ideas and asking questions. Individual solution-focused coaching enables teams to adopt themselves appropriate tools and techniques for their specific context and to gain more nontechnical, social skills. A. Dehlii et al. [14] describe, "Incremental deliveries of *'Done'* learning results ensure that a potentially good result towards the learning goals is always achievable." and checks the learning process by using the *Definition of Fun* [14], which describes the "Definition of Happiness". The future concept of Scrum LPC substantiates a *Definition of Flow* for the *Retro*. In this model, students seem to experience flow because the requirements of the tasks in the present sprints correspond well with the abilities of the individuals, i.e., when the estimated possibilities for action offered by the Sprint tasks match the students' own abilities and there is an high expectation of self-efficacy. Thus, the *Scrum Master* as a solution-focused coach concentrates on the perceived competence as a central element of intrinsically motivated actions - the best prerequisite for the actual learning process. The verification of optimal challenges by a value-based and success-oriented SFC requires a concept of flow [30] and value-oriented communication in an atmosphere of trust. This provides the best basis for the individual's behavior to change during the next sprint. It seemed as if the curiosity would be motived, because they ask many questions and discuss new multivariate solution ideas.

A *Scrum Master* could use a catalogue of dedicated questions and devoted methods for *Retrospectives* [31] in order to lead oneself, to lead students and to lead changes in higher education, so-called Transformative Leadership [32]. Some further guiding principles and useful approaches explore [20]: "It requires critical reflection on questions about for whom the system is working ...calls for critical analysis of beliefs, values...." As already mentioned, evidence through this study shows that excellent qualified SFC knowing tools of value-based orientation could be autonomy-supportive. It is important to remember that no team is ever the same. If there is something which has been useful to the SFC, in most cases it has been a curious, playful, experimental and agile approach in helping teams to learn to take ownership of the Daily Scrum means also ownership of their individual daily life.

Moreover, this study gives further impacts for research with future perspectives developing value-based team working and self-learning competence in higher education. It is a thriving way of experiencing oneself when one is fully engaged and uses one's abilities to the utmost to achieve something that one has previously consciously valued as personal values [33]. Scrum LPC is the process of experiencing self-efficacy [33].

This contribution analyses the relevant references in IEEE-papers between 2014 and 2018 and we could compare other relevant literature for papers of engineers in ACM, Web of Sciences, etc. The value-based guidance of students in their development into holistic personalities is the prerequisite for science to make a significant contribution to social responsibility based on deeply rooted ethical principles. Some open research questions foster success factors, which deserves didactical principles by future design-based research.

Acknowledgment. This work is part of the EVELIN project, which is funded by the German Ministry of Education and Research (Bundesministerium für Bildung und Forschung) with the grant no. 01PL17022C. Solely the authors are responsible for the content of this publication.

References

1. Schwaber, K., Sutherland, J.: The Scrum Guide, November 2017. https://www.scrumguides. org/docs/scrumguide/v2017/2017-Scrum-Guide-US.pdf, pp. 3–5. Accessed 01 Sep 2020
2. Hurbungs, V., Nagowah, S.D.: Practical approach to teaching agile methodologies and principles at tertiary level using student centred activities. In: Parsons, D., MacCallum, K. (eds.) Agile and Lean Concepts for Teaching and Learning-Bringing Methodologies from Industry to the Classroom, pp. 355–390. Springer, Singapore (2019)
3. Chatley, R.: Applying lean learning to software engineering education. In: Parsons, D., MacCallum, K. (eds.) Agile and Lean Concepts for Teaching and Learning, pp. 285–302. Springer, Singapore (2019). https://doi.org/10.1007/978-981-13-2751-3_14
4. Kluckhohn, C.: Values and value orientations in the theory of action. In: Parsons, T., Shields, F.A. (eds.) Toward a General Theory of Action, pp. 388–433. Harvard University Press, Cambridge, MA (1951)
5. Frey, D.: Psychologisches Know-how für eine Gesellschaft im Umbruch – Spitzenunternehmen der Wirtschaft als Vorbild. In: Honegger, C., Gabriel, J.M., Hirsig, R., Pfaff-Czarnecka, J., Poglia, E. (Hrsg.) Gesellschaften im Umbau. Identitäten, Konflikte, Differenzen, pp. 75–98, Seismo, Zürich (1996)
6. Frey, D., Peus, C., Traut-Mattausch, E.: Innovative Unternehmenskultur und professionelle Führung – entscheidende Bedingungen für eine erfolgreiche Zukunft? In: Kudernatsch, D., Fleschhut, P. (Hrsg.) Management Excellence, pp. 351–376, Schäffer-Poeschel, Stuttgart (2005)
7. Opaschowski, H.W.: Von der Geldkultur zur Zeitkultur. Neue Formen der Arbeitsmotivation für zukunftsorientiertes Management. In: Schanz, G. (Hrsg.) Handbuch Anreizsysteme in Wirtschaft und Verwaltung, pp. 32–52, Stuttgart, Schäffer-Poeschel (1987)
8. Wenninger, G. (ed.): Lexikon der Psychologie in fünf Bänden (4). Spektrum Akademischer Verlag, Heidelberg, Berlin (2001)
9. Schwartz, S.H.: Universals in the content and structure of values: theoretical advances and empirical tests in 20 countries. Adv. Exp. Soc. Psychol. **25**(1), 1–65 (1992). https://doi.org/ 10.1016/S0065-2601(08)60281-6
10. Barysch, K.N.: Selbstwirksamkeit. In: Frey, D. (Hrsg.) Psychologie der Werte – Von der Achtsamkeit bis Zivilcourage – Basiswissen aus Psychologie und Philosophie. Springer Verlag, Berlin, Heidelberg (2016). https://doi.org/10.1007/978-3-658-04434-3_5
11. Kricke, M., Reich, K.: Teamteaching. Eine neue Kultur des Lehrens und Lernens. Beltz Verlag, Weinheim, Basel (2016)
12. Hattie, J.: Visible Learning. A Synthesis of Over 800 Meta-Analyses Relating to Achievement. London/New York (2009)
13. Hattie, J.: Visible Learning for Teachers. Maximizing Impact on Learning. London/New York (2012)
14. Delhii, A., van Solingen, R., Wijnands, W.: The EduScrum Guide. https://www.eduscrum.nl/ img/The_eduScrum_guide_English_2.pdf. Accessed 01 Sep 2020

15. Hans, R.T.: Work in progress - the impact of the student scrum master on quality and delivery time on students' projects. In: Fifth International Conference on Learning and Teaching in Computing and Engineering. LaTiCE 2017, Conference Publishing Services, pp. 87–90. IEEE Computer Society, Hong Kong (2017)

16. Müller-Amthor, M., et al: Scrum higher education – the scrum master supports as solution-focused coach. In: IEEE Global Engineering Education Conference (EDUCON), Porto, pp. 948–952 (2020). https://ieeexplore.ieee.org/document/9125304. Accessed 13 Nov 2020

17. Paasivaara, M., et al.: Do high and low performing student teams use scrum differently in capstone projects? In: Claudia, W. (Hg.) 2017 IEEE/ACM 39th International Conference on Software Engineering, pp. 146–149. IEEE, Buenos Aires (2019)

18. Rodriguez, G., Soria, Á., Campo, M.: Measuring the impact of agile coaching on student' performance. IEEE Trans. Educ. **59**(3), 202–209 (2016)

19. Yuen, T.T.: Scrumming with educators, cross-departmental collaboration for a summer software engineering capstone. In: International Conference on Learning and Teaching in Computing and Engineering, pp. 124–127. IEEE 2015, Taiwan (2015)

20. Besser, R.: The reflexionstool - value cards, vol. 2, besser wie gut GmbH, Bremen (2016)

21. EFIL - European Federation for Intercultural Learning, Five Finger Feedback. http://intercult ural-learning.eu/evaluationmethods-2/. Accessed 01 Sep 2020

22. Ryan, R.M., Deci, E.L.: Self-Determination Theory – Basic Psychological Needs in Motivation, Development and Wellness, pp. 239–381. The Guilford Press, New York (2018)

23. de Shazer, S.: Contemporary Case Studies in School Counceling, pp. 143–157. Rowman & Littlefield, Lanham (2019)

24. Bamberger, G.G.: Lösungsorientierte Beratung, Beltz (2015)

25. Bartel, P., Hagel, G.: Lösungsorientierte Beratung in der Hochschullehre. In: Didaktik-nachrichten - DiNa 2019(02). https://www.diz-bayern.de/publikationen/dina-und-tagung sbaende/473-dina-02-2019-kompetenzprofile-und-orientierung-in-der-lehre-loesungsorienti erte-beratung, pp. 18–30. Accessed 01 Sep 2020

26. Anderson, N.R., West, M.A.: Measuring climate for work group innovation, development and validation of the team climate inventory. J. Organ. Behav. **19**, 235–258. https://onlinelibrary.wiley.com/doi/10.1002/(SICI)1099-1379(199805)19%3A3% 3C235%3A%3AAID-JO. Accessed 01 Sep 2020

27. Brodbeck, F.C., Anderson, N., West, M.A.: The Team Climate Inventory: Manual and Validation of the German Version. Hofgrefe, Heidelberg (2000)

28. Antoni, C.H.: Review of 'Teamklima-Inventar (TKI)' by Brodbeck, F.C.; Anderson, N.; West, M.A. In: Zeitschrift für Arbeits- und Organisationspsychologie A&O, vol. 47, no. 1, pp. 45–50. Hofgrefe, Heidelberg (2003)

29. The German Qualifications Framework for Lifelong Learning, adopted by the "German Qualifications Framework Working Group" (AKDQR) Status: 22 March 2011. https://www.dqr.de/media/content/The_German_Qualifications_Framework_for_Lif elong_Learning.pdf. Accessed 01 Sep 2020

30. Csikszentmihalyi, M.: Flow. The Psychology of Optimal Experience. Haper & Row, New York (1990)

31. Andresen, J.: Retrospektiven in agilen Projekten. Carl Hanser, München (2014)

32. Shields, C.M.: Transformative Leadership in Education – Equitable and Socially Just Change in an Uncertain and Complex World, 2nd edn. Routledge, New York (2018)

33. Dweck, C.S.: Self-theories: their role in motivation, personality, and development. In: Essays in Social Psychology. Taylor & Francis, Philadelphia (1999)

A Study on Performance Characteristics of Immune System for Practical Application

Dong Hwa Kim[1]([✉]), T. Y. Tefera[2], and Dae Hee Won[3]

[1] EPCE, ASTU, Adama, Ethiopia
worldhucare@gmail.com
[2] ASTU, Adama, Ethiopia
tefera06@gmail.com
[3] WonKwang University, Iksan, South Korea
Oneday06@wku.ac.kr

Abstract. This paper deals with the characteristics of performance of Immune System (IS) for practical application. Research builds immune based control model for pendulum with nonlinear characteristic and compare its characteristics with GA. IS always has a new parallel decentralized processing mechanism for various situations by using the antibody communication function. Antibody has huge communication system function among different species of antibodies B-cells through the stimulation and suppression chains among antibodies that form a large-scaled network. In addition to that, the structure of the network is not fixed, but varies continuously. That is, IS has a flexibly self-organizes according to dynamic changes of external situation. From the above facts, this paper studies performance of controller of IS and compare its control function with GA.

Keywords: Genetic algorithm · Immune algorithm · AI · Nonlinear · Pendulum control

1 Introduction

Recently, IS has been influencing on everywhere such as agriculture, design, literature, drawing, art, management, and etc. as well as high technologies of manufacturing, smart city, power system, semiconductor, robot, drone, and medical. The turning point of AI was play go by Alphago of Google of 2016. From that time, many countries and global companies have been recognizing the importance of AI and investing. The AI in the site has been developing into an emerging technology, so-called 'Industrial intelligent system'. Basic theory of Alphago is deep learning and it is organized from neural network that is getting and dealing with well information. Also, many researchers are interesting in developing AI tool and deep learning is one of strong AI tool. A combined learning-based artificial intelligence (Hybrid AI) NN (neural network), GA (genetic algorithm), and AIS (immune network system) have been interested in studying much attention using their advantage [1–3]. AI related technologies or application are highly multi-disciplinary systems, which is composed of operations research, artificial intelligence,

M. A. Delele et al. (Eds.): ICAST 2020, LNICST 384, pp. 534–545, 2021.
https://doi.org/10.1007/978-3-030-80621-7_38

information and signal processing, computer software and production background [1–3]. Each theory such as fuzzy, neural, and neuro-fuzzy has been offering new possibilities and making intelligent system even more versatile and applicable in an ever-increasing range of industrial applications. Over the past decade or so, significant advances have been made in two distinct technological area: fuzzy logic (FL) and neural networks (NNs) [1, 8, 16, 18]. Of course, there have been considerable interests for the past few years in exploring the application of fuzzy or neural network (FNN) systems to deal with uncertain information, nonlinearities, and uncertainties of systems. On the other hand, biological information processing systems such as human beings have many interesting functions and are expected to provide various feasible ideas to engineering fields such as intelligent control, robotics, power system, etc. Biological information in living organisms can be mainly classified into the following four systems: brain nervous, genetic system, endocrine system, and immune system.

Brain nervous and genetic systems have already been applied to engineering fields by modeling as neural network and genetic algorithms, they have been widely used in various fields. The aim of immune network system (IS) is to implement a learning technique inspired by the human immune system which is a remarkable natural defense mechanism that learns about foreign substances. However, the immune system has not attracted the same kind of interest from the computing field as the neural operation of the brain or the evolutionary forces used in learning classifier systems [8, 22]. This paper provides the characteristics of AINS as AI tool through comparing GA (Genetic Algorithm) and IS in nonlinear system.

2 The Characteristics of IS as AI Tool

A study of the models that have been performed for various computational aspects of the immune system and their applications to real world problems are available in [12, 15, 19, 20]. There are many intelligent approaches for their purpose as shown in Table 1. The AIN has many merits for engineering and herein it has been attracting for control, computer and network security.

The learning characteristic of the immune system is a distributed function with no central controller, since it has behavior which is consisted of an enormous number and diversity of cells throughout our bodies.

2.1 The Characteristics of Information Processing of IS

IS application implements a learning technique inspired by the human immune system, which is a remarkable natural defense mechanism that learns about foreign substances. Its main function is the clonal selection. That is, biological information processing systems such as human beings and natural systems have many advantages and function for AI tool. Therefore, many have been interesting in functions and expecting to provide various feasible ideas to engineering fields [2, 4–6, 11, 19, 20]. Biological information in living organisms can be classified into the following four systems: brain nervous, genetic system, endocrine system, and immune system [6, 9, 10]. Brain nervous and genetic systems have already been applied to many engineering fields [7–9]. Table 1 is the results of comparison to each AI tools.

Table 1. Comparison of characteristics of AI tools [16–22].

			Purpose of intelligence ○: Best ●: Good					
Control	Diagnosis	Pattern Recognition	Control	Plan	Decision	Design	Identify	Focast
Fuzzy	●	●	○	○	○		○	●
NN	●	○	●				○	○
GA	●			○	○	○		
Chaos	○	●	●				○	○
Classical Control			●	●		○		●

However, only a little attention has been paid to application of immune algorithm in engineering, not to mention their important characteristics. The AIS uses a learning technique inspired by the human immune system which is a remarkable natural defense mechanism that learns about foreign substances as shown in Fig. 1. Therefore, currently, there are many the characteristics of the immune system [1, 3, 5, 12, 19, 20] and summarized;

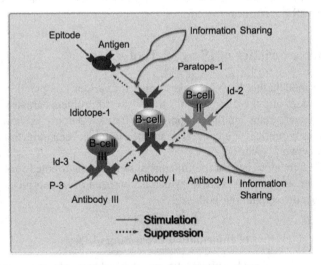

Fig. 1. The role antibody and antigen in IS.

The learning rule of the immune system is a distributed system with no central controller, since the immune system consists of an enormous number and diversity of cells throughout our bodies; The immune system has a naturally occurring event-response system which can quickly adapt to changing situations and shares the property with the central nervous system; The immune system possesses a self-organizing and distributed memory. Therefore, it is thus adaptive to its external environment and allows a PDP (parallel distributed processing) network to complete patterns against the environmental situation. Immune system has various interesting features such as immunological memory, immunological tolerance since it can play an important role to maintain own system dynamically changing environments. Therefore, immune system would be expected to provide a new paradigm suitable for dynamic problem dealing with unknown environments their rather than static system. Brooks, a pioneer of the approaches, has presented architecture for behavior arbitration of autonomous robots [15]. He has argued that intelligence should emerge from mutual interactions among competence modules, and interactions between a robot and its environment. Some researchers particularly focused on the new decentralized consensus-making system [2, 3, 5, 10] because facts that IS can maintain its own system against dynamically changing environments.

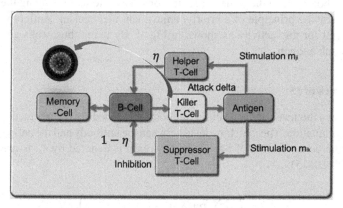

Fig. 2. Dynamic the role of antibody and antigen in IS.

2.2 The Response Mechanism in IS

The IS has two types of response: primary and secondary. The primary response is reaction process when the clonal selection system encounters the antigen for the first time. At this point the AIS learns about the antigen, thus preparing the body for any further invasion from that antigen. This learning mechanism creates the immune system's memory. The secondary response occurs when the same antigen encountered again. This has response characterized by a more rapid and more abundant production of antibody resulting from the priming of the B-cells in the primary response [9, 10]. Life of the memory B-cells has a long term they work continuously to the external agents [16, 20].

2.3 The Role of Antibodies

The antibodies of IS has actually three-dimensional Y shaped molecules, which consist of two types of protein chain: light and heavy. It has two paratopes to match the antigen [9, 10].

2.4 Interactions Between Antibodies

The antigen antibody interaction is similar to that of enzyme substrate interaction. The reaction between an antigen and antibody is noncovalent type, where the antigenic determinants or epitodes interact with domain of the antibody molecule. The noncovalent interaction between antigen and antibody is brought about by hydrogen bonds, vander Waals interactions, ionic bonds and hydrophobic interactions. Therefore, a strong affinity interaction should occur between antigen and antibody to form a stable complex. The interaction among antibodies is important to understand dynamic characteristics of clonal selection system. Figure 1 shows behavior the three antibodies (I, II, III) that respond to the antigens (Virus), respectively. When the antigens come in, it stimulates the antibodies. When the antigens do not come in (no interaction between antibody (II) and antibody (III)), the antibodies have the same concentrations. The interaction among the antibody has behavior by the principle of a priority adjustment mechanism. Antibody has killer and helper cell for this activity as shown in Fig. 2. By using these cells antibody can promptly attack antigen.

2.5 Dynamics of IS

Figure 1 shows the level of each cell in antibody is defined by the interaction between antibodies stimulation. The matching level between the antibody and the antigen decides. Therefore, the concentration of i-*th* antibody, which is denoted by δ_i, is calculated as follows [1, 9, 10, 15]:

$$\frac{dS_i(t)}{dt} = \left(\begin{array}{c} \alpha \sum_{j=1}^{N} m_{ji} \delta_j(t) \\ -\alpha \sum_{k=1}^{N} m_{ik} \delta_k(t) + \beta m_i - \gamma_i \end{array} \right) \delta_i(t) \tag{1}$$

$$\frac{d\delta_i(t)}{dt} = \frac{1}{1 + \exp\left(0.5 - \frac{dS_i(t)}{dt}\right)} \tag{2}$$

From Eqs. (1) and (2), N shows the number of antibodies and positive constants. m_{ji} represents affinities between antibody j and antibody i (i.e. the degree of interaction), m_i is affinities between the detected antigens and antibody i, respectively. Figure 2 shows the dynamic relation operated by antibodies and antigen.

2.6 Selection Mechanism

Selection mechanism is to calculate affinity between antibodies among several antibody groups and antigen. Therefore, there are two methods in mechanism: One thing is to compute between antibody and antibody; another thing is to calculate between antibody and antigen. Response of IS is quite different depends on these selection mechanisms and its mechanism is decided by designer's idea. That is, there can be several possibilities in selection mechanism. Here this paper uses selection method obtained in lymphocyte population [4–6, 13]:

$$\Omega_j(N) = \sum_{i=1}^{S} -x_{ij} \log x_{ij} \tag{3}$$

Here, N is the antibody size, S is the allete variety, and x_{ij} has the probability. Therefore, the means of information $\Omega_{ave}(N)$ is obtained as the following equation [5, 6, 13]:

$$\Omega_{ave}(N) = \frac{1}{M} \sum_{j=1}^{M} \Omega_j(N)$$
$$= \frac{1}{M} \sum_{j=1}^{M} \left\{ \sum_{i=1}^{S} -x_{ij} \log x_{ij} \right\}. \tag{4}$$

where M is the size of the gene in an antibody.
The affinity $m_{\alpha\beta}$ between antibody α and antibody β is given as follows:

$$m_{\alpha\beta} = \frac{1}{\{1 + \Omega(\alpha\beta)\}} \tag{5}$$

$$\Omega(\alpha\beta) = H_s(x) = \left[f_1(x) + f_2(x) + f_3(x)\right].$$

where $\Omega(\alpha\beta)$ is an information which obtained by antibody α and antibody β. If $\Omega(\alpha\beta) = 0$, the antibody α and antibody β match completely. Generally, $m_{\alpha\beta}$ is given by range of 0–1. In this paper, we propose controller that can control by intelligent controller by using immune algorithm and by using membership function for antibody concentration and affinity to antigen. This paper suggests a novel controller structure which has a characteristic mentioned above.

3   Simulation and Results

This paper built a model to obtain the characteristics of IS and compare with GA. The comparison of GA and AINS is obtained from structure that is composed by Simulink and pendulum, which is so much nonlinear function, as shown in Fig. 3. Figures 4 shows model of pendulum (mass, 2 kg and pendulum length, 2 m), which is given state equation and car moves from set point to current position while experiment (simulation).

Figure 5 illustrates variation of objective function to GA (Genetic) and IM (Immune), Fig. 6 represents angle variation of pendulum position to concentration of antibody.

It means when we adjust the concentration of antibody, we can obtain response that we are going to apply to plant control. Usually, antibody concentration is quite delicate and can adjust easily because of chemical area. Figure 7 is variation of controller gain K_i. The fluctuation of AINS is bigger than that of GA. It means IS tries to adjust parameter to plant variation. Figure 8 is variation of controller gain k_p. It has also bigger

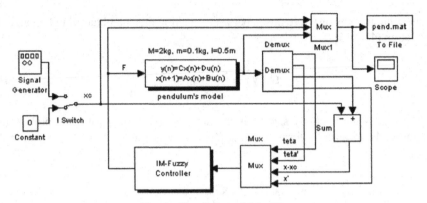

Fig. 3. Simulink model for IS.

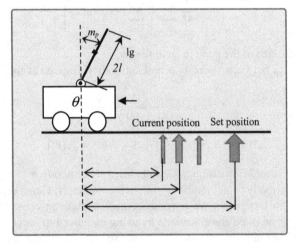

Fig. 4. Nonlinear Pendulum system for control performance of IS.

fluctuation that that of GA. From these two Fig., we can see IS has a dynamically changing behavior to find target value. Figure 9 shows variation of position (θ, θ') by IS. Figure 10 is variation of position to concentration of IS. Figure 10 reveals that we can obtain response through adjusting concentration. To express effectively the characteristics of IS, this paper compares its characteristics on the control performances with GA as shown from Fig. 5, Fig. 6, Fig. 7, Fig. 8, Fig. 9, Fig. 10, Fig. 11, Fig. 12, Fig. 13, Fig. 14, Fig. 15 and Fig. 16.

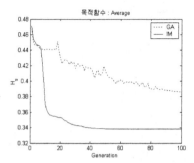

Fig. 5. Variation of objective function.

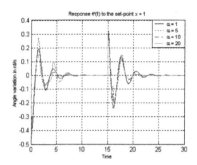

Fig. 6. Angle variation of pendulum to concentration of antibody.

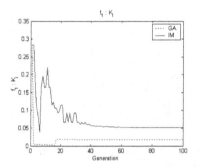

Fig. 7. Variation of controller gain k_i by GA and IM.

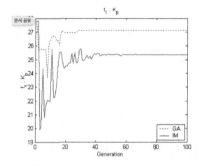

Fig. 8. Variation of controller gain k_p by GA and IM.

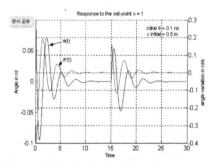

Fig. 9. Variation of position (θ, $\theta\prime$) by GA and IM.

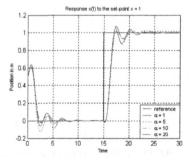

Fig. 10. Variation of position to concentration.

Figures 11 and 12 shows the variation of parameter K_p and K_i. From these two Fig, we can see that IS has a good searching function to new situation. It reveals the characteristics of AINS, which has search and attack external substrate (antigen: bacteria). Figure 13 illustrates variation of fitness function in GA and IS. Figure 14 shows control results by GA and IS selected parameter value after simulation. Figure 15 and Fig. 16 represent variation of parameter K_p, T_i, T_d by GA and IS, respectively. In case of T_i, T_d, the

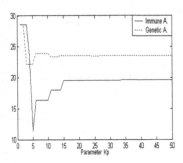

Fig. 11. Variation of parameter K$_p$.

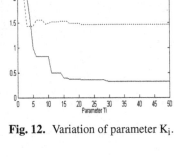

Fig. 12. Variation of parameter K$_i$.

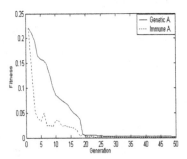

Fig. 13. Variation of fitness function.

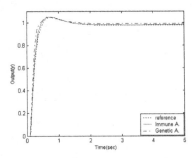

Fig. 14. Response by selected control parameter.

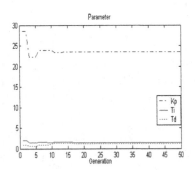

Fig. 15. Variation of parameter by GA.

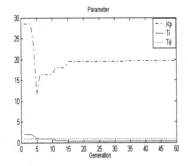

Fig. 16. Variation of parameter by IM.

value is very similar but K$_p$ has a different shape. That is very important remaining topic to research in the future. In Fig. 16, variation of K$_p$ has very wide width. It means that AINS has a dynamically searching function to new target. It is very similar to the results of Fig. 11 and 12. Figure 17 shows variation of angle and position pendulum to concentration of antibody 50. After 15 s, all system is stable position. Figure 18 is variation of angle and position pendulum to concentration of antibody 100. It means the concentration of antibody is too strong. So, we should adjust slowly and weaker to control system at this stage. Figure 19 represents variation of fitness to lamda, which

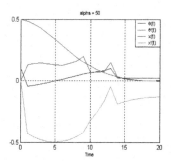

Fig. 17. Variation of angle and position to concentration 50.

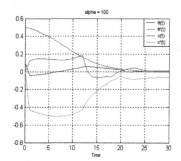

Fig. 18. Variation of angle and position to concentration 100.

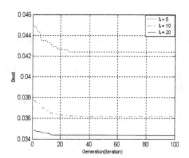

Fig. 19. Variation of fitness to lamda.

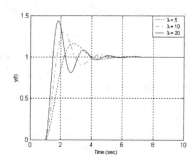

Fig. 20. Response to selected lamda.

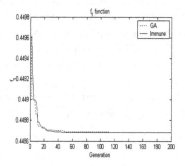

Fig. 21. Response to f_1.

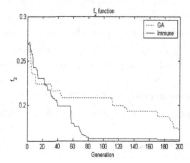

Fig. 22. Response to f_2.

is concentration between antibody and antigen. Figure 20 is response by using lamda selected in Fig. 19. The response of control system is different depends on value of lamda. Figure 21, Fig. 22, and Fig. 23 is variation to generation given by selection mechanism Eq. (5) the above.

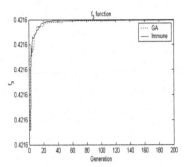

Fig. 23. Response to f_3.

4   Conclusion and Future Works

This paper deals with the characteristics of the control performance of IS through comparing with GA. Basically, both neural networks and immunity-based systems are biologically inspired techniques that have the capability of identifying patterns of interest. They use learning, memory, and associative retrieval to solve recognition and classification tasks. But the underlying mechanisms of recognition and learning are very different. However, the immune system provides diversification instead of converging to local or global optimization. The immune system possesses self-organizing memory and it remembers its categorizations over long periods of time [7, 8, 13, 14]. The IS is best artificial tool for artificial intelligence because it has many advantages such as no leader processing, distribution function, and networking function between antibodies in information processing. Some papers studied that genetic algorithms (GAs) are only an efficient and robust tool for generating AI tools and optimization function. The IS studied in this paper also has many advantages due to the optimal behavior, information sharing networking function, PDP computing processing, and memory function. These can also have a possibility to be used for many cases of nonlinear system as well as security, control, and application for other AI. The results of this research reveal well the characteristics of IS. Unfortunately, due to the limited time, all detailed results do not present in this paper. If there is a chance, authors will publish soon.

References

1. Sohl, E., Bobrow, J.E.: Experiments and simulations on the nonlinear control of a hydraulic servo system. Trans. Control Syst. Techol. 7(2), 238–247 (1999)
2. Mori, K., Tsukiyama, M., Fukuda, T.: Immune algorithm with searching diversity and its application to resource allocation problem. Trans. JIEE **113** – C (10), 872–878 (1993)
3. Kim, D.H.: Auto-tuning of reference model based PID controller using immune algorithm. In: IEEE International Conference on Evolutionary Computation, May 12–17, Hawaii (2002)
4. Kim, D.H.: Intelligent tuning of a PID controller using an immune algorithm. Trans. KIEE **51**-D (1), (2002)
5. Kim, D.H.: PID controller tuning of a boiler control system using immune algorithm typed neural network. In: Bubak, M., van Albada, G.D., Sloot, P.M.A., Dongarra, J. (eds.) ICCS 2004. LNCS, vol. 3037, pp. 695–698. Springer, Heidelberg (2004). https://doi.org/10.1007/978-3-540-24687-9_105

6. Dasgupta, D.: Using immunological principles in anomaly detection. In: Proceedings of the Artificial Neural Networks in Engineering (ANNIE 1996), St. Louis, USA (1996)
7. Farmer, J.D.: A rosetta stone for connectionism. Physica D **42**, 153–187 (1990)
8. Forrest, S., Perelson, A.S., Allen, L., Cherukuri, R.: lf-nonself discrimination in a computer. In proceedings if IEEE Symposium in Research in Security and Privacy, Oakland, CA, pp. 202–212 (1994)
9. Perelson, A.S.: Immune network theory. Immunol. Rev. **10**, 5–36 (1989)
10. Vertosick, F.T., Kelly, R.H.: Immune network theory: a role for parallel distributed processing? Immunology **66**, 1–7 (1989)
11. Vertosick, F.T., Kelly, R.H.: The immune system as a neural network: a multi-epitope approach. J. Theor. Biol. **150**, 225–237 (1991)
12. Ishiguro, A., Kondo, T., Watanabe, Y., Uchikawa, Y.: Dynamic behavior arbitration of autonomous mobile robots using immune networks. Proc. ICEC' **95**(2), 722–727 (1995)
13. Kim, D.H., Cho, J.H.: Design of Robust PID Controller With Disturbance Rejection For Motor Using Immune Algorithm, Japan 2004 (2003)
14. Farmer, J.D., Packard, N.H., Perelson, A.S.: The immune system, adaptation, and machine learning. Physica D **22**, 187–204 (1986)
15. Brooks, R.: A robust layered control system for a mobile robot. IEEE J. R&A **2**, 14–23 (1986)
16. Limin, F.: Neural networks in Computer Intelligence. McGraw-Hill, Inc. (1994)
17. Rowe, G.W.: The Theoretical Models in Biology, first edn. Oxford University Press (1994)
18. Vemuri, V.: Artificial neural networks in control applications. Adv. Comput. **36**, 203–254 (1993)
19. IEEE Computation 2019: The 2019 IEEE Symposium on Immune Computation
20. Zuccolotto, M.: Proceedings of the 19th World Congress, IFAC7116Artificial Immune Intelligent Maintenance System – Diagnostic Agents, Cape Town, South Africa (2019)
21. Ng, T.S., Hung, Y.S.: Safety, Reliability and Applications of Emerging Intelligent Control Technologies (eBook ISBN: 9781483296968) (1995)
22. Genetic algorithms (GA) are a method of optimization involving iterative search procedures based on an analogy with the process of natural selection (Darwinism) and evolutionary genetics. https://www.sciencedirect.com/topics/engineering/genetic-algorithm

Author Index

Printed in the United States
by Baker & Taylor Publisher Services